GENDER
TALK

•

GENDER
TALK

THE STRUGGLE FOR
WOMEN'S EQUALITY IN
AFRICAN AMERICAN
COMMUNITIES

•

JOHNNETTA BETSCH COLE
BEVERLY GUY-SHEFTALL

ONE WORLD
BALLANTINE BOOKS • NEW YORK

A One World Book
Published by The Ballantine Publishing Group

Grateful acknowledgment is made to the following for permission to reprint previously published material: BMI, Lil'Joe Wein Music, Inc.: "Me So Horny" by The 2 Live Crew.

www.ballantinebooks.com/one/

Library of Congress Cataloging-in-Publication Data
Cole, Johnnetta.
    Gender talk : the struggle for women's equality in African American communities / Johnnetta Cole, Beverly Guy-Sheftall.—1st ed.
        p. cm.
    Includes bibliographical references and index.
    ISBN 0-345-45412X (hc)
    1. African American women—Social conditions. 2. African American women—Civil rights. 3. African Americans—Social conditions—1975- 4. Women's rights—United States. 5. Sex role—United States. 6. Sex role—Political aspects—United States. 7. Sexism—United States. I. Guy-Sheftall, Beverly. II. Title.

E185.86 .C58154 2003
305.48'896073—dc21   2002040875

Manufactured in the United States of America

First Edition: February 2003

10   9   8   7   6   5   4   3   2

*For our fathers, John Thomas Betsch, Sr., and
Walter Peabody Guy, Jr., who were ahead of their times
in knowing that their daughters have the right to
be free from racial and gender biases and to follow
their own dreams*

●

CONTENTS

•

ACKNOWLEDGMENTS

•

Expressing gratitude should never be just a ritual, and if it is sincerely felt, then it is not possible to make too much of it. The gratitude we feel toward each of the individuals who has helped to move *Gender Talk* from an idea in our heads to publication is enormous and comes straight from our hearts.

In 1999, Ruth Simmons, at that time the Sister President of Smith College, and now at the helm of Brown University, warmly welcomed us to Smith and provided us with office space and other support that we needed to prepare the proposal for *Gender Talk*. Ruth Simmons also gave us steady doses of sisterly encouragement. Beginning in 2001, another Sister President, Dolores E. Cross, who was the president of Morris Brown College, gave us office spaces to which we could "steal away" from our regular responsibilities. We certainly appreciate having sister-friends in high places.

We are especially thankful to our sisters and brothers who agreed to be interviewed and who were honest and forthcoming with us about their personal lives and perspectives on Black America, especially where gender matters are concerned. Their voices can be heard throughout this book.

Without the support of the Ford Foundation, especially Alison Bernstein, Susan Berresford, and Margaret Wilkerson, we would have been unable to convene a large group of "informants" whose contributions to the "Multilogue on Gender Relations Within African American Communities" were crucial to our thinking about the project. A special thanks goes to Professors Rudolph P. Byrd and Frances Smith Foster, former chairs of African American Studies and the Institute for Women's Studies at Emory University, for all their support in the planning and implementation of the multilogue. A word of thanks to Sherie Randolph, then associate director of the

Women's Research and Resource Center at Spelman College, for her help with logistics leading up to and including the day of the multilogue.

The chapter on hip-hop was the most difficult of the chapters for us to write. And we would not have managed to do so without the assistance of three folks who shared with us their intellectual take on this particular form of popular culture: Ethan Cole took on the role of teacher for his mom, Johnnetta, and "Auntie" Beverly as he made available to us an enormous amount of research on a style of music and a way of looking at the world that are more closely associated with his generation than with ours. Our colleague, Irma McClaurin, a professor of anthropology at the University of Florida at Gainesville, encouraged us to look through anthropological lenses to see more clearly the complexities of a cultural phenomenon that now circulates far beyond the young Black folks who first created it. And TaRessa Stovall brought insights to us about hip-hop that came from her own experience with the media *and* from conversations with her eleven-year-old son, Calvin, and nine-year-old daughter, Mariah, who represent the generation to whom we must pass on only the best that there is about hip-hop. And thanks as well, TaRessa, for the help you gave us as we worked feverishly to meet the final deadline for completing *Gender Talk*.

Our undergraduate research assistant from Emory University was Rama Mulukutla, who willingly and ever so efficiently met every challenge we put before her to find materials in the library or on the Internet.

Our graduate research assistant, Jennifer Lynn Freeman (now a doctoral student at Emory University in women's studies), was absolutely invaluable. Without the level of her commitment of time and intellect, our book would simply not have been written. She painstakingly transcribed all of the interviews and provided feedback on how we might make more effective use of what twenty-two insightful women and men shared with us. Jennifer also handled the logistical arrangements for the multilogue and, even more important, helped us analyze that rich body of material and understand its many meanings. During the many days and nights that we worked on *Gender Talk*, Jennifer offered valuable analysis and specific suggestions that always made the text better.

We are profoundly grateful to Marie Dutton Brown, our literary agent, for believing in us and in this project, and for leading us to an extraordinary editor, Elisabeth Kallick Dyssegaard, whose patience with us, dedication to our book project, and professional know-how in getting *Gender Talk* between two covers we applaud.

Finally, but ever so sincerely, we thank each other for the collegial and sisterly relationship out of which this book was conceived; and for the ever deepening friendship that brings joy to our personal and professional lives.

Johnnetta Betsch Cole
Beverly Guy-Sheftall

July 2002

PREFACE

•

What is most important to me must be spoken, made verbal and shared, even at the risk of having it bruised or misunderstood.

> Audre Lorde, "The Transformation of Silence into Language and Action," *Sister Outsider,* 1984

In all of their lives in America . . . Black women have felt torn between the loyalties that bind them to race on one hand, and sex on the other . . . yet they have almost always chosen race over the other: a sacrifice of their selfhood as women and of full humanity, in favor of the race.

> Nellie McKay, "Remembering Anita Hill and Clarence Thomas: What Really Happened When One Black Woman Spoke Out," 1992

This was a difficult book to write. In many ways it was the inevitable consequence of our long involvement in both Black Studies and Women's Studies, and an evolving friendship, though it was not until Johnnetta became a candidate for the presidency of Spelman College during the spring of 1987 that our lives became intertwined in ways that neither of us could have predicted. Beverly had been teaching at Spelman since 1971 and directing the Women's Research and Resource Center since 1981. During the first few years of Johnnetta's presidency, we cotaught Introduction to Women's Studies classes three times.

The idea for the book was born while we were coteaching; engaging in heated discussions outside the classroom about the state of the race; witnessing and debating a number of gender-related issues on and off campus—such as the founding of a new lesbian/bisexual student organization at Spelman, Anita Hill's visit to the campus in the aftermath of the Clarence Thomas Supreme Court hearings, and a highly publicized case in the fall of 1996 involving a Spelman student who alleged that she was raped by several Morehouse students; watching O. J. Simpson's trial for the alleged murder of his wife, Nicole Simpson, and her friend Ron Goldman; and sitting around girl-talking about trivial and serious issues in our personal and professional lives.

When Johnnetta left the Spelman presidency and assumed a professorship at Emory University in 1998, we thought there would be time, finally, to embark upon what we knew would be an ambitious and controversial book project. Put very simply, we wanted to reflect upon the knowledge we'd gained from our years of study and what we had experienced as African American women. We also wanted to explore intraracial gender matters with a broader audience and write a probing analysis of gender politics within African American communities, especially in the contemporary period.

Coauthoring this book would be a daunting task because we knew we would be entering territory, in some instances, far from our own professional expertise, such as hip-hop culture. We knew it would be challenging to see Black America from the vantage points of young people whose worlds were radically different from two middle-aged women who had grown up in the Jim Crow South during the forties and fifties. More unsettling was our awareness of the cultural taboos against airing "dirty racial linen" in public and the potential charge that we were race traitors and Black male bashers. Paula Giddings, who wrote the first feminist history of Black women, has written one of the most cogent analyses of the perils of engaging in frank public discourse about intraracial gender matters, particularly within a cultural milieu where African Americans are already judged harshly and haunted by damaging racial stereotypes.

In her insightful essay "The Last Taboo," she discusses the Clarence Thomas Supreme Court hearings and analyzes the impact of persistent silences within the Black community on issues relating to sexuality.[1]

Similarly, in her enlightening essay on "the sexual politics of Black womanhood," sociologist Patricia Hill Collins explains the imperatives of racial solidarity that dictate that Black women remain silent about certain intraracial issues but are free to speak publicly about others:

> White men's rape of Black women during slavery can be discussed whereas Black men's rape of Black women today cannot. . . . Rape, incest, misogyny in Black cultural practices, and other painful topics that might implicate Black men remain taboo.[2]

We also agonized over the nature of the "data" for this project since we wanted to include as many voices as we could. We knew we would be drawing upon our own experiences as feminist scholars who had spent all of our professional lives within higher education. Johnnetta started teaching when she was twenty-seven, and Beverly at age twenty-three. We have spoken at high schools, colleges, churches, women's groups, sororities, community organizations, and corporations. Our extensive travel throughout the United States under a variety of circumstances has exposed us to different audiences within Black communities. Our friendships and collegial relationships with various women and men, some progressive and others not so progressive, have also kept us informed about a range of gender attitudes and behaviors among African Americans.

In preparation for *Gender Talk* we have continued to read, much more intensely over the past five years, a broad range of scholarly and popular writing about violence within African American communities, hip-hop, Black masculinities, Black gays and lesbians, sexuality within the African diaspora, Black nationalism, and Black feminism. While carrying out this research, we were surprised by the sheer quantity and complexity of the material we would now characterize as Black gender discourse. Giving appropriate attention to this rich scholarship required a tremendous amount of time and reflection on our part. Throughout *Gender Talk* we felt it important to include these voices.

We have read familiar and influential texts with radically different positions, such as Eldridge Cleaver's *Soul on Ice*, Daniel Patrick Moynihan's *The Negro Family: The Case for National Action*— hereafter referred to as the Moynihan Report—and Dr. Frances Cress Welsing's *The Isis Papers: The Keys to the Colors*. We read autobiographies by young African Americans, including rappers, well-known public figures such as Elaine Brown, Shirley Chisholm, John Lewis, and Andrew Young, as well as writers such as Amiri Baraka (formerly LeRoi Jones), Samuel R. Delany, bell hooks, and June Jordan. We read biographies of civil rights activists such as Ella Baker, Fannie Lou Hamer, Ruby Doris Smith Robinson, and Bayard Rustin. We immersed ourselves in the voluminous and immensely popular self-help literature about Black male-female relationships and perused old copies of Nathan Hare and Julia Hare's short-lived journal *Black Male/Female Relationships* and their blatantly antifeminist polemic, *The Endangered Black Family: Coping with the Unisexualization and Coming Extinction of the Black Race*. We read all the books on the Clarence Thomas–Anita Hill saga, and the lengthy Mission Statement for The Million Man March/Day of Absence, which took place in the nation's capital on October 16, 1995. We read interviews with James Baldwin, bell hooks, Toni Morrison, Marlon Riggs, Ruth Simmons, and Alice Walker. We sifted through numerous articles in *Ebony* (including Martin Luther King, Jr.'s "Advice for Living" column and "For Brothers Only"), *Essence* (including "Brothers"), *Emerge*, *Today's Black Woman*, and hip-hop magazines such as *The Source*.

We listened with amazement to the gangsta rap lyrics of Tupac Shakur, Snoop Doggy Dogg, and Ice T, and sat like schoolchildren for an informative mini-lecture/demonstration about rap music at writer Pearl Cleage's home one summer afternoon. We read about Bishop T. D. Jakes's stunning performance at his "Women Thou Art Loosed!" conference before a screaming crowd of 52,000 women, almost all of whom were Black, at the Atlanta Dome on a hot summer night in July 2000, and we read his hugely popular books. We viewed videos, sometimes in anger, occasionally laughing uncontrollably, which included comedy routines by Chris Rock, "Fallen Champ: The Untold Story of Mike Tyson" and "Sister, I'm Sorry: An Apology to Our African American Queens." We previewed a documentary in progress, "NO!," about rape within Black communities, produced, written, and directed by a young independent filmmaker, Aisha Shahidah Simmons. We were puzzled by Toni Morrison's stance on domestic violence in her provocative introduction to her anthology on the O. J. Simpson saga and wished we could have interviewed her. We wept during our interview with Kimberly Tyler when she shared with us the most heart-wrenching and incredible narrative about spousal abuse that we had ever heard. We learned new things about ourselves when we interviewed each other about the impact of our mothers and close friends on our own development. We attended the Nineteenth Annual Awards Banquet of the National Association of Black and White Men Together in Philadelphia with writer Sonia Sanchez, their keynote speaker. We perused D. Anne Browne's new Web site, www.agoodblackman.com, which honors the contributions of Black men and works to overcome negative stereotypes about them.

We lingered over the precious material we gathered at a historic but poorly attended conference at Morehouse College in September of 1996, "Black, Male and Feminist/Womanist," sponsored by an unusual, now-defunct Morehouse student organization, Black Men for the Eradication of Sexism. These gender-progressive young Black students organized workshops on "Confronting Homophobia," "Parenting to Combat Sexism," and "Sexism in the Black Liberation Movement."[3] We attended a mandatory education session in Georgia at the DeKalb County Courthouse for men who had been arrested for domestic violence, facilitated by Sulaiman Nuriddin of Men Stopping Violence. More than ever before, we listened to the voices and observed the public behaviors of young African Americans whenever and wherever we could.

We also wanted to engage in our own "gender talk" and decided to conduct a series of interviews with Black women and men during the summer of 1999. Our criteria for selection of the twenty-three persons we interviewed were fairly precise. We wanted a range of persons with respect to gender, age, sexual orientation, professional status, class, regional identification, and political perspectives. We also wanted to include a substantial number of persons who had spent a significant amount of their professional energies engaged in reflection, writing, researching, teaching, and organizing around race/gender issues and/or whose life histories had something to teach us about gender issues. We were not interested in engaging in intense dialogue with persons for whom gender talk was uncomfortable or who had not thought about these issues very deeply. We didn't want to talk only with academics; we wanted an equal mix of women and men and we wanted to be sure to include some young folk. We also wanted class diversity, though most of the interviewees were professionals with college degrees. We wanted persons with close connections to the Black church because of its role in shaping gender attitudes within African American communities.

While most of the interviewees could be labeled gender progressive, they had a broad range of ideological perspectives with respect to issues such as Black nationalism, male-female relationships, and homosexuality. Some were high achievers and had grown up poor; they had lived in two-parent, single-parent, and polygamous (in one case) households, and were without children or were the parents of a gay son or a lesbian daughter. Several had experienced or witnessed family violence, sometimes both, or engaged in abusive behaviors themselves. They had satisfying marriages, counseled about-to-be married couples, were divorced, chose to remain single, or looked forward to not being single much longer. They were ministers, nationalists, feminists, gay, straight, Muslim, Christian, journalists, community organizers, freelance writers, and scholars. They had headed organizations as diverse as The Black Panther Party and the National Council of Negro Women, and ranged in age from twenty-seven to eighty-seven. They taught law students, worked in rape crisis centers, struggled with Black churches to end domestic violence, and edited both a popular Black women's magazine (*Essence*) and subsequently a major feminist magazine (*Ms.*).

In the Appendix, the name and professional affiliation are given for each of the individuals we interviewed. The methodology we used in conducting the twenty-three interviews is also found in the Appendix.

Near the end of our interviews, we decided that it would be instructive to expand our dialogue, hear more voices, and engage in group sessions that would help us clarify some of the issues that had surfaced during the interviews. We approached Alison Bernstein, vice president of the Ford Foundation, about our desire to facilitate a daylong "Multilogue on Gender Issues and African American Communities." We received a grant from the Ford Foundation that allowed us to invite two of our Emory University colleagues, Professor Frances Smith Foster, then director of the Institute for Women's Studies, and Professor Rudolph Byrd, then director of African American Studies, to join us in convening the multilogue at the Foundation on November 19, 1999.

All of the eighteen African American women and men who participated in the daylong conference have spent their professional lives working, in some capacity, on gender issues; and they represented a range of professional backgrounds in the academy, and in the private and not-for-profit sectors. All of the participants in the multilogue freely brought their diverse experiences to our rich and enlightening discussion about gender in African American communities. Each participant's name and professional affiliation appear in the Appendix.

The morning and afternoon sessions were organized around responses to four questions that we posed to the participants.

1. What, in your opinion, are the most urgent gender issues within African American communities at the present time?
2. Could you help us understand gender dynamics among our youth, including, but not limited to, hip-hop culture?
3. A number of identity markers, particularly gender, race, sexual orientation, and class, are important in understanding U.S. culture. How do you respond to and organize your life around these constructs?
4. What shifts/transformations have you undergone as an adult in your own thinking and behavior around gender?

The lively and highly insightful responses of the participants to these four questions have significantly informed our thinking about gender matters in Black communities. While the voices of the women and men we interviewed and those who participated in the multilogue are heard primarily in Chapter 2, "Having Their Say: Conversations with Sisters and Brothers," we actually hear from them throughout *Gender Talk*. We also hear from many of them through their own writings about gender, which are also included here.

In our attempt to avoid the isolation that frequently accompanies the writing of a book, we made the decision to engage in a methodology that is more public and interactive. We participated in two well-attended forums about *Gender Talk* at Emory University: one in October 1999 at the beginning of the project, and a second one in December 1999 following the multilogue at the Ford Foundation. At both of these gatherings we described the project, made formal presentations, and then engaged the audience in dialogue.

We have been ever mindful of the complexity of this project. Rather than avoiding the controversial and participating in the perpetuation of silences around these complicated matters—what writer Jill Nelson calls "race secrets," which inspired one of the book's chapter headings—we've explored a number of highly contentious intracommunity issues. When *Gender Talk* was nearly done, we reluctantly made the decision to speak about painful aspects of our own personal lives that were intimately connected with the book's themes. Each of us speaks about one of our own gender-related traumas because to remain silent would have compromised the very integrity of this project. We also hope that by telling some of the details of our own stories as two public, professional Black women who identify ourselves as feminists, several myths will be exploded.

Finally, this book is not a comprehensive analysis of contemporary Black sexual politics. It probes a carefully selected number of gender-specific issues involving African Americans over the past several decades. Our decision to engage in dialogue with others during the process was perhaps the wisest choice we made. We also thought it would be instructive to begin with our own lives since our understanding of the importance of gender politics within African American communities has been profoundly shaped by our own social and professional locations. At the end, we provide a vision of what community transformation might look like if gender were more central to analytic frameworks. We also suggest specific strategies for the creation of progressive Black communities as committed to the eradication of gender inequality and heterosexism as we've been to struggles against racism and poverty.

Johnnetta Betsch Cole and Beverly Guy-Sheftall
July 2002
Atlanta, Georgia

INTRODUCTION

•

We have a collective obsession with fronting and posturing for white people, not airing dirty laundry, which frequently comes down to not facing or dealing with reality. . . . Black people are big on keeping race secrets. . . . This keeping of secrets operates in every area of our lives. . . . It's time we started talking.

Jill Nelson, *Straight, No Chaser,* 1997

Afro-American gender relations have always been in crisis. This crisis is the major internal source of the wider problems of Afro-Americans. Even more tragically, this internal wound is the main means by which the externally originating problems are magnified and transmitted.

Orlando Patterson, *Rituals of Blood,* 1998

Ask most African Americans about the state of our race, and the responses, over and over again, are likely to call attention to the impact of racism, and perhaps poverty, as explanations for our contemporary situation. During informal talk at parties and around dinner tables; in beauty parlors, barbershops, and at church suppers; in magazines for African American markets; in scholarly and popular books written by Black authors, the point is repeated that *race* still matters. Cornel West's enormously successful *Race Matters* (1993) was the first in a long line of books by Black scholars, writers, and journalists to interrogate contemporary race issues from a variety of ideological perspectives. As the mainstream Black community ponders our most urgent problems at the beginning of this new century, it is likely to name the deterioration of the Black family or the increase in the Black male prison population, both of which it links to the persistence of racism.

Rarely, except among a small group of feminists and other gender-progressives, is there serious consideration of the importance of moving beyond a race-only analysis in understanding the complexities of African American communities and the challenges we face.[1] While we are certain that institutionalized racism and the persistence of economic injustices are responsible for our contemporary plight as second-class citizens, we boldly assert that *gender* matters too. When we use the term *gender* we are referring not solely to women or sexism, but also to the experiences of men, cultural definitions of womanhood and manhood, and the interconnections between race, gender, sexual orientation, age, class, and other oppressions.

Gender Talk makes the case that an understanding of sexual politics (a term popularized by the women's movement)—how patriarchy is manifested within African American communities, and how we define appropriate roles for Black women and men—helps illuminate the status of Black America in the twenty-first century. We will articulate how gender dynamics are embedded in the very structure of Black society, and explain the complex manifestations and consequences of sexism within African American communities. We have been helped in this challenging task by a range of cross-generational Black women and men who have had insightful things to say about gender matters. Their voices are here, along with ours, as we've struggled to make sense of a subject about which there continues to be tremendous confusion and controversy.

There is perhaps no intracommunity topic about which there has been more contentious debate than the issue of gender relations in Black America. We also believe that the proverbial "battle between the sexes" has caused deep ruptures in the cohesiveness of African American communities that have not gone unnoticed. In the aftermath of the popularity of Ntozake Shange's 1975 award-winning play *for colored girls who have considered suicide/when the rainbow is enuf*, and the release of Michele Wallace's controversial book *Black Macho and the Myth of the Superwoman* three years later, *Newsweek* published a stunning article, "A New Black Struggle" (August 17, 1979). Its authors, Diane Weathers, Diane Camper, Vern E. Smith, Brenda Russell, and Sylvester Monroe, analyzed the fallout within the African American community of Shange's and Wallace's "airing of the race's dirty linen" and the palpable crisis in Black male-female relationships that these feminist writings uncovered. Nearly a decade earlier Toni Cade asserted in her groundbreaking anthology, *The Black Woman* (1970), that "it doesn't take any particular expertise to observe that one of the most characteristic features of our community is the antagonism between our men and women."[2]

In 1971, Calvin Hernton, author of the well-known *Sex and Racism in America* (1965), unleashed a scathing, blatantly sexist analysis of the impact of "sexual racism" on interpersonal relations between Black women and men in the United States in the provocatively entitled *Coming Together: Black Power, White Hatred, and Sexual Hang-Ups* (1971). Here he blamed the devastating sexual alienation and conflict between Black men and women on the tortured history of U.S. race relations and complicated relationships between white men and Black women during slavery. He accused enslaved Black women of castrating Black men, of being complicit with white men in destroying "the black man as a Man," and of internalizing negative white attitudes toward Black men. "She . . . came to believe that her man was a rapist of white women, and she acted out, all at once, emotions of hatred and jealousy and repulsion toward black men."[3] He even goes so far as to assert, within the context of his discussion of slavery, one of the most shocking Black woman-blaming statements we have ever read: "No man can really rape a woman; the woman has to submit at some point. Black women have *let* white men have intercourse with them. All a rapist can do is kill a woman—did not the black woman have the guts to die?" (50). Though Hernton holds whites (including the mass media) primarily accountable for this persistent "love and hate among Black men and women," he also sounds the alarm for a deepening crisis in Black gender relations.[4] Later in his career, Hernton underwent profound shifts in his thinking about gender matters and asserts that white racism isn't the only culprit. This evolution is most apparent in *The Sexual Mountain and Black Women Writers: Adventures in Sex, Literature, and Real Life* (1987), in which he discusses the centuries-long oppression of Black women, and Black men's culpability in this process:

> In the name of white supremacy, every imaginable act of human atrocity was perpetrated against blacks. Now, in an all-black situation, we witness a chillingly similar type of oppression, we see sundry acts of inhumanity leveled against black females ... the centuries of slavery and racism, and the struggle to overcome them, have not informed the humanity of black men when it comes to black women ... the oppressive experiences of black men have not deterred them from being oppressors themselves.[5]

In 1996, Elsie Washington adds her voice to the chorus in *Uncivil War: The Struggle Between Black Men and Women*. Here, she announces unequivocally to Black audiences—"we are at war."[6] Unlike Hernton, however, she believes, as we do, that *internal* factors are very much responsible for our "self-inflicted battle wounds," despite the complicit behavior of the white media and its perpetuation of negative Black stereotypes. She harps upon a theme that is reiterated over and over again in the increasingly popular Black self-help literature. While there has always been tension between sexes of all races, for African Americans, "the discord has reached crisis proportions."[7] This sentiment is captured at a deep personal level in a 2001 *Ms.* article by Angela Ards, "Where Is the Love?" in which she reveals that she is haunted by the spectre of failed relationships with men. "If racism results in thwarted opportunities, then I've felt its reach most in my relationships with black men. ... the sense that my choices are fewer, chances dimmer, comes mainly because I am a black woman trying to love a black man."[8]

Three decades later, public discourse about a continuing crisis among African American men and women has not abated. In fact, there is every reason to believe that the situation has actually worsened. The majority of Black children (54 percent) now live in single-parent, largely female-headed households, as compared with one in four American children in the general population. Sixty-eight percent of African American children are born to unmarried mothers. These are also the families most likely to be living in poverty (49 percent). Only 40 percent of African Americans are married. It is important to remember that as late as 1960, "78 percent of all black families with children were headed by married couples" and that "the core of the traditional African American family system has been the nuclear family."[9] The decline in Black marriages, increases in women raising children alone, and higher divorce rates can be explained to some extent by increases in Black male joblessness and other economic factors, but this is only part of the story.[10] Blacks are less likely to marry than either whites or Hispanics, and two out of three Black marriages end in divorce.[11] There is a decrease in "marriageable" Black men due to an imbalanced sex ratio, unemployment, low wages, violent crime, homicide, drugs, incarceration (Blacks, mostly men, account for 47 percent of the prison population and 29 percent of those confined to mental hospitals), and early deaths. In fact, few scholars studying the dramatic changes that have taken place among American families more broadly over the past fifty years would disagree that "getting married and staying married may become relatively rare events among Black Americans if current trends in family organization, and in the economic marginalization of young Black men, continue."[12]

We hasten to add that white families (and those of other ethnic groups) are experiencing transformations as well, but not with the same devastating consequences as among African American families, because poverty and unemployment are less of an issue. To illustrate, when fathers are absent in Black families, more than half of the families are poor compared with less than one quarter in father-absent white families.[13] A decrease in nuclear families and out-of-wedlock births among the general population has resulted in contentious debates about the decline in traditional family values.

During the past decade nearly one third of all babies were born to unmarried women, and the prediction is that more than half of those born in the nineties, including two-parent homes, will spend some portion of their childhood in a single-parent home. We believe that in the case of Black America, analyses of social policies and other structural issues impacting single-parent African American families are imperative if we are to more fully understand the pervasiveness of unwed motherhood in our communities.

In the most disturbing scholarly treatment of Black family/gender relations to date or what he calls the internal gender environment, sociologist Orlando Patterson, using census and national survey data, makes the case in *Rituals of Blood: Consequences of Slavery in Two American Centuries* (1998) that our sexual relations are "fraught with distrust and conflict." The origins of the crisis, he argues, can only be understood by a penetrating examination of slavery and its consequences. In his lengthy chapter "Broken Bloodlines: Gender Relations and the Crisis of Marriages and Families Among Afro-Americans," he attempts to explain, among other dilemmas, the "unpartnered" state of African Americans: why nearly a third of Black women are dissatisfied with their sexual partners, and why "Afro-Americans are today the loneliest of all Americans."[14] *Rituals of Blood* is perhaps the most depressing scholarly analysis ever of contemporary Black male-female relationships. Patterson sees the state of Black families as equally dire—exacerbated by over 60 percent of Black children having been abandoned by their fathers; declining rates of marriages; and increased divorce rates.

When we interviewed sociologist Delores B. Aldridge, who has written about Black male-female relationships, she shared with us her vision of contemporary Black gender relations: "They're in chaos, and tears come to my eyes when I think about the deterioration we've experienced over the past several decades. There are communication problems and serious respect issues among our men and women. Economics is certainly an issue, which exacerbates our gender problems, as well as the way Black people, especially women, are portrayed in the popular media. I'm thinking in particular of rap music lyrics which construct us as bitches and sexual objects." Professor Aldridge is also convinced that the difficulties we face addressing these urgent matters are connected to our not wanting to "air our dirty linen in public," though she quickly asserts that people outside our communities are aware of what's going on despite our silences. "Folk *know!* We have no secrets."

In *Mad at Miles: A Blackwoman's Guide to Truth* (1989), Pearl Cleage lays bare the damaging evils of sexism and the crimes Black women suffer at the hands of Black men. Calling names and taking no prisoners, she sends a wake-up call to Black communities about stopping the violence. Her questions are haunting: How can they hit us and still be our heroes? How can they hit us and still be our leaders? Our husbands? Our lovers? Our geniuses? Our friends? And the answer is . . . they can't. *Can they?*[15]

Continuing a tradition of Black feminist writing that began in the 1830s with Maria Stewart's speeches, there is a significant body of contemporary scholarly and popular writing by African American women and men that has helped shape our own thinking about gender issues within Black communities. Some of these publications criticize the lack of gender-informed analyses of African American communities and attempt to advance a more complex, less unidimensional way of understanding our condition. This body of work is predictably smaller and less well known than the proliferation of writing in the popular press, and in what is a growing profusion of books (and writing on the World Wide Web) that oversimplifies the status of Black women versus Black men and blames all our problems on racism. The popular notion that Black men are an "endangered species" has given the impression that all is well with Black women. The metaphor of "the endangered Black male" calls attention to a number of demographic realities. For example, one in four Black males is in some way involved with the criminal justice system. There are more Black men of college age in the cells of America's jails and prisons than in the dormitories of our colleges and universities. Black male-on-male homicide is the leading cause of death among young Blacks between the ages of seventeen and twenty-six. This image of the endangered Black male unfortunately reinforces the notion that improving the status of Black men will single-handedly solve all the complex problems facing African American communities.

We assert the equal importance of improving the status of Black women and believe that without attention to gender matters, there can be no long-lasting solutions to many of our race problems. We are also concerned about the effects of outmoded and narrow definitions of masculinity on Black men's self-perceptions and their impact on relationships with African American women and children.

As a result of our involvement in both the civil rights and women's movements, we have been committed to the eradication of racism, sexism, class privilege, and heterosexism for most of our professional lives. We have been engaged in difficult dialogues with white feminists about the importance of understanding the particular experiences of women of color, and the need to take seriously the intersection of race, class, and gender in the lives of all women, not just women of color. We have argued that affirmative action, gun control, antiracism, and welfare reform are as important as legalized abortion, battered women's shelters, and laws against sexual harassment. We have also been engaged in difficult dialogues with Black men about their sexism, problematic conceptions of Black manhood, and their own gender privilege, even within a culture that continues to be deeply racist and demonizes them. Violence against Black people wears several faces. There's a much needed focus on police brutality and Black male-on-male homicide, but too little attention to rape, spousal abuse, and incest. We have often been in contentious debates as well with other Black women about the impact of gender oppression within our own communities, how we treat one another, and our hasty defense of Black men no matter how offensive their behavior. Many Black women have been convinced that there is a conspiracy by white America to destroy Black men, and as a result they remain silent about the physical and emotional abuse women suffer within our communities.

Judging from the positive reactions of Blacks to the influential work of sociologist E. Franklin Frazier, there appears to be a double standard regarding the airing of dirty racial linen in public. Black men may violate the cultural taboo; Black women may not. In Frazier's 1957 scathing critique of the "Black bourgeoisie"—who reportedly suffer from deep-seated inferiority and matriarchal households—he attributes the frustrations of the middle-class Black woman to "her unsatisfactory sexual life," because she may be married to a " 'glamorous' male who neglects her for other women."[16] Bourgeois Black women are "idle" and "overfed," so they become overweight and, like their male counterparts, are boring because they "read very little and have no interest in music, art or the theater" (223). Frazier even argues that Black women's insecurities relative to white women are justified since, in addition to having presumably beautiful, fair skin and straight hair, white women are "generally more sophisticated and interesting because she has read more widely and has a wider view of the world" (218–219).

The Black community's negative responses to airing dirty racial linen also appear to be more muted when the objects of the attack are Black women rather than Black men. A startling example of this phenomenon is the enormous popularity of Shahrazad Ali's slanderous and damaging book, *The Blackman's Guide to Understanding the Blackwoman* (1990) and its sequel, *The Blackwoman's Guide to Understanding the Blackman* (1992), both of which were self-published and are reputed to have sold over a million copies. Given the Black community's abhorrence of "airing dirty racial linen," we wonder why there was no attack on the white media that was responsible for much of the books' popularity and their brisk sales in our communities? Beverly recalls the numerous telephone calls she received from local and national television stations asking her to debate Ali—which she agreed to do, regrettably, on one occasion. With the exception of Haki Madhubuti's edited collection, *Confusion by Any Other Name* (1990) and Elsie Washington's *Uncivil War*, there was no serious critique in the 1990s of the Black woman–hating venom that was spewed throughout our communities as a result of Ali's book.

Despite Ali's criticism of many Western ideas, she embraces its most problematic gender notions. Her bold pronouncements about appropriate roles for Black men and women are totally consistent, for example, with Western patriarchal attitudes about male dominance and female submission. Though she castigates Black women for having adopted Western ideas about how to behave, Ali embraces uncritically the central ideas of Western patriarchy—men must rule, and women must limit themselves to their God-given roles as wives and mothers, and submit happily to the will, and even tyranny, of men. Since African American women already are more likely to be victims of gender-specific violence than other women in the United States, perhaps the most inexcusable, outrageous, and potentially harmful portions of Ali's narrative involve her encouraging Black men to put Black women in their places by "soundly slapping her in the mouth."[17] Though she indicates that it would be wrong to beat Black women to a "bloody pulp" or to "daily beat the hell" out of them, she indicates that a little bit of violence is justifiable "if she ignores the authority and superiority of the Black man." Ali's embrace of the most negative aspects of patriarchy are unmistakable when she reminds Black men that they will never be able to excel until they get their women under control and force them into submission. Similarly, she argues, the Black family will not survive until Black women are tamed, like animals. Attacks on the savagery of Black people in general, and in this case Black women, are perennial themes in the Western literary and intellectual tradition. Ali's voice joins a loud, more often male, chorus of Black woman-blaming.

Now is a particularly critical time for *Gender Talk* because of what we perceive to be an embattled Black, mostly male leadership, a deepening crisis in Black male-female relationships, an embrace of patriarchal family values, and a backlash against feminism and Black feminists. Rabid anti-Black feminist discourse initially surfaced most vehemently in the 1970s and 80s in response to the writings of Michele Wallace, Ntozake Shange, and Alice Walker, mainly because of their portrayal of Black men. Now the backlash is rampant in the popular press, including the Black media, rap music, films, sitcoms, talk shows, and self-help literature. A concrete intracommunity example involved the trashing in the broadly circulated, Harlem-based *Amsterdam News* (October 21, 1995) of Black feminist activist Angela Davis because of her public criticism of the Million Man March, which took place in Washington, D.C., October 16, 1995.[18] Accusing Davis of being "married to another woman," Abiola Sinclair, in the regular column "Media Watch," knew that whatever positive attitudes the Black community might have harbored toward this revered revolutionary figure would be compromised by this sly and obviously erroneous reference to her personal life (this would be impossible legally). Despite Davis's critically important work on behalf of Black communities, including imprisoned men and women, Dr. Lenora Fulani labels her "a political has-been who has meant nothing to the African American people for decades." As we travel to college campuses, we frequently hear among Black students, female and male, strong attacks against anything which they perceive to be feminist. This might include discussions about taking a Women's Studies course, challenges to homophobia, or simply the need for all-female gatherings.

There is a great deal of anger within Black communities about the so-called trashing of successful Black men or "Black male bashing." Accusations about the "demonization" of upwardly mobile Black men abound as a result of the high visibility of the Clarence Thomas–Anita Hill hearings; the FBI handling of former Mayor Marion Barry's alleged drug use; and the trials of O. J. Simpson, Mike Tyson, Congressman Gus Savage, and the Reverend Henry Lyons. Black feminists are often targeted for particular scorn because of their public pronouncements and writings about the problems of sexism within Black communities and the behavior of particular Black men. Beverly experienced hostility on a regular basis from Black women and men when she lectured on college campuses about what we might learn from the Clarence Thomas or O. J. Simpson sagas. On a particular university campus, she was challenged publicly by a male professor in the crowded interracial audience before she began to speak, presumably because of references to Thomas, Simpson, and the Million Man March in the brochure title. He asked, facetiously, if she had been a juror at O. J.'s trial or if she had attended the Million Man March, to which she responded, "no," since she had not been invited to the march and if she had been a juror the verdict might have been different. Beverly's response resulted in his leaving the lecture hall before her talk began. The story doesn't end here, however. Shortly after Beverly's return to the Spelman campus, President Johnnetta Cole received a letter dated November 5, 1995, from a Black female journalist criticizing Beverly for having indicated publicly that the professor's behavior was not a good role model for students. She then described the professor's considerable contributions to the Black community, his admirable behavior as a family man, and his commitment to the rights of Black women as full participating citizens in our community and the nation. Beverly had been very clear in her response to the professor's behavior that one listens to an argument in an academic context before dismissing it, so she did not feel she had unfairly judged his behavior or that she was making a generic statement about his character. The most revealing part of the letter was the journalist's assertion that "whatever differences that we have as Black brothers and sisters should and can be worked out behind closed doors, and not aired in public as though we need to be validated by whites or the white media." What this complaint underscores, yet again, is the anger Black women are likely to experience when we speak publicly, especially in mixed audiences, about problems within the community, especially if Black men are criticized. In fact, feminist viewpoints are frequently blamed for the problems that confront Black America rather than the behaviors that generate gender critiques.

Within this woman-blaming climate, there is a proliferation of books designed to cure what ails Black communities. Many of them focus on strengthening Black families and healing male-female relationships. They include rigidly prescriptive narratives to assist "good" Black women (meaning "not feminist") who are engaged in what is considered a righteous search for a decent Black man. An example is Denene Millner's *The Sistahs' Rules: Secrets for Meeting, Getting, and Keeping a Good Black Man* (1997). Popular magazines like *Ebony* frequently include articles such as Nicole Walker's "The Ten Biggest Mistakes Women Make in Relationships" (May 1998), which repeat old stereotypes about evil Black women and remind readers that "hell hath no fury like a Black woman scorned" (166). To illustrate: "Whatever you care to call it—dissin', putting in check, low-rating, fronting off, downing—all the names stand for the same thing, disrespect" (166).

There is also the tenacious myth of the emasculating Black woman, which Black sociologist E. Franklin Frazier popularized in the 1930s and which the popular radio and later television show *Amos 'n' Andy* made unforgettable in the character of Sapphire.[19] *Amos 'n' Andy*, the radio serial first known as *Sam 'n'*

Henry, premiered in 1926. Two white actors portrayed southern Black men who had migrated north to Chicago. This racist radio show had its roots in nineteenth-century minstrel shows and Black-face vaudeville acts. Two years later, after becoming a regional hit, the main characters were renamed Amos and Andy and, in 1929, *Amos 'n' Andy* joined NBC and eventually became the country's most popular radio show and something of a national obsession. Two characters were added: Kingfish, head of a fraternal order, and his wife, Sapphire.

In June 1951, *Amos 'n' Andy* premiered on television, and the broadcast was shown at the annual convention of the NAACP in Atlanta, Georgia. After the broadcast, the convention passed a unanimous resolution condemning the show for its derogatory stereotypes of Black people. Despite the controversy, however, the show remained enormously popular, both within and beyond the Black community, and won an Emmy nomination in 1952. CBS canceled *Amos 'n' Andy* after its second season, but it was syndicated to hundreds of local stations and remained a staple of television entertainment until the mid 60s. It was popular in Black homes largely because it was the only show on television featuring Black people. Johnnetta and Beverly recall watching the show with their families on a regular basis. In 1929, Ernestine Wade, a Black actress and musician, took on the part of Kingfish's wife. As a result of Wade's handling of the role, Sapphire would later become the most popular and the most stereotypical character in the series, the very embodiment of what's wrong with so-called matriarchal Black families. Kingfish's domineering wife reinforced many of the most prevalent stereotypes about Black women—overbearing, bossy, sharp-tongued, loud-mouthed, controlling and, of course, emasculating—which lingered in the national psyche, also among Blacks, long after the show left the air. Sapphire constantly scolded Kingfish, especially about his dishonesty, laziness, and unreliability—prevalent stereotypes about Black men. Their relationship conformed to the stereotype of the matriarchal Black family that influential Black scholar Frazier immortalized in his classic *The Negro Family in the United States* (1939). "Sapphire" would become, long after an association with the program had faded, an acceptable and unquestioned

term for so-called "ball-busting" Black women. Sapphire also became a pervasive image in the folk culture of African Americans
and one of the most damaging and tenacious stereotypes of Black
women, which still has currency in contemporary conceptions of
Black womanhood.

Though not as iconographic or influential as Sapphire, Kingfish
would become the stereotypical unreliable Black male, the bane of
Black women's existence and the alleged source of dysfunctional
Black families. In a June 1958 issue of *Ebony*, alias Daisy Disgusted, speaking for the generic Black woman, responds to the
query, "What's Wrong With Negro Men?" with the mildly tongue-
in-cheek response that included a litany of familiar accusations to
insiders: 1) They are egotistical; 2) They believe in male superiority;
3) They are demanding; 4) They are insincere; 5) They are uninhib-
ited; 6) They are philanderers; 7) They are weak (2–3). While she
does not intend to be a Black male basher by reminding readers that
"our men are probably no bigger liars or better philanderers than
other men," Daisy Disgusted does want them to understand the authenticity of her claims: "I am a colored woman concerned right
now with the faults of colored men." She also distances herself
from what she would call a feminist agenda and reaffirms her faith
in enlightened patriarchy: "We don't want to wear the pants or
carry the dinner bucket. There is not one of us who would not
gladly exchange her diploma for a marriage certificate, who prefers
pounding a typewriter in somebody's office to burping a baby in her
own home. We work because single or (and especially) married, we
too, must eat."

There is still no shortage in Black popular culture of blatant
calls for Black women to be subservient to the wishes and demands
of Black men. In the December 1999 issue of *Ebony*, in the "For
Brothers Only" column, Kevin Chappell teaches Black men how to
"tame the dragon in your lady." He begins by describing a pitiful
scene, reminiscent of Sapphire's perpetual treatment of her husband
Kingfish, in which a particular Black woman's eruption was "not of
the neck-rolling, finger-snapping, hand-on-the-hip variety," but
scornful and emasculating just the same, though she barely raised
her voice. Witnessing this closeted "fire-breathing dragon" reminds
him that "in this power struggle for control of relationships, Broth-

ers are losing ground at such a rate that, as a group, we are beginning to look as pitiful as the Brother at the mall" (40).

Ebony's propensity to include advice from Black men about gender relations is not new and has been consistent, in many cases, with mainstream attitudes about relationships between the sexes. In a surprising though revelatory "Advice for Living" column by the Reverend Dr. Martin Luther King, Jr. (which appeared in *Ebony* in the late fifties), there is the familiar woman-blaming refrain in some of his advice, and clearly sexist views about women's familial roles, particularly his assertion that "the primary obligation of the woman is that of motherhood." One wife complained about her churchgoing husband who became a complete tyrant when he came home and seemed to "hate me and the children, too." King's advice to her was to examine herself and to "analyze the whole situation and see if there is anything within your personality that arouses this tyrannical response from your husband." To be consistent, King also advised a complaining husband to examine himself to see if he was doing anything to cause his wife to demonstrate unwifely behavior. Some years later, in a more sustained argument, King reveals his traditional views about gender roles and his acceptance of stereotypes about the matriarchal Black family. In a speech delivered at Abbott House in Westchester County, New York, on October 29, 1965, five months after the release of Daniel Patrick Moynihan's controversial report, *The Negro Family: The Case for National Action,* King paints a familiar portrait of the devastating impact of slavery on Black families. "There were polygamous relationships, fragile, monogamous relationships, illegitimacies, abandonment, and most of all, the tearing apart of families as children, husbands, or wives were sold to other plantations . . . Masters and their sons used Negro women to satisfy their spontaneous lust or, when a more humane attitude prevailed, as concubines."[20] He goes on to assert that the most damaging legacies of slavery were fragile, deprived, and psychopathic families, and the development of a Black matriarchy reinforced in large part by Black women's greater access to jobs and their ability to support the household. "The Negro male existed in a larger society which was patriarchal while he was the subordinate in a matriarchy" (40).

What we desperately need are not more warnings about the dire state of Black gender relations and masculinist solutions that maintain the status quo. What we do need are sustained discussions within our communities about the creation of new and egalitarian models of relationships between the sexes. As we look toward the future, we need to conceptualize race loyalty differently. Audre Lorde reminds us of the problem of difference within African American communities, and the courage we need to address a range of intracommunity issues despite our history of racial oppression and a self-imposed conspiracy of silence about exposing "race secrets." She reminds us that "sexual hostility against Black women is practiced not only by the white racist society, but implemented within our Black communities as well. It is a disease striking the heart of black nationhood, and silence will not make it disappear."[21]

Gender Talk explores the necessity of seriously considering gender matters in our strategies for improving the race. And while our work focuses on African American communities, our analysis also underscores what ails us as a nation, still deeply committed to hierarchies based on race, ethnicity, gender, class, and sexual orientation. We believe that this "truth-telling" about issues within Black America will also unmask the ugliness and complexity of race, gender, and class matters in the broader body politic.

1

•

THE PERSONAL IS POLITICAL

You can't know where you're going if you don't know where you've been.

African proverb

Growing up in the fifties, I never thought much about the issue of gender; race was too overwhelming.

Leith Mullings, *On Our Own Terms: Race, Class, and Gender in the Lives of African American Women,* 1997

We are actively committed to struggling against racial, sexual, heterosexual, and class oppression, and see as our particular task the development of integrated analysis and practice based upon the fact that the major systems of oppression are interlocking.

Combahee River Collective, 1983

When we finally met in 1987 at Hunter College in New York City, it seemed like a long overdue meeting. We knew a great deal about each other and had read each other's work. We also knew that we viewed gender differently from many African American men and women who ignored, trivialized, or denied its significance. The question we pose here is *why*? In particular, we wanted to explore those factors in our own lives that significantly influenced our gender attitudes. How did we come to the conclusion that in order to understand Black America we must confront how deeply race matters—but also how gender matters—and how both race and gender intersect in the lives of women and men, girls and boys?

In this autobiographical chapter we describe pivotal moments in our own personal histories, which shaped our perspectives on gender and led us to call ourselves Black feminists and to work in the women's movement. We believe that our own stories, like the stories of the men and women whose lives we share in Chapter 2, "Having Their Say: Conversations with Brothers and Sisters," can help illuminate some of the themes that emerge in subsequent chapters. Over the course of our evolving friendship, we began to realize how similar many of our experiences had been, though there were also many differences; Johnnetta's coming of age in the fifties and Beverly's coming of age in the sixties was a major factor in this regard. But our respective journeys to feminism had begun in similar places. We begin, therefore, with our family backgrounds and the influence of our mothers in particular. We probe how we came to have certain views on religion, sexuality, homophobia, and interpersonal relationships, especially marriage and friendships. We articulate the circumstances under which we came to ally ourselves with African American Studies and Women's Studies and the nature of our activism around race and gender issues. And we give voice to painful personal experiences that connect us to what countless women—including Black women—have endured because of the reign of patriarchy in American society and throughout the world. Examining certain aspects of our lives underscored for us once again how the personal is indeed political.

We begin this chapter with a reminder of what U.S. women's struggles over the past forty years have been about, despite the ways in which they've been trivialized:

> They started women's shelters; they changed how the police interview rape survivors. They deeply reformed birthing

and other health practices. They demanded control of their bodies in all kinds of different situations—in sex, in reproduction, on the street, and at work. They put preschool child care on the national agenda. They criticized images everywhere . . . They were interested in making divorce no-fault and marriage rather better . . . They fought for the participation of women and girls in sports. They struggled for expansion of female opportunities in the workforce. They proposed equal pay for jobs of comparable worth. . . . They recovered the biographies, issues, and works of under-appreciated women once active in history and culture. They worked for family leave for birth and adoption.[1]

The women's movement also created a climate in which women, perhaps for the first time in large numbers, could choose whether they would marry or become mothers. Certainly we have both witnessed and experienced the positive transformations brought about by the women's movement. We are also aware of how few African American women's voices there are in the voluminous literature on the history and impact of the women's movement. This erasure of Black women in popular and scholarly histories, television documentaries, and magazine articles in retrospectives about the "second-wave" women's liberation movement perpetuates the myth that we were absent from the development of contemporary feminism rather than being critical to its formulations.[2] Three African American women—Shirley Chisholm, Pauli Murray, attorney and member of President Kennedy's Commission on the Status of Women, 1961–1963, and Aileen Hernandez, union organizer and second president of the National Organization of Women (NOW)—were involved with twenty-six other women in the creation of the mostly white feminist organization NOW in 1966.

Black feminists were especially insightful about the connections between race and gender and how differences between women made it difficult for them to bond on the basis of their common womanhood. Even more scarce are the voices of Native American, Chicana/Latina, Asian American and Arab American women in these narratives. Ignoring or devaluing the unique and often oppositional perspectives of women of color during the Movement, it is not surprising that mainstream feminists would "white-out," marginalize, or even forget these contributions in reconstructions of "their" Movement some years later. Despite these silences, however, the promise of feminism—that women can live better lives with a wider range of choices and resources—is in fact a reality four decades after the beginning of the "second wave" of the women's movement. It has enabled women and girls, even those victimized by poverty and racism, to inhabit a world different from the worlds of our grandmothers and great-grandmothers. This is not to suggest, however, that profound differences do not continue to be a reality among women with respect to our experiences, choices, resources, and life chances.

Our decision to discuss very personal aspects of our respective lives is very much a reflection of a proposition that is closely associated with the "second wave" of the women's movement—"the personal is political." In the late 1960s and early 1970s small groups of radical women involved in the development of feminist organizations gathered together in meetings and shared their personal stories of being female and oppressed. In these "consciousness-raising" sessions, described as the movement's most effective organizing tool, the details of one's particular story were echoed in the story of another woman, and another, and another.[3] While this term has been attributed to feminist activist Kathie Sarachild, a member of New York Radical Women, she acknowledges that she learned the practice of "telling it like it is" during her involvement with the Student Nonviolent Coordinating Committee (SNCC) in the civil rights movement in Mississippi.[4] What became clear fairly soon in analyses of male supremacy was that what an individual woman had assumed was peculiar to her was in reality a rather common experience in the lives of women. What was assumed to be personal was in fact generalizable, and could therefore be acted upon in an organized and collective way. In short, the personal was seen to be political.

These consciousness-raising sessions were intended to foster sisterhood among women who named their common enemies and bonded on the basis of their common oppressions. Women's movement scholars have tended to assume that these sessions took place

primarily among middle-class white women who did not work outside their homes, and therefore had the luxury of sitting around
talking and drinking coffee after they had taken their children to
school. This image of privileged, unemployed white women—the
stereotypical vanguard of the newly emerging women's liberation
movement—needs to be challenged, however, because both middle-
and working-class Black women also gathered around kitchen tables and elsewhere and discovered commonalities with women
both different from and like themselves. Less economically privileged Black women also made similar discoveries about their collective plight during coffee breaks at their factory jobs, sitting in
Laundromats waiting for their families' clothes to dry, and in
church basements as they fried chicken and made potato salad
for the annual church picnic. It is also important to note that
consciousness-raising was an important strategy of Black feminist
organizations, including the little known National Black Feminist
Organization (NBFO) which began in May 1973 when about thirty
Black women gathered in New York for a day-long meeting to
discuss their experiences. Six months later they convened the first
national conference of Black feminists in New York City; the organization was interested in exposing media stereotypes and the
sexual abuse and rape of Black women, and securing the minimum
wage for domestic workers, as well as underscoring the need of the
Black and women's communities to address both racism and sexism
simultaneously.[5] Among its five hundred attendees were Shirley
Chisholm, Eleanor Holmes Norton, Flo Kennedy, Barbara Smith,
Alice Walker, Michele Wallace, and Margaret Sloan, its first and
only president.

An acknowledgment that the personal is political was a dramatic departure from what most men and many women had been
thinking or saying. For most men, especially middle-class white
men, the world was neatly dichotomized into the private (women's
spheres) and the public (men's spheres). The personal (women's domain) and the political (the public arena of power and action) were
disconnected. For many women, there was an outward accommodation to this bifurcated view of the world, although many of their
experiences suggested something very different.

Each of us also participated in "consciousness-raising" sessions and came to see multiple ways in which we were connected to other women. In 1968, when Beverly was a graduate student at Atlanta University studying literature, she was one of a small group of young Black women who met on Sunday afternoons at Sandra Flowers's small apartment in a working-class neighborhood near the campus. Beverly came to realize much later that these were consciousness-raising sessions. In the late 1960s and early 70s, Johnnetta was involved in periodic gatherings with women in the university town of Pullman, Washington, where common and different experiences with gender matters were discussed and debated.

Though our lives took divergent paths and ten years separate us in age, each of us grew up largely in the separate world of Black people in the Deep South. Johnnetta was born in 1936 in Jacksonville, Florida, and Beverly was born in 1946 in Memphis, Tennessee. We each grew up with two siblings (Beverly is the oldest of three daughters, and Johnnetta has an older sister and a younger brother); in two-parent households (until Beverly was eleven and her parents separated, and Johnnetta was fifteen and her father died); in middle- and upper-middle-class extended families. After Beverly's parents separated, her mother moved with her three daughters around the corner to her parents' home. Beverly's grandfather was a Baptist minister and her grandmother a stay-at-home mother. Johnnetta did not live with her grandparents, but her grandfather and his second wife were very much a part of her early life; and into her young adulthood, her grandfather was a central figure in her life. This was also the case with her great-grandfather until he died when Johnnetta was eleven years old.

In the South of the 1940s and 50s, every aspect of our public lives was defined by the socially constructed notion of "race." Being Black determined where one sat on a bus or at the movies, from which water fountain one drank, on which day one went to the zoo or circus, in which cemetery one was buried, where one attended school, worshiped, or played. Class could soften some of the persistent inequities and painful humiliations that African Americans endured in the apartheid South before the civil rights movement, but no amount of money would enable Black people to fully escape the indignities of Jim Crow. Although Johnnetta's maternal great-grandfather was Abraham Lincoln Lewis, Jacksonville's first Black millionaire, he was unable to shield his family from racism. His material wealth and prestige and the resources of her middle-class nuclear family spared Johnnetta some of the most egregious consequences of being Black in Jacksonville—she could travel by car and avoid the back of the bus—but there was no way around attending "colored" schools and no way to gain entrance to "for whites only" concerts, art galleries, and theaters. To be sure, each of us at an early age was conscious of the racially stratified society in which we were living and we barely noticed the highly gendered rules of the Jim Crow South. Later, when Beverly arrived at Spelman College in Atlanta, Georgia, in 1962, she did notice how different the rules governing the lives of women students were from the rules for the male students at Morehouse. Spelman women were subjected to rigid curfews and dress codes that were absent at their nearby brother institution, Morehouse College.

Both of us were fortunate to have grown up in homes where not only notions of white racial superiority were challenged, but many widely held notions about male superiority were as well. Perhaps the most important similarity in our upbringing was that we were raised in relatively gender-progressive homes, which may not have been the norm within southern Black families, despite the myth of the matriarchal Black household. In recent published interviews with feminist writer bell hooks and with Ruth Simmons, president of Brown University, both of these southern women describe growing up in male-dominant households. bell hooks describes a household in which her father's word was absolute law and where she grew up "seeing male power as something for which no reason or argument had to be given. It was simply the power vested in the father by virtue of his maleness," which she would come to resist.[6] Ruth Simmons's description of her patriarchal household captures the "gender divide" that bell hooks asserts characterizes many southern Black families like her own:

> I grew up in a family completely dominated by males. There were seven brothers and, of course, my father, who was a typical Southern parent in most respects, though not all. He

was dictatorial, although I say that lovingly because it was thought proper for the head of the household to be that way. My mother served him, as one would have in the old days. We all paid homage to him in this very typical African American Southern household in that time. Girls were expected to be of service to men. They were not expected to have independent lives. It was not proper to harbor goals independent of what our husbands wanted or independent of what the men of the family dictated. All the emphasis was placed on the boys, on what they did and what they could achieve. Girls were expected to get married and raise a family, but little more than that. The expectation was that we would preserve our place in the social order and support our men.[7]

Like hooks, Simmons, following the lead of her older sister, resisted familial and societal admonitions to be subordinate to men and instead "developed strong independent streaks."

Both Beverly and Johnnetta benefitted from their families having relatively egalitarian gender attitudes. When Beverly was in the eighth grade, her mother left her father and, with her three daughters, moved in around the corner with her parents. When Johnnetta was fifteen, her father died. Neither of our mothers remarried. During those formative years, fathers whom we would now describe as liberal on gender matters raised us. Beverly's father was noncontrolling and unobtrusive. He never spanked his daughters and felt that no male, including a father, should ever strike a female, including his own daughters. Beverly remembers that her father never raised his voice at home. Johnnetta's father would sometimes braid her and her sister's hair and would take them shopping for clothes. Neither father exercised a "command and control" presence in the household. They were neither physically nor verbally aggressive.

Neither of our parents communicated to us rigid definitions of gender roles. Neither of our mothers liked or did much cooking, and housework was defined as necessary for sanitary purposes but not as the fulfillment of one's creativity and value as a woman. Each of our mothers worked at jobs outside the homes from which they derived a great deal of satisfaction. Beverly's mother was a public school math teacher but later decided to spend the rest of her professional career as an accountant in the business office of two Black colleges in Memphis. Johnnetta's mother began her professional career as a professor of English and the registrar at Edward Waters College, a small historically Black college in Jacksonville, Florida. She later worked in the family's insurance business, the Afro-American Life Insurance Company, and eventually served as its vice president and treasurer.

We were aware of class differences within Black communities. Although no woman in either of our families worked as a domestic, we each recall seeing lines of Black women waiting at bus stops to go off to work in the homes of white people; and we remember hearing that many Black women who worked for whites were subjected to sexual harassment by the men in those households and suffered inhumane treatment by the women. Each of our mothers explicitly taught us that we must respect all Black women and be sensitive to their different economic circumstances. They demonstrated such sensitivity by insisting that as children we address all Black women by their last name, rather than by a first name only, which was the norm among southern white children. Mrs. Hines was the housekeeper in Beverly's maternal grandfather's home. She and her sisters were instructed over and over again by their mother that Mrs. Hines was not their servant, and that she was not to be treated as such by the three young girls who happened to be living with their grandparents because their mother could not afford to live comfortably elsewhere. Johnnetta's maternal grand-aunt—affectionately but respectfully called Na-Na—was the caretaker, housekeeper, and cook during much of Johnnetta's childhood. Few if any rules were laid out by Johnnetta's mother that were as rigid as the importance of respecting Na-Na. In those stern lessons about respect were obvious messages about a notion of sisterhood, that is, a sense of solidarity across class and age. We believe that our mothers were also expressing some degree of feminist consciousness as they taught us the importance of respect and dignity for all women, including those who did domestic work.

Our mothers conveyed other feminist messages to us as well,

not only through their clear rules but also by their behaviors. When Beverly was in the ninth grade, her mother petitioned the Memphis public schools to waive their home economics requirement for female students and demanded that Beverly be allowed to take typing, which was reserved for juniors and seniors. This act of "feminist" defiance on her part sent several clear messages to Beverly early on: that learning to be a homemaker was relatively unimportant; that the skills of a typist would be more useful to a serious, college-bound student; and that one could resist white and patriarchal authority. In a 1998 Salon.com interview, Toni Morrison recalled the tough, aggressive Black women with whom she grew up and the transgressive behavior of her mother in particular.

> My mother would walk down to a theater in that little town that had just opened, to make sure that they were not segregating the population—black on this side, white on that. And as soon as it opened up, she would go in there first, and see where the usher put her, and look around and complain to someone. That was just daily activity for her, and the men as well. So it never occurred to me that she should withdraw from that kind of confrontation with the world at large. And the fact that she was a woman wouldn't deter her. . . . Later, it was called "feminist" behavior.[8]

When Beverly read Toni Cade Bambara's tribute to her mother on the acknowledgments page of *The Salt Eaters* (1980), she thought about her own influential mother who would excuse Beverly from housework if she were reading or doing school work: ". . . dedicated to my first friend, teacher, map maker, landscape aide Mama Helen Brent Henderson Cade Brehon who in 1948, having come upon me daydreaming in the middle of the kitchen floor, mopped around me."[9] Mary Frances Lewis Betsch and Ernestine Varnado Guy were vehement about the need for their girl children to be educated, economically independent, and self-reliant. They insisted that a woman must never be dependent on men, even if she is married. Our mothers valued education deeply and took enormous pride in saying that their grown-up daughters had doctoral degrees. Johnnetta's mother firmly defended her decision to study anthropology, a field in which very few Black women were involved. When at the conclusion of two years of field work in Liberia, West Africa, Johnnetta delivered her first son under challenging circumstances, her mother traveled to Liberia to be a part of that special event. And for many years afterward, she delighted in telling the story of how her daughter, the anthropologist, delivered her first grandson. Johnnetta's mother also often gave advice on how Johnnetta could continue to advance her career while married and the mother of three sons. She believed that giving up her career was not an option for her daughter.

Beverly's mother prompted Beverly (whose husband was also in a doctoral program) to pursue a Ph.D. while she was teaching at Spelman, and reminded her that her husband's attainment of a doctorate should not preclude her getting one as well. Although she could not understand Beverly's decision to not have children, she was clearly proud of her daughter's academic accomplishments over the years, which was apparent in her assertion that her daughter "prefers to produce books." Beverly recalls her mother's joy during a few poignant moments while she was visiting her for the last time in the hospital. Though she was losing her battle with breast cancer and would not survive another week, she wanted Beverly to tell her all about her latest book, a centennial history of Spelman College that was hot off the press.

We each grew up with loud and unequivocal messages from our mothers that women in general, and we in particular, were equal to men. We were told that we were smart and could have control over our lives, despite our race and gender, if we made wise choices. Beverly's mother shared with her how she carefully spaced her three children so that they would be born two years apart and delivered before the hot summer months of Memphis. Her plan was that they would all have May birthdays. Almost on schedule, Beverly and Francine came the first week in June, and Carmella came the last week in April. Beverly's nosy intrusion into her mother's top left dresser drawer revealed a diaphragm, which helped to explain her mother's ability to control the circumstances under which she would become pregnant.

Feminist was certainly not a word that either of our mothers ever used to define themselves, but on one cutting-edge feminist issue—reproductive rights—they were clear. Both Mary Betsch and Ernestine Guy believed that one of the most unfortunate burdens to befall a woman was an unwanted pregnancy, especially in their teens. And while each was deeply Christian and probably would have felt uncomfortable with a public, generalized pro-abortion posture, they instructed us as teenagers, in no uncertain terms, that should we ever become pregnant we were to come to them before it was too late so that they could "take care of things." This instruction took place before women had a right to legal abortions. Beverly's mother also shared with her, unashamedly, that one of her best married friends had had several abortions, and that a neighbor who lived only a few doors down from them was skilled at performing abortions, which were, of course, illegal at that time.

Our experiences with marriage, mothering and "othermothering," and divorce have been shaped by and in turn have helped to shape our experiences with race and gender in America. We again note how many similarities there are in these personal aspects of our lives. Marriage as an institution is frequently problematic for feminists, including some of us who are African Americans. For it is so often a site where patriarchy is generated and expressed. Neither of us had arrived at a fully developed feminist identity when we first married; however, looking back on our lives from where we are now, it seems that our choices of husbands, how our domestic arrangements were lived out, and how and why our respective marriages were dissolved reflect our own feminist values even if we were not altogether aware of them.

The commonalities in Johnnetta's first marriage and Beverly's only marriage are striking. Just as we had gone to college at an early age (Johnnetta was fifteen and Beverly was sixteen), we also married at a fairly early age (Johnnetta at twenty-two, Beverly at twenty-three); and both of us married men we met while we were graduate students. The men we married were both economists. Because they acknowledged that their wives were smart women, there was constant engagement around intellectual issues. The politics of each of our former husbands could best be described as progressive or liberal; however, Johnnetta's first husband was also very much an activist. While neither of our households operated on the basis of an equal division of the domestic chores between husbands and wives, in each case, the men did participate in domestic duties far more than was usual for men to do in the 1960s and 70s.

There are also important differences between Johnnetta's first and Beverly's only marriage. Johnnetta and her husband had three sons, whereas Beverly and her husband agreed from the beginning of their marriage that they would not have children. Beverly's marriage was dissolved after eleven years, and Johnnetta's first marriage lasted twenty-two years. Beverly married a man with whom she shared being African American and Southern. Johnnetta and her husband, a white man from the Midwest, shared neither "race" nor geographical origin.

Beverly's marriage was definitively nontraditional, and in sharp contrast to the household in which her husband grew up, where his mother carried out the roles of wife and mother in highly traditional ways. From the beginning of their courtship, while they were both pursuing master's degrees at Atlanta University, they voiced a shared view that marriage is a flawed institution, and should therefore be embraced with caution. As early as when he was twelve years old, Beverly's husband concluded that he did not want to be responsible for bringing any children into the world, and Beverly was indifferent to biological motherhood. She was also among that first generation of women who had been impacted by messages from the women's movement that proclaimed the joys of voluntary motherhood. She was comfortable with bypassing the trap of societally imposed motherhood and felt free to remain childless. She also recalls never liking to play with dolls or baby-sitting, which she did throughout high school for her mother's married friends. In retrospect, she realizes how fortunate she was to have married a man whose notions of masculinity were not tied to his ability to father children.

The conclusion that Beverly reached from their joint decision not to have children was perhaps unexpected for her husband. She reasoned that since they were not going to have children, they didn't need to do a number of other things that are traditionally associated with American families. For example, Beverly rarely cooked and didn't establish regular routines for household work. In the first two years of the marriage, they ate their big meal during lunch in the faculty dining room at Alabama State University, where they both were professors. Then Beverly and her husband ate a light, easy to prepare supper later at home. An important aspect of the marriage was that Beverly was able to pursue her professional interests free from most of the demands of wifehood and motherhood. She entered a doctoral program, traveled around the world, and published her first book, with no husbandly pressure to assume traditional gender roles.

Although Beverly does not have a simple explanation for why she and her husband divorced, it became increasingly clear that they were growing apart despite their similarities and the strength of their friendship. Having different needs and expectations from the marriage was certainly relevant. Beverly's unconventional notions of wifehood also might have been a factor. For her husband, the marriage was no longer fulfilling, and the close friendship and intellectual bond that they had developed over the years were simply not enough. Notwithstanding the complex set of reasons for dissolving their marriage, they carried out the decision in a remarkably amicable manner and have remained friends for the past twenty years. Over the years Beverly has concluded that she's better suited for friendship within the context of a relationship than wifehood.

Johnnetta's first marriage was also nontraditional in that it was interracial. Neither Johnnetta's mother nor her husband's parents were initially happy about this union, although over time they came to be supportive of their respective children's spouses and they clearly loved their grandchildren. The marriage was also atypical in the sense that shortly after it began, Johnnetta and her husband went off to Liberia, West Africa, to engage in two years of research that would form the basis of their doctoral dissertations. Living as a married couple in a West African country put Johnnetta and her first husband in an interesting situation of role reversal—for, as a white man, for the first time in his life he was in the minority, and Johnnetta, as a Black woman, was for the first time in her life in the majority.

The three sons that Johnnetta and her first husband brought into the world are four years apart, a conscious decision of planned births (reminiscent of Beverly's mother's planning) to avoid two children in college at the same time. Johnnetta's first husband was very much involved with the raising of their sons; and much of the time that he spent with his sons revolved around the kinds of things that American men and boys tend to do together, such as sports and camping trips. He also made it clear through his own actions and what he said to their sons that Johnnetta was not to be treated as the maid, and they were to actively participate in household chores and the care of the yard. The three sons also witnessed their parents' collaboration not only in terms of sharing an interest in African and African American Studies, but in participating in social justice causes that revolved around the civil rights and Black Power movements and the movement against the war in Vietnam.

For Johnnetta, the decision to end a twenty-two-year marriage was certainly precipitated by the discovery of her husband's infidelity. Anthropologist Mary Catherine Bateson has written very insightfully on the possibility that such a revelation is not so much a cause as a catalyst for the breakup of a marriage:

> In recent years I have begun asking people, when the break-up of a marriage is attributed to adultery, whether there was not something deeply wrong before the affair was discovered . . . Often, I believe, sexual infidelity is used by one partner or another as a trigger to end a relationship that has already become unsatisfactory.[10]

Throughout most of the twenty-two years of their marriage, Johnnetta's upward career trajectory, when compared with her husband's horizontal one, was a source of growing tension. This was especially the case because American patriarchy and racism are built on the notion that a man is always to be more successful—as represented by size of salary and prestige of post—than a woman; and white people are always to be in career and professional positions that are "above" those of Black people.

After her divorce in 1982, Johnnetta concluded that she was not interested in marrying again. This conclusion was reinforced during the four years that she taught at Hunter College and became more and more immersed in Women's Studies, and the women's movement. From the literature and ideas of Women's Studies and through the lives of women friends and associates, Johnnetta came face-to-face with a challenge to the deeply entrenched patriarchal notion that *every* woman wants and needs a man.

Beverly always thought of marriage as something that she would do only once, no matter how satisfactory it might be, and after her divorce, she became even more convinced that she would not marry again because it would require too many adjustments, many of which she didn't have to make in her first marriage. She could not see how a marriage would enhance her full and productive life or how she could find time for a husband on a full-time basis because of the self-imposed demands of her professional life. She also could not imagine finding another husband who would be easier to live with than her first one. She did not feel, as many women do, that two incomes would make her life more comfortable. She didn't want children, and she did not feel that intimacy or happiness were possible only within a marriage. She was becoming more convinced as well that friendship was what she was better at than wifehood. She also suspected that her evolving feminist politics would make it more difficult to find a husband whose gender attitudes were compatible with her own.

In 1987, two weeks after Johnnetta had begun her presidency at Spelman College, a telephone call of congratulations from a childhood friend put into motion a series of events that caused her to reevaluate her decision to remain single. The two of them had been childhood friends who lived one house apart in Washington, D.C., when they were eight, nine, and ten years old; but they had not seen each other since they were fifteen. Between that time and 1987, thirty-five years had passed. For Johnnetta, his seeming ability to be comfortable with a highly visible professional woman was significant. From the beginning of their adult relationship, they talked about this frequently. From the start of their adult relationship, Beverly was close to each of them—becoming over time Johnnetta's closest friend and building a friendship as well with her husband. The special friendship that we share has clearly been shaped in large measure by our feminist worldview, one that rejected the notion that a married woman and a single woman cannot be close; that a single woman cannot be a buddy to the husband of a married woman; and that a close friendship between two women must then block out all other friendships that each might have with other women.

Our friendship is also situated within our shared intellectual fields and political perspectives. Although trained in different fields as the primary focus of our academic work—Johnnetta in anthropology and Beverly in American Studies and English—we share expertise in Women's Studies and African American Studies. Cast in political terms, each of us is a "race woman" and a feminist.

Yet another way in which our feminist politics shape our relationships with each other and our extended family is how we practice caretaking, which is not confined to biological kin. Johnnetta has developed a caring relationship with Beverly's sisters, and Beverly has an auntie/friend relationship with Johnnetta's three sons. Beverly has shared Johnnetta's extensive caretaking responsibilities even further, as she related closely with Johnnetta's second husband's father and, before her death, his mother. Beverly also relates well with the range of Johnnetta's biological kin, and with Johnnetta's "little sister" through the Big Brothers Big Sisters program. The way that Johnnetta lives her life involves nurturing and support, which extends far beyond her maternal obligations to her three sons. And for each of us, there is a constant version of "othermothering" that occurs as we mentor countless young Black women and other women who are our students or who simply reach out to us for academic and personal guidance.

Growing up in the Jim Crow South, we each were surrounded by the beliefs and rituals of a Black church. Beverly's paternal grandfather was a Baptist minister with whom her family lived after her parents separated. Her mother was a loyal member of Metropolitan Baptist Church and sang in the choir every Sunday. Her father did not attend church, but belonged to a family that was attached to Avery Chapel Colored Methodist Episcopal (CME) Church. Johnnetta's family was deeply involved with Mt. Olive African Methodist Episcopal (AME) Church in Jacksonville, Florida.

Her maternal great-grandfather was the superintendent of the Sunday school and was a deacon, as were his son and grandson. Johnnetta's father was also a deacon and chaired the church's Finance Committee, and her mother played the organ and piano and directed all of Mt. Olive's choirs.

The gender-appropriate roles of the women and men in our respective churches were typical for Black Baptist and Methodist churches of that era and haven't changed very much. History was made in August 2000 when the Reverend Vashti Murphy McKenzie, of Baltimore, Maryland, was elected the first female bishop in the 213-year history of the African Episcopal Methodist Church.[11] More typically, the top leadership roles of minister and deacon are reserved for men while women are ushers, organists, deaconesses, and choir members.

Today, Johnnetta is a practicing Christian. Beverly, who is not, suspects that too much mandatory churchgoing during her childhood has led to her lack of enthusiasm for organized religion. However, similar college experiences strongly contributed to our tolerance and understanding of different religious traditions about which we were unaware during our youth. After one year of an early college entrance program at Fisk University, Johnnetta went to Oberlin College, an institution with a liberal tradition and one that took pride in the diversity of its students with respect to race, ethnicity, religion, and gender. It was at Oberlin that she first came into sustained contact with individuals of Jewish, Muslim, Hindu, and other faiths. Religious ecumenicalism, which in Johnnetta's Southern Black community meant Baptists mingling with Methodists, took on new meaning during her college years. Beverly remembers the profound impact on her worldview of a World Religions course she took during her sophomore year at Spelman College. She began to question the supremacy of Christianity as advanced in the rhetoric of Black fundamentalist churches—and most Christian churches, for that matter. She realized that if she had been born in India rather than Memphis she would probably be Hindu or Muslim. For both of us, college was the place where we most definitively began to see Christianity as one religion in the world, not *the* religion, and certainly not the religion that most people practiced.

Once you learn to think in terms of multiplicity in one arena, it is easier to think pluralistically about other important matters. Once you are able to challenge the superiority of one form of religion, for example, it is easier to challenge the superiority of other societal norms.

Our mothers were typical of their generation in terms of what they communicated to their daughters about sex. They said very little, except: Don't have sex and don't get pregnant before you marry. They also made it clear to us as we moved up the education ladder that an unplanned pregnancy would present a barrier to our reaching the next rung. In the minds of our mothers, not getting a substantial education was a sure way to put us at the mercy of a man on whom we would be dependent. Strong, independent-minded career women in their own right, Mary Betsch and Ernestine Guy wanted no less for their daughters.

Although our mothers said little about sex, each had a great deal to say about males. The list of dos and don'ts was substantial: Be very careful, for boys will lead unsuspecting girls down the wrong path; you must never be financially dependent on a husband, so always have a job and your own money; men like loose women for sex, but they don't marry them; don't accept expensive gifts from boyfriends, because they will expect something, usually sex, in return; there are good men and ones to be avoided, but even the good ones are not monogamous because "No man is educated below the belt."

From our mothers we frequently heard complimentary comments about decent and responsible Black men, including those in our families. These reliable and marriageable men were compared with those whom our mothers (and other Black women) labeled "sorry," and therefore to be avoided at any cost. Neither of us ever heard our mothers "put down" our fathers. Even after Beverly's mother separated from her husband, she was careful about not negatively influencing her daughters' perceptions of their father, who would continue to transport them daily to and from the school where he taught and which they attended. Because Beverly's mother wanted him to be close to his daughters, she also allowed him easy access to their home; he could even come to visit unannounced. She also made the decision not to entertain dates at 430 Lucy (or openly see other men), so that their new home remained a place where "daddy" would always feel comfortable visiting his three daughters. Beverly realizes in retrospect what a sacrifice this was on the part of her single mother and is now aware of how difficult raising three daughters alone must have been without regular male companionship or support. Johnnetta's mother as well never married again, and never had—to her children's knowledge, at least—a male companion. She not only finished raising her two college-age daughters and her young son, who was only seven years old when her husband died, but Johnnetta's mother also became the principal caretaker for her own father.

As we grew up in our respective hometowns of Jacksonville, Florida, and Memphis, Tennessee, each of us was aware of gay and lesbian persons in our communities. And while we each recall hearing derogatory references to "sissies," "faggots," and "bulldaggers," neither of us recalls hearing our parents make homophobic comments. During Johnnetta's teenage years, she was close to two of her mother's friends who were homosexuals and who rented her family's garage apartment. The first tenant/friend was a lesbian, the second, a gay man; and each interacted regularly with Johnnetta and her family. However, it was not until each of us was out of college that we became sensitized about homosexuality in a direct way. During the 1972–73 academic year when Beverly was a newly married young professor at Spelman, she met a young Black female history professor who only stayed at the college one year but who became a lifelong friend. Beverly recalls that when she met Ruby, she had not thought much about homosexuality, although she had certainly grown up hearing mildly negative comments from adults about "sissies"—homosexual men in the community who were hairdressers, choir directors, and music teachers. She heard less about lesbians, though her mother hinted, as Beverly got older, that one of her own closest unmarried female friends might have been the subject of rumors about being a lesbian. The most memorable part of what her mother shared with Beverly was that this friend had chosen not to marry and still lived a fulfilling life. What Beverly always remembered about these messages as she got older was that women could remain single and still be happy.

Drawn to Ruby because of her wisdom, progressive racial politics, and unconventional values (she did not seem to care very much about clothes, decorating, or talking incessantly about men), Beverly developed a friendship with a woman in many ways very different from herself and her other female friends. Within a short period of time, Beverly came to know that Ruby was a lesbian and, because of the trust that had developed between them, Ruby allowed her to ask whatever stupid questions she had about women loving other women. In her important role as teacher within the parameters of the evolving friendship, Ruby enabled Beverly to understand the limitations of her heterosexist notions (which would have been almost impossible to escape), and the complexities of being lesbian, especially in African American communities.

For Johnnetta, the first serious acknowledgment of her own heterosexism occurred in the early 1970s when she was team teaching a course called "the Black Woman" at the University of Massachusetts. One of the students in that course, who was also a staff person in the Women's Studies program, respectfully but firmly "called out" Johnnetta, her coinstructor, and the other students, almost all of whom were African American women. She challenged their exclusionary statements, erroneous assumptions about sexuality, and blatant and unapologetic homophobic comments. It was not long after that course that Johnnetta met her former student's partner, and developed a close friendship with the two of them that has continued for over thirty years.

For both of us, our extensive involvement with Women's Studies and the women's movement in the 1970s and 1980s put sexuality issues on our intellectual and personal agendas. Johnnetta lived in Amherst, Massachusetts, from 1970 to 1983, next to Northampton, Massachusetts—a town with a large lesbian community. In 1983, when she left Amherst and began teaching at Hunter College in New York City, her association with the Women's Studies program and the presence of Audre Lorde kept issues of heterosexism front and center. During this same period Beverly was a young professor at Spelman College, where her work in establishing the Women's Research and Resource Center brought her into close contact with a range of women, including lesbians. Some of the earliest speakers at the center were self-identified feminist lesbians such as

Barbara Smith, coeditor of *All the Women Are White, All the Blacks Are Men, but Some of Us Are Brave: Black Women's Studies* (1982), a groundbreaking Black Women's Studies anthology.

In 1987, Johnnetta came to Spelman as its first Black woman president and it was during that first year on campus that her friendship with Beverly, who had been teaching Women's Studies for over a decade, began. Within the context of an evolving friendship, we spoke about a number of complex gender issues, and began to openly challenge heterosexism. In the fall of 1993, Johnnetta wrote an open letter to the Spelman College community in which she joined the debate about the recently chartered Lesbian and Bisexual Alliance (LBA). Her goal was to affirm her commitment to diversity and to help create a "beloved community" at Spelman, including students who were different:

> . . . each member of the community has the right to work, to study, to live, and to learn without interference to their well being, their safety, and their peace of mind. We must have as our cardinal rule that our own individual beliefs and values do not give us license to dictate those beliefs and values to others. Most importantly, our own individual beliefs and values do not give us license to discriminate against those whose beliefs and values are different, nor to impede in any way their ability to participate fully in campus life.[12]

Beverly was saddened when she read an article in the student newspaper some six years later about the inactivity of Afrekete (they changed their name from Lesbian and Bisexual Alliance to avoid immediate scrutiny) because of "constant opposition from the Spelman community,"[13] and wondered how she could do more in her role as director of the Women's Studies program to bring about a more loving community at her alma mater.

Throughout our professional lives we have had a number of close gay and lesbian friends who were "out" and with whom we were in solidarity around a number of issues related to difference. The charge has been made by some that we are lesbians and even lovers, which is not an unusual occurrence in the lives of heterosexual women who self-identify as feminists and maintain close friendships with lesbians. On separate occasions Johnnetta and Beverly have been asked in public if they were lesbians. Speculation about our sexual orientation is fueled, we believe, by the homophobic assumption that any Black woman who is a feminist is also a lesbian. We are also convinced that many Black women and other women of color (as well as white women) reject the label of "feminist" for fear of being labeled a lesbian.

Our engagement with gender issues has been greatly influenced by our location within the academy, as well as professional lives that are connected to the study of racism and sexism and other systems of inequality. Johnnetta recalls that in her discovery of anthropology as a college student in the late fifties, she was pleased to learn of the role of women anthropologists such as Margaret Mead, Ruth Benedict, and Hortense Powdermaker, but most importantly, a Black woman, Zora Neale Hurston.

Johnnetta's first publication, an annotated bibliography that appeared in the December 1971 issue of *The Black Scholar*, criticized the paucity of written material on Black women. A decade later, Black women continued to be invisible in mainstream scholarship, which motivated Beverly (along with Roseann Bell, a colleague in the English department at Spelman) to publish the first anthology of Black women's literature, *Sturdy Black Bridges* (1979). In noting our own involvement with the production of scholarship on African American women early on, we must pay tribute to the giants in the field of Black Women's Studies whose early work informed and inspired us. We each recall the powerful impact on our thinking of Toni Cade [Bambara]'s groundbreaking anthology, *The Black Woman* (1970); Sharon Harley and Rosalyn Terborg-Penn's *The Afro-American Woman* (1978); bell hooks's first book, *Ain't I a Woman? Black Women and Feminism* (1981); Barbara Smith's *Home Girls: A Black Feminist Anthology* (1983); and Paula Giddings's *When and Where I Enter: The Impact of Black Women on Race and Sex in America* (1984). We also remember the impact of reading the memoirs of other Black feminists, in whose narratives about the development of their feminist consciousness we heard echoes of our own. The earliest of these was Michele Wallace's 1975 *Village Voice* essay, "Anger in Isolation: A Black Feminist's Search for Sisterhood," which appeared before her path-breaking but much maligned book *Black Macho and the Myth of the Superwoman* (1978). Three autobiographies by politically active Black women helped make us feel that we were not alone in being both Black and feminist. They were Shirley Chisholm's *Unbossed and Unbought* (1970), in which she asserted that "of my two 'handicaps,' being female put many more obstacles in my path than being black" (12); Flo Kennedy's radical Black feminist manifesto, *Color Me Flo: My Hard Life and Good Times* (1976); and Pauli Murray's *Song in a Weary Throat* (1987). Most recently, anthropologist Leith Mullings's familiar description of her evolving engagement with gender matters and its impact on her personal and political development in *On Our Own Terms: Race, Class, and Gender in the Lives of African American Women* (1997) reminded us of the power of autobiography as we thought about how we would begin this project.

Being together at Spelman presented many challenges, for even though we were at a historically Black college for women, it appeared as if race rather than gender was the more urgent issue among many faculty, staff, and students. Our late-night discussions about a range of compelling intraracial gender issues got us thinking about eventually writing a book together about our collective understanding of the intersection of race and gender within Black communities.

By examining particular aspects of our respective pasts, we are clearer about where we've been and where we need to go as we continue a journey we began many years ago. One of the most difficult aspects of this journey was engaging in some "truth telling" with respect to our own gender-related traumas. For Beverly it was making the decision to write for the first time about her own experience with violence, which occurred during the year before Johnnetta arrived on the Spelman campus. Because the man was also a professor at Spelman, Johnnetta was pulled into the incident during the first year of her presidency. The case ended with a felony conviction and is therefore on public record. For Johnnetta, it was making the decision to speak here about a gender-related trauma that led her to file for divorce from her second husband. We briefly tell these stories because of their relevance to the overall goal of the project, which is exploring gender matters within Black communities. We are convinced that in the telling of these stories, as two highly visible, professional Black women, several myths will be exploded. One is that such nightmares only happen to poor or unsophisticated Black women, and that one is less likely to experience gender trouble or domestic turmoil with middle-class, professional men. Another is that it would be irresponsible to air dirty linen in public for fear of perpetuating dangerous racial stereotypes.

Shortly after her fortieth birthday, Beverly made the decision to terminate a short-term relationship with a Spelman professor because of his obsessive possessiveness, invasions of her privacy, and extreme distrust of women. Having never experienced harsh or physically abusive treatment in any of her previous relationships, she never could have imagined or predicted the terrorism to which she would be subjected for one seemingly endless year. This year from hell would include physical assault, car theft, setting her car afire under the carport, late-night and all-night surveillance of her home, breaking and entering, and other life-threatening behaviors, the most aggressive and dangerous of which was placing her name, telephone number, and address in numerous public telephone booths and men's bathrooms throughout Atlanta with the invitation, "I have good p———y." This blatant public announcement of her alleged sexual availability resulted in a series of telephone calls by strange men at all times of the day and night indicating their desire to accommodate this bogus invitation. A particularly embarrassing moment occurred when Beverly's former husband called to inform her that the men's bathroom at Paschal's Restaurant (a popular place among Atlanta University Center faculty and students) included such an invitation. Beverly was grateful for the call and his removal of her name, but worried that he would wonder about her dating criteria!

For nearly a year, Beverly was in and out of Atlanta courts attempting to have this ex-boyfriend prosecuted for simple battery, car theft, and finally arson. Eventually, he was found guilty of arson, a felony in the state of Georgia, but the other charges were dropped. Because he was a college professor and a first offender, he was put on probation for five years rather than imprisoned. No doubt he would have landed in jail if he'd been a factory worker or auto mechanic. Throughout this crisis, Beverly relied on friends, both women and men. Her closest friend, Vicki, and her husband, Jimmy, hurried to her house on the night of the physical attack and tried to restrain him before the police arrived; Barbara, a Spelman administrator and friend, supported Beverly throughout the entire ordeal, which may have resulted in her condo being vandalized after the college fired the professor because of his felony conviction; Leah, a close friend, went to court with Beverly for the three day arson trial and held her hand during two of the most stressful days of her life, which included taking the witness stand for the first time; her cousin, Levi, flew to Atlanta and spent the day listening to Beverly talk instead of performing his usual heart surgery duties; and her friend, bell hooks, visiting Atlanta for the National Women's Studies Association Conference at Spelman (which the Women's Center hosted), interrogated male callers from whom she learned the locations of several public phone booths in Beverly's neighborhood. Armed with paper towels and Windex, Beverly and bell struck out late at night that week to remove the "evidence" of Beverly's existence. Beverly was particularly grateful for the help of another male chemistry professor at Spelman who identified the chemical, which had been taken from the college's chemistry lab and used to set her car afire. The supportive Black detective who worked diligently to solve this difficult arson case (there were no witnesses) described how hard it would have been to get a guilty conviction without expert testimony at the trial from Beverly's faculty colleague. His willingness to testify against another male professor and to corroborate Beverly's testimony in court was critical to the case.

The betrayal, which Johnnetta would experience during her second marriage, was nothing short of a nightmare. It pierced the core of so much that she had spoken about publicly, written about, and worked against throughout her professional life as a feminist and strong advocate for the rights of women and girls.

There are two aspects of what Johnnetta experienced, in comparison with Beverly, that have led her to hold back on speaking in specific terms about what led her to end what had been "a good marriage" for thirteen years. First, the events took place recently, whereas in Beverly's case, the events occurred sixteen years ago. More importantly, in Beverly's case, what she has revealed only involves exposing the man who engaged in acts of violence against her. In the situation in which Johnnetta found herself, revealing anything except the most general information about her former husband would seriously jeopardize innocent people. For these two reasons, Johnnetta will only say that her former husband carried out a gender-related abuse involving someone outside the family, which had devastating consequences for everyone involved.

What was it like for a woman of Johnnetta's high visibility to live through such a nightmare? At the end of the day, it was not fundamentally different from what is experienced all over the world by countless women despite their racial, class, and cultural differences. Indeed, gender-related traumas lead to a blurring of boundaries that might otherwise separate a middle-class suburban "housewife" from a poor woman in an inner-city neighborhood. When violent acts are committed against a woman or a girl, differences in the religious beliefs, nationality, age, or sexual orientation of the individuals do not disappear, but they clearly lose much of the weight they exert in the daily lives of the victimized.

What Johnnetta was pulled into as a consequence of her former husband's actions continues to occur in the lives of women and girls who are the victims of abuse or abuse-related crimes. No matter how horrific the act that is committed by a man, there is the tendency, even if it is said or felt only temporarily, to excuse the victimizer and blame the victim. How familiar is the refrain "*She* must have provoked *him* to do such a thing!" The implication is that by what she said or did, what she wore, how she walked or where she was, *she* brought the behavior on herself. Johnnetta also went through what is perhaps the most destructive way in which patriarchy writes the narrative about gender-related traumas. She found herself thinking and acting as if it were she who had carried out the abusive act. In short, Johnnetta fell into the trap of owning the act that had been done by her then husband. The process of disowning what happened, living through this intensely painful and humiliating experience, and moving on to reinvent her life has certainly not been easy for Johnnetta. Healing from the hurt of what her husband did and finding a place of peace is a process, a long process. It is not an event. But Johnnetta is in this process and gives thanks for where she is in her journey to strong, compassionate, and effective spiritual counseling; psychological counseling under the guidance of a highly skilled and sensitive Black woman therapist; the love and support of her three sons (who went into a kind of role reversal whereby they became her parents), other family members, and ever so wonderful friends.

We are deliberately refraining from providing more of the day-to-day details of these traumatic and life-altering incidents in our lives. We believe that it is more important for us to share what we learned about the nature of patriarchy, which might be instructive for other women and men. What we learned is that every woman is a potential victim of abuse and betrayal, regardless of her class status, level of maturity, or the care with which she chooses a particular partner. We also learned that despite our familiarity with theories about male aggression and control, and even the specificity of gender-specific violence, understanding these issues theoretically is very different from dealing with them on a personal level.

One of the most painful lessons Beverly learned is how deeply entrenched is the notion that violent behavior by a man is inevitably provoked by something that a female is doing. The question Beverly was asked most often was what did you do to cause such bizarre behavior on the part of an ostensibly nice, professional young man? In an unusual moment of candor, Beverly shared her experience of violence, both physical and psychological, with a small group of Black women at a three-day Black Feminist Seminar in May 1990 at the University of Wisconsin at Madison organized by Professor Stanlie James and sponsored by the Department of Afro-American Studies.

Seminar participants shared their work in a supportive, sisterly atmosphere, which included intense discussions about the future of Black feminism. Though it was extremely painful, Beverly shared with the group how difficult it was initially for her to get some people to believe the details of her story; the assumption was that she was exaggerating. In her retelling of what Beverly experienced at the seminar, Professor Abena Busia captures how women continue to be victimized very often by the very women whom you would assume would be empathetic:

> . . . when retelling the story in the room that had for us become almost a sacred space, she [Beverly] had to relive, even amongst a community of supposedly sympathetic Black women, the terror of that rejection of her version of the story, and thus, of her. It was difficult for us, as a group, to go through the experience of the division that Beverly's story caused. Some of us understood immediately the implications of her situation and why she had spoken. Others took her through the "third degree," and were relentless in their interrogation until one of them stopped in mid-sentence when she finally heard herself asking, "Well how many times and how badly did he beat you?" By the time she heard herself ask this . . . we were all too emotionally drained to make the excruciating choice between recognizing the betrayal of a sister that even *thinking* that question represented, and the collective growth and transformation that *stopping* asking in mid-sentence illuminated.[14]

Some of the responses to both our situations underscore how deep and pervasive woman-blaming is throughout society, including our own communities.

What we learned about ourselves during and following these life-changing circumstances is perhaps equally as instructive. We believe that both of us have emerged from these personal violations as whole women because of our ability to engage in feminist analyses of what occurred. Without our gender politics, we may well have fallen into the trap that ensnares so many women and girls who are victims of physical, psychological, and sexual abuse—namely, blaming the victim. Beverly learned something about her own resilience amidst the only trauma she had ever experienced in her life. She remembers that very little about her professional life was impacted—she continued to focus on her work—and that very few people on the job, even those closest to her, knew what was happening to her. For the first time in her life, she also came to understand how precious life is and how suddenly one's security can be threatened. There were even moments when she thought she might not survive.

Johnnetta learned how fragile *and* how resilient she is. Perceived by herself and others as a strong Black woman, Johnnetta sometimes found herself, however, immobilized by the very thought of what her husband had done, and at other times sobbing uncontrollably over it all. But Johnnetta also learned how healing it is to reject ownership of something she did not do, and how much that rejection rebuilds a sense of strength.

We are convinced that breaking our respective silences about two horrific experiences will help Beverly finally put to rest what was clearly the most traumatic series of incidents in her life; and as Johnnetta moves to Greensboro, North Carolina, to serve as the president of Bennett College, she is convinced that having written here about the most traumatic experience in her life will help her to leave it where it belongs. We certainly hope that our truth telling, as painful as it has been, will provide some degree of courage and comfort to women who have known and felt pain similar to our own.

2

•

HAVING THEIR SAY: CONVERSATIONS WITH SISTERS AND BROTHERS

We need to hear from Black men who are interrogating sexism, who are striving to create different and oppositional visions of masculinity. Their experience is the concrete practice that may influence others.

bell hooks, *Talking Back,* 1990

I think that if Black men can acknowledge the sins of our fathers and can work to correct the effects of them and not repeat the sins, if we can do those things, then life in the Black community will be just the most peaceful thing in the world. If we fix ourselves, everything else will fall in line like a linchpin. I think we have to straighten out the misbehavin' men. And I don't think Black men are worse or better than white men.

Zaron Burnett, Interview, 1999

In the Black community talking about issues of gender is seen as a kind of anti-Black discourse, that is to say outside of the context of Blackness, and anti-Black because it takes the focus away from the "real" issue which is race. Blackness is also defined in heterosexist ways, so that if you're gay you clearly can't be Black.

Manning Marable, Interview 1999

Having Our Say is the riveting story of the Delany sisters, Sarah L. and Elizabeth A., ages 102 and 100 respectively when they began sharing their life histories with Amy Hill Hearth in the living room of their home in Mount Vernon, New York.[1] Though they never thought they'd see the day "when people would be interested in hearing what two old Negro women have to say," their narratives and many others' have taught us the importance of passing along knowledge and experience from one generation to another. To be sure, many of the stories African Americans share with the world have been about our racial journeys. There are far fewer reflections on gender and sexuality, especially from Black men, though there are some exceptions, including Michael Awkward's *Scenes of Instruction: A Memoir* (1999), Samuel R. Delany's *The Motion of Light in Water* (1988), and Essex Hemphill's *Ceremonies* (1992).

Having had our say about how our own life experiences shaped our perspectives on gender, we turn now to the stories of a range of Black women and men that illuminate how gender matters in their individual and collective identities as African Americans. Some of the voices in this chapter are those of women and men whom we interviewed. Other voices are those of participants in the multilogue on gender issues in African American communities. These autobiographical narratives are a rich source of information on how a diverse, highly selective group of Black women and men came to gender consciousness, including feminism. Not unlike our own stories, they reveal how people's parents and extended families provided examples of nontraditional expressions of gender roles. As they "have their say," we witness their personal and political struggles with hierarchical gender and racial roles.

THE IMPACT OF KINFOLKS

Like other communities in the United States, African American communities are shaped by normative attitudes about gender that impact our relationships within and beyond our families. These pervasive and largely unexamined beliefs about gender—men should be dominant, women subservient—are so "natural" that they often go unchallenged, even in communities that believe passionately in the "unnaturalness" of racial oppression. Farai Chideya, a young journalist, told us that "my issues with race have been public and my issues with gender have been private." Like many other young college-age African American women, Nikki Stewart (her race-progressive mother named her after the popular poet Nikki Giovanni), tells us that her mother didn't talk to her about gender, despite her difficult marriage, but rather, "my mother has learned about gender from me." These assertions help to explain why issues of gender have been more hidden, more resistant to analysis and intervention in African American communities. Black folks learn sex roles, as do white folks, at an early age—earlier than our consciousness of "race" differences and racial oppression. Byllye Avery, founder of the National Black Women's Health Project, describes her first inklings of gender oppression:

> The overriding thing that I have always seen, ever since I was a little girl—and I hadn't heard the word feminism, didn't have any idea about it—was how there were always differences in the way I was treated and my brother was treated, the way my mother was treated and the way my daddy was treated. And when questions were asked, the response was, "It's because he's a man," or "It's because she's a woman or you're a girl." I think that internalized sexism is rooted so deep in our society; in fact, some things seem to be even bigger in our community and among our people, or maybe they hurt more, or maybe I pay more attention to them.[2]

Over and over again we heard stories from the women we interviewed that revealed what we call an "everyday feminism," an awareness on the part of African American women of gender oppression. It emerged in accounts of their determination to take care of their families, sometimes as single parents, and in their commitment to teach their sons as well as their daughters to question and challenge male privilege. This "everyday feminism" came out of the context of Black women's daily lives in a racist society. Marcia Gillespie, then editor of *Ms.* magazine, described several childhood incidents that shaped her understanding of gender oppression. Her mother and grandmother were models of feminist resistance in the Black community.

> My Nana had such an enormous impact on my life; she lived at the other end of the block. I came home from school and went to my Nana's who took care of me until Mommy and Dad came home. So she was *big* in my life. Here was a woman widowed in 1917 who raised her children on her own, never married again—never acted like she needed to be married again. She had a real strong sense of herself, of her independence, of her intelligence. You know all of these things were so empowering. This model didn't fit with the patriarchal model, never did. That stuff that I saw on television of the "little woman"—that "little woman" who was supposed to be the ideal, I didn't know any women like that! They didn't live in my neighborhood. It made no sense to me. So what were we? How did we define our experience? Well, feminism helped me see it. We were women who empowered ourselves. Women who made rules, who weren't afraid to say, "No, that's my rule!" Women who demanded respect. Maybe there may have been hostility out there in the world, but within their communities they demanded respect. It was about what you represented and the way you carried yourself and what you valued and the work that you did. I grew up with a mother and a father who were both activists and it wasn't like, I defer to you honey. Mama did what she decided she was going to do.[3]

Aubra Love, director of the Atlanta-based Black Church and Domestic Violence Institute, says she first knew she was a feminist when she observed feminism in process at Cornell University in 1971. The experience of "watching women fully actualized" inspired her to read more about the women's movement, to build alliances with other women, to attend a Women's Conference in Albany, New York, and to join the National Black Feminist Organization in New York, which was founded in 1973. However, it was her experiences as an adolescent that predisposed her to have a positive response to feminism.

> I didn't know the word feminist. But you know, I was raised by a single mother who was divorced when I was very young, and she always worked. The expectation was that I would always be able to support myself and that (nobody said this to me very explicitly) my choice of a mate would not be based on my economic condition. The expectation was that I would at least finish undergraduate school and after that I would get to make a decision, because at that point I would have to be self-supporting anyway, so we always talked about school as K through 16 in a sense, and that was very helpful to me. The expectation was that I would work as a teenager. I had a mother who respected herself and was defined in church as a teacher, but was in fact a preacher herself. But, you know, "God suffered not a woman to preach." So, I think my mom was probably the strongest role model around and I had two sisters. And then I went to Black schools in Atlanta where I saw women who were really self-empowering, the kind of women who would drop some bit of womanly wisdom that would carry me through.[4]

Ruby Sales, a former civil rights activist who grew up in the Deep South, credits her mother and father with living lives that challenged normative sex roles:

> I grew up with a father who is very atypical in that community because my father, a Baptist minister, would hang out clothes, wash, iron, cook, and on Saturday he would say to my mother, "Mrs. Sales you'll have breakfast in bed today and I'll do everything." My mother didn't cook dinner for us; my dad was the cook in our family so therefore all my brothers do the same thing. My father braided our hair and my divorced brother braids his daughter's hair. When I got to be a young adult my father and I traded clothes. So, in

retrospect, I realize I grew up in a very androgynous household where there were very fluid roles for women and men.[5]

By contrast, writer Pearl Cleage describes having grown up in a
"male reverential" and politically radical family in Detroit, Michigan, with a "big race man" father who longed for sons (he had two
daughters) and eventually founded an alternative Black church,
The Shrine of the Black Madonna.

> Gender was never a big discussion in our household. Race
> was twenty-four hours a day. Always, always we talked
> about race. Any kind of effort to inject anything about
> gender issues into the discussion was immediately conde-
> scended to by my father and uncles. My aunts were always
> angry at their brothers because if they are all sitting around
> eating, my father would say, "I sure would like some water"
> and my grandmother would instantly say to one of his sis-
> ters, "Go get your brother a glass of water." Whatever it
> was that any of those four men wanted, the sisters would
> serve them in the same way my grandmother served them.[6]

Her maternal grandparents' household was even more traditional.
"My grandfather came to Detroit to work at Ford. My grandmother was a very smart woman who wanted to work, wanted to
teach. But my grandfather thought that would be a real slap at him
because there is no reason his wife would have been working if he
could take care of her. So, he never allowed her to work."

African American men, privileged by their gender and their potential power over women (Black women in particular), have been
influenced by society's normative ideas about gender, though there
have certainly been men like Ruby's father who have rejected these
norms. Haki Madhubuti, founder of Third World Press, articulates
eloquently his understanding of the sex role socialization to which
men in the U.S. have been subjected and likens it to the "seasoning"
process that befell enslaved Africans in the New World, and the
Eurocentric "miseducation" that African Americans experience in
schools.

Male acculturation (or a better description would be male "seasoning") is antifemale, antiwoman/feminist, and anti-reason when it comes to woman's equal measure and place in society. This flawed socialization of men is not confined to the West but permeates most, if not all cultures in the modern world. Most men have been taught to treat, respond, listen, and react to women from a male's point of view. Black men are not an exception here; we too, are imprisoned with an intellectual/spiritual/sexual understanding of women based upon antiquated male culture and sexist orientation—or should I say miseducation. For example, sex or sexuality is hardly ever discussed, debated, or taught to Black men in a nonthreatening or nonembarrassing family or community setting.[7]

African American men who had struggled with patriarchal gender norms that privilege them within African American communities presented especially provocative and refreshing narratives. Family upbringing was a crucial variable in shaping their understanding of gender, especially more progressive interpretations. Some men talked about receiving "feminist" messages from their mothers and other female family members. Thandabantu Iverson, a labor organizer and professor, recounted one of his earliest memories of such a message:

When I was about 11 years old I remember something from my mother, a poor little black girl from a family of nine in Painesville, Ohio, whose life in a number of ways was curtailed and constrained by this system. She called me to her side and asked me to look at my little sister, who at that point probably was two years old. She said, "Do you love your little sister?" And I said, "Mama, you know I love her," even though we fought all the time. So she said, "Well, if you love your sister, I want you to remember one thing. That every woman you meet in your life will be someone's sister, someone's daughter. And I want you to learn how to live so that you will not treat any woman the way I have been treated." Gender for me is both a process in our communities making for great pain, but it is also, as my mother tried to show me that day, a potential pathway for becoming better and different as humans in community.[8]

Other men described relatively progressive fathers who taught them that their status as men did not require that they harbor sexist attitudes about women or behave in "unmanly" ways. Atlanta writer Zaron Burnett, who was involved in radical organizations during the sixties and seventies, told us that his "feminist mother" and "nonoppressive" father addressed gender issues directly. Burnett also found that seeing gender oppression as analogous to racial oppression enabled him to better understand the phenomenon of male privilege and how it functions in the subordination of women. Born in Virginia and raised in New Jersey, he moved back and forth between his family's home in New Jersey, and that of his great-grandmother in North Carolina. Both of his parents were school teachers, and Burnett felt his parents' respect for education contributed to an environment where he and his siblings were encouraged, especially by his mother, to ask questions, also about gender:

> My mother wouldn't claim to be a feminist but by all definitions she is one. She made all of us understand—that everything we were being told by men about women was all wrong! She encouraged us to test all the information with her. She said anything that's too odious for you to talk to me about, you shouldn't talk to any female about. She said if I can take it they can too. And if it's wrong, I'll tell you why. And my Dad was very nonoppressive. He was very masculine in the traditional sense, but he wasn't a mean person and he didn't take unfair advantage of situations or people. There was no presumption that women did this or men did that. There were jobs to do and everybody had to do them.[9]

An activist in the Black nationalist movement—during which "we were always arguing about the woman's question"—Burnett also felt that his understanding of racism helped him understand sexism.

Because he could "always put myself in the position of the white person," it was not difficult for him to put himself in the position of women who were also different from himself. Married to feminist writer Pearl Cleage, Burnett believes that his sensitivity to gender helped him in their relationship. In a moving portrait of their special marriage, Pearl shares with a national audience her long list of what she likes about Burnett (whom she affectionately calls Zeke), a few items of which we repeat here: "He always tells the truth. He knows how to listen. He appreciates my intelligence. He never makes me feel guilty. He values and encourages my work. He is consistent. He loves his family. He laughs a lot. He loves Black people and works for our liberation. He solicits and respects my opinions. He doesn't fuss."[10]

Historian Manning Marable (born in 1949) taught a course on Black women's history in 1981 that resulted in a groundbreaking essay on the need to eradicate patriarchy in the Black community.[4] Like Zaron Burnett, he describes being raised by a feminist mother and credits her for the development of his own feminist consciousness. June Marable, the salutatorian of the first graduating class at Central State University in Wilberforce, Ohio, in 1948, also passed along her passion for history to her son who was reading college history texts by the time he was in the eighth grade. While a college student, she worked as a maid in the home of Professor Charles H. Wesley, the preeminent historian and the head of The Association for the Study of Negro Life and History for many years. Manning's mother decided that if she ever got married, one of her children would become a historian. As a kid Manning got history books for his birthday and Christmas from his public school teacher mother who demanded that he write little book reports for her and engage in discussions with her about her assigned readings. He suspects that the seeds for his evolving feminist consciousness were being sown in this process and that his later contact with particular Black women also profoundly impacted his intellectual development.

> I encountered Black women in Black history through the books my mother encouraged me to read. By the time I went to college I was thinking about Black history. I wasn't

a feminist but I thought about Black history not in simplis-
tic, male dominated ways or male confined ways. So she put
me on the correct path. The other thing that happened is
that there were a whole series of Black women intellectuals
and activists who had a very positive impact upon my development. One of them was you, Johnnetta. Johnnella Butler
and Angela Davis had a tremendous impact on my intellectual growth and sisters like Barbara Smith.[11]

Manning describes his paternal grandmother, Fanny Marable, who
was born in 1898, raised in Tuskegee, Alabama, and the mother of
thirteen children, as another "feminist" role model. "I learned
about the history of my family through my grandmother and I became fascinated with history. Between June Marable and Fanny
Marable, I had no choice. The history that my grandmother told
was a fully gender-balanced history in that it focused on the roles of
women and men in the making of an American family."

During our interview with Manning we were struck by the similarities between his and our own personal stories. The three of us
were born in the Deep South and were raised among educators with
"feminist" mothers and fathers who in some ways were gender-
progressive in their child-rearing practices. Manning's description
of his family was familiar to us:

As patriarchal and as conservative as Black civil society was
in the early and mid–twentieth century, one of the common
factors in the production of a Black feminist sensibility and
scholarship and activism is that if you go back to those so-
called traditional Black households, there was, paradoxically, a kind of protofeminist position of Black men as they
related to sisters in a household. My dad's view was that my
mom should achieve the highest goals she wanted; she had a
master's degree and taught science in high school. He
worked in a tire factory for a decade before he became ill,
but he really believed that Mom's career should go forward.
Later she went back to school, took three years off and got
a Ph.D. at the age of fifty and Dad was very supportive

through it all. He was not a feminist. And yet . . . you can
see that in that kind of a household where there was a real
sharing of responsibility and a commitment to personal
growth that the family would be supportive of Mom and all
of us did that. I never really thought before about the
Marables being protofeminist, but it now occurs to me that
you wouldn't see a more politically progressive, intellectu-
ally progressive group of folk.[12]

A generation later Nikki Stewart, a former student of Beverly's
and presently a doctoral student in Women's Studies at the University of Maryland, describes the breakup of her parents' marriage
when her "brilliant" mother decided to pursue a doctorate in history at the University of Chicago under Dr. John Hope Franklin's
tutelage. During her mother's matriculation, Nikki's father simply
left (he accused her of sleeping too much), which wrecked her
family's financial situation and caused her mother to drop out of
the doctoral program, "which was the biggest heartbreak of her
life." To make matters worse, she attempted to get a job at the Center for Urban Studies, where she had previously obtained a master's
degree, but was told by the Black male director, "I'm sorry Barbara,
we had to give it to a brother." Nikki struggled as a fifteen-year-old
to make sense out of the devastating situation in which the family
found itself: "You know, man leaves, we plunge into poverty, my
mother was brilliant, but she couldn't get a job."[13]
    While Burnett and Marable suggested that having educated
mothers greatly influenced their awareness of gender issues, professor and Baptist preacher Michael Eric Dyson's personal narrative
provides a contrasting experience that nonetheless created in him a
similar sensitivity to women's issues. He is very clear about the cen-
trality of gender as an issue for Black men even though it remains
unacknowledged. "Gender is at the heart of the Black male preoccupation with their own self-expression. Whether we're talking
about hip-hop culture, the Black church, or Black institutions of
higher learning, the gender issue is front and center. But Black men
don't see their gender in the same ways that white men don't see
they have a race. Gender is a central but invisible function in the

psychic and material operations of Black male life. When I think about gender I'm forced to come to grips as a Black man with the privilege of male supremacy, and as I've evolved, I've tried to confront my own male supremacist perspectives and biases."[14] Dyson describes his awareness of gender issues as beginning in childhood with the example of his mother's hard work in the home and the oppression she endured because she was female. Unfortunately, she was prevented from continuing her education beyond high school because her father thought college was only for men. What Dyson observed about his mother's life led him to question the treatment of women in general, the particular burdens of Black women, and the negative consequences of Black patriarchy. His exposure to Black women writers eventually led him to feminism while he was in college and preaching in Knoxville, Tennessee, in 1983.

> I had to come to grips with the gender issue when I became a pastor in the South. I ran up against a powerful barrier when I tried to link the race issue to the gender issue because I had been reading. I remember these Black preachers. They took tremendous offense at this young Black woman [Michele Wallace]. I will never forget the furor that her *Black Macho and the Myth of the Superwoman* created. How dare she speak about these issues, how dare she articulate in public space the denigration of Black female identity by Black men! I began to understand the double jeopardy of Black women from reading books by Michele Wallace, then bell hooks. What I began to see is that—Wow!!—all this time I've been taking a whole lot of cultural and intellectual capital from my masculinity. And I didn't want to do it anymore. I wanted to be a traitor to patriarchy. In one sense I began to see that to be a traitor to a sort of narrow form of masculinity was to be loyal to the greater forms of humanity. I saw my mother do so much of the work with my father. My father was from Georgia and was a laborer all of his life. My mother was a paraprofessional with the Detroit Public Schools. And I saw my mother giving up stuff so we could have clothes, the Sunday stuff, the Easter stuff; she

would never have any clothes. I never will forget being told the story of why she didn't go to college. She was a straight "A" student. A brilliant woman! But she was the youngest of several children in Alabama—Hyssop, Alabama. And the short of it is that she couldn't go to school—she was offered a scholarship to college but she was a cotton picker—literally—and her father didn't think that women should go to college, but that they should fall in love.[15]

Dyson's account runs counter to the widely held and mythical notion in Black communities that in most Black families, where higher education was possible for the children, females were encouraged to go to college rather than their brothers.

For Rudolph Byrd, a professor of African American Studies at Emory University, his father's abuse of his mother set the stage for his disloyalty to patriarchy and his abhorrence of the oppression of women.

There are experiences that I can point to that have sensitized me to thinking about human beings in all their complexity. It involves my relationships with the women in my family, my mother and my sisters. At an early age there was one instance with my father. I love my father, but my father was like many men of his generation and he was abusive of my mother. When I was ten, my father came home after a lengthy disappearance and my mother questioned him. Where have you been? He said I don't have to explain and she said yes you do. And he said no I don't. And then he hit her. I was in the next room in our two bedroom apartment. And I could hear the fight escalating because they had been at the point before, and I just said to myself, I'm not going to do nothing about it this time. So when he hit her, I went right to the kitchen, got the biggest knife I could find, then went to the bedroom and I pointed it at my father and I said, "Get out and leave my mother alone." Then there was silence; my father stopped, my mother stopped, and my mother said to him, "See what you have done." And my father took the knife, put it in the kitchen and went away. He came back about two hours later. Didn't apologize, but all of his gestures pointed towards remorse. So we went to the zoo, but I stood on the outside of that. I said it's not going to be that easy for you. And so in that instance I really declared war on my father and on that kind of behavior. And I maintained that position with my father until I was nineteen or twenty. We reconciled about a year before he died. But I was very clear from that moment on that this was not acceptable and that I would not tolerate this in my family, and that I would not treat other women that way.[16]

NEGOTIATING INTERPERSONAL RELATIONSHIPS

Some men spoke of relationships with wives and girlfriends who taught them to look more intensely at their assumptions about women's roles. Others talked about how successions of "failed" marriages or relationships led them to examine their behavior in an attempt to get it right the next time. In some instances they admitted to being victimized by patriarchy as children, only to grow up and repeat behaviors that they knew to be wrong, including violence against the women closest to them. In all of their stories we found an eventual willingness to accept a status that for many is very difficult to face: the role of oppressor. Many of the Black men we interviewed and who participated in the multilogue came of age during the civil rights movement and made personal commitments to the fight against racial oppression as evidenced in their political, educational, and grassroots activism. They so completely identified the image of the oppressor with the white male that the image of themselves as potential oppressors of Black women was an unreconcilable one. And so many struggled with the painful question: "How could I, so committed to fighting racism and who feels so deeply oppressed myself, be accused of oppressing someone Black like me?" As Faye Wattleton stated, "We like to think that an oppressed people does not oppress its own, and that's just not the case." Writer, lecturer, and young hip-hop journalist Kevin Powell grew up in New York in a "matriarchal family," raised primarily by his mother, who had only finished the sixth grade and never married, and an extended family of aunts and his grandmother. Despite the absence of his father, whom he hasn't seen for twenty-five years, he also realizes that he grew up "in a very patriarchal environment on my block."[17] He attributes his "internalized sexism" to the strong influence of popular culture and his male peers among whom their "paradigm of Black manhood or masculinity is basically how many women can you conquer." The lack of positive male role models and an absent father impacted him profoundly as well. As a young adult in college, he sought examples of strong men in Black empowerment organizations, but he realized that their definitions of Black manhood often depended in part on the subjugation of Black women. Both positive and negative personal relationships with women, including his physical abuse of a former girlfriend, eventually led him to further analyze his behavior and to publicly question sexism and male privilege:

> Why do we resist a gender analysis? There's something about Black manhood in the context of this country which every day of our existence makes us feel we're under siege. Does that justify being oppressive, being sexist, being misogynistic? Definitely not. But I think there's a feeling with a lot of Black men that I know, young ones and old ones—as I'm coming to find out—50- and 60-year-olds, 70-year-olds act the same way a lot of the times—that we are under siege. And I think a lot of us are so insecure that the last thing we want to do is confront something negative about ourselves. It's like Zora Neale Hurston said, "women are the mules of the earth" and y'all the easiest, as sisters, as Black women, to oppress because we can't do nothing to nobody else. Or we're too cowardly to respond to anything else. I don't think many of us would put it in that language but that's my observation and my experience. I would say I have spent most of my life wallowing in blatant sexism.[18]

Powell's comments remind us that his hip-hop generation inherited oppressive gender attitudes about women and what it means to be a Black man from the patriarchal discourse of brothers during the sixties as well as mainstream society. He recalls his college days in the eighties when Black student organizations relegated women to supporting roles:

> We called our Black Student Union the African Student Congress and there was a whole group of sisters . . . They used to say, well what about the women's issues. And at the time I also was leaning towards and I eventually joined the Nation of Islam—patriarchy manifested. And so I said, "Sister you got to understand, this is about the Black man, you know what I'm saying. Y'all just got to support us . . . And of course, as y'all know the sisters were doing all the work. They were making the flyers, passing out the flyers, the whole nine yards. But we were the dynamic spokespersons. We were baby Stokely Carmichael and H. Rap Brown up in there. There is the anti-apartheid movement going on in the eighties too and so Jesse was running for president and Farrakhan was on the rise and it was like Black men are back! And we felt good about ourselves and we all were sleeping with all these sisters and being just blatantly disrespectful . . . I think that the socialization I experienced as a child that was intensified in college set the stage for me pushing my girlfriend in June 1991 into a bathroom door. All the stuff was already there.[19]

The incident described above, which he narrates with refreshing honesty, challenged Powell to confront his deeply held sexist attitudes about women. He described the process as one initially fraught with denial, until he was challenged by female friends and Black feminist writings and eventually came to see himself as a hypocritical brother who wasn't practicing what he espoused as he continued the psychological abuse:

> I saw her in the streets. She actually let me live with her again after that. That's the pattern that a lot of women who've been abused take. I ended up cursing her out in the street, and she's a very dark-skinned sister, and called her

"black" in a derogatory manner, and so much for my Black nationalist thing. My afrocentricity! Here's the biggest hypocrite around.[20]

Powell's subsequent association with a group of sisters who encouraged him to read Black feminist writers such as bell hooks and Pearl Cleage, specifically *Mad at Miles* because of its discussion of violence against women, resulted in him confronting the consequences of his adolescent socialization and his later disrespectful treatment of women.

And I remember picking up bell hooks's book again and it's amazing how one book can really affect your life. I went back to reread Miles Davis's book and I thought about what he had said about Cicely Tyson and what he had done to her and I started replaying it in my mind—just like I had when I became conscious of racism as a college freshman and replayed all the instances. Wow, my mother's relationship with my father. How I related to my female teachers. How I related to the girls in my grammar school. How I thought about women in high school. How I thought about all those high school boys running to 42nd street in NY to the peep show, not realizing that we were participating in the objectification of women. And out of that tragedy, and I call it a tragedy because since that day, that time, I've never really talked to that sister. And I would love to one day just be able to say to her face-to-face I'm really sorry for what I did and I can't begin to tell you how much it changed the course of my life because I never thought about gender oppression until that time. . . . really thought about it. But that was the beginning of my thinking about it.[21]

This painful process, Powell notes, ultimately helped him to become more sympathetic about his mother as he realized that "here's a working class Black woman who has had to deal with racism and sexism and classism her entire life."

Black men who see themselves as reformed sexists (or, as Powell describes himself in *Ms.*, as a "recovering misogynist"[22]) must struggle to overcome traditional gender role socialization and become better men. James Early described his own process of reformation:

> One of the things that I try always to return to almost every moment in my life is who am I personally? Because if I don't, I won't live my life fully as a professional or activist. So one of the things about my transformation, which is still in progress, is I've imposed a certain discipline on some of my desires. I have come to understand, and I certainly dialogue with my sons about it, that I am still growing and I now understand that I have the capacity to keep growing. For example, in my dealings with women, I admit that I treat them in the most traditional and bad ways, as men often do. But I'm also able to impose discipline on myself and admit that certain desires are not totally gone, but I won't act on them.[23]

With unusual candor, Sulaiman Nuriddin (formerly a member of the Nation of Islam), who works with Men Stopping Violence in Atlanta, Georgia, described the way in which his growing understanding of male privilege, through personal struggles in several partnerships, led him to healthier relationships:

> I know that I bring to my present relationship a Sulaiman that's unlike any Sulaiman that's ever existed before because of what I've learned about myself and how to be in a relationship. And what I've learned about how to give and share in a way that's not about possessing another human being. I would even venture to say that had I had this knowledge early on, Kadijah and I might still be together. Transitions, experiences, life—have all been good for me. I don't regret any bit of it because it's brought me where I am today and I give thanks for that. I listen to women today in a way I've never listened before. And I'm not caught up in this thing that it has to be my way. There are times when Mira and I disagree. But we respectfully disagree with each other and it's okay, you know? And I didn't know how to

do that before. I don't even know if I realized how dominating and controlling and possessive I was because it was so ingrained in me. Imelda didn't have to do anything, Kadijah didn't have to do anything, I did it all. That was what I was taught. Dad did it all. Mom didn't work, she stayed at home with the children. That's the way I did it too.[24]

Even within the context years earlier of a polygamous relationship that he embraced during his Rastafarian phase, Sulaiman was committed to the idea of fairness and equity in relationships and accepted, with difficulty, one of his female partner's proposal to bring her new male partner into the household.

RETHINKING MANHOOD AND WOMANHOOD

Several women and men we interviewed challenged normative beliefs about what it means to be a man or a woman and revealed a range of attitudes about gender. Some rejected traditional notions about masculinity and femininity; others violated taboos about homosexuality. Accounts of experiences with sexism and heterosexism were sometimes painful and etched deeply in the psyche. Rudolph Byrd, a forty-five-year-old professor at Emory University, associates his sensitivity to gender issues with relationships with his mother, aunts, and close friendships with women. Witnessing the physical abuse of his mother at the hands of his father, even though he was only ten or eleven years old, was particularly transformative with respect to his understanding of male dominance:

When my father raised his hand and struck my mother's face the world as I knew it changed completely. It was in this moment that my commitment to gender equality crystalized. Such a commitment placed me, inevitably, in opposition to my father who held, like many men of his generation, deeply flawed and patriarchal views of family and society.[25]

For Byrd, intervening in the incident of his father's abuse of his mother, as well as his own experience of rejection in college because of his presumed homosexuality, underscored for him the link between women's oppression in a patriarchal society and the oppression of gays in a homophobic society. Ironically, his heart-wrenching experience of ostracism took place within the context of questions about his Black identity:

> I could relate to the oppression of women and the oppression that I was beginning to feel as a gay man. I understood where this stuff was coming from. Because of how they're socialized, men want to prove two things—that they are not girls and they are not faggots. Males did not want to be like me. And because they didn't want to be like me, I paid more attention to the other people they were dismissing (females) and understood that they were interesting people. That we had things in common.
>
> In college my first year I was hypersensitive to what Blackness meant. But I was resistant to thinking monolithically about Blackness because of the work that I had done around gender. And I also knew that I embodied all of the contradictions.
>
> The experience that made this clear in terms of race and sexuality took place during my sophomore year in college. You know how at white institutions all the Black students eat at the same table. And I had been struggling all my freshman year to get along with these Black folk, doing everything I could. Hosting birthday parties for people I did not like. I mean I was just brownnosing up a storm. And then I went to a dinner; I went to the dining room one Saturday night and there were about forty Black students all seated at the same table. And I remember approaching the table wondering if I could sit there. Would they let me sit here? And they did not make room for me. And I just stood there. Everybody looked and it was clear to me that there was a consensus—he cannot sit here. And I thought I have done all this work within the framework of the Black Students Association (BSA). I have gotten you all money. I have gone out on a limb. And I can't sit here and have a meal with you. Nothing was said. And

this happened within about a minute or two, but it was clear. I said fine to myself and went and sat with some white friends.

The following Monday a sister came to me and indicated that she wanted to tell me something. She was at dinner and saw what happened to me and wanted to tell me why it had happened. There was a BSA meeting, she explained, and the leadership of the BSA meeting said Rudolph Byrd and so and so are faggots. And we will have nothing else to do with them. And I thanked her for telling me that and really appreciated her honesty. I decided not to waste any more time with those folks because I understood that I could never be Black enough for them since I was not going to block those other parts of myself. And so it was my experience with homophobia and the rejection of my blackness that caused me to empathize with women. I understood that we occupied the same position. So that early experience with my father and my experience in college were pivotal in my understanding of the connections between the oppression of women and homosexuals.[26]

Kendall Thomas also describes an experience he had with a young Black male member of the Nation of Islam at a conference on Black masculinity at Princeton University during which he revealed that he was gay. The response on the part of the young man was "How can a black man be a homosexual?"—which caused Thomas to reflect upon the reality that "in that position, in that place, gender was very much a mechanism for policing who I could be, and still be Black."[27]

We were struck by the number of men whose views about gender had been shaped by their witnessing violence within their families. Haki Madhubuti described his long years of struggle for Black liberation having been motivated by childhood experiences. "I came from a very violent home. At twelve years old, I pulled my stepfather off my mother as he was about to beat her into some unknown world."[28] Referring to her own abuse by her husband, Iverson's mother insisted that he learn how to live as a man, "so that

you will not treat any woman the way I have been treated."[29] Gary
Lemons describes himself as "a survivor of domestic violence": it
has taken "all the courage that I can muster to begin to speak about
that in my life. To actually say that I have survived conditions
which have destroyed many men of African descent."[30]

Pearl Cleage's experience with an abusive boyfriend in college
provided a catalyst for her evolving gender consciousness and a
professional career in which feminist themes permeate her writing
and activist life. She grew up in a peaceful two-parent household
before her parents divorced (when she was six), so that she was utterly unprepared for what she experienced during her freshman
year at Howard University.

> He started out a really nice kind of straight guy. And then he
> became incredibly jealous and controlling and abusive, and
> eventually tied me up and did just awful, awful, horrible
> stuff. Nobody had ever hit me. My family didn't hit. My
> mother had never talked to me about abuse at all. So I as-
> sumed it was something I had done. I must have done some-
> thing to make him react this way. So I thought that for at
> least a year and a half . . . until I really thought he was going
> to kill me. I had never said anything to anyone about him
> being abusive. I went to his house one day for something
> and he was mad about something and he had to go to
> class and he said I'm going to make sure that you're here
> when I get back. So he took all of my clothes, everything I
> was wearing and tied me to a desk so that I could not leave.
> And I'm sitting there stark naked, a block from Howard
> University, saying to myself, you are over your head, you do
> not know how to handle this, you need to call your Daddy.
> So I called my dad and said I'm engaged to a guy. I know I
> told you he was great and I was going to marry him. I was
> lying. He's abusive, he's going to kill me, please come and
> get me.[31]

It's not surprising that Pearl's first book, which she self-published,
Mad at Miles: A Blackwoman's Guide to Truth, would begin with
"the problem" of the physical abuse of Black women. She quotes

from Shahrazad Ali's *The Blackman's Guide to Understanding Black Woman*, in which Ali boldly asserts, "When she [the black woman] crosses this line and becomes viciously insulting it is time for the Blackman to soundly slap her in the mouth." Then Pearl moves on to an interview with Ike Turner in the September 3, 1990, issue of *People* magazine during which he calmly reveals that he whacked his wife, Tina Turner, across the face prior to a performance after which she asked him to take her to the hospital because she thought her jaw was broken. "She did the whole show without me being able to detect it."[32]

In the chapter entitled "The Other Facts of Life," Pearl contextualizes gender-specific violence against women as part and parcel of the fabric of American life:

> In America, they *admit* that five women a day are killed by their husbands, boyfriends, ex-husbands, ex-boyfriends, or lovers. That doesn't count the women killed during random rapes, murders, robberies, and kidnappings. In America, the main reason women are ever hospitalized is because they've been beaten and tortured by men. More than for childbirth. More than for cancer care. More than from heart attacks. In America, thousands of women a day are raped and/or tortured and abused by men in as many ways as you can think of, and don't want to, including beating, shooting, scalding, stabbing, shaking, and starving. The facts indicate that we are under siege, incredibly vulnerable, totally unprepared and *too busy denying the truth to collectively figure out what to do about it. . . .* All men are *capable* of abusing women, no matter what they tell you or what they call it, so don't kid yourself about this one or that one being different.[33]

After some sound advice to women about warning signals, she reminds them that "*Violence is never justified*. It should *never* be forgiven. Apologies and pleas for forgiveness should fall on deaf ears. If a man beats you/hits you/shoves you/slaps you/torments you once, *he will do it again*. Cut him loose" (29).

Ruby Sales describes having had more healthy personal

experiences in her family and community that shaped her views about gender and sexuality and resulted in a positive sense of self as she came to maturity. They include strong female (heterosexual, lesbian, and bisexual) role models, which she describes with a remarkable sense of ease, as well as an atypical father and mother whom she describes as "androgynous" in their nonconformity to traditional gender roles:

> I think the moment you make a decision that you're going to step outside of the safety of what it means to be a female, you make some very conscious, intentional decisions about how you see yourself. I made those decisions in Columbus, Georgia, when I used to sneak to the public library and read books on what it meant to be a lesbian because somewhere I was struggling with real issues of bisexuality. Now the interesting thing is that I didn't feel threatened by the question of bisexuality because many of my teachers were bisexuals and what I had learned about them was that it wasn't the act that was wrong . . . it was the indiscretion.[34]

Supported by a community of women who themselves challenged normative gender roles, Sales understood that her sexuality did not have to determine her expression of femininity.

> I know that I didn't want to be like Alice Holt who was somewhere out there trying to act like a man and standing on the corner—I was too much invested in the culture of my teachers and women whom I deeply admired. I came to lesbianism, I came to bisexuality emulating women like Bertha Manns who wore rakish hats and was actually one of the prettiest women in our town. I knew that you could be a bisexual woman and be really attractive. So I didn't think that in order to work out gender issues, I had to act like a man or look like a man.[35]

Others shared with us their personal struggles around gender and their commitment to challenging attitudes about normative masculinity and homophobia in African American communities. Gary Lemons, a professor and minister in the Church of God in Christ, asserted:

> I'd say that what I have to do as a man who is always contesting the construction of heteronormative masculinity is to go right to the heterosexist idea of what manhood and masculinity are supposed to be. And then I act out against it. This results in assumptions about my sexuality, which is always fine with me, but I don't allow that to be the stopping point of our conversation.[36]

Others expressed how their own homophobia "imprisoned" them and that the process of challenging their homophobia enabled them to understand the links between heterosexism, misogyny, patriarchy, and painful experiences they had as children. Thandabantu Iverson described how the experience of reading Audre Lorde while he was a graduate student helped him to confront at a deep, personal level the complex scripts about masculinity and sexuality that circulate within African American communities and our complicity with perpetuating systems of oppression:

> It was difficult for me to walk into a bookstore and be seen buying a book by Audre Lorde. I wondered what will people think of me, tall, Black, masculine, buying a book by this Black lesbian. When I got home, I locked my door, and closed my windows and went in my room . . . Somehow I had to shut myself up because I didn't want anybody else to know that I was doing this. And I could not read beyond where she talked about how she was trying to raise her son to be a non-oppressive male. And it all came together and I was awash in tears. Something happened to me in that room. Since that, I have begun to try to think differently and live my life differently. It moved me from a point of simply seeing these different kinds of discrimination or oppression as separate things and began to make me understand that our realities as African American people are complex.[37]

Robin Kelley (reminiscent of Ruby Sales) discussed how his unusually progressive, antihomophobic mother, despite her economic plight, exposed her son and daughter to a belief system and diverse community that encouraged the idea of gender as chosen identity rather than natural behavior.

> My mother used to quote the Bagavad-Gita and she would talk about Shiva and talk about these nongendered gods . . . and my mom's best friends were anyone who was marginal— so all the lesbians in the community were her best friends, all the gay men in the community were her best friends—And so it was my sister, my mom and me living on a very marginal economic existence, in a world where I just assumed that I could pretty much choose my own gender identity—that it's not even a question of society's definitions of masculinity.[38]

In one of the most extraordinary tributes we've ever read to a Black mother, Kelley describes his mother's ability to transform the world in which they lived through her capacity to dream and her refusal to accept societal definitions of race, class, and gender:

> In the quiet darkness of her bedroom, her third eye opens onto a new world, a beautiful, light-filled place as peaceful as her state of mind . . . Her other two eyes never let her forget where we lived. The cops, drug dealers, social workers, the rusty tap water, the roaches and rodents, the urine-scented hallways, and the piles of garbage were constant reminders that our world began and ended in a battered Harlem/Washington Heights tenement apartment . . . Yet she would not allow us to live as victims. Instead, we were a family of caretakers who inherited this earth. We were expected to help any living creature in need, even if that meant giving up our last piece of bread . . . She simply wanted us to live through our third eyes, to see life as possibility. She wanted us to imagine a world free of patriarchy, a world where gender and sexual relations could be reconstructed . . . She wanted us to visualize a more expansive, fluid, "cosmopolitan" definition of blackness.[39]

Feeling as if he was raised to be a feminist by his mother, Kelley describes the most painful interlude of his childhood when he (along with his sister) was kidnapped by his father at age nine and kept in a world for six long years that was antithetical to the value system in which he was reared:

> My father who now lived in white Seattle kidnapped us from our safe world in Harlem. So here he is playing patriarch, not a patriarch in a capitalist sense but more like a feudal patriarch in the precapitalist sense, thinking he was doing the right thing. My father kept us against our will in prison and presented to us a completely dysfunctional notion of black masculinity because it involved violence from the first moment. My father becomes a monster and I'm prepared to be a feminist.[40]

After many years, Kelley's mother, who didn't have resources to hire a lawyer, moved to Los Angeles, California, and engineered her children's daring escape. "My father's got people chasing after us; it's a harrowing experience. But I get to my mom when I'm fifteen years old and my sister and I become feminists again." Kelley's and his sister's feminist identity never leave them because of the profound influence of their mother: "My sister and I are at UCLA together. She was active, I was active. She taught me a lot of things. We always raised the question of feminism and gender and then she would give me things to read and I would give her things to read. I read bell hooks the second year of college. No one had to tell me, look for black feminism, because it was part of the agenda and my mom's reading that stuff. My mom also had Simone de Beauvoir in the house. I remember as a kid picking up the book (I was seven) and I could read and I knew it said sex (*The Second Sex*) but I didn't know what sex was!"[41] Thinking about his mother and father, Kelley also critiques the notion prevalent among some segments of the Black community that fathers are better at raising sons than mothers:

> I'm disturbed by the idea that black men should raise boys and that black women can't raise boys. In fact, I feel that

black women, like my mother, were better prepared to raise me as a boy than anyone else. Because my mother questioned what boyhood was and told me that there are other models. That's why I'm weird, but I'm proud that my mother raised me.[42]

He is also convinced that unconventional child-rearing practices where gender matters are concerned help produce children who question societal norms and are freer in their expressions of femininity or masculinity.

Echoing Kelley, Gary Lemons, a professor at The New School in New York City, asserted, "I am weird and very proud of it." Raised by a traditional father with respect to gender roles, Lemons raises his son differently because of the suffering he experienced at home:

I was not a child who was liked by my father. I think he thought that the kind of man he was was the kind of man he was going to make me into. I could not live up to those expectations. My son laughs at me because I can't dribble a ball. I've taught my son that it's not a problem to be a different kind of male child. But in my own life, I have been positioned at the margins because I didn't fit into a traditional black male model. My father said I actually hate you because you're not the son I wanted you to be. There were also beatings.[43]

Raised by an abused mother, who told him, "You are right the way you are," Lemons (like Rudolph Byrd) told himself that when he grew up, he would be different from his father. He also found "sanctuary in the margin" and found peace "being a [so-called] freak." As a graduate student he would learn that there are Black men who bond with Black women in struggles for gender equality, with whom he could identify: "I found in those men feminist fathers. I call them my feminist forefathers, men like Du Bois, Frederick Douglass, Calvin Hernton." Rejecting and "acting out" against heterosexist, normative concepts of masculinity, Lemons realizes that his sexuality is often in question and that he might be rejected by men because he doesn't adhere to the party line. "But I'm not going to live out, nor align myself with a kind of misogyny that is about us males bonding in a way that is about the objectification, subjugation of women."[44]

Like Kelley's extraordinary mother and others, redefining masculinity and femininity was seen as an important task for some within African American communities. The men and women with whom we spoke were also aware that while African Americans abhorred the racial attitudes and behavior of mainstream society, we were less reluctant as a community to distance ourselves from its oppressive gender attitudes and practices. Legal scholar Derrick Bell asserts that "because sexism and patriarchy are deeply rooted in this society, all too many black men have fallen into patterns of physical and emotional abuse of women."[45] He also demonstrated a remarkable degree of commitment to gender equality when he resigned in protest from his tenured post as Weld Professor of Law at Harvard Law School because it refused to hire a woman of color for their law school faculty.

THE INTERSECTION OF CLASS AND GENDER

Class also plays a part in the shaping of gender roles. This connection was succinctly articulated by Elaine Brown, former head of the Black Panther Party. For Brown, poverty most strongly impacted her experiences and attitudes around gender. The women in her family greatly influenced her particular sense of female independence; she saw the oppression they had to deal with as a result of their class. It was impossible to believe in the inferiority of women in the face of Black women's racial experiences, according to Brown: "These women who have worked like dogs, who have also been lynched, it didn't even occur to me that they were less than men."[46] The women with whom she grew up were almost invincible in spite of their overwhelming economic plight:

I didn't know men in my childhood. I only knew women. And these women were tough. They were the backbone of the community. These were some bad women, including my mother. My Aunt Mary told me when my mother died recently that she was so proud she could buy that house for her mother. She had a good job; she was twenty-two years old and she bought that house in 1939 and she was working as a washer at the Navy yard. So for me there are three sources of our oppression: patriarchy, capitalism, and racism. But for me the most important thing has been poverty.[47]

Poverty, an extended family of mainly women, and her education in an all-girls high school provided Elaine Brown with a unique gender lens that would later shape her response to the sexism she encountered in the Black Panther Party:

I didn't know I was supposed to take on a gender role. One of the great things about my individual experience was that I had gone to a girls' high school. That's why I told my daughter, "You don't understand the power of that four years I had at Girls High." There was no male principal. The president of every class was a woman; the everything of everything was a woman. It never occurred to us that women were powerless.[48]

She and her high school girlfriends envisioned a life for themselves predicated on their development as highly self-actualized individuals, free from the constraints of conventional gender roles:

I was going to France or something; whatever it was we wanted to do, we would just do these fabulous things, and we never thought that we would get married. It didn't even occur to us that we would become "the wife of . . ." We were never trained for wifehood, and I went in there at fourteen years old. The second thing that shaped my identity was I had a mother who worshiped me. I was the ghetto princess. I was living in the ghetto but I was like the most beautiful girl in the world. It never occurred to me that I wasn't this fabulous person. So when I went to Girls' High, it was just an extension of how fabulous I was. And I took

Latin and we were smart. And being smart was more important to me than anything.

Fast forwarding to the Black Panther Party; it didn't occur to me that I had a role to play with men. I swear to you it didn't! It didn't even occur to me 'cause I didn't cook. So when I was in the Black Panther Party, it's like, "Cooking breakfast? Fine, let them do it." Let whoever does cooking, do the breakfast. I write articles myself! I will learn to shoot a gun, but I will not cook because I don't cook! Why would I be cooking? So the gender thing came into play really in the sixties for me—with this whole notion that liberation was a man's thing. I didn't get it! I was never the little woman. No woman I knew was the little woman. So I fought this and we became known as the clique.[49]

She also reminded us that Angela Davis was run out of the Party because of her refusal to be deferential to the men.

Like Elaine Brown, Audree Irons, an administrative assistant at Spelman, described Black women in her family and community as feminist role models. Irons recalls that having a strong work ethic was an important message passed on to her by her mother and grandmother. She remembers the history of self-reliance that African American working-class and poor women *had* to practice:

They taught me a work ethic; they taught me spirituality, they taught me how to make it without a man because I was looking at these women who were making it without men. In fact, my grandmother taught her sons how to shoot a gun. You know that's the way you had to live in the country, you went out and hunted your food. I learned a lot from just watching my mother and my grandmother being strong women and I didn't know what all of that was called, I just thought that's what women do. Men leave, we keep going. We don't miss a beat. Like later for them. That's basically the attitude my mother and grandmother had. It was like we'll throw them out like garbage and we'll just keep on going; they assumed the role of both male and female. And naturally I picked up some of that too. I had three children, but I'm not with any of the fathers. I have two sets of children (by two men) and I basically knew I didn't have to put up with either of them. My mother and grandmother showed me how to cope, so I just kick them to the curb and keep on going.[50]

Irons described her class status as strongly mediating her experiences as a Black woman. When asked about her biggest challenges as a young single Black woman, she quickly responded:

I think economics. I think at times I'm constantly in this little box that I didn't choose to put myself in. I'm just there. I'm constantly fighting to tear every wall down and I'm wondering if somebody is going to let me tear this down. I tried a chisel, now I got a hammer. Maybe I should try some dynamite now, I mean that. I just want to be who I want to be and not even worry about all that other stuff. And it's a constant battle. How to make enough money to take care of the kids. What do I do to prepare them for their education? Where am I going to get the money from? How are we going to eat today? Where's the gas coming from for the car? You're working two jobs and you're getting maybe three hours of sleep a night and it's like this is crazy. I just feel so trapped but I'm like I can't give up, I've got to break this box apart. Economics is the main thing. And I would say at times I'm more fortunate than some of my other sisters. I've graduated from high school. I've been to college for a year and a half. Ever since I've been working at Spelman I've been taking classes to try and lift myself up economically. And I have sympathy for the women who are caught in housing projects who're going through the same struggles as I am but they don't even see a way out. They don't have time. They are too caught in the daily things of how do I feed my kids?[51]

Clearly, class oppression magnifies Black women's experience of gender oppression.

Kimberly Tyler's compelling life story, like that of Audree Irons, is a testament to the struggles of poor Black women as they attempt to realize their dreams in the face of seemingly insurmountable obstacles. Tyler struggled through growing up the daughter of a prostitute and a pimp, domestic violence, drug abuse, molestation, rape, homelessness, and unemployment. Notice the way she introduced herself at the start of what was clearly one of the most disturbing and moving of all of the interviews that we conducted.

Well, I'm Kimberly Tyler. I was born October 31, 1966, Halloween. My mother was a prostitute. My father was a pimp. They were married and had four children, I was the third one to be born—pretty much in poverty. I saw my mother turn tricks for a living and I saw my father beat my mother for not bringing home the amount of money he thought she should bring home. I've seen my mother pass out from being drunk. She was an alcoholic and she did drugs. At an early age I was molested by my uncles and cousins.[52]

Although Tyler desperately wanted to avoid repeating in her later life all that she had witnessed and experienced as a young girl, she endured similar incidences of physical and sexual abuse as a young woman.

At the age of eighteen, I married a man who was very abusive to me. A lot of things happened in that marriage, but I tried to stay in it because I had Deandria and Garret, my oldest son, and I always wanted my children to have a mother and a father. But then the abuse started. The fights started. The stabbings—one doctor said twelve times, one doctor said twenty-two times. I'm not really sure how many times. I was thrown downstairs. My head was gashed open. And at that time, I did not know that my husband was molesting my daughter, Deandria. And she didn't tell me. I guess because he told her that if she told me he would kill us. So for a long time, for many years, he molested my daughter.[53]

Kimberly found herself in and out of welfare and work. It was during the time that she was working at Wheeler County Hospital in Glenwood, Georgia, that her husband subjected her to the most horrific physical and sexual abuse in their marriage:

> One night, while I was working at the hospital and got off at 11:00 at night I didn't have a way home because my husband would not come to get me. One of the paramedics, a white guy, said he did not want to see me walk home by myself at that hour, and he gave me a ride in an ambulance. When I got home, my husband started asking me why this man had brought me home, and I asked him why he didn't pick me up. He then said he wanted me to have sex with him and I said no. And from there it went into stabbing and beatings. I remember picking up an iron to hit him with it but somehow he got the iron and started beating me with it. Finally, he left the apartment. I remember holding my guts so that they would not fall on the floor. And I went to the door of some neighbors and they took me to the hospital.[54]

Kimberly Tyler miraculously survived that merciless physical beating by her husband, only to then be raped by him while she lay in her hospital bed.

> He came into the hospital while I was all stitched up and bandaged up and could not move because my hands were tied so that I could not pull out the tubes they had in me. They had me strapped to the bed. While I was in that condition, he actually came into the hospital room and got on top of me and forced having sex with me. Then he told me if I tried to leave him he would kill me. I believed him. And when I was released from the hospital, I went back to him. When I think about it, I did the same thing that my mother did, because I remember my father beating my mother and putting her in a tub to die, and she went back to him. She kept going back. So I found myself doing some of the same things that my mom did.[55]

But over time, Kimberly Tyler found a way to leave her husband. She is now married to a man whom she describes as the antithesis of her first husband. Kimberly managed to enroll in a United Way–sponsored program that helped her to get off welfare. She is now working in a hospital in a social service position where she helps young Black women whose life conditions are similar to what hers were. Today, Kimberly Tyler is also enrolled at Georgia State University. But managing to reinvent her life has certainly not been easy for Kimberly. She shared with us how she had to battle a welfare system that treated her as a second-class citizen even as she tried to improve her life:

> It's still a nightmare with the Department of Family and Child Services (DFACS). You got to show all this stuff. Justify every dime they give you and if you don't spend every dime you got to give it back. So I made up in my mind I was going to be one of these women who was going to change the system. I knew that I wanted to work for DFACS so that I could kind of change the system because I had been talked down to all of my life and told, you don't want to be nothing, you're not going to be anything. I remember the day I graduated, the next month which was May '98, they had sent me a welfare check for $378 and I took it back to DFACS and told Ms. Bennett, I don't need this check. You give it to someone else. And she looked at me like I was crazy! I think that's when Bankhead realized that I was their big success story.
>
> And believe it or not, I started working for them. And I worked there and I had my little case load but I still was not satisfied. I was a people person. I had learned a lot through all my experiences of being molested, being raped, my daughter being molested, my daughter being raped; mom prostituting, dad pimping. Drugs coming in and out my family. I just did not want to sit behind a desk. I said now Lord, I want to do something. I want to help your people. I heard other case workers talk to their clients so ugly and I got mad because I thought we are human. Sometimes we are thrown in

these situations not because we want to be but because of circumstances.

Then I started thinking that I was not my circumstances, I was all my possibilities, anything that I wanted to be. Well I decided I want to go for another job. At this point I said I'm moving up to the east side like the Jeffersons. So I put in my mind that I was gonna move up. Like I said, I worked for DFACS for a month. One of my job duties at Bankhead was to help place other welfare recipients on jobs. Something came through my office about Grady Health Care Systems and about working with teenage mothers and adolescents, educating them about welfare reform, and having girls linked to our family planning clinic so they wouldn't get pregnant. Then I knew every welfare law. I decided to learn every law concerning welfare and Black women. I just wanted this to be a mission of mine, educating our Black women about welfare laws. I had already told God, if you allow me to work with people, I'll do it in your name and I'll reach everyone that I can because I have this big testimony about my life and I knew that there were other women who were being battered, and other children who were being molested, and other children who don't have mothers, whose mothers' boyfriends and husbands are messing with them. That was real touching to me and I knew other women on welfare just needed somebody to say, I've been there and I've done that but I made it and I'm going to help you to make it.[58]

FIGHTING FOR SOCIAL JUSTICE

Difficult life experiences not only encouraged the women and men we interviewed to develop a stronger gender consciousness, but in many cases also led to activist struggle in their communities around racism, sexism, class oppression, and homophobia. For some, the path led to teaching, research, and writing books that would make a difference in knowledge and attitudes about African American women and men; for others, the path of activism led them to engage in work that educated women and men about the deleterious effects of patriarchy such as domestic violence; some managed to do both. For others, like Kimberly Tyler, the path to activism came directly from her commitment to changing her status as a victim of poverty, racism, and sexism to a life of struggle in the very institutions that had once marginalized her.

For the Reverend Aubra Love, her clergy activist work as director of the Black Church and Domestic Violence Project came out of her personal experience with domestic abuse:

> When I talk about the history of the project, I'm reminded that there are particular ways that people talk about social change and because I've been an activist all my life I have to start with that history from my own experience because that's where I do the work from. It all began for me as a mature woman in seminary. I met a pastor, we dated for a couple of years, I married him, and he was physically abusive. He was a perfect gentleman during the two years we dated. But we had done the Christian model of dating—going to revivals and going to dinner—and all our time was very structured. But in unstructured time, he was a completely different person.
>
> When the abuse started, I was faced with a serious dilemma since I belonged to a church with a Black congregation and whites at the top. What does it mean to go to a white district superintendent about a brother? What a challenge it was trying to get some understanding and help from the church. Lots of things happened in the process, from involving the criminal justice system to actually fleeing from home and having him transferred to another parish out of state. When I went to community agencies/shelters, I learned a lot of things. Such as, if you have a male child over twelve there are usually no accommodations for him within a battered woman's shelter. So, he is stuck with wherever chronically homeless adult men go, which is really the business of our churches and community. You don't take your

fifteen year old to a shelter of chronically homeless men. This was my situation because my son was older than twelve. And I realized that we need to find housing money to construct transitional housing so that the woman's authority is not undermined within her household, that the family stays connected. That's when I applied for the McKinney funds and proposed transitional housing for women fleeing domestic violence in Asheville, North Carolina. The church then asked me to be their interim pastor. So that's where I started doing this work.[57]

Understanding that her clergy experiences were complicated by race and gender, Love decided to focus her interventions within African American communities in order to confront the silence around the issue of intraracial violence against women:

Initially I was pastoring at a white church, but I was compelled to historically Black churches and teach this work around domestic violence. I wanted to stay in community with other black people, to talk about the experience of my own healing and recovery, to break the silence for women in the pews who felt nobody would listen to what they were talking about. And I started to go to other churches. I'd get invited to speak on Mother's Day and I'd preach about domestic violence. We'd have a mother/daughter banquet, and I'd talk about domestic violence. And eventually I got some press coverage and met Marie Fortune, who had assembled a national group of African Americans around domestic violence. I was invited to come to Seattle and work with her in a program that was funded through the Ford Foundation. I did that for a year and a half, and later applied for separate non-profit status for the newly founded Black Church & Domestic Violence Institute, because what was apparent to me was that this work must be defined within our own communities.[58]

The link between critical engagement with one's lived experiences, political activism, and progressive ideas about gender was articulated repeatedly by the women and men with whom we spoke. For them the personal is political, as it has been for the two of us. They are also explicit about the meanings of their gendered, racial, and class identities as African Americans. They refuse to be silent about the consequences of racism *and* sexism in our lives, even if it means airing dirty linen in public. Hard-hitting, unapologetic Pearl Cleage has chosen the pen as her weapon in the struggle for an infusion of feminist values in Black communities and the eradication of everything we do to each other that is destructive. "My friend the well respected public servant comes to work with sunglasses to hide the two black eyes her husband gave her by beating her head against the wall while their children slept in the next room. My sisterwriter with the three young children tells horror stories of being scalded with boiled water and forced to suck the barrel of a gun as if it was her husband's penis." Cleage must never forget what she knows, but like the griot, give voice to it: "I own no weapons and have never been in a fight in my life. I am not an organizer and I have no troops to marshal with marching songs and battle plans. What I do is write about what I see and what I feel and what I know in the hope that it will help the people who read it see more and feel more and know more."[59] Cleage is explicit about her motives and her audience:

> I am writing because nobody even said the word sexism to me until I was thirty years old and I want to know why. I am writing because I have seen my friends bleed to death from illegal abortions. I am writing because I have seen my sisters tortured and tormented by the fathers of their children. I am writing because I almost married a man who beat me regularly and with no remorse. . . . I am writing to find solutions and pass them on.[60]

She is convinced, as we are, that what we know about slavery and racism can help us understand gender injustice if we ever figure out a way to use our racial knowledge for different purposes. The crucial question for her is: "How do we transfer racial understanding to a discussion of sexism?" We would make it "sexism" *and* heterosexism?

We are writing because we believe it is possible to free ourselves as a community from the traps of sexism and heterosexism even as we continue our struggle against the ever present threats of racial inequality and poverty. We believe that hearing all our voices and telling the truths of all our lives will help to undermine patriarchal dominance that is "no less virulent and deadly than racism," in the wise words of Pearl Cleage. We believe that our collective wisdom and historical commitment to social justice are crucial in our continued journey toward emancipation for all of us, women and men, gay and straight. Those among us who embrace Black feminist politics in all its forms are convinced that a revolution in gender relations is possible within our communities. We have had our say. Take this sisterly and brotherly medicine and pass it on.

3

•

COLLISIONS:

BLACK LIBERATION VERSUS

WOMEN'S LIBERATION

When feminism does not explicitly oppose racism, and when antiracism does not incorporate opposition to patriarchy, race and gender politics often end up being antagonistic to each other and both interests lose.

Kimberlé Crenshaw, "Whose Story Is It Anyway? Feminist and Antiracist Appropriations of Anita Hill," 1992

The sex war and the race war in the United States have always been ruled by the politics of a common ideology—the Ideology of Race First and Sex Second. . . . racial equality between white and black men is more important than the "lesser question" of sex equality . . . the politics of sex and the politics of race are one and the same politics.

Calvin Hernton, "Breaking Silences," 1992

Is our attainment of patriarchal power through the oppression of women any less insidious than white people's perpetuation of a system of racial oppression to dehumanize us? Many of us have become so obsessed with fighting racism as a battle for the right to be patriarchal men that we have been willing to deploy the same strategies to disempower black women as white supremacists have employed to institutionalize racism.

Gary Lemons, "To Be Black, Male,
and Feminist," 1998

On October 11, 1991, Professor Anita Faye Hill appeared before the United States Senate Judiciary Committee and accused Judge Clarence Thomas, a fellow African American and the Republican nominee to the Supreme Court, of sexually harassing her while they both worked at the Department of Education and the Equal Employment Opportunity Commission. That unforgettable day, captured on prime-time national television, was described by linguist Geneva Smitherman as "a unique and extraordinarily complex moment in U.S. history, the reverberations of which will continue to resound for years."[1] Barely a week later, on October 17, psychologists Nathan and Julia Hare appeared in a talk show on Black Entertainment Television (BET) and, using predictable antifeminist rhetoric, informed their largely Black audience about a long, destructive history of Black women's betrayal of the race that began when slave women collaborated with their white masters. In direct contrast, historian Paula Giddings applauded Anita Hill in her analysis of the divisive impact on the Black community of this courageous young Black woman who forced a "mandate on gender" by refusing to remain silent and publicly rejecting demands for racial loyalty. "For many, what was *inappropriate* was that a black woman's commitment to a gender issue superseded what was largely perceived as racial solidarity."[2] Remembering the history of Black America, we are mindful of other watershed events during which race and gender collide and where, according to Cornel West, African Americans feel compelled to "close ranks for survival in a hostile country."[3] In these perennial struggles of a people under siege, the interests and perspectives of Black women are often ignored, as was the case with Anita Hill.

Nearly a century earlier, in 1892, educator Anna Julia Cooper broke rank and wrote eloquently about the "voiceless Black woman of America" who is "confronted by both a woman question and a race problem" and, like Anita Hill, is expected to choose between the well being of her race and her own needs as a woman.[4] Despite their marginalization, nineteenth-century Black women leaders waged a valiant battle against sexism within their communities, were openly critical of Black male leadership, and spoke with remarkable candor about intraracial gender tensions. According to historian Deborah Gray White, these Black women were "convinced that black female issues and race issues were identical," and that throughout their gender struggles, "it was not dirty laundry they were airing, it was just cold hard truth."[5] Cooper's *A Voice from the South* (1892) engages in frank public discourse about intraracial gender politics and anticipates some of the questions that preoccupy us in *Gender Talk*. She asks and we echo her: What would a vision of Black community transformation look like if gender were more central to our analytic frameworks? What might we learn from engaging in more systematic analyses of the struggles between race and gender within African American communities? What would we gain from conceptualizing race loyalty differently so that the needs of both Black women and men could be more fully realized?

In order to more fully understand the contemporary context of gender relations within African American communities, we want to call attention in this chapter to several important moments in U.S. history in which the collision of race and gender issues had a divisive impact on the Black community. During each of these episodes the issue of race loyalty became a prominent feature of the ensuing public discourse. There were also profound differences between Black women and men *and* among Black women about how to deal with these crises. This is particularly true in the more recent past, when a series of highly public and controversial events—the Clarence Thomas–Anita Hill Supreme Court hearings; the Mike Tyson, O. J. Simpson, and the Reverend Henry Lyons trials—forced the Black community to respond to what they perceived to be harmful airing of dirty linen in public. We have our own memories of these debates, but also a range of writings that help us make sense of the Black community's complicated responses.

Twenty-one years removed from slavery and preoccupied by the challenges of "race regeneration" after the long nightmare of slavery, Anna Julia Cooper was unapologetic in her feminist analysis of Black America about the urgency of analyzing our past failures and achievements, our present "difficulties and embarrassments," and our "mingled hopes and fears for the future." She boldly asserted that it was now time "to pause a moment for retrospection, introspection and prospection." In addition to analyzing the pervasive legacy of slavery and the racism of the white women's movement, Cooper also provided what we would now call an internal critique, an analysis of sexism *within* the Black community. She was particularly perturbed that "while our men seem thoroughly abreast of the times on almost every other subject, when they strike the woman question they drop back into sixteenth century logic."[6] This preoccupation with race matters and blindness to gender concerns would characterize mainstream Black political thought until the mid-sixties, when a radical Black feminist discourse and practice emerged within the context of the civil rights movement.[7]

Certainly, it is time again to pause for retrospection and introspection. There is a growing body of work by Black women, which, in the tradition of Cooper, analyzes intracommunity issues and arrives at diagnoses and solutions that are frequently at odds with the more popular and influential Black male discourse about the state of Black America.[8] Fortunately, there is also a growing body of work by Black men, some of whom self-identify as feminists, in which gender and sexuality are central.[9]

LOOKING BACK

Following in Anna Julia Cooper's footsteps, we begin our own historical retrospective with the debate over the Fifteenth Amendment to the Constitution in 1870 which, like the Thomas-Hill saga, was a watershed event whose reverberations with respect to Black gender politics have continued for over a century. This contentious discussion over granting suffrage to Black men and not to Black women precipitated a major split within the women's movement and rancorous debate within the Black community as well. The famous debate between abolitionist Frederick Douglass and white suffragists occurred in New York City in 1869 at the annual convention of the American Equal Rights Association (AERA), which was founded in 1866 to obtain the vote for Black men and all women. Douglass argued for the greater urgency of race over gender. He believed it was the "Negro's hour," and that women's rights could wait, since linking woman suffrage to Negro suffrage at this historical juncture would seriously reduce the chances of securing the ballot for Black men. For Black people, Douglass insisted, the ballot was more urgent since it was a matter of life and death. He reiterated that the plight of women (he most assuredly meant white women) and freed persons (men and women) was simply incomparable in his eloquent and riveting litany of the differences between being Black and being female in America:

> When women, because they are women, are hunted down through the cities of New York and New Orleans; when they are dragged from their houses and hung upon lampposts; when their children are torn from their arms, and their brains dashed out upon the pavement; when they are objects of insult and outrage at every turn; when they are in danger of having their homes burnt down over their heads; when their children are not allowed to enter schools; then they will have an urgency to obtain the ballot equal to our own.[10]

When asked by an unidentified person in the audience whether this was true for Black women as well—that is, the urgency of the right to vote for Blacks—he responded, "Yes, yes, yes . . . but not because she is a woman, but because she is black."[11]

Frances E. W. Harper, a prominent Black abolitionist, suffragist, and writer, supported Douglass, while Sojourner Truth supported white suffragists, believing that if Black men got the vote, they would continue to dominate Black women. In a speech at the same 1869 meeting, Harper argued for greater urgency of the struggle against racism: "When it was a question of race, she [Harper] let the lesser question of sex go. But the white women all go for sex, letting race occupy a minor position."[12] Two years earlier, Sojourner Truth, speaking at the 1867 meeting of the AERA, articulated her fears about Black men getting the vote: "There is a great stir about colored men getting their rights, but not a word about the colored women; and if colored men get their rights, and not colored women get theirs, there will be a bad time about it."[13] Granting political rights to Black women would alter existing power imbalances between them and their men, Truth believed: "When we get our rights, we shall not have to come to you for money . . . You have been having our right so long, that you think, like a slaveholder, that you own us."[14]

From our perspective over a century later, what is perhaps more important to consider is not whose argument was the most convincing, but how we might reinterpret this historic debate. Historian Darlene Clark Hine provides a useful way of assessing the meaning of this race/gender divide in the late nineteenth century. She argues that with few exceptions, Black women and men certainly applauded the adoption of the Fifteenth Amendment, but that "inauspiciously, this amendment in some ways cemented a gender breach in black culture," because it created a fundamental inequality between Black men and women.[15] "Once black men gained the right to vote," Hine reminds us, "black women had no alternative but to negotiate with and convince their male relatives to use the ballot to advance group as opposed to individual interests."[16] Hine argues that what was perhaps even more problematic from Black women's perspectives was that this differential power base "allowed black men the latitude to determine the public agenda in the struggle against racism" (344). In other words, the political agendas of the race continued to be shaped by Black men; thus the perspectives of Black women could be ignored entirely or relegated to the back burner.

Debates about Black women in the public sphere included issues other than suffrage, such as the feasibility of higher education, the nature of their role in the work force, and even whether they should be ordained in the ministry. In an era in which the prevailing opinion was that a woman's natural sphere of activity was the home and her roles as wife and mother were her most important functions, it is not surprising that many discussions about women, including Black women, focused on the domestic sphere. Intense debates centered around the nature of Black womanhood itself. At the center of these debates were arguments about her moral character, which was a reflection of the general preoccupation with women's moral nature on the part of Victorian society. The most persistent theme in the writings of late-nineteenth-century white men is the devaluation of Black women in opposition to their ideal- ization of white women as chaste and virtuous. A much repeated re- frain in white racist political discourse among men and women is the immorality and promiscuity of Black women, especially in dis- cussions of the deteriorated condition of Black families and the criminality of the race.

Although it is not surprising, given the acceptance by white so- ciety of the inherent inferiority of the Black race, that whites would advance the thesis that Black women were morally defective, it is important to point out that some African Americans also accepted the dominant culture's stereotypical definitions of Black woman- hood; many were sensitive as well to the peculiar plight of African American women. Though there is celebration then of Black woman- hood, Black-woman bashing also has a long history within Black political discourse dating back to the post-Reconstruction era, as was the case in mainstream racial discourse, though it would defi- nitely worsen over time.[17] Literary critic Robert Reid-Pharr cap- tures the paradoxical nature of responses to the generic Black woman by asserting that she "is a creature who readily provokes great reverence *and* icy hot hostility" among Black people.[18] The most extreme example of the latter phenomenon can be found dur- ing the late nineteenth century in a scathing attack on Black women by William Hannibal Thomas, born in 1843 in Ohio to free par- ents. In 1871 he came south to teach former slaves, and in 1873 he received a license to practice law in South Carolina, where he later became a trial justice and a member of the state legislature. Remi- niscent of Justice Clarence Thomas and other contemporary Black conservatives, he was frequently cited by racist whites in support of their anti-Black arguments. The sins of the Black woman that Wil- liam Hannibal Thomas enumerated were presumably more difficult to deny since they had been observed by a Black man. Echoing mainstream nineteenth-century gender discourse, Thomas argued that the destiny of a people is tied to its women and therefore Blacks are doomed because:

> . . . not only are fully ninety percent of the negro women of America lascivious by instinct and in bondage to physical pleasure, but . . . the social degradation of our freed-women is without parallel in modern civilization. . . . as moral rectitude is not a predominant trait in negro nature, female chastity is not one of its endowments.[19]

Black women's alleged sexual immorality is particularly offensive to Thomas: "Innate modesty is not a characteristic of the American Negro woman. . . . Marriage is no barrier to illicit sexual indulgence" (183–84). Black women, Thomas argued, even fail as wives and mothers, their most important function, which renders the race weak and ineffectual.

In his most damaging indictment, Thomas blames Black women for whatever differences exist between the races and in the process makes the argument for white supremacy, the dominant racial ideology of the period:

> There is a fundamental difference in the racial character, habits, integrity, courage, and strength of negro and white Americans. What makes it? The answer lies in one word— their women. . . . Girls of the two races will grow up side by side . . . yet the chances are two to one that the negro girl at twenty will be a giggling idiot and lascivious wreck, while her white companion . . . has blossomed out into chaste womanhood, intelligent in mind . . .(200)

Thomas has obviously accepted the dominant culture's notion that not only are Black women hopelessly degenerate, but that white women are paragons of virtue and models of womanhood whom they should emulate. His racist views did not go unnoticed, however, and several prominent Black males such as Charles Chesnutt, Booker T. Washington, William E. B. Du Bois, and Kelley

Miller criticized him publicly. Such Black woman-blaming dia-
tribes, no matter how atypical or despised among some Black
men,[20] were responses, we believe, to criticisms on the part of Black
women contemporaries like Cooper who chastised Black male leaders for their disloyalty to the race. Comparing Black women to
Black men, Cooper asserts that Black women are "always sound
and orthodox on questions affecting the well-being of the race. You
do not find the colored woman selling her birthright for a mess of
pottage."[21]

THE MASCULINE SIXTIES

Gender conflicts would intensify and become more palpable during
the civil rights movement, especially after 1965, with the popularity of
the Moynihan Report, the emergence of militant Black nationalism,
and a fledgling though visible Black women's liberation movement.[22]
To be sure, conservative gender ideologies would characterize the
more radical and influential cultural nationalist politics of the sixties which, paradoxically, harked back to the patriarchal Victorian
ethos of the late nineteenth century in some respects. While cultural
nationalism has promoted critically important positive, oppositional racial ideologies, such as self-reliance and independence for
oppressed African peoples, it failed to distance itself from the most
traditional gender attitudes of the dominant white culture. Describing the sixties as "the masculine decade," historian Paula Giddings
reminds us that the late sixties theme of "Black Power" became "a
metaphor for the male consciousness of the era."[23] Imamu Amiri
Baraka (formerly LeRoi Jones), one of the most influential architects and spokespersons for militant Black nationalism during the
mid and late sixties, articulates its philosophy of Black familyhood
within the context of "nation building" in an essay written for
Black World in 1970. His analysis of an African-derived ideology
of complementarity between the sexes is remarkably reminiscent,
ironically, of nineteenth-century Euro-American notions of a benevolent patriarchy based on normative definitions of manhood
and womanhood:

... we do not believe in equality of men and women. ...
we could never be equals ... nature has not provided
thus. ... we will complement each other ... there is no
house without a man and his wife ... When we say complement, completes, we mean that we have certain functions
which are more natural to us, and you have certain graces
that are yours alone. We say that a Black woman must first
be able to inspire her man, then she must be able to teach
our children, and contribute to the social development of
the nation.[24]

The racial discourse of other influential cultural nationalists involved in Black liberation struggles during the "machismo" sixties includes an embrace of a biologically based natural order with respect
to gender roles. Maulana Ron Karenga, founder of the radical Los
Angeles–based organization US (he is also responsible for Kwanzaa),
and a major proponent of African traditions, has endorsed patriarchal
gender norms, within the body of his work, which he calls "kawaida
theory"; this theory asserts the importance of Black people embracing
their own definition of self or a collective self-consciousness that is
shaped by our own cultural values and norms rather than those of the
oppressor. In this regard, he embraces the African-centered ideology
of complementarity in his analyses of Black familyhood, one of the
legacies presumably of African familial relations before the onslaught
of European colonialism. But his notion of separate but unequal roles
for men and women is also an unmistakable articulation of male supremacy, though his views would evolve significantly over time.

What makes a woman appealing is femininity and she
can't be feminine without being submissive. A man has to
be a leader ... There is no virtue in independence. The
only virtue is interdependence. Black women ... should
remember this. The role of the woman is to inspire her man,
educate their children and participate in social development. ... We say male supremacy is based on three things:
tradition, acceptance, and reason. Equality is false; it's the
devil's concept. Our concept is complimentary [sic].[25]

Leith Mullings reminds us that for cultural nationalists, "women are associated primarily with the domestic sphere. Their reproductive capacity is essentialized and becomes the primary aspect of their identity."[26] She is particularly insightful in her explanation of why these nation-building messages are so attractive to many Black women. "To women of African descent, who have historically borne the double burdens of work and home, a language of complementarity, protection, or even frank patriarchy may be very seductive" (140). Psychologist Na'im Akbar associates our acceptance of traditional gender roles with "the degree to which we have internalized many of the alien and destructive attitudes that are prevalent in Euro American society," the two most destructive of which are materialism and sexism.[27]

The extent to which many African Americans embrace the gender ideologies of white patriarchal culture and its attitudes about manhood and womanhood is revealed in various racial debates during the sixties. In a special issue of *Ebony* on "The Negro Woman" (August 1966), C. Eric Lincoln reaffirms Moynihan's thesis about the pathological Black family:

> So it was that the headship of the Negro family was thrust upon the Negro mother by the viciousness of a slave system which consciously sought the psychological castration of the Negro male. . . . The truth is that despite the fact that the Negro woman has done so much to bring the race so far, it has been done at the expense of the psychological health of the Negro male who has frequently been forced by circumstances into the position of a drone.[28]

The composite portrait of C. Eric Lincoln's all-powerful Negro woman is different from the one Pauli Murray describes in an essay that appeared a few years later.[29] In painstaking detail she exposes the myth of the Black matriarchy and Black women's more privileged status vis-à-vis Black men, pervasive themes in the racial discourse of the sixties. She reminds us that female-headed households at that point constitute only one-fourth of Black families, so that numbers alone would demonstrate that the majority of these families conform to the ideal American type in terms of structure. To Lincoln's assertion that traditionally Black women have been better educated, Murray concedes that in March 1968 there were 86,000 more nonwhite women college graduates than nonwhite male graduates, but that in March 1966 the median years of school completed by Black females (10.1) was only slightly higher than that for Black males (9.4). More significant, she finds that "the percentage of both sexes in the Negro population eighteen years of age and over in 1966 who had completed four years of college was roughly equivalent (males: 2.2 percent; females: 2.3 percent), but that Black males are slightly more educated (3.3 percent) than Black females (3.2 percent) with respect to graduate training." She also reminds readers that in 1968 there were 688,000 more Black women than men, which may account for the larger number of college-trained Black women. Emphasizing their persistent poverty, Murray tells us that six of every ten Black women were in private household employment or other service jobs, which are relatively low-paying, and that the median wage of nonwhite women workers was $3,268. This is only 71 percent of the median income of white women workers.[30] While Lincoln focuses on the difficulties Black men face finding jobs and supporting their families, Murray debunks the widespread myth of the privileged economic position of Black females:

> The 1966 median earnings of full-time year-around nonwhite female workers was only 65 percent of that of nonwhite males. The unemployment rate for adult nonwhite women (6.6) was higher than for their male counterparts (4.9). Among nonwhite teenagers, the unemployment rate for girls was 31.1 as compared with 21.2 for boys (196).

Two competing and contradictory ideologies emerged within African American political circles and scholarly studies on Black families, which Lincoln's and Murray's divergent points of view illustrate. At the center of these debates were radically different attitudes about the impact of white racism on African American men and women. It was widely accepted that racism had emasculated

Black men, prevented their legitimate claims to manhood, and compelled them to demand their rightful place as men (even patriarchs) in a white male–dominated society that had rendered them powerless. Secondly, Black women, more privileged by the racial social order because they are less threatening, are powerful matriarchs who need to step back and support Black men's long overdue quest for manhood. In other words, racism privileges Black women and situates Black men at the bottom of the heap, reversing the natural order of things with respect to manhood and womanhood. Since Black women are on the top, presumably, efforts must be made to restore Black men to their rightful places. The twin myths of Black emasculation and the Black matriarchy have contributed to serious polarization within African American communities around the politics of gender, and the assumption is that the latter is the greater evil. Contributors to *The Black Woman*, Jean Carey Bond and Patricia Peery explain:

> The emasculation theory, as interpreted by Blacks is two-pronged, one version being primarily followed by women, the other . . . of both men and women. Version number one alleges that Black men have failed throughout our history to shield their women and families from the scourge of American racism and have failed to produce a foolproof strategy for liberating black people . . . black men are weak . . . who must be brushed aside and overcome by women in the big push toward freedom. Version number two also arrives at the point that Black men are weak via the route that Black women have castrated them . . .[31]

During the sixties, Black nationalist sentiment permeated racial discourse, which was replete with admonitions to Black women to "abandon their 'matriarchal' behavior, learn to speak only when they are spoken to, and take up positions three paces (or is it ten) behind their men."[32] When Bond and Peery attempted to answer the question "Is the Black male castrated?"—a prevalent theme in the writings of Black nationalist women and men—their response was unequivocal: "In reality Black women, domineering or not, have not had the power in this male-dominated culture to effect a coup against anyone's manhood—in spite of their oft-cited economic 'advantage' over the Black man."[33] There was an explicit message in Black nationalist discourse about the destructive aspects of feminism and Black women's quest for liberation. It was very simple. Feminism is a white middle-class movement that retards racial unity and draws Black women from their more urgent work— eradicating racial oppression. Affirming Moynihan's thesis about the negative consequences of a Black matriarchy, the Black Power movement was in large part dedicated to the restoration of Black manhood, without which the liberation struggle was doomed. Psychologist, cultural nationalist, and one-time coeditor of *The Black Scholar* Nathan Hare revealed the extent to which Moynihan's problematic assumptions about gender and Black families had been embraced by Black activists: "In the struggle to reassert our black manhood, we must sidestep the trap of turning against our women and they, in retaliation, turning against us. The black woman is, can be, the black man's helper, an undying collaborator, standing up with him, beside her man."[34] Black men were not the only ones making this argument, however.

In the first issue of *The Black Scholar*, published the same year as *The Black Woman* (1970), Linda La Rue trivializes the goals of the women's movement, which is being led by suburban white women whose only problem is "boredom, genteel repression, and dishpan hands." She ignores the involvement of a small group of Black women and is intent on persuading others not to form alliances with white women in the newly emerging women's liberation movement. She also resents analogies between the common oppression of Blacks and women. "Any attempt to analogize black oppression with the plight of the American white woman has the validity of comparing the neck of a hanging man with the hands of an amateur mountain climber with rope burns."[35] Despite her assertions about the irrelevance of the white women's liberation movement to Black women, especially poor ones, La Rue is also critical of the Black liberation movement's embrace of "unsatisfactory male-female role relationship[s] which we adopted from whites as the paradigm of the good family" (4). She refers to

Stokely Carmichael's alleged statement, "the only place in the black movement for black women is prone," as "sexual capitalism or sexual colonialism."[36]

A stark illustration of the overall marginalization of Black women in the Black liberation struggle, despite their intense involvement, is manifest in the decision on the part of civil rights leaders not to allow a Black woman to speak at the March on Washington in 1963.[37] In her 1964 autobiography, *The Trumpet Sounds*, Anna Arnold Hedgeman describes her feelings about the male-dominant civil rights leadership and her experiences as the only woman on the planning committee for the March on Washington, which was the brainchild of A. Philip Randolph, founder of the Brotherhood of Sleeping Car Porters (1925) and, at age seventy-four, chair of the Negro American Labor Council. When Hedgeman discovered that women were not speaking on the program, she wrote a letter to Randolph in which she emphasized Black women's important roles in the civil rights movement. She also argued that "since the 'Big Six' [had] not given women the quality of participation which they [had] earned through the years," it was even more imperative that Black women be allowed to speak. By the "Big Six," as this elite group was popularly known, she meant the male leadership of the civil rights movement—A. Philip Randolph, Martin Luther King, Jr. (SCLC), Roy Wilkins (NAACP), John Lewis or James Forman (SNCC), James Farmer (CORE), and Whitney Young (National Urban League). The patriarchal response of the architects of the march was to allow the wives of the civil rights leaders and a few other Black women freedom fighters to sit on the dais. A hastily planned "Tribute to Women" was added to the agenda. It included Rosa Parks, Daisy Bates, Diane Nash, and Gloria Richardson, who were introduced but were not allowed to speak or even march in the vanguard with the male leaders. None of the movement women, some of whom had risked their lives, was invited to the White House to meet with President Kennedy following the march.

There is some confusion about the composition of the "Big Six." Beginning in 1963, according to James Farmer's autobiography, *Lay Bare the Heart*, the white philanthropist Stephen Currier, head of the Taconic Foundation, assembled the leaders of the six major civil rights organizations in New York City.[38] Calling themselves the Council on United Civil Rights Leadership (CUCRL), the group also included a token female, Dorothy Irene Height, president of the National Council of Negro Women (NCNW), which was founded by Mary McLeod Bethune in 1935. Farmer reminds us that the mainstream press frequently ignored both Height and Lewis, due to gender in the first case and age in the second case, and sometimes referred to the group as the "Big Four." Yet he also notes that though the world of civil rights leadership in the sixties was a man's world, Height managed to negotiate this terrain effectively.

We interviewed Dr. Height in her NCNW offices in August 1999, forty-two years after she had assumed its helm, and asked her about her experiences as the lone female among influential Black male leaders for much of her professional career. She spoke to us about the beginnings of the "Big Six," Currier's agenda for the Black community following NAACP leader Medgar Evers's assassination in 1963,[39] and fondly steered us to Farmer's autobiography because of its frank, though sparse, discussion of gender politics among the group. The "Big Six," who had managed to overcome their personal and organizational rivalries, met on a regular basis in New York City at the behest of Currier. While the group had a serious agenda and accomplished a great deal, Height stressed that "the thing that I think always bothered me was there was not equal concern about women and gender as there was about race." She reminded us that while the leadership was male, the backbone of the civil rights movement was most certainly women and youth. With a tinge of resentment, she described having always been relegated to the margins in meetings with the "Big Six." At one important meeting at the White House, Clifford Alexander and Roger Wilkins decided that she should sit near the president for a change. When Roy Wilkins came in, however, he took the seat reserved for her. Rather than protesting, she thought: "In the presence of the President, you're not going to fight," she assured us. She wanted us to understand her dilemma: she was obliged to respect the men's leadership roles and not take it personally.

In order to maintain her dignity, she repeatedly told herself that you have "to take your task seriously and yourself more lightly."

She assured us that her philosophy in this regard didn't mean that "you are giving in." It seemed very important to her that we understood her predicament. "You see what I mean?" was a constant refrain during the interview. She underscored the importance of her always maintaining a respectable stance. "I wouldn't want to be there fighting with the men," she said, and laughed heartily! In the *Report of Consultation of Problems of Negro Women*, convened by President Kennedy's Commission on the Status of Women during the same year, Dr. Height reveals her acceptance, at least publicly, of conventional gender roles for Black men and her acceptance of tacit patriarchal Black families:[40] "If the Negro woman has a major underlying concern, it is the status of the Negro man and his position in the community and his need for feeling himself an important person, free and able to make his contribution to the whole society in order that he may strengthen his home."[41]

Despite her loyalty to the Black male leadership, Dr. Height was particularly critical of Whitney Young and Roy Wilkins, who were apparently very resentful of the young students in the vanguard of the sit-in movement. Height argued that young people should be around the table but was told that they would be disruptive. "Finally, I just said well as a woman it's hard for me to think we can sit around the table and not have young people. I said we need to have them here." This was apparently the reason James Forman and later John Lewis were invited to join the CUCRL group. Dr. Height then turned to the intransigence of the male leadership with respect to a woman speaking at the March on Washington. The women pleaded to be included, especially Anna Hedgeman, Dr. Height told us. [The women kept saying,] "Well could we have just one person? We didn't care who it was." Dr. Height then summoned her assistant to share with us a cherished photograph that captured the marginalization of women at the march, and she described that infamous day in 1963 as if it were only yesterday. "The only female voices that were really *heard* were Mahalia Jackson and Marian Anderson," she said, offering up for us, Exhibit A, a photograph that is seldom seen of the March on Washington. The standard image of the march includes Martin Luther King, Jr., overseeing the crowd, and the wives sitting on the dais. In Dr. Height's picture, we see her, the head of a major organization of Black women, sitting off to the side, invisible to the public. She told us that some of the women who had been involved in the march, including Hedgeman, were so insulted that they refused to attend the march! The women reminded the men that they sounded no different from white people who justify the inclusion of a token Black person. "They couldn't even hear that they were doing to us what the white folks do to us, do to all of us." They kept repeating that Black women were being included because Mahalia Jackson was singing. The women quickly responded, when Mahalia Jackson sings "The Star Spangled Banner," these are not her words. Black women still are not speaking. No matter what arguments they put forward, however, "We couldn't get through. We did everything, I tell you, but picket." Finally, a compromise was struck; they would have seats on the platform. The photograph Dr. Height showed us is a visible reminder, however, that in fact, in the end, women leaders were not allowed to sit on the dais!

Dr. Height also shared with us a little known story about the women's response to their humiliation at the march. Under the auspices of NCNW, they met as a group in an "After the March, What?" session at a local hotel "that they told us we couldn't have." The number one theme of the session was "never again will they have such a thing." A memorable outcome of the meeting was Pauli Murray's classic essay, "The Negro Woman in the Quest for Equality," published the following year, in which she articulates the double burden that Black women shoulder, which she metaphorically calls Jim Crow and Jane Crow. Alluding to the gender politics surrounding the march, Murray is the first to write publicly about what she describes as a new Black male aggressiveness toward Black women.

> What emerges most clearly from events of the past several months is the tendency to assign women to a secondary, ornamental or "honoree" role instead of the partnership role in the civil rights movement which they have earned by their courage, intelligence and dedication. It was bitterly humiliating for Negro women on August 28 to see themselves ac-

corded little more than token recognition in the historic March on Washington. Not a single woman was invited to make one of the major speeches or to be part of the delegation of leaders who went to the White House. This omission was deliberate.[42] (596)

In Jervis Anderson's biography of Bayard Rustin, a prominent gay civil rights leader, adviser to King, SCLC staffer, and the march's chief strategist, he describes the careful behind-the-scenes negotiations and compromises among the various civil rights organizations who had not previously collaborated on a national project. Anderson discusses the "brooding feminist rebellion behind the scenes."[43] He reports that Black women activists resented that no woman—not even Dorothy Height, the most powerful Black woman civil rights leader on the national scene—had been invited to deliver a major address. Daisy Bates, who was a leader in the desegregation of Little Rock's Central High School in 1957, was allowed a brief moment at the platform to introduce five "Negro women fighters for freedom"—among them Rosa Parks, whose refusal to give up her seat on a Montgomery bus in 1955 had provided the catalyst for the Montgomery bus boycott.[44]

Similarly, civil rights attorney and feminist activist Pauli Murray sent a letter to Randolph a week before the march in which she wrote:

I have been increasingly perturbed over the blatant disparity between the major role which Negro women have played and are playing at the crucial grass-roots levels of our struggle and the minor role of leadership they have been assigned in the national policy-making decisions . . . It is indefensible to call a national March on Washington and send out a Call which contains the name of not a single woman leader. Nor can this glaring omission be glossed over by inviting several Negro women to appear on the August 28 program. The time has come to say to you quite candidly, Mr. Randolph, that "tokenism" is as offensive when applied to women as when applied to Negroes, and that I have

not devoted the greater part of my adult life to the implementation of human rights to [now] condone any policy
which is not inclusive.[45]

A decade later, Black women activists, many of whom were
SNCC (the Student Nonviolent Coordinating Committee) workers,
helped to catalyze a women's movement that would generate sustained discourse within the Black community about the relevance
of women's liberation to the Black struggle. Separate Black feminist
organizations began to emerge in the mid-sixties which contradict
the widely held assumption that Black women were hostile to feminism during the "second-wave" women's rights movement. Much
of what we associate with the emergence of Black feminist activism
during the sixties can be traced to the women of SNCC.

SNCC was organized in the wake of the first college student sit-
in at a lunch counter in Greensboro, North Carolina, in 1960. Its
founding conference, organized by Ella Baker, executive director of
SCLC (Southern Christian Leadership Conference), brought more
than a hundred student activists from mostly southern colleges and
high schools to Raleigh, North Carolina, April 16–19, 1960.[46]
Gender politics came to the surface at a staff retreat in Waveland, Mississippi, four years later in November 1964, during which
thirty-seven position papers were presented by staff covering a range
of topics related to the future of SNCC.[47] One of these, "SNCC Position Paper: Women in the Movement," was unsigned, but later discovered to have been written by two white staffers, Casey Hayden
and Mary King, who objected to what they perceived to be gender
inequality within the organization.[48] Many Black women denied
that they were oppressed in SNCC or prohibited from assuming
leadership positions. At a SNCC reunion conference at Trinity College in 1988, Jean Wheeler Smith asserts, "I wasn't subordinate, I
was high functioning. I did anything I was big enough to do . . ."
She indicated that while Stokely might have wanted to be a male
chauvinist, he just wouldn't have been able to get away with it given
the strength of the Black women around him like Ella Baker, Fannie
Lou Hamer, Victoria Gray, and Ruby Doris Smith-Robinson.[49]

We also interviewed Zoharah Simmons, who, under the name

Gwendolyn Robinson, had been a scared nineteen-year-old project director in Laurel, Mississippi, for eighteen months after dropping out of Spelman as a sophomore in 1964. Simmons described the "Amazon Project" she created to deal with complicated gender matters. Gwen had been sexually attacked by SNCC trainees at the orientation session before going to Mississippi and she received no response after reporting it. She also observed other male behavior that was offensive to her, so she decided that she must establish strict sexual rules for the protection of female SNCC volunteers. Her requirements for the men were simple: "*Any* unwanted sexual attention to *any* woman (black or white), in the project, in the town, in any way, and you were out of the project immediately." She was sensitive to complex interracial sexual politics and the demand, in some cases, that white women sleep with Black men to prove they weren't racist. For Gwen this was psychologically coercive and not consensual sex. Girls under eighteen were also off-limits as far as Gwen was concerned. She said that when SNCC staffers became aware of her rules, the word went out that "she's running some kind of an Amazon camp down there and none of the seasoned SNCC men would work with me." She attests, as well, to the strength of the SNCC field women (there were three in Mississippi at the time) and their ability to deal with tough gender-related issues.[50]

Remembering her mother's heroism, filmmaker Aisha Shahidah Simmons recalls the significance of Gwen's sexual harassment policy, which earned her the sarcastic title of "Amazon" for refusing to acquiesce to men. The term *Amazon* has two reference points. According to Greek myth, Amazons were a group of warrior women who only tolerated men in order that the race would continue. Amazon meant "breastless" in the Greek context; the myth asserted that a woman's right breast was removed so that she could use the arm for a sling or an arrow. There is also an African version, supposedly confirmed by historical records, which relates the story of armed regiments of women in the late nineteenth century kingdom of Dahomey (now Benin, West Africa) who guarded the king's palace, fought in battles, and were also referred to as Amazons. Within African American culture, strong, independent, aggressive Black women are sometimes called "Amazons," which is a link to our ancestral past, even if the specific legend of women warriors in Dahomey has been lost. Gwen/Zoharah's daughter Aisha recently completed a controversial documentary film *NO!* about the silences surrounding the intraracial rape of Black women and girls.[51] She recalls the irony of SNCC women having to resist sexual assault and harassment by Black male comrades while at the same time struggling with them against racism under the serious threat of death.[52]

Elaine Brown speaks candidly as well about the sexual harassment and violence she experienced and witnessed as a Black Panther. Reminiscent of Gwen/Zoharah's story, she described "the clique," which Panther men called a group of women, including herself, who defied male control in the organization; they were "smart bitches" who needed to be silenced.[53] Despite the derogatory label, however, Brown recalls the group fondly as "some bad sisters." She also explains the paradoxical nature of women's involvement in the Movement:

> A woman in the Black Power movement was considered, at best irrelevant. A woman asserting herself was a pariah. A woman attempting the role of leadership was, to my proud black Brothers, making an alliance with the "counter-revolutionary, man-hating, lesbian, feminist white bitches." It was a violation of some Black Power principle that was left undefined. If a black woman assumed a role of leadership, she was said to be eroding black manhood, to be hindering the progress of the black race. She was an enemy of black people.[54]

Sociologist Joyce Ladner recalls her Movement days on the occasion of SNCC's twenty-fifth anniversary at Trinity College in Connecticut (1988) during their first reunion: "We assumed we were equal. When we got into SNCC I would have been ready to fight some guy if he said, 'You can't do this because you're a woman.' I would have said, 'What the hell are you talking about?' A lot of the women in SNCC were very, very tough and independent minded."[55] Before 1964, Ladner added, the enemy was external, not internal. Civil rights activist Prathia Hall agrees with

Ladner and inserts that "something *did* happen in our community after 1965, something *did* happen as we moved to Black Power and as we moved to black nationalism and as the Black Muslims became very prominent in terms of their attitude toward women."[56]

Rancorous debates surrounding Black sexual politics became more public and more visible with the release in 1978 of Michele Wallace's controversial book *Black Macho and the Myth of the Superwoman* (excerpts appeared in *Ms.*), in which she analyzed Black male sexism and the patriarchal discourse of the Black liberation movement, especially militant Black nationalism. Echoing Wallace, the August 27, 1979, issue of *Newsweek* chronicled a new Black struggle that underscored intraracial tensions based on gender: "It's the newest wrinkle in the black experience in America—a growing distrust, if not antagonism between black men and women that is tearing apart marriages and fracturing personal relationships" (58). This "wake-up call," which also contributed to fears about airing dirty racial linen in public, came on the heels of Ntozake Shange's award-winning Broadway play, *for colored girls who have considered suicide/when the rainbow is enuf* (1976), and Wallace's polemic, *Black Macho*. Both Shange and Wallace were demonized by many Black men and women for their Black male-bashing and violation of cultural taboos about keeping family secrets.

It is important to recall that at the beginning of the twentieth century, some Black women leaders had a different conception of race loyalty; they did not feel obligated to keep "race secrets." Ida Wells Barnett, prominent antilynching crusader and journalist, describes in her autobiography an incident she wrote about when she was editor (and part owner) of *Free Speech*. It involved a Memphis minister who had left his church services one Sunday night, gone to the home of a married member, and been caught by her husband in a compromising situation. Despite the fact that the Reverend Nightingale was a previous owner of the newspaper, Wells exposed him to the Black community and made generic comments about "that type of minister." The ministers' alliance was incensed by her reference to the incident, and voted to boycott the newspaper and discredit the paper in their churches. Ignoring their warnings, the editors' retort was swift, courageous, and unapologetic: "We answered this threat by publishing the names of every minister who belonged to the alliance in the next issue . . . and told the community that these men upheld the immoral conduct of one of their number and asked if they were willing to support preachers who would sneak into their homes when their backs were turned and debauch their wives. Needless to say we never heard any more about the boycott . . ."[57] For Wells and her coworker, loyalty to the race meant protecting the community from one of its respected male members and exposing others who would condone such behavior. Remaining silent about situations outside *or* inside the community would not promote the well-being of the race, Wells believed.

BLACK WOMEN'S LIBERATION

Accusations of disloyalty to the race on the part of Black women would become more widespread and hostile during the sixties as Black nationalism and feminism competed for hegemony within African American activist and intellectual circles. Black women were being admonished to choose between loyalty to the race and their own liberation agendas. In 1969, political activist-writer Toni Cade delivered a lecture to the Rutgers University's Livingston College's Black Woman's Seminar in which she called attention to Black nationalist demands that women be subservient to men and warned Black women to be aware: "There is a dangerous trend . . . to program Sapphire out of her 'evil' ways into a cover-up, shut-up, lay-back-and-be-cool obedience role. She is being assigned an unreal role of mute servant that supposedly neutralizes the acidic tension that exists between Black men and Black women. She is being encouraged—in the name of the revolution no less—to cultivate 'virtues' that if listed would sound like the personality traits of slaves."[58] The following year, Cade published one of the most important collections of feminist writings by Black women, *The Black Woman*. This pathbreaking anthology includes SNCC activist Frances Beale's essay, "Double Jeopardy: To Be Black and Female," which highlights Black women's sexual and economic exploitation, mainstream culture's stifling gender roles, Black male sexism, the need for reproductive freedom, and the evils of capitalism.

Beale criticizes Black nationalists who demand that women be subordinate to men and assert that women's most important contribution to Black revolutionary struggle is having babies. "Those who are exerting their 'manhood' by telling black women to step back into a domestic, submissive role are assuming a counter-revolutionary position" (93). In fact, one of the most divisive issues generated by Black nationalists was the idea that since Black people were being threatened by genocide, women's main contribution to the revolution would be refusing to take birth control pills and procreating. In a collectively written letter to brothers dated September 11, 1968, entitled "Birth Control Pills and Black Children: The Sisters Reply," six mostly working-class women speak up for poor Black women who would be the victims of such a proposal:

> Poor black women in the U.S. have to fight back out of our own experience of oppression. Having too many babies stops us from supporting our children, teaching them the truth or stopping the brainwashing as you say, and fighting black men who still want to use and exploit us. . . . You'll run the black community with your kind of black power—you on top![59]

Employing a sophisticated class analysis, these women pen a similar letter to embattled women in North Vietnam in which they assert, "the poor Black woman is the lowest in the capitalist social and economic hierarchy. A few are beginning to see their oppressors as those who mean to keep them barefoot, pregnant, and ignorant of male oppression."[60]

Echoing Anna Julia Cooper, Beale, like these revolutionary poor women, acknowledges Black men's progressive *racial* views, but bemoans their acceptance of outmoded gender ideologies: "He sees the system for what it really is for the most part, but where he rejects its values and mores on many issues, when it comes to women, he seems to take his guidelines from the pages of the *Ladies' Home Journal*" (92). She rejects the myth of the Black woman as emasculator and the notion that Black men have been more victimized by racism than Black women: "Certain black men are maintaining that they have been castrated by society but that black women somehow escaped this persecution and even contributed to this emasculation. . . . It is true that our husbands, fathers, brothers, and sons have been emasculated, lynched, and brutalized. They have suffered from the cruelest assault on mankind that the world has ever known. However, it is a gross distortion of fact that black women have oppressed black men" (92).

In 1968, Beale recommended that SNCC form a Black Women's Liberation Caucus, which a year later split from SNCC and became an autonomous organization, the Black Women's Alliance (BWA),[61] and eventually the Third World Women's Alliance (TWWA), which existed from 1968 to 1979. According to Kimberly Springer, Beale's "increasing awareness of the gap between SNCC's espoused democratic ideals and the sexual division of labor in the organization" (117) and her growing frustration about SNCC's "inattention to Black women's gender oppression" (118) led to her petition for a Black women's caucus within SNCC and eventually the founding of TWWA, the first explicitly Black feminist organization to emerge in the sixties.

The issue of sexual politics within the African American community was a hotly debated topic in the 70s in journals such as *The Black Scholar*, *Freedomways*, and *Black Books Bulletin*, and provided the catalyst for the founding of a short-lived, bimonthly magazine by psychologists Nathan and Julia Hare, *Black Male/ Female Relationships*. A misogynist, Black-woman-as-traitor-to-the-race theme began to emerge, and this scapegoating of Black women for all of the race's problems helped to fuel increased hostility between Black men and women. *The Black Scholar* would provide the most balanced treatment of the Black sexism debate that had been generated by the 1965 Moynihan Report, the emergence of the Black Women's Liberation movement, and Michele Wallace's and Ntozake Shange's controversial feminist writings. The first of five groundbreaking issues focused on "Black Women's Liberation" (April 1973). It underscored tensions between the agendas of the Black liberation movement and the newly emerging women's movement. Robert Chrisman's editorial supported the embryonic "global movement to free men and women from racial, sexual and class oppression," and criticized the male-dominated Black liberation struggle that ran the risk of becoming a "carbon copy of white male chauvinism." Barbara Sizemore's lead essay, "Sexism and the Black Male," articulates the reality of institutionalized sexism in American society, the economic marginalization and powerlessness of Black women, the myth of the Black matriarchy, and the ways in which African American men have been socialized to adopt dominant cultural values with respect to male superiority and dominance. She makes an important distinction between a household headed by a female and a matriarchal household. "Just what kind of rule does she exert? She has little money-making ability, no control and absolutely no power to protect her family. She is subject to the same limitations which face the black man but on an even lower level of subjugation."[62]

Sizemore is especially critical of the gender ideologies of Black nationalism and the Nation of Islam, as they are articulated by Elijah Muhammad throughout his book, *Message to the Blackman in America* (1965). He calls women property, who must be isolated and controlled. Malcolm X's views about women were impacted by his embrace of Islam and Elijah Muhammad, who taught him about the true natures of men and women: "Now Islam has very strict laws and teachings about women, the core of them being that the true nature of man is to be strong, and a woman's true nature is to be weak, and while a man must at all times respect his woman, at the same time he needs to understand that he must control her if he expects to get her respect."[63] It is interesting to note, however, that after Malcolm X left the Nation of Islam and traveled more broadly, he repudiated his sexist past and questioned some of his earlier gender attitudes. In addition to distrusting women because they were "tricky," and "deceitful," he accepted Islamic beliefs about gender differences, which he taught in his classes at Temple Seven in Chicago.[64] During an interview in Paris three months before he was assassinated, Malcolm X made statements about women that illustrate significant shifts in his thinking:

> In every country you go to, usually the degree of progress can never be separated from the woman. If you're in a country

that's progressive, the woman is progressive . . . I am proud of the contributions that our women have made in the struggle for freedom.[65]

Sizemore also quotes from *Mwanamke Mwananchi*, a seventies guidebook for the nationalist woman, which advocates patriarchal gender relationships and women's submissiveness, and is reminiscent of the gender ideologies of the Nation of Islam:

We understand that it is and has been traditional that the man is the head of the house. . . . Women cannot do the same things as men—they are made by nature to function differently. Equality of men and women is something that cannot happen even in the abstract world. . . . Nature has made women submissive—she must submit to man's creation in order for it to exist.[66]

In the same issue there is an interview with Queen Mother Moore, a prominent spokesperson for Black nationalism, in which she urges Black women to stay away from the white women's liberation movement and sympathize with the plight of Black men, whom she believes have been more victimized by racism than Black women.

The special April 1978 issue of *The Black Scholar*, "Blacks and the Sexual Revolution," includes a predictable, rambling critique of the "middle-class white women's liberation movement" by Black nationalist Nathan Hare. He describes it as antimale, antimaternal, "a diversionary alternative to black rebellion,"[67] and the major culprit in the destruction of the Black family and "the alienation and disunity of black male and black female." Ironically, in the same issue Audre Lorde presents a feminist vision of the Black community in which self-defined Black women are recognized as "a vital component in the war for black liberation"[68] and homophobia and lesbian-baiting are not tolerated. Calling attention to misplaced antilesbian hysteria, she asserts boldly, "within the homes of our black communities today, it is *not* [our emphasis] the black lesbian who is battering and raping our under-age girl-children, out of displaced and sickening frustration" (33).

The March/April 1979 "Black Sexism Debate" issue featured sociologist Robert Staples's antifeminist essay, "The Myth of Black Macho: A Response to Angry Black Feminists," which spawned a range of responses a month later in the May/June issue, including a profeminist manifesto, "Women's Rights Are Human Rights," by Black nationalist writer Kalamu a Salaam, who had been inspired by the women's rights activism of Frederick Douglass. He asserts unequivocally, "I am striving to be a revolutionary, and without the eradication of sexism there will be no true and thorough going revolution." He supports the goals of the women's liberation movement, which he believes are not antithetical to Black liberation. In these debates the question of speaking publicly about controversial issues *within* Black communities remained contested.

BATTLE ROYAL

We began this chapter with Anita Hill and have returned to her at the end. There is no incident in the history of African Americans that illustrates more clearly how vehemently Blacks (across class, gender, and region) are opposed to sharing racial secrets than their opposition to Anita Hill's public exposure of Clarence Thomas's alleged sexually inappropriate conduct. Anita Hill's violation of this deeply held Black cultural taboo unleashed a storm of controversy the likes of which we had not witnessed before. When Black women "break the silence" about our experiences with Black men, especially sexual ones, there is intense anger in our communities. In other words, racial disloyalty is a more serious transgression when Black women expose Black men. Black feminist social critic and historian of science Evelynn Hammonds notes:

> Black women must always put duty to the race first. No mention was made of how Clarence Thomas had failed in his duty to the race, especially to Black women. This deeply held ethic that Black women have a duty to the race while Black men are allowed to have a duty only to themselves can only be challenged by a Black feminist analysis that emphasizes the importance of Black women's lives.[69]

Hammonds reminds us that Thomas's race loyalty is not challenged, either, when he erroneously portrays his sister, Emma Mae Martin, as a welfare cheat, one of the most damaging contemporary stereotypes of poor Black women. In a *Village Voice* article, Lisa Jones reveals that Thomas's sister had only been on welfare temporarily. Normally she held down two minimum-wage jobs while supporting four children, but when her aunt had a stroke she took care of her and was unable to afford child care and work at the same time. Historian Nell Painter provides a brilliant gendered analysis of the differential plight of Thomas and his sister, which makes his construction of his sister as a "welfare queen" even more disgusting:

> He seemed not to have appreciated that he was the favored boy-child who was protected and sent to private schools and that she was the girl who stayed behind, married early, and cared for a relative who had fallen ill. If he realized how common his family's decisions had been, he gave no indication of seeing those choices as gendered. . . . Even though as a hospital worker his sister was a symbol of Jesse Jackson's masses of black folk who work every day, her life as a worker counted for naught in Thomas's story. His eagerness to shine on a conservative stage allowed him to obscure the actual circumstances of her life and her finances and to disregard her vulnerability as a poor, black woman.[70]

Literary critic Nellie McKay uttered perhaps the most poignant statement about what is to be gained from refusing to air racial secrets:

> . . . perhaps the greatest beneficiaries (besides herself) of Anita Hill's publicly uttering her allegations of sexual harassment against Clarence Thomas, a black man (one with influence and power), are the millions of black women for whom her action represented a further breaking of the bonds of generations of black women's silence on and denial of their differences with black men, because of gender

issues, and their right to be full human beings despite the conflicts of race and sex.[71]

We concur with progressive Black women and men that our communities are not served by any of us keeping racial secrets. We will fare much better when we commit ourselves to dealing openly and honestly with what harms us—whether it is racism in the majority culture or sexism in our own backyards. We must "talk back," in bell hooks's terms, about the suffering we experience, no matter who the victimizer might be. In our quest for both racial and gender equality, we must heed Audre Lorde's wise words: "So it is better to speak remembering we were never meant to survive."[72]

4

•

THE BLACK CHURCH:
WHAT'S THE WORD?

"If it wasn't for the women, you wouldn't have a church!"

Cheryl Townsend Gilkes,
If It Wasn't for the Women, 2001

To be a woman, black, and active in religious institutions in the American scene is to labor under triple jeopardy.

Theressa Hoover, "Black Women and the Churches:
Triple Jeopardy," 1990

We need to talk about these things. . . . For issues of sexuality are turning out to be a spiritual fault line threatening the stability and the unity of the Church.

The Reverend Dr. James A. Forbes, Jr., 1999

Historically, religion has served as a liberating force in the African American community . . . The organized black church, however, has itself oppressed its constituents, as evidenced by its historical practice of sexism.

Charles I. Nero,
"Toward a Black Gay Aesthetic," 1991

Like the majority of African American youngsters, each of us grew up in a Black church—Beverly in Metropolitan Baptist Church in Memphis, Tennessee, and Johnnetta in Mt. Olive African Methodist Episcopal Church in Jacksonville, Florida. In ways that are clearly representative of the experiences of countless African American girls and boys, it was in a church that we were taught a good deal about gender issues. There was certainly ample time to learn these lessons, for despite differences in the theology, ritual, and practices of the Baptist and AME denominations, each of us spent a good deal of time in church and doing church-related activities.

Beverly recalls that every Sunday belonged to church. After Sunday school at 9:30 A.M., there was a church service that began at 11:00 that often lasted until 2:00 in the afternoon. Because her mother sang in the choir, Beverly was required to wait at church until a post–Sunday service choir rehearsal was over. Following a trip home for Sunday afternoon dinner, Beverly and her two sisters would return to church for Baptist Training Union (BTU) meetings that would go from 6:00 to 8:00 P.M. In the summertime, Beverly would be sent to Vacation Bible School.

Johnnetta's experiences at Mt. Olive AME church were quite similar. Sunday morning Sunday school was not to be missed, especially since her great-grandfather was the superintendent of the Sunday school. Then followed the regular Sunday morning service that began at 11:00 A.M. and, depending on how many "extras" there were—such as a christening, or the number of people who responded to the invitation to join the church, or just how long it took for the minister to deliver his sermon, or how many people "got happy" (that is, received the holy spirit) and for how long—the service could last until 2:30 or 3:00 in the afternoon.

Johnnetta's mother played the piano and the organ and directed all of the choirs, and her father was a deacon in the church. Thus it was not unusual for one or both of her parents to have an after-church meeting that would keep Johnnetta and her sister at church beyond the time when other members had left for their Sunday afternoon meal.

From the ages of four to eight, Johnnetta and her sister would have their Sunday dinner at their great-grandfather's home, where his wife would prepare her specialty of fried chicken cooked in olive oil, with some combination of the trimmings that are lumped under the category of African American soul food: black-eyed peas and rice, collard greens, potato salad, macaroni and cheese, and corn bread. After dinner, Johnnetta and her sister were allowed to play at their great-grandfather's desk, where only two games were permissible: "regular" school or Sunday school.

Johnnetta also recalls the special children's programs at Easter and Christmas that were highly effective in teaching her and her peers oratorical skills, as well as a good deal about African American history and biblical lore. For the two of us, as was and remains the case for many African American children, the church was a major site for activities as well as for direct instruction about how to live "the good life," which included gender matters. Even when a parent or parents did not routinely go to church, as Beverly's father did not, they required their children to do so.

What were the principal lessons about gender that we were taught and indeed that countless African American children learn in Sunday school, church services, and the year-round church activities in which they participate? That God is a male and that Jesus is both white and male; that the relationship between women and men in everyday life is to be like that between God and His church, for God is the head of the church, and all members are to follow Him; and that God and all of His people will look down on a "bad woman" (for example, one who gets pregnant out of wedlock) and praise "a virtuous woman" (for example, one who is a loyal helpmate to her husband and a good mother to her children).

For our respective peer groups—that is, youngsters who grew up in Black churches in the 1940s and 1950s—these notions about women and gender relations were rarely, if ever, challenged.

In this chapter on the Black church, we explore the ramifications of such ideas and values about gender, as they are continuously expressed in the patriarchal ideology, ritual, and daily practices of African American Christians. But we will also examine patterns of resistance to patriarchy that date back to early church women and continue in contemporary womanist and feminist theologies and progressive Black churches.

Of course, this chapter cannot fully capture the range and complexity of what is meant by "the Black church," which refers generally to organized Christian religious institutions to which African Americans have been attached since slavery. For here is an institution forged from the retention of complex African beliefs and rituals that were reinterpreted in a "New World" setting that involved slavery, Jim Crow segregation, and persistent racism as well as other systems of inequality. The Black church is an institution that is a critical site for the subordination of women and the perpetuation of conservative gender ideologies on the one hand; and a place where womanist and feminist theologians challenge such ideas and practices of inequality and envision the kind of "beloved community" that is constructed on principles of gender equality.

However, distinctive characteristics set the Black church aside from other forms of organized religion. Sociologist, religious scholar, and ordained Baptist minister Professor Cheryl Townsend Gilkes identifies the four pillars of the Afro-Christian religious tradition as preaching, praying, singing, and testifying.[1] She is not suggesting that these components are peculiar to Black churches, but rather that the way in which they are expressed distinguishes them from mainstream Christian churches. This chapter focuses on Protestant churches, for that is where the majority of Black women and men are affiliated and carry out their organized religious life.

Throughout our history in the United States, the Black church has been the most important and influential institution in the Black community, and the one we've always been able to control. It instilled values; dictated how we should and should not behave, often on the basis of gender; provided a safe space for worship given the dictates of segregation; and was an important site of resistance to racism as it challenged the limitations that the dominant society placed on African Americans. Social critic, religious scholar, and ordained Baptist minister Michael Eric Dyson argues that the Black church "continues to occupy the center of Black culture," and "remains our most precious institution."[2]

During the long years of slavery, it was against the law for Black folks to learn to read and to write. And once emancipation came, the schools that educated Black people were grounded in Christian ideology and practice. As Gilkes notes, "After reflection on their own experience, the most important critical tool used by Black people has been the Bible."[3]

While Christianity is not the sole source of Western gender-role ideologies for Black Americans, it is a major one. And it is certainly the case that patriarchy is a protected modus operandi, a visible if unacknowledged tradition, and one of the most cherished and tenacious values in the Black church. How did this come to be? Any response to the question must recall the African continent and the early days of the Black church in America when patriarchy was first established as a near-sacred ideal.

Debate continues over the extent to which West African cultures were or were not patriarchal. The most reliable scholarship underscores profound differences between the gender ideologies and practices of Europeans and what they encountered in those West African societies they plundered for slaves. While not resolving the debate, we can say the following: In most West African societies, residence was set by women coming to live in their husband's geographical area (patrilocal residence); kinship was traced through one's father (patrilineal descent), and much of the public and political life was in the hands of men. However, the absence of dependence on males was related to the fact that women carried out much of the physical labor, and because they controlled the marketplaces, they were often economically independent. Women also exercised political power as they "expressed their disapproval and secured their demands by collective public demonstrations, including ridicules, satirical singing and dancing, and group strikes."[4] What these varied gender roles indicate is that the status of West African women involved a more complex and fluid situation than is captured in terms that would describe them as either liberated or oppressed.[5] In other words, "while patriarchy may have been present in West Africa, the world view of African slaves did *not* exclude women from religious and political society."[6]

As African women and men were forced into slavery, this more fluid gender ideology and the dual-sex political systems collided head on with the more static gender ideology of the West, especially Christianity, where a woman's place was more clearly defined as in the home and outside the pulpit. This meeting of two distinct gender ideologies first took place within the "peculiar institution" of slavery.

How could the dominant group maintain the cult of white womanhood while subjecting the dark members of that sex to unrelenting, backbreaking free labor? One solution was to generate images and stereotypes of Black women that removed them from the standard definitions and descriptions of womanhood. In this process, Black women lost their gender identity in the minds of the dominant culture in fundamental ways. Images of white women as pure, fragile, and emotional were juxtaposed with images of Black women as oversexed, strong beasts of burden. Gilkes summarizes the situation for Black women under slavery this way: "Early in their history, black women learned that American society would not provide them the protection and privileges of the pedestal. . . . [they] were *never* treated as white women were."[7] Indeed, during slavery, Black women and men endured many of the same hardships. "Black women were overworked, flogged, and otherwise exploited, just like black men."[8] However, they retained their female gender role in other ways. Enslaved women were considered fair game for any white man's sexual desires, and in the process lost control of their bodies and their reproductive rights. Within the community of slaves, they were expected to perform wifely duties such as gardening and cooking and had the primary responsibility of child rearing.

Professor Angela Davis captures poignantly the complexity of slave women's gender identity. Paradoxically, because they were prohibited from conforming to conventional notions of womanhood, they were "free" to construct their own gender identity, which included the power to resist. Angela Davis makes this important point when she says:

> Black women were equal to their men in the oppression they suffered. They were their men's social equals within the slave community; and they resisted slavery with a passion equal to their men's. This was one of the greatest ironies of the slave system; in subjecting women to the most

ruthless exploitation conceivable, exploitation which knew
no sex distinctions, the groundwork was created not only
for Black women to assert their equality through their social relations, but also to express it through their acts of
resistance.[9]

The fluid gender ideology that Africans brought with them and
the distinctive model of Black womanhood that was fashioned during slavery were not always welcome within Black communities,
which over time were influenced by patriarchal gender norms
within the dominant culture. In fact, white society's disavowal of
"Black manhood," which is captured in the widely held notion of
"the emasculated Black man," produced a yearning for Black patriarchy that would enable Black men to take their rightful places in
the American body politic. This embrace of patriarchal ideals did
not take place without resistance by some African American women,
however.

As early as 1789, Black women joined Black men in organizations that worked to end slavery and "lift up the race."[10] While the
preachers in their churches were almost always Black men, who
were recognized as leaders by white men, in those early days, Black
women were prayer warriors, singers, teachers, catechizers, and
storytellers. There were a few Black women preachers, and their experience with sexism in Black churches has been well documented.
For example, Jarena Lee, a free Black, struggled to become a
preacher against the wishes of her husband.[11]

Around the beginning of the twentieth century, Black women
lost access to pulpits and their leadership in churches became even
more seriously challenged. This "silencing" of Black women's voices
coincided with "regularizing" the presence of Black male preachers.
One response by Black women was the emergence between 1885
and 1900 of what historian Evelyn Brooks Higginbotham calls a
"feminist theology," which "contested the masculinism that threatened them with silence and marginality."[12] Black Baptist women
formed the Women's Auxiliary Convention of the National Baptist
Convention. Other women moved into the Holiness Movement of
the nineteenth century and the Pentecostal Movement of the twen-

tieth century. Another avenue pursued by some Black women in response to their suppression within Black churches was the formation of the National Association of Colored Women—a club movement of prophetic Christian women.[13]

Perhaps it is not surprising that African American men, who were prohibited from exercising power in other public arenas, would be adamant about maintaining authority in the one institution they did manage to control, Black churches. Their embrace of patriarchy in Black churches was aided by passages in the Bible that support the subordination of women.

Male dominance in African American churches was expressed most clearly by the fact that Black women were forbidden to be ordained and to preach from a pulpit. These prohibitions continue to be "justified" by reference to biblical sources. At a Black Methodist preachers meeting of the Washington annual conference in 1890, the question was posed: "Is woman inferior to man?" The chairman of the meeting replied: "Sad as it may be, woman is as inferior to man as man is to God."[14]

Keeping Black women out of the pulpit of certain churches constitutes what Michael Eric Dyson calls ecclesiastical apartheid, and is surely connected to the reality that preaching, as Gilkes puts it, "is the most masculine aspect of black religious ritual. In spite of the progress of women in ministry, preaching remains overwhelmingly a form of male discourse."[15] There may also be a deep psychological resistance to the very idea that a group of men (even though they will be in the numerical minority in most Black churches) should have to sit and listen to a woman (preacher) telling them what to do and what not to do.

Subtle and not so subtle notions that Black women, like children, are best seen and not heard, and that a Black woman should stand several paces behind her man permeated religious circles, and were also present in prescriptions for proper behavior by Black women in civil society. For example, in a 1966 *Ebony* magazine special issue on Black women, in which women were contributors, the editorial declared, "The immediate goal of the Negro woman today should be the establishment of a strong family unit in which the father is the dominant person." The editorial went on to say that Black women would be advised to follow the example of the Jewish mother "who pushed" her husband to success, educated her male children first, and engineered good marriages for her daughters." And to the career woman, the advice was given that she "should be willing to postpone her aspirations until her children, too, are old enough to be on their own."[16]

In many Black churches, Black women have resisted words and actions that call for them to be subservient to men. Gilkes notes:

> The cultural maxim, "If it wasn't for the women, you wouldn't have a church," rises up against male attempts to exclude, ignore, trivialize, or marginalize women in a number of capacities.[17]

From the very beginning of the African Methodist Episcopal church to the present, there have been expressions of patriarchy *and* resistance to it. For example, the founder of the AME Church, Richard Allen, had to face the issue of women preachers when his own wife objected to their church's gender practices. Despite the loud cries of AME church women through the years, however, it was only in 2000 that the Reverend Vashti M. McKenzie, was elected the first Black woman bishop in the AME church.[18]

Some Black women directly challenged biblical arguments. As early as the 1830s, Maria Stewart was the first woman of any race to give a public lecture and leave a manuscript record. In 1833 after a brief career on the lecture circuit, however, she delivered a farewell speech to the Black community, especially ministers, in which she expressed resentment and hurt about its negative response to her defiance of gender conventions as a public lecturer. She called attention to their hypocrisy and unwillingness to honor her talents:

> I find it is no use for me as an individual to try and make myself useful among my color in this city. It was contempt for my moral and religious opinions in private that drove me thus before a public . . . my respected friends, let us no longer talk of prejudice, till prejudice becomes extinct at

home. Let us no longer talk of opposition, till we cease to oppose our own. . . . Men of eminence have mostly risen from obscurity; nor will I, although a female of a darker hue, and far more obscure than they, bend my head or hang my harp upon willows.[19]

Her passionate defense of women's right to speak in public invokes biblical heroines and wise women throughout history in her query:

What if I am a woman . . . Did he [God] not raise up Deborah, to be mother and a judge in Israel? Did not Queen Esther save the lives of the Jews? And Mary Magdelene first declare the resurrection of Christ from the dead? . . . . Did St. Paul but know of our wrongs and deprivations, I presume he would make no objections to our pleading in public for our rights . . . holy women ministered unto Christ and the apostles; and women. . . . have had a voice in moral, religious and political subjects . . . why the Almighty hath imparted unto me the power of speaking thus, I cannot tell. . . . Among the Greeks, women delivered the Oracles. . . . The prediction of the Egyptian women obtained much credit at Rome. . . . Why cannot we become divines and scholars? (198).

Itinerant preacher and abolitionist Sojourner Truth also used biblical references to defend her preaching and support for women. To a man who said that women couldn't have as many rights as men because Christ wasn't a woman, she retorted at an 1851 Akron, Ohio, women's rights convention: "Where did your Christ come from? From God and a woman! Man had nothing to do with Him![20]

Black women also challenged sexist ideas and practices in the church early on through their innovative organizational strategies. Nannie Helen Burroughs is an extraordinary example. She had an important impact on the Black Baptist church, though her significance in African American history has not been adequately documented.[21] An educator, writer, and activist, Burroughs is responsible for the establishment of National Woman's Day, having instituted in

1907 a "Women's Day" in Black Baptist churches that eventually
spread to nearly every Black church denomination and to some
white denominations. This special day was "a glorious opportunity
for women to learn to speak for themselves."[22] Born in Orange,
Virginia, in May 1878, to John Burroughs, an itinerant preacher,
and Jennie Poindexter Burroughs, Nannie Burroughs grew up in
Washington, D.C., and attended the Colored High School (later
M Street and Dunbar High), where Mary Church Terrell and Anna
Julia Cooper taught and became her role models. She was also influenced by her pastor, the Reverend Walter Brooks, at Nineteenth
Street Baptist Church, who had been active in the formation of the
National Baptist Convention, founded by ministers in 1895 to
unite Black Baptist churches under one umbrella. Following gradua-
tion from high school, Burroughs found clerical work in Philadelphia in the office of the *Christian Banner* and later relocated to
Louisville, Kentucky, with the Reverend Lewis Jordan, an officer of
the Foreign Mission Board of the National Baptist Convention
(NBC). While working in Louisville, she traveled to Richmond, Virginia, in 1900 for the annual meeting of the NBC and became one
of the founders of the Women's Convention (WC), an auxiliary to
the NBC. When she was only nineteen years old she delivered her
inaugural speech, "How the Sisters Are Hindered from Helping."
This feminist critique of sexism within the church catapulted her
into national prominence. After the founding of the Women's Convention, she became its first corresponding secretary. During her
first year in office, she reported having worked 365 days, traveled
22,125 miles, delivered 215 speeches, organized 12 societies, written 9,235 letters, and received 4,820 letters.[23] Until her death in
May 1961, she remained at the helm of the Women's Convention
succeeding to its presidency in 1948 after having been corresponding secretary for forty-seven years.

For Burroughs, the church was a site of resistance and an important outlet for the political empowerment of Black women,
though she constantly battled the Black male leadership about their
insensitivity to women's needs. She also criticized the church for
failing to assist in the political development of women, and argued
in the August 1915 issue of the *Crisis*, the official organ for the

NAACP, that suffrage would enable women to fight male domi-nance and sexual abuse. In 1909 she founded the National Training School for Women and Girls in Washington, D.C., for which she is perhaps better known. It stressed industrial education because she wanted to prepare Black women for employment in areas that were open to them—nurses, cooks, maids, housekeepers, and clerks, for example. The National Training School was renamed the Nannie Helen Burroughs School and is now an elementary school.

In the annals of Black church history, Burroughs should also be remembered for *The Slabtown District Convention*. Gilkes credits this feminist play with providing useful advice to educated women in their community and criticizing the misbehavior of male leaders and women's complicity with such behavior.[24]

Despite serious resistance, Black women have continuously cre-ated roles for themselves that become essential for the functioning of the church. For example, in the nineteenth century, women were not permitted ordination in the AME church. They could only ex-hort and preach without a license. But because they insisted that God had called them to preach, the office of stewardess was created in 1869, and the office of deaconess in 1900. Once the AME church officially permitted the licensing of women to preach, their preach-ing was limited to the subordinate office of "evangelist." Today, in many denominations, Black women exercise substantial influence through the positions of deaconess and stewardess.

"Church mothers" have also challenged patriarchy in the church. Addressed by the minister and members of the congrega-tion as "Mother," she is an older woman who is looked up to as a sterling example of Christian morality. She may be the leader of the adult class and is surely an expert on the Bible. Some church moth-ers are said to speak in little sermons, and the words of Mother Pol-lard who participated in the Montgomery bus boycott are well known: "My feet are tired but my soul is rested." The opinions of a church mother can sometimes prevail over the views of a male preacher.

Yet another way in which Black women have shown their oppo-sition to the sexism of Black preachers is by "voting with their feet," and leaving a church—sometimes to found one of their own.

This willingness to "vote with their feet" may or may not be accompanied by identification with feminism. Indeed, within church circles, many Black women exhibit profound ambivalence toward feminism—even when they are vehemently opposed to sexism. Often Black church women distance themselves even further from an ideology, a movement, which they associate with problematic moral values and which they believe advocates inappropriate behavior for Christian women, especially in the sexual arena. We think it is fair to say that persons with strong religious beliefs are likely to be more conservative, especially where gender norms are concerned. While many Black women have rejected patriarchal ideas in their churches, many have not, choosing instead to internalize the gender roles put forth by the prevailing church authority.

SEXUALITY AND THE BLACK CHURCH

Serious gender talk about the Black church must inevitably turn to a discussion of sexuality. Dyson offers a helpful list of related challenges:

> Earlier and earlier, black boys and girls are becoming sexually active. Teen pregnancy continues to escalate. Besides these problems, there are all sorts of sexual challenges that black Christians face. The sexual exploitation of black female members by male clergy. The guilt and shame that result from unresolved conflicts about the virtues of black sexuality. The continued rule of black churches by a mainly male leadership. The role of eroticism in a healthy black Christian sexuality. The revulsion to and exploitation of homosexuals. The rise of AIDS in black communities. The sexual and physical abuse of black women and children by black male church members. The resistance to myths of super black sexuality.[25]

Certainly, some of the most hush-hush race secrets in African American communities revolve around issues of sexuality and the church. It is not that preachers fail to talk about sex. And it is certainly not that parishioners and preachers are not engaging in sex. What lies at the heart of these "secrets" is the hypocritical disconnect between what is said about sex—with whom it should take place among Christian folks and under what circumstances—and the realities of people's sexual lives.

How did it come about that Sunday after Sunday in Black church after Black church, ministers warn their congregations about succumbing to carnal desires, and yet some of these same ministers are involved in sexual exploits with women parishioners and others in the community? Though this is not peculiar to Black churches, it is important to raise these issues as we probe the dissonances between what we as Black Americans practice and what we preach. How do we explain the hypocritical behavior of some Black ministers (some of whom are closeted gay men) who rant from their pulpits about the sinfulness of homosexuality, and yet turn to the choir directors (some of whom are "secretly known" to be gay) to lift a song? What do we imagine are the feelings of other gay parishioners who worship in churches where their sexual choices are demonized?

The explanation for such contradictions can be found in the convoluted history of Black sexuality, which began during slavery and continues to define Black-white and Black-Black relations in America. This history is so distorted, it is little wonder that for many Black Christian women and men, a healthy sense of sexuality is hard to come by. Dyson raises the rhetorical question: "How can [we] have a healthy sense of black Christian sexual identity in a world where being black has been a sin, where black sexuality has been viewed as pathology, and where the inability to own—and to own up to—our black bodies has led us to devalue our own flesh?"[26]

Europe's images of Africa have not been constant. When European travelers first saw Africans, they praised the majestic stance of the men, and the regal beauty of the women. Many years later when Europeans again encountered African people, this time with the determination to enslave them to satisfy their greed, Africans were described quite differently. The men were said to have genitals that were so large, they were burdensome to them; and the women were said to be so oversexed that they fornicated with gorillas. Numerous reports from European travelers described the sexual behavior of Africans that usually focused on their "immorality." In his history of Jamaica, Edward Long, a so-called authority on African slaves whose work was highly valued, characterized Blacks as animals. Their "faculties of smell are truly bestial, nor less their commerce with the other sexes; in these acts they are libidinous and shameless as monkeys, or baboons. The equally hot temperament of their women has given probability to the charge of their admitting these animals frequently to their embrace."[27] The involvement of white missionaries in slavery rested on the fallacious assumption that the souls of Black folks were like their bodies, inferior to those of white Christians; and in addition to saving their souls, it was the duty of white people to tame the crude carnal desires of Black women and men. The interlocking interests of missionaries and slave owners were such that an African saying is painfully accurate: "When the whites came we had the land and they had the Bible. Now we have the Bible and they have the land."

From the very beginning, a conservative view of sexuality was advanced in the churches Blacks founded. One explanation points to the conservative theologies of white Christianity, which was steeped in Victorian repression. It became imperative for African Americans to refute all of the negative beliefs about their sexuality; so the Black church became a major site for the rehabilitation of Black people's morality.

One such expression of patriarchy that is writ large in Black churches is the double standard of sexual morality. Put bluntly, this double standard privileges men when it says, "We want the women to be virgins, but the men should have experience."[28] One result of this double standard is that "in our loving churches teenage girls are condemned for out-of-wedlock pregnancies. They are often re-quired to confess their sins and ask for forgiveness in front of the entire congregation, and they may be expelled from the choir or kept from participating in other public church functions. But the (usually older) men who impregnate them are overlooked and hence implicitly excused. Sometimes the father of the child sits on the deacons' row or in the pulpit."[29]

This double standard privileges male ministers. Bishop Vashti McKenzie, the first woman to become bishop of the African Methodist Episcopal Church, indicates that women clergy are subject to far more scrutiny than their male counterparts. Furthermore, the church is far more unforgiving concerning the indiscretions of woman ministers. Bishop McKenzie also speaks of a double standard outside the realm of sexual behavior. Women in the ministry are under constant pressure to explain and defend their call to the ministry, and their success or failure affects the women clergy who follow them.

One of the most blatant manifestations of male privilege in Black churches occurs when, to use Marcia Dyson's language, preachers prey on women parishioners for sexual favors.[30] Such behavior is certainly not restricted to Black preachers. It occurs in white churches, the White House, and other places of worship outside the Christian tradition. Some men of the cloth consider such sexual exploits their right. This point is worth considering with respect to Dr. Martin Luther King, Jr.—one of the world's greatest champions for civil and human rights. Dyson situates Dr. King's behavior within the rampant patriarchy of the Black church:

> Only advocates of moral perfection will seek to deny King his high place in history because of his sexual sins. This does not mean that we cannot or should not criticize King for his rampant womanizing and his relentless infidelity. . . . King was certainly reared in a preacherly culture where good sex is pursued with nearly the same fervor as believers seek to be filled with the Holy Ghost. And the war against white supremacy in which King participated was thoroughly sexist and often raucous. . . . King's sexual practices were nourished within a powerful pocket of the church. His sexual habits grew in part out of a subculture of promiscuity that is rampant among clergy and religious figures in every faith.[31]

Dyson's observations reminded Beverly of a painful incident experienced by her sister Carmella in Atlanta. During the early eighties, Carmella went to a prominent Baptist minister's church one afternoon for advice about a pending separation from her husband during which he literally chased her around his office and offered sexual solace rather than marital counseling. What transpired in his office was unbelievable to Carmella, since she had deliberately chosen not her own pastor but one of the best-known and respected Black ministers in Atlanta. The anger and disgust she experienced that afternoon resulted in a temporary withdrawal from the church and cynical feelings about predatory ministers who take advantage of women in distress, which she was clearly experiencing as a result of the break-up of her marriage. Though over twenty years have passed, Carmella recalls this afternoon as if it were just yesterday. She has returned to the church in Memphis where she and Beverly were nurtured, however.

Given the sexual vulnerability of Black women in the larger society and their feeling that there's nowhere to turn—no place they can be safe except in church—they sometimes experience sexual exploitation there by the very individuals they think they can trust. Marcia L. Dyson, who describes an experience similar to Carmella's when she sought counsel about marital problems from her own pastor, puts it this way:

> Black women are so often called upon to appear strong, independent and self-confident. Church is the one place we feel safe enough to wear our vulnerability on the sleeves of our designer dresses. We feel secure in stitching our neediness into the hems of our softly tailored suits. When we share our tears and fears with our male ministers, we forge one of the most intimate relationships possible between two human beings. If we're the least bit careless about our principles and prayers, it becomes easy to confuse spiritual and emotional needs with erotic desires and to act on them inappropriately.[32]

After candidly discussing the phenomenon of "preying preachers," Marcia Dyson does not assume that unholy alliances among church folks are "just the way things are" and that we simply have to put up with them. Instead, she offers very basic suggestions for helping to correct this widespread pattern of sexual exploitation of women, even when they are complicit with "preying" ministers. First, women must be encouraged to seek counseling and therapy within *and* outside the church, and congregations need to be encouraged to develop a female ministry. Second, Dyson, who herself behaved indiscreetly with a minister, urges women to stop playing house in God's house and transferring their desire for a husband or lover onto the married minister. Finally, churches must develop and follow guidelines to address sexual misconduct by pastors and other members of the church. The Black church, in other words, needs to move beyond hypocrisy. The recent crisis within the Catholic church with respect to the sexual abuse of youngsters by priests, especially boys, is the most blatant example in recent years of how men in power exploit, in this case, vulnerable, innocent parishioners.

The Black church is also generally speaking hypocritical about homosexuality. Lesbian theologian Reverend Dr. Irene Moore is more unequivocal: "Our black churches, both denominational and storefront, are fertile soils for planting and cultivating homo hatred."[33] We devote a chapter to other aspects of what Delroy Constantine-Simms calls "the greatest taboo in Black communities," but here we focus on how this "race secret" is handled and mishandled in Black churches.

The African American church's attitude about homosexuality has been strongly influenced by the dominant culture's attitudes. Homophobia and heterosexism are so deeply entrenched in "mainstream" American culture that it would be impossible for the Black church to have immunized itself against it. Many white Christians have declared homosexuality to be a perversion and have boldly indicated that they hate the sin but love the sinner. However, as Kelley Brown Douglas, the first theologian to seriously address sexuality and homophobia in the Black church, observes: ". . . the Bible does not present as clear a position on homosexuality as is often self-righteously asserted. The meaning of the biblical stories customarily referred to as proof against homosexual practices has generally been misconstrued or distorted. Biblical scholars have painstakingly shown that the Leviticus Holiness Codes (Lev. 18: 22; 20:13), the story of Sodom and Gomorrah (Gen. 19: 1-9), and Paul's Epistle to the Romans (1:26–27) do not present a compelling case against homoeroticism. These scholars have also pointed out that neither the words nor the actions of Jews, as recorded in the Gospels, suggest an anti-gay or anti-lesbian stance. In fact the New Testament shows Jesus to be virtually indifferent about matters of sexuality."[34]

Just as white people have misused biblical texts to argue that God supported slavery, and that being Black was a curse, the Bible has been misused by African Americans to justify the oppression of homosexuals. It is ironic that while they easily dismiss the Bible's problematic references to Black people, they accept without question what they perceive to be its condemnation of homosexuals.

Today's preachers who make speaking out against homosexuality a centerpiece of their moral crusades can find precedence for such behavior in the work of one of the most powerful Black ministers in American history, the Reverend Adam Clayton Powell, Sr. He was the pastor of Abyssinian Baptist Church in Harlem from 1908 to 1937 and the father of the legendary Congressperson Adam Clayton Powell, Jr., who succeeded his father as pastor of Abyssinian. An influential leader in Harlem, Adam Clayton Powell, Sr., was also a self-appointed campaigner against what he considered to be immorality in Black society, particularly prostitution, gambling, and homosexuality.

Because of his close and positive relationship with the Black press, Powell received full coverage for his scathing attacks on homosexuality, which were delivered from the Abyssinian pulpit.[35] It is noteworthy that "womanizing" was not among the sins he identified for removing a pastor from his post.

The opposite of the Powell approach of "calling out" and exposing gay and lesbian people in the church is the practice of stamping out homosexuality through silence. Tragically, such silence also means ministers' ignoring HIV/AIDS and its impact on the women, men, and children in their very congregations and surrounding communities. Kelley Brown Douglas notes how serious such silences can be when she reminds us that while African Americans make up 13 percent of the U.S. population, they account for about 57 percent of all new HIV/AIDS infections; Black women now have the highest incidence of new HIV infections. Moreover, while the death rate from AIDS is decreasing in the overall population, AIDS remains a leading cause of death among Black people ages twenty-five to forty-five. Among Black women, who make up 56 percent of the total female HIV/AIDS cases, heterosexual sex is the most common route to infection. Despite overwhelming evidence to the contrary, however, far too many in the Black church community continue to consider AIDS a "gay" disease.[36] Even if this were the case, we argue, it would still deserve the attention of faith communities. Devastating realities such as these statistics on the HIV/AIDS epidemic in African American communities, and startling contradictions such as "preying preachers" have compelled progressive ministers like the Reverend Dr. James Forbes, Jr. to assert that "issues of sexuality are turning out to be a spiritual fault line threatening the stability and the unity of the church."[37] The words of a womanist theologian and professor of religion at Howard University, the Reverend Dr. Kelley Brown Douglas, are even more chilling:

> There is a life-defying brokenness in the Black community . . . [which] is ravaged by teenage pregnancies, homicide, HIV/AIDS, domestic violence, and even sexual misconduct among clergy and other Black leaders. . . . The Black church, which has traditionally been a sanctuary of life and freedom for Black people, has been shamefully unresponsive to these issues even while it provides a sacred canopy for sexist and heterosexist structures and behavior.[38]

NEW DIRECTIONS

Throughout African American communities, common parlance about the Black church is that it remains a critical institution; it has contributed to our very survival as a people; and it is "a place of refuge in a mighty storm." Gender talk about the Black church continues to proliferate; it identifies the institution as both a site of male-centeredness and power *and* a site of resistance to male domination. But happily there are ongoing challenges to long-standing and persistent patriarchal attitudes and behaviors in the Black church.

While there are some "everyday folks" in Black churches who continue to speak out against sexism in their faith communities, there is an even more significant impact when Black religious and spiritual leaders address this question. Those religious and spiritual leaders who challenge the Black church to change its ways fall into one or more of the following categories: progressive theologians/ministers; academic ordained ministers; womanist theologians/ministers; openly gay and lesbian ministers; ministers of independent churches; ministers of mega churches; and spiritual gurus.

Today, as is the case throughout the history of the Black church, men dominate in the pulpit, in published religious scholarship, and in leadership in both the sacred and profane worlds. A small subset stands out because of their progressive views on "the woman question" and other social and political issues—men such as Drs. James H. Cone, James A. Forbes, Jr., James Washington, Vincent Harding, Cornel West, Michael Eric Dyson, and Mark Chapman. Among them, the radical and pioneering Black liberation theology of Cone, professor of systematic theology at Union Theological Seminary, included an early critique of sexism in the Black church: "Although black male theologians and church leaders have progressive and often revolutionary ideas regarding the equality of blacks in American society, they do not have similar ideas regarding the equality of women in the black church and community."[39] In an unusual appeal to Black male ministers, Cone urges them to take the issue of women's liberation seriously and understand the depth of sexism in Black churches as well as the connection between racism and sexism; learn how to really listen to women's stories of pain and struggle; and support women's leadership roles in the church, including that of minister. He boldly advocates affirmative action strategies for Black women in churches so that they will be represented equally in all positions of responsibility. And finally, he calls for serious discussion of the role of Black women in the church and asserts passionately that "The black church cannot regain its Christian integrity unless it is willing to face head-on the evil of patriarchy and seek to eliminate it" (139).

The sermons, published works, and community activism of the Reverend Dr. James Forbes, Jr., the first Black senior minister at The

Riverside Church in New York City (1989), consistently stand in opposition to much that is preached and practiced in thousands and thousands of Black churches. The Reverend Forbes, who grew up in a Black Pentecostal church, is also a professor at Union Theological Center in New York City. And while he is known as a great and highly effective preacher, his messages are often antithetical to standard Black religious rhetoric, especially on such issues as the role of women in the church, homosexuality, and AIDS. One of his bold ideas is that churches should assume responsibility for providing youngsters with effective sex education, which he discusses in a collection of interviews with twenty Black religious leaders who speak out against homophobia and are welcoming of lesbians and gays in their congregations.[40] His proposal is the establishment of Tender Loving Care clubs for children in churches, which would provide them with sophisticated knowledge about sexuality so that they can behave responsibly as adults.

There is a growing body of preachers and seminary scholar-teachers whose work is grounded in womanist philosophy and practice—that is, a belief in gender equality and a theology of liberation, which is attentive to the particular experiences of African American women. Among these preacher-teacher-scholar-activists is the Reverend Dr. Jacquelyn Grant, a professor at the Interdenominational Theological Center (ITC), an ordained AME minister, and founding director of the Office of Black Women in Church and Society; Kelley Brown Douglas, professor of theology at Howard University Divinity School; and Vashti McKenzie, the first woman bishop elected in the history of the African Methodist Episcopal church, who is now serving in Africa. These women directly address issues of male dominance and female resistance to that dominance in and outside of Black churches. These sister religious leaders also openly take on issues of sexuality and sexual violence.

The deafening silence on or open condemnation of homosexuals in many Black churches, including their refusal to confront the AIDS epidemic, is vigorously challenged by individuals like the late Reverend Dr. James S. Tinney, founder in 1982 of Faith Temple, a Black gay church in Washington, D.C.; the Reverend Renee McCoy, pastor of the Black gay Harlem Metropolitan Community

Church; and the Reverend Dr. Renee Hill—all of whom are founders/leaders of predominantly Black gay/lesbian churches or progressive mainstream churches. Some of these "out" homosexual preachers not only engage in gender talk about "straight" Black churches, they also take on controversial gender issues within their own congregations and the wider homosexual, bisexual, and trans-gendered communities. Tinney, who adamantly supported same-gender marriages, has written that gay Black churches will make it possible for the first time for Black gay Christians "to hear the gospel in their own 'language of the Spirit,' respond to the gospel in their own ways, and reinterpret the gospel in their own cultural context—taking into account both race and sexual orientation at every step in this process."[41] The Reverend Dr. Renee Hill, senior associate minister for peace and justice at All Saints Episcopal Church in Pasadena, California, is committed to inclusiveness. She is part of an "out" lesbian family in the church and her partner is in charge of children and family ministry; they are parents of a daughter. Having been influenced by the pioneering theological work of Dr. James Cone, she notices "who is not there, who is silent, who is present in the church but not coming forward and why. How is this community constructed in a way that anybody is being left out or made silent?"[42]

A growing phenomenon in African American religious life is churches which, while Christian in theology and practice, are independent of any denomination. Not all such nondenominational congregations are led by ministers who speak on gender matters, however. Among those who do is the Reverend Dr. Barbara Lewis King, the founding minister and chief executive officer of Hillside International Truth Center in Atlanta, Georgia. From the language she offers in prayers—"Dear Mother/Father God"—to the openness with which she addresses gender matters that are central to what she calls the ability of a woman or a man to transform their lives, Barbara King works outside of many of the limits of organized denominations. Hers is not a ministry exclusively focused on women, but she frequently addresses issues of special concern to African American women.

Then there are the Black mega-churches. They have congregations of 10,000 to 25,000; have huge physical structures that contain day-care facilities, health centers, and bookstores; and they often own businesses that reach out beyond their own congregations. Some of the mega-churches also reach enormous radio and television audiences and hold revivalist-style gatherings.

Bishop T. D. Jakes stands out among such mega-church pastors in terms of his specific appeal to Black women. At his gatherings in places like the Georgia Dome in Atlanta, and at The Potter's House in Dallas, Texas, his 26,000-membership church, in his televised programs, and his numerous books, T. D. Jakes mixes Christian theology with commonsense therapy and a Pentecostal preaching style. While Black feminists would seriously challenge his analysis of gender issues and suggested cures, no one can challenge the fact that many of Bishop Jakes's messages and the core of his unique ministry include gender talk and other race secrets. As the back cover of his best-selling self-help book *Woman, Thou Art Loosed! Healing the Wounds of the Past* (1993) proclaims: "For the single parent and the battered wife, for the abused girls and the insecure woman, there is a cure for the crisis!" Rejecting the cultural taboo against airing dirty racial linen, he alludes to the sexual abuse of boys as well as rape and violence against women, and asserts "that our silence contributes to the shame and secrecy that [is attached] to these victimized persons." Despite his helpful admonitions about the dangers of silence, however, there is an attachment to traditional Christian gender norms that ultimately renders his healing philosophy suspect. His problematic, stereotypical gender attitudes are most evident in his disturbing chapter on "Origins of Femininity":

> Women were made like receptacles. They were made to be receivers. Men were made to be givers, physically, sexually and emotionally, and by providing for others ... The woman was made, fashioned out of the man, to be a help meet. ... Women are open by nature and design. Men are closed. You must be careful what you allow to plug into you and draw strength from you.[43]

We affirm Bishop Jakes's commitment to treating the wounds of African American women but we are also mindful of the narrow framework in which he dispenses his healing medicine and the potential for a relapse.

Within the enormously influential community of self-help practitioners there are women who ground their counsel in notions of spirituality. One scholar, Akasha Gloria Hull, labels this communal work "soul talk" or "soul process."[44] Like the organized Black church, they are involved in healing our collective wounds, but call upon in much more explicit ways their wisdom as women who've navigated difficult life journeys. Two of the most visible and popular Black women whom some would describe as contemporary community "healers" are Susan Taylor and Iyanla Vanzant. Each has built a large following among Black women seeking help for the problems that plague them and their families, and counsel on how to transform their lives. Susan Taylor, the former editor-in-chief of *Essence* magazine, has a very large following of Black women because of her monthly *Essence* column, "In the Spirit," her books, speaking engagements around the country, especially on college campuses, and the seminars she leads for Black women. Now editorial director of the magazine, she periodically writes a column under the title of "In the Spirit," and enjoys great respect and admiration among African American women for her wise words and spiritual grounding.

Iyanla Vanzant has created a national following that has propelled her to the status of best-selling author, popular speaker, and television personality. Much of what Vanzant writes and talks about references her own struggles to build and maintain a healthy relationship with her husband, sustain the best possible relationships with her children, and affirm herself as a self-actualized Black woman.

In their writings and public appearances, both Taylor and Vanzant shy away from what might be labeled as "feminism," but they center their teachings on issues that haunt many African American women. The "medicine" they prescribe for problems that range from sexual abuse to low self-esteem are grounded in Afrocentric notions of healing and personal empowerment through spiritual growth.

Dr. Barbara King, founding pastor of Atlanta-based Hillside

Truth International Center, brings to her large congregation a fusion of womanist and Afrocentric theology. In our interview with her, she spoke about the resistance of many male preachers to the presence of women in the pulpit, and of the many difficulties she faced personally in her quest to become a minister within mainstream denominations. These struggles motivated her to found her own church and chart her own journey as an activist minister committed to addressing openly pressing issues facing contemporary, including younger, congregations.

We opened this chapter by recalling our own upbringing in Black churches placing us solidly within the long-standing tradition of churchgoing and church-related activities in African American life. We were struck by the fact that every woman and man who participated in the multilogue at the Ford Foundation (described in the Appendix) continued to reference the Black church even if they were no longer members of a particular congregation. This widespread association of Black folks with "the Church" means that centuries-old patterns of patriarchal attitudes and behavior could continue. Or, ideally, these institutions to which millions of Black people are attached in varying degrees could become sites for the transformation of fundamental ideas and values about gender.

We call for and indeed hope for sustained gender talk on the part of various religious and spiritual leaders that will reach broad audiences within and outside of the church. For it is such gender talk that is a prerequisite to the change in consciousness and then the action that will allow us to grapple with whatever ails us physically, spiritually, and sexually. And we remain convinced of the unique power of Black feminist/womanist analyses, whether generated by women or men, as we move beyond the silences that have exacted far too high a price in our communities.

5

•

RACE SECRETS AND
THE BODY POLITIC

The way out is to tell: speak the acts perpetrated upon us, speak the atrocities, speak the injustices, speak the personal violations of the soul. Someone will listen, someone will believe our stories, someone will join us. And until there are more who will bear witness to our truths as black women, we will do it for one another.

> Charlotte Pierce-Baker, *Surviving the Silence:*
> *Black Women's Stories of Rape,* 1998

Our community has been a place of contradiction in the matter of protecting us women. Black men risked life and limb to save us from being battered and raped by white men during slavery. This makes the brutalizing of sisters by brothers today all the more painful.

> Susan Taylor, *Essence,* 2002

We may not yet be able to stop the violence of the racist state, but self-inflicted violence in our communities we can stop. . . . Black men must hold each other responsible for challenging sexism in our community as we all challenge the racism of white America.

> Robert L. Allen, "Stopping Sexual Harassment," 1995

When we consider the history of the exploitation of Black bodies within the cultural terrain of the United States, we speak volumes about the politics of race and the ways in which gender and class also impact what it means to be Black. The physical and psychic brutality that characterizes African American experience has been unrelenting. We have been chained, branded, burned, bought, sold, lynched, castrated, raped, beaten, stalked, and profiled. Racially speaking, the public spectacle of lynching, especially images of Black male bodies hanging from trees, sometimes castrated, is perhaps our most familiar association with the horrific consequences of racism in the American landscape and the vulnerability of Black bodies. It is probably our most vivid reminder of the power of white racism to terrorize, mutilate, torture, and wreak havoc on a "minority" community.

But there have been other assaults on Black bodies. The forty-year Tuskegee experiment, "one of the most notorious episodes in the history of human subjects research in the United States,"[1] is an egregious example of the involvement of the Federal government in medical experimentation on unsuspecting Black men.[2] Less well known is the Elmer Allen case, which involved a lone Black man who was also used as a human guinea pig, this time for testing plutonium in humans during the development of the atom bomb in 1947. As disturbing in the annals of U.S. medical history, but even less well known, is the use of slave women as human guinea pigs by white male doctors perfecting their gynecological surgery skills.[3] Dr. James Marion Sims was known primarily as the father of gynecology because of his invention of a precursor to the modern speculum. For four years in Montgomery, Alabama (1845–49), he performed painful surgery on several slave women suffering from injuries to the vagina and rectum sustained during childbirth. The most victimized was Anarcha, on whom thirty operations were performed before he finally repaired her "female disorder."

Historian Elsa Barkley Brown reminds us that the issue of violence against women is one of the most underanalyzed aspects of African American history. The existence of Black female lynch victims, for example, has not been a part of the discussion of racial violence in the American body politic. While the rape of Black women and girls is perhaps the second most obvious manifestation of racial violence, it has not been as prominent in our collective memories of the horrors of racism. At the 1893 Colombia Exposition in Chicago, Anna Julia Cooper spoke eloquently about the sexual exploitation of Black females and the "painful, patient and silent toil of mothers to gain a fee simple title [sic] to the bodies of their daughters."[4] This relative lack of attention to the myriad forms of violence that Black women experience perpetuates the idea that Black male bodies are more at risk than those of Black women and children. We do not have, although we know she existed, a Black female counterpart, for example, to the graphic visual images conjured up by our memories of the lynching death of fourteen-year-old Emmett Till in Money, Mississippi, that awful August 28, 1955, when his bloated, mutilated body was plucked from the Tallahatchie River.

The story of the Turner family painfully illustrates the extent to which Black men, women, and children have been perpetual victims of domestic terrorism in the United States. It remains one of the most unimaginable episodes in the saga of white lynch mob violence that reached epidemic proportions in the late nineteenth-century Reconstruction South. This graphic and almost unreadable description of the lynching of Hayes Turner and his pregnant wife, Mary, in Valdosta, Georgia, in 1915 is a reminder of the fact that whites consider Black bodies worthless, but also of the way in which history "wipes out, ignores, disremembers violence against Black women."[5] We became aware of the Turner family saga while reading historian Lerone Bennett's riveting, though sparsely rendered account in *Before the Mayflower: A History of Black America* (1982). It stayed in our memories throughout the writing of *Gender Talk*.[6]

Walter White's study of lynching describes in even more painstaking and horrifying detail the circumstances surrounding the mob violence visited upon the entire Turner family:

> To Turner's wife . . . was brought the news of her husband's death. She cried out in her sorrow, pouring maledictions upon the heads of those who had thrust widowhood upon

her so abruptly and cruelly. Word of her threat to swear out warrants for the arrest of her husband's murders came to her. "We'll teach the damn' nigger wench some sense," was their answer, as they began to seek her. Fearful, her friends secreted the sorrowing woman on an obscure farm, miles away. Sunday morning, with a hot May sun beating down, they found her. Securely they bound her ankles together and by them, hanged her to a tree. Gasoline and motor oil were thrown upon her dangling clothes; a match wrapped her in sudden flames. Mocking, ribald laughter from her tormentors answered the helpless woman's screams of pain and terror. "Mister, you ought to've heard the nigger wench howl!" a member of the mob boasted to me a few days later as we stood at the place of Mary Turner's death. The clothes burned from her crisply toasted body, in which unfortunately, life still lingered, a man stepped towards the woman and, with his knife, ripped open the abdomen in a crude Cesarean operation. Out tumbled the prematurely born child.[7]

Despite our collective racial memory of lynching as a "masculine experience" (102), the brutal murder of Mary Turner was not an isolated case. Between 1880 and 1940 more than eighty Black women were lynched.[8]

The centuries-long history of physical and sexual exploitation of Black women, which began during the Middle Passage, bears repeating. We continue to be haunted by the questions Elsa Barkley Brown raised when she discovered images of Black women lynch victims in her father's political cartoons: Why is it that people don't remember the lynching of Black women and the brutality of that experience? Why is it that Black women's other experiences of violence—rape, sexual and other forms of physical abuse in white homes, and elsewhere—are not remembered as vividly, if at all, when we ponder the history of African American experience in general? Is it possible for us to imagine the lynching of Mary Turner, her husband, Hayes, and their unborn child?

I Am a Man[9]

In order to more fully understand the complexity of Black gender politics, especially around issues of violence, we need to explore constructions of masculinity, Black male identity formation, and Black male's sexual attitudes and behaviors.[10] Over the past decade, discussions of Black masculinity as well as Black male experience have become more intense. Probing these complex issues has been useful in our ongoing analysis of intraracial gender politics. We have found the work of a handful of Black male scholars critical to our efforts, even though we do not always agree with them. While we understand at a profound level the particular plight of Black men and the hostile world they inhabit, we do not believe that "black males have been the principal victims of the legacy of racial discrimination and prejudice in American society,"[11] or that Black men have been prohibited from being men or denied a gender identity. Despite their relative economic and political powerlessness in white male–dominated society, Black men also benefit from the gender privilege that operates in some manner for all males in male-dominant cultures such as the United States, though clearly white men as a group are the most privileged. This is the case for Black men even if that power is only able to be exercised *within* their own marginalized communities and within their families. This is not to say that power and privilege are shared equally by men within racial/ethnic communities since poverty, sexual orientation, color, and professional status impact the nature of the power all men are able to exercise in patriarchal societies. The point we are making is that no men are entirely without gender privilege in relation to certain women in patriarchal societies.

Despite their disadvantaged economic status, which has worsened over the past two decades,[12] African American men have not entirely rejected mainstream definitions of patriarchal masculinity. Even though they may be unable because of racism and other social factors to perform the traditional gender roles of provider and protector or display the "masculine" traits of power, autonomy, dominance, and control, they still cling to notions of manhood that permeate the larger culture. In an interview Noel Cazenave conducted with Black fathers who were mailmen, a large percentage identified being responsible, working hard, and having ambition as major characteristics of being a man and the role of economic provider as their most important gender role.[13] Influential rapper/ activist Sister Souljah's description of her hardworking, generous, responsible father underscores the impact of mainstream patriarchal definitions of gender roles on Black men's conceptions of masculinity and femininity. Having rejected his own father as a role model, he turns to the media for lessons about how to be a better family man, not realizing the bankrupt nature of mainstream definitions of masculinity; Sister Souljah writes:

> My father drew his understanding of what it meant to have a family from television. He wanted to be a man's man. He believed that it was solely the man's responsibility to bring home the bacon and rule the household. He believed that the woman must work hard at being beautiful; that she make her husband as comfortable as a king in his own castle; that she perfect her skills of housecleaning and cooking and have a lot of babies. . . . Most of all, he demanded that she be fully dependent on him. No driving, traveling alone, taking classes. . . . He must be the source of her money, love, sex, and strength, and the center of her existence.[14]

Being a responsible family man is only one way of conceptualizing Black masculinity. There are multiple other ways. Despite their persistent second-class status, many men in our father's and grandfather's generations came to manhood under a different set of circumstances than is the case with many of today's Black youth trapped in a world of drugs, unemployment, AIDS, gangs, and devastating poverty, without extended families and stable community anchors. Black social scientists have also attempted to explain the dire consequences, in many instances, of Black men not being able to "head" their families, get and keep a good job, and control their own lives or the lives of those they love—traditional markers of manhood in this society.

Black men's perception of their emasculated status also impacts their sexual identity in ways that may explain other aspects of their behavior. In fact, several Black male sociologists and psychologists, among others, have argued compellingly that there is a link between the social marginalization of Black males and their sexual attitudes and behaviors. In this chapter, we argue that the persistence of racism must be understood in any analysis of Black definitions of masculinity that certainly impact Black gender politics as well. Sociologist Robert Staples, a pioneer in the study of Black masculinity, argues that it is more difficult in this culture for Black men to achieve appropriate gender roles than it is for Black women, and this "role failure" results in conceptions of manhood that are available to them—impregnating females, fathering many children, especially boys, and having many sexual conquests and sexual relationships.[15] Sociologist Clyde W. Franklin II, an expert on Black male gender roles and a pioneering architect of Black Men's Studies, argues that any exploration of Black masculinity must take into consideration the legacy of slavery when Black men were property and rendered submissive, nonprotective, powerless, and studs supreme.[16] Franklin also asserts that Black men have had few legitimate outlets for the normative masculine roles of dominance and control. We disagree with Franklin's assertion that "Black male slaves had no gender" because they were perceived to be inhuman, or that Black males have been "men" for only the past twenty years.[17] Sociologist Benjamin P. Bowser, an expert on community-based AIDS prevention, echoes this argument in his discussion of "exaggerated Black sexuality": when men in a male-dominated society are prevented from enacting the normative masculine social and economic roles they resort to overcompensating behaviors in other arenas. "I would propose that men in all social classes who experience frustrated instrumental and expressive roles place more emphasis on their sexuality."[18] When Black men are unable to be men in traditional ways, what Bowser calls "male role attrition," they compensate by exaggerating what's left of normative gender roles. "And that is sex. . . . what is left of his manhood demands that he control this last frontier. The result is exaggerated sexuality."[19]

Bowser goes on to argue that one consequence of this exaggerated sexuality is competition with other Black men, which often leads to violence. Bowser thus offers a much needed gender analysis of an urgent social problem that has been framed primarily within racial terms. Criminologist William Oliver, an expert on Black-on-Black violence, and member of the Institute on Domestic Violence in the African American Community, refers to this same phenomenon as the "compulsive masculine alternative," a process he identifies among low-income Black males, in particular, in which manhood is reimagined employing a different set of values and norms that encompasses "toughness, sexual promiscuity, manipulation, thrill seeking and a willing use of violence to resolve interpersonal conflict."[20] This compensatory behavior, which Oliver refers to as dysfunctional adaptations to the denial of manhood, enables Black men to feel good about themselves even though they are unable to live up to hegemonic notions of masculinity. Gary Lemons puts it even more bluntly when he asserts that Black men's fear of emasculation or feminization "has led us to overdetermine our sexuality, believing that our identity as men resides only in the power of our penises."[21]

These alternative avenues to masculinity have problematic consequences, according to the influential work of psychologist Richard Majors, cofounder of the National Council of African Men (1990), who has written extensively on the dilemmas of Black masculinity.[22] Majors identifies "cool pose" as a survival strategy employed by *some* Black men, which has cost them and society an enormous price while it has also enabled them to ward off the most damaging effects of racism. Majors reveals its negative side:

> Cool helps to explain the fact that African American males die earlier and faster than white males from suicide, homicide, accidents, and stress-related illnesses; that black males are more deeply involved in criminal and delinquent activities; that they drop out of school and are suspended more often than white children; and that they have more volatile relationships with women.[23]

Other Black male scholars have also argued that certain components of Black male gender identity and their culturally sanctioned sex role may explain the violence which "brothers" inflict on other "brothers."[24] In other words, Black men's perpetual quest for manhood in a society that would render them boys—or worse, girls—predisposes them to violent behavior not because of individual pathology but because of social factors stemming from both institutionalized racism and sexism. Psychologist Ricky L. Jones attempts to illustrate his theory of violent Black masculinity in an analysis of a highly publicized Black fraternity hazing incident that resulted in the brutal killing of Michael Davis while he was pledging Kappa Alpha Psi at Southeast Missouri State University in 1994. In order to understand the behavior of Davis's fraternity brothers, Jones argues that "identity contributes to violence (and vice-versa) and identity is not intrinsic, but is a social construct largely external to individuals."[25]

We were drawn to Jones's work because of his mention of an earlier hazing incident that resulted in the death of Morehouse College freshman Joel Harris, who was pledging Alpha Phi Alpha. Joel enrolled in the Introduction to Women's Studies class Johnnetta and Beverly were coteaching at Spelman in 1989. We remember the first day of class when Joel and another Morehouse student huddled close to the two of us, nervously, feeling somewhat more secure and protected near us, we presumed, in their first Women's Studies class; frequently male students assume that Women's Studies classes are male-bashing classes and that they will be targeted for abuse. Within three weeks, however, Joel was talking openly about his new ideas about being a good father, especially as it related to raising a daughter, which he admitted he now preferred to raising a son. Beverly still recalls even more vividly the last day of young Joel's life, and his mother's remarkable composure at the funeral a few days later in New York City. On the evening of his death, Joel wandered into Beverly's office, more excited than she had ever seen him; he told her that he wanted to talk with her briefly before rushing off to a fraternity meeting. During their short conversation, he told her how much he was enjoying the class, how he was sharing his books with his mother, and how much he was looking forward to the rest of the semester.[26] Within a few hours he was dead.

Jones connects the violence that sometimes occurs within Black Greek fraternity contexts to cultural notions of masculinity that

emphasize power over others and aggression. Jones is not excus-
ing Black male violence, but is asking us to see the link between
certain Black male identities and the particularities of Black men's
sojourn in America. "This identity is acted upon by multiple factors: race, class, gender, and historical political, economic, and
social disenfranchisement. . . . Black male violence—at its core,
when all illusions are stripped away—is about attempts to achieve
manhood."[27]

Despite Black men's attachment to traditional male values,
there are some culturally specific aspects of Black masculinity that
distinguish it from normative white masculinity. Influenced by the
work of Majors, other Black social scientists have amplified his pre-
liminary discussion of "cool pose," especially the masculine imperative of toughness. This aspect of Black male behavior is
connected to what Michele Wallace identified as "black macho" in
her controversial polemic on the sexism of the civil rights movement. Clinical psychologist Merlin Langley argues that coolness is
"a fundamental character trait of the African American male in his
struggle to assert his masculinity."[28] By "cool pose," these scholars
mean a clearly identifiable array of coping behaviors and psychological defenses, both positive and negative, that some Black males
in particular employ to deal with the persistent stressors of an oppressive society. Noel Cazenave argues that some Black males believe they can demonstrate their manhood and garner respect mainly
by being tough, violent, and exerting control over others.[29] Without
the conventional trappings of masculinity—social status, money,
prestige, fancy jobs—Black males resort to exaggerated masculinity
and toughness in order to be respected.

We found autobiographical narratives of "tough" Black males
a useful source of "data" on the extent to which Black men explicitly embrace the more problematic aspects of mainstream definitions of manhood. These include Claude Brown's extremely popular
Manchild and the Promised Land (1990), Robert Beck's *The Naked
Soul of Iceberg Slim* (1968), Monster Kody Scott's *Monster: The
Autobiography of an L.A. Gang Member* (1993), and Ice T's *The
Ice Opinion* (1994). The hypermasculinity that many Black social
scientists attempt to explain is especially apparent in the masculinity-

obsessed culture of Black gangs. The following description of a Los Angeles gang's membership requirement captures this reality:

> An individual must buy a pair of khaki pants, "sag" the waist, and "put on the look." Next [he] has to "jump-in" and fight three gang members all at once. If [he] still stands after ten minutes, he is considered "tough" and thus is accepted into the gang.[30]

William Oliver's ideas about compulsive masculinity, the requisite "tough guy" role, and violence among Black males are certainly illustrated in the lives of Black gang members whom Majors and his collaborators describe as the epitome of "the frustrated Black male in this country."[31] In his delineation of "the jungle creed," former gang member and gangsta rapper Ice T captures the frustration, despair, and rage among inner-city Black youth that lead to gangs characterized by obsessive masculinity and dangerous, self-destructive, risk-taking behaviors:

> "Who gives a fuck?" is one of the first questions a kid will ask himself growing up in the ghetto. He'll look around at the broken-down buildings, the shabby projects, the cracked schoolyard playgrounds, and it doesn't look like anybody gives a fuck. . . . Everybody he sees is just trying to survive. . . . The successful people you see in the ghetto are the drug dealers, the pimps—the brothers driving around in the flashy cars. Your role models are those fly guys because everybody else is struggling. . . . *In the jungle, masculinity is at a premium* [emphasis ours]. Anybody weaker than the next man will be victimized by the stronger. . . . Displays of strength and aggression are prized . . . In the 'hood, violence and even murder become something honorable. The most violent person, the most defiant person, will get the highest ranking.[32]

Ice T understands the rules of hegemonic masculinity, even though he realizes how elusive it is for disadvantaged Black youth (29). He reveals as well the extent to which heterosexist attitudes prevail within "the jungle creed."

> You don't understand anyone who is weak. You look at gay people as prey. There isn't anybody in the ghetto teaching that some people's sexual preferences are predisposed. You're just ignorant. You got to get educated, you got to get out of that jail cell called the ghetto to really begin to understand. All you see is a sissy. A soft dude. A punk.[33]

Ice T knows that sexual conquest, the quintessential sign of American masculinity, is one of the ways that men, especially disempowered Black males, assert their manhood.

> I can't speak for women, but I know what men are about. I know about muthafuckin' men: They want to fuck. Men are dogs. . . . Why do men want to become successful? To get women. (71–72)

LL Cool J (which stands for Ladies Love Cool J), born in 1968 on Long Island as James Todd Smith, describes a troubled childhood permeated by violence, within and outside his family, and the lure of "cool pose" as he struggled to become a man. The most traumatic event of his young boyhood occurred four years after his mother left her abusive husband and moved in with her loving parents. When James was only four years old, his father, angry that his wife would not return to the marriage, stormed James's grandparent's house and shot her and her father, who came to her rescue, with a twelve-gauge shotgun. Both miraculously survived, though James's mother sustained more life-threatening injuries, which would require hospitalization for several months. The family chose not to file criminal charges and eventually returned to some sense of normalcy, but little James would bear deep emotional scars that would be exacerbated by his mother's new boyfriend Roscoe, who abused her both physically and psychologically. Having witnessed his father's habitual abuse of his mother before she left him, and having endured Roscoe's unrelenting cruelty, James would become by age thirteen the angry, out-of-control Black boy about whom Black scholars have written with painful frequency. Filled with rage and with no role models (except for his grandfather), he replicated the very behavior he despised in his father and the man with whom he spent the most time:

> What I see now is that Roscoe's constant beating changed me. I went from this normal kid who got straight A's and loved school to a troublemaker. . . . I was angry in my school. I was always fighting in the neighborhood . . . I was a bully. I didn't care who I fought or why. I was turning into a prepubescent Roscoe.[34]

Though James escapes poverty and its devastating consequences— "my family pretty much gave me what I wanted"—he finds it difficult to reject his community's norms of masculinity:

> I would carry guns just waiting for someone to mess with me so I could put a cap to them. . . . having them gave me a sense of protection and a sense of power. Fighting also gave me that power. So did terrorizing and abusing others, I'm ashamed to say. . . . I was really a confused kid who wanted to be cool, who wanted to fit in and simply didn't know how to. I wanted to be down, to be part of the crew. And I thought being cool meant I had to drink a few forties, rob a couple of people, carry a knife, carry a gun, and be menacing. Now, how ridiculous was I? (53)

In an astute analysis of the ways in which he was complicit in his own emasculation, James describes his embrace of unhealthy masculine traits. "I know now I was far from being cool. The way I used to act was real corny. *It was impotent* [our emphasis]. I became powerless to control the violence that had taken hold of me. I became the same impotent demon that was abusing me . . . I wasn't just abusing other people, though, I was also abusing myself . . . And at the end of the day, I started hating myself" (53–54).

Homicide is the leading cause of death among Black males between the ages of fifteen and twenty-four (and the leading cause of death for both Black men and women ages twenty-five to thirty-four!). Most of them will be killed by other Black males, usually relatives or acquaintances. It is certainly true that the historical legacy of racism may be the most crucial variable in understanding this disturbing phenomenon since most of these homicides occur in urban areas where there are huge ghettos and high poverty, crime, and unemployment rates. However, it is imperative that we consider other explanations as well for Black-on-Black violence and other self-destructive behaviors that are wreaking havoc on Black communities. While the literature on the relationship between anger, rage, and violence is substantial,[35] more attention needs to be paid to the gendered aspects of Black male on male violence, and Black male on Black female violence since the primary victims are lovers, wives, acquaintances, and children.[36]

BREAKING SILENCES

While the problem of Black-on-Black homicide has been widely acknowledged in the media, it has been more difficult for us to break our silence about the sexual abuse of children and intimate partner violence. Gradually Black social scientists have begun to deal with these serious problems with greater frequency. *Essence* and *Ebony* must also be credited with enabling Black communities to deal more effectively with controversial issues within our communities such as incest, rape, wife-battering, mental illness, bisexuality, and homosexuality—including Black women married to gay men, and the growing phenomenon of ostensibly heterosexual Black men who have sex with other men, a phenomenon called "down under," which has profound implications for the the AIDS epidemic in African American communities.[37] A recent *Ebony* article includes the sad narrative of a professional Black woman who was infected with AIDS by her closeted husband who was sleeping with other men ("M-S-M," he called it) and eventually died of AIDS.[38]

We begin this discussion by asserting that violence against women is encouraged in many cultures and is a reflection of societal beliefs about women's subordinate status and the notion that women are the property of men to be treated however they deem appropriate. In other words, our discussion of Black family violence proceeds from our understanding of the larger social structure that is characterized by systemic gender oppression. But as activist/scholar Robert L. Allen argues, "It is a tragedy that many of us [Black men] have internalized the violence of this oppressive system and brought it in our communities and our homes."[39] It is important, as well, to focus on our own communities, since William Oliver reminds us that conflicts between Black men and women lead to a greater frequency of assault and murder of females than among any other racial/ethnic group in the United States. Black women also kill Black men at higher rates than other women do in the United States, which Oliver attributes to sexual infidelity, emotional and physical abuse, jealousy, and self-defense.[40] We have been able to maintain denial about this crisis because of the absence of any "sustained, social scientific studies of violence in Black families."[41] While incest occurs within Black families—as it does in other families irrespective of race, ethnicity, or class—it remains perhaps our biggest "race secret" and the sexual crime we seem to be least able to deal with publicly. It is in the fiction and autobiographies of Black writers—Ralph Ellison's *Invisible Man*, Maya Angelou's *I Know Why the Caged Bird Sings*, Toni Morrison's *The Bluest Eye*, Alice Walker's *The Color Purple*, and Sapphire's *Push* (1997)—that these "race secrets" are more likely to be explored. Among these texts, *Push* is the most extreme example of the sexual vulnerability of young Black girls in the sense that the protagonist, Precious Jones, is sexually and physically abused by both her biological father and mother.

Beverly became aware of the serious problem of sexual abuse within African American communities as a result of her early involvement with the National Black Women's Health Project (NBWHP), a community-based, grassroots, self-help organization founded by Byllye Avery in 1983. She met Byllye when she came to Spelman College in 1982 to organize the first national conference on Black women's health issues, which took place in June 1983 and attracted over two thousand women to the campus. Despite Beverly's knowledge about the global realities of violence against women, which she discusses in her women's studies classes, she was unprepared for the stories Black women shared over and over again at NBWHP weekend retreats, conferences, and workshops, especially "Black and Female: What Is the Reality?" Often for the first time in their lives they would speak with tremendous pain and shame about sexual abuse within their families. During the early years of the project, Black women broke the conspiracy of silence and dared to speak about the race secrets they'd been programmed to keep. Byllye Avery recalls: "The number one issue for most of our sisters is violence—battering, sexual abuse. Same thing for their daughters, whether they are twelve or four. We have to look at how violence is used, how violence and sexism go hand and hand . . . We have to stop it, because violence is the training ground for us."[42] These women's willingness to defy Black cultural taboos prompted Beverly to ponder more deeply our denials about the prevalence of violence in Black families. She recalled, in particular, the vitriolic responses to Alice Walker's novel, *The Color Purple* (1982), because of its handling of incest, marital rape, and wife battering. Black scholars have certainly dealt to some extent with Black family violence but many of them have tended to identify racism and other socioeconomic factors as the major culprits.[43]

We want to broaden the discussion by offering a more gendered analysis of the prevalence of interpersonal violence in our communities. It is important to assert unequivocally that abuse is not the normative experience in or peculiar to Black families. By abuse we mean the exercise of power within families that results in inappropriate and damaging behaviors such as violence against women and children, including boys and adolescents, and between partners or spouses and among siblings.[44] Since nearly 30 percent of American children experience sexual abuse of some sort, it is fair to say that Black men, like other men, also resort to violence for some of the same reasons that other men do—for purposes of control and as a means of exerting power. It is also the case that intervening factors, such as unemployment, poverty, and drug and alcohol abuse, also contribute to family violence in Black communities.

In one of the first books to be written by a Black woman incest survivor, *Crossing the Boundaries: Black Women Survive Incest* (1994), Melba Wilson speaks openly about her father's abuse that began when she was eleven or twelve. She discusses the special burdens Black women victims of child sexual abuse experience because in addition to dealing with the trauma of incest, they are also encouraged to remain silent since many in the community believe that exposing dirty linen will reinforce racist stereotypes about us. However, Wilson's truth-telling narrative is not only a collection of Black women's incest stories—as important as that would have been. It is also an examination of the influences which led to this abuse, including the persistence of myths about Black female sexuality and the gender- and race-based stereotypes to which Black women and men are subjected and which impact the ways we relate to each other. Wilson is passionate about her mission: "I write . . . for all those young black girls (and boys) who have not yet made it to adulthood, who are still being abused . . . who are equally trapped within their walls of silence because of unwritten, spoken and unspoken taboos about what should or should not happen; what should or should not be said about what does or does not happen in our communities of colour."[45] On a personal note, she also writes for a niece who was "savagely raped by a male relative whom she loved and trusted, and who, because of her mental state, still doesn't know what happened to her" (5).

Silences about the sexual abuse of Black boys is even more profound in our communities. Certainly, more scholarship is needed about this understudied phenomenon which, in the U.S. population at large, appears to be "common, underreported, underrecognized, and undertreated," according to one scholar who painstakingly examined all the relevant studies from 1985 to 1997.[46] His overall findings were that boys at highest risk were younger than thirteen, nonwhite, poor, living with only one parent—especially the mother—having a family member who had been sexually abused, and being away from home; perpetrators tended to be known but non-kin, and to self-identify as heterosexual. Boys less than six years of age were at greatest risk by family members and acquaintances, and boys older than twelve years of age were more vulnerable to abuse by strangers. Boys were less likely to report sexual abuse than girls.

Though it is impossible to make definitive statements about the sexual victimization of African American boys by men, what research there is, though sparse, clearly indicates that there's cause for concern and some of the inexplicable and dysfunctional behaviors we observe in adult Black males may be traceable to childhood sexual abuse.[47] Evidence of sexual abuse would include post-traumatic stress disorder, major depression, aggression, low self-esteem, sexual dysfunction or hypersexuality, gender role confusion, and substance abuse. Sexually abused men were also more likely than nonabused males to engage in high-risk sexual behaviors. As youngsters, victims might perform poorly in school, run away from home, and get in trouble with the law. Studies also indicate that Black boys are less likely to be sexually abused by Black women than is the case with white boys and white women. In our discussions with Black therapists, we learned that Black males are increasingly beginning to reveal their painful experiences with sexual abuse, but it is a topic that remains largely unexplored even among the Black therapeutic community. One explanation is that the discussion of sexuality in general has been such a taboo topic in Black communities, and the issue of homophobia makes it more difficult for Black males to disclose their sexual abuse. In a case study, Calvin (not his real name) revealed that he had been sexually abused by his grandfather from age five through seventeen, and that he was afraid to speak about it for fear it would tear his family apart and that "it was a strongly held belief in his family that you did not take familial situations outside the family, especially if it would cause a member of the family to face 'the system.' "[48]

A story shared by one of Johnnetta's male friends echoes the major findings which we've just discussed. As a young boy from the age of eight through eleven, he was routinely sexually abused by an older man who was a neighbor and friend of the family. The abuser was married and appeared to be heterosexual. Now in therapy to try to process and put away years of torment and confusion that are the result of this unreported childhood abuse, Johnnetta's friend also manifests some of the other findings mentioned in Dr. Holmes's study: he continues to be unsure of his sexual identity and he has deep-seated anger and resentment not only toward the abuser but toward his family, who he feels failed to protect him. In recalling the trauma of those early years, he speaks of a fear of "telling on the man," some of which centered around a concern that he himself would be identified as a sissy; that no one would believe him; and that he would suffer worse consequences for breaking the silence about the abuse than for not speaking out.

SEEING GENDER

To underscore the importance of moving beyond a narrow race analysis when taking into consideration the complexity of African American experience, including in the sexual arena, let us return to where we began. What would it mean to look more closely at Black men through the prism of gender? What would we gain from employing a gender analysis of the impact of racism on African American women and men? What difference, for example, would it make if we acknowledged that Black women *and* men were lynched, which means that lynching was not an exclusively male racial experience? The significance of this departure from conventional antiracist discourse is manifest in legal scholar Devon Carbado's gendered analysis of the Clarence Thomas–Anita Hill case. Carbado argues that Thomas, who constructed himself as a racial victim, was able to garner support among a broad cross section of Blacks by accusing the all-white male judiciary committee of a "high-tech lynching," as he answered charges of sexual harassment by Professor Anita Hill. Hill should have been able to "represent" the race as well because of the historical sexual abuse of Black women, but we do not attach the same significance to the racial experiences of Black women. The lynching of Black males remains the quintessential marker of racial subordination and the undeniable evidence of the "truth" that Black men are the primary victims of white supremacy. In a patriarchal culture, "emasculation," which lynching symbolizes, is the worst fate possible. Anita Hill was unable to "use her race to muster support from the Black community because Clarence Thomas as a Black man held the political ace."[49] Thomas's support in the Black community actually increased after Hill's charges of sexual misconduct. He became yet another example of a Black man targeted by the system presumably for sexual crimes he did not commit; the fact that the accuser was not a white woman was irrelevant. Hill could not mobilize the Black community, including women, against a successful Black man for the "lesser" crime of sexual harassment—even if they were willing to acknowledge that Thomas was guilty. In other words, Black men's experiences with racism, especially lynching and police brutality, are more damaging than Black women's experiences with sexism, including rape and lynching! Our gendered experiences within our own communities (which are not conceptualized as "racial" experiences) are marginalized if they appear at all in narratives about the history of race in America.

In his gender-sensitive analysis of the masculinist nature of anti-racist discourse, Carbado also reminds us that Black men (and the broader community) respond differently to accusations about sexual assaults of Black women when the perpetrator is white:

> They are up in arms when white men abuse Black women because they want it known that Black women's bodies will no longer be the terrain for white male physical or sexual aggression . . . any white man who violates a Black woman's body violates Black men and their "property interest" in that Black woman's body. However, when the abuser is a Black male, the response is less politically strident, and often politically defensive, because the assault on the Black woman . . . is sometimes understood to represent an assertion of Black male masculinity, which, it is argued, is a response to white male racism.[50]

In other words, Black male perpetrators of violence against Black women are likely to experience gender privilege within Black communities, including the presumption of innocence which white men are rarely granted.

In February 1992, heavyweight champion Mike Tyson was

convicted of raping the 1991 Miss Black America contestant, Desiree Washington, and shortly thereafter the Reverend Theodore
Jimerson, president of the National Baptist Convention, launched a
national drive to obtain 100,000 signatures so that Tyson could receive a suspended sentence in order that he could avoid prison. His
supporters constructed him as a victim who had experienced a similar fate as Clarence Thomas, Mayor Marion Barry, and other high-
profile Black male leaders.[51] Marcia Gillespie, former editor of
Essence and *Ms.*, expressed her outrage about violence against
Black women in an interview with us during which she blasted
Black leaders and celebrities for shamelessly planning a "Welcome
Home Mike Tyson" march in Harlem after the former heavyweight
champion had served three years in prison for the rape of Desiree
Washington. In her chapter on "Everyday Violence" in *Straight, No
Chaser* (which inspired the title of this chapter), journalist Jill Nelson describes the alternative rally: a vigil for victims of violence and
abuse, which took place on June 19, the day before the Tyson parade was to have occurred. Gillespie calls this event the first "Take
Back the Night" march ever to be held in Harlem. It was planned
by a coalition of Black women and men who formed African Americans Against Violence (AAAV), which said "no," loudly and publicly to treating Tyson as the heroic prodigal son. They came to
realize that their efforts to stop the parade would also provide them
a rare opportunity to focus the community's attention on the pervasive problem of violence against Black women. Nelson credits the
Reverend Calvin O. Butts, pastor of Abyssinian Baptist Church,
with being the only local religious leader who supported their efforts. Echoing Carbado, Gillespie reminded us that "the only time
sexual assault becomes an issue in our community is if the penis is
white!"

In order to demonstrate Black America's insensitivity to the issue of violence against women, even Black women, Nelson takes us
behind the scenes to late May 1995, when a group of Black men
(Don King, Congressman Charlie Rangel, the Reverend Al Sharp-
ton, Conrad Muhammed) and Roberta Flack formed a planning
committee to stage a welcome-home parade for convicted rapist
Mike Tyson, an event Nelson labels TysonFest. More importantly,

she seizes this opportunity to preach about Black male on Black female violence, another "race secret," but locates the issue within
the broader context of the misogynist culture of the United States.
"What makes black men think they can be born and raised in a culture that has profound contempt for all women and places black
women at the bottom, and escape unaffected? . . . Too often black
men seek to fit themselves into tired white patriarchal modes of behavior."[52] Psychologist Aaronette White offers an equally compelling
description of an unnamed local grassroots Black feminist collective's
mobilization against the sexual abuse of Black females. They worked
to mobilize Black communities against rape in St. Louis, Missouri,
in the aftermath of the Mike Tyson conviction (1992) and subsequent appeal in Gary, Indiana. They were especially outraged by the
Free Mike Tyson campaign, which was being supported by prominent Black men such as the Reverend T. J. Jimerson, former president
of the National Baptist Convention, and filmmaker Spike Lee. The
Black women's self-help group's first ad appeared in a local weekly
Black newspaper, the *St. Louis American*, on April 15, 1993, and
included the names of ninety-two Black women. By the time the
second ad appeared on October 21, 1993, it included an additional
142 Black male supporters. The purpose of the lengthy ad was to
provide critically needed sociopolitical antirape education in Black
communities. The ad exposed destructive rape myths and coun-
tered misunderstandings about the seriousness of rape in Black communities.[53] Echoing other gender-progressive Black scholars and
activists, the ad underscores the importance of a more complex
analysis of racial violence: "When Black-on-Black crime is mentioned,
rarely do we discuss the sexual brutalization of Black women. Missing from the Black liberation movement is an understanding of rape
and the physical and emotional scars it leaves on Black girls and
women. . . . If a woman uses poor judgment, that does not mean
she deserves to be raped. . . . We are concerned about the historical
vulnerability of Black women that includes the idea that the sexual
abuse of a Black woman is not really a crime" (213).

Mindful of the success of an earlier effort on the part of Black
women to be heard in high profile cases involving accusations
against Black men, the group borrowed the model used by African

American Women In Defense of Ourselves (spearheaded by Elsa Barkley Brown, Barbara Ransby, and Deborah King), which generated the ad supporting Anita Hill with 1,600 signatures by Black women (including ours). A historic gesture of Black feminist resistance, the ad appeared in *The New York Times* and six Black newspapers on November 17, 1991.[54]

Social critic and writer Pearl Cleage self-published one of the most heartbreaking and hardhitting analyses of Black sexism and violence against Black women, *Mad at Miles: A Blackwoman's Guide to Truth*, in 1990 and circulated it throughout Black communities. Her Black feminist manifesto was a wake-up call to Black America in which she provided painful personal testimony about the violence that Black women she knew had experienced, as well as her own experiences with her abusive college boyfriend while she was an undergraduate at Howard University in the sixties. The title reflects the anger she feels toward the legendary Miles Davis, one of the great musical geniuses of all time, because of his abuse of women, including his famous wife, Cicely Tyson, which he reveals and attempts to justify in his autobiography.[55]

Cleage's admonition to Black men to assume responsibility for their violent behavior runs counter to the racial party line, which shifts the blame elsewhere. The predictable script goes something like this: White racism victimizes Black men, Black men then mistreat Black women. This shameless and largely unexamined argument—that Black men's violent behaviors are solely the fault of white men—was stated most strikingly in 1968 by Black Panther leader Eldridge Cleaver in one of the most shocking expressions of misogyny you're likely to read.

> I became a rapist. To refine my technique and *modus operandi*, I started out by practicing on black girls in the ghetto—in the black ghetto where dark and vicious deeds appear not as aberrations or deviations from the norm, but as part of the sufficiency of the Evil of a day—and when I considered myself smooth enough, I crossed the tracks and sought out white prey. I did this consciously, deliberately, willfully, methodically . . . Rape was an insurrectionary act.

It delighted me that I was defying and trampling upon the white man's law, upon his system of values, and that I was defiling his women—and this point, I believe was the most satisfying to me because I was very resentful over the historical fact of how the white man has used the black woman. I felt I was getting revenge.[56]

Cultural critic Wahneema Lubiana cites Black nationalism's failures with respect to sexual politics—despite its usefulness as a politics of racial resistance. Paradoxically, "its most hegemonic appearances and manifestations have been masculinist and homophobic . . . its circulation has acted both as a bulwark against racism and as disciplinary activity within the group."[57] While it has certainly demanded racial loyalty from Black women, it has permitted, as the Cleaver case demonstrates, offensive airings of dirty laundry by Black men who rarely receive the label of race traitor. We begin again where we started, always aware of charges likely to be hurled at us about exposing race secrets. So we proceed cautiously here in calling attention to this aspect of African American history. In the nineteenth century South, at the height of savage white mob violence that claimed over two thousand Black lives (1880–1930), there was the phenomenon of intraracial lynchings, a manifestation perhaps of the Black community's willingness to punish "race traitors" who violated the community's norms.[58] Though same-race lynchings are largely unknown to contemporary audiences, Professors E. M. Beck and Stewart E. Tolnay, who have written extensively on lynching,[59] analyzed 129 Black-on-Black lynchings and the range of behaviors that motivated Blacks to resort to mob violence. These included very few cases of Black collaboration with whites. The more frequent cases involved Blacks committing serious crimes within the community. According to Beck and Tolnay, nearly three-fourths of the victims of Black mobs were believed to have committed murder, sexual assault, or rape-murder. They document the case of Sam Wilson, who was shot and hanged by a group of Black men on December 17, 1885, in Jones County, Mississippi, having been accused of murdering his half sister and brother and their mother.

We were particularly interested in those cases that involved family members, which Beck and Tolnay reveal were less common in white-on-white lynchings. To our surprise, incest was the most common offense among the intrafamilial lynchings described by Beck and Tolnay. According to the *Little Rock Daily Gazette*, on July 15, 1885, David Scruggs of Jefferson County, Arkansas, was abducted by a Black mob for having allegedly sexually abused his daughter. What these startling cases may reveal is the sanctity of the Black family for freedpersons who were prohibited from protecting their family members during the long nightmare of slavery. While it would be impossible at this juncture to say with certainty what these cases really mean (though Beck and Tolnay offer some feasible speculations), it is not unreasonable to assume that at the very least there were strong Black community sanctions against rape and incest. The extent to which Blacks appear to be enraged by violence against women can be gauged by the brutal lynching of Anderson Moreland in Monroe County, Georgia, for his alleged rape of a young Black girl. According to the *Atlanta Journal*, on June 8, 1892, "he was stripped of his clothes and beaten into [in]sensibility and dropped into a hot tub of salt water."[60]

We do not believe that Black men shed or completely abandoned whatever gender identities they brought with them from Africa, though their struggles to retain their manhood during and in the aftermath of slavery would be unrelenting. The community's outrage at the persistent victimization of Black women helps to explain, we would argue, the Black-on-Black lynchings just described in Southern newspapers during Reconstruction. It didn't matter to these Black men that the perpetrators were their "brothers." Perhaps they shared William E. B. Du Bois's painful memories of what he and others believed was the most egregious crime of slavery, which was not the emasculation of Black men:

> I shall forgive the white South much in its final judgement day; I shall forgive its slavery, for slavery is a world-old habit. . . . I shall forgive its so-called "pride of race," the passion of its hot blood, and even its dear, old laughable strutting and posing; but one thing I shall never forgive . . .

its wanton and continued and persistent insulting of the black womanhood which it sought and seeks to prostitute to its lust.

What we hope is that the injustices visited upon Black women and men, no matter who the victimizer might be, are seared into our collective consciousness. Remembering the Turner family—Hayes, Mary, and their unborn child—is a good start.

6

•

BLACK, LESBIAN, AND GAY:
SPEAKING THE UNSPEAKABLE

It is not difference which immobilizes us but silence. And there are so many silences to be broken.

Audre Lorde, *Sister Outsider,* 1984

Because of our homosexuality, the Black community casts us out as outsiders. We are the poor relations, the proverbial black sheep, without a history, a literature, a religion, or a community.

Joseph Beam, *In the Life,* 1986

Homophobia divides black people as allies, it cuts off political growth, stifles revolution, and perpetuates patriarchal domination.

Cheryl Clarke, "The Failure to Transform: Homophobia in the Black Community," 1983

One of the most pernicious consequences of white supremacist ideology has been the perpetuation of damaging myths about Black sexuality that have portrayed us as lascivious, lewd, hypersexual, degenerate, and bestial. The most persistent and denigrating gender-specific racial stereotypes construct Black women as sexually insatiable and morally depraved, and Black men as predatory rapists whose main targets are virtuous white women. Cornel West, among others, has argued that in order to distance ourselves from these stigmatizing racial stereotypes, sexuality has become a virtually taboo subject in Black public discourse.[1] Historian Paula Giddings asserts that sexuality is in fact "the last taboo in the Black community."[2] If this is true of Black sexuality in general, then it is even more the case for homosexuality within African American communities.[3]

One manifestation of Black America's attempts to accommodate itself to mainstream gender ideologies and resist constructions of ourselves as sexually deviant or pathological has been what one Black theologian describes as "cultural homophobia." Similarly, another scholar argues that Black homosexuals "betray the quest for healthy black families, a regulated and normalized black sexuality."[4] Cultural homophobia is linked, then, to our acceptance of traditional notions of manhood/womanhood and our embrace of Western, especially Christian, antihomosexual biases:

> It's a Black machismo that is very much related to images of athletes, entertainment, and rap artists. It's supposed to represent what it is to be a man in the Black community, and that is to be anti-gay, physically very strong, and to demonstrate male sexual prowess. It's a cluster of myths regarding the Black male, and embedded in the heart of it is hatred of people who are specifically gay and lesbian. That was the model that was held up and that many people bought into.[5]

In fact, this assertion of a hypermasculine sexuality—a barely disguised Black machismo identity—which is openly hostile to Black gays (the antithesis of authentic Black masculinity), characterizes the cultural nationalist politics of the sixties and is another manifestation of its conservative, mainstream gender ideologies that were analyzed in Chapter 3. Maulana Karenga, the founder in 1965 of the radical California-based US organization, was the most influential proponent of cultural nationalism. It asserts that a strong Black nation is contingent upon the development of an African-based culture among Black Americans and a rejection of all things culturally white. An essential component of cultural nationalism is the idea that there is a distinct African American culture "with identifiable traits, customs, ceremonies, and beliefs."[6] Like literary critic Wahneema Lubiano, we are aware of the strengths and limitations of Black nationalism and the paradoxical manner in which it "has acted both as a bulwark against racism and as disciplinary activity within the group," especially in "its most hegemonic appearances [which] have been masculinist and homophobic."[7]

A virulent homophobic discourse emerged in Black nationalist literature and certain strains of Afrocentric thought during the sixties that was in many ways at odds with how many Black communities dealt with homosexuals historically. There was a kind of tolerance of these "open secrets" in many African American communities as long as it wasn't named or made too much of publicly. West recalls the community in which he was raised, where there was closeted homosexuality and a kind of "don't ask, don't tell" attitude:

> I know when I was growing up in the black community, most people knew that, let's say the brother in the church was a gay brother. People would say, oh, that's so and so's child. You know, *he's that way* (my emphasis). And they'd just keep moving. There wasn't an attempt to focus on his sexuality; he was an integral part of the community. It wasn't a matter of trying to target him and somehow pester him or openly, publicly degrade him. Those who said he's "that way" didn't believe that was desirable, but they just figured that's just the way he was, that's just his thing, you know.[8]

In a candid discussion of the paradoxical gay-friendliness of the Black Pentecostal church, which he describes as being an "earthly haven" for closeted homosexuals, the Reverend James S. Tinney describes why he feels comfortable as an "out" Pentecostalist.

> Despite the anti-sexual theme which characterizes much of Pentecostal preaching, a certain tolerance of variant sexual

activities . . . exuded itself. The conscious way in which the presence of homosexuality was recognized (whether approved or not) contributed to a feeling that it was really no worse than women wearing open-toe shoes or saints missing a mid-week prayer meeting.[9]

Similarly, gay activist Keith Boykin, former executive director of the National Black Gay and Lesbian Leadership Forum, describes his own family's tolerance of homosexuality, which is reminiscent of that of Johnnetta's and Beverly's families:

A popular church organist and gospel musician, Uncle Michael was a flamboyant gay man. Although he had lived in my grandmother's house all his life and often brought men home with him, I never heard anyone say a disparaging word about him. My parents never told me to avoid him when they would drop me and my sister off at our grandmother's house for long weekends or other occasions. In fact, I did not even know at the time that he was gay or, for that matter, what it meant to be gay. I only knew that his hair was processed and that he wore tight-fitting colorful pants, and shirts unbuttoned to his waist.[10]

Though these references are to gay Black men in the church, gay activist-writer Joseph Beam reminds us that "we have been ministers, hairdressers, entertainers, sales clerks, civil rights activists, teachers, playwrights, trash collectors, dancers, government officials, choir masters, and dishwashers."[11]

RACE TRAITORS

West's and Boykin's recollections of tolerant attitudes about sexual difference within some Black communities is important to bear in mind when we examine the racial discourse of particular scholar-activists. Gay theologian Elias Farajaje-Jones is especially critical of Afrocentrists such as Molefi Asante and Frances Cress Welsing, who perpetuate the very Eurocentric values they claim to abhor in their own heteropatriarchal/homophobic discourse: "These writers accept the premise that homosexuality and bisexuality are negative values. They never question the origin of their bias. They accept a negative Eurocentric definition of homosexuality/bisexuality."[12] Echoing Farajaje-Jones, lesbian feminist critic Barbara Smith asserts that "the conservative agendas of some Afrocentric or Black nationalist scholarship encourage condemnation of what they define as European-inspired perversion, a conspiracy to destroy the Black family and the race."[13] Ironically, there is very little difference in the manner in which Afrocentric and Western discourses both pathologize homosexuality. Furthermore, though cultural nationalists seek to debunk damaging racial stigmas, they fall into the trap of colluding with "whitey" by advocating normative notions of sexuality and narrow definitions of blackness which privilege heterosexual families and relationships.[14]

In Eldridge Cleaver's enormously popular *Soul on Ice* (1968), written while he was in prison serving time for rape, there is a vicious attack on James Baldwin's sexuality, which Cleaver characterizes as a "racial death-wish." Here we find one of the most blatant examples of the association between homosexuality and pathology in Black nationalist discourse. "Homosexuality is a sickness, just as are baby-rape or wanting to become the head of General Motors."[15] In her analysis of the crisis in Black male-female relationships, psychiatrist Frances Cress Welsing bemoans "Black male passivity, effeminization, bisexuality, and homosexuality," which, she asserts, were nonexistent among indigenous Black Africans. These evils are attributable, in other words, to the emasculating behaviors of white supremacists with respect to Black men and are part of a white plot to destroy the race, a familiar argument in Cleaver as well. Furthermore, Welsing asserts, this involuntary loss of manhood in Black communities is responsible for "Black racial suicide."[16]

The masculinist, heterosexist rhetoric of Black nationalism also permeates Molefi Asante's negative commentary on homosexuality in his manifesto on Afrocentricity, which we applaud, nevertheless, for its oppositional stance on the evils of white supremacy and Eurocentricism. Here, homosexuality (defined as non-African) is associated with dysfunctional Black manhood (Black lesbians appear to be nonexistent). He uses derogatory terminology such as selfishness, unhealthiness, whiteness, unconsciousness, decadence, and metaphors associated with disease to describe homosexuality. Though it is an unfortunate condition, Asante assures his readers, homosexuality can be "cured" by an embrace of Afrocentricity:

> Homosexuality is a deviation from Afrocentric thought. . . . The time has come for us to redeem our manhood through planned Afrocentric action. . . . Guard your minds and you shall save your bodies . . . The homosexual shall find the redemptive power of Afrocentricity to be the magnet which pulls him back to his center.[17]

A persistent theme in post-fifties Black nationalist/Afrocentric discourse is that African Americans, especially males, become homosexuals as a result of adopting decadent white values or having been exposed to the disgusting behavior in prison. Explanations by Black scholars and lay persons alike that assign blame to external factors help perpetuate the myth that homosexuals are deviant, degenerate, and unmanly. The most despised category for a Black man is "faggot." In his statement in support of the women's liberation and gay liberation movements, Black Panther Huey Newton was the lone voice among influential Black male leaders during the sixties who espoused "a revolutionary value system" that is opposed to all oppressions, including sexism and heterosexism. In this regard, he urges his fellow Black Panther sisters and brothers to rid themselves of homophobia and to stop using the derogatory "f" word. "The terms 'faggot' and 'punk' should be deleted from our vocabulary," and "homosexuals are not enemies of the people," Huey insisted unequivocally.[18] Judging from the absence of pro-gay discourse among other influential Black political figures, Huey's message presumably fell on deaf ears.

Minister Louis Farrakhan (Nation of Islam) gave one of the most mean-spirited and hyperhomophobic speeches ever uttered by a Black leader, "The Time and What Must Be Done," in Oakland, California, on May, 20, 1990. He asserted that decadent homosexuality (like incest, adultery, and rape) is a crime that deserves the death penalty.[19]

> Now brothers, in the Holy world you can't switch. [Farrakhan walks across the stage like an effeminate man] No, no, no . . . in the Holy world you better hide that stuff 'cause see if God made you for a woman, you can't go with a man . . . you know what the penalty of that is in the Holy land? Death . . . They don't play with that . . . [he laughs] Sister get to going with another sister—Both women [are decapitated].[20]

His denunciation of lesbians and gays or "homo-hating" is not entirely surprising given the responsibility of religious leaders to safeguard what they consider to be the moral values of their communities, which included eliminating prostitutes, drugs, gambling, homosexuality, and other vices. In his November 3, 1929, sermon, "Lifting Up a Standard for the People," the Reverend Adam Clayton Powell, Sr., pastor of Abyssinian Baptist Church in Harlem from 1908 to 1937, linked homosexuality with other "sexual perversions," including the sexual abuse of boys and girls.[21] Airing dirty racial linen, he railed against ministers who preyed on boys in their churches and castigated the congregations for sheltering their morally degenerate, presumably gay, pastors. Whatever judgments one reaches ultimately about the Reverend Powell's behavior with respect to ridding the community of gays or "outing" abusive gay ministers, one thing is clear: He is not in denial about the complexity of sexual behaviors among African Americans.

BACK TO AFRICA

In an attempt to distance ourselves from racial stereotypes that construct us as sexual deviants, it has been imperative to assert our "normality" in the sexual arena. One of the myths Black America perpetuates about itself in this regard, especially publicly, is that same-sex desires, behaviors, and relationships are alien to African

cultures and when we exhibit such practices, they are a manifestation of pathological behaviors we learned from decadent whites.
Crucial to the maintenance of the myth of the absence of homosexuality in African American communities has been our lack of information or denials (which includes Africans on the continent as
well) about same-sex behavior in Africa, our ancestral home. Eugene J. Patton's essay "Heart of Lavender" (reminiscent of the title
of Joseph Conrad's racist novel, *Heart of Darkness*), which appears
in a groundbreaking anthology, *The Greatest Taboo* (2000), asserts
that "homosexuality is often thrown onto the pile of artifacts left
over from the legacy of European and Arab colonialism rather than
being indigenous to African societies themselves."[22] Or to put it another way, same-sex practices did not occur in sub-Saharan Africa
until the arrival of Arabs and Europeans, so that indigenous
African history is essentially heterosexual.

Despite the premises of African-centered philosophies, many of
which romanticize Africa and its gender relations, a growing body of
scholarship about same-sex practices outside the West points to the
complexity of sexual cultures throughout the African continent, including sub-Saharan societies before the arrival of the Europeans.[23]

In order to contextualize the debate about "homosexuality" in
Africa, it is important to take into consideration the complexity
of same-sex practices in cultural contexts around the world and to
recall the reality of "homoerotic" practices among most human
cultures, according to scholars.[24] In other words, what cultures
consider to be normal and natural in the sexual arena varies considerably around the globe. In one of the most extensive discussions of
male-to-male sexual behavior outside the West, William Eskridge
defines same-sex unions as "any kind of culturally or legally recognized institution whereby people of the same sex are bonded together in relationships for sexual or other reasons of affinity."[25]
David F. Greenberg's *The Construction of Homosexuality* (1988)
explains in painstaking detail divergent attitudes about "homosexuality" around the globe and over time. Some societies deny its
existence, he argues, some are relatively hostile to it, others tolerate
or even accept it, and still others institutionalize it. There are societies

in which same-sex erotic behavior is frequent, though they lack a concept of the "homosexual" person or homosexual identity. In other words, a connection is not made between who one *is* and what one *does*. Being involved in an intimate or erotic relationship with a person of the same gender does not necessarily result in the society attaching a "homosexual" label. It is mainly in the West, and only since about 1700, that we have divided human beings into two oppositional categories: heterosexual and homosexual. As Greenberg reminds us, "our sexual culture is not universal to the human species," since there are many societies that do not categorize people on the basis of sexual behaviors alone.

Rather than perpetually trying to *prove* that sexual practices in Africa are radically different from Europe and the United States, or asking whether "homosexuality" exists among peoples of African descent around the globe, we might ask a different set of questions: What is the nature of the sexual universe that Africans inhabited prior to the transatlantic slave trade and colonization? What concepts of gender and sexuality did enslaved Africans bring with them to the Americas? What were their ideas about the differences between men and women, and how did these differ from European gender constructs?[26] Though it is difficult to generalize about the diverse cultures of sub-Saharan Africa, what did they consider to be normal or natural expressions of sexual desire? Did they consider same-sex erotic behavior to be deviant?

Despite widespread notions about the decadence of the West, including having "invented" homosexuality, some scholars argue that "Western societies have been far more repressive toward homosexuality than the indigenous cultures of Asia, Africa, and the Americas."[27] Furthermore, while scholarship on sexual practices among enslaved Africans in the Americas has been sparse, as one scholar put it, "Africans, like Europeans, brought complex ideas about sexuality to the New World. And like Native American societies, the West African cultures from which most Africans came exhibited a wide range of sexual practices and attitudes . . . some fostered greater sexual expressiveness than was characteristic of the dominant European societies."[28] Many cultures outside the West institutionalize "transgenderal" unions that involve people of the same sex, one of whom assumes some of the roles and behaviors that have been defined by the culture for the opposite sex.[29]

In an informative anthropological text by Ifi Amadiume, *Male Daughters, Female Husbands: Gender and Sex in an African Society* (1987), an example of what Greenberg would describe as "transgenderal" unions is discussed. Amadiume's analysis of Igbo women in southeastern Nigeria during the precolonial era underscores the flexibility of gender constructs in West Africa where women could become husbands in woman-to-woman marriages.[30] In various parts of Africa, woman-to-woman marriages in the precolonial context included the securing of a wife or wives by affluent females. Thus, within certain African kinship systems, one did not have to be a biological male to function in the role of husband. Certain women were permitted to perform male roles, including taking a wife. This practice enabled the female husband to exercise rights over another woman's labor and reproductive capacity.[31] A woman-to-woman marriage enabled the female husband to have heirs, because her wife could also have been married or continue to have sexual relationships with men for the purpose of procreation. Female husbands could also have male husbands. There was a variety of circumstances that led to women's marrying other women. Wealthy women took wives in order to project power and authority. If they were married and childless, securing a wife enabled them to provide their male husband with heirs for his lineage group.[32] Additional wives also assisted female husbands with other household responsibilities. Like Amadiume, most scholars studying African kinship systems insist that these woman-to-woman marriages were not sexual, though these assertions may not be based on empirical evidence. In any case, these relationships should not be analyzed as an illustration of lesbianism within the African context but rather as an example of the flexibility of gender constructs in certain non-Western cultures.

In our discussion of the complex issue of African sexualities in various cultural contexts, it is helpful to employ alternative lenses. Gloria Wekker, an Afro-Surinamese anthropologist, suggests how scholars might better analyze same-sex behavior cross-culturally. She has written about the institution of *matiism* among descendants of enslaved African women (and men) in Paramaribo, Suriname. *Mati* is the Sranan Tongo word used to describe "women who have sexual relations with other women but who typically also will have had or still have relationships with men, simultaneously."[33] In her insightful discussion of a widespread institution among Creole working-class women in Suriname called the *mati* work (women who engage in sexual relationships with women and men, either simultaneously or consecutively), Wekker situates the practice within its historical and cultural context and avoids language that would attribute a homosexual *identity* to these women, most of whom are mothers and single heads of their own households. Wekker does not, therefore, use Western labels such as heterosexual, homosexual, or bisexual in her analysis of *mati*. In her description of the sexual universe these Afro-Caribbean working-class women inhabit, Wekker reveals that they consider their sexual activity with other women pleasurable, but they do not identify as "lesbian."

Similarly, in *Singing Away from the Hunger* (1996), an autobiography by Mpho'M'Atsepo Nthunya (born in 1930), a domestic worker who cleans houses at the National University of Lesotho, there is evidence of same-sex relationships among women that does not violate marriage norms in this tiny southern African country.[34] While women in Lesotho do not identify as "lesbians" in the Western sense of the term, erotic relationships among them do exist. They do not conceptualize these relationships as sexual, however, because "sex" in their culture is defined as phallic penetration. In her autobiography, Nthunya describes her affectionate marriage with her husband and her long-term intimate, though not sexual, relationship with a woman, "M"alineo, though she indicates that the custom of such close female friendships is gone. Among the Mosotho, *motsoalle* are close friendships between women that are recognized within the culture, and by husbands, with ritual feasts akin to marriage feasts. This is how Nthunya describes the relationship: "It's like when a man chooses you for a wife, except when a man chooses, it's because he wants to share the blankets with you. The woman chooses you the same way, but she doesn't want to share the blankets. She wants love only."[35] There is no evidence in Nthunya's narrative that the women of her generation in Lesotho chose female partners exclusively. Again, what these practices underscore is the need to analyze relationships among African women in different cultural contexts without imposing Western-based sexual categories.

What Wekker's and other scholars' work emphasizes is that sexual behaviors have different meanings in various cultures. Therefore, interpretations of same-gender sexual and emotional bondings among persons of African descent on the continent and in the African diaspora need to take into consideration the cultural specificity of Western categories of sexual identity such as "heterosexual," "homosexual," "lesbian," and "bisexual," which have particular meanings in a U.S. context. Such an approach would change the terms of the debate about sexuality among Afrocentrists and other scholars doing African/African American history. Solid research also needs to be conducted on same-sex relations in various cultural contexts in Africa, because we know so little about them. Anthropologist E. E. Evans-Pritchard, who studied indigenous African cultures, was the first scholar to describe sexual relationships between older men and younger boys among the Azande warriors in southern Sudan during the precolonial era. Other scholars have characterized these relationships as age-graded or age-structured forms of homoerotic relations. Evans-Pritchard's research suggests that a range of sexual practices was tolerated on the continent, though the widespread assumption continues to be that Black Africa is heterosexual. Ironically, this idea was perpetuated initially by European scholars who assumed that primitive peoples such as Africans were too unsophisticated to practice homosexuality:[36]

> Among the myths Europeans have created about Africa, the myth that homosexuality is absent or incidental is the oldest and most enduring. For Europeans, black Africans—of all the native peoples of the world—most epitomized "primitive man." Since primitive man is supposed to be close to nature, ruled by instinct, and culturally unsophisticated, he had to be heterosexual, his sexual energies and outlets devoted exclusively to their "natural" purpose: biological reproduction. If black Africans were the the most primitive people in all humanity—if they were, indeed, human, which some debated—then they had to be the most heterosexual.[37]

This racist explanation for the absence of "homosexuality" in sub-Saharan Africa is repeated, with a different set of arguments to be sure, in the pro-Black discourse of Africans and African Americans alike who feel compelled to distance themselves from the taint of deviant sexuality. Rejecting racist constructions of themselves as primitive, they claim an exclusive heterosexuality as proof of their humanity! Paradoxically, the idea of the "disease" of homosexuality is not necessarily consistent with the belief systems of indigenous non-Western cultures but is rather an idea perpetuated and exported by colonizing Christian Europeans to cultures they deemed inferior.

SAME-SEX RELATIONS IN THE NEW WORLD

Although historical accounts of African American gay and lesbian experience have been sparse, it is clear that our sexual desires and behaviors have been far more varied and complex than we have been willing to admit publicly.[38] Silences abound in historical accounts of sexual practices among African slaves, and there continues to be controversy about the sexual abuse of slave men by their white masters or homosexual behavior among slave men.[39] An examination of legal documents from the colonial period in New Netherland Colony (now Manhattan), New York, reveals an example in 1646 of complex sexual practices among males during slavery. In his massive documentary of the history of gays in the United States, Jonathan Katz reports an incident in which a "negro," Jan Creoli, is accused of committing the crime of sodomy with Manuel Congo, a ten-year-old African boy. Creoli was choked to death and burned at the stake while Congo was flogged at the execution site.[40]

Some years later there is mention of sexual relations among Black male slaves in various parts of the African diaspora. Esteban Montejo, a nineteenth-century runaway slave from Cuba, indicated in his autobiography that sodomy did occur on plantations in Cuba among African slaves, including perhaps the rape of young Black boys by slave masters. There was voluntary sex as well among slave men who "had sex among themselves and did not want to know

anything of women."[41] Without doubt, there is much to be investi-
gated by scholars about the sexual practices of our slave ancestors
before we can make any definitive statements about whether homosexuality is alien to African cultures.[42]

In her collection of essays, *Dark Continent of Our Bodies*
(2001), feminist scholar E. Frances White wonders why Black scholars of slavery haven't explored the issue of homosexual rape of slave
men by their owners. Toni Morrison's novel *Beloved* (1982) raises
the possibility of such rape, according to White, in a scene in which
there is the suggestion of involuntary oral sex between white guards
and slave men on a chain gang (108–109). While White is not suggesting in her analysis of *Beloved* that there is evidence of the rape
of Black slave men (though she indicates there was certainly the *potential* for it), she does make a compelling case for our need "to ask
why we [scholars] persist in seeing the sexual emasculation of black
men as stemming from their actual castration or their inability to
protect black women from rape rather than also from their inability
to protect *themselves* from rape."[43] And then White speculates
about the more taboo question: Was there homosexual desire
among enslaved men? She cites William S. McFeely's biography of
Frederick Douglass (1991), in which he speculates that Edward
Covey raped the male slaves whom he controlled in Eastern Shore,
Maryland, perhaps even Frederick Douglass himself.[44]

A startling discovery concerning the complex erotic lives of
Black women during the nineteenth century occurred when the letters (about 120 of them written between 1854 and 1868) of Addie
Brown, a domestic worker, to Rebecca Primus, a teacher, came to
the attention of a scholar conducting research at the Connecticut
Historical Society on the prominent Primus family of Hartford,
Connecticut.[45] Clearly these letters, which began when Addie was
eighteen, reveal a close, emotionally charged, romantic friendship
between two ordinary nineteenth-century free Black women, one of
whom (Addie) is much less educated than her "beloved sister," and
is five years younger. In a letter dated August 30, 1859, from Addie
to Rebecca in Hartford, Connecticut, Addie's passionate love for
her friend is unmistakable: "You are the first girl that I ever *love* so
and you are the *last* one. Dear Rebecca, do not say anything against

me *loving* you so, for I mean just what I say. O Rebecca, it seem I can see you now, casting those loving eyes at me. If you was a man, what would things come to? They would after come to something very quick."[46]

It is important to underscore that their passionate friendship was in the open and, according to scholar Karen Hansen, "was recognized, facilitated, and sanctioned by their kin and friends within the African-American community."[47] She speculates about their reasons:

> Although they appeared to harbor no misgivings about the passion the women felt for each other, [their] kin tried to assist them in negotiating their relationships with men. While supporting the friendship, they warned that it should not interfere with male-female courtship. . . . their ties were not regarded as exclusive, but rather as compatible with social obligations and heterosexual partnership, as long as they finessed the situation skillfully. (193–94)

Both women were also involved with men and eventually married. Addie married first, after which her letters to Rebecca stopped and she died not long after her marriage. A few years later, Rebecca married; she died in 1932, at age ninety-five. We mention their relationship because it raises a number of questions that we cannot answer about African American attitudes toward sexuality in the aftermath of slavery. What is certain, as is the case in the African context, is that many of our assumptions about Black people may not be verifiable due to the lack of substantial empirical evidence.

Growing Up Homosexual

There is considerable evidence, however, of negative attitudes toward homosexuality within African American communities that have complex origins and manifestations. What we are interested in discussing are the consequences of these complex and evolving attitudes. Commenting on his own homophobia, because he "grew up in the black community, in the black church, [and] on the black block," where "there's a lot of homophobia," Cornel West speaks passionately about the plight of his gay brothers and sisters and the connections between racism, patriarchy, and heterosexism.[48] Despite these connections, however, it has been difficult for a community under siege because of racial terrorism to acknowledge how "cultural homophobia" might be contributing to the oppression of gays and lesbians and other gender-based antagonisms within Black communities. Amidst the continuing debates about the origins of Black homosexuality, Ronn Simmons reminds us that Black men are not gay because of white supremacy or incarceration, a major charge of some Black leaders. On the contrary, "too many of us realized we were 'different' during preadolescence before we knew what racism was or who white people were."[49] Many gays and lesbians also experienced a tremendous amount of hurt and confusion about their "abnormal" sexual desires.

The legendary choreographer Alvin Ailey, born poor in Texas in 1931, describes his inexplicable sexual urges as a young boy in his candid autobiography, *Revelations*:

> I had a lot of homosexual fantasies before I ever got into doing anything physical. Once, when I was fifteen, I dressed in drag. There was a Halloween party going on across the street, and something possessed me. My mother was at work, and I went home, dressed in her clothes, and returned to the party in makeup, high-heeled shoes—the works. And yet I can honestly say at that stage of my life I had no idea what was happening.[50]

James S. Tinney, born in Kansas City, Missouri in 1942, would marry, have two children, become an "out" Pentecostal minister, found a gay church, and become a passionate and well-known advocate for the rights of gays and lesbians among progressive faith communities. He indicates that "as early as I can remember, even at the age of four, I was emotively and sexually drawn to men."[51]

Similarly, the gay poet-activist Essex Hemphill recalls his early, uncontrollable sexual urges (he knew from age five that he would love men) and trying to find books in the library about homosexuals when he was in the sixth grade:

I approached the swirling vortex of my adolescent sexuality as a wide-eyed, scrawny teenager, intensely feeling the power of a budding sexual drive. . . . it became apparent that what I was or what I was becoming—in spite of myself—could be ridiculed, harassed, or even murdered with impunity. The male code of the streets where I grew up made this very clear: Sissies, punks, and faggots were not "cool" with the boys. . . . If I was clear about no other identity, I knew, year by year, that I was becoming a "homo." A Black homo.[52]

Born in 1942, in New York, Samuel R. Delany, a prolific science fiction writer, is perhaps the Black writer who has written most candidly and graphically about his homosexuality. He describes his earliest sexual experience as an eleven-year-old summer camper and his having lived an active gay life since he was seventeen. In a lengthy autobiographical narrative, "Coming/Out," which appeared in a collection of his essays, *Short Views: Queer Thoughts and the Politics of the Paraliterary* (1999), Delany recalls having put together "a list of some twenty-two incidents involving sex that happened to me between age seven (1949) and age fifteen (1957), including the 1953 incident with Joel":

"Joel," I said, "do you remember when we had the fight where we all made Billy suck our cocks?"
    "Yeah," Joel said. "Sure."
    "We really *liked* that, didn't we?
    "Huh? Yea, I guess we did."
    "I could see it. I mean. I liked it too." Then I said: "I think that's because we're homosexual."
    ". . . It's funny," I said. "You and me. We're both homosexual. We're both Negro . . ."[53]

Louis Williams, born in 1950 in Harlem to a middle-class family, describes his inexplicable journey to homosexuality in a book on gay Black men in Harlem, *One of the Children* (1996):

Louis and Billy attended the same elementary school. . . . They used to walk to and from school every day. . . . Another friend, Johnny, whom Louis had met at school, would join them on the way. . . . Louis notes that around about sixth grade he realized that his feelings for his two closest friends were different from the feelings he had toward a lot of his other friends . . . He didn't understand it at the time, but at some point, in a bathroom at school, Johnny approached him and touched him. Louis recalls, "I always remember how good that felt. I mean I felt sick inside, you know. I suddenly felt I was in love or something. I just know I felt wonderful." At some point over the next few months, as their sexual involvement increased, Louis told Johnny that he was in love with him and wanted to marry him.[54]

Ron Vernon, a founding member of Chicago's Third World Gay Revolution (1970), describes his early awareness that he was homosexual and the responses in his community:

I think I first realized I was a homosexual when people started calling me a faggot . . . I think people started calling me faggot because of the way I acted . . . always being with girls . . . and eventually the word "sissy" arose, and I was classified. And that's when I really became aware that something was different about me. I was about 7 or 8 years.[55]

Silences also surround what we believe has been the "unspeakable" sexual abuse of Black boys in our communities. The well-known gay writer James Baldwin, born poor in Harlem in 1924, describes an experience when he was only six or seven, which reveals the sexual vulnerability of Black boys:

My father kept me in short pants longer than he should have, and I had been told, and I believed that I was ugly. This means that the idea of myself as a sexual possibility, or target, as a creature capable of desire, had never entered my mind. And it entered my mind, finally, by means of the rent made in my short boy-scout pants by a man who had lured me into a hallway, saying that he wanted to send me to the store. That was the very last time I agreed to run an errand for any stranger.[56]

A life in the streets and in downtown New York City taught Baldwin very early in life that the labels *queer/gay* and *heterosexual/straight* had very little meaning in the urban world he was beginning to inhabit. A frequent visitor to the Apollo movie theater on Forty-second Street, he encountered heterosexual, mostly white men—"they looked like cops, football players, soldiers, sailors, Marines, or bank presidents [with] wives, mistresses, and children"—who were after quick, impersonal sex with other males. Their behavior taught him that irrespective of one's sexual identity or marital status, "the male desire for a male roams everywhere, avid, desperate" (683) and that it had very little to do with one's self-identification or sexual preference. In other words a man could consider himself a heterosexual and still desire men sexually.

A recent manifestation of the reality of Black men, in particular, living dual sexual lives (which would not have surprised Baldwin) was revealed in a startling *Essence* article, "Men Who Sleep with Men," in which the author discusses a clandestine phenomenon called "on the down low," in which ostensibly heterosexual men regularly have sex with other men.[57] Because of the alarming increase in HIV/AIDS among heterosexual Black women, the secret world of men sleeping with men is generating more attention and should generate brisk sales for J. L. King's *Secrets: Life on the Down Low* (2003). We should also point out another "open secret" in Black communities, which is the phenomenon of gay or bisexual men who marry women, father children, and lead dual lives. The Reverend James S. Tinney writes openly about having married, fathering two children, and revealing he was gay to his wife after they had been married for three years. Because they were active members of the same church, his wife's response was to seek counsel with their pastor, his wife, and other trusted church members in the hopes that her husband would "exorcise" his demons; needless to say, the events surrounding the eventual divorce were tragic for everyone involved.[58] While she was growing up in Memphis, Beverly's mother shared with Beverly her "secrets" about which Black men were closeted and married. Some of these men were prominent, well-respected members in the community and others were close friends of the family. Not understanding the reality of over-lapping identities at that point in her development, Beverly recalls being confused, since she assumed that married men, especially fathers, were by definition heterosexual. Her mother spoke rather casually and without judgment, as if it was fairly common and didn't bother to explain the situations. Essex Hemphill poignantly describes the reality of the closet, especially for the Black middle class, and the necessity of staying there:

> We constitute the invisible brothers in our communities, those of us who live "in the life"; the choir boys harboring secrets, the uncle living in an impeccable flat with a room-mate who sleeps down the hall when family visits; men of power and humble peasantry, reduced to silence and invisibility for the safety they procure from these constructions. Men emasculated in the complicity of not speaking out, rendered mute by the middle-class aspirations of a people trying hard to forget the shame and cruelties of slavery and ghettos. Through denials and abbreviated histories riddled with omissions, the middle class sets about whitewashing and fixing up the race to impress each other *and* the racists who don't give a damn.[59]

Though invisible in the scholarly literature on Black families, *Essence* discussed the phenomenon in an article entitled "Cover Girls." Here, wives married to gay men revealed how they cope with being married to gay men, why they struggle to keep their family secrets, and the value of the support groups they meet with on a monthly basis.[60]

Given the reality of what we've just described about the complexity of sexual behavior, much of which is hidden, it is sad but not surprising that many Black homosexuals, or men who appear to be effeminate, experience ostracism, name-calling, and sometimes outright hatred, in their own communities. Paradoxically, there is "acceptance" of sexual difference as long as it remains invisible. Black people's intense hatred of racism and their knowledge of the pain it causes has not kept many of them from subjecting their gay brothers and sisters to a range of indignities. If homosexuals are open about their sexuality, they frequently experience homophobia inside and outside the community; sometimes they experience rejection by their own families, and if they choose to remain closeted, they live with fear of exposure. In a widely discussed article in the May 1991 issue of *Essence* (it provoked the most reader response in the history of the magazine), Clara and Linda Villarosa described the difficulties they faced as mother and daughter when Linda revealed for the first time that she was a lesbian. Though Clara had suspected it for some time, Clara and her husband were devastated—like many Black parents—when Linda brought her partner, Laura, home. "I couldn't accept the fact that my daughter was lesbian—I just couldn't believe it. I assumed it was a phase she was going through and that it would go away like an unpleasant dream. This was the seventies, when homosexuals were thought of as sick."[61] Eventually, Linda's mother came to accept her. They strengthened their bonds, and she could acknowledge, "even though having a lesbian daughter is not what I would have chosen, I've learned to accept Linda for who she is, not what I wanted her to be. Now I can look at my daughter with a sense of pride and a sense of peace" (125).

Many such narratives don't have a happy ending. Gay activist Ron Vernon describes continual harassment by his male classmates that ended in a fight and eventually a stay in a juvenile correctional facility, although his attackers went unpunished. Joseph Beam, gay activist writer, utters a painful assessment in the early eighties of the plight of Black homosexuals: "Because of our homosexuality the Black community casts us as outsiders. We are the poor relations, the proverbial black sheep, without a history, a literature, a religion, or a community."[62] Loneliness, shame, anger, self-hatred, and depression were frequently the price Black homosexuals paid for being different. Beauford Delaney, a well-known artist, who was born in Knoxville, Tennessee, in 1901, provides one example of the tragic life of a gay Black man. Plagued by alcoholism and mental illness for much of his adult life, he attempted suicide on several occasions despite treatments in mental hospitals in France. He never resolved his guilt about his homosexuality, according to his biographer, David Leeming:

He was supportive of the many homosexuals who became part of his circle . . . instead of forming erotic relationships with these friends, he depended on them to find him anonymous street boys with whom he could have sex that did not "pollute" friendship. This process depressed him, and he was often "in love" with the very people who procured sex for him.[63]

Pauli Murray, feminist lawyer-theorist, poet, African American Studies professor, ordained Episcopalian priest, and one of the co-founders of the National Organization for Women (NOW), was born in 1910 and raised in Durham, North Carolina. She remained closeted throughout her distinguished professional life. There is no mention of her sexuality in her family biography, *Proud Shoes: The Story of an American Family* (1956), or in her detailed autobiography, *Song in a Weary Throat: An American Pilgrimage* (1987). Both are primarily racial narratives of a family, and of an individual who played an important role in the women's movement, involved herself in the gender politics of Black communities, and chronicled the evolution of her feminist consciousness but chose not to reveal much about her private life. Murray's biographer, Sarah Cable, reveals a hidden aspect of her tortured lesbian life during which she spent seventeen years (1937–1954) trying to cure her pathological disorder (sexual attraction to women) by appealing to psychiatrists and doctors and even committing herself to a mental institution and seeking testosterone implants during the thirties.[64]

Pioneering feminist activist-writer Anita Cornwell came out as a young lesbian in the fifties and, unlike Murray, was comfortable with her sexuality. Born poor in the Deep South and raised to be independent by her "feminist" mother, she made peace with her personal and political choices early on:

It wasn't until after I had had my fourth Lesbian relationship—sometime during the early sixties—that I decided that, for better or worse, I was irrevocably Gay. And from that time onward, I began to withdraw as much as possible from the heterosexual world. I found most straight men too sexist, and I was tired of listening to straight womyn [sic] complain about the problems they were eternally having with their men . . . even then I was baffled as to why so many heterosexual womyn continued to let men use and abuse them in the same manner that their mothers, grandmothers, and even their great-grandmothers . . . had done.[65]

Barbara Smith describes the relative ease with which she embraced a lesbian identity as a young woman and the comfort she always felt with women:

I have never been very comfortable around men. Although I had male lovers when I was straight, they were few and far between. . . . Long before I came out I was most familiar and comfortable with a world of women. Although I was intrigued by males' sexual potential when I reached adolescence and found some boys attractive, I found girls attractive too. Men were in general scary and unknown and the older I got the more frightening and incomprehensible they became. . . . What a relief it was to come out finally and be done with the whole mess.[66]

HOMOPHOBIA IN BLACK

It is tempting to assume that such deeply entrenched and damaging attitudes about homosexuality are less rampant in Black communities in the aftermath of nearly four decades of lesbian and gay/feminist activism at the national level. Rap artist and actor Ice T provides a chilling description, however, of the impact of the cult of hypermasculinity and its connection with "cultural homophobia" (theologian Raymond East's terminology) in many urban ghettos. In these communities there is no awareness of the antihomophobic discourse of the academy and progressive activist circles:

In the jungle, masculinity is at a premium. Anybody weaker than the next man will be victimized by the stronger. . . .

The white knight is not the hero. Displays of strength and aggression are prized because you're always walking like a prison inmate. In the 'hood, violence and even murder become something honorable. . . . You don't understand anybody who is weak. You look at gay people as prey. There isn't anybody in the ghetto teaching that some people's sexual preferences are pre-disposed. You're just ignorant . . . All you see is a sissy. A soft dude. A punk.[67]

Despite the reality of persistent homophobia within and without Black communities, it is important to recall the successes of an influential Black gay and lesbian movement that began in the eighties and was fueled in large part by writer-activists such as Audre Lorde, Barbara Smith, Joseph Beam, Essex Hemphill, Craig Harris, Marlon Riggs, and Mandy Carter, and the theological work of "out" gay and lesbian preacher-scholars such as James S. Tinney, Renee L. Hill, Elias Farajaje-Jones, and Irene Moore. The Black press has for the most part ignored the movement, though it is committed to eradicating all oppressions, including racism *and* homophobia.[68] Allies within the larger Black community include civil rights leaders such as the Reverend Jesse Jackson, the Reverend Joseph Lowery, John Lewis (Democrat, Georgia), Eleanor Holmes Norton, Coretta Scott King, Kweisi Mfume; theologians such as James Cone and Kelley Brown Douglas; well-known writers such as Maya Angelou, Sonia Sanchez, and bell hooks; as well as organizations like the Congressional Black Caucus and NAACP.[69] Coretta Scott King has been especially outspoken, and in a speech in Atlanta was urgent in her demand for a "national campaign against homophobia in the black community."

Progressive Blacks of all sexual orientations are increasingly concerned, however, about what appears to be a resurgence of the kind of virulent homophobia that characterized the racial discourse of the sixties. This has been apparent in the Black community's initial response to HIV/AIDS, the silences about sexuality that characterize national gatherings focused on "The State of Black America," and the in-your-face homophobic rantings of rap music. Very disturbing more recently have been efforts on the part of the white right wing to engage segments of the African American community in their antigay/lesbian projects. In the wake of the April 1993 March on Washington for Lesbian, Gay and Bi Equal Rights (similar marches took place in 1979 and 1987) and the federal civil rights bill HB 431, a group of conservative Black ministers in Cleveland, Ohio, issued in Cleveland's Black newspaper a profoundly homophobic article, "The Black Church Position Statement on Homosexuality." It condemned homosexuality as being anti-Christian, and cited a publication of a right-wing Christian organization, the Traditional Values Coalition, as support for their argument.[70] Mandy Carter is actively involved in a project of the National Black Lesbian and Gay Leadership Forum to mobilize the Black community against the Christian right wing's antihomosexual agendas as well as similar Black-led campaigns.

There is no more blatant manifestation of the negative consequences of our perpetual silences around sexuality, especially bisexuality, than the Black community's response to the AIDS crisis.[71] According to a *Newsweek* article, AIDS is the leading cause of death for Black men in the United States between the ages of twenty-five and forty-four (surpassing homicide), and the leading cause of death for Black women. Shockingly, nearly one in fifty African American men is infected with HIV (three times the rate for white men), and one in 160 Black women is HIV-positive (compared with one in three thousand for white women). Black men and women are ten times more likely than whites to be diagnosed with AIDS, and ten times more likely to die from it. Though Blacks constitute only 12 percent of the population in the United States, in 2000 we were half of the new forty thousand AIDS cases.[72] Now half of new HIV cases occur in people under twenty-five, and a large percentage of them are young African American men or adolescents. Black gay or bisexual men are more likely to become HIV-infected than their white counterparts, and a recent survey of young men in six U.S. cities found that while 30 percent of gay black men aged twenty-three to twenty-nine were HIV-positive, less than one-third knew they were living with the disease. Worldwide, there are 40 million people living with HIV/AIDS, 70 percent of whom live in sub-Saharan Africa. The most recent estimates are that by the year

2010, the average life expectancy for persons living in sub-Saharan Africa will be only forty years of age, and for Botswana and Mozambique it will be twenty-seven because of the AIDS pandemic. In Zimbabwe, one-third of all adults are infected, and Botswana, the worst hit, now has an alarming 39 percent of adults infected with HIV/AIDS.

Historian of science Evelynn Hammonds spoke eloquently at the Ford multilogue about the cost of turning away from issues of gender in our community, including the devastating impact of our silences and shame around HIV/AIDS. In her scholarship on HIV/AIDS in Black communities, she pays attention to the ways in which this epidemic has resulted in significant ruptures in our most treasured rituals, "like people refusing to have public funerals for their children because they died of AIDS." In a conversation with her father, she reminded him that "We have funerals for ax murderers, but Black parents are frequently ashamed to have funerals for their children who die of AIDS!" Hammonds' research has convinced her that HIV/AIDS is really a disease which provides a window "into some of our deepest and most troubling feelings about our bodies, sexuality, and gender."

Dazon Dixon Diallo, founder of SisterLove, an Atlanta-based AIDS-advocacy organization for women of color, preaches the gospel of self-help by urging women to practice safe sex and not sleep with men who refuse to wear condoms. Phill Wilson, HIV-positive, openly gay, and one of the most outspoken Black voices on AIDS, invokes the provocative metaphor, "Our house is on fire!" in his sermons at the Holy Name of Jesus Church in Los Angeles. He has chosen as his life's mission getting African Americans to face the grim and worsening reality of AIDS. Founded in 1999, his African American AIDS Policy and Training Institute is the first think tank devoted to prevention strategies designed especially for African Americans. Like the New York–based Balm in Gilead, which works with Black churches, Wilson's organization is a cry in the dark, and despite its righteous work has met with resistance from some segments of the Black community. When Black ministers gathered at a conference in 1980, there was the unbelievable charge: "AIDS is not our problem. We're not going to let them [whites] blame this on us," which confirmed the charge among many Black gay activists that at the beginning of the epidemic the Black church had turned a deaf ear on one of our most devastating problems.[73]

Twenty years later there are some churches that are responding more aggressively to the ravages of AIDS in African American communities. In the spring of 2001, ten thousand Black churches joined Balm in Gilead in a week of prayer against AIDS. The New York–based group also convened 350 Blacks, many of them ministers, at a training institute in Tuskegee, Alabama, to discuss how Black churches could become more involved. The Reverend George McRae, the sixty-year-old pastor of Miami's Mt. Tabor Missionary Baptist Church, which is located in a neighborhood plagued by poverty, crime, and drugs, says that "every black church should have an AIDS ministry," so he visits other churches advising them about starting AIDS programs.[74] Under his bold leadership, his church has weekly condom giveaways during Sunday services and provides free breakfast for drug addicts, some of whom are HIV-positive. Though some in his congregation have been resistant to these moves, the Reverend McRae is determined to attack "the Triangle of Death in the black community: drugs, crime, and HIV."[75] Over time he has had a positive impact, which is apparent in the words of one church member, James Copeland, age seventy-six. "He taught us that the church had to go into the neighborhood to deal with its problems and quit hiding things" (86). Not surprisingly, while the church has dealt with the connection between drug addiction and HIV/AIDS, it has not dealt with the issue of AIDS and homosexuality. Although the organization the Reverend McRae founded, MOVERS (Minorities Overcoming the Virus through Education, Responsibility and Spirituality), is an AIDS advocacy group, he is clear about the difficulties of addressing homosexuality in the Black church. He realizes that homosexuality is "an unforgivable sin" in Black communities, and something that's "deeper than the church's stance on it." Part of the explanation is the issue of Black masculinity. "Once you admit you're gay, it puts a question mark behind your manhood."

What exacerbates an already devastating crisis is the level of closeted sexuality that exists in Black communities and the high-risk behaviors that accompany it (living "on the down low"); rampant homophobia that forces many to deny their sexual behaviors; and poverty that limits access to adequate health care. In a compelling editorial, "By Ignoring AIDS, Blacks Dig Own Grave," Atlanta-based Cynthia Tucker issues yet another wake-up call to our communities and leaders: "With black preachers denouncing homosexuality from the pulpits and black families shunning gay sons, few gay black men are out of the closet . . . You'd think a deadly plague ravaging black communities across the nation would have provoked prayer vigils, community crusades and countless community-based counseling programs . . . As long as black homosexuality lives in the shadows and denial hovers in the air, HIV will continue to stalk black America. The killer lives among us, nurtured by bigotry, ignorance and apathy."[76] In a spirit of solidarity, we want to remember the thousands of nameless African Americans who've lost their lives to AIDS and a number of gay male activists whose names we do know: Essex Hemphill, Joseph Beam, Marlon Riggs, Melvin Dixon, Craig G. Harris, Assotto Saint, James S. Tinney, and Steven Corbin.

Ongoing discussion of Black homosexuality, bisexuality, and the deadly consequences of denial about its prevalence can broaden our analysis of what ails our communities. In so doing, we might reconnect with the vision of Audre Lorde, who lost her battle with breast cancer in 1992. She remains one of the most important, though still largely ignored, figures in Black America. Despite her significance, we continue to encounter, in a broad range of Black circles, people who never heard her name. This was even the case at a faculty development workshop Beverly conducted for Black academics a few years ago. Audre Lorde, more than anyone else, encouraged Black lesbians and gays to come out of the shadows. She also compelled all of us to be clear about the devastating consequences of hating difference. Her plea for us to speak out—because our silences will not protect us—is now more urgent than ever.

7

•

NO RESPECT:

GENDER POLITICS AND HIP-HOP

Despite the "dangerous" edge of so much hip-hop culture, all of its most disturbing themes are rooted in this country's dysfunctional values. Anti-Semitism, racism, violence, and sexism are hardly unique to rap stars but are the most sinister aspects of the national character.

Nelson George, *Hip Hop America*, 1998

The lyrics of many rap songs promote sexual aggression, woman hatred and remorseless violence in the African-American community. They stoke and fuel behavior we can ill afford in a racist society that already has a stranglehold on our collective necks.

Evelyn C. White, *Chain, Chain, Change*, 1985

Hip-hop reflects the intent of the entire culture: to reduce black female sexuality to its crudest, most stereotypical common denominator . . . If hip-hop has any virtue in this regard, it is that it uncovers what the larger culture attempts to mask. The bitch-ho nexus in hip-hop is but the visible extension of mainstream society's complicated, and often troubling, gender beliefs.

Michael Eric Dyson, *Holler If You Hear Me*, 2001

Why discuss hip-hop in a book on gender? Because there has been a major war brewing (simmering, erupting—back to simmering again) between Black men and women since the sixties, and hip-hop is a significant and influential site of contemporary gender battles.[1] According to hip-hop critic-historian Nelson George, this cultural war between the sexes has been fought with words, books, magazines, movies, and rap music. One example of the hip-hop generation's take on male-female relationships is put forth in the smash hit song "Me So Horny" by the once popular and controversial group The 2 Live Crew:

> *I'll play with your heart just like it's a game*
> *I'll be blowin' your mind while you're blowin' my brain*
>   [veiled reference to oral sex]
> *I'm just like the man they call Georgie Puddin' Pie*
> *I fuck all the girls and I make 'em cry*
> *I'm like a dog in heat, a greak without warning*
> *I have an appetite for sex 'cause me so horny.*

While it is certainly true that if you've heard one rap artist or group you haven't heard them all, the frequent characterization of Black women as "hos" and "bitches," along with the sexual posturing of Black men, seems to have become generic and all too acceptable in rap music, especially California-based "gangsta rap" and Miami-based "booty rap."[2] While all rap music is not misogynist, a sampling of just a few song titles underscores its preoccupation with sex, violent overtones, and the denigration of women: "Pop That Coochie" and "Give Me Some Pussy" (2 Live Crew); "One Less Bitch" (Eazy-E); "Get Off My Dick Nigger—and Tell Yo' Bitch to Come Here" and "It's a Man's World" (Ice Cube); "To Kill a Hooker" (NWA); "Treat Her Like a Prostitute" (Slick Rick); "Bitch Betta Have My Money (Jason Lewis); and "Pregnant Pussy" (UGK). Some female rappers are mired as well in the sex-obsessed culture their male counterparts have generated, and what they choose to call themselves is instructive: "Fuck a Man" and "Is the Pussy Still Good?" (HWA, Hoez with Attitude); "Two Minute Brother" (BWP, Bytches with Problems).

Rap music began reaching huge audiences with the emergence of music videos in the early eighties. In 2001, over 89 million hip-hop CDs were sold. Suburban white youth are now purchasing approximately 60 percent of rap CDs. Custodians of a billion-dollar global hip-hop music market, multinational conglomerates (Sony, Warner Brothers, EMI, MCA, BMG, and Polygram), only one of which is U.S.–owned, are now major players in the packaging and distribution of damaging racial/sexual images, and the overriding goal is profits, according to hip-hop critic Bakari Kitwana:

> Often highlighted are those aspects of rap which . . . do not threaten the status quo, reinforce negative stereotypes about Blacks, [and] manipulate those stereotypes to increase sales. . . . Countless artists in search of securing record deals report that they are often told that their message is not hard enough, that they are too cleancut, that "hardcore" is what is selling now . . . essentially the message is that "gangsta" rap is "in."[3]

Echoing Kitwana, bell hooks underscores the extent to which gangsta rap does not appear out of nowhere, but is rather "expressive of the cultural crossing, mixing, and engagement of black youth culture with the values, attitudes and concerns of the white majority" and its "misogynist, patriarchal ways of thinking."[4] Similarly, hip-hop historian and writer Kevin Powell makes the connection between patriarchal American values and constructions of Black manhood in rap lyrics:

> Many of us men of color have held tightly to white patriarchal notions of manhood—that is, the way to be a man is to have power. Within hip-hop culture . . . that power translates into material possessions, provocative and often foul language, flashes of violence, and blatant objectification of and disrespect for women. Patriarchy, as manifested in hip-hop, is where we can have our version of power within this very oppressive society.[5]

This chapter is not a history of hip-hop; other books try to sort out the contested and complex history of hip-hop's origins.[6] Nor do we align ourselves with the conservative moral brigade that seeks to lay the responsibility for all forms of social violence, sexism, and homophobia at the doorstep of hip-hop, and in the process unites some pretty strange bedfellows, such as Tipper Gore, wife of former Vice President Al Gore; entertainer Dionne Warwick; and C. Delores Tucker, head of the National Political Congress of Black Women (NPCBW). Tucker's group has a strong alliance with Empower America, a conservative think tank founded by William Bennett in 1993. We are also not out to scapegoat all of rap music, for as a musical form it has proven itself to be innovative and a cutting-edge example of popular culture as resistance. We are also convinced that rap music enables us to better understand the perspectives of America's disenfranchised youth, even though it is not always a mirror of their everyday lives.

But a critical discussion of the gender politics of the music that in profound ways defines the hip-hop generation certainly opens up the possibility of a long-overdue cross-generational dialogue between our women and men, our youth and elders. In his book *The Hip Hop Generation* (2002), cultural critic Bakari Kitwana defines the demographic segment with which we are concerned in this chapter as African Americans born between 1965 and 1984, and he uses the term *hip-hop generation* interchangeably with *Black youth culture*. Contrasting the different worlds of "them" and "us," he asserts:

> For our parents' generation, the political ideals of civil rights and Black power are central to their worldview. Our parents' generation placed family, spirituality, social responsibility, and Black pride at the center of their identity as Black Americans. They, like their parents before them looked to their elders for values and identity. The core set of values shared by a large segment of the hip-hop generation . . . stands in contrast to our parents' worldview. For the most part, we have turned to ourselves, our peers, global images and products, and the new realities we face

for guidance . . . Central to our identity is a severe sense of alienation between the sexes.[7]

This severe sense of alienation between the sexes is most notably reflected in the frequent descriptions of Black girls and women as "bitches," "hos," "skeezers," "freaks," "gold diggers," "chickenheads," and "pigeons." Rap music videos are notorious for featuring half-clothed young Black women gyrating obscenely and functioning as backdrops, props, and objects of lust for rap artists who sometimes behave as predators. While gangsta rap, which emerged in the late eighties, is often described as a contemporary expression of youthful political radicalism, it seems as though the resentment, hostility, and disdain that many young Black men feel toward the police and "the System" have been directed at Black females. It appears that too many of our young men are blaming young women and treating them as part of the problem, rather than as cherished lovers and potential life partners. Kitwana suggests that the continuing popularity of rappers' women-hating lyrics and the gender conflicts they disclose are a disturbing reflection of the tension brewing between young Black women and men. He is not suggesting, however, that this "gender divide" began with the hip-hop generation: "The persistence of old attitudes about gender roles, rooted deep in American and Black cultures and strongly shaped by popular culture and Judeo-Christian ethics, has helped to breed cynicism between young Black men and women."[8]

We are aware that rap music is where many young Blacks get their problematic gender messages and that "due to its role in shaping a whole generation's worldview, including [their] ideas about sex, love, friendship, dating, and marriage, rap music is critical to any understanding of the hip-hop generation's gender crisis."[9] We are concerned because we believe that hip-hop is more misogynist and disrespectful of Black girls and women than other popular music genres. The casual references to rape and other forms of violence and the soft-porn visuals and messages of many rap music videos are seared into the consciousness of young Black boys and girls at an early age. The lyrics, images—and attitudes that undergird them—

are potentially harmful to Black girls and women in a culture that is already negative about our humanity, our sexuality, and our overall worth. They are also harmful to Black boys and men because they encourage misogynistic attitudes and behaviors.

We are also aware that contentious debates will continue about whether in fact certain forms of rap music, which Los Angeles–based gangsta rapper, actor, and former gang member Ice T calls simply "the art of shit talking," are harmful. He defends the music (he's sold over 10 million CDs all over the world since 1987) by indicating that it is harmless boasting on the part of ghetto men with few outlets for expression, and has very little connection to reality. He also says he learned early on that telling a nasty story, especially about sex, would get him more listeners than rhyming and rapping about politics.

> From the nasty tales of Stagolee in the 1800s to H. Rap Brown in the '60s, most of rap is nothing more than straight-up bravado . . . in the ghetto, a black man will say, "I'll take my dick and wrap it around this room three times and fuck yo' mama." Now this man cannot wrap his dick around the room three times, and he probably doesn't want to fuck your mother, but this is how he's gonna talk to another brother. It's a black thang. It's machismo. It doesn't mean anything.[10]

Contradicting himself, he also says that his rap is reality-based, and that what he says is "real" because it is a reflection of how he lives and talks, and how disempowered men in his neighborhood live and talk. Whether what rappers sing about is "real" or fantasy, we do not believe, as Ice T argues, that it has no meaning. We remain unconvinced, as well, by Ice T's argument that the use of derogatory language such as "bitch" (which he says is non-gender-specific) among certain classes of women is unproblematic:

> A black girl . . . will say, "Yeah, I'm a bitch. Straight up."
> Shit talkin' doesn't piss off ghetto women, 'cause anything I

can issue to a ghetto girl she's got an answer for. They'll answer all the shit we talk with a "fuck you, Ice." And that's it. They don't say, "You're sexist." They respond with their own rap (105).

At the very least we are convinced that his unacknowledged class biases with respect to women have consequences in the "real" world and are manifest in the attitudes of many young women and men who believe it's all right to treat *certain* women disrespectfully and label them "bitches" and "hos" because that's who they are and that's what they deserve. In other words, classism and sexism are the twin burdens of poor Black women.

Cultural critic Michael Eric Dyson writes about the most disturbing and destructive aspects of hip-hop culture in the compelling chapter "Do We Hate Our Women?" from his book on Tupac Shakur:

> Poor black urban culture seems to nurture *femiphobia*—the fear and disdain of the female expressed in the verbal abuse and protracted resentment of women. . . . Hip-hop culture has been particularly virulent in its femiphobic sentiments. . . . femiphobia has become the rhetorical reflex of rap. . . . [it] influences the lyrics of hip-hop artists, measures authentic rap—and hence, male—identity, specifies a pervasive machismo, and forges masculine bonds within the culture.[11]

In the culture at large, including popular culture, white women do not have the ongoing historical constructions of themselves as worthless, subhuman, promiscuous, predatory, and hypersexual. This has been the burden of Black women since slavery, and hip-hop music participates in and is complicit with these stereotypical and damaging depictions of Black girls and women.

Since the connection between machismo and homophobia in rap music is barely acknowledged, it is not surprising that women-bashing and gay-bashing are part of the culture of violence that pervades some rap music genres. Reggae rapper Buju Banton's album *Boom Bye Bye* (1992) contains one of the most lethal manifestations of the hatred of gay men. He exhorts homeboys to shoot "nasty men" with an automatic or an Uzi.

The refrain, urging faggots to run or get shot, is a painful reminder of the ease with which guns are employed as a solution to urban social ills.

We are not suggesting that frank sexual references or violence are unique to rap music. Like rappers, male blues singers celebrate the sexual prowess of Black men and blame Black women for their problems. Blues lyrics are blatantly raunchy and make references to the seductive nature of women. But usually the blues were not played in the presence of or listened to by children or even teens; it was considered primarily "grown folks' music." While many female blues singers sang about low-down, unfaithful, unreliable men, and male singers wailed about how my baby done left me, took all my money and run away with another man, there was also love (often unrequited) expressed about these relationships, even when they were seriously flawed. Blues lyrics, while they make references to physical abuse, do not celebrate violence against women to the same extent that rap music does, nor do they feature women as primarily sexual targets. Furthermore, the blues have been a much-needed avenue of emotional expression, venting and healing for African American women and men. Above all, as we know from the scholarship of Ralph Ellison and Albert Murray, the blues is an art form as well as a means to transcendence.

The coming-of-age songs of the baby boomer generation were heavily influenced by the Motown Sound, a vibrant expression of youthful innocence, yearning, desire, and love's ups and downs. This music was embraced because it truly celebrated romance and relationships, even when they were elusive and hard to keep. The love lyrics were poignant, heartfelt, and inspirational. Sexual references were relatively vague or veiled when they occurred, and women were presented for the most part as desirable rather than as sex objects and worthless. The cumulative effect of the music was that many of us could not wait to fall in love, hold hands, and enjoy sweet, tender embraces, kisses, and honeyed words of romance.

Another hip-hop critic comments on the popular music of previous generations that he recalls fondly as a site for hearing "beautiful harmonies and lyrics propagating images of love and longing," as well as inspiring "hopes and dreams rather than . . . violence, competition and naked aggression."[12] The sexual revolution of the late sixties would have a profound impact on American culture, however, one manifestation of which was the pervasiveness of more sexually explicit lyrics in popular music and more in-your-face sexual images in print media.

A compelling question for us is whether relationships between Black women and men and gender conflicts within our communities have worsened over time. Refusing to be nostalgic about romantic love among previous generations, Toni Morrison is nevertheless insightful in her observations about what Black communities have lost:

> I know my mother and father, my grandmother and grandfather, and the people that lived around me, they thought they were doing something important. And I don't know if they "loved" each other or not, but they took careful care of one another and there was something clear and common about what they were doing. They worked with each other. Sometimes they complained about things, but you always knew that there was some central thing that was bigger than they were, that they were doing. It had to do with raising children, with being morally coherent people.[13]

The tensions between today's young men and women, which we interpret as a lack of respect, must be resolved or they will imperil our families and communities for generations to come.

BREAK TO BEGINNINGS

There is nothing blatantly sexist or misogynistic in the origins of hip-hop or rap, which began in 1974 in the South Bronx. Jamaican-born deejay Clive Campbell, aka "Kool Herc," combined some of the patterns of reggae with his ability to manipulate turntable equipment to create a new music form known as breakbeats. Herc combined this with the blending of several records together utilizing the same musical break, which many credit as "the blueprint for hip-hop."

That was the new music. Early hip-hop lyrics were often concerned with limiting and ending gang violence. Kool Herc gained his popularity by playing music at the behest of his sister in recreation halls as a way to channel the energy of neighborhood youth and distract them from the prevailing gang culture of the time. Afrika Bambaataa, a former gang member, institutionalized this antigang perspective when he founded the cultural group Zulu Nation. Influenced by the nationalist ideology of the Black Panthers and the self-help activities of the Nation of Islam, Bambaataa created a Black cultural arts community organization made up of former and potential gang members. Their weapon of choice became dancing, and with break dancing young men dueled with their feet and their dance moves rather than fists, knives, or guns.

One of the ironies of rap/hip-hop music is that the form is not entirely new. It combines pulsating, compelling beats to grab your attention and hypnotically seduce listeners just as drums have been a primary means of communication in many traditional cultures. The interweaving of spoken word with rhythmic beats laid the foundation for hip-hop. Its origins can be traced to the folk cultural forms of signifying; the innovative styles of Black radio DJs; the politically confrontational 1960s and 70s music of composers/ performers, The Last Poets and Gil Scott-Heron; as well as the stylistic and performance innovations of Black Aesthetics movement poets such as Larry Neal, June Jordan, Amiri Baraka, Haki Madhubuti and Sonia Sanchez.[14]

Given the countercultural roots of hip-hop, the compelling question is: At what point did violence, sexism, and homophobia become core elements of a subculture that once was predicated on a rejection of gang violence and the negative aspects of street life? And when did Black women become the enemy of Black male rappers and the hip-hop generation?

In his brilliant analysis of gangsta rap, historian Robin D. G.

Kelley acknowledges on the positive side how it exposes the media's criminalization of Black youth, police repression, and the racism of the criminal justice system, including the warehousing of Black bodies by the prison industrial complex. He is also quick to point out, on the other hand, how its misogynistic, violent characteristics have antecedents in the sexist tendencies of African American vernacular culture where the term *bitch* was commonplace. To make his point, Kelley alludes to a mid-sixties toast (an improvised, narrative poem performed on street corners and in barber shops) entitled "The Lame and the Whore," in which a seasoned pimp instructs a pimp-in-training about how to treat his "bitches."

> *Say, you got to rule that bitch,*
> *you got to school that bitch,*
> *you got to teach her the Golden Rule,*
> *you got to stomp that bitch,*
> *you got to tromp that bitch,*
> *and use her like you would a tool*
> *You got to drive that bitch*
> *And got to ride that bitch*
> *Like you would a motherfucken mule*
>
> *Then take the bitch out on the highway and drag her*
> *until she's damn near dead.*
> *Then take your pistol and shoot her*
> *Right through her motherfucken head.*[15]

COMMERCIALIZATION AND THE CHANGING IMAGE OF HIP-HOP

Hip-hop remained part of an underground culture up until the end of the 1970s, making its mark mostly in nightclubs, schoolyards, and public parks. The commercial success of the entrepreneurial Sugar Hill Records and the breakthrough hit "Rapper's Delight" drew the attention of major record companies, and by the early 1980s, hip-hop had crossed over and established itself as a major cultural expression of Generation X. As hip-hop gained greater control of public space, record companies acknowledged that the phenomenon was more than just a passing fad. Record producers took different routes to capitalizing on the hip-hop craze. One path emphasized soft rap, music that Bakari Kitwana describes as "diluted" and repackaged until it became "a variation of R&B artists, focused on singing, dancing and/or 'profiling.' "[16] The other path emphasized "hardcore" music—labeled "gangsta rap"—that expressed the frustration, suffering, conflicts, and perpetual crises facing young Black urban men who frequently viewed an underground, criminally oriented lifestyle as the only way out of unending poverty and hopelessness.

All rap is not created equal, however. While the corporate music industry, which still controls distribution for even independent record companies, promotes the more lucrative hard core over the softer forms of rap, some hard core and gangsta rap artists consider themselves politically progressive and spiritually committed to "keeping it real." This makes separating out "authentic" rap from a commodification of blackness extremely difficult. Gangsta rappers feel they are the voice of the people and agents of change. Yet their messages, which may seem to rail against the establishment, are generally controlled by commercial interests and pose no real threat to the white power structure. Angry young men hurling epithets at their homeboys and female counterparts, and hypnotic songs and videos depicting mindless violence, conspicuous material excess, and hostile sexism may be closer to representing New Jack stereotypes of Black buffoonery than paving the way to Black progress. And those stereotypes have always made money for their white creators.

In fact, hip-hop culture now permeates popular sports, particularly basketball, as well as television and radio commercials for everything from fast food to trendy, urban-style clothing to cars. Hard-driving hip-hop songs are an integral part of many of Hollywood's mainstream films for audiences from toddlers to baby boomers. It is precisely this fusion of grassroots energy and sensibility and savvy social marketing that gives hip-hop its power. The mass marketing and acceptance of hip-hop have made it a political lightning rod in contemporary politics as it dresses up the discontent of socially marginalized youth in glib, glittery packaging that has come to be synonymous with urban cool.

Rapper Chuck D (Public Enemy) has referred to rap as "Black folks' CNN." Its simultaneously subversive and subjective interpretations of social reality, especially the plight of poor and working-class Blacks in urban America, is fused with technological sophistication that puts the music in everyone's head through radio, television, films, and the Internet.[17] Yet for all its mass appeal, for all the attention hip-hop has brought to the plight of the young, urban disenfranchised, the music's subversive messages still contain problematic content, continually drawing fire from those who support it as well as from conservatives who view it as the modern-day equivalent of the Tower of Babel.

PUTTING THE MESSAGE IN RAP

As hip-hop grew in the 1980s, so did the spread of the highly addictive new drug, crack cocaine, and the socially destructive policies of Reaganomics. It is no surprise that this branch of popular culture commented on the rapid disintegration of a Black community squeezed by the flood of potent new drugs and guns on the one hand, and a web of despair and disempowerment by government policies on the other.

Some trace the introduction of social commentary into hip-hop to "The Message," by Grandmaster Flash and the Furious Five in 1982. The song's refrain, "It's like a jungle sometimes; it makes me wonder how I keep from going under," struck a major chord within Black, Latino, and other disenfranchised communities and gave the beats of hip-hop a new level of social relevance and power.

The marriage of message to dance music added yet another dimension to the complexity and appeal of hip-hop culture. Message rap provided the explicit political text for underscoring the previously visual and implicit expressions of discontent. Like their predecessors, rap artists with a message took up a socially conscious musical agenda that valorized the plight of the discontented and disenfranchised. For the most part, message rap has represented it-self as the "authentic" voice of consciousness for the urban under-class, in particular offering social critique of the "predatory and oppressive" world that Black males inhabit. This is a world where police brutality, drugs, and violence related to gangs and drug deal-ing dominate the social landscape. With its strident and striking so-cial commentary on the urban experiences of young Black men (later joined by Latino, Asian, and other disenfranchised youth), gangsta rap provides what Charles Lusane calls "a form of politi-cal, economic and ideological empowerment."[18]

But rap has many serious problems. According to Ernest Allen, Jr., it carries with it serious antisocial baggage and fosters a malevolent, self-destructive discontent. Our primary concern is with its misogy-nist tendencies and its routine denigration of Black women. We know its potential to influence the attitudes and behaviors of its male and female audiences with respect to the sexual objectification and abuse of Black women and girls. If hip-hop's message is that Black females deserve to be devalued, denigrated, and abused be-cause they are in fact "bitches and hos," then it is clear we have an urgent community problem that must be addressed with haste.

What's Love Got to Do with It?

At the core of the gender politics of hip-hop is a pervasive and pro-found ambivalence toward Black women and the portrayal of rela-tions between the sexes as primarily conflictual. In an important study of gangsta rap's influence on college students' actual atti-tudes, and potentially their behavior, Professor Bruce Wade and his student Cynthia Thomas-Gunnar present a compelling argument that "explicit [rap] lyrics are generally inappropriate and harmful to society."[19] They discovered that contemporary Black college stu-dents, especially men, believe that rap music accurately portrays gender relations. Is it any wonder then, since the music frequently communicates a general hostility, distrust, and disregard for Black women as anything other than atomized body parts and sex ob-jects, that the study concluded that men who listen to rap music

favorably were more likely to harbor attitudes that could be described as rape-prone?

Given the enormous popularity of hip-hop and gangsta rap, this
is certainly a frightening and explosive finding. It confirms many
critics' beliefs that rap music has an undeniable and adverse influence on its young listeners. Certain rap music lyrics, particularly
gangsta rap, are apparently effective at communicating a dangerous
message: that the enemy of Black urban youth is not just the police
or poverty, not only an unjust system, but Black women and girls as
well. Songs like "Trust No Bitch, Trust No Hoe" and "Bitch Betta
Have My Money" portray Black women as predatory, untrustworthy, and worthless.

In many of these music videos, women are stripped of any hu-
manizing subjective identity, since the viewer observes only body
parts, and the script is usually what social critic Michael Eric Dyson
refers to as the rappers' "subterranean, pornographic fantasies."[20]
Often described as "booty rap," this form of rap is "characterized
by an obsession with sex and perverted eroticism, visually backed
by scantily clothed women mimicking sex and sometimes actually
performing it on stage," according to Perkins.[21] As evidenced by the
lyrics of Underground Kingz (UKG), even pedophilia becomes fair
game in this distorted and unreal world of rap, sex, and violence.
In an *Essence* article that asks "Are Music Videos Pimping Our
Girls?" self-described hip-hop feminist Joan Morgan believes "it's
up to us to identify these videos for what they are—adult content
that shouldn't be shown in prime time."

What is the danger of gangsta rap's *femiphobia*, borrowing
Dyson's terminology? What happens when a young man's perceptions of women have been shaped by the misogynistic messages he's
heard for most of his life and what he has seen on countless music
videos? To be sure, women are likely to be robbed of their humanity
and viewed both artistically and perhaps in real life mainly as objects of male sexual fantasies. The line between hyperbolic lyrics
and real hate language has become increasingly blurred in gangsta
rap. Moreover, the celebrated "thug life" does not just provide a
creative source for rap lyrics, it actually intrudes upon the lives of
rappers like Tupac Shakur and Notorious B.I.G. as their jail sen-

tences, drug charges, gun shoot-outs, and ultimately their deaths reveal. Another danger is that the symbolic violence portrayed in the music and accompanying videos can become all too real, as was the case in rap star Dr. Dre's 1991 brutal nightclub beating of MTV rap deejay Dee Barnes; hip-hop legend's Tupac Shakur's 1993 alleged sexual assault of a twenty-year-old female fan, which Dyson describes in some detail and is inclined to disavow; and boxing superstar Mike Tyson's 1991 rape of eighteen-year-old Desiree Washington, a Miss Black America beauty pageant contestant. Both Shakur and Tyson were found guilty, though they continued to be supported by many segments of the Black community irrespective of class or age. In early June 2002, R&B singer R. Kelley (whose vulgar songs "Feelin' on Yo Booty," "Bump and Grind," and "Your Body's Calling" are reminiscent of many rap lyrics) was indicted by a Chicago grand jury on twenty-one counts of child pornography and expects support from the Black community during his legal battles, which will probably be forthcoming.[22] In the aftermath of Dr. Dre's beating of Dee Barnes, during which he slammed her against the wall of a dance club, tried to throw her down the stairs, and punched her in the head, the members of his group, NWA (Niggas with Attitude), asserted in an MTV interview that "the bitch deserved it." Barnes filed a multimillion-dollar lawsuit against Dr. Dre, who is widely regarded as one of the principal architects of West Coast gangsta rap.

Despite the violent nature of the incidents in which Tyson, Shakur, and Dr. Dre have been involved, many young Black men and women hold the celebrities blameless and criticize the victims instead. This manifestation of male-to-male loyalty is rampant in the society at large, as well as among African Americans. America's patriarchal cultural script demands that a male's first allegiance should be to his *homies* or *boys*, to use the language of hip-hop. In his recollections of the Black community's support of Mike Tyson, Tupak Shakur, and O. J. Simpson, hip-hop chronicler Nelson George is critical of unwarranted support of indefensible male behavior:

There is an intense knee-jerk defense of black male privilege loose in the African-American community that can be irrational and destructive. Usually the stance is supported by paranoia that this particular black man . . . is being targeted by white people because of his public profile. Often they are right. There are many whites who love to pull black icons off whatever pedestal they've climbed upon. But not all brothers have that excuse . . . the truth is some of these brothers have seriously fucked up and deserve both the censure from our community and jail time.[23]

Bakari Kitwana reminds us that when it comes to gender issues, the hip-hop generation is frequently willing to disregard the more sinister side of their heroes. Some of the most blatantly misogynistic rap stars continue to have devoted male and female fans that do not seem to be bothered by the degrading behavior these stars display in both their private lives and their performances. In fact, those who criticize the rappers in question are often derided for not understanding that the artists are simply "keeping it real," which means staying true to authentic Black experience, especially real ghetto experience.

Clearly not enough young men of the hip-hop generation have been positively impacted by the progressive gender ideologies of contemporary feminism, even though its influence can be seen in the broader society. While they have grown up in households with struggling women in many instances, they have also been immersed in the deeply rooted sexism of American and African American culture. Strong, capable women are often viewed as emasculating, disempowering, or derisively labeled as lesbians. The women many hip-hop songs celebrate are valued primarily for satisfying their men sexually and providing whatever support they need. Tragically, many young women even pass the ultimate test of loyalty by endangering themselves and their futures, including the risk of incarceration, through drug use, burglary, or prostitution, all in the name of "love."

While examining the values that many young men and women are encouraged to embrace, we are mindful of the fact that they have come of age in a time when women—especially young, sexually desirable women—are viewed by a sex-obsessed dominant culture as sex objects rather than as multidimensional beings deserving of love and respect. When males and the male-controlled media treat young women as objects, they often see themselves in the same manner. This insidious dynamic is certainly not entirely new, but with so much of popular culture representing young women as half-naked, promiscuous, man-hungry, and lacking in self-esteem, internalized sexism is one likely result. Poet and social critic Sonia Sanchez describes this phenomenon as the country trying to "asphyxiate our daughters in a state of undress, and convince them that they're hos. Even in college they [try to make them] hos. Any place [young women] walk, the country says, 'I'm going to take you back to hoedom.'"[24]

Similarly, young people are ensconced in a mass culture of crass materialism that places financial gain and the mindless consumption of material goods over healthy, productive, loving relationships. Some rappers have made millions rapping about women giving up sex in exchange for liquor, jewelry, and less. The message that young Black women's bodies can be purchased cheaply on the open market is a grim, modern-day reminder of slavery. In some ways, Black women are still on the auction block! What makes this scenario so devastating, however, is that it is our own men, the young ones to whom our future will soon be entrusted, who are frequently doing the bidding and buying in this century. And much too often our young women are selling themselves, metaphorically speaking, in a desperate and misguided search for love and "security."

While Mike Tyson, Tupac Shakur, and Dr. Dre's behavior can be viewed as emblematic in many ways of the gender violence that Black girls and women have faced historically, especially at the hands of white men, we are reminded more broadly of the schizophrenia of this country's sexual value system and how it is reflected increasingly in tragic intraracial dramas.

THE VIRGIN/WHORE SPLIT

Given mainstream culture's simple classification of women as virgins or whores—or, as Dyson puts it, angels or demons—it is not surprising, although it is disappointing, that contemporary African

American culture has internalized a general animosity and ambivalence toward women. We believe strongly that the overwhelmingly sexist representations of Black women in gangsta rap and hip-hop are linked to persistent negative images of Black womanhood in mainstream American culture. While African American culture is distinct in many ways from white culture, it is not immune to external influences. To be sure, the misogyny in hip-hop/gangsta rap is not entirely different in its impact from the woman-hating messages of the dominant culture. As one critic of hip-hop rightly points out, "The misogynist lyrics of gangsta rap are hateful indeed, but they do not represent a new trend in Black popular culture, nor do they differ fundamentally from woman-hating discourses that are common among White men."[25] To understand this hostility, we have to begin with an analysis of the larger American cultural framework. A consideration of the legacy of slavery is a good place to begin a serious examination of the root causes of the gender conflicts that can be highlighted in hip-hop.

Under slavery, Black women's bodies were viewed as commodities, and used as a breeding ground for the reproduction of a slave population. Enslaved Black women were also raped for the illicit pleasure of predatory white slave masters. Lacking control of their sexuality and unable as mothers to protect their children from being sold, Black women have always occupied a precarious social space in American society.

Paradoxically, Black women have long represented the asexual, caretaking "mammy"; the seductive and licentious siren; as well as the long-suffering or emasculating matriarch. The deeply held belief that Black women are less valuable than women of other races/cultural groups—a legacy of slavery—pervades all aspects of American culture. Because their bodies have been devalued and unprotected, it is appalling but not surprising that exploitative surgical procedures were perfected using the bodies of enslaved women in the American South. Anthropologist and writer Zora Neale Hurston captures the devalued status of Black women in her famous novel, *Their Eyes Were Watching God* (1937). Here, she creates a strong female protagonist, Janie Crawford, who struggles to assert her personal and sexual independence in the face of criticism from a visible Black community and an invisible white world. As Janie comes of age, her grandmother cautions her against trying to establish her own identity and place in the world because "Black women is de mules of deh earth."

Ironically, Black communities have also been complicit in the production of damaging images of Black womanhood, including the Black woman-as-whore stereotype, especially in hip-hop, where young, business-savvy artists maintain a great deal more control over the content and direction of their products, especially early on, than African American artists did in the past.

The contemporary desire of Black men to control Black women, especially our sexuality, has palpable roots in certain strands of the Black nationalist politics of the 1960s. In the blatantly patriarchal gender politics of the Nation of Islam, Black women have been construed as out-of-control sexual beings that must be brought under the wings of their men. In the guise of protecting Black women, the Honorable Elijah Muhammad called for the complete domination of women:

> The woman is man's field to produce his nation. . . . Until we learn to love and protect our woman, we will never be a fit and recognized people on the earth. . . . Our women are allowed to walk or ride the streets all night long, with any strange men they desire. They are allowed to frequent any tavern or dance hall that they like. . . . Islam will not only elevate your women but will also give you the power to control and protect them.[26]

Controlling, restraining, and dominating Black women was a popular theme in the blaxploitation films of the sixties. Here, Black women were portrayed as helpless, hopeless, pitiful victims, always at the disposal of a powerful hypersexual Black male figure, such as Shaft, Sweetback, and even Blacula.

Similar themes are evident in the Black pimp narratives of Robert Beck, aka Iceberg Slim, particularly *Pimp: The Story of My Life* (1967). Beck produced numerous works of pulp fiction between 1967 and 1977 that influenced many hip-hop artists with

respect to their woman-blaming attitudes. Iceberg Slim was a blatant misogynist who held his mother responsible for his having become a pimp. He perceived women in general as promiscuous,
money-hungry, "ball-busters" who controlled and damaged men's
sexuality by lying, cheating, and being untrustworthy or overly
ambitious. The negative characteristics of Iceberg Slim's women
were replicated almost verbatim in the hip-hop lyrics of rappers like
Ice T. While not every hip-hop artist cites a literary lineage, Ice T acknowledges his indebtedness to Iceberg Slim for providing him with
definitive perspectives on women. While three of the songs on his
1992 album *Body Count* emphasize some form of violence against
women, it was his "Cop Killa" song that attracted the attention and
ire of right-wing critics.

Devaluation and violence are twin enemies of Black women.
The belief that they are unworthy of respect is a recurrent American
refrain. And while it is true that gangsta rap did not invent the denigration of Black women, it has, with a vengeance, picked up on the
chorus line, transformed it into an enticing mantra of Black women
as "bitches" and "hos," and released it for mass consumption to an
audience already receptive because of rap's other seductive social
messages and their realistic scenarios about life in the 'hood. Young
Black and white men and women consume these problematic gender messages without much question, and without understanding
that progressive messages of racial liberation can also contain heavy
doses of misogyny that, in the end, reaffirm patriarchal power at the
expense of women.

The 1968 publication of Eldridge Cleaver's *Soul on Ice*, written
while he was in prison for rape, made visible what had perhaps
been invisible before—the devaluation of Black women by Black
men as well as white men. Cleaver's confession that he raped Black
women as practice for raping white women was a chilling revelation, one that reinforced in America's mind that Black women were
of value to no one. The blatant disregard for the humanity of Black
women continues to weave itself as a recurring theme not only in
rap, but in other arenas of popular culture.

Certainly there is evidence of how little Black life is valued in
America, and in many ways because of their race and gender, Black

women's lives are valued even less. Children Now, a child research and advocacy group, recently issued a press release in which they evaluated electronic games for their sensitivity to gender and diversity. Most of the games failed on both counts. What was most disturbing in the report was the finding that "the makers of top-selling video games portray almost all Black women as victims of violence. . . . Video makers design the games so that 86 percent of the Black women in them are harmed violently."[27]

Clearly some radical intervention is needed. If we believe that Black men are becoming "endangered" through imprisonment, drugs, and violence (from the police and one another), we need to consider that Black women are also "endangered" from acts of violence perpetrated by Black and white men and their growing incarceration rates due to their involvement with drugs. Privileging racism over sexism has not worked well in the past, and it will not solve the current problems Black America faces. The harsh reality is that Black women are often victimized by the sexism of Black men who may be compensating for the ways in which racism disempowers them and makes them feel unmanly. Rather than striking out at those who may be responsible for their oppression, some Black men lash out at Black women because they are accessible and vulnerable targets who lack the power to protect themselves or to retaliate.

Black communities are in crisis. In the midst of debilitating poverty and racism, drug abuse, HIV/AIDS, outrageous incarceration rates, hopelessness, and violence among Black youth, there is also a ticking time bomb of hostility between the sexes that, left unchecked, has the power to erode some of the progress we have made since the civil rights and Black Power movements. What is needed is a multilayered, community-based attack on sexism in Black popular culture. We must pose the difficult question of whether all forms of artistic license are socially acceptable if they threaten our basic humanity. We are especially concerned that impressionable young folks who consume problematic gender messages day after day run the risk of internalizing these messages and acting out what they've observed.

The vulgar language of hip-hop culture is reflected in the everyday speech of many Black youth, irrespective of class. Young girls

in housing projects and on college campuses are sometimes indistinguishable from one another in terms of the language they employ. It was frequently the case that Black females in previous
generations, irrespective of their class status, took great offense at
anyone who dared call them a "bitch" or a "ho." Many young girls
today casually refer to themselves as "bitches" and "hos." Hip-hop
chronicler Nelson George recalls a disturbing experience he had at
Spelman College in 1989 as a speaker on a panel dealing with hip-
hop during which he was castigated by Morehouse and Spelman students for his criticism of Luther "Luke" Campbell and
his Miami-based 2 Live Crew's group's "lyrical violence toward
women."[28] A year earlier the rap group had made history when it
sold over 500,000 copies of its *Live Is What We Are* album. A cur-
sory review of some of their song titles helps to explain George's
denigration of their vulgar chants: "Give Me Some Pussy"; "Throw
the Dick"; "Me So Horny"; and "The Fuck Shop." Nelson George
is bewildered for years by the students' defense of Luke, and a
decade passes before he attempts to make sense of that confusing
evening. What this situation perhaps illustrates is that the generation gap (between Nelson and the students) is far greater than the
gender gap among hip-hop generationers. A year later a federal judge
in Florida would ban 2 Live Crew's album *Nasty as They Wanna Be*
on obscenity charges that would later be dropped, although they still
have the distinction of being the first recording group in the United
States to have their albums prohibited from being sold to minors until the ban was released. A prominent Harvard professor, Henry
Louis Gates, Jr., would testify as an expert witness on their behalf at
the trial, which resulted in a storm of controversy and contentious
debates within the Black academic community.[29]

The way in which some Black women actually embrace the use
of the terms *bitches* and *hos* creates controversy within Black communities similar to the one surrounding the use of the term *nigga*.
Some women consider their embrace of the term *ho* as a transgressive gesture because they are encroaching on male territory and reclaiming a derogatory term as something affirming of their sexuality.
This defiance is also seen as exposing a double standard, whereby
men's expression of their sexuality is celebrated, while women's
naming of *their* sexual desires generates shock and moral indict-

ment. The latter was the intent of the female gangsta rappers "Bytches With Problems" (BWP), who said they embraced the term because they were angry with the way women were portrayed and wanted to make fun of double standards. The question we raise is whether BWP is really being transgressive by embracing a word that has no positive connotations.

In *The Source*, hip-hop's most popular magazine, Harvard professor Randall Kennedy, author of *Nigger: The Strange Career of a Troublesome Word*, says that hip-hop "has probably been the greatest vehicle for promulgating" the use of the N-word in America today. The trend of young Black men publicly calling one another "nigga" and "my nigga" in song lyrics, comedy routines, film, and television underscores the self-image dilemmas of African Americans. If these young men embrace a word that just a generation ago was a potent weapon of hatred and oppression, it isn't such a stretch for them to routinely refer to women as "bitches" and "hos."

At coronations on many college campuses, including Miss Maroon and White at the all-male Morehouse College in Atlanta, Georgia, queens, sometimes scantily clad, look and behave like strippers. In fact, many aspects of stripper culture permeate hip-hop music videos and the public performances and values of Black youth, including on college campuses. The most blatant example of the convergence of stripper culture with Black youth culture occurs during Freaknik (which is almost defunct), when thousands of Black college students converge in Atlanta for their annual spring break. What we witnessed or read about the public behavior of many college men and women on the streets of Atlanta during that second weekend in April is appalling—topless coeds riding in cars; attempted gang rapes; videotaping of sex acts; vulgar language; stalking; and young men and women hanging out of cars with buttocks in full view. This lewd behavior, in addition to being dangerous, is yet another example of the confluence of the rap video world and the everyday worlds of many Black youth.

Some major housecleaning is in order. Kitwana, who has profoundly influenced our own thinking about the implications of misogynistic rap, reminds us that the hip-hop generation is the first to grow up in an environment of women's rights and the notion of gender equality, even if those values aren't always embraced or made explicit in our communities. At the same time, it seems obvious that few young men of the hip-hop generation care much about feminism or find it useful in their own lives. This is certainly not peculiar to their age group. While female-headed households are very familiar to many of them, they may have been impacted negatively by the deeply rooted sexism of contemporary American and African American culture that makes it difficult for them to empathize with the rights of women and their desires to be treated with dignity and respect. Strong, capable women are often viewed as emasculating or derisively labeled as lesbians. These young people have also grown up amidst legal battles around gender issues, including Anita Hill's charges of sexual harassment against Supreme Court Justice nominee Clarence Thomas, Senator Robert Packwood's expulsion from Congress after allegedly molesting dozens of women, and President Bill Clinton's near-impeachment for his inappropriate sexual relationship with former White House intern Monica Lewinsky. Similarly, this generation has lived with contentious debates surrounding gays in the U.S. military, antigay/lesbian hate crimes, and movements to legalize same-sex marriages and permit gays and lesbians to adopt children.[30] With these evolving gender shifts and family configurations, one might assume that the hip-hop generation has developed a more progressive attitude about gender roles and more egalitarian views about interpersonal relationships than would have been the case with their parents and grandparents.

In the aftermath of public disclosure concerning Jesse Jackson's extramarital affair and "outside" child, we are reminded as well of mixed messages the older generation sends our youth—do what we tell you to do, not what you see us doing! This hypocrisy does not go unnoticed by them, including poor black youth who are often the target of venomous commentary by mainstream and more privileged adults. Lisa Y. Sullivan, founder of the Black Student Leadership Network, describes a compelling and revealing scene in a neighborhood barber shop in Washington, D.C., following news about Jackson's "baby scandal": "A young brother told me, 'he [Jackson] got child care issues! The only difference . . . is that he can pay for his and I can't pay for mine. I've never listened to those cats, politicians and preachers, telling me to stop making babies outside marriage. Brothers like me see them out here in the wee hours of the morning creeping around getting their sex on and they ain't with their wives. Why I got to stop getting my groove on but they can do their dirt.' "[31] Sullivan reminds us that despite the older Black community's discomfort about airing racial dirty linen (rather than changing our behavior), we have failed in many ways, because of our double standard, to set a good example with respect to practicing what we preach:

> Poor black youth have known for a while that the moral authority of black leadership was at best co-opted and at worst bankrupt. Preachers and pimps, I have been told too many times by black youth, are cut from the same cloth. Try having a conversation with an inner-city teen or young adult about established black leadership. . . . Many black youth feel a loathing, even disdain toward black leaders who have made careers out of judging black youth morally unfit and worthy of tongue lashings about their values and 'dysfunctional' behavior. (15)

Sullivan, risking charges of being a race-traitor, is swift with a solution to this dilemma: "Dirty linen and all, it's time black leadership examined its behavior and the impact it's having on the moral development of black youth . . . black leaders need to stop browbeating black youth for behavior they still engage in" (15).

It is instructive to recall those young Black women (our generation) in the Black liberation movements of the sixties who accepted the rampant sexism of Black men and the organizations they created because their "warrior brothers" needed understanding and support. Many Black women believed they had to put their own issues on the back burner or abandon them altogether. Some took a back seat reluctantly, but they believed that once Blacks eliminated the overt racism and oppression that kept us down, our men would suddenly become enlightened, view us as equals, and fight for women's liberation. They were also reluctant to publicly disclose behaviors they found offensive in a racist society too quick to judge and punish Black men for similar or worse behaviors on the part of white men.

Perhaps Black women's willingness to put men's interests first also set the stage for today's gender wars. Ntozake Shange, Michele Wallace, and Alice Walker were challenged and attacked in the media by Black men and women for revealing the gender fault lines within our communities. They took the heat for being "race traitors," as they waved ugly truths about sexism and abuse in our collective faces. Many responded with anger and sometimes outright rage. Both Walker and Wallace have written candidly about the pain they experienced in the aftermath of these sometimes vicious community onslaughts. Women rappers and hip-hop feminists, like their literary foremothers, may be cause for optimism in these continuing battles between the sexes.

"Ladies First": Toward a Feminist Agenda for Hip-Hop

In contrast to their female counterparts in heavy metal and rock and roll, Black and Latina women have been involved in hip-hop culture from its beginning. However, as Queen Latifah indicates in her autobiography *Ladies First: Revelations of a Strong Woman*, they were generally relegated to a marginal supporting cast in what was an overwhelmingly male-dominated arena. In a candid interview with Tricia Rose, Carmen Ashhurst-Watson speaks about what it's like to work behind the scenes in the music business. With over twenty years of experience in media, film, and television, she is one of the few female executives to make it to the top of the music industry and is former president of Russell Simmons's Rush Communications, then the second-largest Black entertainment company in the United States.

> It's a very macho industry across the board, not just with rappers. There's a lot of foul and sexist language that is routine. The things that Anita Hill said she heard from

Clarence Thomas over a four-year period, I might hear in a morning. My boss, if he wants to tell me I did a good job, he'll call me up and say, "Carmen, I'm on your dick!" Should I say, "Look, this is sexual harassment, I shouldn't have to hear that," or do I take the props (praise)? That's the kind of decision that women have to make literally by the hour—not by the day, not by the week. . . . It's at that level of conversation all the time. Rappers also use verbal disrespect. So you as a woman executive . . . might be asked to cover for the rocker who leaves some girl drunk and battered in the back of the car. Part of your job can require you to cover for really blatant sexism, sexual harassment and abuse. It's hard to fight because it is so routine for the rockers to abuse women on that level. In my experience, rappers are not often that physically abusive.[32]

What this narrative illustrates is the blatantly sexist atmosphere of this particular male-dominated industry and the way in which there is a connection between the music and the behavior of its creators.

Even though Lady B is credited as the first female rapper with her 1979 song "To the Beat, Y'all," it was female rappers' "hit and dismiss" responses to Brooklyn-based rapper group UTFO's recording of "Roxanne, Roxanne" (1985) that helped them gain greater visibility. The original song was about a young ghetto girl who "dissed" (rejected) three male suitors. Fourteen-year-old b-girl Lolita Shante Gooden, using the stage name Roxanne Shante, and a New York City waitress named Joan Martinez, who called herself "The Real Roxanne," took umbrage at the male sexual bravado that the first Roxanne song celebrated. What followed was a barrage of lyrical responses, referred to as "hit and dis" recordings, by a number of female rappers. In fact, over one hundred Roxanne-related records were recorded. According to Perkins, "the Roxanne cycle pitted b-boys against b-girls in the eternal battle of the sexes" and "injected a feminist current into the rap mainstream."[33] Perkins notes that these women rappers would call attention to the problems of inner-city women who routinely battle what the fictional Roxanne rhymes about—sexual harassment on the streets and predatory behavior by male suitors. It was also an answer-back record that launched the career of one of rap's most popular and enduring female groups, Salt-N-Pepa.

Some of the seemingly more progressive female rap artists have also taken on some of the more sexually explicit overtures of male rappers, leading some critics to ponder whether they actually challenge the sexual stereotypes of Black women promulgated by male rappers, or whether they in fact embody such stereotypes through their own attire, body language, and sexual candor. Do sexually empowered female entertainers such as Salt-N-Pepa, TLC, L'il Kim, and Foxy Brown and the provocative nature of their music and performances actually contribute to sexual objectification or even violence against Black women?

We believe this viewpoint reintroduces the old problem of blaming the victim. The suggestion that women "invite" violence because of how they dress not only makes women appear responsible for their own rape or sexual assault, but casts men as victims of their own "primal" instincts who are merely responding to external stimuli. However you read it, this interpretation is problematic. What makes people human is their ability to make choices and to distinguish between right and wrong. Otherwise, we become victims of our own instincts and urges.

Following in the footsteps of Salt-N-Pepa, other women rappers such as M. C. Lyte and YoYo, having also been influenced by hardcore rap, seem to walk a thin line between tough, streetwise girl and "good" girl. Jamison observes that rapper Queen Latifah also broke through what had been a man's world with her celebratory lyrics about Black womanhood. At age nineteen, she not only challenged the emerging hardcore hip-hop toward which record companies seem to gravitate, but she also challenged the dominant stereotypes of Black women as "bitches" and "hos." With the release of her album *All Hail the Queen*, Queen Latifah insisted on regal images in hip-hop's representation of Black women. Her second song from the album *Ladies First* introduced female British rapper Monie Love, and celebrated Black women without disrespecting or dismissing Black men.

While Queen Latifah's rise to stardom was swift, other female rappers have had to carve out a space for themselves at a much slower pace. In the process, they have encountered glass ceilings and brick walls in their attempts to exercise economic and artistic control over their work. Freestyle artist Toni Blackman says that it was hard for her to claim her own space in hip-hop, which is dominated by males and misogynistic values. At freestyle jam sessions, she was often the only woman artist in the room who was not the girlfriend of one of the guys.

Although many women sang vocals on hip-hop sound tracks, few were in the producer's seat. While more women are taking greater creative control of their work behind the scenes, and a few such as Lauryn Hill, Missy Elliott, and Lil' Mo are also producers, the world of hip-hop music has been primarily a boys' club where women are presumed to be singers and nothing more. In this respect, little has changed from the early days of hip-hop where, according to Nancy Guevara, the media, like other cultural institutions, routinely display a tendency to ignore, negate, stereotype, or trivialize women's participation.[34] Despite this resistance, however, Black women have made more advances in hip-hop than white women in rock and roll and heavy metal. Female hip-hop artists do create and perform songs with healthy messages, such as BWP's "NO Means NO!", which assails date rape. Unfortunately, the song received little airplay. Women rappers are certainly an important force in the Black community's struggle to reshape the agendas of the hip-hop industry. They are claiming their right to trample upon the sacred cows in rap music as they critique some of its more destructive elements. Women rappers are not without their contradictions, inconsistencies, and challenges, however, as is the case as well with self-defined hip-hop feminists—not a label all women rappers embrace. They present a complex array of responses to hip-hop culture in general and gangsta rap in particular. They offer varying views on gender politics that are sometimes at odds with each other.

In Joan Morgan's provocative and popular narrative of her life as a hip-hop feminist, she acknowledges that "the black community had to include its women" and that "sexism stood stubbornly in the way of black men and women loving each other or sistas loving themselves;"[35] that Black women are suffering from "exorbitant rates of solo parenting, domestic violence, drug abuse, incarceration, AIDS, and cancer" (53); and that many Black women were, where Black men are concerned, "misguidedly over-protective, hopelessly male-identified, and all too often self-sacrificing" (55).

In more revealing confessions about her own personal sexual politics, however, Morgan's attachment to feminism, despite her self-designation, seems less certain:

> As liberated women we may revel in our ability to pay our own way but we're not likely to fall for the men who let us. The one boyfriend I had who actually took the 'feminist' approach of splitting all our dating expenses . . . couldn't win for trying. Since he made almost three times my salary, my 'feminist' mind had trouble processing his actions as anything but cheap. Hypocritical as it was, the sight of him calculating the bill had the undesirable effect of waterhosing my libido. . . . Men have long figured out what us liberated supersistas have been loath to admit: Men are not the only ones with a vested interest in sexism. When it comes to equality, most of us are only willing to go but so far. Equal pay for equal work, yes . . . But complete and total equality? Not hardly. Because while we recognize sexism's evils, we also fully enjoy its privileges (214–215).

Morgan is also explicit about women using their "erotic power"—what some female rappers call "pussy power"—in the battle against sexism. What is clear to us is that hip-hop generationers have a different conception of feminism than we do, or are perhaps more suspicious of its value, especially with respect to what women might have to surrender in these gender wars. There is comfort in the idea of patriarchal protection, even if it means fewer freedoms for women.

As long as female hip-hop artists are willing to break down barriers and challenge misogyny in hip-hop culture, there is reasonable hope for progress. And when a lone male dares to go against the pack, there is cause for celebration as well. Writer and cultural critic Kevin Powell asserted in his "Confessions of a Recovering

Misogynist": "These days I am a hip-hopper-in-exile. I dress, talk, and walk like a hip-hopper, yet I cannot listen to rap radio or digest music videos without commenting on the pervasive sexism . . . I constantly 'pick on the men' and myself, because I truly wonder how many men actually listen to the concerns of women."[36]

The range of gender ideologies in hip-hop, whether deployed by men or women, requires much greater scrutiny as well as a commitment by hip-hop artists and producers to healing the rift between the sexes that is becoming harder-edged and more mean-spirited than ever before. We hope that rap artists who create this powerful music, which is now exported around the globe, can be persuaded to respond positively to critiques about its potentially negative impact on young people. The historic hip-hop summit that took place in New York City in June of 2001 and brought together hip-hop artists with influential leaders, mostly male, from many segments of the Black community, was a welcome intervention. Organized by rap music mogul Russell Simmons (Rush Communications/Def Jam Recordings), the summit participants included Kweisi Mfume (NAACP), Minister Louis Farrakhan (Nation of Islam), Representative Cynthia McKinney (Democrat-Georgia), scholars Manning Marable, Cornel West, and Michael Eric Dyson, as well as hip-hop artists such as Sean (Puffy) Combs (Bad Boy Records).[37] Rap music has the artistic space to accommodate competing and complementary views. But if the more positive, progressive voices are to be heard and have an impact, rap artists must gain greater control over the production of their work and the dissemination of their messages. This is a challenge when the mostly white, greedy corporate world controls the production and distribution processes with no regard for promoting positive social values or healing the social rifts between Black men and women.

To be sure, the ultimate responsibility for shifting the language and images now pervasive in some strands of rap music lies within Black communities. Several African American leaders are committed to continuing meeting with leading hip-hop producers and superstar performers with hopes of persuading them to use the power of their lyrics to communicate more positive, empowering messages. The most prominent leader to wage war on rap music while also calling for dialogue with rap artists has been the Reverend Calvin Butts, pastor of Harlem's famous Abyssinian Baptist Church. An outspoken organizer at the 1993 protest rally in New York City during which he called for censorship, the Reverend Butts continues his advocacy efforts for major reforms in the rap community despite their First Amendment rights to free speech. More of us, on an individual and collective level, must challenge degrading images of women, boycott music that perpetuates hate and gratuitous violence, and talk, talk, talk with one another in our schools, universities, churches, mosques, and community centers about how we can move a more solution-oriented gender debate into the public arena. We must continue to dialogue with artists and producers of rap about creating more affirming, socially conscious messages. We must demand that songs with countermessages get more air time, such as BWP's "NO means NO!" and A Tribe Called Quest's "Date Rape," which assails acquaintance violence. We must address ways of countering the low self-esteem that plagues many of our young people to the point where they demean themselves with words and images as powerful as shackles, whips, and nooses.

We must engage in active resistance to the more toxic aspects of hip-hop. At the annual NAACP conference in Houston, Texas, during the first week of July in 2002, President Kweisi Mfume denounced "song lyrics [that] defame our struggle, demean our ancestors, denigrate our women, and disrespect our culture."[38] Of all the problems facing Black America that he delineated—incarceration, breast cancer, prostate cancer, HIV/AIDS—his reference to hip-hop received the most rousing response from the audience, suggesting that many Black people are fed up with certain aspects of this music. It is imperative that we seriously consider that the negative consequences of our young people being exposed to a steady stream of antisocial messages, pornographic images, and destructive behaviors will continue to erode our communities from within. And the ticking time bomb of corrosive gender relations will inevitably explode in our faces.

In the October 2002 issue of *Ebony*, editor Lerone Bennett, Jr.'s hard-hitting article, "Sex and Music: Has It Gone Too Far?," labels this sexually explicit music "macho-macho," and articulates the ways in which it is harmful to Black communities. He is also clear about what we must do: "We also need a new understanding—in the media, in the entertainment industry, in our churches, schools and organizations—that popular songs are as important as civil rights bills and that a society that pays pipers to corrupt its young and to defame its women and mothers will soon discover that it has no civil rights to defend and no songs to sing" (150).

The power of words—and the attitudes they reflect—cannot be ignored. The hateful and harsh gender talk in too much of rap music and American popular culture must be addressed by socially conscious women and men who deplore violence and misogyny, and understand the damage it does within our communities and around the world.

8

•

WHERE DO WE GO FROM HERE?

If there is one thing we can learn from the 60s it is how infinitely complex any move for liberation must be. For we must move against not only those forces which dehumanize us from outside, but also against those oppressive values which we have been forced to take into ourselves.

Audre Lorde, *Sister Outsider*, 1984

We will continue to fail to transform ourselves until we reconcile the unequal distribution of power in our political community accorded on the basis of gender and sexual choice.

Cheryl Clarke, "The Failure to Transform," 1983

In trying to understand the complex web of Black gender relations and some of the causes and effects of the "isms" that inform those relations, we gathered and consulted with some of the best African American minds of our time. They shared their insights with amazing grace and enormous generosity. Although their viewpoints sometimes varied, they agreed that this conversation was for naught unless we were committed to finding solutions to the problems we explored and discussed at length.

We want to draw on an experience Johnnetta had that puts the need for next steps into perspective. She was giving a speech and was 'on message.' Johnnetta critiqued racism and sexism and heterosexism. She harped on ageism and ableism as she defied every 'ism' on earth. At the end of the talk an African American brother came up to her and said, "You know, sister, I'm going to tell you something. You really ought to start practicing the Noah Principle."

Having grown up in a very Southern, Black, AME church–related family, she thought she knew something about the Bible. So she said, "The Noah Principle?" He said, "Yeah. There will be no more credit for predicting the rain. *It's time to build the ark.*"

Building this particular ark is a multifaceted challenge, and each of us has a role to play. Working together, we can begin to bridge the gender-relations gap and strengthen the foundation of our families and communities. We can turn disrespect into self-respect, which translates into higher regard and better treatment for our women, our men, and our children. This will not be easy. It will require a great deal of time and effort as well as the willingness to confront some very uncomfortable truths. The rapidly increasing toll of HIV/AIDS and violence against women, men, and youth have reached intolerable proportions and the alternative, to let our people drown in a tidal wave of needless destruction, is neither acceptable nor inevitable. We simply *must* act now.

FROM PATRIARCHY TO PARTNERSHIP

If there is no struggle there is no progress. . . .
Power concedes nothing without a demand.
It never has and it never will.

Frederick Douglass

Our first step is to transform the patriarchy that ascribes power to men over women and divides us along gender lines into a more humane, equitable form of empowerment that benefits us all. The problem with patriarchy, which is based on male superiority and supremacy, is that it comes at the expense of women, children and, ultimately, other men. The notion of the man as the one, true king of the house, head of the family, and leader in the community turns our homes and neighborhoods into hostile territories. It gives African American men a false sense of power based on dominance and control. Domestic violence is often triggered when a man with this false sense of power feels threatened or challenged and moves to regain a sense of control through beating, raping, or berating his partner and/or children.

Domestic violence has ramifications beyond the immediate trauma that is inflicted. We know that children of both genders who witness domestic violence are very likely to continue the cycle—as perpetrator, victim, or both—generation after generation.

The only cure for fractured families and hostile gender relations is a new model of partnerships in which we work together rather than against one another. Ironically, African American gender relations may have been more equitable under slavery. Because neither male nor female slaves had power or control—over their own bodies, lives, or families—they didn't have the luxury of male-female power struggles. Or when they did, those struggles were dwarfed by the greater violence and everyday trauma of master-slave power dynamics.

But as Frederick Douglass reminds us, we cannot expect the brothers to simply awaken one day and magically agree that patriarchy is outmoded, and volunteer to share the power with sisters. The roots of this patriarchal belief system are so deep, so strong, so inextricably intertwined with our cultural values that we are talking about a major undertaking. It dominates our churches in particular, and is the foundation of many of our collective spiritual and family traditions.

Much of the work to change patriarchy to partnership must begin within ourselves as women. We must replace the old patterns that have become so destructive with a new way of thinking, feeling, seeing, and believing that offers us the possibility of healing and positive change. We must be prepared for resistance and fortified for long-term struggle within our own households, families, and communities. This is nothing less than a revolution.

By revolution we mean a movement for radical change. We know that change is not only possible, it is inevitable. Gender relations in our communities have been changing *for the worse* for a very long time. Now we must take the reins and turn our collective attitudes and behaviors around so they can be transformed for the better.

We believe that it will be very difficult to dislodge the very deep and tenacious belief among many African American men that they do not have any power to relinquish under a racist, capitalist system. They are likely to argue that more African American women are educated and employed than African American men. They will try to overpower our cries of sexism with references to the racism that oppresses all of us, but especially them. They will undoubtedly remind us of all the ways that they are "an endangered species," as if we are not also "endangered"—not only from the greater society, but in many cases, because of them!

INDIVIDUAL CHANGE

"We'd better take time to fashion revolutionary selves, revolutionary lives, revolutionary relationships."

—Toni Cade Bambara

To be effective, change must occur on two levels: within individuals and within the system. As individuals, we must educate ourselves not only about the problem, but also about solutions. What have other communities done to achieve greater gender equity? What are we willing to give up to achieve this change? What can we do in the short-term and finally over the long haul?

Individual change begins with greater awareness, which can be painful. Sometimes it hurts to open our eyes and face reality about ourselves, our homes, and our communities. But we must look unflinchingly at what ails us—domestic violence, the sexual abuse of girls and boys, incest, rape, homicide—and do what we can to stop it. We must not avert our gaze from the horrors of the HIV/AIDS epidemic that is slaughtering people of all races, but especially people of African descent at a terrifying rate all over the world. We cannot afford to let ourselves or our children engage in unprotected sex or pretend that they will just say "no!" We should turn down the volume, remove the headphones, or change the station when we hear song lyrics or conversation, or see music videos and other media portrayals that denigrate us or our loved ones *in any way*. We must speak up and speak out over and over again until the message gets through: that this foul, hateful language and behavior are a twenty-first-century form of self-imposed slavery and we must free ourselves or continue to suffer the needlessly tragic consequences.

The sixties slogan "Each One Teach One" is as relevant today as it was during the civil rights and Black Power movements. Our first task then is to change our own behaviors. As we evolve, those around us will notice and respond to the changes. There will be questions, confusion, criticism, and resistance. Many will claim that they would like to change, but simply "can't." We can encourage them, we can teach by example, and we can model the behavior that will create positive change.

As Black women, we can:

- Call sexism as we see it and experience it.
- Teach ourselves, our children, our friends, our loved ones, and everyone we come in contact with that it is time for a change and the time is now.
- Raise feminist sons and daughters who regard one another as equals rather than as enemies.
- Remind ourselves and our children that we are not "niggaz," "bitches," "dawgs," and "hos."
- Remember that we—not the celluloid celebrities—are our children's truest role models. Therefore, we must demonstrate that men and women can respect one another, love one another, and be kind to one another.
- Use our positions as teachers in elementary, middle, high, and Sunday schools and other religious institutions, and colleges and universities. We can practice gender equity in our classrooms and use what we know to demonstrate new attitudes to our students.

But women cannot "build the ark" alone. There are several ways in which individual Black men can challenge patriarchal dominance and gender inequity.

- Each brother can monitor his own individual language, gender attitudes, and behaviors that suggest a belief in male dominance and the idea that only men should be in control of families, churches, organizations, and "their" women.
- Each brother can challenge other Black men who exhibit sexist/homophobic behaviors.
- Black men are most often the heads of Black churches. Imagine if these preachers began to speak out against sexism from the pulpit.
- As parents, Black men can begin to model different and nonsexist behaviors.
- Black men should cease buying and supporting profoundly misogynist services and products such as gangsta rap and pornography.
- Black men should acknowledge their gender privileges and work to challenge the sexist oppression of Black women.
- Gender-progressive African American men can help to construct healthier, more humane definitions of "manhood" and "maleness" than those currently dominating popular culture. They can serve as role models for other men.

When Black men publicly disavow sexist attitudes and behaviors that are rampant in both the African American and the larger community, they play a powerful role in replacing patriarchy with partnership and struggling for positive change. And of course there is much that all of us—Black women and Black men—can do.

- Black women and men need to pose this question with respect to any experience with oppression: Is the fundamental cause racism, or is the problem also coming from within our communities?
- Because knowledge is the prerequisite for action in the interest of positive change, Black men and women need to learn more about gender/sexuality issues. We need to read books such as bell hooks's *Feminism Is for Everyone*, Paula Giddings's *When and Where I Enter*, Rudolph Byrd's and Beverly Guy-Sheftall's *Traps: African American Men on Gender and Sexuality*, Michael Eric Dyson's *Race Rules*, and Cathy Cohen's *The Boundaries of Blackness: AIDS and the Breakdown of Black Politics*. Then we need to talk *with one another* about the

nature of sexism, racism, classism, and heterosexism and how they are interrelated.

- Black women and men must work together to heighten awareness and activism around issues such as domestic violence, sexual harassment, the prison-industrial complex, HIV/AIDS, and the abuse of children.

SYSTEMIC CHANGE

"I freed thousands of slaves. I could have freed thousands more, if they had known they were slaves."

Harriet Tubman

Patriarchy and gender wars are grounded in a male sense of power, making them as systemic as they are individual; as political as they are personal. Our battle is not to wrestle power *from* Black men, but rather to lift up the benefits and advantages of authentic partnerships that enable us to work together rather than against one another.

While patriarchy is old behavior, the phenomenon of African Americans loudly and proudly calling themselves and one another "niggas," "bitches," "dawgs," and "hos" is relatively new behavior—fueled and spread worldwide by mass media. Hip-hop culture is now urban youth rebellion gone corporate.

Individual action can enable systemic change. As a result of private, individual tragedies that sparked public awareness campaigns, more people wear seat belts; fewer people smoke; more women have mammograms; fewer people drink and drive; more pregnant teens receive prenatal care; and fewer teens get pregnant.

From comments made throughout the interviews we conducted, from suggestions made during the daylong multilogue we facilitated, and from our own heads come these specific actions that African American women and men can do together:

- Create media with new gender messages—in books, music, Web sites, videos and DVDs, billboards, radio and television programs, ads and public service announcements.

- Involve the messengers. Enlist the support of writers; artists; rap stars; filmmakers; television, music, and video writers; producers and directors. Imagine what might happen if we could get some big-name stars engaged in capturing the public's imagination and making gender talk trendy.
- Engage the hip-hop community, the young men on urban basketball courts, as well as those in colleges, prisons, and churches. We must also find ways to reach out to young women who display their bodies in strip clubs, music videos, and on the streets.
- Persuade religious leaders to include more gender matters in their preaching, teaching, and writing.
- Insist that school curricula and extracurricular activities appropriately address gender issues.
- Create gender talk presentations that can be used in middle and high schools, youth programs, churches, and community centers.
- Encourage young men to form and become involved in groups such as Black Men for the Eradication of Sexism, which was started at Morehouse College but is now defunct.
- Hold a series of public dialogues at colleges and universities to engage our communities in cross-generational gender talk.
- Tell our stories. Write new, gender-progressive books for future generations, including children's books.
- Arrange for a 1-800 or 1-900 telephone number, directed primarily to young people, which features sensible gender information.
- Encourage our leaders—politicians, academics, ministers, activists, policy makers, entrepreneurs, and others—to speak out more explicitly and boldly about gender matters.

This list is just a beginning. You certainly have your own ideas and resources. We urge you to put them to work for the cause of gender justice in African American communities. We *can* build the ark of better gender relations, stronger families, and safer communities. As a very first step, we need to do as Jill Nelson urges us to do: We need to start talking. Indeed, we need more gender talk!

APPENDIX

•

What follows is a brief description of the data we collected for *Gender Talk*, which included face-to-face interviews, and a daylong symposium at the Ford Foundation on November 19, 1999, whose topic was "Gender Issues and African American Communities."

INTERVIEWS

A major premise underlying this book project was that soliciting the opinions of a broad range of African Americans about gender matters would help us determine the overall framework of *Gender Talk*. We want to underscore the importance of trust between those we interviewed and ourselves. The interview methodology can be problematic if there is insufficient trust between the parties involved. It became clear to both of us that every person we interviewed trusted our motives, understood the overall significance of the project, and felt they could be open and candid.

We conducted all twenty-three of the interviews together, for the most part, in the summer and fall of 1999. This work was done in the homes of interviewees, or in Beverly's home in Atlanta, or in our hotel rooms when were away from Georgia. Following each interview, we reflected upon what we had learned and what issues we needed to explore further. We began each session by asking the interviewee to make a brief autobiographical statement, keeping in mind our desire to probe a broad range of gender-related issues related to African American communities. We asked the same set of questions at the beginning of every interview: (1) In summary terms, how would you characterize the present condition of African

Americans, and include in your response the impact of gender on our present situation? (2) How would you describe the present condition of our youth? (3) Which has had the greater impact on your life, race or gender, or both? [During the course of the interviews, as a result of one respondent, we inserted "class."] (4) Within African American communities, what do you consider to be the major, most pressing gender issues? (5) How would you describe the present situation of African American women/men, especially women/men of your age?

Following these general questions, we proceeded to a series of carefully constructed questions that had been crafted for each individual based on our knowledge of their personal histories, professional affiliations, writings, or activist projects. We asked Beverly's administrative assistant, Audree Irons, for example, what she thought had been her greatest challenges as a single parent, and what her opinions were about the major concerns of our students since she had spent nearly a decade working at a Black women's college. We asked Sulaiman Nuriddin to share with us the circumstances that led to his working with men to stop violence against women. At the very end of the interviews, which lasted from two to four hours, we asked respondents to share with us anything else they thought was relevant for the book project.

What follows is a list of the persons we interviewed and their professional affiliations at the time of the interview:

1. Dr. Joyce Ladner, senior fellow, government studies, The Brookings Institute, Washington, D.C.; former interim president and professor of sociology, Howard University.
2. Marcia Gillespie, editor-in-chief, *Ms.* magazine; former editor, *Essence* magazine.
3. Dr. Michael Eric Dyson, Ida B. Wells Barnett professor, DePaul University, Chicago, Illinois.
4. Dr. Dorothy I. Height, chair of the board, National Council of Negro Women.
5. Audree Irons, administrative assistant, Women's Research and Resource Center, Spelman College.
6. Attorney Derrick Bell, visiting professor of law, New York University Law School.

7. The Reverend Calvin Butts, pastor, Abyssinian Baptist Church, New York City.
8. Farai Chideya, journalist and author, New York City.
9. Kimberly Tyler, Grady Hospital, Atlanta, Georgia.
10. The Reverend Barbara King, pastor, Hillside Truth International Center, Atlanta, Georgia.
11. Pearl Cleage, writer, playwright, Atlanta, Georgia.
12. Zaron Burnett, writer, Atlanta, Georgia.
13. Dr. Rudolph Byrd, associate professor, the Graduate Institute of the Liberal Arts and Director of African American Studies, Emory University.
14. Dr. Delores Aldridge, Grace Towns Hamilton professor of sociology and African American Studies, Emory University.
15. Kevin Powell, writer, lecturer, journalist, Brooklyn, New York.
16. Ruby Sales, community organizer.
17. Dr. Manning Marable, founding director, Institute for Research in African American Studies and professor of history and political science, Columbia University.
18. Elaine Brown, former chair, Black Panther Party; writer and community organizer.
19. Aubra Love, executive director, Black Church and Domestic Violence Institute, Atlanta, Georgia, ordained minister.
20. Sulaiman Nuriddin, Batterers Intervention Program Team Manager, Men Stopping Violence, Atlanta, Georgia.
21. Gwendolyn Zoharah Simmons, assistant professor of religious studies, University of Florida at Gainesville, and former SNCC activist.
22. Barbara Smith, writer and activist.
23. Nikki Stewart, Director of Community Education, Washington D.C. Rape Crisis Center.

MULTILOGUE

When we had conducted most of the interviews, we decided it would be instructive to expand our dialogue, hear more voices, and engage in a group session that would help us clarify some of the issues that had surfaced during the interviews. The overall goal was to provide an opportunity for a focused discussion on gender issues among a particular group of women and men. The discussion would serve as research data for *Gender Talk* and hopefully generate useful suggestions for the final chapter of the book. We approached Alison Bernstein, vice president of the Ford Foundation, about our desire to facilitate a daylong "Multilogue on Gender Issues and African American Communities" at the Foundation, which took place on November 19, 1999, in New York City, and was taped. It included eighteen participants, four conveners (two of whom served as facilitators), and a research assistant. It was cosponsored by Emory University's Institute for Women's Studies and the African American Studies program, and was coconvened by their respective directors, Dr. Frances Smith Foster and Dr. Rudolph Byrd. We served as facilitators for the day.

In our opening remarks, following greetings by our program officer, Dr. Margaret Wilkerson, we reflected upon the uniqueness of this historic occasion. We believe that there has never been a group of African American women and men, experts on race and gender matters, gathered in one place for the express purpose of talking about gender issues and African American communities. We are even more certain that there has never been a gathering of Black women and men quite like the group assembled at the Ford Foundation. They were unquestionably a special group, having spent a considerable amount of their professional lives studying, debating, writing about, organizing around and, perhaps most importantly, trying to do something meaningful about the complex problems we face as a community. The very focused agenda for the day, which was carefully constructed by Frances Smith Foster, Rudolph P. Byrd, and the two of us, included a morning session during which each participant, as a way of introducing him/herself, was asked to offer an insight about how he or she viewed gender issues within African American communities. During the remainder of the morning session, participants engaged in dialogue about two questions: (1) What, in your opinion, are the most *urgent* gender issues within African American communities at the present time? and (2) How would you describe gender dynamics among our youth, including, but not limited to, hip-hop generationers? The afternoon session was designed in such a way that participants could reflect more deeply upon their own views and were asked to engage in dialogue about two questions: A number of identity markers, particularly gender, race, sexual orientation, and class, are important in understanding U.S. culture. How do you respond to and organize your life around these constructs, and what shifts or transformations have you undergone as an adult in your own thinking *and* behavior around gender? Following an open discussion among participants, we concluded our formal deliberations and gathered for dinner during which Professors Foster and Byrd provided carefully crafted summary remarks. At the end of the dinner, we brainstormed about how we might continue our dialogue, and agreed to reconvene after *Gender Talk* was published to discuss additional activities that would be useful for the project.

A list of participants follows:

1. Byllye Y. Avery, founder, National Black Women's Health Project.
2. Kimberlé Williams Crenshaw, professor of law at Columbia University School of Law and the UCLA School of Law.
3. Dazon Dixon Diallo, founder and president of SisterLove, Inc., Atlanta, Georgia, the first and largest women's AIDS organization for women of color in the Southeast; also national program director for the Center for Human Rights Education.
4. James Early, director of Cultural Heritage Policy at the Smithsonian Center for Folklife and Cultural Heritage, Washington, D.C.
5. Dr. Jacquelyn Grant, Fuller E. Callaway professor of systematic theology at the Interdenominational Theological Center, Atlanta, Georgia; also assistant minister, Victory African Methodist Episcopal Church, Atlanta, Georgia.
6. Dr. Evelynn Hammonds, associate professor of the history of science in the program in science, technology, and society at the Massachusetts Institute of Technology.
7. Calvin Hernton, emeritus professor of African American Studies, Oberlin College, now deceased.

8. bell hooks, distinguished professor of English at the City College of New York.
9. M. Thandabantu Iverson, lecturer in the division of labor studies, Indiana University, Gary, Indiana.
10. Dr. Robin D. G. Kelley, professor of history and Africana Studies at New York University.
11. Dr. Gary Lemons, director of Race, Ethnicity, and Post-colonial Studies at Eugene Lang College of the New School University, New York City.
12. Haki R. Madhubuti, founder/publisher and chair of the board of Third World Press; also professor of English, Chicago State University.
13. Dr. Tricia Rose, associate professor of Africana Studies and history and director of Graduate Studies, New York University.
14. André Willis, doctoral student in the philosophy of religion, Harvard University.
15. Sherie Randolph, assistant director, Women's Research and Resource Center, Spelman College.
16. Kevin Powell, writer, lecturer, journalist, activist, cultural critic, Brooklyn, New York.
17. Faye Wattleton, former president of Planned Parenthood Federation of America; now president of the Center for Gender Equality, New York City.
18. Kendall Thomas, professor of law, Columbia University, New York City.

PRINT AND NON-PRINT SOURCES

The following print sources and non-print sources were helpful to us in the writing of *Gender Talk* as well:

Periodicals:

Black Male/Female Relationships
The Black Scholar

Challenge: A Journal of Research on African American Men

The Crisis Magazine

Ebony

Emerge

Essence

Journal of African American Men

Ms.

Sage: A Scholarly Journal on Black Women

Souls: A Critical Journal of Black Politics, Culture & Society

Voice of the Negro

Videotapes:

Black Nations/Queer Nations?, Third World Newsreel, 1995

Chris Rock: Bigger and Blacker, HBO Home Video, 1999

Chris Rock: Bring the Pain, HBO Home Video, 1996

Fallen Champ: The Untold Story of Mike Tyson, ETC Productions, Inc., 1993

No! A Work in Progress, AfroLez Productions, 2000, PO Box 58085, Philadelphia, Pennsylvania 19102-8005

Sister, I'm Sorry: An Apology to Our African American Queens, Freedom AGJ and Quiet Fury, 1997

Woman! Thou Art Loosed 2002: God's Leading Ladies Series, The Potter's House, T.D. Jakes Ministries

NOTES

•

PREFACE

[1] Paula Giddings, "The Last Taboo," in *Race-ing Justice, En-gendering Power,* ed., Toni Morrison (New York: Pantheon Books, 1992), 441–465.

[2] Patricia Hill Collins, *Black Feminist Thought,* 2nd ed. (New York: Routledge, 1990), 124.

[3] See Rudolph P. Byrd and Beverly Guy-Sheftall, eds., *Traps: African American Men in Gender and Sexuality* (Bloomington, In.: Indiana University Press, 2001), for a copy of the Mission Statement for Black Men for the Eradication of Sexism, 200–204.

INTRODUCTION

[1] The works of several Black feminist scholars have been especially useful to us because of their insightful gender analyses of particular aspects of African American experience. These include Paula Giddings, *When and Where I Enter: The Impact of Black Women in Race and Sex in America* (New York: Morrow, 1984); bell hooks, *Ain't I a Woman: Black Women and Feminism* (Boston: South End Press, 1981), *Feminist Theory: From Margin to Center* (Boston: South End Press, 1984), and *Killing Rage: Ending Racism* (New York: Henry Holt and Co., 1995); Angela Davis, *Women, Race and Class* (New York: Random House, 1981), *Women, Culture, and Politics* (New York: Random House, 1989), and *Blues Legacies and Black Feminism: Gertrude "Ma" Rainey, Bessie Smith and Billie Holiday* (New York: Vintage Books, 1998); Patricia Hill Collins, *Black Feminist Thought: Knowledge, Consciousness, and the Politics of Empowerment,* rev. ed. (New York: Routledge, 2000) and *Fighting Words: Black Women and the Search for Justice* (Minneapolis: University of Minnesota Press, 1998); Leith Mullings, *On Our Own Terms: Race, Class, and Gender in the Lives of African American Women* (New York: Routledge, 1997); Barbara Omolade, *The Rising Song of African American Women* (New York: Routledge, 1994); Kimberly Springer, ed., *Still Lifting, Still Climbing: African American Women's Contemporary Activism* (New York: New York University Press, 1999); Joy James, *Shadowboxing: Representations of Black Feminist Politics* (New York: St. Martin's Press, 1999); E. Frances White, *Dark Continent of Our Bodies: Black Feminism and the Politics of Respectability* (Philadelphia: Temple University Press, 2001); and Sheila Radford-Hill, *Further to Fly: Black Women and the Politics of Empowerment* (Minneapolis: University of Minnesota Press, 2000).

[2] Toni Cade, ed., *The Black Woman: An Anthology* (New York: Signet, 1970), 10. In the second edition of *Black Feminist Thought* (New York: Routledge, 2000), Patricia

Hill Collins devotes a chapter, "Black Women's Love Relationships," to her analysis of "love and trouble" (borrowing from the title of a short story collection by Alice Walker), which characterizes intimate relationships between Black women and men.

[3] Calvin C. Hernton, *Coming Together* (New York: Random House, 1971), 14.

[4] Ibid., 180.

[5] Calvin C. Hernton, *The Sexual Mountain and Black Women Writers: Adventures in Sex, Literature and Real Life* (New York: Anchor Press, 1987), 7–8.

[6] Elsie B. Washington, *Uncivil War* (Chicago: The Noble Press, 1996), 1.

[7] Ibid., 2.

[8] Angela Ards, "Where Is the Love?," *Ms.*, August/September 2001, 55.

[9] Andrew Billingsley, *Jacob's Ladder: The Enduring Legacy of African-American Families* (New York: Simon & Schuster, 1992).

[10] William Julius Wilson, *The Truly Disadvantaged: The Inner City, the Underclass, and Public Policy* (Chicago: University of Chicago Press, 1987) and *When Work Disappears: The World of The New Urban Poor* (New York: Vintage Books, 1997).

[11] M. Belinda Tucker and Claudia Mitchell Kernan, eds., *The Decline in Marriage Among African Americans: Causes, Consequences, and Policy Implications* (New York: Russell Sage Foundation, 1995), 12.

[12] Ibid., 177.

[13] Donna L. Franklin, *Ensuring Inequality: The Structural Transformation of the African-American Family* (New York: Oxford University Press, 1997), xxi.

[14] Orlando Patterson, *Rituals of Blood: Consequences of Slavery in Two American Centuries* (Washington, D.C.: Civitas, 1998), xii.

[15] Pearl Cleage, *Mad at Miles: A Blackwoman's Guide to Truth* (Southfield, Michigan: The Cleage Group, Inc., 1990), 21.

[16] E. Franklin Frazier, *Black Bourgoisie* (New York: Simon & Schuster, 1957), 222.

[17] Shahrazad Ali, *The Blackman's Guide to Understanding the Blackwoman* (Philadelphia: Civilized Publications, 1989). One year later she published *The Blackwoman's Guide to Understanding the Blackman.*

[18] Abiola Sinclair, "Will the Media be Fair to the Million Man March?," in the *Amsterdam News*, vol. 86, October 21, 1995, 26. In the same issue, Dr. Lenora Fulani, chair of the Committee for a Unified Independent Party, also makes disparaging remarks about Davis, 13.

[19] See Melvin Patrick Kelly, *The Adventures of Amos 'n' Andy: A Social History of an American Phenomenon* (New York: The Free Press, 1991), for a comprehensive discussion of this American saga.

[20] "An Address by Dr. Martin Luther King, Jr.," in *The Moynihan Report and the Politics of Controversy*, eds. Lee Rainwater and William L. Yancey, (Cambridge: The M.I.T. Press, 1967), 405. King's address appears in Chapter 15, "Reaction of Civil Rights Leaders."

[21] Audre Lorde, *Sister Outsider* (Trumansburg, N.Y.: Crossing Press, 1984), 119–120.

1 THE PERSONAL IS POLITICAL

[1] Rachel Blau Du Plessis and Ann Snitow, eds., *The Feminist Memoir Project: Voices from Women's Liberation* (New York: Three Rivers Press, 1998), 11–12.

[2] Revisionist narratives which include the involvement of African American women in the development of modern feminism include Paula Giddings, *When and Where I*

Enter (New York: Morrow & Co, 1984); Sara Evans, *Personal Politics: The Roots of Women's Liberation in the Civil Rights Movement and the New Left* (New York: Knopf, 1979); *Daring to be Bad* (Minneapolis: University of Minnesota Press, 1989); Beverly Guy-Sheftall, ed., *Words of Fire: African American Feminist Thought* (New York: New Press, 1995); Du Plessis and Snitow, eds., *The Feminist Memoir Project: Voices from Women's Liberation* (1988); Estelle B. Freedman, *The History of Feminism and the Future of Women* (New York: Ballantine Books, 2002).

3 Alice Echols, *Daring to be Bad: Radical Feminism in America, 1967–1975* (Minneapolis: University of Minnesota Press, 1989), 4.

4 Ibid., 84. In this chapter there is also a lengthy discussion of the debates which took place within various feminist organizations about the value and limitations of consciousness-raising as an organizing tool for the women's movement.

5 For a comprehensive analysis of the earliest Black feminist organizations, see Kimberly Springer, *Living for the Revolution: Black Feminist Organizations, 1968–1980*, forthcoming 2003, in which she also discusses their consciousness-raising process as an important tool for personal transformation. See also Duchess Harris, "From the Kennedy Commission to the Combahee Collective: Black Feminist Organizing, 1960–1980, in *Sisters in Struggle: African American Women in the Civil Rights-Black Power Movement*, eds., Bettye Collier-Thomas and V. P. Franklin (New York: New York University Press, 2001) for a discussion of consciousness-raising in NBFO, one of its many goals being "raising the feminist consciousness of black women" (291).

6 Mary S. Hartman, ed., *Talking Leadership: Conversations with Powerful Women* (New Brunswick: Rutgers University Press, 1999), 100–101.

7 Ibid., 242–243.

8 2000 Salon.com.

9 Toni Cade Bambara, *The Salt Eaters* (New York: Random House, 1980).

10 Mary Catherine Bateson, *Composing a Life* (New York: The Atlantic Monthly Press), 138.

11 See *Ebony*, September 2000, 185–89, for coverage of this historic event.

12 The President's Open Line, September 17, 1993.

13 Phylicia Fant, "Afrekete Unwelcome at Spelman," *The Spelman Spotlight*, April 9, 1999, 1.

14 Stanlie James and Abena P.A. Busia, eds., *Theorizing Black Feminisms* (New York: Routledge & Kegan Paul, 1994), 289.

2 HAVING THEIR SAY: CONVERSATIONS WITH SISTERS AND BROTHERS

1 Sarah L. Delany and Elizabeth Delany with Amy Hill Hearth, *Having Our Say: The Delany Sisters' First 100 Years* (New York: Dell, 1993).

2 Multilogue, Ford Foundation, New York City, November 19, 1999.

3 Interview with Johnnetta Cole and Beverly Guy-Sheftall, New York City, August 8, 1999.

4 Interview with Cole and Guy-Sheftall, Atlanta, Georgia, August 2, 1999.

5 Interview with Cole and Guy-Sheftall, Washington, D.C., August 10, 1999.

6 Interview with Cole and Guy-Sheftall, Atlanta, Georgia, August 19, 1999.

7 See Haki Madhubuti's essay, "On Becoming Anti-Rapist," in *Traps: African American Men on Gender and Sexuality*, eds., Rudolph P. Byrd and Beverly Guy-Sheftall, 159.

[8] Multilogue, Ford Foundation, New York City, November 19, 1999.

[9] Interview with Cole and Guy-Sheftall, Atlanta, Georgia, August 17, 1999.

[10] Pearl Cleage, "Zeke's Wife: A Meditation on Marriage," *Essence,* May 1998, 97.

[11] Interview with Cole and Guy-Sheftall, New York City, July 28, 1999. See also Manning Marable's "Groundings With My Sisters," *How Capitalism Underdeveloped Black America* (Boston: South End Press, 1983), 69–103.

[12] Interview with Cole and Guy-Sheftall, New York City, July 28, 1999.

[13] Interview with Cole and Guy-Sheftall, Washington, D.C., August 9, 1999.

[14] Interview with Cole and Guy-Sheftall, New York City, August 6, 1999.

[15] Ibid.

[16] Interview with Cole and Guy-Sheftall, Atlanta, Georgia, August 18, 1999.

[17] Interview with Cole and Guy-Sheftall, New York City, August 4, 1999.

[18] Ibid.

[19] Ibid.

[20] Ibid.

[21] Ibid.

[22] Kevin Powell, "Confessions of a Recovering Misogynist," *Ms.,* April/May 2000, 72–77.

[23] Multilogue, Ford Foundation, New York City, November 19, 1999.

[24] Interview with Cole and Guy-Sheftall, Atlanta, Georgia, August 19, 1999.

[25] Interview with Cole and Guy-Sheftall, Atlanta, Georgia, August 18, 1999.

[26] Ibid.

[27] Multilogue, Ford Foundation, New York City, November 19, 1999.

[28] Ibid.

[29] Ibid.

[30] Ibid.

[31] Interview with Cole and Guy-Sheftall, Atlanta, Georgia, August 19, 1999.

[32] Pearl Cleage, *Mad At Miles* (Southfield, Michigan: The Cleage Group, 1990), no page number.

[33] Ibid., 27–28

[34] Interview with Cole and Guy-Sheftall, Washington, D.C., August 10, 1999.

[35] Ibid.

[36] Multilogue, Ford Foundation, New York City, November 19, 1999.

[37] Ibid.

[38] Interview with Cole and Guy-Sheftall, August 10, 1999.

[39] Robin D. G. Kelley, *Freedom Dreams: The Black Radical Imagination* (Boston: Beacon Press, 2002), 1–2.

[40] Multilogue, Ford Foundation, New York City, November 19, 1999.

[41] Ibid.

[42] Ibid.

[43] Ibid.

[44] Ibid.

[45] Derrick Bell, "The Sexual Diversion: The Black Man/Black Woman Debate in Context," in *Traps: African Men on Gender and Sexuality*, 169–170. For a discussion of the circumstances leading to his departure and eventual resignation from the law school faculty at Harvard, see his *Confronting Authority: Reflections of an Ardent Protester* (Boston: Beacon Press, 1994).

[46] Interview with Cole and Guy-Sheftall, Atlanta, Georgia, August 21, 1999.

[47] Ibid.

[48] Ibid.

[49] Ibid.

[50] Interview with Cole and Guy-Sheftall, Atlanta, Georgia, August 20, 1999.

[51] Ibid.

[52] Interview with Cole and Guy-Sheftall, Atlanta, Georgia, August 19, 1999.

[53] Ibid.

[54] Ibid.

[55] Ibid.

[56] Ibid.

[57] Interview with Cole and Guy-Sheftall, Atlanta, Georgia, August 2, 1999.

[58] Ibid.

[59] *Mad at Miles*, 4.

[60] Ibid., 5.

3   COLLISIONS: BLACK LIBERATION VERSUS WOMEN'S LIBERATION

[1] See Geneva Smitherman, ed., *African American Women Speak Out on Anita Hill-Clarence Thomas* (Detroit: Wayne University Press, 1995), 7.

[2] Paula Giddings, "The Last Taboo," in *Race-ing Justice, En-gendering Power: Essays on Anita Hill, Clarence Thomas, and the Construction of Social Reality*, ed., Toni Morrison (New York: Pantheon, 1992), 442.

[3] Cornel West, "Black Leadership and the Pitfalls of Racial Reasoning," in *Race-ing Justice, En-gendering Power*, 392.

[4] Anna Julia Cooper, *A Voice from the South*, The Schomburg Library of Nineteenth Century Black Women Writers, ed., Henry Louis Gates, Jr. (New York: Oxford University Press, 1988), 134.

[5] Deborah Gray White, *Too Heavy a Load: Black Women in Defense of Themselves, 1894–1994* (New York: W. W. Norton & Company, 1999), 54.

[6] Anna Julia Cooper, *A Voice from the South: By a Black Woman of the South* (Xenia, Ohio: Aldine Printing House, 1892), 26–27.

[7] Cogent analyses of the emergence of Black feminist discourse and activism during the sixties can be found in Toni Cade, ed., *The Black Woman* (1970); Paula Giddings, *When and Where I Enter* (1984); Kimberly Springer, ed., *Still Lifting, Still Climbing*, and her unpublished dissertation, "Our Politics Was Black Women: Black Feminist Organizations, 1968–1980," Emory University, 1999; Beverly Guy-Sheftall, *Words of Fire: An Anthology of African American Feminist Thought* (New York: New Press, 1995); Deborah Gray White, *Too Heavy a Load: Black Women in Defense of Themselves, 1894–1994* (1999).

[8] Especially useful in this regard is a large body of work by bell hooks, which began in 1981 with the publication of her first book, *Ain't I A Woman: Black Women and Feminism*; Jill Nelson, *Straight, No Chaser*; Patricia Hill Collins, *Fighting Words*; Leith Mullings, *On Our Own Terms: Race, Class and Gender in the Lives of African American Women* (New York: Routledge, 1997); Donna L. Franklin, *What's Love Got to Do With It*.

[9] These include two recently published anthologies—Devon Carbado, ed., *Black Men on Race, Gender, and Sexuality: A Critical Reader* (New York: New York Uni-

versity Press, 1999) and Rudolph Byrd and Beverly Guy-Sheftall, eds., *Traps: African American Men on Gender and Sexuality* (Bloomington: Indiana University Press, 2001).

[10] Philip S. Foner, ed., *Frederick Douglass on Women's Rights* (New York: Da Capo Press, 1992), 87.

[11] Ibid.

[12] Stanton, et al, *The History of Woman Suffrage* (New York, 1881–1886), vol. II., 391.

[13] Eric Foner, ed., *Major Speeches by Negroes in the U.S., 1797–1971* (New York: Simon & Schuster), 345–346.

[14] Ibid., 345.

[15] Darlene Clark Hine, " 'In the Kingdom of Culture': Black Women and the Intersection of Race, Gender, and Class," in *Lure and Loathing: Essays on Race, Identity, and the Ambivalence of Assimilation*, ed., Gerald Early (New York: Penguin Books, 1993), 34.

[16] Ibid.

[17] One of the most insightful essays about this long-standing hostility against Black women, which he calls misogynist, is Robert F. Reid-Pharr's "At Home in America," in his *Black Gay Man: Essays* (New York: New York University Press, 2001). He also reminds us that Angela Davis's "The Black Woman's Role in the Community of Slaves," *Black Scholar*, vol. 3, no. 4 (December 1971), 2–15, includes an insightful, but largely ignored, analysis of the ways in which some segments of the Black community demonize slave women for their alleged complicity with the system of slavery.

[18] *Black Gay Man*, 81.

[19] William Hannibal Thomas, *The American Negro, What He Was, What He Is, and What He May Become* (Boston: Macmillan, 1901), 183–184.

[20] For an analysis of northern freedmen like William Hannibal Thomas, see William Toll's "Free Men, Freedmen, and Race: Black Social Theory in the Gilded Age," *Journal of Southern History*, 54 (November 1978), 571–596. See also James M. McPherson, *The Abolitionist Legacy: From Reconstruction to the NAACP* (Princeton: Princeton University Press, 1975), who attributes Thomas's extreme racist attitudes to his "sick mind," mixed blood, and hatred of Blacks. A contemporary, Professor Kelley Miller of Howard University, wrote an extensive critique of Thomas's book for *Hampton Negro Conference*, vol. 5 (July 1901).

[21] *A Voice from the South*, 139.

[22] When Stokely Carmichael was elected chair of SNCC in May 1966 (unseating John Lewis), the organization was experiencing contentious internal debates and a major ideological shift toward black separatism and self-determination, having been impacted by the newly emerging black consciousness movement. His use of the "Black Power" slogan signaled a new SNCC.

[23] Paula Giddings, *When and Where I Enter*, 316.

[24] Reprinted as "Black Woman" in Imamu Amiri Baraka (LeRoi Jones), *Raise Race Rays Raze: Essays Since 1965* (New York: Random House, 1969), 148.

[25] Clyde Halisi and James Mtume, eds., *The Quotable Karenga* (Los Angeles: Saidi Publications, 1967), 27–28. See also his *Essays on Struggle: Position and Analysis* (Los Angeles: Kawaida Publications, 1978); *Kawaida Theory: An Introductory Outline* (Los Angeles, CA: Kawaida Publications, 1980); *Introduction to Black Studies* (Los Angeles:

Kawaida Publications, 1982), especially the chapter on "Black Social Organization," which includes a discussion of the Black family and Black male-female relationships. His essay "In Love and Struggle: Toward a Greater Togetherness," *Black Scholar,* vol. 6, no. 6 (March 1975), 16–28, rejects the idea of the Black matriarch, which he attributes to divisive tactics on the part of white oppressors; here he also espouses more egalitarian notions about relationships between Black men and women. "We must struggle against domination by the oppressor and we must not dominate each other" (22).

[26] Leith Mullings, *On Our Own Terms,* 139.

[27] Na'im Akbar, "Materialism and Chauvinism: Black Internalization of White Values," in *Crisis in Black Sexual Politics,* eds., Nathan Hare and Julia Hare (San Francisco: Black Think Tank, 1989), 50.

[28] C. Eric Lincoln, "A Look Beyond the 'Matriarchy,' " *Ebony,* vol. 21, no. 10 (August 1966), 112–113. He is happy to report that Black middle-class families "are turning from the traditional pattern of the matriarchal family to the American ideal of masculine headship" (114), but bemoans poor Blacks who have not embraced mainstream middle-class values, are not interested in assimilation or integration, and cling, unfortunately, to "their traditional styles of life."

[29] Pauli Murray, "The Liberation of Black Women," *Voices of the New Feminism,* ed., Mary Lou Thompson (Boston: Beacon Press, 1970). Reprinted in *Words of Fire: An Anthology of African American Feminist Thought,* ed. Beverly Guy-Sheftall, 195.

[30] Ibid., 195.

[31] Jean Carey Bond and Patricia Peery, "Is the Black Male Castrated?" in *The Black Woman* (New York: Signet, 1970), 114–115. Originally published as "Has the Black Male Been Castrated?" in *Liberator* magazine, vol. 9, no. 5 (May 1969), 4–8.

[32] Ibid., 113.

[33] Ibid., 116–117.

[34] Nathan Hare, "Will the Real Black Man Please Stand Up?" *The Black Scholar* vol. 2, no. 7 (June 1971), 32–35.

[35] Linda LaRue, "The Black Movement and Women's Liberation," *The Black Scholar* (May 1970), 2.

[36] There are different versions of Carmichael's controversial statement among scholars. See Sarah Evans, *Personal Politics* (1979); Clayborne Carson, *In Struggle;* Cheryl Lynn Greenberg, ed., *A Circle of Trust: Remembering SNCC* (New Brunswick: Rutgers University Press, 1998); Cynthia Griggs Fleming, *Soon We Will Not Cry* (Lanham, MD: Rowman & Littlefield Publishers, 1998); Belinda Robnett, *How Long? How Long?* (New York: Oxford University Press, 1997); and Lynne Olson, *Freedom's Daughters: The Unsung Heroines of the Civil Rights Movement from 1830 to 1970* (New York: Scribner, 2001). There is a consensus among SNCC workers present that he made the statement one evening, in jest, at the Waveland Retreat in response to his own question to Mary King: "What is the position of women in SNCC?" His answer was, "The position of women in SNCC is prone!" Olson includes a detailed rendering of the incident in which she includes Mary King's statement that Carmichael's joking that evening had been taken out of context and was not evidence that SNCC had been a misogynist organization. Quite to the contrary, it had been an organization where women had been in authority, had exercised tremendous responsibility, and were certainly valued for more than their bodies. In the early years of SNCC, at least, women

felt a sense of empowerment, which Carmichael's statement, if taken at face value, would have contradicted. Fleming has the most extensive discussion of the debate about whether SNCC was a fundamentally sexist organization in the aftermath of Carmichael's statement. Robnett explains that white women and Black women had differential work experiences, and that King's and Hayden's position paper on sexism in SNCC was less about their status in SNCC but more about their fears of SNCC becoming a hierarchal, patriarchal organization (like SCLC), given discussions about a more centralized power structure.

[37] The most useful books on gender politics within the civil rights and Black Power movements are Toni Cade, ed., *The Black Woman: An Anthology* (New York: Penguin Books, 1970); Michele Wallace, *Black Macho and the Myth of the Superwoman* (New York: Dial, 1979); Sarah Evans, *Personal Politics: The Roots of Women's Liberation in the Civil Rights Movement and the New Left* (New York: Knopf, 1979); Paula Giddings, *When and Where I Enter* (1984); Cynthia Stokes Brown, ed., *Ready from Within: Septima Clark and the Civil Rights Movement* (CA: Wild Trees Press, 1986); Vicki Crawford, Jacqueline Rouse, and Barbara Woods, eds., *Women in the Civil Rights Movement* (Brooklyn: Carlson Publishing, 1990); Peter J. Ling and Sharon Monteith, eds., *Gender in the Civil Rights Movement* (New York: Garland Publishing, 1999); Donna L. Franklin, *What's Love Got to Do With It* (2000); Deborah Gray White, *Too Heavy a Load: Black Women in Defense of Themselves, 1894–1994* (New York: W. W. Norton, 1999); Belinda Robnett, *How Long? How Long?: African American Women in the Struggle for Civil Rights* (New York: Oxford University Press, 1997); Kimberly Springer, ed., *Still Lifting, Still Climbing: African American Women's Contemporary Activism* (New York: New York University Press, 1991); Elaine Brown, *A Taste of Power: A Black Woman's Story* (New York: Pantheon Books, 1992); Cynthia Griggs Fleming, *Soon We Will Not Cry: The Liberation of Ruby Doris Smith Robinson* (Lanham, MD: Rowman & Littlefield, 1998); Lynne Olson, *Freedom's Daughters: The Unsung Heroes of the Civil Rights Movement from 1830 to 1970* (New York: Scribner, 2001); Michael Eric Dyson, *I May Not Get There with You: The True Martin Luther King, Jr.* (New York: The Free Press, 2000).

[38] Historian Clayborne Carson also discusses Currier and the role of the Taconic Foundation in the Movement in *In Struggle: SNCC and the Black Awakening of the 1960s* (Cambridge: Harvard University Press, 1981).

[39] In her interview with Radcliffe College's Black Women Oral History Project, Dr. Height recalls the evolution of the Taconic Foundation somewhat differently. According to her, it began in 1960 or 1961, when Stephen Currier assembled a group of civil rights leaders in New York who met on a regular basis to discuss the status of Black people in the United States. It included Whitney Young, A. Philip Randolph, Roy Wilkins, Jack Greenberg (NAACP Legal Defense Fund), Dr. Martin Luther King, Jr., C. Eric Lincoln (who had written about the Black Muslims), James Farmer, and herself. At her behest, SNCC was asked to join later, and John Lewis or James Forman was invited. After the assassination of Medgar Evers in 1963, Currier felt even more urgency about addressing race problems, and called for additional input from leaders he had assembled at a breakfast meeting in June 1963, the same morning Evers was buried in Arlington Cemetery. The outcome of this gathering was the United Civil Rights Leadership. It is interesting to note that during these interviews, Dr. Height did not mention

the complicated gender politics surrounding the March on Washington, and while she does discuss the follow-up meeting called by the Council for women in various organizations to discuss racial issues which surfaced during the march, she does not allude to the problems of women not being allowed to speak. She does reveal that she saw her role in the movement as representing the particular concerns of women and youth, which were ignored on the civil rights agenda.

40 In *Too Heavy a Load*, historian Deborah Gray White is very critical of Dr. Height's conservative stance on Black families and her failure to provide leadership with respect to the championing of Black women's rights as President of NCNW.

41 Lee Rainwater and William L. Yancey, *The Moynihan Report and the Politics of Controversy* (Cambridge: The M.I.T. Press, 1967), 34. This text is the most comprehensive coverage of the controversies surrounding the report and includes behind-the-scenes strategies preceding the release of the report; discussion of President Lyndon Johnson's commencement speech (drafted by Moynihan and Richard N. Goodwin and approved by civil rights leaders King, Wilkins, and Young) at Howard University, June 4, 1995, which reflected some of the confidential report before its release; and divergent responses to the report, including civil rights leaders, as well as the debates that swirled around it. Several months after the release of the controversial report (March), a White House Conference, "To Fulfill These Rights," was held in November to develop programs that would support the goals of the report; civil rights leaders objected to discussions about the Black family and argued that the subject of the conference should be jobs, protecting civil rights workers, and the implementation of the 1964 and 1965 Civil Rights Acts. Prior to the conference there were two planning meetings between civil rights leaders and government representatives. Dr. Height, as usual, was the lone female among the group and was a participant at the conference.

42 Pauli Murray, "The Liberation of Black Women," in *Voices of the New Feminism*, ed., Mary L. Thompson (Boston: Beacon Press, 1970), 354–55. A significant figure in the emergence of the modern women's movement, Murray indicates in her autobiography, *Song in a Weary Throat* (New York: Harper & Row, 1987), that her interest in women's rights began in the 40s, when she entered law school at Howard University (1941). Convinced that a legal education would better equip her to combat racism, she experienced blatant sexism there and asserted, "Ironically, if Howard Law School equipped me for effective struggle against Jim Crow, it was also the place where I first became conscious of the twin evil of discriminatory race bias, which I quickly labeled Jane Crow," 183. She was a member of President Kennedy's Commission on the Status of Women (1961–63) and was also involved in the struggle to pass Title VII of the landmark 1964 Civil Rights Act, which mandated equal employment opportunities for women. She, with twenty-eight other women, became a founding member of the National Organization for Women (1966), which signaled "a historic development in the women's movement" (182). Reprinted as "Jim Crow and Jane Crow" in *Black Women in White America: A Documentary History*, ed., Gerda Lerner (New York: Vintage Books, 1973), 59.

43 Jervis Anderson, *Bayard Rustin: Troubles I've Seen, A Biography* (New York: HarperCollins Publishers, 1997), 258.

44 For a discussion of the critical role of women in the Montgomery Bus Boycott, which remains marginal in narratives of the civil rights movement, see Jo Ann Gibson

Robinson, *The Montgomery Boycott and the Women Who Started It* (Knoxville: University of Tennessee Press, 1987).

[45] Excerpts from Pauli Murray's letter to Randolph are included in Jervis Anderson's biography of Bayard Rustin, 259.

[46] Excellent histories of SNCC include Clayborne Carson, *In Struggle: SNCC and the Black Awakening of the 1960s* (Cambridge: Harvard University Press, 1981); Mary Aiken Rothschild, *A Case of Black and White: Northern Volunteers and the Southern Freedom Summers, 1964–65* (Westport, CT: Greenwood Press, 1982); Howard Zinn, *SNCC: The New Abolitionists* (Boston: Beacon Press, 1965); Joanne Grant, *Ella Baker: Freedom Bound* (John Wiley & Sons, 1998); Cheryl Lynn, ed., *A Circle of Trust: Remembering SNCC* (New Brunswick: Rutgers University Press, 1998); Mary King, *Freedom Song: A Personal History of the 1960s Civil Rights Movement* (New York: Morrow, 1987); John Lewis, *Walking with the Wind: A Memoir of the Movement* (New York: Simon & Schuster, 1998).

[47] See Christen Anderson Bicker, " 'Triple Jeopardy': Black Women and the Growth of Feminist Consciousness in SNCC, 1964–1975," in Kimberly Springer's *Keep Lifting, Keep Climbing* for a comprehensive analysis of the evolution of gender politics within SNCC.

[48] See Clayborne Carson's *In Struggle*, chapter 10, Sarah Evans's *Personal Politics*, Belinda Robnett's *How Long? How Long?*, Cynthia Griggs Fleming's *Soon We'll Not Cry* for discussions on the Waveland retreat and the complaints of white female staffers. Later that evening Stokely Carmichael uttered his infamous and widely circulated statement about women's position in SNCC.

[49] Greenberg, 136–137.

[50] Interview with Gwendolyn Zouharah Simmons, Philadelphia, July 24, 1999.

[51] Contact AfroLez Productions, P.O. Box 58085, Philadelphia, PA 19102 for information about the film.

[52] Aishah Simmons, "Creating a Sacred Space of Our Own," *Just Sex: Students Rewrite the Rules on Sex, Violence, Activism, and Equality,* eds., Jodi Gold and Susan Villari (Boulder, CO: Rowman and Littlefield Publishers, 2000).

[53] Elaine Brown, *A Taste of Power: A Black Woman's Story* (New York: Pantheon Books, 1992).

[54] Ibid., 357.

[55] See the chapter "SNCC Women and the Stirrings of Feminism," in *A Circle of Trust: Remembering SNCC*, ed., Cheryl Lynn Greenberg (New Brunswick, NJ: Rutgers University Press, 1998), 143.

[56] Ibid., 146.

[57] Alfreda M. Duster, ed., *Crusade for Justice: The Autobiography of Ida B. Wells* (Chicago: University of Chicago Press, 1970), 40–41.

[58] Toni Cade, *The Black Woman* (New York: Penguin, 1970), 102–103.

[59] "The Sisters Reply," in *The Sixties Papers: Documents of a Rebellious Decade*, eds., Judith Clavir Albert and Stewart Edward Albert (New York: Praeger, 1984), 479–480. The letter was signed from Mr. Vernon, New York, by Patricia Haden, a welfare recipient; Sue Rudolph, a housewife; Joyce Hoyt, a domestic; Rita Van Lew, a welfare recipient; Catherine Hoyt, a grandmother; and Patricia Robinson, a housewife and psychotherapist. She appears in Toni Cade's *The Black Woman* (1970) as the co-

author of study papers by poor Black women in Mt. Vernon that reveal their commitment to women's rights and Black empowerment. They are critical of the Black Power movement, which they see as elitist and insensitive to the needs of poor people.

[60] Pat Robinson and Group, "Poor Black Women's Study Papers," in *The Black Woman*, 193.

[61] Kimberly Springer, "The Interstitial Politics of Black Feminist Organizations," in *Meridians: Feminism, Race, Transnationalism*, vol. 1, no. 2 (Spring 2001), 164–65.

[62] Barbara A. Sizemore, "Sexism and the Black Male," *The Black Scholar*, vol. 4, nos. 6 and 7 (March–April 1973), 3.

[63] *The Autobiography of Malcolm X* (New York: Ballantine Books, 1992), 260.

[64] Ibid.

[65] George Brietman, ed., *By Any Means Necessary* (New York: Pathfinder Press, 1970), 179.

[66] Numininas of Committee for Unified Newark, 1971, 7.

[67] Nathan Hare, "Revolution Without a Revolution: The Psychology of Sex and Race," *The Black Scholar*, vol. 9, no. 7 (April 1978), 3.

[68] Audre Lorde, "Scratching the Surface: Some Notes on Barriers to Women and Loving," *The Black Scholar*, vol. 9, no. 7 (April 1978), 31.

[69] Evelynn Hammonds, "Viewpoint: Who Speaks for Black Women?" *Sojourner: The Women's Forum*, November 1991, 7–8.

[70] Nell Irvin Painter, "Hill, Thomas, and the Use of Racial Stereotype," in *Race-ing Justice, En-gendering Power: Essays on Anita Hill, Clarence Thomas, and the Construction of Social Reality*, ed. Toni Morrison (New York: Pantheon Books, 1992), 202–203.

[71] Nellie Y. McKay, "Remembering Anita Hill and Clarence Thomas: What Really Happened When One Black Woman Spoke Out," in *Race-ing Justice*, 277–78.

[72] Audre Lorde, "A Litany for Survival," in *The Black Unicorn: Poems* (New York: W.W. Norton, 1978), 32.

4   THE BLACK CHURCH

[1] Cheryl Towsend Gilkes, *"If It Wasn't for the Women": Black Women's Experience and Womanist Culture in Church and Community* (Maryknoll, NY: Orbis Books, 1991), 125. This text is the most comprehensive and cogent black feminist analysis of the gender politics of the Black church. Similarly, Kelley Brown Douglas's *Sexuality and the Black Church: A Womanist Perspective* (Maryknoll, NY: Orbis Books, 1999), is the definitive work on the underanalyzed topic of the Black church's engagement or lack thereof with issues of sexuality. Michael Eric Dyson has provided the most scathing critiques of the Black church and the sexual behavior of ministers in particular in *Race Rules: Navigating the Color Line* (Vintage, 1996) and his controversial treatment of Martin Luther King, Jr., in *I May Not Get There with You* (New York: The Free Press, 2000). His wife, the Reverend Marcia L. Dyson, has written courageously and autobiographically about the predatory behavior of some Black ministers.

[2] Michael Eric Dyson, "When You Divide Body and Soul, Problems Multiply: The Black Church and Sex," in *Traps: African Men on Gender and Sexuality*, eds., Rudolph Byrd and Beverly Guy-Sheftall (Bloomington: Indiana University Press), 32.

3 Gilkes, 127.

4 Quoted in Gilkes, 64.

5 Niara Sudarkasa, "The Status of Women in Indigenous Africa," *Feminist Studies* 12 (1986), 91–103. See also Ifi Amadiume, *Reinventing Africa: Matriarchy, Religion, and Culture* (London: Zed Books, 1997), 110–112.

6 Gilkes, 75.

7 Gilkes, 73, 75.

8 Gilkes, 75.

9 Angela Y. Davis, *Women, Race and Class* (New York: Random House, 1981), 29.

10 Rosalyn Terborg-Penn, "Discrimination Against Afro-American Women in the Women's Movement, 1830–1920," in *The Afro-American Woman: Struggles and Images*, eds., Sharon Harley and Rosalyn Terborg-Penn (Port Washington, NY: Kennikat Press, 1978), 29–34.

11 Jarena Lee, "The Life and Religious Experience of Jarena Lee, a Coloured Lady," in *Sisters of the Spirit: Three Black Women's Autobiographies*, ed., William L. Andrews (Bloomington, IN: Indiana University Press, 1986). Originally published in 1849.

12 Gilkes, 200.

13 Important studies of the Black women's club movement include Deborah Gray White, *Too Heavy a Load: Black Women in Defense of Themselves, 1894–1994* (New York: Norton, 1999).

14 Bettye Collier-Thomas's documentary history *Daughters of Thunder: Black Women Preachers and Their Sermons, 1850–1979* (San Fransisco: Jossey-Bass Publishers, 1998) is the most comprehensive discussion of Black women preachers and debates over the ordination of women ministers within the Black church, which began in the antebellum period.

15 Gilkes, 129–130.

16 "For a Better Future," *Ebony,* August 1966, 15a.

17 Gilkes, 141.

18 See Vashti M. McKenzie, *Not Without a Struggle: Leadership Development for African-American Women in Ministry* (Cleveland: The Pilgrim Press, 1996).

19 "Mrs. Stewart's Farewell Address to Her Friends in the City of Boston," September 21, 1833. Quoted in *Black Women in Nineteenth-Century American Life: Their Words, Their Thoughts, Their Feelings*, eds., Bert James Loewenberg and Ruth Bogin (University Park, PA: Pennsylvania State University Press, 1976), 200.

20 Sojourner Truth quote appears in *Black Women in Nineteenth-Century American Life*, 236. Originally published in *History of Woman Suffrage*, eds., Elizabeth Cady Stanton et al., (Rochester, NY, 1881), vol. 1, 116.

21 See Evelyn Brooks Higginbotham's *Righteous Discontent: The Women's Movement in the Black Baptist Church, 1880–1920* (Cambridge: Harvard University Press, 1993), for a lengthy discussion of Burroughs's impact on the Black Baptist church, and Cheryl Gilkes's discussion of Burroughs in Chapter 8 of *If It Wasn't for the Women*.

22 Quoted in Gilkes, 33.

23 Higginbotham, 158.

24 Gilkes, 143.

25 Michael Dyson, "When You Divide Body and Soul Problems Multiply: The Black Church and Sex," in *Race Rules: Navigating the Color Line* (New York: Vintage, 1996), 87.

26 Dyson, 83.

[27] Edward Long, *The History of Jamaica* (London, 1774), 240.

[28] James A. Forbes, Jr., "Introduction," in *Homosexuality and Christian Faith*, ed., Walter Wink (Minneapolis: Fortress Press, 1999), 8.

[29] Marcia Dyson, "When Preachers Prey," *Essence*, 192.

[30] Ibid.

[31] Michael Eric Dyson, *I May Not Get There with You*, 157, 160.

[32] Marcia Dyson, 190, 192.

[33] Rev. Irene Moore, "A Garden of Homophobia," *The Advocate*, December 9, 1997, 9.

[34] Kelley Brown Douglas, *Sexuality and the Black Church*, 90.

[35] George Chauncey, *Gay New York* (New York: Basic Books, 1984), 254–255.

[36] Brown, 2–3.

[37] Forbes, 1999, 2.

[38] Brown, 142.

[39] James H. Cone, *For My People: Black Theology and the Black Church* (Maryknoll, NY: Orbis Books, 1984), 139; see also *Black Theology: A Documentary History*, vol. 2, 1980–1992, eds., James H. Cone and Gayraud S. Wilmore (Maryknoll, NY: Orbis Books, 1999). Mark L. Chapman's *Christianity on Trial: African-American Religous Thoughts Before and After Black Power* (Maryknoll, NY: Orbis Books, 1996) contains a sustained and useful discussion of Christianity and sexism, 135–167, which is grounded in womanist theology.

[40] Gary David Comstock, *A Whosoever Church* (Louisville: Westminister John Knox Press, 2001), 170.

[41] James S. Tinney, "Why a Black Gay Church?" in *In the Life: A Black Gay Anthology*, ed., Joseph Beam (Boston: Alyson Publications, 1986), 7.

[42] Comstock, 199. See also Renee Hill's pathbreaking essay, "Who Are We for Each Other: Sexism, Sexuality and Womanist Theology," in James H. Cone and Gayraud S. Wilmore, eds., *Black Theology: A Documentary History*, vol. 2, 1980–1992, 345–351.

[43] T. D. Jakes, *Woman Thou Art Loosed!* (Shippensburg, PA: Destiny Image Publishers, 1993), 7.

[44] Akasha Gloria Hull, *Soul Talk: The New Spirituality of African-American Women* (Rochester, VT: Inner Traditions, 2001), 151.

5   RACE SECRETS AND THE BODY POLITIC

[1] Floyd D. Weatherspoon, *African American Males and the Law: Cases and Materials* (Lanham, MD: University Press of America, 1998), 319.

[2] See James Howard Jones, *Bad Blood: The Tuskegee Syphilis Experiment* (New York: Free Press, 1993) for an analysis of this national tragedy.

[3] This "unspeakable" saga in American history was first mentioned in G. J. Barker-Benfield, *The Horrors of the Half-Known Life: Male Attitudes Toward Women and Sexuality in Nineteenth Century America* (New York: Harper & Row, 1976); for a fuller discussion, see Diana E. Axelsen, "Women as Victims of Medical Experimentation: J. Marion Sims's Surgery on Slave Women, 1845–1850," *Sage: A Scholarly Journal on Black Women*, vol. 2, no. 2 (Fall 1985), 10–13; Deborah K. MacGregor, *Sexual Surgery and the Origins of Gynecology: J. Marion Sims, His Hospital, and His Patients* (New York: Garland Publishing, 1989); Todd L. Savitt, "The Use of Blacks for Medical Experimentation and Demonstration in the Old South," *Journal of Southern History*

48, no. 3 (August 1982), 332; Evelynn Hammonds, *The Logic of Difference: A History of Race in Science and Medicine in the United States, 1850–1990,* forthcoming from the University of North Carolina Press.

⁴ Cooper's speech was delivered at the World's Congress of Representative Women and was reprinted in *Black Women in Nineteenth-Century Life,* eds., Bert James Lowenberg and Ruth Bogin (University Park: Pennsylvania State University Press, 1977), 329.

⁵ Elsa Barkley Brown, "Imaging Lynching: African American Women, Communities of Struggle, and Collective Memory," in *African American Women Speak Out on Anita Hill-Clarence Thomas,* ed., Geneva Smitherman (Detroit: Wayne State University Press, 1995), 102.

⁶ Lerone Bennett, Jr., *Before the Mayflower: A History of Black America,* 5th edition (Chicago: Johnson Publications, 1982), 352.

⁷ Walter White, *Rope and Faggot: A Biography of Judge Lynch* (New York: Knopf, 1929), 28–29.

⁸ The most useful historical texts on lynching include James Cameron, *A Time of Terror* (Baltimore: Black Classic Press, 1994); Dennis B. Downey and Raymond M. Hyser, *No Crooked Death: Coatesville, Pennsylvania and the Lynching of Zacharia Walker* (Chicago: University of Illinois Press, 1991); Howard Smead, *Blood Justice: The Lynching of Mack Charles Parker* (New York: Oxford University Press, 1986); James R. McGovern, *Anatomy of a Lynching: The Killing of Claude Neal* (Baton Rouge: Louisiana State University Press, 1982); Stewart E. Tolnay and E. M. Beck, *A Festival of Violence: An Analysis of the Lynching of African-Americans in the American South, 1882–1930* (Chicago: University of Illinois Press, 1995); Walter White, *Rope and Faggot: A Biography of Judge Lynch* (New York: Knopf, 1929); Philip Dray, *At the Hands of Persons Unknown: The Lynching of Black America* (New York: Random House, 2002).

⁹ In a riveting photograph of Black men protesters wearing placards around their necks that read, "I Am A Man," Ernest Withers documents the garbage workers' strike in Memphis, Tennessee, which brought Martin Luther King, Jr. to the city where he would be assassinated in 1968. This photograph appears on the cover of Devon W. Carbado's *Black Men on Race, Gender, and Sexuality* (1999).

¹⁰ Useful texts in this regard include Lawrence E. Gary, ed., *Black Men* (Beverly Hills: Sage, 1991); Robert Staples, *Black Masculinity: The Black Man's Role in American Society* (San Francisco: The Black Scholars Press, 1982); Jewelle Taylor Gibbs, ed. *Young, Black and Male in America: An Endangered Species* (Dover, Mass.: Auburn House, 1988); Richard G. Majors and Jacob U. Gordon, eds., *The American Black Male: His Present Status and His Future* (Chicago: Nelson-Hall Publishers, 1994); Richard Majors and J. M. Billson, *Cool Pose: Dilemmas of Black Manhood in America* (New York: Lexington, 1992); Benjamin P. Bowser, ed., *Black Male Adolescents* (Lanham, MD: University Press of America, 1994); Haki Madhubuti, *Black Men: Obsolete, Single, Dangerous?* (Chicago: Third World Press, 1990); Lawrence E. Gary, Christopher B. Booker, and Abeda Fekade, *African American Males: An Analysis of Contemporary Values, Attitudes and Perceptions of Manhood* (Washington, D.C.: Howard University School of Social Work, 1993); William Oliver, *The Violent Social World of African American Men* (New York: Lexington Books, 1994); E. Hutchinson, *The Assassination of the Black Male Image* (Los Angeles: Middle Passage Press, 1994); J. Lemelle, *Black Male Deviance* (Westport, CT: Praeger, 1995); Ernestine Jenkins and Darlene Clark Hine, eds. *A Question of Manhood: A Reader in U.S. Black Men's History and*

Masculinity, vols. 1 & 2 (Bloomington: Indiana University Press, 2000 and 2001); Donald Belton, ed. *Speak My Name: Black Men on Masculinity and the American Dream* (Boston: Beacon Press, 1995); George Edmond Smith, *More Than Sex: Reinventing the Black Male Image* (New York: Kensington Books, 2000); Christopher B. Booker, *"I Will Wear No Chain!": A Social History of African American Males* (Westport, Conn.: Praeger, 2000); Daniel Black, *Dismantling Black Manhood: An Historical and Literary Analysis of the Legacy of Slavery* (New York: Garland Publishing, 1997); Herb Boyd and Robert L. Allen, eds. *Brotherman: The Odyssey of Black Men in America* (New York: Ballantine Books, 1995); Floyd D. Witherspoon, *African American Males and the Law: Case and Materials* (Lanham, MD: University Press of America, 1998); Ellis Cose, *The Envy of the World: On Being a Black Man in America* (New York: Washington Square Press, 2002).

[11] Jewelle Taylor Gibbs, "Anger in Young Black Males: Victims or Victimizers?," in *The American Black Male*, 129.

[12] See Charles A. Murray, *Losing Ground, American Social Policy, 1950–1980* (New York: Basic Books, 1984) and William Julius Wilson, *The Truly Disadvantaged: The Inner City, the Underclass and Public Policy* (Chicago: University of Chicago Press, 1987) for thorough discussions of the deteriorating status of Black men, especially Black youth, due to unemployment, involvement with the criminal justice system, homelessness, and persistent poverty.

[13] Cazenave, 1979.

[14] Sister Souljah, *No Disrespect* (New York: Random House, 1994), 5–6.

[15] Robert Staples, "Masculinity and Race: The Dual Dilemma of Black Men," *Journal of Social Issues* 34 (1978), 169–83.

[16] Clyde W. Franklin, II, "Ain't I a Man? The Efficacy of Black Masculinities for Men's Studies in the 1990s," in *The American Black Male*, 273–275.

[17] Ibid., 275.

[18] Benjamin P. Bowser, "Black Men and AIDS: Prevention and Black Sexuality," in *The American Black Male*, 123.

[19] Ibid., 125.

[20] Richard Majors, Richard Tyler, et al., "Cool Pose: A Symbolic Mechanism for Masculine Role Enactment and Coping by Black Males," in *The American Black Male*, 249–250.

[21] Gary Lemons, "To Be Black, Male, and Feminist," in *Feminism and Men: Reconstructing Gender Relations* (New York: New York University Press, 1998), 4.

[22] *Journal of African American Men*, published in collaboration with the David Walker Research Institute at Michigan State University, is the official journal of the National Council of African American Men (NCAAM), and provides the catalyst for the development of Black Men's Studies, a much needed intervention in the field of African American Studies.

[23] Richard Majors and Janet Mancini Billson, *Cool Pose: The Dilemmas of Black Manhood in America* (New York: Lexington Books, 1992), 2.

[24] Ricky L. Jones, "Violence and the Politics of Black Male Identity in Post Modern America," *African American Men* 3.2 (Fall 1997), 80–107.

[25] Ibid., 87.

[26] See H. Nuwer, *Broken Pledges: The Deadly Rite of Hazing* (Marietta: Longstreet Press, 1990).

[27] Jones, 104.

[28] Merlin R. Langley, "The Cool Pose: An Africentric Analysis," in *The American Black Male*, 237.

[29] Noel Cazenave, "Black Men in America: The Quest for Manhood," in *Black Families*, ed. Harriet McAdoo, 1981.

[30] "Cool Pose: A Symbolic Mechanism . . . ," 254.

[31] Ibid.

[32] Ice T, *The Ice Opinion* (New York: St. Martin's Press, 1994), 3–10.

[33] Ibid, 10.

[34] LL Cool J, *I Make My Own Rules* (New York, St. Martin's Press, 1998), 4–47.

[35] See W. Grier and P. Cobbs, *Black Rage* (New York: Basic Books, 1968); Lee Rainwater, *Behind Ghetto Walls: Black Families in a Federal Slum* (Chicago: Aldine, 1970); E. Liebow, *Tally's Corner* (Boston: Little Brown, 1967); D. Glasgow, *The Black Underclass* (New York: Knopf 1981).

[36] As we examine the gendered aspects of Black masculinity, it is imperative that we imagine new modes of Black masculinity that serve as an intervention to what we earlier termed hegemonic masculinity or to what Ice T recalls as the "jungle creed." Rudolph P. Byrd has theorized such a mode of Black masculinity in *Traps: African American Men on Gender and Sexuality*. In his prologue to this anthology he co-edited with Beverly, he theorizes a new mode of Black masculinity called the Ideal of John, based upon the figure of High John the Conquerer in African American folklore. The Ideal of John is a mode of Black masculinity that is antisexist and antihomophobic, a mode of Black masculinity that functions as an antidote against emasculating forms of masculinity that plagued Ice T and LL Cool J.

[37] Especially insightful have been the following *Essence* articles: Tamala Edwards, "Men Who Sleep With Men," October 2001, 76–78, 187–88; Robin D. Stone, "Silent No More," August 2001, 122–26, 153–56; "Cover Girls," March 1992, 69ff.

[38] Kevin Chappell, "The Truth About Bisexuality in Black America," *Ebony,* August 2002, 158.

[39] Robert L. Allen, "Stopping Sexual Harassment: A Challenge for Community Education," in *Race, Gender, and Power in America: The Legacy of the Hill-Thomas Hearing*, eds., Anita Faye Hill and Emma Coleman Jordan (New York: Oxford University Press, 1995), 137.

[40] Robert Hampton, *Violence in the Family: Correlates and Consequences* (Lexington: Lexington Books, 1987).

[41] Toinette M. Eugene and James Newton Poling, *Balm in Gilead: Pastoral Care for African American Families Experiencing Abuse* (Nashville: Abingdon Press, 1988), 54. See also the works of the premier researcher on Black family violence, Robert Hampton, including his edited collection, *Violence in the Black Family: Correlates and Consequences* (Lexington, MA: Lexington Books, 1987); *Black Family Violence: Current Research & Theory* (Lexington, MA: Lexington Books, 1991); *Family Violence: Prevention and Treatment,* 1993; and *Preventing Violence in America,* 1996. Works that focus on black women and violence include Beth E. Richie, *Compelled to Crime: The Gender Entrapment of Battered Black Women* (New York: Routledge, 1996); Evelyn White, *Chain Chain Change: For Black Women in Abusive Relationships* (Seattle: Seal Press, 1985); Melba Wilson, *Crossing the Boundary: Black Women Survive Incest* (Seattle: Seal Press, 1994); Victoria King, *Manhandled Black Females* (Nashville: Winston-Derek Publishers, 1992); Traci C. West, *Wounds of the Spirit: Black Women, Violence, and Resistance Ethics* (New York: New York University Press, 1999).

42 Byllye Y. Avery, "Breathing Life into Ourselves: The Evolution of the Black Women's Health Project," in *The Black Women's Health Book: Speaking for Ourselves* (Seattle: Seal Press), 8.

43 The devastating impact of racism on Black families, as well as their strengths, has been documented with extraordinary precision by solid social science researchers, including Robert Bernard Hill, *The Strengths of Black Families* (New York: Emerson Hall, 1972); Robert Staples, ed., *The Black Family* (Belmont, CA: Wadsworth, 1991), and *The Black Family: Essays and Studies* (Belmont, CA: Wadsworth, 1986); Andrew Billingsley, *Black Families in White America* (Englewood Cliffs, NJ: Emerson Hall, 1968), *Black Families and the Struggle for Survival* (New York: Friendship Press, 1974), and *Climbing Jacob's Ladder: The Enduring Legacy of African American Families* (New York: Simon & Schuster, 1994); Harriette Pipes McAdoo, *Black Families* (Beverly Hills, CA: Sage, 1996).

44 An even more taboo subject is the sexual abuse of Black male children and women who abuse children. See William C. Holmes, "Sexual Abuse of Boys: Definition, Prevalence, Correlates, Sequelae, and Management," *Journal of the American Medical Association* 21 (December 1998), 1855–62; R. Mathews, J. K. Matthews, and K. Speltz, *Female Sexual Offencers: An Exploratory Study* (Vermont: Safer Society Press, 1989), for a discussion that also includes three black women.

45 Melba Wilson, *Crossing the Boundary: Black Women Survive Incest* (Seattle: Seal Press, 1994), 4–5. Originally published in London by Virago Press, Ltd, in 1993.

46 William C. Holmes, MD, "Sexual Abuse of Boys: Definition, Prevalence, Correlates, Sequelae, and Management," *The Journal of the American Medical Association*, vol. 280, no. 21 (December 2, 1998), 1855–1862.

47 See Veronica B. Abney and Ronnie Priest, "African Americans and Sexual Abuse," in *Sexual Abuse in Nine North American Cultures: Treatment and Preventions*, ed., Lisa Aronson Fontes (Thousand Oaks, CA: Sage Publications, 1995), 11–30; L. H. and R. L. Pierce, "Race as a Factor in the Sexual Abuse of Children," *Social Work Research and Abstracts* 20 (1984), 9–14; G. E. Wyatt and G. J. Powell, eds., *Lasting Effects of Child Sexual Abuse* (Newbury Park, CA: Sage, 1988), 119–134; G. E. Wyatt, "The Sexual Abuse of Afro-American and White-American Women in Childhood," *Child Abuse and Neglect* 9 (1985), 507–519; G. E. Wyatt, "Sexual Abuse of Ethnic Minority Children: Identifying Dimensions of Victimization," *Professional Psychology: Research and Practice,* vol. 2, no. 1 (1990), 338–343.

48 Abney and Priest, 26.

49 Devon W. Carbado, ed., *Black Men on Race, Gender and Sexuality* (New York: New York University Press, 1999), 1.

50 Devon W. Carbado, "The Construction of O. J. Simpson as a Racial Victim," in *Black Men,* 171.

51 See Michael Awkward " 'You're Turning Me On': The Boxer, the Beauty Queen, and the Rituals of Gender," and Charles R. Lawrence III, "The Message of the Verdict: A Three-Act Morality Play Starring Clarence Thomas, Willie Smith, and Mike Tyson," in *Black Men on Race, Gender and Sexuality* for a discussion of the Tyson saga.

52 Jill Nelson, *Straight, No Chaser,* 157–58.

53 A brilliant analysis of this broadbased coalition can be found in White's essay "Talking Black, Talking Feminist: Gendered Micromobilization Processes in a Collective Protest Against Rape," in *Still Lifting, Still Climbing: African American Women's Contemporary Activism,* ed., Kimberly Springer (New York: New York University Press, 1999), 189–218. The appendix includes the copy for both ads.

⁵⁴ See Barbara Ransby's "A Righteous Rage and a Grassroots Mobilization," in *African American Women Speak Out on Anita Hill-Clarence Thomas*, ed. Geneva Smitherman (Detroit: Wayne University Press, 1995), 45–52, for further discussion.

⁵⁵ Miles Davis (with Quincy Troupe), *Miles: The Autobiography* (New York: Simon & Schuster, 1989).

⁵⁶ *Soul on Ice* (New York: Dell, 1968), 14.

⁵⁷ Wahneema Lubiano, "Black Nationalism and Black Common Sense," in *The House That Race Built*, ed. Wahneema Lubiano (New York: Vintage Books, 1998), 232.

⁵⁸ E. M. Beck and Stewart E. Tolnay, "When Race Didn't Matter: Black and White Mob Violence Against Their Own Color," in *Under Sentence of Death: Lynching in the South*, ed., W. Fitzhugh Brundage (Chapel Hill: University of North Carolina Press, 1997), 132–154.

⁵⁹ See their book, *A Festival of Violence: An Analysis of Southern Lynchings, 1882–1930* (1995).

⁶⁰ "When Race Didn't Matter," 144.

⁶¹ William E. B. Du Bois, "The Damnation of Women," reprinted in *Traps: African American Men on Gender and Sexuality*, eds., Rudolph P. Byrd and Beverly Guy-Sheftall (Bloomington: Indiana University Press), 63. Originally published in 1920 in *Darkwater: Voices from the Veil*. This collection of pro-feminist writings by Black men illustrates their commitments to the eradication of both racism and sexism in their vision of a just world. See also the November/December 2000 special issue of *Crisis*, 1–16, which includes a round-table discussion on Du Bois's "The Damnation of Women," in which Cole and Guy-Sheftall participated.

6 BLACK, LESBIAN, AND GAY: SPEAKING THE UNSPEAKABLE

¹ Cornel West, *Race Matters* (Boston: Beacon Press, 1993), 83.

² Paula Giddings, "The Last Taboo," in *Race-ing Justice, En-gendering Power*, 442. See also Delroy Constantine-Simms, ed., *The Greatest Taboo: Homosexuality in Black Communities* (Los Angeles: Alyson Books, 2000) for the most comprehensive book-length treatment of Black homosexuality within the United States and beyond, and Keith Boykin's chapter on "Black Homophobia," which includes antilesbianism in his book *One More River to Cross: Black and Gay in America* (New York: Anchor Books, 1996).

³ At present there is no history of African American gays and lesbians, though Barbara Smith is completing a long overdue history that will chronicle "the last four hundred years of homosexual, homoemotional, and homosocial experiences in African American life," and explore what the reality of Black homosexuality has meant to Black people of various sexual orientations. This is a challenging project for many reasons, according to Smith, including the fact that many contemporary Blacks are unwilling to acknowledge their sexual orientation, though they are well known in gay and lesbian circles. See her essay, "African American Lesbian and Gay History: An Exploration" in *The Truth That Never Hurts* (New Brunswick, NJ: Rutgers University Press, 1998), 82–92. What Black lesbian and gay history there is occurs largely in works in which white lesbian and gay history is the major focus, such as Jonathan Ned Katz's *Gay/Lesbian Almanac* (New York: Harper Colophon, 1983) and *Gay American His-*

tory: Lesbians and Gay Men in the U.S.A. (New York: Thomas Y. Crowell, 1976); Elizabeth Kennedy and Madeline Davis, *Boots of Leather, Slippers of Gold* (New York: Routledge, 1993); George Chauncey, *Gay New York: Gender, Urban Culture, and the Making of the Gay Male World, 1890–1940* (New York: Basic Books, 1994); Lillian Faderman, *Odd Girls and Twilight Lovers: A History of Lesbian Life in Twentieth-Century America* (New York: Penguin, 1991), and *To Believe in Women: What Lesbians Have Done for America, a History* (Boston: Houghton Mifflin, 1999). An exception would be the introductory chapters in Devon W. Carbado et al, eds., *Black Like Us: A Century of Lesbian, Gay and Bisexual African American Fiction*, which cover three historical periods beginning with the Harlem Renaissance and ending with the contemporary period, 1980–2000.

[4] Rhonda W. Williams, "Living at the Crossroads: Explorations in Race, Nationality, Sexuality, and Gender," in *The House That Race Built*, ed., Wahneema Lubiano (New York: Vintage Books, 1998), 144.

[5] Interview with the Rev. Msgr. Raymond G. East in Gary David Comstock, *A Whosoever Church* (Louisville: Westminster John Knox Press, 2001), 94–95.

[6] Molefi Kete Asante, "On Cultural Nationalism and Criticism," in *Malcolm X as Cultural Hero and Other Afrocentric Essays* (Trenton, NJ: Africa World Press, 1993), 42.

[7] Wahneema Lubiano, "Black Nationalism and Black Common Sense: Policing Ourselves and Others," in *The House That Race Built*, 232. This essay is a cogent analysis of Black nationalism and the ways in which it both rejects and mimics Euro-American cultural traditions, especially patriarchal, familial constructs. Insightful critiques of the masculinist, patriarchal, and heterosexist ideologies of Black nationalist discourse can also be found in Robert L. Allen, *Black Awakening in Capitalist America* (New York: Doubleday, 1969), which is perhaps the first critique of the sexist politics of contemporary Black nationalism; Madhu Duby, " 'I Am a New Man': Black Nationalism and the Black Aesthetic," in *Black Women Novelists and the Nationalist Aesthetic* (Bloomington: Indiana University Press, 1994); Deborah McDowell, "Reading Family Matters," in *Changing Our Own Words*, ed. Cheryl Wall (New Brunswick, NJ: Rutgers University Press, 1989); E. Frances White, "Africa on My Mind: Gender, Counter Discourse, and African American Nationalism," in *Dark Continent of Our Bodies: Black Feminism and the Politics of Respectability* (Philadelphia: Temple University Press, 2001); Valerie Smith, "Gender and Afro-Americanism Literary Theory and Criticism," in *Speaking of Gender*, ed. Elaine Showalter (New York: Routledge, 1989); Patricia Hill Collins, "When Fighting Words Are Not Enough: The Gendered Content of Afrocentrism," in *Fighting Words: Black Women and the Search for Justice* (Minneapolis: University of Minnesota Press, 1998), which includes an informative discussion of the cultural nationalism that emerged during the Black Power movement of the sixties.

[8] "Christian Love and Heterosexism," *The Cornel West Reader* (New York: Basic Civitas Books, 1999), 404.

[9] James S. Tinney, "Struggles of a Black Pentecostal," *Black Men/White Men: Afro-American Gay Life & Culture,* ed., Michael J. Smith (San Francisco: Gay Sunshine Press, 1983), 170.

[10] Keith Boykin, *One More River to Cross: Black and Gay in America* (New York: Anchor Books, 1996), 8–9.

[11] Joseph Beam, ed., *In the Life: A Black Gay Anthology* (Boston: Alyson Publications, 1986), 16.

[12] Elias Farajaje-Jones, "Breaking the Silence: Toward an In-the-Life-Theology," in *Black Theology*, vol. 2, 1980–1992, eds., James H. Cone and Gayraud S. Wilmore (Maryknoll, NY: Orbis Books, 1999), 153.

[13] *The Truth That Never Hurts*, 89.

[14] Rhonda W. Williams, 145.

[15] Eldridge Cleaver, *Soul on Ice* (New York: Random House, 1992 [1968]), 13.

[16] Frances Cress Welsing, *The Isis Papers: The Keys to the Colors* (Chicago: Third World Press, 1991), 81, 275–277.

[17] Molefi Kete Asante, *Afrocentricity: The Theory of Social Change* (Buffalo: Amulefi Publishing Company, 1980), 4–5.

[18] Huey P. Newton, "A Letter from Huey to the Revolutionary Brothers and Sisters About the Women's Liberation and Gay Liberation Movements," reprinted in *Traps: African American Men on Gender and Sexuality*, eds. Rudolph P. Byrd and Beverly Guy-Sheftall (Bloomington: Indiana University Press, 2001), 281–83. Originally published in *Gay Flames Pamphlet*, no. 7, 1970.

[19] Ron Simmons, "Some Thoughts on the Challenges Facing Black Gay Intellectuals," in *Brother to Brother*, ed., Essex Hemphill (Boston: Alyson Publications, 1991), describes the videotape of Farrakhan's speech "The Time and What Must Be Done," which was released by Final Call, Inc., Chicago, Illinois, 222–23. This essay is a hard-hitting critique of the homophobic writings of numerous Black writers, scholars, and leaders. See also Dwight A. McBride's essay, "Can the Queen Speak: Racial Essentialism, Sexuality, and the Problem of Authority," in *The Greatest Taboo*, 24–43, for a similar critique of a range of Black thinkers' views on what he calls "Black lesbigay" experience, including bell hooks, Dr. Frances Cress Welsing, Essex Hemphill, and James Baldwin. His detailed analysis of Welsing's denigrating writings on homosexuality is especially enlightening. See also Irene Monroe, "Louis Farrakhan's Ministry of Misogyny and Homophobia," in *The Farrakhan Factor: African American Writers on Leadership, Nationhood, and Minister Louis Farrakhan*, ed. Amy Alexander (New York: Grove Press, 1999), 275–298.

[20] Quoted in Ron Simmons, 214.

[21] Adam Clayton Powell, Sr., *Against the Tide: An Autobiography* (Salem, NH: Ayer Company Publishers, 1938), 209–220. See a discussion of Adam Clayton Powell Sr.'s crusade against homosexuals in Harlem during the thirties in George Chauncey's *Gay New York* (1994), 254–56, and the cultural context in which it took place.

[22] *The Greatest Taboo: Homosexuality in Black Communities*, 124.

[23] Marriage and kinship have been the focus of gender-based scholarship about African societies. Though there have been very few studies of sexual practices and ideologies in sub-Saharan Africa, even among Western ethnographers, it is now possible to explore the subject of same-sex behaviors, desires, and relationships in African cultures. See Stephen O. Murray and Will Roscoe, eds., *Boy-Wives and Female Husbands: Studies of African Homosexualities* (New York: St. Martin's Press, 1998), the most comprehensive treatment of the controversial topic; Evelyn Blackwood and Saskia E. Wieringa, eds., *Female Desires: Same-Sex Relations and Transgender Practices Across Cultures* (New York: Columbia University Press, 1999); Mark Gevisser and Edwin

Cameron, eds., *Defiant Desire: Gay and Lesbian Lives in South Africa* (New York: Routledge, 1995); Wayne Dynes and S. Donaldson, *Ethnographic Studies of Homosexuality* (New York: Garland, 1992); William Eskridge, Jr., "A History of Same-Sex Marriage," *Virginia Law Review* 79, no. 7 (October 1993), 1419–1513; Wayne Dynes, "Homosexuality in Sub-Saharan Africa: An Unnecessary Question," *Gay Books Bulletin* 9 (1983), 20–21; Arlene Swidler, ed. *Homosexuality and World Religions* (Harrisburg, PA: Trinity Press, International, 1993); Evelyn Blackwood, ed., *The Many Faces of Homosexuality* (New York: Harrington Park Press, 1986); Thomas O. Beidelman, *The Cool Knife: Imagery of Gender, Sexuality and Moral Education in Kaguru Initiation Ritual* (Washington, D.C.: Smithsonian Institution Press, 1997); Rudi C. Bleys, *The Geography of Perversion: Male-to-Male Sexual Behavior Outside the West and the Ethnographic Imagination, 1750–1918* (New York: New York University Press, 1995); Eugene Patton, "Africa: Heart of Lavender," in *The Greatest Taboo: Homosexuality in Black Communities*, ed., Delroy Constantine-Simms (Los Angeles: Alyson Books, 2001), 124–31; Terence J. Deakin, "Evidence for Homosexuality in Ancient Egypt," *International Journal of Greek Love* 1 (19), 31–38; Esther Newton, "Of Yams, Grinders, and Gays," *Outlook: National Lesbian and Gay Quarterly* 1 (Summer 1988), 28–37; Cary Alan Johnson, "Inside Gay Africa," *Black/Out: The Magazine of the National Coalition of Black Lesbians and Gays* 1, no. 2 (Fall 1986), 18–21.

[24] Important studies on the anthropology of sexuality include Gilbert Herdt's pioneering work on ritualized homosexuality in Melanesia, *Ritualized Homosexuality in Melanesia* (Berkeley: University of California Press, 1984); *Guardians of the Flutes: Idioms of Masculinity,* (New York: McGraw-Hill, 1981) and *The Sambia: Ritual and Gender in New Guinea* (New York: Holt, Rinehart and Winston, 1987); Walter L. Williams's work on the berdache tradition among North American Indians, *The Spirit and the Flesh: Sexual Diversity in American Indian Culture* (Boston: Beacon Press, 1986).

[25] William N. Eskridge, Jr., "A History of Same Sex Marriage," *Virginia Law Review* 79 (1993), 1419–1513.

[26] Considerable controversy with widely divergent perspectives continues about the nature of gender constructs in Africa prior to the arrival of Europeans. For discussions of gender in the precolonial African context, see Cheikh Anta Diop, *The Cultural Unity of Black Africa: The Domains of Patriarchy and Matriarchy in Classical Antiquity* (Chicago: Third World Press, 1990); Onaiwu W. Ogbomo, *When Men and Women Mattered: A History of Gender Relations Among the Owan of Nigeria* (Rochester, NY: University of Rochester Press, 1997); Oyeronke Oyewumi, *The Invention of Women: Making an African Sense of Western Gender Discourses* (Minneapolis: University of Minnesota Press, 1997); Ifi Amadiume, *Male Daughters, Female Husbands: Gender and Sex in an African Society* (London: Zed Books, 1987); Claire C. Robertson and M. A. Klein, eds., *Women and Slavery in Africa* (Madison: University of Wisconsin Press, 1983).

[27] Greenberg, 12.

[28] Leila J. Rupp, 24–25.

[29] Greenberg, 26–65. See the following texts for discussions of same-sex unions in the Americas, especially within Native American cultures prior to contact with Europeans. This tradition has been referred to as *berdache* or more recently the cross-gender

role, third sex, or two-spirit, which are men or women who deviated from their traditional gender roles and are permitted to marry persons of the same sex. Walter L. Williams, *The Spirit and the Flesh: Sexual Diversity in American Indian Culture* (Boston: Beacon Press, 1986); Sue Ellen Jacobs, Wesley Thomas, and Sabine Lang, eds., *Two-Spirit People: Native American Gender Identity, Sexuality, and Spirituality* (Urbana: University of Illinois Press, 1997); Sabine Lang, *Men As Women, Women As Men: Changing Gender in Native American Cultures* (Austin: University of Texas Press, 1998); Will Roscoe, *Changing Ones: Third and Fourth Genders in Native North America* (New York: St. Martin's, 1998); Lester Brown, ed., *Two-Spirit People: American Indian Lesbian Women and Gay Men* (New York: Harrington Park Press, 1997); Will Roscoe, *The Zuni Man-Woman* (Albuquerque: University of New Mexico Press, 1991); Frederick Manfred, *The Manly-Hearted Woman* (Lincoln: University of Nebraska Press, 1975).

[30] The existence of "female husbands" came to the attention of Western anthropologists such as Melville Herskovits and E. E. Evans-Pritchard in the 1930s.

[31] Niara Sudarkasa, "The Status of Women in Indigenous African Societies," in *Women in Africa and the African Diaspora*, eds. Rosalyn Terborg-Penn, Sharon Harley, and Andrea Benton Rushing (Washington, D.C.: Howard University Press, 1987), xi, 32.

[32] Ifi Amadiume, *Male Daughters, Female Husbands: Gender and Sex in an African Society* (London: Zed Books, 1987), 72.

[33] Gloria Wekker, "Matiism and Black Lesbianism: Two Idealtypical Expressions of Female Homosexuality in Black Communities of the Diaspora," in *The Greatest Taboo: Homosexuality in Black Communities*, ed., Delroy Constantine Simms (Los Angeles: Alyson Books, 2001), 149. Another version of this essay, "One Finger Does Not Drink Okra Soup: Afro-Surinamese Women and Critical Agency," appears in *Feminist Geneaologies, Colonial Legacies, Democratic Futures*, eds., M. Jacqui Alexander and Chandra Talpade Mohanty (New York: Routledge, 1997), 330–352.

[34] K. Limakatso Kendall, ed., *Singing Away the Hunger: The Autobiography of an African Woman* (Bloomington: Indiana University Press, 1997). See also Kendall, " 'When a Woman Loves a Woman' in Lesotho: Love, Sex, and the (Western) Construction of Homophobia," *Boy-Wives and Female Husbands*, 224–241.

[35] *Singing Away the Hunger,* 69. The work of anthropologist Judith Gay analyzes "mummy-baby" relationships in Lesotho, which are romantic and sexual friendships among older and younger females. See " 'Mummies and Babies' and Friends and Lovers in Lesotho," in *The Many Faces of Homosexuality: Anthropological Approaches to Homosexual Behavior*, ed., Evelyn Blackwood (New York: Harrington Park Press, 1986), 97–116; this text also includes articles on sexuality in the Afro-Brazilian context.

[36] See E. E. Evans-Pritchard, "Sexual Inversion Among the Azande," *American Anthropologist* 72 (1970), 1428–34. Gilbert Herdt's chapter on "Same-Gender Relations in Nonwestern Cultures," in his book *Same Sex, Different Cultures* (1997) is very useful. See Stephen O. Murray and Will Roscoe's discussion of European attitudes toward African sexuality in their anthology, *Boy-Wives and Female Husbands: Studies of African Homosexualities* (1998), xi–xxii. David Greenberg's *The Construction of Homosexuality* indicates that a range of mostly European scholars going back to the

nineteenth century discuss what he calls "transgenderal homosexuality" among the following sub-Saharan societies: the pastoral Nandi (Kenya); the Dinka and Nuer (Sudan); the Konso and Amhara (Ethiopia); the Ottoro (Nubia); the Fanti (Ghana); the Ovimbundo (Angola); the Thonga (Rhodesia); the Tanala and Bara (Madagascar); the Wolof (Senegal); and the Lango, Iteso, Gisu and Sebei (Uganda), 61.

[37] *Boy-Wives and Female Husbands*, xi.

[38] What substantive historical scholarship there is on homosexuality/bisexuality in African American communities focuses on the vibrant subculture of gay and lesbian life in Harlem during the twenties and thirties, including the lives and work of the Harlem Renaissance's gay writers, not all of whom would have used this label, such as Langston Hughes, Countee Cullen, Claude McKay, Richard Bruce Nugent (whose short story "Smoke, Lilies and Jade," which appeared in *Fire!!* November 1926, is supposedly the first Black writing to deal with homosexual desire), Wallace Thurman, Alain Locke, and Alice Dunbar-Nelson, as well as entertainers such as Mabel Hampton, Alberta Hunter, Gladys Bentley, and Bessie Smith. The earliest novels by Black writers with homosexual themes include Wallace Thurman, *The Blacker the Berry* (1929) and *Infants of the Spring* (1932); twenty years would pass before the publication of Owen Dodson's *Boy at the Window* (1951) followed by James Baldwin's *Giovanni's Room* (1956) and Ann Allen Shockley's *Loving Her* (1974), the first novel with a black lesbian protagonist.

For sources about gay Harlem, see George Chauncey's *Gay New York* (1994); Eric Garber, "A Spectacle in Color: The Lesbian and Gay Subculture of Jazz Age Harlem," in *Hidden from History: Reclaiming the Gay and Lesbian Past*, eds. Martin Duberman, Martha Vicinus, and George Chauncey (New York: New American Library, 1989), 318–33; Gloria T. Hull, *Color, Sex, and Poetry: Three Women Writers of the Harlem Renaissance* (Bloomington: Indiana University Press, 1987); Leila J. Rupp, *A Desired Past: A Short History of Same Sex Love in America* (Chicago: University of Chicago Press, 1999); David Levering Lewis, *When Harlem Was in Vogue* (New York: Knopf, 1981); Joseph Beam, ed. *In the Life: A Black Gay Anthology* (Boston: Alyson Publications, 1986); Eric Garber, "Gladys Bentley: The Bulldagger Who Sang the Blues," *Out/look* (Spring 1988), 52–61; Angela Y. Davis, *Blues Legacies and Black Feminism: Gertrude "Ma" Rainey, Bessie Smith, and Billie Holiday* (New York: Pantheon Books, 1998); Hazel Carby, " 'It Jus Be's Dat Way Sometime': The Sexual Politics of Black Women's Blues," *Radical America* (1986), 9–22; the chapter on "Iconic Signifiers of the Gay Harlem Renaissance" in *The Greatest Taboo*; Section I, 1900–1950: The Harlem Renaissance, in *Black Like Us: A Century of Lesbian, Gay and Bisexual African American Fiction*, eds., Devon W. Carbado, Dwight A. McBride, and Donald Weise (San Francisco: Cleis Press Inc., 2002).

Sources relating to the contemporary period include John L. Peterson, "Black Men and Their Same-Sex Desires and Behaviors," in *Gay Culture in America: Essays from the Field*, ed., Gilbert Herdt (Boston: Beacon Press, 1992), 147–162; Larry Icard, "Black Gay Men and Conflicting Social Identities: Sexual Orientation versus Racial Identity," *Journal of Social Work and Human Sexuality* 4 (1985–1986), 83–93; Robert Staples, "Homosexuality and the Black Male," in *The Material Queer: A LesBiGay Cultural Studies Reader*, ed., Donald Morton (Boulder, Co: Westview Press, 1996), 229–35; Alan P. Bell and Martin S. Weinberg, *Homosexualities: A Study of Diversity among*

Men and Women (New York: Simon & Schuster, 1978); Emmanuel S. Nelson, ed., *Critical Essays: Gay and Lesbian Writers of Color* (New York: Harrington Park Press, 1993); Keith Boykin, *One More River to Cross: Black and Gay in America*, 1996; Gregory M. Herek and John P. Capitanio, "Black Heterosexuals' Attitudes Toward Lesbians and Gay Men in the United States," *The Journal of Sex Research,* vol. 32, no. 2 (1995), 95–105; Alycee J. Lane, "Black Bodies/Gay Bodies: The Politics of Race in the Gay/Military Battle," *Callaloo,* vol. 17, no. 4 (1994), 1074–1088; Judith Halberstam, "Mackdaddy, Superfly, Rapper: Gender, Race, and Masculinity in the Drag King Scene," *Social Text,* vol. 15, nos. 3 & 4 (Fall/Winter 1997), 24–28; Rochelle Thorpe, " 'A House Where Queers Go': African-American Lesbian Nightlife in Detroit, 1940–1975," in *Inventing Lesbian Cultures in America,* ed., Ellen Lewin (Boston: Beacon Press, 1996).

[39] See Charles I. Nero, "Toward a Black Gay Aesthetic: Signifying in Contemporary Black Gay Literature," in *Brother to Brother,* 229–52, for a discussion of homosexual desire among slave men in the Americas, particularly Cuban Esteban Montejo's *The Autobiography of a Runaway Slave,* ed. Miguel Barnet (New York: Random House, 1968); A. Leon Higginbotham, Jr.,'s *In the Matter of Color: Race and the American Legal Process* (New York: Oxford University Press, 1978), which uncovers laws forbidding homosexual practices among Black men during the colonial period; and Jonathan Katz's *Gay/Lesbian Almanac: A New Documentary* (New York: Harper and Row, 1983) and *Gay American History* (New York: Avon Books, 1976), which document two legal cases involving sexual crimes committed by Black slave men.

[40] Jonathan Katz, *Gay American History,* 22–23. Kendall Thomas also discusses the incident in " 'Ain't Nothin' Like the Real Thing': Black Masculinity, Gay Sexuality, and the Jargon of Authenticity," in *The House That Race Built,* ed. Wahneema Lubiano, 125–6.

[41] Esteban Montejo, 41.

[42] Charles I. Nero, 234.

[43] E. Frances White, *Dark Continent of Our Bodies: Black Feminism and the Politics of Respectability* (Philadelphia: Temple University Press, 2001), 163.

[44] See White's footnote 2 at the end of her chapter, "The Evidence of Things Not Seen: The Alchemy of Race and Sexuality," 183, in which she alludes to McFeely's biography, *Frederick Douglass.*

[45] For an analysis of the letters that were written between 1854 and 1868, see Karen V. Hansen, " 'No Kisses Is Like Youres': An Erotic Friendship Between Two African-American Women During the Mid-Nineteenth Century," in *Lesbian Subjects: A Feminist Studies Reader,* ed. Martha Vicinus (Bloomington: Indiana University Press, 1996), 178–207, and Farah Jasmine Griffin's edited collection of the letters, *Beloved Sisters and Loving Friends* (New York: Alfred Knopf, 1999).

[46] *Beloved Sisters and Loving Friends,* 21.

[47] Hansen, 189.

[48] "Christian Love and Heterosexism," *The Cornel West Reader* (New York: Basic Civitas Books, 1999), 403.

[49] Ron Simmons, 215–21. While the literature on Black gay men is not exhaustive, a number of sources capture the realities of their lives. See Cary Alan Johnson, Colin Robinson, and Terence Taylor, eds., *Other Countries: Black Gay Voices,* vol. 1 (New

York: Other Countries, 1988); Larry D. Icard, "Assessing the Psychosocial Well-Being of African American Gays: A Multidimensional Perspective," in *Men of Color: A Context for Service to Homosexually Active Men*, ed. John F. Longres (New York: Harrington Park Press, 1996), 25–47; Joseph Beam, ed., *In the Life: A Black Gay Anthology* (1989); Essex Hemphill, *Brother to Brother* (Boston: Alyson Publications, 1991); Bruce Morrow and Charles H. Rowell, eds., *Shade: An Anthology of Fiction by Gay Men of African Descent* (New York: Avon Books, 1996); William G. Hawkeswood, *One of the Children: Gay Black Men in Harlem* (Berkeley: University of California Press, 1996); Michael J. Smith, ed. *Black Men/White Men: Afro-American Gay Life and Culture* (San Francisco: Gay Sunshine Press, 1999); B. Michael Hunter, ed., *Sojourner: Black Gay Voices in the Age of AIDS* (New York: Other Countries, 1988); Robert F. Reid-Parr, *Black Gay Man: Essays* (New York: New York University Press, 2001); Keith Boykin, *One More River to Cross: Black and Gay in America* (New York: Anchor Books, 1996); Charles Michael Smith, ed., *Fighting Words: Personal Essays by Black Gay Men* (New York: Avon Books, 1999).

[50] Alvin Ailey, *Revelations* (New York: Carol Publishing Company, 1995), 19.

[51] James S. Tinney, "Struggles of a Black Pentecostal," *Black Men/White Men: Afro-American Gay Life & Culture,* 167–168.

[52] Essex Hemphill, Introduction, *Brother to Brother*, ed. Essex Hemphill (Boston: Alyson Publications, 1991), xv. See his *Ceremonies: Prose and Poetry* (New York: Penguin Books, 1992), especially the title chapter, "Ceremonies," for a detailed discussion of his earliest sexual encounter, which occurred with an older white male store owner, George, in the neighborhood of a Washington, D.C. ghetto. Hemphill also reveals that George had "initiated most of the boys I knew, and some of their older brothers, one by one, into the pleasures of homo sex" (96). See Hemphill's ("The Other Invisible Man"), Samuel R. Delany's (Coming/Out"), Rodney Christopher ("Explaining It to Dad") and Carl Phillips's ("Sea Level")—"coming out" narratives in *Boys Like Us: Gay Writers Tell Their Coming Out Stories*, ed. Patrick Merla (New York: Avon Books, 1996).

[53] Samuel R. Delany, *Short Views: Queer Thoughts and the Politics of the Paraliterary* (Hanover: Wesleyan University Press, 1999), 72, 74.

[54] William G. Hawkeswood, *One of the Children*, 129.

[55] Ron Vernon, "Growing Up in Chicago Black and Gay," *Black Men/White Men,* 33.

[56] James Baldwin, "Here Be Dragons," *The Price of the Ticket: Collected Fiction, 1948–1985* (New York: St. Martin's Press, 1985), 681.

[57] See Tamala Edwards, "Men Who Sleep With Men," *Essence*, October 2001, 76–78 ff.

[58] "Struggles of a Black Pentacostal," 170.

[59] Essex Hemphill, *Ceremonies: Prose and Poetry* (New York: Penguin Books, 1992), 63–64.

[60] Patricia Elam Ruff, "Cover Girls," *Essence,* March 1992, 69 ff.

[61] "Coming Out," *Essence*, May 1990, 82–84. See also Linda Villarosa's "Revelations," in *Afrekete: An Anthology of Black Lesbian Writing*, eds. Catherine E. McKinley and L. Joyce DeLaney (New York: Doubleday, 1995), 215–227, for a discussion of their confessional essay and what she experienced among Black people during her

speaking engagements following the publication of her coming-out story. Other anthologies and autobiographies that explore Black lesbian experience include Barbara Smith, ed., *Homegirls: A Black Feminist Anthology* (New York: Kitchen Table Women of Color Press, 1983); Makeda Silvera, ed., *Piece of My Heart: A Lesbian of Color Anthology* (Toronto: Sister Vision Press, 1991); Audre Lorde, *Zami: A New Spelling of My Name* (Freedom, CA: The Crossing Press, 1982); Anita Cornwell, *Black Lesbian in White America* (Tallahassee: Naiad Press, 1983); Hilda Hidalgo, ed., *Lesbians of Color: Social and Human Services* (New York: Haworth Press, 1995); Shawn Stewart Ruff, ed., *Go the Way Your Blood Beats: An Anthology of Lesbian and Gay Fiction by African-American Writers* (New York: Henry Holt & Co., 1996); *Black Like Us: A Century of Lesbian, Gay and Bisexual African American Fiction*, eds., Devon W. Carbado, Dwight A. McBride, and Donald Weise (San Francisco: Cleis Press, 2002).

[62] Joseph Beam, ed., *In the Life*, 17.

[63] David Leeming, *Amazing Grace: A Life of Beauford Delaney* (New York: Oxford University Press, 1998), 5.

[64] See Lillian Faderman, *To Believe in Women*, 325, which alludes to Cable's unpublished manuscript, "Biology as Social Identity: How the Medical Discourse on Sexuality During the Early Twentieth Century Influenced Pauli Murray's Conception of Her Identity in American Society," Schlesinger Library, Radcliffe College. See also Heather Phillips, "I Feel in My Bones That You Are Making History: The Life and Leadership of Pauli Murray," Senior Honors Thesis, Radcliffe College, 1977.

[65] Anita Cornwall, *Black Lesbian in White America* (Minneapolis: Naiad Press, 1983), 8–9.

[66] Barbara Smith, *The Truth That Never Hurts: Writings on Race, Gender and Freedom*, 162–63.

[67] Ice T, *The Ice Opinion* (New York: St. Martin's Press, 1994), 10.

[68] We are referring to the founding of a number of Black gay and lesbian organizations since the 1970s and the convening of various national conferences since 1987, such as Salsa Soul Sisters, which was founded in 1974 and was the oldest Black lesbian organization in the United States; it published the first periodical for lesbians of color, *Third World Women's Gay-zette* (1976), and eventually changed its name to African Ancestral Lesbians United for Societal Change; the National Coalition of Black Gays (NCBG, 1978), which was renamed the National Coalition of Black Lesbians and Gays (1985), and hosted the first National Third World Lesbian and Gay Conference in 1979 during the first March on Washington for Lesbian and Gays; Gay Men of African Descent, and Black Gay Men United; the proliferation of Black gay and lesbian publications such as *Blacklight: A Journal of Writings and Graphics by Black Gay Men*, BLK, B&G, *Black/Out: The Magazine of the National Coalition of Black Lesbians and Gays*, *Blackheart*, *Ache*, *Moja: Black and Gay*, *Rafiki: The Journal of the Association of Black Gays* (some of which are defunct), as well as the publication of numerous articles and books by and about Black lesbians and gays; the founding of Black gay churches, such as the Harlem Metropolitan Community Church and the Washington, D.C.–based Faith Temple, and the emergence of queer Black theology. A Black gay literary renaissance began with the publication of Adrian Stanford's poetry collection, *Black and Queer* (Boston: Good Gay Poets, 1977) and continued with the publication of several groundbreaking anthologies, *In the Life* (1986) and *Brother to Brother*,

whose introduction by Essex Hemphill chronicles this literary outpouring; self-published volumes of poetry; films, such as Marlon Rigg's *Tongues Untied*; and novels by Samuel Delany, Randall Kenan, Melvin Dixon, and Larry Duplechan. See Rodney Christopher's "Becoming a Movement" and Cary Alan Johnson's "The Emergence of an African Gay and Lesbian Movement" (which includes a global perspective) for retrospectives on the emergence of a Black gay liberation movement in the United States and Africa.

69 Barbara Smith in her essay "Blacks and Gays: Healing the Great Divide," 124, in *The Truth That Never Hurts*, credits the National Black Caucus with having the most impressive record of all members of Congress with respect to supporting legislation for gays and lesbians.

70 Ibid., 128–29.

71 The most enlightening analysis of the responses to HIV/AIDS on the part of African American communities can be found in Cathy J. Cohen, *The Boundaries of Blackness: AIDS and the Breakdown of Black Politics* (Chicago: University of Chicago Press, 1999). Here she examines why the issue of HIV/AIDS has been neglected by Blacks and why traditional leaders have been relatively silent about the disease, despite the fact that African Americans now account for more than 55 percent of all newly diagnosed HIV infections.

72 June Dubbs Butts, "Fighting AIDS With Sexual Honesty," *The Washington Post*, July 19, 1992, C2.

73 Lynette Clemetson, " 'Our House Is on Fire!': Special Report on AIDS at 20," *Newsweek*, June 11, 2001, 50–51.

74 Miranda Ward, "Sex in the AU City," *Club AUC Magazine*, March 2002, 16.

75 Ibid., 51.

76 "Healing Hands," *Savoy* magazine, September 2002, 83. For a comprehensive discussion of the responses of the Black church to HIV/AIDS, see Reginald Glenn Blaxton, " 'Jesus Wept': Reflections on HIV Dis-ease and the Churches of Black Folk," in *Dangerous Liaisons* (1999), 102–141; see Gary David Comstock, " 'Whosoever' Is Welcome Here: An Interview with Reverend Edwin C. Sanders II," in *Dangerous Liaisons*, 142–157, for a discussion of Rev. Sanders' HIV/AIDS ministry at the church he founded in a working class neighborhood in Nashville, Tennessee, Metropolitan Interdenominational Church.

77 Ibid., 84.

78 *The Atlanta Journal-Constitution*, July 10, 2002, A16.

7   No Respect: Hip-Hop and Gender Politics

1 See Bakari Kitwana, *The Rap on Gangsta Rap* (Chicago: Third World Press, 1994), in which he describes hip-hop culture as "graffiti art, break dancing, rap music, style of dress, attitude, verbal language, body language, and urban-influenced lifestyles," 12. See also *Black Enterprise*'s four-part series on the Hip-Hop Economy, which begins with the May 2002 issue.

2 Hip-hop critic William Eric Perkins, in his analysis of rap's second wave characterizes "gangster rap" as the product of gang culture and street wars in South Central Los Angeles and the "retro-mack culture" of East Oakland, which is perhaps most associ-

ated with the defunct group Compton's NWA (Niggas with Attitude), Houston's Geto Boys, and rappers Dr. Dre, Easy-E, MC Ren, Ice Cube, and Too Short; Perkins characterizes Miami-based "booty rap," most associated with 2 Live Crew and Luther Campbell, as "obsessed with sex and perverted eroticism." Female booty rap groups include New York–based Bytches With Problems (BWP) and Los Angeles–based Hoez with Attitude (HWA). See his edited collection, *Droppin' Science: Critical Essays on Rap Music and Hip Hop Culture* (Philadelphia: Temple University Press, 1996), 18–28.

3 *The Rap on Gangsta Rap,* 23.

4 bell hooks, "Sexism and Misogyny: Who Takes the Rap? Misogyny, Gangsta Rap and the Piano," Z magazine, February 1994, 26.

5 Kevin Powell, "Confessions of a Recovering Misogynist," *Ms.,* April/May 2000, 77.

6 See Fred Goodman, *Hip Hop: The Illustrated History of Break Dancing, Rap Music, and Graffiti* (New York: St. Martin's, 1984); David Toop, *The Rap Attack: African Jive to New York Hip Hop* (Boston: South End Press, 1984); Havelock Nelson and Michael A. Gonzales, *Bring the Noise: A Guide to Rap Music and Hip Hop Culture* (New York: Harmony Books, 1991); Alex Ogg with David Upshal, *The Hip Hop Years: A History of Rap* (1999); Tricia Rose, *Black Noise: Rap Music and Black Culture in Contemporary America* (Hanover, NH: University Press of New England, 1994); Nelson George, *Hip Hop America* (1998); William Eric Perkins, ed., *Droppin' Science: Critical Essays on Rap Music and Hip Hop Culture* (1996); Brian Cross, *It's Not about a Salary: Rap, Race and Resistance in Los Angeles* (New York: Verso, 1993).

7 Bakari Kitwana, *The Hip Hop Generation: Young Blacks and the Crisis in African-American Culture* (New York: Basic Civitas Books, 2002), 6–8.

8 Ibid., 92.

9 Ibid., 87.

10 Ice T, *The Ice Opinion: Who Gives a Fuck?* (New York: St. Martin's Press, 1994), 94.

11 We have been greatly influenced by insightful analyses of the gender politics of rap music and other aspects of hip-hop culture, especially the scholarly work of Tricia Rose. See in particular Nelson George's chapter "Too Live," in *Hip Hop America* (New York: Penguin Books, 1998); William Eric Perkins's introductory chapter to his edited collection, *Droppin' Science: Critical Essays on Rap Music and Hip Hop Culture;* Tricia Rose's "Never Trust a Bug Butt and a Smile," *Camera Obscura,* May 1991, 109–131, and *Black Noise: Rap Music and Black Culture in Contemporary America* (Hanover and London: Wesleyan University Press, 1994); Paula Ebron, "Rapping Between Men: Performing Gender," *Radical America* 24 (October–December 1989), 23–27; Robin Roberts, "Music Videos, Performance, and Resistance: Feminist Rappers," *Journal of Popular Culture* 25 (Fall 1991), 141–52; Eithne Quinn, " 'It's a Doggy-Dogg World': Black Cultural Politics, Gangsta Rap and the 'Post-Soul Man,' " in *Gender and the Civil Rights Movement,* eds., Peter J. Ling and Sharon Monteith (New York: Garland Publishing, 1999), 169–213; Robin D. G. Kelley's chapter, "Kickin' Reality, Kickin' Ballistics: 'Gangsta Rap' and Postindustrial Los Angeles," in *Race Rebels: Culture, Politics and the Black Working Class* (New York: Free Press, 1994); Michael Eric Dyson, *Holler if You Hear Me: Searching for Tupac Shakur* (New York: Basic Books, 2001); Bakari Kitwana, *The Rap on Gangsta Rap* and *The Hip Hop Generation: Young Blacks and the Crisis in African-American Culture* (New York:

Basic Civitas Books, 2002); Leola Johnson, *Radical America,* 26, no. 3 (1992), 7–19; Kimberlé Crenshaw, "Beyond Racism and Misogyny: Black Feminism and 2 Live Crew," *Boston Review* 16, no. 6 (December 1991), 6, 30–32; Jeffrey Louis Decker, "The State of Rap: Time and Place in Hip-Hop Nationalism," in *Microphone Friends: Youth Music and Youth Culture,* eds., Andrew Ross and Tricia Rose (New York: Routledge, 1994).

[12] Mark Naison, "Why Does Rap Dis Romance?," quoted by Eithne Quinn in *Gender in the Civil Rights Movement,* eds., Peter J. Ling and Sharon Monteith (New York and London: Garland Publishing Inc., 1999), 199.

[13] Danille Taylor-Guthrie, ed., *Conversations with Toni Morrison* (Jackson: University Press of Mississippi, 1994), 72–73.

[14] Ernest Allen, Jr., "Making the Strong Survive: The Contours and Contradictions of Message Rap," in *Droppin' Science,* 161.

[15] Robin Kelley, *Race Rebels,* 215–16. Bruce Jackson's *"Get Your Ass in the Water and Swim Like Me": Narrative Poetry from Black Oral Tradition* (Cambridge: Harvard University Press, 1974) is the source of Kelley's examples from Black vernacular culture, which includes toasts, the dozens, and Baadman narratives.

[16] Bakari Kitwani, *The Rap on Gangsta Rap,* 18.

[17] *Black Scholar* 23, no. 2 (Winter/Spring 1993), 37.

[18] Clarence Lusane, 38.

[19] Bruce Wade and Cynthia Thomas-Gunnar, "Explicit Rap Music Lyrics and Attitudes Toward Rape: The Perceived Effects on African American College Student's Attitudes," *Challenge: A Journal of Research on African American Men* (October 1993), 58.

[20] Dyson, *Holler if You Hear Me,* 1993.

[21] William Eric Perkins, ed., *Droppin' Science: Critical Essays on Rap Music and Hip Hop Culture* (Philadelphia: Temple University Press, 1996), 24.

[22] See Jim De Rogatis, "Like a Freak," *GQ,* September 2002, 349–357, for a profile of R. Kelley.

[23] *Hip Hop America,* 183.

[24] Quoted in Dyson, *Holler If You Hear Me,* 187.

[25] Leola Johnson, "Rap, Misogyny and Racism," *Radical America,* vol. 26, no. 3, (1992), 10.

[26] Elijah Muhammad, *Message to the Blackman in America* (Atlanta: M.E.M.P.S., 1965), 58–60.

[27] See www.childrenow.org/media/video-games/2001.

[28] See Nelson George's chapter, "Too Live," in *Hip Hop America* for a detailed description of his encounter with students at the Atlanta University Center over their defense of offensive rap music, which he critiques harshly.

[29] See Kimberle Crenshaw, "Beyond Racism and Misogyny: Black Feminism and 2 Live Crew," *Boston Review* 16, no. 6 (December 1991), 6, 30–32. See Gates's defense of his position in "2 Live Crew Decoded," *The New York Times,* June 19, 1990, A31.

[30] See Bakari Kitwani's enlightening chapter on the gender politics of rap, "Where Did Our Love Go?" in his *The Hip Hop Generation,* especially 90–92.

[31] Lisa Y. Sullivan, "Not Walking the Talk," *Sojourners Magazine,* vol. 31, no. 3 (May–June 2001), 15. She is also founder and president of LISTEN Inc., and former director of the field division of the Children's Defense Fund.

32 Tricia Rose, "Contracting Rap," in *Microphone Friends: Youth Music and Youth Culture*, eds., Andrew Ross and Tricia Rose (New York: Routledge, 1994), 142.

33 William Eric Perkins, *Droppin' Science: Critical Essays on Rap Music and Youth Culture*, 16.

34 Nancy Guevara, "Women Writin' Rappin' Breakin'," in *Droppin' Science*, 49–61. This is one of the first treatments of the serious involvement of Black and Latina women in hip-hop (rap music, graffiti art, and break dancing) from the beginning.

35 Joan Morgan, *When Chickenheads Come Home to Roost: My Life as a Hip-Hop Feminist* (New York: Simon & Schuster, 1999), 44.

36 Kevin Powell, "Confessions of a Recovering Misogynist," *Ms.*, April/May 2000, 77.

37 See Kevin Chappell, "Hip-Hop at the Crossroads: Will Lyrics and Perceptions Change," *Ebony*, September 2001, 111–114.

38 The Honorable Kweisi Mfume, Keynote Address, 2002 NAACP Annual Convention, Houston, Texas, July 2002. Quoted in *The Atlanta Journal-Constitution*, July 9, 2002, A3.

BIBLIOGRAPHY

•

PREFACE

Byrd, Rudolph and Beverly Guy-Sheftall, eds. *Traps: African American Men on Gender and Sexuality.* Bloomington: Indiana University Press, 2001.

Collins, Patricia Hill. *Black Feminist Thought.* 2nd edition. New York: Routledge, 1990.

Giddings, Paula. "The Last Taboo," in *Race-ing Justice, En-gendering Power: Essays on Anita Hill, Clarence Thomas, and the Construction of Social Reality.* ed., Toni Morrison. New York: Pantheon Books, 1992.

Lorde, Audre. "The Transformation of Silence into Language and Action." *Sister Outsider: Essays & Speeches.* Freedom, CA: The Crossing Press, 1984.

McKay, Nellie Y. "Remembering Anita Hill and Clarence Thomas: What Really Happened When One Black Woman Spoke Out," in *Race-ing Justice, En-gendering Power.*

INTRODUCTION

Alexander, Eleanor. *Lyrics of Sunshine and Shadow: The Tragic Courtship and Marriage of Paul Laurence Dunbar and Alice Ruth Moore.* New York: New York University Press, 2001.

Ali, Shahrazad. *The Blackman's Guide to Understanding the Black Woman.* Philadelphia: Civilized Publications, 1989.

Blee, Kathleen and Ann Tickmayer. "Racial Differences in Men's Attitudes About Gender Roles," *Journal of Marriage and the Family* 57 (1995), 21–30.

Cade, Toni, ed. *The Black Woman: An Anthology.* New York: Signet, 1970.

Cazenave, Noel. "A Woman's Place: The Attitudes of Middle-Class Black Men," *Phylon* 94, no. 1 (1983), 12–32.

——— and R. Smith. "Gender Differences in the Perception of Black Male-Female Relationships and Stereotypes," in *Black Families: Interdisciplinary Perspectives*, eds. Howard Chatham and James Stewart. New Brunswick, NJ: Transaction Books, 1991.

Cleage, Pearl. *Mad at Miles: A Blackwoman's Guide to Truth.* Southfield, Michigan: The Cleage Group, Inc., 1990.

Collins, Patricia Hill. *Black Feminist Thought.* 2nd edition. New York: Routledge, 2000 [1990].

The Combahee River Collective. "A Black Feminist Statement," in *Words of Fire: An Anthology of African-American Feminist Thought.* ed., Beverly Guy-Sheftall. New York: New Press, 1995 [1982].

Figueira-McDonough, Josefina. "Gender, Race, and Class: Differences in Levels of Feminist Orientation." *Journal of Applied Behavioral Science* 21, no. 2 (1985), 121–142.

Franklin, Donna L. *Ensuring Inequality: The Structural Transformation of the African-American Family.* New York: Oxford University Press, 1997.

Frazier, E. Franklin. *Black Bourgeoisie.* New York: Simon & Schuster, 1957.

Harris, Laura Alexandra. "Queer Black Feminism: The Pleasure Principle," in *Feminist Review*, no. 54 (Autumn 1996), 3–30.

Hernton, Calvin. *Coming Together.* New York: Random House, 1971.

———. *The Sexual Mountain and Black Women Writers: Adventures in Sex, Literature and Real Life.* New York: Anchor Press, 1987.

Hunter, Andrea and James Davis. "Constructing Gender: An Exploration of Afro-American Men's Conception of Manhood." *Gender and Society* 6, no. 3 (1992), 464–479.

Kane, Emily. "Race, Gender, and Attitudes Toward Gender Stratification." *Social Psychology Quarterly* 55, no. 3 (1992), 311–320.

——— and Laura Sanchez. "Family Status and Criticism of Gender Inequality at Home and at Work," *Social Forces* 72, no. 4 (1994), 1079–1102.

Kelly, Melvin Patrick. *The Adventures of Amos 'n' Andy: A Social History of an American Phenomenon.* New York: The Free Press, 1991.

Lorde Audre. *Sister Outsider: Essays and Speeches.* Trumansburg, N.Y: Crossing Press, 1984.

Martin, Juanita and Gordon Hall. "Thinking Black, Thinking Internal, Thinking Feminist," *Journal of Counseling Psychology* 39 (1994), 509–514.

Mullings, Leith. *On Our Own Terms: Race, Class, and Gender in the Lives of African American Women.* New York: Routledge, 1997.

Nelson, Jill. *Straight, No Chaser: How I Became a Grown-Up Black Woman.* New York: G.P. Putnam's Sons, 1997.

Patterson, Orlando. *Rituals of Blood: Consequences of Slavery in Two American Centuries.* Washington, D.C.: Civitas, 1998.

Rainwater, Lee and William L. Yancey, eds. *The Moynihan Report and the Politics of Controversy.* Cambridge: The M.I.T. Press, 1967.

Sinclair, Abiola, "Will the Media Be Fair to the Million Man March: Media Watch." *The New York Amsterdam News*, October 21, 1995.

Tucker, M. Belinda and Claudia Mitchell Kernan, eds. *The Decline in Marriage Among African Americans: Causes, Consequences, and Policy Implications.* New York: Russell Sage Foundation, 1995.

Wade, Jay C. "Gender Role Perceptions and Gender Role Conflicts of Middle-Class African American Men." *Journal of African-American Men,* vol. 1, no. 2 (Fall 1995). 103–120.

Washington, Elsie B. *Uncivil War.* Chicago: The Noble Press, 1996.

Wilcox, Clyde. "Race, Gender Role Attitudes and Support for Feminism." *Western Political Quarterly* 43 (1989), 113–121.

———. "Black Women and Feminism." *Women and Politics,* vol. 10, no. 3 (1990), 65–84.

Wilson, William Julius. *The Truly Disadvantaged: The Inner City, the Underclass, and Public Policy.* Chicago: University of Chicago Press, 1987.

———. *When Work Disappears: The World of the Urban Poor.* New York: Vintage Books, 1997.

1 THE PERSONAL IS POLITICAL

Bambara, Toni Cade. *The Salt-Eaters*. New York: Random House, 1980.

Bateson, Mary Catherine. *Composing A Life*. New York: The Atlantic Monthly Press, 1989.

Du Plessis, Rachel Blau and Ann Snitow, eds. *The Feminist Memoir Project: Voices from Women's Liberation*. New York: Three Rivers Press, 1998.

Ebony, September 2000, 185–189.

Echols, Alice. *Daring to be Bad: Radical Feminism in America, 1967–1975*. Minneapolis: University of Minnesota Press, 1989.

Fant, Phylicia. "Afrekete Unwelcome at Spelman." *The Spelman Spotlight*, April 9, 1999.

Freedman, Estelle B. *No Turning Back: The History of Feminism and the Future of Women*. New York: Ballantine Books, 2002.

Hartman, Mary S., ed. *Talking Leadership: Conversations with Powerful Women*. New Brunswick: Rutgers University Press, 1999.

Hull, Gloria T., Patricia Bell Scott, and Barbara Smith, eds. *All the Women Are White, All the Blacks Are Men, But Some of Us Are Brave: Black Women's Studies*. Old Westbury, N.Y.: Feminist Press, 1982.

James, Stanlie and Abena P.A. Busia, eds. *Theorizing Black Feminisms: The Visionary Pragmatism of Black Women*. New York: Routledge and Kegan Paul, 1994.

Mullings, Leith. *On Our Own Terms: Race, Class, and Gender in the Lives of African American Women*. New York: Routledge, 1997.

Thomas, Bettye Collier and V.P. Franklin, eds. *Sisters in the Struggle: African American Women in the Civil Rights-Black Power Movement*. New York: New York University Press, 2001.

2 HAVING THEIR SAY: CONVERSATIONS WITH SISTERS AND BROTHERS

Aldridge, Delores, ed. *Black Male-Female Relationships: A Resource Book of Selected Materials*. Dubuque, Iowa: Kendall/Hunt, 1989.

———— and Carlene Young, eds. *Out of the Revolution: The Development of Africana Studies*. Lanham, MD.: Lexington Books, 2000.

Bell, Derrick. "The Sexual Diversion: The Black Man/Black Woman Debate in Context," in *Speak My Name: Black Men on Masculinity and the American Dream*. ed., Don Belton. Boston: Beacon Press, 1995.

————. *Confronting Authority: Reflections of an Ardent Protester*. Boston: Beacon Press, 1994.

————. *Ethical Ambition: Living a Life of Meaning and Worth*. New York: Bloomsbury USA, 2002.

Brown, Elaine. *The Condemnation of Little B*. Boston: Beacon Press, 2002.

Cleage, Pearl. *Mad At Miles*. Southfield, Michigan: The Cleage Group, 1990.

————. "Zeke's Wife: A Meditation on Marriage," *Essence,* May 1998.

Delany, Sarah L. and Elizabeth Delany with Amy Hill Hearth. *Having Our Say: The Delany Sisters' First 100 Years*. New York: Dell, 1993.

Hunter, Andrea G. and Sherrill L. Sellers. "Feminist Attitudes among African American Women and Men." *Gender and Society* 12 (1998), 81–100.

Kelley, Robin D. G. *Freedom Dreams: The Black Radical Imagination*. Boston: Beacon Press, 2002.

Lemons, Gary. "To Be Black, Male and Feminist: Making Womanist Space for Black Men on the Eve of a New Millennium," in *Feminism and Men: Reconstructing Gender Relations*. eds., Steven P. Schacht and Doris W. Ewing. New York: New York University Press, 1998.

Madhubuti, Haki R. "On Becoming Anti-Sexist," in *Traps: African Men on Gender and Sexuality*. eds., Rudolph P. Byrd and Beverly Guy-Sheftall. Bloomington: Indiana University Press, 2001.

Marable, Manning. "Groundings With My Sisters: Patriarchy and the Exploitation of Black Women," in *How Capitalism Underdeveloped Black America*. Boston: South End Press, 1983.

Phillips, Layli. " 'But Some of Us Are Brave': The Courage and Vision of the Sister-Love Women's AIDS Project." *Womanist: Theory and Research,* vol. 2, no. 1 (Fall 1999), 1–2.

Powell, Kevin. "Confessions of a Recovering Misogynist." *Ms.*, April/May 2000.

3   COLLISIONS: BLACK LIBERATION VERSUS WOMEN'S LIBERATION

Albert, Judith Clavir and Stewart Edward Albert, eds. *The Sixties Papers: Documents of a Rebellious Decade*. New York: Praegar, 1984.

Anderson, Jervis. *Bayard Rustin: Troubles I've Seen, A Biography*. New York: HarperCollins Publishers, 1997.

Anderson-Bricker, Kristen. " 'Triple Jeopardy': Black Women and the Growth of Feminist Consciousness in SNCC, 1914 -1975," in *Keep Lifting, Keep Climbing: African American Women's Contemporary Activism*. ed. Kimberly Springer. New York: New York University Press, 1999.

Asante, Molefi. *The Afrocentric Idea*. Philadelphia: Temple University Press, 1987.

Baraka, Imamu Amiri. "Black Woman," *Raise Race Rays Raze: Essays Since 1965*. New York: Random House, 1969.

Baxandall, Rosalyn and Linda Gordon, eds. *Dear Sisters: From the Women's Liberation*. New York: Basic Books, 2000.

The Black Scholar. "Blacks & the Sexual Revolution." vol. 9, no. 7, April 1978.

The Black Scholar. "Black Sexism Debate." March/April 1979.

The Black Scholar. "The Black Woman." vol. 6, no. 6, March 1975.

The Black Scholar. "The Black Woman III." vol. 14, no. 5, September/October 1983.

The Black Scholar. "Black Women and Feminism." 1986.

The Black Scholar. "Black Women's Liberation." vol. 4, nos. 6–7, March/April 1973.

The Black Scholar. "The Black Woman." vol. 3, no. 4, December 1971.

Bond, Jean Carey and Patricia Peery. "Is the Black Male Castrated?" in *The Black Woman*. New York: Signet, 1970.

Breitman, George, ed. *By Any Means Necessary*. New York: Pathfinder Press, 1970.

Brown, Cynthia, ed. *Ready From Within: Septima Clark and the Civil Rights Movement*. Navarro, CA: Wild Trees Press, 1986.

Brown, Elaine. *A Taste of Power: A Black Woman's Story*. New York: Pantheon Books, 1992.

Byrd, Rudolph and Beverly Guy-Sheftall, eds. *Traps: African American Men on Gender and Sexuality*. Bloomington: Indiana University Press, 2001.

Cade, Toni. *The Black Woman: An Anthology.* New York: Penguin, 1970.

Carson, Clayborne. *In Struggle: SNCC and the Black Awakening of the 1960's.* Cambridge: Harvard University Press, 1981.

Caton, Simone M. "Birth Control and the Black Community in the 1960s: Genocide or Power Politics?" *Journal of Social History* 31 (1998), 545–569.

Chisholm, Shirley. *Unbought and Unbossed.* New York: Avon, 1970.

Chrisman, Robert and Robert I. Allen, eds. *Court of Appeal: The Black Community Speaks Out on the Racial and Sexual Politics of Clarence Thomas vs. Anita Hill.* New York: Ballantine Books, 1992.

Cooper, Anna Julia. *A Voice from the South.* The Schomburg Library of Nineteenth Century Black Women Writers. ed., Henry Louis Gates, Jr. New York: Oxford University Press, 1988. Originally published in 1892 by Aldine Publishers, Xenia, Ohio.

Collier-Thomas, Bettye and V. P. Franklin, eds. *Sisters in the Struggle: African American Women in the Civil Rights-Black Power Movement.* New York: New York University Press, 2002.

Collins, Patricia Hill. *Black Feminist Thought: Knowledge, Consciousness and the Politics of Empowerment.* New York: Unwin Hyman, 1990.

———. *Fighting Words: Black Women & the Search for Justice.* Minneapolis: University of Minnesota Press, 1998.

Crawford Vicki et al., eds. *Women in the Civil Rights Movement: Trailblazers and Torchbearers, 1941–1965.* Brooklyn: Carlson Publishing, 1990.

Davis, Angela Y. *Women, Race and Class.* New York: Random House, 1981.

Duster, Alfreda M., ed. *Crusade for Justice: The Autobiography of Ida B. Wells.* Chicago: University of Chicago Press, 1970.

Eichelberger, Brenda. "Voices on Black Feminism." *Quest* 3.4 (Spring 1977), 16–28.

Evans, Sarah. *Personal Politics: The Roots of Women's Liberation in the Civil Rights Movement and the New Left.* New York: Vintage Books, 1979.

Fleming, Cynthia Griggs. *Soon We Will Not Cry: The Liberation of Ruby Doris Smith Robinson.* Lanham, MD: Rowman & Littlefield Publishers, 1998.

Foner, Eric, ed. *Major Speeches by Negroes in the U.S., 1797–1971.* New York: Simon & Schuster, 1972.

Foner, Philip S., ed. *Frederick Douglass on Women's Rights.* New York: Da Capo Press, 1992.

Frazier, E. Franklin. *Black Bourgeoisie.* New York: Free Press, 1957.

———. *The Negro Family in the United States.* Chicago: University of Chicago Press, 1939.

Freedman, Estelle B. *No Turning Back: The History of Feminism and the Future of Women.* New York: Ballantine Books, 2002.

Gaines, Kevin. *Uplifting the Race: Black Politics and Culture in the United States Since the Turn of the Century.* Chapel Hill: University of North Carolina Press, 1995.

Giddings, Paula. "The Last Taboo," in *Race-ing Justice, En-gendering Power: Essays on Anita Hill, Clarence Thomas, and the Construction of Social Reality,* ed., Toni Morrison. New York: Pantheon, 1992.

———. *When and Where I Enter: The Impact of Black Women on Race and Sex in America.* New York: William Morrow, 1984.

Grant, Joanne. *Ella Baker: Freedom Bound*. New York: John Wiley, 1998.

Greenberg, Cheryl Lynn. *A Circle of Trust: Remembering SNCC*. New Brunswick: Rutgers University Press, 1998.

Guy-Sheftall, Beverly, ed. *Words of Fire: An Anthology of African American Feminist Thought*. New York: New Press, 1995.

Haley, Alex. *The Autobiography of Malcolm X*. New York: Ballantine, 1992.

Halisi, Clyde, ed. *The Quotable Karenga*. Los Angeles: US Organization, 1967.

Hammonds, Evelynn. "Viewpoint: Who Speaks for Black Women?" *Sojourner: The Women's Forum*, November 1991, 7–8.

Hare, Nathan. "Will the Real Black Man Stand Up?" *The Black Scholar* vol. 2, no. 10 (June 1971), 32–35.

———. "Revolution Without a Revolution: The Psychology of Sex and Race." *The Black Scholar*, vol. 9, no. 7 (April 1978), 2–7.

Hare, Nathan and Julia Hare, eds. *Crisis in Black Sexual Politics*. San Francisco: Black Think Tank, 1989.

Harris, Duchess. " 'All of Who I Am in the Same Place,' The Combahee River Collective." *Womanist: Theory and Research*, vol. 2, no. 1 (Fall 1999), 9–21.

Heath, G. Louis, ed. *Off the Pigs: The History and Literature of the Black Panther Party*. Metuchen, NJ: Scarecrow Press, 1976.

Hedgeman, Anna Arnold. *The Trumphet Sounds: A Memoir of Negro Leadership*. New York: Holt, Rinehart & Winston, 1964.

Hernton, Calvin. *Coming Together: Black Power, White Hatred, and Sexual Hang-Ups*. New York: Random House, 1981.

———. *Sex and Racism in America*. New York: Grove Press, 1965.

Hill, Anita Faye and Emma Coleman Jordan, eds. *Race, Gender, and Power in America: The Legacy of the Hill-Thomas Hearings*. New York: Oxford University Press, 1995.

Hine, Darlene Clark. " 'In the Kingdom of Culture': Black Women and the Intersection of Race, Gender, and Class," in *Lure and Loathing: Essays on Race, Identity, and the Ambivalence of Assimilation*. ed., Gerald Early. New York: Penguin Books, 1993.

hooks, bell. *Ain't I a Woman: Black Women and Feminism*. Boston: South End Press, 1981.

———. *Feminist Theory: From Margin to Center*. Boston: South End Press, 1984.

———. *Killing Rage: Ending Racism*. New York: Henry Holt and Company, 1995.

———. *Talking Back: Thinking Feminist, Thinking Black*. Boston: South End Press, 1989.

Hull Gloria T., Patricia Bell Scott and Beverly Smith, eds. *All the Women Are White, All the Blacks Are Men, But Some of Us Are Brave: Black Women's Studies*. New York: Feminist Press, 1982.

James, Joy. *Race, Women, and Revolution: Black Female Militancy and the Praxis of Ella Baker*. Lanham, MD: Rowman & Littlefield, 1999.

———. "Radicalising Feminism." *Race & Class*, vol. 40, no. 4 (1999), 15–31.

———. *Transcending the Talented Tenth: Black Leaders and American Intellectuals*. New York: Routledge, 1997.

Jones, Charles E., ed. *The Black Party (Reconsidered)*. Baltimore: Black Classic Press, 1998.

Karenga, Maulana. *Essays on Struggle: Position and Analysis*. Los Angeles: Kawaida Publications, 1978.

———. *Introduction to Black Studies*. Los Angeles: Kawaida Publications, 1982.

———. *Kawaida Theory: An Introductory Outline*. Los Angeles: Kawaida Publications, 1980.

———. "In Love and Struggle: Toward a Greater Togetherness." *The Black Scholar*. vol. no. 6 (March 1975), 16–28.

La Rue, Linda. "The Black Movement and Women's Liberation." *The Black Scholar* (May 1970), 2.

Lerner, Gerda, ed. *Black Women in White America: A Documentary History*. New York: Oxford University Press, 1972.

Lincoln, Eric C. "A Look Beyond the 'Matriarchy.'" *Ebony*, vol. 21, no. 10 (August 1966), 112–114.

Ling, Peter J. and Sharon Monteith, eds. *Gender in the Civil Rights Movement*. New York: Garland Publishing, 1999.

Lomax, Pearl. "Black Women's Liberation." *Essence*, August 1972, 68.

Lorde, Audre. *Sister Outsider: Essays and Speeches*. Trumansburg, N.Y.: Crossing Press, 1984.

Lubiano, Wahneema, ed. *The House That Race Built*. New York: Vintage Books, 1998.

McKay, Nellie Y. "Remembering Anita Hill and Clarence Thomas: What Really Happened When One Black Woman Spoke Out," in *Race-ing Justice, En-gendering Power: Essays on Anita Hill, Clarence Thomas, and the Construction of Social Reality*. ed., Toni Morrison. New York: Pantheon Books, 1992.

Morris, Aldon. *Origins of the Civil Rights Movement: Black Communities Organizing for Change*. New York: The Free Press, 1984.

Moynihan, Daniel Patrick. *The Negro Family: The Case for National Action*. Washington, D.C.: U.S. Department of Labor, 1965.

Mullings, Leith. *On Our Own Terms: Race, Class and Gender in the Lives of African American Women*. New York: Routledge, 1997.

Murray, Pauli. "The Liberation of Black Women," in *Voices of the New Feminism*. ed.,Mary Lou Thompson. Boston: Beacon Press, 1970.

———. *Song in a Weary Throat: An American Pilgrimage*. New York: Harper & Row, 1987.

Newton, Huey. *To Die for the People: The Writings of Huey Newton*. New York: Vintage Books, 1972.

———. *Revolutionary Suicide*. New York: Harcourt Brace Jovanovich, 1973.

Norton, Eleanor Holmes. *Fire in My Soul: Joan Steinau Lester in Conversation with Eleanor Holmes Norton*. New York: Atria Books, 2003.

Olson, Lynne. *Freedom's Daughters: The Unsung Heroines of the Civil Rights Movement from 1830 to 1970*. New York: Scribner, 2001.

Omolade, Barbara. *The Rising Song of African American Women*. New York: Routledge, 1994.

Painter, Nell Irvin. "Hill, Thomas, and the Use of Racial Stereotype," in *Race-ing Justice, En-gendering Power: Essays on Anita Hill, Clarence Thomas, and the Construction of Social Reality*. ed., Toni Morrison. New York: Pantheon Books, 1992.

"Panther Sisters on Women's Liberation," in *Off the Pigs: The History and Literature of the Black Panther Party.* ed., G. Louis Heath. Metuchen, NJ: Scarecrow Press, 1976.

Petry, Ann. "What's Wrong with Negro Men?," *The Negro Digest,* 1947

Radford-Hill, Sheila. *Further to Fly: Black Women and the Politics of Empowerment.* Minneapolis: University of Minnesota Press, 2001.

Rainwater, Lee and William L. Yancey. *The Moynihan Report and the Politics of Controversy.* Cambridge: The M.I.T. Press, 1967.

Robinson, Jo Ann Gibson. *The Montgomery Bus Boycott and the Women Who Started It.* Knoxville, TN: University of Tennessee Press, 1987.

Robnett, Belinda. *How Long? How Long?: African American Women in the Struggle for Civil Rights.* New York: Oxford University Press, 1997.

Roth, Benita. "Race, Class and the Emergence of Black Feminism in the 1960s and 1970s." *Womanist: Theory and Research,* vol. 2, no. 1 (Fall 1999), 3–9.

Scott, Joyce Hoe. "From Foreground to Margin: Female Configurations and Masculine Self-Representation in Black Nationalist Fiction," in *Nationalisms and Sexualities.* eds., Andrew Parker, et al. New York: Routledge, 1992.

Simmons, Aishah. "Creating a Sacred Space of Our Own," in *Just Sex: Students Rewrite the Rules on Sex, Violence, Activism, and Equality* eds., Jodi Gold and Susan Villari. Boulder: Rowman & Littlefield Publishers, 2000.

Sizemore, Barbara A. "Sexism and the Black Male." *The Black Scholar,* vol. 4, nos. 6 & 7 (March-April 1973), 3.

Smith, Barbara, ed. *Home Girls: A Black Feminist Anthology.* New York: Kitchen Table Women of Color Press, 1983.

Smitherman, Geneva, ed. *African American Women Speak Out on Anita Hill-Clarence Thomas.* Detroit: Wayne State University Press, 1995.

Springer, Kimberly. "The Interstitial Politics of Black Feminist Organizations." *Meridians: Feminism, Race, Transnationalism,* vol. 1, no.2 (Spring 2001), 164–165.

———. " 'Our Politics Was Black Women': Black Feminist Organizations, 1968–1980." Unpublished doctoral dissertation. Emory University, 1999.

———, ed. *Still Lifting, Still Climbing: African American Women's Contemporary Activism.* New York: New York University Press, 1999.

Stanton, Elizabeth Cady et al., eds. *The History of Woman Suffrage,* vol. 2. Rochester, NY: Fowler and Wells, 1881–1922.

Tanner, Leslie, ed. *Voices of Women's Liberation.* New York: New American Library, 1970.

Thomas, William Hannibal. *The American Negro, What He Was, What He Is, and What He May Become.* Boston: Macmillan, 1901.

Taylor, Ula Yvette. *The Veiled Garvey: The Life and Times of Amy Jacques Garvey.* Chapel Hill: University of North Carolina Press, 2002.

Van Deberg, William, ed. *Modern Black Nationalism: From Marcus Garvey to Louis Farrakhan.* New York: New York University Press, 1997.

Weber, Shirley. "Black Power in the 1960s: A Study of Its Impact on Women's Liberation." *Journal of Black Studies* 11(1981), 483–498.

Wallace, Michele. *Black Macho and the Myth of the Superwoman.* New York: Dial, 1979.

White, Aaronette M. "Talking Black, Talking Feminist: Gendered Micromobilization Processes in a Collective Protest Against Rape," in *Still Lifting, Still Climbing.*

———. "Ain't I A Feminist? Black Men as Advocates of Feminism." *Womanist: Theory and Research*. Vol. 3.2/4.1 (2001–2002), 28–34.

White, Deborah Gray. *Too Heavy A Load: Black Women in Defense of Themselves, 1894–1994*. New York: W.W. Norton & Company, 1999.

4 THE BLACK CHURCH:

Angell, Stephen W. and Anthony B. Pinn, eds. "Women's Identities within the A.M.E. Church," in *Social Protest Thought in the African Methodist Episcopal Church, 1862–1939*. Knoxville: University of Tennessee Press, 2000.

Baker-Fletcher, Karen. *Sisters of Dust, Sisters of Spirit: Womanist Wordings on God and Creation*. Minneapolis: Fortress Press, 1998.

Cannon, Katie Geneva. *Womanism and the Soul of the Black Community*. Lexington, NY: The Continuum Publishing Company, 1995.

———. *Black Womanist Ethics*. Atlanta: Scholars Press, 1988.

Chapman, Mark. *Christianity on Trial: African-American Religious Thought Before and After Black Power*. Maryknoll, NY: Orbis Books, 1996.

Collier-Thomas, Bettye. *Daughters of Thunder: Black Women Preachers and Their Sermons, 1850–1979*. San Francisco: Jossey-Bass Publishers, 1998.

Comstock, Gary David and Susan E. Henking, eds. *Que(e)ring Religion: A Critical Anthology*. New York: Continuum, 1997.

Comstock, Gary David. *A Whosoever Church: Welcoming Lesbians and Gay Men Into African American Congregations*. Louisville: Westminster John Knox Press, 2001.

Cone, James H. and Gayraud S. Wilmore, eds. *Black Theology: A Documentary History*, vol. 2, 1980–1992. Maryknoll, NY: Orbis Books, 1993.

Cone, James H. "Black Theology, Black Churches, and Black Women," in *For My People: Black Theology and the Black Church*. Maryknoll, NY: Orbis Books, 1984.

———. *My Soul Looks Back*. Nashville: Abingdon Press, 1982.

Dodson, Jualynne E. *Engendering Church: Women, Power, and the AME Church*. Lanham, MD: Rowman & Littlefield Publishers, 2002.

Douglas, Kelly Brown. *Sexuality and the Black Church: A Womanist Perspective*. Maryknoll, NY: Orbis Books, 1999.

Dyson, Michael Eric. *I May Not Get There With You*. New York: The Free Press, 2000.

———. *Race Rules: Navigating the Color Line*. New York: Vintage, 1996.

Dyson, Marcia. "When Preachers Prey," *Essence*, May 1998, 120–122ff.

Farajaje-Jones, Elias. "Breaking Silence: Toward An In-The-Life Theology," in *Black Theology: A Documentary History*, vol. 2, 139–159.

Forbes, James A. Jr. "More Light from the Spirit on Sexuality" in *Homosexuality and Christian Faith: Questions of Conscience for the Churches*. ed., Walter Wink. Minneapolis: Fortress Press, 1999.

Gilkes, Cheryl Townsend. *"If It Wasn't for the Women": Black Women's Experience and Womanist Culture in Church and Community*. Maryknoll, NY: Orbis Books, 2001.

Grant, Jacquelyn. "Black Theology and the Black Woman," in *Words of Fire: An Anthology of African American Feminist Thought*. New York: New Press, 1995.

———. *White Women's Christ and Black Women's Jesus: Feminist Christology and Womanist Reponse*. Atlanta: Scholars Press, 1989.

———, ed. *Perspectives on Womanist Theology*. Black Church Scholars Series, vol. 7. Atlanta: ITC Press, 1995.

Higginbotham, Evelyn Brooks. *Righteous Discontent: The Women's Movement in the Black Baptist Church, 1880–1920*. Cambridge: Harvard University Press, 1983.

Hill, Renee L. "Who Are We for Each Other?: Sexism, Sexuality and Womanist Theology," in *Black Theology: A Documentary History, 1980–1992*, vol. 2. eds., James H. Cone & Gayraud S. Wilmore. Maryknoll, NY: Orbis Books, 1993. pp. 345–351.

Hoover, Theressa. "Black Women and the Churches: Triple Jeopardy," in *Black Theology: A Documentary History, 1966–1979*. eds., Gayraud S. Wilmore and James H. Cone. Maryknoll, NY: Orbis Books, 1979.

Hull, Akasha Gloria. *Soul Talk: The New Spirituality of African American Women*. Rochester, Vermont: Inner Traditions, 2001.

Jakes, T.D. *Woman Thou Art Loosed!* Shippensburg, PA: Destiny Image Publishers, 1993.

Lakey, Othal Hawthorne and Betty Benne Stephens. *God In My Mama's House: The Women's Movement in the CME Church*. Memphis: CME Publishing House, 1994.

Lee, Jarena. *The Life and Religious Experience of Jarena Lee*. Philadelphia, 1849.

McKenzie, Vashti M. *Not Without a Struggle: Leadership Development for African American Women in Ministry*. Cleveland: The Pilgrim Press, 1996.

Mitchell, Doris J. and Jewell H. Bell. *The Black Woman: Myths and Realities*. Cambridge: Radcliffe College, 1978.

Nero, Charles I. "Toward a Black Gay Aesthetic: Signifying in Contemporary Black Gay Literature," in *Brother to Brother*. ed., Essex Hemphill. Boston: Alyson Publications, 1991.

Painter, Nell Irvin. *Sojourner Truth: A Life, a Symbol*. New York: W.W. Norton & Company, 1996.

Powell, Sr., Adam Clayton. *Against the Tide: An Autobiography*. New York: Richard R. Smith, 1938.

Riggs, Marcia Y. *Awake, Arise & Act: A Womanist Call for Black Liberation*. Cleveland, Ohio: The Pilgrim Press, 1994.

———, ed. *Can I Get A Witness?: Prophetic Religious Voices of African American Women in An Anthology*. Maryknoll, NY: Orbis Books, 1997.

Sanders, Cheryl J., ed. *Living the Intersection: Womanism and Afrocentrism in Theology*. Minneapolis: Fortress Press, 1995.

Sudarkasa, Niara. "The Status of Women in Indigenous Africa." *Feminist Studies* 12 (1986), 91–103.

Terborg-Penn Rosalyn and Sharon Harley, eds. *The Afro-American Woman: Struggles and Images*. Port Washington, NY: Kennikat Press, 1978.

Tinney, James S. "Struggles of a Black Pentecostal," in *Black Men/White Men: Afro-American Gay Life and Culture*. ed. Michael J. Smith. San Francisco: Bay Sunshine Press, 1999.

———. "Why a Black Gay Church?" *In the Life: A Black Gay Anthology*. ed., Joseph Beam. Boston: Alyson Publications, 1986.

Townes, Emilie M., ed. *A Troubling in My Soul: Womanist Perspectives on Evil and Suffering*. Maryknoll, NY: Orbis Books, 1993.

———. *Embracing the Spirit: Womanist Perspectives on Hope, Salvation, and Transformation*. Maryknoll, NY: Orbis Books, 1997.

———. *Womanist Justice, Womanist Hope*. Atlanta: Scholars Press, 1993.

van Allen, Judith. " 'Aba Riots' or Ibo 'Women's War'?: Ideology, Stratification and the

Invisibility of Women," in *Women in Africa: Studies in Social and Economic Change*. eds., Nancy J. Hafkin and Edna Bay. Stanford: Stanford University Press, 1976.

Weems, Renita J. *Just a Sister Away: A Womanist Vision of Women's Relationships in the Bible*. Philadelphia: Innisfree Press, 1991.

Williams, Delores S. *Sisters in the Wilderness: The Challenge of Womanist God-Talk*. Maryknoll, NY: Orbis Books, 1993.

5   RACE SECRETS AND THE BODY POLITIC

Allen, Robert L. "Stopping Sexual Harassment: A Challenge for Community Education," in *Race, Gender and Power in America: The Legacy of the Hill-Thomas Hearings*. eds., Anita Faye Hill and Emma Coleman Jordan. New York: Oxford University Press, 1995.

Asante, Molefi K. *Afrocentricity*. Trenton: African World Press, 1991.

———. *The Afrocentric Idea*. Philadelphia: Temple University Press, 1987.

Baraka, Imamu Amiri. *Raise Race Rays Raze: Essays Since 1965*. New York: Random House, 1969.

Beck, Robert. *The Story of My Life*. Los Angeles: Holloway House, 1969.

Belton, Don, ed. *Speak My Name: Black Men on Masculinity and the American Dream*. Boston: Beacon Press, 1995.

Bennett, Michael, and Vanessa D. Dickerson, eds. *Recovering the Black Female Body: Self Representations by African American Women*. New Brunswick: Rutgers University Press, 2001.

Bennett, Jr., Lerone. *Before the Mayflower: A History of the Negro in America, 1619–1964*. Baltimore: Penguin Books, 1966.

Black, Daniel P. *Dismantling Black Manhood: An Historical and Literary Analysis of the Legacy of Slavery*. New York: Garland Publishing, 1997.

Booker, Christopher B. *"I Will Wear No Chain!": A Social History of African American Males*. Westport, CT: Praeger, 2000.

Boyd, Herb, and Robert L. Allen, eds., *Brotherman: The Odyssey of Black Men in America*. New York: Ballantine Books, 1995.

Brown, Elsa Barkley. "Negotiating and Transforming the Public Sphere: African American Political Life in the Transition from Slavery to Freedom." *Public Culture* 7 (1994), 107–46.

Brown, Claude. *Manchild in the Promised Land*. New York: Macmillan, 1965.

Brundage, W. Fitzhugh, ed. *Under Sentence of Death: Lynching in the South*. Chapel Hill: University of North Carolina Press, 1997.

Buchwald, Emilie, Pamela R. Fletcher, and Martha Roth, eds. *Transforming A Rape Culture*. Minneapolis: Milkweed Editions, 1993.

Cameron, James. *A Time of Terror: A Survivor's Story*. Baltimore: Black Classic Press, 1994.

Carbado, Devon W., ed. *Black Men on Race, Gender, and Sexuality: A Critical Reader*. New York: New York University Press, 1999.

Carby, Hazel V. *Reconstructing Womanhood: The Emergence of the Afro-American Woman Novelist*. New York: Oxford University Press, 1987.

———. " 'On the Threshold of Woman's Era': Lynching, Empire, and Sexuality in

Black Feminist Theory," in *"Race," Writing, and Difference* ed. Henry Louis Gates, Jr. Chicago: University of Chicago Press, 1986.

———. "It Jus Be's Dat Way Sometime: The Sexual Politics of Women's Blues," *Radical America*, vol. 20, no. 4 (February 1987), 238–49.

———. *Race Men: The W.E.B.Du Bois Lectures.* Cambridge: Harvard University Press, 1998.

Hemphill, Essex. "If Freud Had Been a Neurotic Colored Woman: Reading Dr. Frances Cress Welsing," in *Ceremonies*. New York: A Plume Book, 1992.

Carillon, Ricardo and Jerry Tello, eds. *Family Violence and Men of Color: Healing the Wounded Male Spirit*. New York: Springer Publishing Company, 1998.

Cazenave, Noel. "Black Men in America: The Quest for Manhood," in *Black Families*. ed., Harriette McAdoo. Beverly Hills, CA: Sage, 1981.

Chapman, Rowena, and Jonathan Rutherford, eds. *Male Order: Unwrapping Masculinity*. London: Lawrence & Wishard Limited, 1988.

Cleage, Pearl. *Mad At Miles: A Blackwoman's Guide to Truth*. Southfield, Michigan: The Cleage Group, 1990.

Cleaver, Eldridge. *Soul on Ice*. New York: Dell, 1968.

Cose, Ellis. *The Envy of the World: On Being a Black Man in America*. New York: Washington Square Press/Pocket Books, 2002.

Crenshaw, Kimberlé Williams. "Mapping the Margins: Intersectionality, Identity Politics, and Violence Against Women of Color," in *The Public Nature of Private Violence*. eds., Martha A. Fineman and Roxanne Mykitiuk. New York: Routledge, 1994.

———. "The Marginalization of Sexual Violence Against Black Women." *National Coalition Against Sexual Assault Journal* 2 (1994), 1–6.

Davis, Angela Y. *Blues Legacies and Black Feminism: Gertrude "Ma" Rainey, Bessie Smith, and Billie Holiday*. New York: Pantheon Books, 1998.

———. "We Do Not Consent: Violence Against Women in a Racist Society," *Women, Culture and Politics*. New York: Random House, 1984.

———. *Women, Race and Class*. New York: Random House, 1981.

Davis, Miles with Quincy Troupe. *The Autobiography of Miles Davis*. New York: Simon & Schuster, 1989.

Edwards, Tamala. "Men Who Sleep With Men," *Essence*, October 2001, 76–78.

Eugene, Toinette M. " 'Swing Low, Swing, Chariot!': A Womanist Response to Sexual Violence and Abuse," in *Violence Against Women and Children: A Christian Theological Sourcebook*. eds., Carol J. Adams and Marie Fortune. New York: Continuum, 1995.

Farrakhan, Louis. "Minister Louis Farrakhan Speaks on Domestic Violence," *Final Call* 2 (June 1995), 1–3.

———. "Allah (God) Hates Divorce-Part Two," *The Final Call*, April 14, 1995, 7–8.

———. "Minister Farrakhan Calls for One Million Man March," *The Final Call*, December 14, 1994, 1.

Felder, Cain Hope. *Stony the Road We Trod: African American Biblical Interpretation*. Minneapolis: Augsburg Fortress, 1991.

Franklin, Clyde W. *The Changing Definition of Masculinity*. New York: Plenum Press, 1984.

Frazier, E. Franklin. *The Negro Family in the United States*. Chicago: University of Chicago Press, 1939.

Gary, Lawrence E., Christopher B. Booker and Abeba Fekade, eds. *African American*

Males: An Analysis of Contemporary Values, Attitudes and Perceptions of Manhood. Washington, DC: Howard University School of Social Work, 1993.

Gibbs, Jewell Taylor. *Young, Black and Male in America: An Endangered Species.* Dover, MA: Auburn House, 1988.

Ginzburg, Ralph. *100 Years of Lynchings.* Baltimore: Black Classic Press, 1988.

Glaude, Eddie Jr., ed. *Is It Nation Time? Contemporary Essays on Black Power and Black Nationalism.* Chicago: University of Chicago Press, 2002.

Grier, William H. and Price M. Cobbs. *Black Rage.* New York: Basic Books, 1968.

Gunning, Sandra. *Race, Rape, and Lynching: The Red Record of American Literature, 1890–1912.* New York: Oxford University Press, 1996.

Hall, Jacquelyn Dowd. " 'The Mind That Burns in Each Body': Women, Rape, and Racial Violence," in *Powers of Desire: The Politics of Sexuality.* eds. Ann Snitow, Christine Stansell, and Sharon Thompson. New York: Monthly Review Press, 1983.

Haley, Alex. *The Autobiography of Malcolm X.* New York: Ballantine, 1973.

Hampton, Robert L., ed. *Violence in the Black Family: Correlates and Consequences.* Lexington, MA: Lexington Books, 1987.

———. *Black Family Violence: Current Research and Theory.* Lexington, Mass.: Lexington Books, 1991.

Hampton, Robert L. and Richard Gelles. "Violence toward Black Women in a Nationally Representative Sample of Black Families." *Journal of Comparative Family Studies* 25, no. 1 (Spring 1994), 105–19.

Hare, Nathan and Julia Hare. *Crisis in Black Sexual Politics.* San Francisco: Black Think Tank, 1989.

Hawkins, Darnell, ed. *Homicide Among Black Americans.* London: University Press of America, 1986.

Higgins, Lynn A., and Brenda R. Silver, eds. *Rape and Representation.* New York: Columbia University Press, 1991.

Holmes, William C. and Gail B. Slap. "Sexual Abuse of Boys: Definition, Prevalence, Correlates, Sequelae, and Management." *Journal of the American Medical Association* 280 (1998), 1855–1862.

Horton, James Oliver, ed. *Free People of Color: Inside the African American Community.* Washington: Smithsonian Institution Press, 1993.

Hunter, Mic. *Abused Boys: The Neglected Victims of Sexual Abuse.* New York: Fawcett, 1991.

Ice T. *The Ice Opinion: Who Gives a Fuck?* New York: St. Martin's Press, 1994.

Jenkins, Earnestine, and Darlene Clark Hine, eds. *A Question of Manhood: A Reader in U.S. Black Men's History and Masculinity.* Vols. 1 and 2. Bloomington: Indiana University Press, 2000 and 2001.

Jones, Charles E., ed. *The Black Panther Party Reconsidered.* Baltimore: Black Classic Press, 1998.

Jones, Dionne J. *African American Males.* New Brunswick, NJ: Transaction Publishers, 1994.

Jones, James Howard. *Bad Blood: The Tuskegee Syphilis Experiment.* New York: Free Press, 1993.

July, William, II. *Brothers, Lust and Love: Thoughts on Manhood, Sex, and Romance.* New York: Doubleday, 1998.

Kaplan, Elaine Bell. *Not Our Kind of Girl: Unraveling the Myths of Black Teenage Motherhood.* Berkeley: University of California Press, 1997.

Kimmel, Michael. *Manhood in America: A Cultural History.* New York: Free Press, 1996.

———, ed. *Changing Men: Directions in Research on Men and Masculinity.* Newbury Park, CA: Sage, 1987.

——— and M. Messner, eds. *Men's Lives: Readings in the Sociology of Men and Masculinity.* New York: Macmillan, 1989.

Kunjufu, Jawanza. *Countering the Conspiracy to Destroy Black Boys.* Chicago: African American Images, 1985.

Lemelle, Anthony J. Jr. *Black Male Deviance.* Westport, CT: Praeger, 1995.

———. "The Political Sociology of Black Masculinity and Types of Domination." *Journal of African American Men,* vol. 1, no. 2 (Fall 1995), 87–101.

Liebow, E. *Tally's Corner.* Boston: Little, Brown & Co., 1967.

Lorde, Audre. *Sister Outsider.* Trumansburg, CA: Crossing Press, 1984.

Lubiano, Wahneema, ed. *The House That Race Built.* New York: Vintage Books, 1998.

Madhubuti, Haki. *Black Men: Obsolete, Single Dangerous?: The African American Family in Transition.* Chicago: Third World Press, 1990.

Magda, Arthur J. *Prophet of Rage: A Life of Louis Farrakhan and His Nation.* New York: Basic Books, 1996.

Majors, R. G., and J. M. Billson. *Cool Pose: The Dilemmas of Black Manhood in America.* New York: Lexington Books, 1992.

Majors, Richard G., and Jacob U. Gordon, eds. *The American Black Male: His Present Status and Future.* Chicago: Nelson-Hall, 1994.

Mann, Susan. "Slavery, Sharecropping, and Sexual Inequality," in *Black Women in America: Social Science Perspectives.* ed. Micheline Malson, et al. Chicago: University of Chicago Press, 1990.

McCall, Nathan. *Make Me Wanna Holler: A Young Black Man in America.* New York: Random House, 1994.

McCloud, Aminah Beverly. *African American Islam.* New York: Routledge, 1995.

McDowell, Deborah E., ed. *"The Changing Same": Black Women's Literature, Criticism and Theory.* Bloomington: Indiana University Press, 1995.

McGovern, James R. *Anatomy of a Lynching: The Killing of Claude Neal.* Baton Rouge, LA: University of Louisiana Press, 1982.

Milner, C. and R. Milner. *The Secret World of Black Pimps.* Boston: Little, Brown, 1972.

Mitchell, Angela with Kennise Herring. *What the Blues Is All About: Black Women Overcoming Stress and Depression.* New York: Penguin Putnam, 1998.

Monroe, Irene. "Louis Farrakhan's Ministry of Misogyny and Homophobia," in *The Farrakhan Factor: African American Writers on Leadership, Nationhood, and Minister Louis Farrakhan.* ed., Amy Alexander. New York: Grove Press, 1998.

Moon, Michael, and Cathy N. Davidson, eds. *Subjects and Citizens: Nation, Race, and Gender from Oroonoko to Anita Hill.* Durham: Duke University Press, 1995.

Muhammad, Elijah. *Message to the Blackman in America.* Atlanta: M.E.M.P.S., 1965.

Nelson, Jill. *Straight, No Chaser: How I Became a Grown-up Black Woman.* New York: G.P. Putnam's Sons, 1997.

Oliver, William. *The Violent Social World of African American Men.* New York: Lexington Books, 1994.

———. "Black Males and the Tough Guy Image: A Dysfunctional Compensatory Adaptation," *Western Journal of Black Studies* 8 (1984), 1999–2202.

———. "Sexual Conquest and Patterns of Black on Black Violence: A Structural-Cultural Perspective," *Violence and Victims*, 4(1989), 257–273.

Ottenberg, Simon. *Boyhood Rituals in an African Society*. Seattle: University of Washington Press, 1989.

Parker, Andrew, and Mary Russo, eds., et al. *Nationalisms and Sexualities*. New York: Routledge, 1992.

Pierce-Baker, Charlotte. *Surviving the Silence: Black Women's Stories of Rape*. New York: W.W. Norton & Co, 1998.

Poussaint, Alvin. *Why Blacks Kill Other Blacks*. New York: Emerson Hall, 1972.

Prothrow-Stith, Deborah. *Deadly Consequences*. New York: HarperCollins, 1991.

Randolph, Laura. "The Hidden Fear: Black Women, Bisexuals and the AIDS Risk," *Ebony*, January 1988.

Reed, Jr., Adolph. *Class Notes: Posing as Politics and Other Thoughts on the American Scene*. New York: The New Press, 2000.

Richie, Beth E. *Compelled to Crime: The Gender Entrapment of Battered Black Women*. New York: Routledge, 1996.

Roberts, Dorothy. *Killing the Black Body: Race, Reproduction, and the Meaning of Liberty*. New York: Vintage Books, 1997.

Satter, Beryl. "Marcus Garvey, Father Divine and the Gender Politics of Race Difference and Race Neutrality," *American Quarterly* 48 (1996), 30–37.

Scarry, Elaine. *The Body in Pain: The Making and Unmaking of the World*. New York: Oxford University Press, 1985.

Shakur, Sanyika, aka Monster Kody Scott. *Monster: The Autobiography of an L.A. Gang Member*. New York: Penguin Books, 1993.

Silverman, Geneva, ed. *African American Women Speak Out on Anita Hill-Clarence Thomas*. Detroit: Wayne State University Press, 1995.

Simmons, Aishah Shahidah. "Creating a Sacred Space of Our Own," in *Just Sex: Students Rewrite the Roles on Sex, Violence, Activism, and Equality*. eds., Jodi Gold and Susan Villari. Lanham, MD: Rowman & Littlefield Publishers, 2000.

Smith, George Edmond. *More Than Sex: Reinventing the Black Male Image*. New York: Kensington Books, 2000.

Staples, Robert. *Black Masculinity: The Black Males' Role in American Society*. San Francisco: Black Scholar Press, 1982.

Stone, Robin D. "Silent No More," *Essence*, August 2001.

Uzzell, Odell and Wilma Peebles-Wilkins. "Black Spousal Abuse: A Focus on Relational Factors and Intervention Strategies." *Western Journal of Black Studies* 13, no. 1 (1989), 10–16.

Wafford, Tony. "Why I Give a Damn!," *Essence*, June 2002.

Walker, Alice. *The Color Purple*. New York: Harcourt Brace Jovanovich, 1983.

Wallace, Michele. *Black Macho and the Myth of the Superwoman*. New York: Warner Books, 1978.

Watts, Roderick J., and Robert J. Jagers, eds. *Manhood Development in Urban African American Communities*. New York: The Haworth Press, 1997.

Weatherspoon, Floyd D. *African American Males and the Law*. Lanham, MD: University Press of America, 1998.

Weinberg, Martin S., and C. J. Williams. "Black Sexuality: A Test of Two Theories," *The Journal of Sex Research* 2 (1988), 197–218.

West, Carolyn, ed. *Violence in the Lives of Black Women: Battered, Black and Blue.* Haworth Press, forthcoming 2003.

West, Traci C. *Wounds of the Spirit: Black Women, Violence and Resistance Ethics.* New York: New York University Press, 1999.

White, Jr., Vibert L. *Inside the Nation of Islam.* Gainesville: University Press of Florida, 2001.

White, Evelyn C. *Chain Chain Change: For Black Women in Abusive Relationships.* Seattle: Seal Press, 1985.

———. *The Black Women's Health Book: Speaking for Ourselves.* Seattle: Seal Press, 1990.

White, Aaronette M. "Talking Black, Talking Feminist: Gendered Micromobilization Processes in a Collective Protest Against Rape," in *Still Lifting, Still Climbing: African American Women's Contemporary Activism.* ed. Kimberly Springer. New York: New York University Press, 1999.

White, Walter. *Rope and Faggot: A Biography of Judge Lynch.* New York: Alfred A. Knopf, 1929.

White, E. Frances. *Dark Continent of Our Bodies: Black Feminsm and the Politics of Respectability.* Philadelphia: Temple University Press, 2001.

Whitfield, Stephen J. *A Death in the Delta: The Story of Emmett Till.* Baltimore: Johns Hopkins University Press, 1988.

Wilson, Melba. *Crossing the Boundary: Black Women Survive Incest.* Seattle: Seal Press, 1994.

Wilson M., Pamela. "Black Culture and Sexuality," *Sexuality, Ethnoculture and Social Work* 1 (1986), 29–46.

Wilson, A. N. *Understanding Black Adolescent Male Violence: Its Remediation and Prevention.* New York: Afrikan World Infosystems, 1992.

Wood, Frances E. " 'Take My Yoke Upon You': The Role of the Church in the Oppression of African-American Women," in *A Troubling in My Soul: Womanist Perspectives on Evil and Suffering,* ed., Emilie M. Townes. Maryknoll, NY: Orbis Books, 1993.

Wyatt, Dr. Gail Elizabeth. "The Aftermath of Child Sexual Abuse of African American and White Women: The Victim's Experience." *Journal of Family Violence* 5, no. 1 (March 1990), 66–81.

———. "The Sexual Abuse of Afro-American and White American Women in Childhood." *Child Abuse and Neglect* 9 (1985), 507–19.

———. *Stolen Women: Reclaiming Our Sexuality, Taking Back Our Lives.* New York: John Wiley & Sons, 1997.

6   BLACK, LESBIAN, AND GAY: SPEAKING THE UNSPEAKABLE

Adam, Barry. "Age, Structure and Sexuality: Reflections on the Anthropological Evidence on Homosexual Relations." *Journal of Homosexuality,* vol. 11, no.1 (1985), 19–33.

Ailey, Alvin. *Revelations.* New York: Carol Publishing Company, 1995.

Alexander, Amy, ed. *The Farrakhan Factor: African American Writers on Leadership, Nationhood and Minister Louis Farrakhan.* New York: Grove Press, 1998.

Alexander, Adele Logan. "Unconventional Sexuality Among the 'Talented Tenth,' " in *Black Women's History at the Intersection of Knowledge and Power.* eds., Rosalyn Terborg-Penn and Janice Sumler-Edmond. Acton, MA: Tapestry Press, Ltd., 2000.

Amadiume, Ifi. *Male Daughters, Female Husbands: Gender and Sex in an African Society.* London: Zed Books, 1987.

Asante, Molefi K. *Afrocentricity.* Trenton: African World Press, 1991.

Baldwin, James. "Preservation of Innocence," *Outlook* 2:2 (Fall 1989), 40–45.

———. *Price of the Ticket: Collected Nonfiction, 1948–1985.* New York: St. Martin's Press, 1985.

Beam, Joseph, ed. *In the Life: A Black Gay Anthology.* Boston: Alyson Publications, 1986.

Beemyn, Brett, ed. *Creating a Place for Ourselves: Lesbian, Gay, and Bisexual Community Histories.* New York: Routledge, 1997.

Belton, Don, ed. *Speak My Name: Black Men on Masculinity and the American Dream.* Boston: Beacon Press, 1995.

Bentley, Gladys. "I Am a Woman Again," *Ebony*, August 1952.

Blackwood, Evelyn and Saskia E. Wieringa, eds. *Female Desires: Same-Sex Relations and Transgender Practices Across Cultures.* New York: Columbia University Press, 1999.

Blackwood, Evelyn, ed. *The Many Faces of Homosexuality: Anthropological Approaches to Homosexual Behavior.* New York: Harrington Park Press, 1996.

Blaxton, Reginald Glenn. " 'Jesus Wept': Reflections on HIV Dis-ease and the Churches of Black Folk," in *Dangerous Liaisons: Blacks, Gays and the Struggle for Equality.* New York: New Press, 1999.

Bleys, Rudi C.. *The Geography of Perversion: Male-to-Male Sexual Behavior Outside the West and the Ethnographic Imagination, 1750–1918.* Washington Square, NY: New York University Press, 1995.

Boykin, Keith. *One More River to Cross: Black & Gay in America.* New York: Anchor Books, 1996.

Brandt, Eric, ed. *Dangerous Liaisons: Blacks, Gays, and the Struggle for Equality.* New York: New Press, 1999.

Butts, June Dobbs. "Fighting AIDS with Sexual Honesty," *The Washington Post,* July 19, 1992.

Byrd, Rudolph and Beverly Guy-Sheftall, eds. *Traps: African American Men on Gender and Sexuality.* Bloomington: Indiana University Press, 2001.

Carbado, Devon W., Dwight A. McBride, and Donald Weise, eds. *Black Like Us: A Lesbian, Gay and Bisexual African American Fiction.* San Francisco: Cleis Press, Inc., 2002.

Chauncey, George. *Gay New York: Gender, Urban Culture, and the Making of the Gay Male World, 1890–1940.* New York: Basic Books, 1984.

Clarke, Cheryl. "The Failure to Transform: Homophobia in the Black Community," in *Homegirls: A Black Feminist Anthology.* ed., Barbara Smith. New York: Kitchen Table Press, 1983.

———. "Transferences and Confluences: Black Poetries, the Black Arts Movement, and Black Lesbian-Feminism," in *Dangerous Liaisons: Blacks, Gays, and the Struggle for Equality.* ed., Eric Brandt. New York: The New Press, 1999.

Comstock, Gary David. *A Whosoever Church: Welcoming Lesbians and Gay Men Into African American Congregations*. Louisville: Westminster John Knox Press, 2001.

―――― and Susan E. Henking, eds. *Que(e)ring Religion: A Critical Anthology*. New York: Continuum, 1997.

Cornwall, Anita. *Black Lesbian in White America*. Tallahassee: Naiad Press, 1983.

Cunningham, M. "Sex Role Influences of African American Males: A Literature Review." *Journal of African American Male Studies* 1(1) (1993), 30–37.

D'Emilio, John. *Sexual Politics, Sexual Communities: The Making of a Homosexual Minority in the United States, 1940–1970*. Chicago: University of Chicago Press, 1983.

―――― and Estelle B. Freedman. *Intimate Matters: A History of Sexuality in America*. New York: Harper and Row, 1988.

Davis, Angela Y. *Blues Legacies and Black Feminism*. New York: Pantheon Books, 1998.

Delany, Samuel R. *Heavenly Breakfast: An Essay on the Winter of Love*. Flint, Michigan: Bamberger Books, 1997.

――――. *Longer Views: Extended Essays*. Hanover: Wesleyan University Press, 1996

――――. *The Motion of Light on Water: Sex and Science Fiction Writing in the East Village, 1960–1965*. New York: Masquerade Books, 1993.

――――. *Shorter Views: Queer Thoughts & The Politics of the Paraliterary*. Hanover: Wesleyan University Press, 1999.

――――. *Silent Interviews: On Language, Race, Sex, Science Fiction and Some Comics*. Hanover: Wesleyan University Press, 1994.

――――. "Some Queer Notions About Race." in *Dangerous Liaisons*. ed., Eric Brandt.

Douglas, Debbie et al, eds. *Má-Ka Diasporic Juks: Contemporary Writing by Queers of African Descent*. Toronto: SisterVision, 1997.

Douglas, Kelly Brown. *Sexuality and the Black Church: A Womanist Perspective*. Maryknoll, NY: Orbis, 1999.

Duberman, Martin, et al., eds. *Hidden From History:Reclaiming the Gay and Lesbian Past*. New York: NAL Books, 1989.

Dynes, Wayne and S. Donaldson. *Ethnographic Studies of Homosexuality*. New York: Garland, 1992.

Dynes, Wayne. "Homosexuality in Sub-Saharan Africa," *Gay Books Bulletin*, Spring/Summer 1983, 20–21.

Edwards, Tamala. "Men Who Sleep With Men," *Essence*, October 2001.

Eichelberger, Brenda. "Voices on Black Feminism," *Quest* 3.4 (Spring 1977), 16–28.

Ernst, F. A. et al. "Condemnation of Homosexuality in the Black Community: A Gender-Specific Phenomenon?" *Archives of Sexual Behavior*, 20.6, 579–85.

Eskridge, William, Jr. "A History of Same-Sex Marriage." *Virginia Law Review*, 79, no. 7, October 1993, 1419–1513.

Evans-Pritchard, E. E. "Sexual Inversion Among the Azande." *American Anthropologist* 72 (1970), 1428–34.

――――. *Man and Woman Among the Azande*. London: Faber & Faber, 1974.

Faderman, Lillian. *To Believe in Women: What Lesbians Have Done for American History*. New York: First Mariner Books, 2000.

Farajaje-Jones, Elias. "Breaking Silence: Toward An In-The-Life Theology," in *Black Theology*, 139–159.

Fone, Byrne. *Homophobia: A History.* New York: Henry Holt & Company, 2000.

Fout, John C. and Maura Shaw Tantilla, eds. *American Sexual Politics: Sex, Gender and Race since the Civil War.* Chicago: University of Chicago Press, 1993.

Garber, Eric. "A Spectacle in Color: The Lesbian and Gay Subculture of Jazz Age Harlem," in *Hidden from History: Reclaiming the Gay and Lesbian Past.* eds., Martin Duberman, Martha Vicinus, and George Chauncey. New York: New American Library, 1989.

Garber, Eric. "Gladys Bentley: The Bulldagger Who Sang the Blues," *Out/Look,* 1.1 (Spring 1988), 52–61.

Gevisser, Mark and Edwin Cameron, eds. *Defiant Desire: Gay and Lesbian Lives in South Africa.* New York: Routledge, 1995.

Greenberg, David G. *The Construction of Homosexuality.* Chicago: University of Chicago Press, 1988.

Halberstam, J. "Mack Daddy, Superfly, Rapper: Gender, Race, and Masculinity in the Drag King Scene," *Social Text 52/53,* vol. 15, nos. 3 & 4 (Fall/Winter 1997), 104–131.

Halperin, David M. *One Hundred Years of Homosexuality.* New York: Routledge, 1990.

Halperin, David M., et al., eds. *Before Sexuality: The Construction of Erotic Experience in the Ancient Greek World.* Princeton: Princeton University Press, 1990.

Hammonds, Evelynn. "Race, Sex, AIDS: The Construction of the 'Other.' " *Radical America,* vol. 20, no. 6 (1986), 28–36.

―――― and Margaret Cerullo. "AIDS in Africa: The Western Imagination and the Dark Continent." *Radical America,* vol. 21, nos. 2–3 (1987), 17–23.

Hansen, Karen V. " 'No Kisses Is Like Youres': An Erotic Friendship Between Two African-American Women During the Mid-Nineteenth Century." *Lesbian Subjects.* ed., Martha Vicinus. Bloomington: Indiana University Press, 1996.

Hardy, James B. *B-Boy Blues.* Boston: Alyson Publications, 1994.

Hare, Nathan and Julia Hare. "The Rise of Homosexuality and Other Diverse Alternatives." *Black Male/Female Relationships,* vol. 5 (1981), 8–15.

Hawkeswood, William G. *One of the Children: Gay Black Men in Harlem.* Berkeley: University of California Press, 1995.

Hemphill, Essex, ed., with Joseph Beam. *Brother to Brother: New Writing by Black Gay Men.* Boston: Alyson Publications, 1991.

Herdt, Gilbert H., ed. *Ritualized Homosexuality in Melanesia.* Berkeley: University of California Press, 1984.

――――. *Same Sex, Different Cultures: Exploring Gay & Lesbian Lives.* Boulder, Colorado: Westview Press, 1997.

――――, ed. *Third Sex, Third Gender: Beyond Sexual Dimorphism in Culture and History.* New York: Zone Books, 1994.

Herek, G. M. and J. P. Capitanio. "Black Heterosexuals' Attitudes Toward Lesbians and Gay Men in the United States." *Journal of Sex Research* 32 (2): 95–105.

Hernton, Calvin. "Breaking Silences," in *Court of Appeal,* 1992.

Hill, Renee L. "Who Are We for Each Other?: Sexism, Sexuality and Womanist Theology," in *Black Theology: A Documentary History, 1980–1992,* vol. 2. eds., James H. Cone & Gayraud S. Wilmore. Maryknoll, NY: Orbis Books, 1993.

Hine, Darlene Clark. "Rape and the Inner Lives of Southern Black Women: Some

Thoughts on the Culture of Dissemblance." *Signs: A Journal of Women in Culture and Society* 14, no. 4 (Summer 1989), 912–20.

Holland, Sharon Patricia. " 'Which Me Will Survive?': Audre Lorde and the Development of a Black Feminist Ideology," *Critical Matrix*, 1(1988), 2–30.

Howard, John, ed. *Carryin' on in the Lesbian and Gay South*. New York: New York University Press, 1997.

Hull, Gloria T. *Color, Sex, and Poetry: Three Women Writers of the Harlem Renaissance*. Bloomington: Indiana University Press, 1987.

Hunter, Michael B., ed. with the Other Countries Collective. *Sojourner: Black Gay Voices in the Age of AIDS*. New York: Other Countries Press, 1993.

Iceberg Slim. *Pimp: the Story of My Life*. Holloway House: Los Angeles, 1967.

———. *The Naked Soul of Iceberg Slim*. Holloway House: Los Angeles, 1971.

Isaacs, G. and McKendrick, B. *Male Homosexuality in South Africa: Identity, Formation, Culture and Crisis*. Cape Town: Oxford University Press, 1992.

Jarrett, Gene. "A Song to Pass On: An Interview with Thomas Glave." *Callaloo* vol. 23, no. 1 (2000), 1227–1240.

Johnson, Leola. "Rap, Misogyny and Racism." *Radical America*, vol. 26, no. 3, 1992, 6–19.

Jones, LeRoi. *Home: Social Essays*. Hopewell, NJ: The Ecco Press, 1961.

Julien, Issac. " 'Black Is, Black Ain't': Notes on De-Essentializing Black Identities," *Black Popular Culture*. ed. Gina Dent. Seattle: Bay Press, 1992.

Katz, Jonathan. *Gay American History: Lesbians and Gay Men in the U.S.A.* New York: Thomas Crowell, 1976.

———. *Gay/Lesbian Almanac: A New Documentary*. New York: Harper and Row, 1983.

———. *The Invention of Heterosexuality*. New York: Dutton, 1995.

Keenan, Randall. *Lives of Notable Gay Men and Lesbians: James Baldwin*. New York: Chelsea House, 1994.

Lane, A.J. *Homosexuality and the Crisis of Black Cultural Particularity*. Los Angeles: University of California, 1997.

Leeming, David. *Amazing Grace: The Life of Beauford Delaney*. New York: Oxford University Press, 1998.

Lewin, Ellen, ed. *Inventing Lesbian Cultures in America*. Boston: Beacon Press, 1996.

Lewis, David Levering. *When Harlem Was In Vogue*. New York: Oxford University Press, 1979.

———. *W. E. B. Du Bois: The Fight for Equality and the American Century, 1919–1963*, vol 2. New York: Henry Holt and Company, 2000.

Loiacano, D. K. "Gay Identity Issues Among Black Americans: Racism, Homophobia, and the Need for Validation," *Journal of Counseling & Development*, 68 (1989), 21–25.

Lomax, Pearl. "Black Women's Liberation," *Essence*, August 1972.

Longres, John F., ed. *Men of Color: A Context for Service to Homosexually Active Men*. New York: Harrington Park Press, 1996.

Lorde, Audre. *Sister Outsider: Essays and Speeches*. Trumansburg, NY: Crossing Press, 1984.

Lumsden, Ian. *Machos, Maricones, and Gays: Cuba and Homosexuality*. Philadelphia: Temple University Press, 1996.

"Man Who Lived 30 Years as a Woman," *Ebony,* October 1951.

Mbiti, John S. *Love and Marriage in Africa.* London: Longman, 1973.

McClintock, Anne. *Imperial Leather: Race, Gender, and Sexuality in the Colonial Contest.* New York: Routledge, 1995.

McFeely, William S. *Frederick Douglass.* New York: W.W. Norton, 1991.

McKinley, Catherine E. & L. Joyce DeLaney, eds. *Afrekete: An Anthology of Black Lesbian Writing.* New York: Doubleday, 1995.

Merla, Patrick, ed. *Boys Like Us: Gay Writers Tell Their Coming Out Stories.* New York: Avon Books, 1996.

Miller, N. *Out in the World: Gay and Lesbian Life from Buenos Aires to Bangkok.* London: Penguin, 1993.

Monroe, Irene. "Louis Farrakhan's Ministry of Misogyny and Homophobia," in *The Farrakhan Factor: African-American Writers on Leadership, Nationhood, and Minister Louis Farrakhan.* ed., Amy Alexander. New York: Grove Press, 1999.

Morrison, Toni, ed. *Race-ing Justice, En-gendering Power: Essays on Anita Hill, Clarence Thomas, and the Social Construction of Reality.* New York: Pantheon Books, 1992.

Morrow, Bruce and Charles H. Rowell, eds. *Shade: An Anthology of Fiction by Gay Men of African Descent.* New York: Avon Books, 1996.

"Muminimas Committee for a Unified Newark." *Mwanamke Mwananchi (The Nationalist Woman).* Newark, NJ: Congress of Afrikan Peoples, 1971.

Munoz, J. E. *Disidentifications: Queers of Color and the Performance of Politics.* Minneapolis: University of Minnesota Press, 1999.

Murray, Stephen O. and Will Roscoe, eds. *Boy-Wives and Female Husbands: Studies of African Homosexualities.* New York: St. Martin's Press, 1998.

Nelson, Emmanuel. "Critical Deviance: Homophobia and the Reception of James Baldwin's Fiction." *Journal of American Culture,* 14, no 3 (1991), 919.

Nelson, Emmanuel, ed. *Critical Essays: Gay and Lesbian Writers of Color.* New York: Harrington Park Press, 1993.

Nugent, B. and W. H. Thurman. "Reclaiming Black Male Same-Sex Sexualities in the New Negro Movement." *In Process,* 1.1., 1996.

Ongiri, A. A. "We Are Family: Black Nationalism, Black Masculinity, and the Black Gay Cultural Imagination." *College Literature,* February 1997, 280–94.

Oppong, Christine, ed. *Female and Male in West Africa.* London: George Allen & Unwin, 1983.

Ottenberg, Simon. *Boyhood Rituals in an African Society: An Interpretation.* Seattle: University of Washington Press, 1989.

Oyewumi, Oyeronke. *The Invention of Women: Making An African Sense of Western Gender Discourses.* Minneapolis: University of Minnesota Press, 1997.

"Panther Sisters on Women's Liberation," in *Off the Pigs: The History and Literature of the Black Panther Party.* ed., G. Louis Heath. Metuchen, NJ: Scarecrow Press, 1976.

Parker, Richard. *Bodies, Pleasures and Passions: Sexual Culture in Contemporary Brazil.* Boston: Beacon Press, 1991.

Patterson, Leonard. "At Ebenezer Baptist Church." *Black Men/White Men: Afro-American Gay Life and Culture.* ed., Michael J. Smith, 1993.

Patton, Cindy and Benigno Sanchez-Eppler, eds. *Queer Diasporas*. Durham: Duke University Press, 2000.

Peddle, Daniel. "The Aggressive: Venturing Outside Society's Usual Grasp of the Feminine." *Trace* 37 (2002), 94–101.

Perkins, Margo V. *Autobiography as Activism: Three Black Women of the Sixties*. Jackson: University Press of Mississippi, 2000.

Peterson, John L. "Black Men and Their Same-Sex Desires and Behaviors," in *Gay Culture in America: Essays from the Field*. ed., Gilbert Herdt. Boston: Beacon Press, 1992.

Plummer, Ken, ed. *Modern Homosexualties: Fragments of Lesbian and Gay Experience*. New York: Routledge, 1992.

Poussaint, Alvin. "An Honest Look at Black Gays and Lesbians." *Ebony*, September 1990.

Powell, Adam Clayton, Sr. *Against the Tide: An Autobiography*. Salem, NH: Ayer Company Publishers, 1938.

Randolph, Laura B. "The Hidden Fear: Black Women, Bisexuals and the AIDS Risk," *Ebony*, January 1988.

Reid-Pharr, Robert F. *Black Gay Man: Essays*. New York: New York University Press, 2001.

———. "Extending Queer Theory to Race and Ethnicity." *The Chronicle Review*, April 16, 2002. B7–9.

Ruff, Patricia Elam. "Cover Girls." *Essence*, March 1992.

Rupp, Leila J. *A Desired Past: A Short History of Same-Sex Love in America*. Chicago: University of Chicago Press, 1999.

Scott, Joyce Hoe. "From Foreground to Margin: Female Configurations and Masculine Self-Representation in Black Nationalist Fiction," in *Nationalisms and Sexualities*. eds., Andrew Parker, et al. New York: Routledge, 1992.

Smith, Michael J. *Black Men/White Men: Afro-American Gay Life & Culture*. San Francisco: Gay Sunshine Press, 1999.

Smith, Charles Michael, ed. *Fighting Words: Personal Essays by Black Gay Men*. New York: Avon Books, 1999.

Smith, Charles Michael. "Bruce Nugent and Wallace Thurman: Reclaiming Black Male Same-Sexualities in the New Negro Movement," *In Process* 1(1996), 53–73.

Smith, Barbara, ed. *Home Girls: A Black Feminist Anthology*. New York: Kitchen Table Women of Color Press, 1983.

Somerville, Siobhan B. *Queering the Color Line: Race and the Invention of Homosexuality in American Culture*. Chapel Hill: Duke University Press, 2000.

Staples, Robert. "Homosexuality and the Black Male." *The Material Queer: A LesBi-Gay Cultural Studies Reader*. ed., Donald Morton. Boulder, Colorado: Westview Press, 1996.

Stokes, Mason. "Strange Fruits: Rethinking the Gay Twenties." *Transition*, vol. 12, no. 2 (92), 56–79.

Swidler, Arlene, ed. *Homosexuality and World Religions*. Harrisburg, Pennsylvania: Trinity Press International, 1993.

Teunis, Niels F. "Homosexuality in Dakar: Is the Bed the Heart of a Sexual Subculture?" *Journal of Gay, Lesbian, and Bisexual Identity*, vol. 1, 1996, 153–76.

Tielman, Rob A.P., et. al, eds. *Bisexuality & HIV/AIDS: A Global Perspective*. Buffalo: Prometheus Books, 1991.

Tirivanho, H.M. "Black Homosexuality in Zimbabwe," *GALZ*, November 1995, 18–19.

Toinette, Eugene. "While Love is Unfashionable: Ethical Implications of Black Spirituality and Sexuality," in *Sexuality and the Sacred*. eds., James B. Nelson and Sandra P. Longfellow. Louisville: Westminster/John Knox Press, 1994.

Trexler, Richard. *Sex and Conquest: Gendered Violence, Political Order, and the European Conquest of the Americas*. Ithaca: Cornell University Press, 1995.

Vicinus, Martha, ed. *Lesbian Subjects: A Feminist Studies Reader*. Bloomington: Indiana University Press, 1996.

Villarosa, Linda. "Coming Out." *Essence*, May 1991.

Washington, Patricia A. "Who Gets to Drink from the Fountain of Freedom?: Homophobia Within Communities of Color." *Journal of Lesbian and Gay Social Services* 13, nos. 1/2(2001), 117–131.

———. "The Second Assault of Male Survivors of Sexual Violence." *Journal of Interpersonal Violence* 14, no. 7 (July 1999), 713–730.

Welsing, Frances Cress. *The Isis Papers: The Keys to the Colors*. Chicago: Third World Press, 1970.

West, Cornel. *Race Matters*. Boston: Beacon Press, 1992.

White, E. Frances. *Dark Continent of Our Bodies: Black Feminism and the Politics of Respectability*. Philadelphia: Temple University Press, 2001.

White, Evelyn. *The Black Women's Health Book: Speaking for Ourselves*. Seattle: Seal Press, 1990.

Wirth, Thomas H., ed. *Gay Rebel of the Harlem Renaissance: Selections from the Work of Richard Bruce Nugent*. Chapel Hill: Duke University Press, 2002.

7   No Respect: Hip-Hop & Gender Politics

Allen, Ernest, Jr. "Making the Strong Survive: The Contours and Contradictions of Message Rap," in *Droppin' Science: Critical Essays on Rap Music and Hip Hop Culture*. ed., William Eric Perkins. Philadelphia: Temple University Press, 1996.

"A Nappy Happy: A Conversation with Ice Cube and Angela Y. Davis," *Transition* 58 (1992), 177–180.

Baker, Houston, Jr. *Black Studies, Rap, and the Academy*. Chicago: University of Chicago Press, 1993.

Bennett, Lerone, Jr. "Sex and Music: Has It Gone Too Far?" *Ebony*, October 2002.

Berry, Venise T. "Feminine or Masculine: The Conflicting Nature of Female Images in Rap Music," in *Cecilia Reclaimed: Feminist Perspectives on Gender and Music*. eds., Susan C. Cook and Judy S. Tsou. Champaign: University of Illinois Press, 1994.

Chappell, Kevin. "Hip-Hop at the Crossroads: Will Lyrics and Perceptions Change?," *Ebony*, September, 2001, 111–114.

Crenshaw, Kimberle. "Beyond Racism and Misogyny: Black Feminism and 2 Live Crew," *Boston Review* 16, no. 6 (December 1991), 6–32.

Cross, Brian. *It's Not About a Salary: Rap, Race and Resistance in Los Angeles*. New York: Verso, 1993.

Davis, Angela Y. *Blues Legacies and Black Feminism*. New York: Pantheon Books, 1998.

De Genoa, Nick. "Gangster Rap and Nihilism in Black America: Some Questions of Life and Death," *Social Text*, 43 (Fall 1995), 89–132.

De Rogatis, Jim. "Like a Freak." *GQ*, September 2002, 349–357.

Dent, Gina, ed. *Black Popular Culture*. Seattle: Bay Press, 1992.

Dyson, Michael Eric. *Between God and Gangsta Rap: Bearing Witness to Black Culture*. New York: Oxford University Press, 1996.

———. *Holler If You Hear Me: Searching for Tupac Shakur*. New York: Basic Books, 2001.

Ebron, Paula. "Rapping Between Men: Performing Gender," *Radical America* 24 (October-December 1989), 23–27.

George, Nelson. *Buppies, B-Boys, Baps & Bohos: Notes on Post-Soul Black Culture*. New York: Harper Perennial, 1992.

———. *Hip Hop America*. New York: Penguin Putnam, Inc., 1998.

———. *Where Did Our Love Go: The Rise and Fall of the Motown Sound*. New York: St. Martin's Press, 1985.

Gonzales, Michael. *Bring the Noise: A Guide to Rap Music and Hip Hop Culture*. New York: Harmony Music, 1991.

Goodman, Fred. *Hip Hop: The Illustrated History of Break Dancing, Rap Music, and Graffiti*. New York: St. Martin's Press, 1984.

Hardy, James Earl . *The Day Eazy-E Died*. Los Angeles: Alyson Books, 2001.

hooks, bell. *Outlaw Culture: Resisting Representation*. New York: Routledge, 1994.

———. *Reel to Real: Race, Sex, and Class at the Movies*. New York: Routledge, 1996.

Hughes, Alan. "Hip-Hop Economy." *Black Enterprise*, May 2002, pp. 70–75.

Ice T. *The Ice Opinion: Who Gives a Fuck?* New York: St. Martin's Press, 1994.

Jackson, Bruce. '*Get Your Ass in the Water and Swim Like Me*': *Narrative Poetry from Black Oral Tradition*. Cambridge: Harvard University Press, 1974.

Johnson, Leola. "Rap, Misogyny and Racism," *Radical America*, vol. 26, no. 3 (1992), 7–19.

Kelley, Robin. *Race Rebels: Culture, Politics, and the Black Working Class*. New York: Free Press, 1994.

Keyes, Cheryl. "The Rap Music Tradition," in *Feminist Messages: Coding in Women's Folk Culture*. ed., Joan Newlon Radner. Champaign: University of Illinois Press, 1993.

Kitwana, Bakari. *The Hip Hop Generation: Young Blacks and the Crisis in African-American Culture*. New York: Basic Civitas Books, 2002.

———. *The Rap on Gangsta Rap: Gangsta Rap and Visions of Black Violence*. Chicago: Third World Press, 1994.

Lusane, Clarence. "Rhapsodic Aspirations: Rap, Race and Power Politics." *Black Scholar*, vol. 23, no. 2 (Winter/Spring 1993), 37–51.

Milner, Christine and Richard Milner. *Black Players: The Secret World of Black Pimps*. New York: Little, Brown, 1973.

Mitchell, Tony, ed. *Global Noise: Rap and Hip-Hop Outside the U.S.A.* Hanover, PA: Wesleyan University Press, 2002.

Morgan, Joan. "Sex, Lies and Videos," *Essence*, June 2002.

———. *When Chickenheads Come Home to Roost*. New York: Simon & Schuster, 1999.

Neal, Mark Anthony. "Keeping It Real: The Hip-Hop Nation on Campus," *Common Quest,* vol. 3, no. 3/vol. 4, no. 1, 10–22.

———. *Soul Babies: Black Popular Culture and the Post-Soul Aesthetic.* New York: Routledge, 2002.

———. *What the Music Said: Black Popular Music and Black Public Culture.* New York: Routledge, 1999.

Nelson, Havelock and Michael A. Gonzales. *Bring the Noise: A Guide to Rap Music and Hip Hop Culture.* New York: Harmony Books, 1991.

Ogg, Alex with David Upshal. *The Hip Hop Years: A History of Rap.* London: Channel 4 Books, 1999.

Perkins, William Eric, ed. *Droppin' Science: Critical Essays on Rap Music and Hip Hop Culture.* Philadelphia: Temple University Press, 1996.

Perry, Imani. "It's My Thang and I'll Swing It the Way That I Feel!: Sexuality and Black Women Rappers," in *Gender, Race and Class in Media: A Text-Reader.* eds., Gail Dines & Jean M. Humez. Thousand Oaks, CA: Sage Publications, 1995.

Potter, Russell. *Spectacular Vernaculars: Hip Hop and the Politics of Postmodernism.* Albany: State University of New York Press, 1995.

Powell, Kevin. "Confessions of a Recovering Misogynist," *Ms.* April/May 2000, 72–77.

Queen Latifah with Karen Hunter. *Ladies First: Revelations of a Strong Woman.* New York: William Morrow, 1999.

Quinn, Eithne. " 'It's a Doggy-Dogg World: Black Cultural Politics, Gangsta Rap and the 'Post-Soul Man,' " in *Gender in the Civil Rights Movement.* eds., Peter J. Ling and Sharon Monteith. New York & London: Garland Publishing, Inc., 1999.

Roberts, Robin. "Music Videos, Performance, and Resistance: Feminist Rappers," *Journal of Popular Culture* 25(Fall 1991), 141–152.

Rose, Tricia. "Contracting Rap: An Interview with Carmen Ashhurst-Watson," in *Microphone Fiends: Youth Music and Youth Culture.* eds. Andrew Ross and Tricia Rose. New York: Routledge, 1994.

———. *Black Noise: Rap Music and Black Culture in Contemporary America.* Hanover: Wesleyan University of Press, 1994.

———. "Never Trust a Big Butt and a Smile," *Camera Obscura,* May 1991, 109–131.

———. " 'Fear of a Black Planet': Rap Music and Black Cultural Politics in the 1990s," in *Gender, Race and Class in Media* eds., Gail Dines & Jean M. Humez. Thousand Oaks, CA: Sage Publications, 1995.

Sister Souljah. *No Disrespect.* New York: Random House, 1994.

Slim, Iceberg. *Pimp: The Story of My Life.* Los Angeles: Holloway House, 1987.

———. *The Naked Soul of Iceberg Slim.* Los Angeles: Holloway House, 1971.

Spruell, Sakina P. "Hip-Hop at the Movies": Hip-Hop Economy, Part 2, *Black Enterprise,* July 2002.

Sullivan, Lisa. "Not Walking the Talk." *Sojourners Magazine,* vol. 31, no. 2, May-June 2001, 15.

Toop, David. *The Rap Attack 2: African Jive to New York Hip Hop.* Boston: South End Press, 1984.

Valdes, Mimi. "Beyond Sucker MCs: Hip-Hop Women," *The Rolling Stone Book of Women in Rock: Trouble Girls.* ed., Barbara O'Dair. New York: Random House, 1997.

Wade, Bruce H. and Cynthia A. Thomas-Gunnar. "Explicit Rap Music Lyrics and Attitudes Toward Rape: The Perceived Effects on African American College Student's Attitudes," *Challenge*, October 1993, 51–60.

Walser, Robert. *Running With the Devil: Power, Gender and Madness in Heavy Metal Music.* Hanover: Wesleyan University Press, 1993.

Ward, Brian. *Just My Soul Responding: Rhythm and Blues, Black Consciousness and Race Relations.* Berkeley: University of California Press, 1998.

———. "Sex Machines and Prisoners of Love: Male Rhythm and Blues, Sexual Politics and the Black Freedom Struggle," in *Gender and the Civil Rights Movement.*

Watkins, S. Craig. *Representing: Hip-Hop Culture and the Production of Black Cinema.* Chicago: University of Chicago Press, 1998.

Werner, Craig Hansen. *A Change is Gonna Come: Music, Race and the Soul of America.* New York: Plume, 1999.

White, Evelyn. *Chain, Chain, Change: For Black Women Dealing with Physical and Emotional Abuse.* Seattle: Seal Press, 1985.

8   WHERE DO WE GO FROM HERE?

Cade, Toni, ed. *The Black Woman: An Anthology.* New York: Signet, 1970.

Clarke, Cheryl. "The Failure to Transform: Homophobia in the Black Community," in *Home Girls: A Black Feminist Anthology.* ed. Barbara Smith. New York: Kitchen Table Press, 1983.

Douglass, Frederick. "The Significance of Emancipation in the West Indies," August 3, 1857, in *The Frederick Douglass Papers: Speeches, Debates, and Interviews.* Series One, 1855–63. edited by John W. Blassingame. New Haven: Yale University Press, 204.

Lorde, Audre. *Sister Outsider: Essays and Speeches.* Freedom, CA: The Crossing Press, 1984.

Tubman, Harriet. Speech, 1857. Quoted in *My Soul Looks Back, 'Less I Forget: A Collection of Quotations by People of Color.* ed., Dorothy Winbush Riley. New York: HarperCollins Publishers, 1993, 148.

INDEX

•

THE
HUNGER
AND THE
HOWLING
OF
KILLIAN
LONE

THERE ARE NO GHOSTS, THERE ARE ONLY
STORIES TOO STUBBORN TO DIE.

*There was a time when everyone in the country
knew my name.*

I was the greatest chef in the world.

But today no-one has heard of Killian Lone.

This is my story. It must be told, now, for the final time.

It begins in my boyhood.

In this very kitchen...

THE
HUNGER
AND THE
HOWLING
OF
KILLIAN
LONE

WILL STORR

First published in 2013 by
Short Books, 3A Exmouth House, Pine Street, EC1R 0JH
This paperback edition was published in 2014

10 9 8 7 6 5 4 3 2 1

A CIP catalogue record for this book
is available from the British Library.

Printed and bound in Great Britain by
CPI Group (UK) Ltd, Croydon, CR0 4YY

Illustrations © Anna Trench
Front cover image © David White/Getty
Small fly images © R. Classen/Shutterstock
Cover design © Leo Nickolls

ISBN 978-1-78072-182-8

For Craig

"I felt like a boat built of hopeless material, of rotten old wood, launched by the shipbuilder onto the stormy sea of life with the words: 'If you sink it will be your own fault, and you will burn in hell for your failure, burn forever in the eternal flames.'"

Edvard Munch (1883–1944)

"Hoot ffir and smoke makith many an angry cook."

15th-century epigram

There are no ghosts, there are only stories too stubborn to die.

That's all that I am today.

I'm the low ache of sadness long forgotten by the living; the tension of hopes unfulfilled. Always here and always watching, I'm a pressure; a shadow; an uneasy corner.

I am a remains.

It's true, of course, that everyone living is surrounded by the unresolved stories of the dead. But my tale lingers with more weight than most. Indeed, the few visitors that make it here, to Kathryn's lonely cottage in East Sussex, tend to sense my presence the moment they walk through the door.

From the day that she arrived, Kathryn has been surrounded by it. It's seen her every dawn and every sunset; witnessed every moment of rage, sorrow and love. It's stayed with her as she's moved through these rooms with the seasons circling around her.

She's never been able to shut my story out because it's her story too. It tells of blood and splendour, of hope and damage and of the love that grew between us, during those long-gone months.

And now, as the paramedics work in a huddle over her body, they can sense it hovering about them. Lifting her stretcher and manoeuvring it gently out of Dor Cottage, they would surely be amazed to hear of the events that have haunted this pale, reduced woman. Indeed, they are too young even to have heard of Killian Lone.

On the night that I left her, I made Kathryn a promise of

loyalty. I meant it to be one final act of goodness; a desperate attempt to erase all the bad. In life, you see, I was a bad man. I did bad things.

And today, here I am – a tale inside whose final scene Kathryn has spent three decades.

A tale that must be told, now, for the last time.

It begins in my boyhood.

In this very kitchen.

Chapter 1

I was born crying on an early day of frost in October 1965 and the first words that my mother ever said to me were "skin and bone". The nurse who had placed me in her arms gently chided her, "Oh really, Mrs Lone, he's perfectly healthy."

"Well, he is breathing," said my mother, with a reluctant nod. "I suppose that's a start..."

She told this story repeatedly throughout my childhood. I'm not entirely sure why. But I know the thought that lay behind those words. After nine and a half months of pregnancy and thirty-six hours of labour, it wasn't me that she wanted to see at all. It was her best friend Margaret's baby, born nine months before me. Margaret had a swimming pool in her garden and the best extension on our cul-de-sac. Everything she wore, drove in or commented upon was discussed jealously in our home. When Margaret gave birth to Mark, he was commonly described as a "belting, strapping little thing", and that is exactly how he was to grow up. Mark House, with his fair hair and his wide shoulders and his handsome smile that triggered a hundred coos from a hundred envious mothers as he was paraded around the Tonbridge Sainsbury's in his John Lewis pushchair. Mark, with his

9

football playing and his athletics medals and his fighting.

To my mother's endlessly replaying disappointment, it was clear that I would never be Mark, even as a newborn. I instinctively turned my head when someone peered down at me with their huge grown-up face, and I cried and cried and didn't stop crying for three weeks following my birth. Doctor Feiglen assured my parents that there was nothing wrong with me, insisting to my sceptical mother that I was "just a bit colicky". Nevertheless, my wailing continued. It did so until the day I was taken on my first visit to my great-aunt Dorothy's peculiar old cottage deep in the Sussex Downs. Dorothy had spent the morning baking loaves and the moment the first warm, woody wafts of the bread leaked from her oven and stroked my nose, I finally stopped bawling and broke out into a gigglish grin.

And so it began. As a little boy, I was only happy when I was eating, cooking or shopping for food. When my mother was in one of her rare good moods, she'd spoil me – sometimes to the point of nausea. My most wonderful memory of her, in that period, was the evening she arrived home early from work and confessed that, as a young girl, she had loved Peach Melba Angel Delight. We drove to the shop and bought packets and packets and packets of it, then made it up in huge serving bowls, sprinkled with hundreds and thousands and Jelly Tots and glacé cherries. We gorged until she was sick. Her vomit, as I held her hand in the bathroom, smelled of the acid-sweet Martini she'd been drinking all afternoon. That night, she insisted that I go to bed with her and hug her until she fell asleep. I lay there, rigid, with my arm around her waist, until I heard her snoring, at which point I climbed over my similarly comatose father and hurried to my room.

But those were the rare times, and they grew ever

more infrequent as I became older. From toddler-hood and towards double figures, I remained skin and bone, pale and nervous and rarely far from tears. I learned to do my crying in private, during the long grind of the chores which my mother – exhausted from her work as the manager of a large team of social workers – would set me on. I found it particularly hard to hold myself firm during the last twenty minutes or so of every day, when she would conduct her brief tour of the rooms I'd been working on. The bony pad of her finger would be pressed along fridge tops and down toilet bowls and my punishment for its gathering any grime would begin with me having to suck that finger clean.

For the aspiring bullies of suburban Tonbridge, I was a mobile amusement park. I was regularly hounded by a pack of boys that lived up our cul-de-sac, led by Mark House. And at school? Well, there's someone like me at every school. Do you remember me? I was the one with his back to the playground's chainlink fence at break-time. I was the one whose dirty coat the popular boys would dare the skipping girls to touch. I was the one whose hair was a greasy thatch because I couldn't stand to look in the mirror and because Mum never had time. I was the one full of tears and piss who could crumble under the force of an unsympathetic comment.

The only times I felt truly safe were when I was in my favourite place with my favourite person – the kitchen of Dor Cottage with my Great-aunt Dorothy. She was a retired cookery teacher who had long since left her small school in the nearby village of Herstmonceux. Having lost her girls for ever, she had taken to lecturing me instead. I loved her lessons. I loved the food we cooked together. And, more than anything, I loved being in her kitchen.

Never before or since have I felt so powerfully that I was in an enchanted bubble, floating above the jags and bumps of real life.

Dor was the subject of an eccentric and rather eerie family legend. I listened to Dorothy recount it as she worked at the table, the flames from the fire burning in her eyes – which were long and lipped with so many folds and bags they seemed like knots in an ancient oak. As she spoke, I could sense something like fear in her, and something like awe as well. It made her stories wonderfully beguiling. It made me love her even more.

"Have I ever told you, Kill, that this place has been in the family since 1676 and it can never be sold?" she asked. "It was built for Mary Dor, your great, great, great – well, a lot of 'greats', believe you me. Mary was the cook for Thomas Lennard, who lived up at the castle. He was the first earl of Sussex." And then she whispered, as if it was all still too dangerous to say, "What a rogue he was! He loved gambling and cricket and eating, of course. Eating more than anything. He loved Mary's food. Declared she was the greatest cook in England. That's why he built this place for her, so near the castle. But it all went wrong, Kill. They began talking about her, down in the village. Saying her broths were so delicious that there must be some sort of devilry involved in it all. They said her recipes could turn anyone who tasted them mad with uncanny desires. The earl didn't listen, not even when his courtiers started whispering. He was too batty about her cooking to care. But then something happened. Something to do with his pretty wife, Anne. Well, you're too young to hear about that part. But anyhow, it was all blamed on poor Mary and they had her burned as a witch. It's still there, in the elm forest – the place where they got her. There's a stone post, about as high as my knee, with strange runes carved all over it. I'll show it to you one day. The tourists who go past that thing, eating their ice creams and walking their dogs, they've got no idea what happened there. No idea about any of it. Anyway," she turned away and said, more quietly still, "just promise to remember what I said. This place cannot leave the family. Under no account. Not ever."

My mother always insisted that Dorothy was crazy, and that the stories about our witch ancestor were ridiculous. And, as in most things, I agreed with Mum. But in a vague and quiet place, I couldn't deny my fears. Even as a very young boy I could sometimes detect an atmosphere of brooding or crowding – a sense of misalignment – in the cottage. And my great-aunt believed the stories, I could tell.

The only room in which you could really feel anything of the power of the building's age was the kitchen. The rest of the cottage was scrupulously neat and dusted. The chairs in the lounge were arranged so that they were all the same distance from the small fire. Pictures on the walls were of hay bales, oast houses and apple orchards. In the bathroom, Dorothy's toothbrush had its own plastic case that sat on the third shelf of the cupboard, next to her unopened packages of Pears soap. The waste bins sat in the dead centre of these sort-of oversized home-knitted doilies. This barren, nursemaid tidiness only heightened the sensation you felt when you first stepped down into the kitchen – shock melting quickly into staggered enchantment. You felt as if you were travelling back in time. Suddenly, you were in a place of stone and wood and raw flames; amongst layers of history that had been built up by cooks stretching back for generations until it was this mad, tumbling mess of excitement. Hundreds of pots, jars and weird implements gave it a feeling of a madman's hoard or a wizard's bazaar. Every space on every wall was used. There were cupboards of all sizes, each of which looked as if it had been hastily built when the last one had become full.

On one wall there were rows and rows of prongs, spines, blades, strainers, peelers, crushers and corers – the fierce weapons of flavour; on another there were shelves stretching right up to the ceiling, whose contents became more dusty and exotic as you increased in altitude. There were glass jars of pickled ephemera, pots of dried goods, bottles of oddly glistening powder. I remember one container in particular that seemed to have some sort of primitive hand in it. It hung in this golden liquid, its reptilian knuckle resting against the brown-stained glass as if it was trying to see out. Although a modern gas oven had been installed, Dorothy still used the range, a fantastic iron contraption of doors and chimneys with a thick window through which you could see the flames.

Whilst the décor in all the other rooms was like a thin, fragile skin on the surface of the cottage, in the kitchen you felt as if you were really in amongst the building's guts; in the workings of its exposed, throbbing heart. When, with a little groan, Aunt Dorothy took the long step down into the room, even she seemed to change, the dark, yellowing shades of age rebounding off the walls onto her face and erasing her paleness, making her seem more alive.

It was on a magical November night in the kitchen, when I was eleven, that Dorothy told me a story that would change me for the rest of my life.

She was roasting beef. She had just lifted the part-cooked meat from the oven and was basting it in its tray, and I could hear the bubbling spray of the liquid and smell its rich, oaken, dark-honey fragrance. When the kitchen at Dor was being worked like this – as if its fires were fuelling a powerful engine rather than a simple range – a kind of spell would come over us. As the scents and the sounds and the heat and the steam built up in that small room, it began to feel as if we'd been transported to a different place; as if all the many sensory detonations of cooking had connected us to something timeless; had tuned us into all the countless happy hours that had been spent there by cooks past.

As she spoke, my wonderful aunty would often disappear into a fascinating monologue, during which her eyes would barely graze over me. I'd sit at the end of the kitchen table, as comforted as it was possible to be by the warmth and safety and the words that sang impatiently from her mouth; the renegade knowledge about food from distant ages and cultures, mixed with stubborn opinion on matters of knotty culinary lore. On that night, I was in my usual place – at the table, facing the range. I can still recall the precise distance between my little feet and the cobbled floor and the quality of the light – golden-brown and secretive – and how the fire threw out a thick pillow of warmth whose limit came abruptly at the always-freezing, always-sinister stairs at the back of the room.

"Did I ever tell you, hundreds of years ago, your descendants used to be employed as spitjacks?" she said, spooning the juices back over the richly sweating beef. "Do you know what spitjacks are, Kill? Well, I'll tell you. They used to work by the fire in the kitchens of knights and kings and so on, turning the spits of meat. That all stopped in the 1500s when some bright spark invented a contraption out of wheels and pulleys which meant the work could be carried out by dogs – dogs that had been bred specially for the job. It was that hard, they had to take it in turns to work – one day on, one day off. Have you heard the phrase 'every dog has its day'? Well, that comes from turnspit dogs.

"Oh, but they were terribly ugly things – all bony with crooked legs and sad eyes. They had an awful time of it. They had to work right next to the fire, and you can only imagine the beating they must've got if they got tired. But," she stopped basting for a moment, her eyes glistening, her spoon raised in the air, "their job could not have been more important. England, back then, was a roast country. On the continent, where the sun was hot, meat would rot in the heat almost straight away. That's why your Italians and your French had to invent all those sauces to mask the smell and why the Spanish cured their pork. None of this was necessary in old England. Here, the rivers would freeze in September and thousands of peasants would have their hearts stopped by the frost every winter. For most of the year, the whole country was one great big living fridge. Can you imagine? All we needed to do to create the most wonderful food was to put an iron pole through a lamb or a pig or a cow and turn it in front of a flame. But that meat was valuable. It had to be done with care, slowly and for hours and hours. And that was the job of the turn-spit dogs, those poor little creatures."

I think she meant it to be a kind of horror story, something grim to boggle the eyes of a young boy. But that's not the way I heard it. When Dorothy described those dogs, what I heard was a description of myself. Ugly, bony, crooked legs, sad eyes. Every word she said lit a bulb in my head, and when her tale was over, what I saw in the accumulated light was me.

"Oh, but they were such a special, special breed," she said. "They had to be small enough to fit in the wheel, strong enough to walk it and loyal enough not to eat the meat. They were noble dogs, strong in mind and body. They might have looked a bit unusual, but on the inside

– I'm telling you, Kill – they were magnificent. No, I've always thought highly of those turnspit dogs, even though they did our forefathers out of a job. I mean, how could you not? They were so loyal! They were heroes. Heroes of the kitchen."

I moved my arm down by my thigh and pushed my hand into a small fist. I didn't know those concepts could go together. Boniness and strength? Ugliness and loyalty? I hadn't known it was possible.

I was only ever talkative when I was with my aunt Dorothy ,and yet that night, as I pushed my knife through the tenderly roasted silverside, I was silent. Dorothy, with her usual sensitivity, seemed to understand that behind my expression of rough-browed concentration something more important than beef was being chewed over. For once she fell quiet and we went about eating our meal listening only to the music of satisfied cutlery.

I don't think I met her eye at all until – honey-sweetened cocoa drunk – it was finally time for bed. I pushed my chair out, and just before looking to the floor to check how far my feet had to drop, I glanced up, seeking from her a final reassurance.

"Ni'night, Kill," she said, elbows deep in washing-up. "Do you want me to tuck you in?"

"No, thanks."

"Good boy." She turned to look at me again. "You sure you're all right, Kill? Nothing you want to talk about?"

I found myself looking at the latest scar from home, up by my left elbow. "I think I'll just go to bed now."

Outside the warm oasis of the kitchen, Dor could be a rather different place. Although most of the days there were soft, bright and charmed, you always had the sense that this bliss was being conferred on you. It was almost as if you were living inside the thoughts and moods of something else; something that was benevolent only because it had decided to be. At dusk, the walls seemed to embrace the end of the day all too greedily, sucking in more night than their due until the weight of the darkness was such that you'd begin to feel its pressure, pushing you out of the rooms. And of all the hostile, watching spaces that came alive in the ancient building after sundown, those old buckled stairs were the worst. Daylight always vanquished the cottage's strangeness, but even on the sunniest afternoons, a certain trace seemed to linger over those sixteen steps.

I'd feel it as my foot hit the first one. It was as if there was something gathering in the air behind me, something that wanted to push me forward, to make me run, and that was a trick; I knew it was a trick, because the moment I started running, the fear would erupt into the back of my neck, like a great hand trying to grab me, and I'd go faster and faster and I'd get more and more scared and run all the way along the corridor and into my bed with the covers all over me, trying not to let my aunty hear me whimper.

But not tonight. Having taken my fortifying glance at Dorothy, I stood, puffed out my ribby chest and walked those stairs without stopping. One step, two steps, three steps, four. I could feel the fear behind me, bending out of the growling air. I refused to rush. Everyone knew that turnspit dogs weren't afraid of the dark.

When I reached my room and closed the door, I heard a fly buzzing around the light. As soon as I saw its darting motion, it came for me, buzzing in and out, infuriatingly close to my skin. I flapped it away again and again, but still it came. It wasn't quite a phobia, my aversion to flies. I'd feel a sense of panic and revulsion at their presence, but also a kind of murderous fury. It was as if there were something personal in their tormenting; as if their sole, born purpose was to pester me.

That night, though, was different. That fly was a test. I turned off the main light, switched on the wobbly old bedside lamp with the green velvet-tasselled shade and removed all my clothes, carefully folding them in a neat pile on the chest of drawers. Then I lay on top of the woollen blanket, rested my arms by the sides of my body and waited.

It didn't take long. I flinched at the sensation of the fly's legs on my stomach and the grotesque understanding, in its hesitant movements, of the small living thing making judgements and decisions. It took off once more and passed my eyes and I could see that it was sleek and nimble with a silvery body and large red eyes – of the type that I had only ever seen at Dor Cottage.

It landed on my cheek. My hands shook as it walked to the edge of my mouth. I thought about the turn-spit dogs that had once worked away downstairs in the kitchen. I thought about Mary Dor and her fraught and magical recipes. I thought about gravy and Eton Mess and Toulouse sausages and fingers of melted cheese-on-toast, made with parmesan and three-year Cheddar and sprin-kled with nutmeg and fresh cracked pepper and tangy Worcester sauce.

It lifted off again and came down at the corner of my eye. I lay there as the fuzzy lump on the border of my vision licked and drank. I willed the strength to come, opening my mouth wide to breathe deeply. In and out went the cold, thick air.

In, hold, and out.

In, hold, and out.

The fly whipped away and landed, again, on the edge

of my lip. I felt the woollen blanket beneath my damp palms and imagined a lake of melted chocolate and tall flowers with caramel petals and marzipan trees and clouds of still-warm vanilla marshmallows.

Not a movement.

Not a single movement.

The fly crawled, with delicate little pricks on my skin, into my mouth. It buzzed, just once, and walked in further. A muscle in my lip contracted involuntarily and then I closed my tongue over it. The insect was pulled in. I felt its twitching incredulity as it was sucked down into my throat.

Coughing and retching, I sat up and ran to the bathroom to wash my mouth out. When I was done, I caught my reflection in the mirror above the sink. For the first time in my life, I studied my face in detail. I had done it. I would be different from now on. They could hurt me as much as they wanted. They could beat me or pity me or act as if I wasn't there. None of it would matter. I might have looked weak and repulsive but I had strength and loyalty. I was a creature of the kitchen; a controlled, ferocious beast.

I was a turnspit dog.

Chapter 2

When I was younger, and she was in her better moods, my mother used to dress me up in costumes. Policeman, Red Indian, ladybird, sailor. During nights in which she had friends around, she would wake me in the early hours and force me to dance about in her underwear, which she would make fit using safety pins to take in the slack. "Be our sexy dancer!" she would say, laughing and clapping, and I would jiggle about on the living-room rug, its colours blurring through tears and cigar-ette smoke. There was a princess dress with a short pink skirt and glittery sleeves that she would make me wear as I cleaned the house, if the previous day's work had been insufficiently thorough. Now and then, she would send me to the shops in it. I would run down the cul-de-sac, my knees feeling as if they might burst open with the effort, in terror of being spotted by Mark. For my seventh birthday, she bought me a king outfit, complete with plastic crown which she would make me wear as I fetched fresh ice from the kitchen and emptied the ashtray of a weekday evening. When things reached a certain point, I would have to stand still as she stared at me. "One day you'll grow up to be my king," she would say. "You'll be my handsome hero. You'll look after me, won't you, darling? Baby darling, tell me, who do you want to marry when you're a big strong man?"

"You, Mummy."

"Who will be your beautiful princess?"

"You, Mummy."

"Such a good boy, you are. Such a good, strong, handsome boy."

And I would stand still and she would stare.

As I entered my adolescence, I grew out of my costumes. She no longer fantasised about me as her king. As time passed, my mother became more likely to remark bitterly that I was turning out to be "mediocre, just like your father". Before the night of the fly, that had made me impossibly sad. After so many safe and wonderful hours at Dor Cottage, I had begun to muster an impossible ambition to one day be a successful cook, just like my hero, the world-famous chef Max Mann. But not now; not any more. I was a dog. And like all good and loyal dogs, I knew my place and was grateful for it. It felt good to finally accept my mother's entirely logical point of view.

Mediocre: it was a release.

At school, I accepted that my level was down in the corner, quiet and obedient, not one of them. When I wasn't daydreaming about food, I'd entertain myself by keeping track of my classmates' internecine battles. It was my own thrilling, real-time soap opera and my love for its latest twists was second only to my obsession with cooking. I'd move about the corridors and locker rooms and hang by the walls pretending to be looking for something in my rucksack when really I was listening. At some point, I acquired the nickname "Eyeballs". Cruel, perhaps, but undoubtedly deserved.

Loyal dog that I was, I came to care about my classmates

deeply. And despite the violent attentions of Mark House, I succeeded in training myself to remain mostly invisible and to never cry no matter what the provocation. The only occasion on which I broke occurred when I was fourteen. By then I had grown used to quietly observing the lives of the boys and girls around me, taking pleasure in seeing what happened to people whose days were filled with friends and events. I would watch them and I would think about them and I thought most of them were amazing; funny and clever and alive. But something happened over the early months of that summer term. A kind of tornado swept up all of my thoughts and carried them away in one direction. In her direction. I had accidentally fallen in love.

I don't know what it was about Sophie, but I do know that I wasn't the only one. Not the prettiest girl in the class, no, but she was beautiful all the same. It was her extraordinary kindness that first attracted me, but it wasn't long before her earthly properties – her hair and her eyes and her smile – burned themselves onto the backs of my eyes.

I had a fantasy about her that, over the course of those months, thickened imperceptibly into a plan. It took weeks of saving ingredients, small and dangerous robberies from my mother's purse and so much imagining that I began literally dreaming up new ideas. My work started a week before Sports Day. Every night, at two thirty, I would creep into the dark kitchen and cook by tea-light, always with the dread of what would happen if my mother was woken by the scents. By five a.m., I would be finished, the room immaculate once more. At the end of seven days, I had them, stored carefully in baking-sheet-lined layers in a metal biscuit tin beneath my bed. Twenty chocolates and twenty sugared jellies. Forty different flavours, all for her.

I never really considered what my gift might achieve.

It wasn't as if I had imagined her doing anything as terrifying as actually speaking to me. The fact of her eating them, of her joy in my creation, of her taking them in and of my giving her bodily delight. That was enough. That was everything.

I knew that, during Sports Day, I wouldn't be missed. I also knew where Sophie's peg was, in the changing rooms. I stuck some heart-patterned wrapping paper to the tin, and had found some red ribbon, which I abandoned, after thirty frustrating minutes spent trying to tie it into a bow. During the lunch break, I hid in a toilet cubicle with my parcel on my lap. I remained there until I was sure everyone would be down on the fields, leaving me in the safe and echoing quiet.

I crept past the library, past the science lab, past Mr Ariely's English class with its chairs pulled out and the sun on the blackboard, the flowerless pot plant, dusty in the corner of the silent room. The corridors were polished and wide and somehow still rang with the cries of the boys and girls in all their missing hundreds. As I turned into the sports block, I heard talking. I stopped. They were in the boys' changing room. I would go slowly.

"Oy!"

It was Colin, in the doorway.

"Watcha, Eyeballs. What you got there?"

And if Colin was there…

"Oy, Mark!" he called behind him. "It's Eyeballs. He's got us a pressie."

I scrambled away, my pursuers primed with their identical Dunlop trainers and their stinking muscle rub. Out of one block, into another and down towards the third-year lockers, they gained on me. I ran into a toilet, hoping to bolt myself back inside a cubicle, but Mark grabbed me by the shoulders and knocked me off balance, my skull bouncing on the floor, my tin falling on its side. Colin popped open the lid.

"Sweets!" said Mark, placing one in his mouth with his free hand. "Do you want one?"

He took a handful of chocolates and jellies, mushed them into a ball and forced them into my mouth. I spat them out, their sticky warmth crawling down my cheek and chin, and he grabbed my neck and forced my head into the urinal's long gutter. My upper lip hit the blue detergent ball and my face was soaked in the spiky stench of boy-piss. Stephan tipped the tin's contents into the porcelain trough and began urinating on them. Yellow-brown liquid trickled millimetres from my face.

"Here, look," Colin screeched, holding up the lid. "It was for Sophie."

"Do you fancy Sophie?" said Mark. "Do you fancy Sophie?" He turned to address the others. "He's spying on Sophie now. Dirty fucking spy. Stephan, you take him."

Stephan took my neck and Mark disappeared, returning minutes later with a large translucent plastic bottle. The label was white and purple and had an orange square with a black cross over it. Utilitarian letters spelled the words: PAINT THINNER. He unscrewed the cap and yanked down my left eyelid. Reflexively, I pulled away. I felt it tear at the corner. Blood was in my eye.

"Dirty bastard spy," said Mark.

"Don't do too much," said Stephan. "He'll go fucking blind."

"Fuck that," said Mark.

I looked up at them; studied them one by one. Then the burning came. Mark bit his lip in concentration; Stephan's mouth was fish-like. Robert and Andy were standing way above me. Colin had ink smudged on his ear and a scab on his jaw.

The liquid inside my eye felt as if it was boiling. I tried to remain apart from what was happening. I stared hard at the smear of blue biro on Colin's ear. It looked like a raindrop; like Africa; like an upside-down comma.

"He's not even struggling," said Colin.

"I fingered Sophie," said Mark.

It looked like Scandinavia.

"I gave her three fucking fingers."

I swallowed.

"Then I sucked her tits."

I felt the heaviness, then. I felt the upset swell. A sob built defiantly in my throat.

"Then I put my finger up her arsehole and I made her suck it. She loved that. She was moaning."

I stared back at the ceiling. I held myself still as a cold tear slid from the outside corner of my eye, down my temple and then lost itself behind my ear, as if hiding in shame.

"Is he dead?" said Stephan.

I lifted my head, blood and chemical spilling onto my cheek, and said, "I'm fine." For some reason, this seemed to terrify them. With a squeak of rubber heels and a piggery of sniggering, they were gone.

I poured water from a tap into my eye and walked home slowly. The moment my mother saw me, she ordered me to hospital. Three hours later, I returned with a white bandage over a blob of cotton wool for a patch.

"What did they say?" asked my mother. She was sitting in her armchair in front of *Coronation Street*, an iceless Martini in a port glass in her right hand.

"It'll be fine," I said, from the open doorway. "Except

that my eyelid might not go back to the same shape it was. But it'll be fine."

The point of her tongue licked slowly along her lower lip.

"Did it hurt?"

"Yes," I said.

"How much?"

"A lot."

"A lot?"

"Yes."

She unfolded her legs, from where she'd been sitting on them. On the television screen, northern actors carried on obliviously.

"Turn that off," she said.

I pushed the heavily springed power button on the bottom of the old Pye set, and took my usual place, standing in front of her. She held her arms out towards me. I walked into them, stiffly, and felt her cold skin wrap around my neck.

"Do you love me, Killian?"

I knew what to say.

"Yes, Mummy, I love you."

"How much?"

I knew exactly how it went.

"I love you more than anything in the whole wide world, Mummy."

I could feel a vein pulsing in her neck; smell the cigarettes and perfume in her skin; feel the pressure around my throat tightening and then releasing as her mind worked on something, over and over and over. Tightening and releasing; tightening and releasing. I wanted her to put me down, but I had to pretend. I knew what happened when I didn't pretend.

"Who did this to you?" she said, eventually.

She released me and I stood there, hands straight down against my sides.

"It was an accident," I said.

"Who did it?" she said.

"Nobody."

"If you loved me, why would you lie to me?"

"Sorry, Mum."

"So why are you lying to me then?"

"Sorry, Mummy."

There was that sense of stirring and strength; the drawing down of trouble.

"If you don't spit it out, so help me God, I'll have you put into a home. Do you *know* what I do for a job? Have you forgotten? One stroke of my pen. Ten seconds' work. You will never see me again. Is that what you want?"

I closed my eyes and whispered, "It was Mark."

"Mark *House?*"

"But I didn't do anything," I said, pleading. "He just *did it.*"

I wanted to tell her that her hair looked nice. She had had it coloured, that day. All her greyness had gone away.

"I was just giving this thing to someone in my class and he – " I said.

"What thing?"

"Just some – "

"What?"

"Chocolates and things."

"Chocolates?"

Her nostrils narrowed.

"Who to?"

"This girl."

"*A girl?*"

28

They had been getting bad, her grey roots. And now they were all gone. All nice. All back to normal.

"God help us. Fourteen years old. Ogling women."

"I'm sorry, Mummy," I said.

"Perving over girls at your age? Pestering them? Disgusting." She leaned forward. "You're as bad as your bloody grandad."

I lowered my head and looked at my socks; my pink toe, the white fringe of its nail poking out of a hole in the material.

"You need to learn something, if you're going to keep living in my house. You don't go bothering women. You don't go treating them like lumps of meat. Do you hear me? *Dirty little boy.* Filthy dirty *rotten.*"

She took her tortoiseshell cigarette lighter and clicked up a flame. Placing a long Belair Menthol cigarette between her lips, she sucked the fire into its tip and then laid it carefully on the edge of the blue cut-glass ashtray.

I would trim that toenail later on, with the nail clippers that I got from the cracker at Aunt Dorothy's on Boxing Day. And then, tomorrow night, I would get the needle and thread and try to darn that hole.

"Come on then, big man…"

She pulled a second cigarette out of the packet and lit that one too, laying it next to the first.

" …take off your shirt…"

And then my sock would be all mended.

" …and come here."

All nice and safe and mended.

* * *

The next morning, my mother met Mark's mum at the school gate and slapped her face. I looked on, my heart bursting with love and pride as she raised her finger in the face of a mortified Margaret House and said, "Nobody touches my bloody son." Mr and Mrs House were never invited around for cocktails again.

And then, four years later, my life changed again.

Chapter 3

West Kent College was a gloomy hustle of 1960s buildings – vandalised, damp and gloweringly concrete – whose catering department had the capacity for fifty-five new students a year. On my first morning, I was one of seventy-nine who gathered in the breeze-block training kitchen underneath the ceiling tiles with the damp, like apple rot, spreading through them. Mr Mayle, our faculty head, told us not to worry too much about the cramped conditions; that the head-count would soon be reduced to a more manageable amount by the inevitable "Malthusian check".

The reason for the course's over-subscription was simple: the rise of Max Mann. During the late seventies I had become intensely fascinated by the ubiquitous chef and his famous London restaurant, King. There were chefs who had more culinary respect in the country – Raymond Blanc, Nico Ladenis, the Roux brothers – but it was Mann who had somehow come to personify the heat and glamour of ultra-fine dining.

They called him "the Gentleman Chef", because of the famously peaceable way in which he managed his kitchen staff. He was known for never shouting at his workers, and was proud of the young juniors he trained into stars and his record of never having fired one – "I'd never give up on an apprentice," he'd often swear on chat show sofas, as if the very idea was heresy. I knew all the facts about him – lines from the many dozens of press clippings that I would cut out and file carefully into my collection. Like: it was Mann's restaurant in which Elton John and his wife ate Sunday lunch; where Mohamed Al Fayed had celebrated his purchase of Harrods; where the singers went for a free meal following the recording of 'Feed The World'. It was Mann, more than anyone, who had a pioneering appetite for the French food movement, "la Nouvelle Cuisine", and, in part, his celebrity was generated by his reputation for small portions on big plates and the pairing of fruits with meat and fish. All the best comedians would do bits on him. There was this *Two Ronnies* sketch, set in a Wimpy bar, in which Corbett was handed a bowl of chips that came with an unpeeled banana sticking out of them before Barker was given a hamburger that had a slim patty of beef and an entire pineapple jammed between the buns. One Spitting Image joke had a starving Ethiopian bursting into tears when a latex caricature of Mann lifted an enormous silver cloche off a King-style square black plate to reveal a chicken wing and half a grape.

He'd appeared on all the chat shows – Parkinson, Wogan, Russell Harty – and always did variations on the same routine, which the students at college would impersonate. He'd start by taking the presenter's predictable jokes about Nouvelle Cuisine with grace, explain to a disbelieving audience that, honestly, no butter at all was used in his cooking and that the meat and fish really were cooked "*au sec*", by being dipped in cold water and heated in a Teflon pan. This would segue into his dryly sarcastic defence of foie gras and then his anecdote about Michael

Jackson's entourage ordering hot dogs. He'd finish by batting away questions about the rumoured OBE and the elusive third Michelin star by laughing and saying "Oh do come on now" in that Etonian accent that was sharper than a January wind.

Whenever you saw photographs in the *Sun* of pop stars or actors walking into King itself, the flash was always on their faces, blacking out the background. But the background was what I wanted to see. I used to examine those pictures during my lunch breaks, my thumb over the faces of Morten Harket or Liza Minnelli, peering into the dead ink behind them. The most you ever saw was a neatly trimmed rectangular hedge and a canopy over a small door. Somehow, that made the place seem all the more magical. This dull façade, behind which worked Max Mann and his brigade; this unassuming building in a low neighbourhood you'd just walk past if you didn't know better.

It would only be a slight exaggeration to say that, by eighteen, I'd grown to love him. I'd had my head shaved to a grade-four crop, to mimic the hairstyle he demanded of his brigade. I studied how he sat on the TV AM sofa and the particular way he had of crossing his legs with his ankle resting imperiously on his knee. I cut out all the pictures of him I could find – even the postage-stamp-sized ones from the listings pages of the *Radio Times* – and super-glued them onto my bedroom wall.

I ended up on the course at West Kent because my mother was determined that I would go to college. To her shame – and having failed the rest of my exams due to my almost total absence of application – cookery was my only realistic option for study. I soon discovered some unwelcome news about the course. Thanks to Mann's superstardom, Mark House – after toying with rock star, photographer and footballer – had apparently decided that he was destined to become a world-famous chef.

* * *

We'd completed our initial classes in theory, hygiene and basic kitchen mathematics and were about to begin the practical work. With the class gathered before him, Mr Mayle announced that before we moved on to the basics – stocks, mirepoix, concasse, tourne – he wanted to test our basic skills by seeing how good we were at domestic cookery. That coming Monday, he said, we were to present our own preparations of lasagne for tasting by the class. By happy accident of his personality, Mayle always managed to co-opt his students into respectful behaviour by matching their natural teenage instinct for cynicism with his air of gently amused detachment. He spoke with a subtle grin that was so barely detectable as to be tantalising: it danced juicily between one or two tiny muscular twitches at the extreme left side of his mouth. "There's a host of basic skills involved in a simple lasagne," he said. "Let's see if any of you rabble have what it takes to out-cook Signore Birds Eye."

On the morning of lasagne day I was surprised to find that I was the only student who'd arrived in class suffi-ciently early to begin the process of cooking ragu which, Aunt Dorothy had always taught me, took at least four hours; one for the sautéing of the soffritto and the browning of the meat, three for the softest simmer it's possible to tempt from your hob. This was the kind of thing I'd learn every weekend and school holiday after Mum, usually complaining of my being "under her feet", had driven me to Dor. On birthdays, Dorothy would take me from my home in Tonbridge to some of London's ethnic areas – the

Bengalis and Bangladeshis in Brick Lane; the Chinese south of Soho; the West Indians in Brixton – where we'd have lunch for inspiration before spending the afternoon shopping for curious and fantastic ingredients – red gram, white miso, kecap manis, Jamaica flowers, West African giant snails. Then we'd putter back from Hailsham Station in her old Peugeot and she'd go through her collection of stockpots and roasting pans, all of which were so ancient and dented and tarnished by fire that I came to recognise each eccentric one of them as if they were characters in a Gothic children's book. We'd spend the evening cooking an experimental birthday meal on her ancient range.

It was on one such birthday that we had concocted the version of lasagne that I was now so familiar with, I'd almost forgotten it could be made any other way. As I worked in the silence of the West Kent kitchen – my coat hanging alone on the row of hooks outside, my bag of condiments placed reassuringly by my feet like a loyal pet – I added star anise to the soffritto and used ham stock instead of chicken or beef. The candied sweetness of the spice, I knew, worked in gorgeous symphony with the baconiness of the stock and three or four light dashes of Spanish sherry vinegar gave a subtle fizz of acid.

Gradually, my new classmates began to filter into the room and soon they were all frantically working away, the spirit of competition having galvanised them into serious-ness. They were as studious as I'd ever seen them, care-fully measuring tablespoons of tomato purée and weighing blocks of mince. Many stopped Mayle as he walked the classroom's aisles and asked earnest questions about dried oregano, sunflower oil and tinned versus fresh tomatoes.

I was stirring hard, the steam from the ragu making a patina of sweat glisten on the back of my hand, when

Mark House bashed his way through the swing doors.

"Hmmm, Eyeballs," he said, peering into my food. "Bit more salt, maybe?"

He picked up my shaker, unscrewed the top and dumped the contents into the pot.

"That's better," he said. "Now it looks like shit *and* tastes like shit. Consistency, yeah?" And he sauntered off in the direction of his stove.

The salt had fallen in a single iglooish pile that was sinking quickly into the ragu. I grabbed a ladle and tried to remove all the sauce that had had the chance to absorb it. As usual, it was Mark's casualness that struck me – that ruining my dish wasn't some act of piqued fury but an entirely unremarkable event; a reflexive twitch.

The pressure in the room built as burners burned and lips pursed to taste and arms became sore with stirring. Eyes drifted to Mayle as he strode up and down behind the cooks. Girls smiled up at him, boys feigned professorial concentration. The bolder amongst the students would stop him with a trembling, sauce-filled spoon and say, "Sir, what do you think of this?" or "Sir, enough mixed herbs?" and each time he would politely decline, insisting it was up to them – that it was a test of *their* judgement of flavour, not his. Everyone became aware of their neighbour's desperation to beat them, and that stoked their own insecurities and drew them into trying yet harder. Around and around it went until the designated time, when we lined our plates up along the blue trestle table that had been erected in front of Mayle's demonstration kitchen.

Having managed to rescue my sauce, I watched from the back as everyone picked out a fork from an old water-filled ice-cream tub. As I retreated back to my station to start clearing down, I passed Mark, who was proudly delivering his dish to Mayle. He'd brought in his own special presentation plate, which he was holding with both hands and gazing at with the pride of a new father. His lasagne was a firm, bright brick of red food with a sprig of parsley on the top. In a nod to the fashionable cooking of the time, he'd made a salad of what looked like red grapes and lightly sweated onion. It all looked neat and attractive and completely different from mine, which I now realised was a disaster – a slipped pile of steaming meat, the mornay sauce I'd used instead of béchamel bleeding into the ragu in little landslides of creamy white.

"Sir, please, sir," said Mark, pushing his plate into Mayle's hands. "I don't want it to get cold, sir."

I turned and watched as Mayle surrendered and took a bite. Mark's gaze flicked between the dish and the teacher's lips, his expression one of gelatinous pride, an eyebrow raised in anticipation of the glory.

"Hmm," said Mayle. "Yes. Interesting texture." He closed his eyes and rubbed his tongue along the roof of his mouth. "There's something almost... pre-masticated about it."

It took the boy a good three seconds to realise that what he was hearing wasn't good.

I was about to take another step towards my dirty pots when I noticed, in the long mirror that was suspended above the demonstration kitchen, that a small clot of students had formed at the far end of the trestle table. They were gathering around my plate. I would wash up. That's what I would do. What did it matter if everyone was laughing at my dish? Why would I care? I was mediocre and happy that way. I didn't care *at all*.

As I carried my knives, chopping board and pans towards the sink, I couldn't help but have one final look at what was happening. Mayle was moving towards the group. I turned on the hot tap, squeezed in a spurt of detergent and held my fingers under the scorching water to distract myself with pain. So what if Mark House had made a better dish than me? Why would *anyone* be surprised about *that*?

In the mirror, I watched, with my fingers held under the hot tap, as the teacher cut into my pasta with the edge of his fork and scooped up a mouthful.

In the reflection, Mayle began to chew. The other students were watching the action, many with tight almost-grins. And then it happened. Mayle's eyelids dropped. Aunt Dorothy always said that that, for a cook, is what laughter is to a comedian or what tears are to a storyteller. When he opened them again and tried to seek out the cook responsible for what he'd just eaten, I'll never forget it. He looked as if he'd been provoked.

"Who made this?" he said.

He must have realised who it was by the colour of my face, or the fact of everyone turning towards me. There were giggles and smirks and whispering. I dried my fingers tenderly on my apron and tried to suck some moisture into my mouth. I had never had so many eyes on me before.

"I don't know exactly what you've done here," said Mayle. "But this lasagne is like none I've ever tasted."

Mark House snorted like a hog that had been unexpectedly mounted.

"It's wonderful, just wonderful," he said. "Beautifully, beautifully deep and rich flavour. And so complex! What's your name, young man? How did you *do* this?"

I was incapable of doing anything but shrugging, uselessly. Mayle, to my eternal relief, smiled and gave me the kindest little nod. I got back to my washing-up and tried to tell myself that I didn't care. But, already, it was too late.

It wasn't until I lay down in bed that night that I realised that something essential had changed. All those years I believed that I had removed myself from the competitiveness of the world, I had been fooling myself. I had been competing with almost everyone I'd known and my fight had been harder and more determined than any of theirs. The only difference was, mine had been a race to the bottom. That was the only battle I believed I could win. As I closed my eyes to sleep, I was sure of only one thing.

It wasn't any more.

That night I dreamed of Dor Cottage under months of ceaseless rain; of a long-caged magic in the garden, in the roof and in the mortar.

I dreamed of the sixteen steps that I'd climbed with courage as a boy. I looked up, from the bottom, over the rims of their crooked wooden surfaces. At the top stood a figure, weak and wordless with dread. Her face half hidden in darkness, she stared through me.

I'd not seen her before, but I knew her. She'd been with me always — in my sleep and back in the dead times.

I saw a dying room, tall with windows. Glass murky with the dirt of a thousand rain storms and the black bones of winter trees. And then, a beautiful girl. Long eyelashes and freckles across her face like a fine spray of milky chocolate. A blood mark on her face. Dogs in a circle, their claws slipping on a hard, smooth floor. She was begging them to stop.

And I believed it, then, about the magic and the ancestor. I understood about the hunger and the howling. I understood that it was real and it would come. All of it would come.

I saw fire and flies and turnspit dogs and boiling bones and blood under the fingernails of men.

It was a dream of past and a dream of future.

It was a dream of horror.

Chapter 4

Around six months after lasagne day, I was summoned, unexpectedly, into Mayle's office. I knocked softly and pushed open the door, which released the usual smell of old books, carpet and Amaretto. An antique-ish standard lamp in the corner cast dull, licentious and yet homely light, of the kind you'd see in an old-fashioned bistro.

"Hullo, Killian," Mayle said. He placed the book he'd been reading, spine down, on his cluttered desk. "Sit down, sit down. I have some good news for you. As you know, in a couple of weeks everyone's going out on their work placements. Trying to place everyone is always a nightmare but we've somehow muddled through as usual. Most of your classmates are off to institutions or big companies. Schools, hospitals, staff kitchens in Safeways – canteen work, in the main. Bean-stirring. Mark House, you might be interested to learn, is spending a fortnight in an oil rig off the north-east coast of Aberdeen."

He paused to let that near-imperceptible smile flicker across his mouth.

"We have had a tiny bit more luck with you, however."

He smiled gently and leaned forward with his hands on his cheeks. The skin on his face bunched around his eyes so that he looked unnaturally delighted.

"But before we go any further, some good news. Your entry into the 1985 Young Saucier of the Year competition."

"Yes, sir," I said, suddenly alert. This was the award once won by Max Mann himself. Flattered as I had been when Mayle had asked me to take part, I realised that it was only because the college felt it should be represented.

"You, young man, are a finalist."

My jaw slackened.

"You may swear," nodded Mayle.

"Fuck!"

He laughed warmly and swept a bit of imaginary dust off his desk with his fingertips.

"Yes, indeed. Needless to say, this is a first for West Kent. An amazing achievement. A high point of my teaching career and I thank you for it, sincerely. You have a huge talent, Killian. A rough diamond, perhaps, but a diamond certainly. I think you'll go far. But you're going to have to learn to be a bit more of a team player. If you have ambitions to be an executive chef and lead a brigade, you do actually have to *talk* to other people, I'm afraid."

"Yes, sir," I said. "I know, sir."

He held my gaze for a moment.

"Anyhow, because of all this, I have managed to pull a few strings. You'll be pleased to hear that I've arranged your work placement for six weeks, rather than four."

"Thank you, sir."

"You are very, very welcome, young man."

I stood and gave Mr Mayle a grateful bow of the head.

"Goodbye!" he said.

I moved across the room and reached for the handle of his door. Just as my fingers made contact, Mayle spoke again.

"Oh, er – Killian?"

"Yes, sir?"

"Don't you want to know where you'll be apprenticing?"

I turned.

"Yes, sir."

"Well, you'll be working your *stage* up in London."

"London?"

"Yes, you will. London."

London. I wondered where. A bank, maybe. A train station café. A cinema, a theatre, an opera house.

"Okay. Great. London. Thank you, sir."

I turned, once more, to leave.

"At... um... a place called... "

I looked around again. Mayle made a show of carefully examining a sheet of paper on his desk.

"Ah, that's it. You'll be working at... "

He met my eyes and grinned.

"King."

Chapter 5

London has a grey-blue tinge to it in the hour after dawn. That's what I remember most about my walk, on that first morning, to the restaurant – the grey-blue tinge as I hurried from Charing Cross Station and how it seemed exactly right, somehow. It was the colour of the empty streets; the colour of frozen air; the colour of the thinness of the world as it is at six a.m. before it becomes bloated by life. I wasn't exactly sure how to find the right place. All I knew was that it was somewhere in the tall maze of streets that runs east of Tottenham Court Road. Back then, it was all discount sex shops, broken pubs and nameless outlets with chipboard doors that sold knock-off T-shirts and posters. An unlikely place to find the chicest eating establishment in the country, I thought, naively, as I strode past an open entranceway, behind which was a staircase and a paper notice that announced the presence of a "model" on the first floor. It was a lesson I'd learn soon enough – filth is inherent to glamour; sin its silent promise.

It was the first time that I'd been to London without Aunt Dorothy, and the city seemed dirty and overwhelming without her. I remember its gigantic indifference, as if the huge stone buildings were turning their backs on me as I walked between them. I had in my back pocket the piece of paper Mr Mayle had passed me in his office. There was no need to look at it, as it contained only scant information: the address, 32 Gresse Street, and the time I was expected – seven a.m.

King was almost exactly as I'd imagined, except for the fact it was next to a pub called the Bricklayers Arms and that it smelled. The dustmen hadn't yet done their rounds, and the restaurant was wearing this rotten beard of rubbish bags. It didn't bother me in the slightest. Neither did it matter that I was nearly an hour early. I was content just to stand on the lowest of the five steps that Max Mann and his customers walked up every day and to breathe the same air.

I peered, open-mouthed, through the glass door. As my eyes became used to the light, I could just make out the famous black walls decorated with mirrors, the matching black tablecloths and the orchid centrepieces. I stayed like that for at least five minutes, drinking in all the details, before studying the incredible menu that was displayed in a small illuminated case next to the door: mousseline of quail livers flavoured with port and cognac and served with a trio of fruit jellies; guinea-fowl in a caramel glaze with fresh mangoes; champagne-poached sweetbreads; golden mousse of foie gras topped with diced foie gras and served with supreme of pigeon in a sauce of meat juices with halves of grape...

The previous weekend, Aunt Dorothy had given me a set of packet-fresh chef's whites. She'd even gone to the trouble of stitching my name into the breast in neat blue cotton. I reached into my little backpack and found the toque, which I placed on my head. I looked at my reflection in the small gold plaque on which the name of the restaurant had been engraved in luxurious script. I looked warped and indistinct, my outline fuzzy, my face an empty oval.

On the pavement nearby, one of the bin liners had been left untied. I picked yesterday's edition of *The Times* out of it and flipped through its damp pages. Scargill and Sellafield and Star Wars and Thatcher enthusiastic about chemical weapons against the Soviets and Israeli jets battering Palestine and one million pounds being spent on fences at Greenham Common. The news was the same as all the other days. None of it held the importance of what was about to happen for me, right here, at 32 Gresse Street.

I sat down on the steps that led to the door. I waited. I spat on my finger and rubbed off a smudge that had appeared on my tunic. A strange temptation began to crawl over me. I found myself going over to one of the bin liners and tearing a small hole in it. A couple of shallot ends and asparagus off-cuts poked out. I took a green, woody stem and rolled it between my fingers. I had this idea, this compulsion, to put it in my mouth and chew down on it – my saliva mixing with this King ingredient, this incredible artefact – it becoming part of me and me part of it.

Just as my teeth were pressing into it, the door opened. I turned to see a chef in his mid-twenties with a black moustache and full, cracked lips, looking at me with all the bewildered fascination I probably deserved. I palmed the stem and dropped my hand down by my side.

"I'm Killian, Chef," I said quietly. "Apprentice. First day."

His expression sagged into one of damp contempt.

"Fuck's sake," he said. "Staff entrance is round the back. Stephen Mews."

With a tilt of his head, he motioned to the alleyway that ran down the side of the restaurant. I thanked the man and ran.

Stephen Mews was a dingy and greasily cobble stoned dead end, surrounded by unpainted four-storey walls. There was an open double fire door, which was framed by a grubby clamour of plastic crates filled with empty bottles of Moët, Perrier and Coca-Cola, a confetti of discarded ring-pulls flattened into the ground around them. A squall of pigeons, perched in the window frames high above me, looked on as I wished myself luck and walked into the golden rectangle of light.

The kitchen was smaller than I was expecting, and fuller. There were twelve chefs, most of whom were busy checking the contents of the morning deliveries. I gawped at the logos and labels on the packages that were stacked on the clean steel surfaces. They were the most thrilling ingredients from all over Europe. There was Valhrona Grand Cru de Terroir chocolate, Xeres vinegar, Beluga caviar, pata negra ham from Iberian pigs who'd been fed purely on acorns, cheese supplied by the lauded Philippe Olivier – even the salt had been imported from the West coast of Sicily. And then, being rushed past me on a large red trolley, I saw something curious. Boxes and boxes and boxes of fresh, delicious, world-renowned Echire butter.

Unloading all of this were the chefs themselves: serious men with careful eyes and conjurers' fingers, awesome in their black clogs and robeish whites. Gods. Dogs.

I stepped deeper into the room and paused to take in the moment. This was it: *his* world; *his* kingdom. This was where Chef Max Mann himself worked every day and made his reputation. These were *his* burners and strainers and sinks and pans and produce.

Directly to the right of the door were four other young apprentices, all lined up along the cold pass, counting out bunches of basil, chervil, parsley and rosemary, trays of mangoes and kiwis and punnets of raspberries, then ticking off the quantities against delivery notes. Their necks were bent at precisely the same angle, their arms and fingers moving in strange synchronicity. I was surprised to find this sight the most beautiful thing of all, even more than the smells and the deliveries of impeccably sourced ingredients. They formed a machine, bent into shape by the will of the kitchen, but they were also something better than that. Because nothing made from cogs or circuit boards, no matter how advanced, could achieve what even those trainees could. It was just as Mayle had once told the class: perfection is out of reach of the automatic. The secret ingredient of unforgettable food is humanity.

The Gentleman Chef wasn't in the kitchen that morning. Perhaps, I thought, he'd arrive closer to lunch service. The *chef de cuisine* appeared to be a man in his thirties, with red hair and acne on his cheeks like gouges made by a peeler. He was busy with something, up amongst the meat, fish and sauce stations where, during service, the chefs would toil at perfection over searing flames, before sending their food to Max Mann at the pass. As I approached him, it registered for the first time how quiet everyone was. I had expected shouts, banter and laughter – those big noises of camaraderie that act as buoyancy aids for packs of men under pressure. But nobody spoke. Nobody even looked at me. "Excuse me? Chef?" I said.

He was leaning over a stove, writing something on a yellow clipboard.

"That's me," he said.

He had nearly-blond eyelashes and the grease in the skin on either of his nose reflected the light from the ceiling. His chin was a pebble of shininess that marked the base of his head, and it looked as if someone had started there and, with the heel of their hand, pushed upwards. His scarlet ears stuck out of the side of his skull like babies' fists. As I'd observe him over the course of the coming day, I'd be constantly aware of his tongue. It was forever making itself known, whether it was wetting his lower lip or appearing as an arched pillow of slimy muscle as he laughed or coughed. Whenever I stood close to him, I'd get a powerful smell of salami.

Right now, though, my attention was fixed on his arms which were covered in a galaxy of burns, scabs and scars.

"I'm…"

"Late," he said, pushing his biro behind a shrivelled ear. "Fucking hell, pal, I can tell your tenure's going to be brief. What's that on your head?" He grabbed my toque. "Good God. Take the hat off and he's even uglier."

He looked over at the nearby chefs, clapped twice and said, "All right, chaps, the AIDS delivery's arrived."

I looked at him; at his eyes and mouth, as he raised his colleagues in a giggle. Those eyes had seen Max Mann. That mouth had spoken to him.

"All right, first job of the morning. Fetch me a bucket of steam."

"Where–"

But by then he had turned around, his great hunched back bending towards me as he leaned over the steel pass. I walked past two chefs who were unloading fish that had just been wheeled in, in an unsteady tower of ice-filled polystyrene crates, and began searching for a bucket. I wondered what it was for; what delicate Nouvelle technique I was about to learn. I knew Max Mann preferred to season his food with herbs rather than salt. The steam, I guessed, would be used to very gently blanch some rare and fragile leaf.

I looked in the wash-station at the back of the kitchen, inside the garde manger where the vegetables were stored, in the cloakroom with its broken lockers and its wooden clog-shelves that were now filled with derelict trainers, inside all the cabinets, underneath all the cabinets. I opened a door beneath a sink and pushed my head in.

I would not ask for help, I decided. Self-sufficient and reliable, like when I was cleaning for Mum. That's what I needed to be. A toiler. A *machine*.

"Where's my bloody bucket?" came a shout.

There was an empty space at the end of the cold pass, next to the door that led to Stephen Mews. Beside it, a young woman cut celery into elegant spears with perfect mechanical rhythm.

"Is this my station?" I asked her.

She nodded quickly, unsmiling, concentrating on her work. But as I was walking off, she whispered, "Bucket of steam?"

I stopped and marvelled, momentarily, at her eyes and wrists and hands which worked together, de-stringing, spreading and cutting perfectly identical fingers from these things that started off as ugly, misshapen limbs. She had freckles on her fingers and a small pink lip-shaped burn on her right wrist, its size and position suggesting it had been inflicted by a hot oven shelf. Up the back of her neck, spilling out of her collar, was a pale-red birthmark.

"Are you *actually* this stupid?" she whispered. "Or are you just pretending?"

"..."

"A bucket. With steam in it," she continued. "A bucket of steam." she said, again, looking at me blankly. "It's a wind-up. Obviously."

"But what should I do?"

50

She had brown hair, tied in a bun, unusually long eyelashes and freckles across her face like a fine spray of milky chocolate.

"The way I see it, you have three choices," she said. "Option one, get a bucket from over in pastry, hold it over some boiling water and see how long it takes Patrick to stop you scalding your fingers."

"Is Patrick—"

"The one that smells of salami?" She nodded. "Option two, save him a job and just walk out of that door because, let's face it, you'll probably not last the day anyway. Option three, kill Patrick."

"But... "

"I have a knife... " she offered.

I looked at the top of the kitchen in disbelief. When I turned back, the girl had already gone back to her chopping.

"And, by the way – stop bloody talking," she whispered. "We're not supposed to be talking."

Chapter 6

The bucket was cheap red plastic and I held it upside down above a stock pot filled with water. It was boiling hard, its bubbles rising in an insistent panic. Patrick turned leerily towards me with his hands on his hips, the scars on his ruined arms like gang tattoos.

As my fingers began to burn, I watched him catching the eye of all the other men at the grill, sauté and sauce stations. One by one, they stopped lifting, counting and chopping and began to snigger, each of them checking with Patrick every few moments: checking he knew they were joining in; that they were a part of the gang; that they were all devoted bricks in the wall that was about to collapse on me. Eventually, he approached in a slow, slouching shuffle. He leaned an elbow on the side of the stove.

"Are you a cook?" he said. "Or a cock?"

I felt the wet burn driving deeper into the skin of my fingers and over the backs of my hands. I looked Patrick in the eye.

"A cook, Chef," I said.

He spoke louder this time, and slower, his neck bending towards me like a chicken examining a strange new thing. His blunt, acned head took on an expression of exaggerated confusion.

"But you don't look like a cook," he said. He came closer and swiped some sweat off my forehead with an extended finger. "And you are leaking piss." The laughter of the brigade burst over me. "So what are you?"

"A cook, Chef," I said.

My hands began to shake with the pain, my fingers becoming redder, my nails feeling as if they were swelling so much that they might pop off. I looked at Patrick's mouth. How much of Max's food had passed through it? Had he eaten the entire menu? It was amazing to think that I was only a couple of feet away from a throat that had swallowed every dish prepared at King. Every dish!

In my hands there was a pure kind of white-blinding agony. I didn't move. As the seconds squeezed past, the smile slowly vanished from Patrick's eyes.

What was the last thing that mouth had said to Max Mann? How many words had it told him? Patrick's face turned paler. I was vaguely aware that the brigade around me had fallen silent. I imagined myself licking his lips. Kissing them. Sucking the Max right out of them.

Patrick shook his head and said, almost under his breath, "Fucking nutcase..."

As he spoke, a fly landed on his upper lip. It was narrow; silvery grey, with rust-red eyes.

"Urgh!" He swiped it away, spitting in disgust. It circled back, returning once more to his lip.

"Argh!" In the confusion, someone took my arm, very softly, from behind. It was the apprentice who'd told me about the wind-up; the girl with the eyelashes and the chocolate freckles.

"You're on stock take in the walk-in," she said, pulling me away.

"Fucking hell," said Patrick. There was a slight catch

in his voice. "Here we go – weirdos of a feather, flocking together. That's right, petal. Have fun with the cock. No doubt it's the first one you've handled." As he turned, he chuntered, "Fucking dyke."

The huge, coffin-like freezer door slid open with a smooth crunk. We walked together into the grainy light.

"You know what you're here for, don't you?" she said.

"To cook."

"Oh dear," she said. "Apprentices don't get to go anywhere near the stoves, not unless they're cooking for the staff. We do the grunt work. You do realise that? Everything possible is done by hand in a place like this. Chopping, peeling, squeezing – everything. Believe me, if they could find a fire-breathing boy to lie with a boiling stockpot on his face for ten hours, he'd be out there." She gently kicked a large brown cardboard box with a delivery note on top of it. "Right, first job. There should be 188 bags of frozen peas in there. You need to count them out. When you've done that, do the veal bones, beef bones, rabbit carcasses. Then, stock rotation. Start with the sorbet."

There was an instant of silence that followed her last word, during which she could have left. But she paused unnecessarily. She watched as I pushed my throbbing fingers deep between the large sacks of peas and exhaled silently with the relief of it.

"Thanks," I said. "I'm Killian, by the way."

I felt as if she was studying me, for a moment; making some quiet judgement.

"Kathryn."

The sleeves of her tunic were too long. She had had to fold them over themselves into large, pillowy cuffs. I imagined her having to do it every morning. Pushing her arms in and then neatly rolling up the material, slowly exposing her expert fingers and delicate wrists.

"So who taught you how to cook, anyway?" she asked. "Josef Mengele?"

"My aunt," I said.

"She was tough, was she? Your aunt? Some sort of torturer? You should probably think about looking after your hands a bit better than Aunty Pinochet taught you. There's a chance you might need them."

The merciful numbness was now spreading towards my knuckles.

"Oh, I see..." I began. "No, my aunt taught me to cook, but my mum – she's the one who always taught me to sort of take the pain, if that's what you mean."

Her mouth made a barely distinct movement.

"Ah, the school of hard mums." Her eyes flickered away. "Yes, well. Welcome. You should probably also think about not standing up to Patrick like that. You know, let the Wookie win? They take pride in how quickly they can get shot of apprentices. It's like a game to them. That's what they're like here. Especially Patrick."

"But not Max Mann?" I said.

Max Mann wouldn't countenance this behaviour. I knew that. It's why they called him "the Gentlemen Chef". Because he never shouts.

"He never shouts," I said.

I knew Max. I knew Max better than anybody.

Kathryn smiled, thinly, and agreed. "He never shouts."

Chapter 7

The room I was working in was eight foot by ten and, according to the thermometer on the wall, minus twenty-four degrees. The shelves were coated in a skin of fine frost and the packing tape on the cardboard boxes had become brittle and dark. Even with the thick orange over-coat and rubber gloves, the pinching air fought its way to my body without difficulty. It scraped the insides of my nostrils and my ears began to sear; so cold they felt hot. I decided to work without gloves to halt the burn in my fingers.

It wouldn't be long now. The first lunch sitting began at midday – less than three hours away – and I'd surely meet Max before then. I didn't know why that girl Kathryn had said what she had about this kitchen, but I knew when he finally arrived things would be all right. He'd want to sit me down, of course, and get to know the new apprentice who'd be cooking with him for the next six weeks – perhaps longer, if he was judged to be sufficiently skilled.

As my mind synched with my body into the rhythm of the counting and my hands began to recover, I relaxed into the daydream I'd been having since the afternoon Mr Mayle passed me the news of my placement. It wasn't a fantasy, exactly – more a hopeful expectation. I'd seen it in my head so often it had come to feel as if there was no other possible sequence of events.

Max would invite me to sit with him on the restaurant floor, at a table near the kitchen. The waiting staff would be polishing silver around us and the chef would be in front of me with his ankle on his knee, his arm draped over the chair next to him, just as it draped over the back of the sofa when he chatted with Parky and Harty and Wogan. He'd ask why I wanted to be a chef and I'd tell him. I'd tell him about the days at Dor Cottage, those weekends and summer holidays when my mum sent me away because she couldn't cope with me always under her feet, always hanging around, and how my great-aunt Dorothy taught me to make a béchamel, and I know, Chef, I know we've gone beyond these heavy, old-fashioned sauces with Nouvelle Cuisine, and that the modern way to dress a dish is with vinegar or lemon juice, but my mum didn't want me under her feet all the time so I was sent away, and I stopped being sad once I became fascinated by the magic of all that, the matching the quantity of butter and flour and how it combined into this greasy roux and how you added those splashes of cold milk and how lumpy it was and ugly and the risk of it all going wrong if you didn't work hard enough, if you didn't whisk and whisk and whisk, and beat the ugliness out of it, with your elbows and forearms burning against the failure of it all, and it didn't matter if you got some sweat in it, that was what my aunt said, it didn't matter that my mum didn't want me under her feet all summer, or that she thought I would only ever be mediocre, what mattered was the work and the fight and the flavour and the silkiness, the thickness, the luxury of it. You could see it, under the light from the bulb in the kitchen, how by sheer will you'd forced the roux and the milk together – they hadn't wanted to go together, but you'd forced them, you'd beaten them, by the fire in your elbow, by the burn in your shoulder – and now, when you stirred, it purred under the light, it ran in slow waves, like the contours of a young body, like hips, it rolled up and down, thickly, smoothly, and I forgot all about home when I saw what I'd created and I grated the nutmeg but also some ground fennel seeds and, one time, some Stilton and some Parmesan and you wouldn't believe how much flavour that sauce could absorb, this sauce that was once so reluctant, so disobedient, so out of my control, swallowing it all until there she was, you couldn't argue with her, this sauce I'd made, this flavour I'd smashed into life, you couldn't deny how it made my great-aunt Dorothy proud and my mum, Chef, the way my mum looked at me when she tasted my food, that sauce wasn't mediocre, she knew it, even though she said I was a typical man and I would only ever be mediocre and that I should want to be something proper that does something good for the world and even though I was always under her feet, there was this moment when she tasted that sauce that her eyelids fell, it was an involuntary reaction, as involuntary as love, if you don't mind me putting it like that, Chef, and I have to tell you about my aunt who would tell me these stories, Chef, these stories about my distant relations. I'll tell you, Max, because then you'll see it's in the blood, you'll see you made a great decision when you chose to hire me, I'm a natural chef, a witch's nephew, and really, as we're talking like this, as we're getting on so well and getting so close, I can tell you that I think you're just like me, and we're going to work together so well because we're the same in lots of ways, just the sa–

"Oy, flid."
It was Patrick.
"Yes, Chef?"
"Le Patron wants to see you," he said. "Upstairs."

Chapter 8

"You're Killian," said Le Patron. He was reading from a letter that was laid in front of him, which I could see was from West Kent College. The tips of his fingers pressed on the edge of his walnut desk, his nails looking slightly yellow, his square-cut ruby ring looking uncomfortably tight on his thumb. His grey hair was thick – combed and oiled into a side-parting – and he wore his maroon braces over a crisp white shirt that exuded such a powerful simplicity that you could tell it was expensive. A pile of five or six identical shirts, wrapped in dry cleaner's plastic shrouds, had been thrown over the leather club chair in the corner. He appeared to be in his early fifties, his eyes old but his skin tight and relatively unlined.

"Saint Killian," he said. "Irish bishop. Informed the local lord he was in violation of sacred law for marrying his brother's widow. Lord had him beheaded in the town square. Doomed himself in the service of his duty."

He searched my face, as if he was trying to find traces of a decapitated bishop. I hadn't a clue what he was talking about.

"I'm Ambrose Rookwood," he said, eventually. "Le Patron. The proprietor. Your teacher at West Kent college,

Robert Mayle. Old friend of mine. Talented cook. Opened my first restaurant with him in 1955. Poor Mayle, couldn't cope. Pace was too much for him. Very sad. He might have told you?"

"No, sir," I said.

"Ah." He peered back down at the letter without focusing on it. "Now, Killian, enlighten me. Tell me what you know about what we do here. What's your take?"

He said the word "take" slowly and loudly, exposing a set of grey teeth. I'd never met anyone like this before and I felt adrift: I couldn't read his cues and unusual tics. My eyes swept across his office, taking in the bare floorboards that became visibly dusty as they neared the walls, the chipped ivory goblet on the mantelpiece, the framed etching of a naked woman riding a sexually excited horse and the ashtray full of the distinctive white butts of Kent cigarettes. I'd always thought of posh people as somehow cleaner than the rest of us; whiter, purer, naturally scrubbed and polished from birth. And even though Ambrose had a grubbiness about him, it felt inherent and perfectly correct. There was something celebratory about it; something expansive and wicked that made me feel intrigued by him, whilst at the same time, utterly terrified.

The problem with giving him my "take" on Nouvelle Cuisine was that Dorothy had taught me classical cooking. I was excited by it and the creativity and the previously unimaginable flavour profiles it promised but I had never actually tasted it. I hadn't even seen it in colour: I'd only looked at the photographs that sometimes appeared in the restaurant reviews in the *Evening Standard* which I'd make a special detour to Tonbridge Station after college to buy. I remember, in particular, a picture of Mann's terrine of vegetables – these blocks of carrot, runner bean and artichoke, surrounded by a velvet ocean of "farce", his red sauce of ham, egg white and arachide oil, famous because all the implements required in its preparation had to be stored in a fridge and used immediately.

I began slowly. "It's definitely revolutionary, Nouvelle Cuisine. You know, everyone goes on about the tiny portions, but it's not about that, it's about lightness, delicacy and taste. Simple ingredients, cooked simply and presented artfully. That classical Escoffier cooking, all those heavy sauces thickened with rouxs, lots of butter, cream, boiled vegetables, over-seasoned meats and over-cooked fish – we've moved on. There are different techniques, now, like steaming, *au sec* and microwave ovens. The ingredients should taste of themselves, not of butter or sauce."

Ambrose lit a cigarette, sat back and nodded for me to carry on.

"Obviously, it started in France, with Fernand Point at La Pyramide. He'd rebelled against spending days and days preparing loads of stocks and mother sauces, so he said he was going to start with a naked kitchen every morning – nothing stored, nothing pre-prepared, nothing left over, no horrible stodgy floury sauces masking the tastes. It was him, wasn't it, that started thickening sauces by reducing instead of using roux? And he had some amazing apprentices working under him – you know, the Troisgros brothers, Alain Chapel, Paul Bocuse. They all got influenced by him. And then you had Michel Guerard and Roger Verge. The 'Young Bulls', they called them. They had this light, fresh way of cooking – took it even further in their restaurants, swapping ideas, seeing how far they could push it. Then in... uh... " I stalled and looked at the ceiling "...1972 the Gault Millau gave it its name.

La Nouvelle Cuisine. But, you know, it's Max Mann that's really brought it to its full potential since then, isn't it? His pan-fried oysters on mango slices with curry sabayon and his deer and tangerine pie are classics and I read in the paper the other day – is it right that he had to take his duck with blackcurrants off the menu because everyone's copied it? Obviously, I've not tasted it yet, but…"

"Cuisine minceur," Ambrose muttered.

He folded his arms across his belly which, now he'd sat back, suddenly popped into existence under his shirt, and looked out of the window. The mid-morning light picked up the smoke from his cigarette and wafted it into his face. He didn't blink.

"Thin cooking," he said. "In more ways than one."

He'd reddened noticeably.

"Fernand Point, the so-called 'Godfather of Nouvelle Cuisine' – he had a little catchphrase. Do you know what it was? 'Butter! Give me butter! Always butter!' Let me tell you, I have had the heavenly pleasure of eating an egg prepared by Monsieur Point. Do you know how he prepared it? He slid a raw egg from a plate into a melted lump of butter, cooked it on an extraordinarily low heat and then melted more butter over the top of it. He then seasoned it. And then? Do you know what he did next? He added *more butter*." He paused, with a sizzle of menace. "And *that*'s your precious godfather of Nouvelle Cuisine! These pop stars and American actors that dine here, they're more interested in their waistlines and being written about in Nigel Dempster than eating a fine meal. They dress for the evening with 'Feed The World' T-shirts beneath their awful Cardin jackets and they can't even feed themselves. Of course, Max is a genius, but –"

He stopped and peered at me curiously, as if I'd just

dropped from the sky into the space in front of him. "Oh dear," he said. "I'm getting carried away, aren't I?"

"N–"

"Yes," he said, nudging a space between the butts in the ashtray with his cigarette and extinguishing it with a push of his yellow-stained fingers. "Yes, I am." His face bore the suggestion of a mischievous smile. "Never mind," he continued. "I'm sure you're the soul of discretion. Now, young man, as you're no doubt aware, the apprenticing programme we run here is highly sought after. If, after your six-week *stage*, you're deemed worthy of it, you'll be offered the opportunity of being employed as an ouvrier cuisinier and then, if you survive another year or so, a commis. It sounds like you know all about Max. He's a wonderful, wonderful man to work under." His eyes left me for a moment. "And it is true, what he says about his programme. He has never, in fifteen years, given up on an apprentice. Some may have left of their own accord, of course. Many, in fact. Most. But he has never asked a single man to leave, for any reason, before their six weeks is up – a fact he takes an enormous amount of pride in. That's testament not only to his patience, commitment and faith in the traditional brigade system, but also our selection process. I should tell you that we wouldn't usually take an apprentice from a college such as West Kent, but Robert wrote to tell me you're something special. And, of course, you have reached the finals of the Young Saucier competition."

"Yes," I said. "The same one Max Mann won in –"

"Yes, yes," he said. "As I'm sure you know, the winner will be announced at a luncheon at Grosvenor House later in the month. I have certain contacts on the panel of judges and, of course, it would be imprudent of me to reveal the outcome early. Perhaps I'll just tell you we don't hire losers, here at King, and leave it at that. So. I'd like you to prepare my lunch. Steak, mashed potatoes and some of this award-winning sauce."

Chapter 9

I arrived back downstairs from Ambrose's office weightless with the news. In the previous twenty years,
there hadn't been a winner of the Young Saucier of the
Year competition that hadn't gone on to be starred in
the Michelin Guide and receive at least a 14/20 in the
Gault Millau. There had certainly never been one that
had come from a low, municipal college like mine. It
was Max Mann's win in 1972 that had given him his first
small taste of national fame. You'd sometimes read about
it in interviews with him; how news of the Young Saucier
rarely breached the mainstream press, but how that
year the papers ran cartoons alongside stories about the
prize that were thickly marinated in irony. Max's father
was Brian Mann, this notoriously nouveau-riche millionaire. He owned the roadside café chain Speedy Sam's
which, even back then, had a reputation for serving unrea-
sonably priced food that, once plated, seemed to have
a miraculous capacity to generate its own flood of water
and grease, rendering what was already barely edible
so soggy that it usually ended up being scraped into an
overflowing bin. But Speedy Sam's thrived regardless, probably due to his monopoly over all the A-roads.
Those same interviews would also note the suicide of his

mother, and how Max was supposedly ashamed of both his culinary and familial roots and how the Gentleman Chef became uncharacteristically prickly when they were mentioned.

I stood by the kitchen door for a time, watching. I had learned at school that if I placed myself in just the right shadow and didn't move, I could remain unnoticed for a length of time that would astonish a normal person. When I'd been there long enough to roughly work out where the necessary pans could be found, I collected them together and returned to my station.

Next to me was that girl, Kathryn. She was julienning mangoes, carefully transferring the matchstick slices into a small steel bowl nesting in a Tupperware container filled with ice.

"I need some ingredients," I said to her, quietly. She flinched at my voice, and ignored me.

"I have to cook Le Patron his lunch," I said.

"On your first day?"

She looked astonished.

"Is that good?"

"Jesus, impressing Ambrose is the best way to get a job here," she whispered. "That's how Patrick started. But don't screw it up. If Ambrose doesn't like your food, you're fucked."

She lowered her head as Patrick walked down the line, in conversation with a rangy cook with a brown food smear on his tunic and biro all over his left hand. I pretended to be busy and, after they'd passed, Kathryn made no effort to speak again. Her eyes had darkened, her lower lip was pushed downwards in a look of blank concentration. Her fingertips, with their gnawed edges, pressed gently into the firm mango flesh. A little crease between her unplucked eyebrows told me that she was annoyed. I wondered if it was because we'd almost been caught talking.

Hers was a very English prettiness. The cream skin, the freckles, the hair that was simultaneously modest and conspicuously beautiful in its gentle curls and lustre. Her irises were startling – green with crumbs of black and dark gold. Her lips held themselves in an arrangement that told of a tough and perhaps dangerous humour and she had that busy, active alertness about her presence that speaks of intelligence; a mind constantly running. The quality of her culinary technique was also evident. She worked with confidence and tenderness; concentration and economy; delicacy and power; not a movement wasted. And her birthmark, it was –

"Can I help you with something?" she whispered. "You appear to be staring at my face. Is my birthmark fascinating you? Pass me some oil and a pan and I can make you one just like it, if you want."

I looked down, my cheeks heating with shame.

"I need some Worcester sauce and some paprika, port and ground fennel," I whispered. "Do we have any ground fennel?"

She looked at me with an expression of apparently genuine confusion and said, "You must stop now. Stop looking at me. Stop speaking to me. Whatever you're thinking, when you're thinking about me, please stop thinking it. Unless it's hatred. Your hatred I can cope with. In fact, I welcome it. I think we'll get on best of all if you hate me. And if you can't manage that, try pretending. Can you cope with that? Do you think?"

"I'm sorry," I said. "But I *have* to make this sauce."

She sighed, deeply, as she carefully lifted the last of the mango sticks with the blade of her knife and pushed them into the tub. "Fuck's sake," she said. "There's no paprika. And definitely no Worcester sauce."

"You're joking," I said, accidentally back to normal speaking volume. Kathryn winced.

"I've got to go to the shop. If Patrick asks, could you tell him I'm still upstairs?"

She closed her eyes and, shaking her head, said: "Be quick."

Chapter 10

I already knew it, as I sprinted out of Stephen Mews, my chef's clogs slipping on the cobbles: I didn't have enough money. I had dropped 15p into my pocket that morning – enough for a sausage roll in the event that lunch wasn't provided. And yet to prepare the sauce I'd created, I'd need extra ingredients that would cost me... one pound? Two?

Even as I ran past the newsagent's on Charlotte Street, I knew what I was going to do. I ran into a branch of Mace and hunted out the paprika and the Worcester sauce. The decision to do what I did next had arrived, predetermined, the moment Kathryn told me there was none in the kitchen. Once it came, I had a vague sensation of ordering myself not to think about it any more, just to go into automatic, to keep any conscious processing to an absolute minimum, lest it trigger doubt or fear or conscience. I hid at the end of an aisle, holding the ingredients down by my side. Checking in the large security mirrors that noone was watching, I slipped them into my pocket. It was easier than I had imagined. I was almost shocked, as I exited the shop, that nothing happened. The world didn't jump; sirens didn't flash; my reflection didn't change.

Kathryn was preparing the staff lunch when I arrived

back in the kitchen. I fired up the burner next to her, fried off some shallots and crushed garlic, added beef stock and port, brought it to a simmer, reduced the heat and stirred in four tablespoons of tomato purée, some Worcester sauce, ground fennel, paprika and began to reduce it down. Soon, it began to release its sweet, rich and aniseed aroma.

Kathryn and I didn't speak as we worked. I had just started to peel and chop the potatoes for the mash, when I heard her whisper, "No!"

I paused with my knife and frowned in her direction. "Fuck, Killian. You need to boil the potatoes with the skins on and peel them afterwards. Otherwise they'll take on too much water and won't absorb enough butter. Ambrose – if you give him watery mash, you might as well start making enquiries at Garfunkel's right now."

"Hello?"

It was Patrick. A flutter of alarm moved through Kathryn's face and body.

"Sorry, Chef," she said.

He walked towards us with a steaming ladle.

"We've got time to stand around and gossip, have we?"

"*Non*, Chef," she said. "Sorry, Chef."

Patrick mimicked Kathryn. "'Non, chef'," he said, pecking at her forehead with the hot ladle. He peered into the bubbling pot of basil and tomato sauce she was preparing for the staff lunch.

"Is this the family meal?"

"*Oui*, Chef," she said.

He stood upright and called, "Brigade!"

Slowly, one chef after another stopped what they were doing and shuffled towards us. They hung back from the scene with their pale, greasy faces and their smiles of anticipatory pleasure. Patrick picked up a spoon, took some sauce, tipped a drop between his teeth and pressed it to the roof of his mouth. A crusted ball of matter hung from a net of little black hairs in his right nostril. It wobbled there, as he considered the flavour. Finally, he gobbed Kathryn's sauce out through a curled tongue. It fell to the floor with a distant splat.

"Fucking disgusting."

He passed the spoon to a lanky chef next to him. "Perhaps Chris can give us a second opinion."

Chris spat his taste at Kathryn's feet and shook his head with an exaggerated grimace. As every cook in the gang tasted and spat, the whites of Kathryn's eyes shattered with red.

"You," said Patrick, addressing me. "AIDS." He nodded towards the pan. "Why don't you have a go?"

I took the spoon, dipped it in the pot and tipped a few drops in my mouth, just as the others had. It was a roasted tomato and basil sauce, with some chicken stock reducing in it and, I thought, a small amount of honey. How could it not be delicious? I glanced over the faces of the cooks who were watching me, impatient for my verdict. In their pallor and in their burns and scabs and cuts I could sense their dedication; their talent. They were the men of King. *Max's* men. They were here. With me. Waiting for me to join them.

Kathryn moved her gaze from the floor to my face. One of her cuffs had slipped down, unrolled. It was covering a part of her hand. She'd need to roll that back up, I thought. She'd need to sort that out, if she was going to cook any more today.

I met Patrick's eyes and took a steadying breath.

"It's fine," I muttered. "It's good."

I swallowed dryly. Patrick blinked. Immediately, his attention shifted to the stitching on my whites that

Dorothy had carefully completed at the weekend.

"What does that say?" he said.

"Killian, Chef," I said. "My name."

As he pushed his nose up to mine. I could smell his faecal coffee breath and the overwhelming damp salami stench of his skin.

"You," he said, "do not have your name on your jacket. You're just a fucking apprentice."

He picked up a cleaver, pinched the blue cotton stitching between two nubby fingers and pulled it towards him. With a sawing motion, he sliced it off, the red tomato juice soaking from the blade into the white fabric. It dropped into a small foamy puddle on the floor.

"Max has a rule. You probably know it. Never sack an apprentice. It's a bit of a shame that Max isn't here this morning, isn't it?"

He gave a leery sniff and rubbed the hanging matter from his nostril with the back of his hand.

"Go on, you little weirdo. Piss off. I don't want to see you in this kitchen again."

Every emotion and every sensation left me.

"Go on, then! Let's have one last demonstration of your award-winning skills," he said. "Show me how to fuck off in under thirty seconds."

I turned slowly and walked down the room, past the rows of apprentices in their clogs and whites, past the empty stations where Kathryn and I had worked so briefly together and out towards the flat grey light of Stephen Mews with its pigeons and cobblestones and high walls, their stoic magnificence humbled by a hundred-year layer of dirt. The door closed behind me with an underwhelming clunk. I was gazing at it in shocked silence when it opened again with a rattle.

"Killian?" Kathryn looked smaller outside the kitchen; tender and hesitant and pale. "I just wanted – thank you." She'd sorted her sleeve out now. She'd rolled it back up. Ready to carry on cooking for Max. Ready for the rest of her life. "I have to get back in," she said. "But… you know. Thanks."

She'd be fine now, with her sleeves all rolled up properly. She'd be fine going back in there and cooking with Max Mann. A cold wind blew through the hole in my tunic.

"I have to go back to Tonbridge," I said.

"Yeah, that's what I'm saying. I'm saying sorry."

"I never even got to meet him." I heard myself whimper. She put her hand out to touch my arm and I threw it back.

"Don't touch me," I said.

Her elbow hit the door. It clattered angrily with the impact.

"Fucking *twat*," she replied. And without pausing to look back, she disappeared into the kitchen.

Chapter 11

I allowed myself to be pulled by the current of the crowd as it drained towards Charing Cross Station. As I drifted past the Hippodrome and the eastern fringe of Chinatown, I made the decision to leave it as long as possible before telling anyone of my dismissal. I imagined standing in front of everyone, absorbing their reactions: my aunt's sadness, my teacher's disappointment, my mother's sour amusement. And then what? Back to Tonbridge, back to college, back to a life of routine smallness.

Arriving at Bridgewater Close, I walked past the near-identical buildings, past the Houses' place with their large extension, and turned into the path that ran up my front garden – an unremarkable rectangle bordered with pretty flowers and shrubs that rang, somehow, with an almighty sense of emptiness. My door key slipped into place with its familiar run of clicks and bumps, I walked through to the kitchen and, for the first time in my life, suddenly understood father.

There it was, right in front of me: defeat in the form of a forty-seven-year-old margarine factory worker. He was looking down in concentrated silence at the salad cream sandwich he was preparing, wearing a tight blue V-neck jumper with a Bell's whisky logo above the heart.

There were grease-gummed crumbs of dandruff glued into the hem of the V and the skin between it and where his hair started was a dull waxen yellow. Everything was forever drawn down with my father – his mouth, his chin, his shoulders, even his flat feet gave the impression that the gravity of life was too much for his narrow bones. I stood there looking at him with the surreal sensation that my emotional self had somehow leaped from my physical body and decided to spread salad cream on some bread with the back of a teaspoon.

From where I was standing, I could hear the television in the lounge next door.

"Been at college?" said Dad, his Irish accent hardly having weakened at all in spite of his thirty-one years in Kent.

"Work experience today," I said. "In the best restaurant in the world."

"That's nice."

He squinted as he worked the unctuous spread into the very corners of his Mighty White.

"Make us a sandwich, Killian," came a shout from the lounge. "Hellmann's and turkey."

"Okay, Mum."

I prepared it carefully, with the halved cherry tomatoes and the pile of salt and vinegar crisps on the side, just as she liked it, and took it to the lounge, on the way quickly rearranging the telephone receiver into a position where it wouldn't ring – I didn't want any awkward calls from college asking what had happened. Mum hadn't turned the light on, and was sitting in her armchair in the dark awaiting the beginning of *Grange Hill*.

I laid the plate on the arm of her chair and, without looking at me, she said, "You're not in London on

Saturday night are you? I told Felicity you'd baby-sit."

"I was going to visit Aunt Dorothy on Saturday," I said.

"That's fine, then. Visiting's five to six," she said. "You'll be back by seven o'clock."

"Visiting?"

She tutted and rolled her eyes.

"Bloody hell, Killian – hospital. Visiting's over by six. You'll be at Felicity's for seven, easily."

The words she was saying bumped around in my head, trying to make sense of each other. As they did – slowly – my mother became visibly delighted. She had that aggressively teasing look; the expression that overtook her when the world proved, yet again, to be crueller and much funnier than she had given it credit for.

"Didn't anyone tell you? She had a fall, a couple of days ago. She's broken her hip."

She was beaming.

"Look at you!" she laughed. "Oh, what a picture!" She sighed contentedly, tutted and went back to the screen. "You and that bloody woman."

"How is she?" I asked.

She shuffled her bony legs, irritably.

"She'll be fine." A pause. A grip in her blood. "She's ninety-two, for God's sake! She should've been put into a home years ago. The stairs in that cottage. Let's be honest, she had it bloody coming."

Chapter 12

I ran to the station and took the next train to Tunbridge Wells. When it pulled in, ten minutes later, I tore across the lonely triangle of common, under the imperious glare of the Victorian hotels that lined Mount Ephraim like so many bankrupt yet still-haughty duchesses, and then paced, breathless, along London Road towards the Kent and Sussex Hospital.

My day looked to be getting even worse when the receptionist informed me, with a kind smile, that I was two minutes late for visiting. I put my hands on the counter and decided to have a try at pleading.

"Please," I said. "I've only just found out what's happened to her."

The receptionist thought for a second.

"I don't know. No harm in seeing," he said, quietly. He adjusted the telephone with the tips of two fingers so it was in perfect symmetry with his desk-pad, before dialling a four-digit number and having a short conversation, the receiver shielded by a tightly cupped hand.

"Thought so," he said, placing the phone softly on its cradle. "Your aunt's on Bev Cowan's ward. Bev's one of the nice ones. She said you can go up as long as you're quiet."

It took me another ten minutes to find Ward 10; running through high corridors and up and down empty stairs that twisted around lift-shafts, only to find myself back where I'd started. When I eventually found the place, I entered silently.

The ward's brick walls were painted a puce white. Pipes ran in all directions. Tall windows, their glass murky with the dirt of a thousand rain storms, looked out onto the black bones of winter trees and a sky erased by cloud. A feeling of déjà vu lowered itself darkly into the room. Rows and rows of strangers lay in steel beds, in all the mess of their vulnerability. I tried not to look. I was aware, though, of clear tubes up noses and ancient lips quivering like a young bird's and a man with what looked to be some sort of yellow discharge or ointment around his ears.

"You all right?"

The nurse appeared from behind a screen holding her hands in front of her, her fingers stretched out as if they were wet.

"Miss Moran," I said, and was about to explain that I had permission to be there when she interrupted me. "Down at the end. She's a little sleepy. Painkillers. She's had quite a nasty break."

"It'll mend okay, though?" I asked.

She moved her head from side to side, unsurely.

"Well, the doctor says it either needs pinning or replacing and she's very old. It's very invasive, that kind of operation. If you ask me, though, she'll be fine. She's been complaining about the food, and that's a good sign. It was spag bol last night and she suggested that we might want to try cooking the spaghetti for ten minutes less. She was very nice about it. Has she got much family?"

"Never married," I said, and I was about to add, "She

never had much of a personal life," but a memory stopped me: my mother saying with an almost proud sneer, "Don't let Dorothy fool you. She might look like a sweet old dear, but that doesn't mean she doesn't have secrets."

"Well, try not to be too long with her," said the nurse. She hurried away, presumably to wash her arms. I watched as she disappeared, long before the echo of her footsteps.

The lights appeared dimmed. It was that gloomy, early-dusk time, when there's not yet enough darkness for the bulbs to shine against. I found Dorothy in the bed at the end of the room, the glow from a green fire escape sign not doing her complexion any favours. It was only later that I considered it notable that she wasn't doing anything when I saw her. She wasn't reading one of her large-print Jeffrey Archer books, she wasn't doing a crossword, she wasn't sleeping, she wasn't listening to the radio or one of her cassettes. She was just lying there, gazing out at the ward.

I sat on the chair beside her bed and waited for her eyes to connect and for her smile, but it took a long time for her life to find her body; as if the levers and dials were some distance away and she had to struggle to get there.

"Hello, Kill," she said, at last. "What a lovely surprise. You really shouldn't have come, you know."

I was taken by how little space her legs took up under the sheets. And her face: it looked different – diminished in a way that I couldn't quite decipher. It somehow wasn't the explosion of meaning a healthy face is. Her arms were laid gently upon herself, one frail hand on top of the other, a tissue scrunched lightly between two fingers. Her left arm, I noticed, appeared to be shaking.

"It was my own silly fault, Kill," she said. "My doctor, Dr Sanjeev, he always says I shouldn't be using the stairs in the cottage. He's been telling me for years and I've not listened. You know me, Kill, I just can't bear to leave that bedroom. It's the sun in the morning. It's so lovely." She looked down towards her hands, but without her glasses I wasn't sure she could actually see that far. "The doctor here, he's not so nice. A Dr Graham, or something. Says I'll have to walk with an aid of some sort. No more stairs for me. It's my own silly fault. But no matter. I'm just happy to see you." She pulled her chin back and rallied a little, relieved to be pushing the attention away from herself. "So, come on! Tell me how it went at King. They let you out early, then? Not on my account, I hope."

I moved my chair forward in an attempt to squeeze as much hospital out of it as possible.

"I'm just on lunch service in my first week," I lied. "They like to start apprentices off slowly."

"Well," she said, with a satisfied nod, "they sound like very nice people."

"They are," I said.

The lift of her smile finally became evident in the thick creases around her eyes.

"Here, do you think they'll keep you on once the apprenticeship is over?"

"I reckon," I said. "Guess what? I've won the Young Saucier of the Year award. They told me today."

And that's when she came fully alive; became my wonderful great-aunt Dorothy. She rolled her eyes in the mock-crazy fashion she always used to and opened her mouth in a comic exaggeration of awe.

"Oh marvellous, Kill," she said. "Oh, that's bloody marvellous, really. Well done. Did they like your outfit?"

"They were all very jealous."

She studied me closely. Her pencilled-on eyebrows took a small dive.

"So what's the matter then? Why are you sad?"

"Oh, it's just Mum," I said. "She didn't tell me you were in hospital. She did it on purpose, I think."

Her jaw muscles mashed as she thought something over.

"You know I don't like to speak badly of family," she said, eventually. "But I know how she treats you, Kill. Well, you're a grown-up now, that's what I say. You've got a job of your own, near as dammit, and the sooner you can move out of there, the better."

"She's only doing her best," I said. "Even if I did get a full-time job, I doubt I could afford to live by myself. The money would be awful, to start with."

"Well," she said. There was an almost imperceptible nod, as if she was measuring a thought. Around me, I became aware of the sounds of shuffling and coughing breaking against the hard, high walls. The busybody striding of a passing nurse added to that almost cruel taint you can feel in hospitals, where bureau-cracy meets agony and work meets death. When she turned towards me again, I noticed her pupils were dancing all over my face: my mouth; my eyes; my cheeks; my hair; my nose. It was as if she was trying to recall something. When she spoke again her voice had the tiniest thread of hardness running through it.

"You'll be fine, Killian. You will. Trust a wise old buzzard. You're going to be a big hit in London. Already are, by the sounds of things. All you need now is to get out of that house. I know you don't tell me the half of it. All these excuses you make for her."

"She doesn't mean it," I said.

She reached over and closed a shaking hand over mine. Her skin looked shiny and hard, like vinyl. I could see the muscles and mechanisms inside it; rods and hinges and thick blue pipes. I could see everything moving about.

"Can I ask you a funny question, Kill?" she asked, carefully. "Do you have dreams sometimes? About the cottage?"

I saw her heartbeat throb inside a vein. I saw the push of the pulse, defiant in the face of her decay.

"No," I said, still looking at her hand. "I don't know. I don't really remember what happens in them."

"You know you're a special lad, don't you, Kill?" she said. "You've got the Dor blood. You've got Mary in you."

With a miniature groan, she sat herself up, just a little.

"I want you to listen to me now. The next year or two – you might find them to be a little testing. What I mean is, you'll probably *be* tested, in ways you can't possibly begin to imagine. Now, I know you think I'm a dotty old thing, with my funny stories about the cottage and all that. But you must understand. There's more to this world than you might think. When it comes, when it happens, you have to be strong enough to be good. And I know you will, my dear."

She looked settled enough, in her bed. Content. I wondered about the painkillers. It was probably the drugs, making her confused.

"Okay, Aunty," I said. "I understand."

"But first things first," she said. "You need to be allowed to grow up. You need to strike out on your own."

"But I'm never going to be able to move out of Mum's house," I said, pulling my hand up from under hers. "Even if they keep me on, I won't be able to afford it."

I had a sudden doubt about her smile.

"Trust a wise old buzzard," she said. "You'll be all right."

And my room was flooded with golden light. The air was simmering, and I was elevated inside it, lifted by the most wonderful of fragrances. Feathers of flavour were stroking the weight from my body, now the scent of strawberry, now thyme, now roasted chicken, now frying shallots, now lemongrass, now tomato, now satsumas, now chocolate, the air blushing with oranges, greens and pinks. It was as if I were dreaming, not with my mind, but with my nose, mouth and tongue. In that moment, as I floated in the ecstasy, I felt in total command of all of nature's gifts.

Chapter 13

Having lied to Mum, I realised that my only option was to take the 06.52 to London as if I hadn't been dismissed at all. I walked around for an hour or two and eventually ended up outside King. There was a post office on the opposite side of the road whose window faced the restaurant. It had a counter running beneath it, upon which customers were supposed to stick stamps and write addresses. I spent a long time leaning there, pretending to read pamphlets about the dole and housing benefit. I filled in four passport applications and applied for road tax twice. But what I was really doing was the thing I did best: watching in the silence. I wanted to see them – Ambrose and Patrick and Chef Max Mann. I wanted to see Kathryn.

During lunch service, I walked some more. I went to Billingsgate, Smithfield and Borough Market. I made pilgrimages to Le Gavroche, Tante Claire and Chez Nico. I peered at the menus in Inigo Jones, Le Caprice and Langan's Brasserie. Halfway through the afternoon, I took the train to Tunbridge Wells. Aunt Dorothy was missing.

"Is she still in Ward 10?" I asked the receptionist when I arrived at the Kent and Sussex. I had been looking forward to her sympathetic company and felt pleased that, this time, I could have a full two hours. The hospital was busy. The people moved with a curious slowness; the tired slouch of cleaners, weary invalids, harassed visitors and doctors wired on 5p machine coffee.

"Do you know when they were operating?" he said, picking up the phone with the same friendly smile he'd greeted me with the day before.

"No," I said. "Not yet, though."

He mumbled into the receiver, then placed his hand over it. There was a pause as he listened to something, then span around in his chair. My legs ached from the day's walking and I leaned my weight against the counter, running my thumbs impatiently along its edge, which was coming away to reveal the chipboard beneath. I glanced about at the plastic signs, plastic chairs and the dusty plastic light fitting that was hanging dangerously above me from the suspended ceiling.

"Is she still in Ward 10?" I asked, again, when he was off the phone.

"Sorry, sir, could you excuse me for a second?" he got up from his seat. "I've just got to check something..."

He went into the back office, through a door marked "Staff Only", and I could just see him talking to someone through the window, which was louvred with mirrors. He glanced at me, fearfully.

I walked as fast as I could without looking conspicuous. I went around the corner and ran – up the stairs, left down the corridor, radiology, Ward 8, Ward 7, hang on, hang on, I'm going in the wrong direction, back past radiology and upstairs and right and straight down the corridor, neonatal, coronary care, intensive care, no, no, no, maybe downstairs, two flights this time, where are the signs, where are the signs, steps, steps, steps, down past the lift, I remember these murals, I remember that cartoon tiger, it was somewhere around here, I know it was definitely somewhere around here, physical therapy, Ward 5, Ward 6, oh no, how could this be?, down there, right down there to the end, more stairs, I'll go up this time, oh God, not Ward 8 again, hang on, hang on, I remember endocrinology, it was here, it was around here, Ward 9, no, no, no, got to be down here, there, there, those green doors, there they are, those green bloody doors – and I ran; I ran as fast as I could.

"Can I help you?" said the nurse. She was standing over the bed of a man with remarkable eyebrows who looked as if he was concentrating very hard on sitting up.

"Dorothy Moran," I said. "Is she down there?"

The nurse moved into the centre of the corridor. She spoke low and tentatively.

"I'm so sorry," she said. "Somebody downstairs should have told you. She went at about half three this morning."

"Went?"

"I'm so sorry, sir. We had your mum down as next of kin but – has your phone been disconnected? It doesn't seem to be working. We've been trying all day."

The nurse took a tiny step away from me and her hips moved towards the nearby door.

"I'm really, really sorry," she said.

I stood there, surrounded by the moment.

"That's okay," I said, trying to look calm. "But she was fine. I saw her. I spoke to her." I glanced towards the bed Dorothy had been in. A single fly circled over the space where her head had lain.

"Actually," she said, "I think she was a little distressed about the operation and about not being able to walk without assistance. I mean, the doctor told her yesterday morning she might not walk again." She took a little step back towards me and allowed her voice to become softer. "I know it sounds weird, but sometimes – when they get to that age – sometimes you just get the feeling they're ready to go. They just decide it's time, you know? You see it a lot on this ward. Sometimes, they just decide."

I didn't cry when I left the hospital and I didn't cry when I got home and I didn't cry when I was alone on my bed trying not to think about anything at all.

Chapter 14

For the first part of the week that followed, I continued to sustain the fiction that I was working the lunch service at King. I'd spend the days watching in the post office or sitting on a bench in Soho Square, before making it home in time to heat up a Findus dinner with chips for my parents.

That Thursday, I walked into the lounge to meet the sharp silence of a conversation abruptly halted. The television was on, but Dad was standing in front of it in his gold-buttoned suit, his navy-blue tie in a wide shiny knot. Mum was in her armchair, having made her usual move of changing out of whatever it was she'd been wearing in the day and putting on her pink Harrods slippers and a thin cotton 'CHOOSE SLEEP' nightdress that went to her knees. Her small round face hung like a failed sun beneath the horizon of her heavy black fringe that was shot through with lightning strikes of grey. A half-smoked Belair Menthol sat glowing in the heavy glass ashtray – a souvenir from a Mediterranean cruise that she had been on with Dad.

She sprang from her throne as I entered – her spine, her upper lip, her finger poking towards me – all curled up and nasty; one great human-sized jab.

"Joy," said Dad, holding his arm out to stop her. His

suit was too short and his gold bracelet clashed with his orange skin and hairs.

"What did you say to her?" she said. "What did you say to her?"

She turned to my father. "It's not right. It's not right." And to me, "You greedy little bastard, what have you been scheming?"

"What's going on?" I said.

"We've come from the solicitor's," said my father.

"Congratulations," Mum said. "Greedy bastard. I hope you're satisfied. You've got what you wanted."

"What do you mean?" I said.

Mum broke free and slapped me around the face.

"Not now, Joy," said Dad.

"You're not too big for an old-fashioned hiding, you know," she said. "I'll get the fucking kettle boiling."

"That's not..." began Dad. "This is not the way to solve this situation."

I looked back at my father, squinting in confusion; surprised by the calm strength he was exhibiting.

"The house," he explained. "The cottage."

"Okay," I said. "Just tell me what's going on."

"As if he doesn't know," said Mum. "Acting the bloody innocent. This is how I get treated, after everything. This is how I'm repaid."

"Sit down, Joy," said Dad. "Let me try."

He lowered himself onto the sofa with a stiff grunt, his slow movement somehow having a calming effect on the room. "Now," he said, looking up through reasonable eyebrows. "At some point, your aunt Dotty changed her will to make it so you got the cottage." He patted the arm of the chair. "You're just a boy, Killian. She didn't know what she was doing."

The only way I could hold myself together was to lean back on the sofa to stare at the ceiling – at the bottle-green tasselled lampshade, the long cracks in the plaster, like spider's legs, and the remains of the twilight leaking through the net curtains.

"It's not right," said Mum with sorry, pleading eyes. "It's not right."

"We've been relying on getting that house," said Dad. "It's supposed to go to us – next of kin. We need the money, son. We've got to sell it. I'll be retiring soon. We've got loans."

I couldn't remember seeing them this *combined* before.

"Come on, son," said Dad. "There are times in life when you've just got to do what's right. For the family. We've brought you up. This is the least you can do for us. You owe it, really."

When Mum spoke again it was with a careful mix of affection and softly spun hurt.

"All those years I raised you," she said. "I've given you everything I've got. You should see some of the cases that come across my desk. You don't know how lucky you are. This is your chance to help us for a change. To help your mother. To show me how much you love me." Her eyes raked me up and down. "If you still do, that is. All grown up now. Big man. Don't need your mum any more."

My eyes flicked back to the ceiling. I remembered Dorothy, lying there. *Trust a wise old buzzard.*

"You can have it," I said. "I don't want it."

I avoided looking at either of them as I stood. I didn't know where I was going. It didn't matter: the only important thing was to leave. I'd just see where my feet wanted to take me. Maybe to the park. Maybe to a pub. Maybe I'd do as my father always did and poison the discomfort with whisky.

"You're a good boy, Killian," said Mum as I passed by. "It's only right, after everything we've done for Dorothy. We loved her. You know we did. She was family."

She was stroking the arm of the chair with the pad of her thumb and peering down at it in a detached sort of gaze. It was a caring, gentle motion. She was watching herself in the act of it. Being caring. Being gentle. I observed her for just a second. For some reason, I lost control.

"Well, that's bullshit," I said.

Her neck twisted towards me. I could see the sinew in it and I could see something pulsing.

"What did you say to me?"

A U-turn, right round to the front of her and I was there, crouching to the height of her face. I was conscious of the pressure in my thighs; the torque in the muscles as I held myself steady. Her legs poked from beneath her black skirt like pistons.

"You wouldn't even let her come for Christmas," I said. "She looked forward to Christmas dinner all year and you wouldn't let her come. Do you know what she ate on Christmas Day, whilst we were eating turkey? I know, because I saw it in her bin. She ate a can of Campbell's tomato soup."

I stuck my face into hers just as Patrick had done to me.

"Campbell's. Fucking. Tomato. Soup."

I stood up to my full height.

"I don't want to be here any more," I said. "I don't want to live here. I want to live on my own. I really think that's best." Silence. "That's what I want. And that's what Aunt Dorothy wanted. What she didn't want was you lot selling the cottage."

"And what have I got?" Mum shouted, rising from her chair. "Who's going to look after me when I get old? Not him. Not that bloody useless sack of a man." She gestured to the sofa behind me, where Dad confirmed her prediction by doing absolutely nothing at all. "We need the house, Killian. We need the money. I need it."

"It's supposed to be mine, Mum, and I'm sorry but I promise, *I'll* look after you," I said. "*Of course* I will. I promise."

She slapped me, aiming her long nails, as was her habit, at my injured left eye. Her nipples hardened beneath her nightshirt. I lurched back and sunk towards the carpet, covering my head. In the background, I could hear a baked beans commercial showing on the lounge television: *"My brother's been really kind to me lately. He's given me all his comics…"*

"Look at me when I'm talking to you, you ungrateful little bastard."

"His magnifying glass, his favourite poster. He's even given me his share of Heinz baked beans."

She kept it coming and coming and coming, shouting, "After everything I've done for you."

"Genuine too! All of them covered in lovely thick tomato sauce."

"You don't give a shit about me. Typical fucking man –"

"Heinz beans are the business! And me? I gave him the –"

"– cunt."

It would be over soon. She would be sorry and she would hold me again just like she used to. It was going to be fine. It was going to be fine.

* * *

When I got home from drinking in Tonbridge Park that night, I found her in the armchair, asleep with a half-drunk bottle of Martini at her feet. I helped her upstairs and put her to bed. I made sure she was warm and comfortable, the quilt tucked up to her chin and the night-light on, her face cast gently in its safe orange glow.

And I felt the caged magic in Dor Cottage. I felt it breathing; moving towards me as I slept. I reached out and touched it with my fingers, sliced with blood, pushed through dreadful undergrowth. They tore at plants as a great fire burned around me.

In the kitchen, the woman I had always known turned to look at me. Gently, she took my hand and pushed my finger into a pot of hot broth. She held it in the thick and roiling red, until my skin peeled off. She said to me, "And now you've come, so. From the land of Uz, all perfect and upright."

Outside, the elms were filled with night and the voices of children. I could hear them chanting, "Earl's heart and earl's leafs and earl's lusts abounding. Earl's fires and earl's grace and earl's witch is burning."

And dogs surrounded the king of all cooks. He pushed them back with his bleeding fingers. "Who's going to stop them barking?"

And I was king of the dogs, dog of the kitchen, dog of the lost.

I was dog of the kitchen, dog of the lost.

Chapter 15

West Kent's catering department was deserted. I walked through the training kitchen, amongst the cold ovens and the unclattered pots and pans. All the students were on their work placements. I would have imagined that Mr Mayle wasn't there either, if it hadn't been for the message I found by the telephone at home that said he wanted to see me in his office.

I knocked on his door and when, upon his cheery "Hello", I pushed it open, I couldn't work out what he'd actually been doing in there. With his blinds pulled down and his standard lamp on, he blinked at me from behind his desk, looking like a startled mole. If I had had to guess, I would have said he'd just been sitting by himself, quite happily.

"You'd better sit down," he said.

He took off his glasses and leaned on his elbows with a sympathetic downward smile.

"Where have you been?" he said. "We've been trying to get hold of you. I heard from Ambrose…"

I pulled the plastic seat back and sat down. Mayle's office was completely unlike that of any other teacher's room I'd been in. It wasn't just the paperbacks or the biscuit tin or the dusty, tassel-fringed standard lamp; the room's aura was such that it could only have come from his long years of treating it, not as a place of work, but as an extension of his home.

"We've had a few family problems," I said. "My aunt. She passed away."

The words felt too big for my throat.

"Sounds like you've had a rough time," he said.

There had always been something reassuring about Mr Mayle; something that made you want to confide all your most secret frailties. He had these masculine, hairy wrists poking out from his cuffs, small sideburns and his hair was a rich biscuity brown. He'd wear smart mock-tweed suits and tan brogues and yet there was always a comfortably scruffy air about him – an unironed wrinkle in a collar; a reminder scrawled in biro on his hand; his consistently odd socks – that loosened any implied rigidity.

"Pretty rough," I said.

"Overdue for the boils, eh?" His smile became broad and warm, like an arm around my shoulder.

"Sorry, sir?" I said.

"Job," he said. "Book of Job. Did you do any RE at school? 'There was a man in the land of Uz and his name was Job and that man was perfect and upright'?"

I felt suddenly unpleasant, as if a cloud had passed over the room.

"It rings a weird kind of bell," I said.

"You should have a read. I think it's your kind of book. Anyhow, Mr Lone, I need to talk to you about a very important decision you have to make."

He folded the arms of his glasses and placed them neatly on the desk in front of him. Meeting my eyes in a sustained way for the first time, he said, "Is this really what you want? To spend the rest of your life in a professional five-star kitchen? I think you can hack it, Killian, I really do. You're tough, there's no doubt about it. It'll take a lot of perseverance and hard work but I think you'll get there. It's not the talent I'm worried about." He gave a small, reluctant sigh. "You know, Killian, personalities are quite infectious. Do you know what I mean by that? We think our characters are fixed – that we are who we are and that's it. But it's not true. We're porous. We absorb the world around us. The company we keep, the people we look up to – eventually, it becomes us. You know, fine dining, it's... it's not a kind world. And if there's anyone I've ever met that could benefit from a spot of kindness, it would probably be you."

"I can hack it," I said.

Mayle drummed the fingers of his left hand once along the tabletop.

"You're a decent guy, Killian," he said. "You're very bright and you're probably the most naturally talented young cook I've ever come across. But to get to the level of someone like Max Mann, there'll be sacrifices. The long hours and low pay, I'm sure you'll be fine with. The work is the easiest part. It's the other sacrifices. If you want to be in the top one per cent... Well, it's rather like serving on the front lines in a war. Nobody survives with their hearts in one piece. Believe me, I've been around. I'm not convinced it's worth it. You might be surprised to hear this, but I could have been in that one per cent. I decided I didn't want it. I know it's not always obvious, but I'm very happy teaching. I enjoy it. And I like the fact I get to go home at night and spend time with my wife and daughter. We cook, me and my family. We're happy. If I'd pursued all my youthful dreams, I'd be up there, executive chef of somewhere like King. But I'd have none of what I've now got, which may seem very dull and pedestrian to a hungry young man like you. But when you get to my age, believe me Killian, it's everything."

"I'm going to win the Young Saucier," I said. "Did Ambrose tell you? I'm going to win the Young Saucier of the Year."

He smiled, flatly, and picked up his glasses again, opening one of the arms and staring at the hinge. "He did tell me," he said. "And I'm delighted for you. I couldn't be more delighted. I'm delighted for me too. I never thought, in all my years, I'd watch one of my students accepting an award like that. It'll be the proudest moment of my teaching career, it really will, when I accompany you to the ceremony. You've got that under your belt, no matter what you decide."

"I want it," I said. "I really do. It's the only thing I've got. I don't have anything else but this."

He turned his telephone around and pushed it towards me.

"Very well," he said. "In that case you should call Ambrose."

I watched him flick through his notebook to find the number. My right foot tapped violently as I dialled. One ring, two rings, "Ambrose Rookwood."

"Hello," I said. "It's Killian Lone. The apprentice. I –"

"Yes," he said. "I'd like you to come and see me."

"When?"

"Well…" He sounded rather insulted. "Now."

Chapter 16

I rushed through the machine, with its blue, white and steel shades and its pots, smells and blades, hoping that nobody would notice me. The chefs were as silent as the job demanded, and as focused. Lifting, chopping, boiling, peeling, never looking up unless necessary, never talking, only communicating – an essential distinction, as I was to discover. As I passed through, I thought I glimpsed something bizarre over by the fish station. A slightly overweight cook, working over lighted burners, who appeared to be naked from the waist up. Convinced I must have been mistaken, I looked away and, as I did I caught sight of her working with her usual intensity. She turned in my direction and, I swear, as soon as she saw it was me, she stopped what she was doing for just a moment, and stared.

Upstairs, outside Ambrose's office, I tried to get comfortable on the springs that were straining beneath the papery leather of the aged chair, whilst watching the passing waitresses, who were arriving in preparation for service. They were famous, these women. Max was oft-quoted as saying he wanted his wait-staff to be "terrifyingly beautiful" and to achieve this effect he clothed them identically in skin-tight black dresses that ended high at the thigh. They wore their hair stretched back into pony-tails, their eyeshadow black and heavy, their lips full, red and glistening under the restaurant's smartly recessed spotlights. There had been grumbles about these uniforms by feminists in the *Evening Standard*, but as I sat there, I couldn't make sense of their logic. These were the least subservient-looking waitresses I'd ever seen. They radi-ated a kind of alien power, taller than was human and almost insectoid, the sheer dark fabric like an exoskeleton, the eyes swollen huge in the inky kohl, the lips glowing a warning colour. Yes, they were terrifyingly beautiful, but to this young man, they were mostly terrifying.

"Sit down, sit down," Ambrose said when I was finally summoned. As I approached his mahogany desk, I almost slipped on the worn rug that lay loose on the floorboards. I wondered, fleetingly, if it might be some sort of test for the apprentices who brought up his meals, and this, in turn, made me wonder what he'd ended up eating for lunch on the day that I disappeared.

"You've been admiring the parade," he said as I sat. He didn't pose it as a question but announced it as fact. The thing his eyebrows were doing made me wonder if I might be missing something about the waitresses: perhaps the feminists had a point after all. I smiled meekly in response and sat forward in my chair. Ambrose was in a bow tie today, his red braces tight over one of his perfect white shirts. His ashtray was perilously full, a recently discarded butt still glowing orange at the edges. There were no paperbacks in this room, I noticed, or homely standard lamps or biscuit tins. In fact, the whole feel of this office was completely unlike that of his old business partner Robert Mayle. I was sure Ambrose felt just as comfortable in this space as Mayle did in his, but with its chandelier resembling a petrified spider's web, its shelf of awards, its sexual etchings and its framed photos of the occupant himself with powerful businessmen (I recognised two from the newspapers as Robert Maxwell and Tiny Rowland), it wasn't a room that was much concerned with making visitors feel safe.

He sat back and folded his hands beneath his chin, the red ruby in his ring dulled and waxy on his thumb.

"Following your dismissal on Monday," he began, "another apprentice – that girl – finished your sauce." The light slid across his thickly lacquered hair as he dipped his head to look down his nose at me. "It was very good indeed. Contemporary, imaginative, really very promising, for a cook your age."

I lowered my head and bit my cheeks until the urge to smile faded.

"I heard about your incident with Chef Patrick. It is unfortunate, I have to say – your decision to leave so quickly. But I assume by your presence here now you that would like a second chance. Well, I have been informed as to what happened and I have to tell you, we simply do not accept that sort of behaviour here."

As he'd said the word "behaviour", he appeared disgusted, as if he could detect a faint odour of vomit in the air.

"You do not undermine your superiors. This isn't some Derbyshire colliery. This is a two-Michelin-starred fine-dining establishment in the centre of one of the greatest cities in the world. We abide by certain rules here. We have a way of doing things that has operated since the time of Escoffier."

He didn't move, as he spoke. In fact, the only movement in the entire room was that of his jaw beneath his pale skin which, in the light that was coming through the sash window behind him, looked dry and withered, as if it had been hung for years in a forgotten smoke-house.

"One might feel, when one works in the brigade's lower orders, that things aren't fair. But if one excels, one very quickly comes to appreciate the absolute necessity of the way we work. A great many lesser kitchens may concern themselves with rights and wrongs and romantic notions of fair play and so on. But you won't be surprised to learn that here at King we don't regard ourselves as a lesser kitchen. Our goal is not merely filling stomachs and cash registers. We're going to earn our third star when *L'Inspecteur* return this year. We have achieved this pre-eminent standard by eliminating all traces of this sort of thing from the kitchen. We've inhibited our own petty and irrelevant needs and wants in service of what we're here for. The pursuit of perfection."

A thin, paternal smile.

"*L'amour du travail bien fait*," he said. "The love of perfect work. At King, this is our minimum requirement."

"Yes," I said. "I understand."

"If you want to concern yourself with rights and wrongs may I suggest you join the social services where your needs will be richly served every moment you spend tramping around the sink estates of Lambeth and Wandsworth, attending to the needs of the illegitimate children of Negroes and the lesbians?"

He leaned forward and spoke in a hush.

"But we know better than that, don't we, Killian?" he said. "So this is your opportunity to tell me. Are you with us? Or the lesbians?"

"I'm with you, sir," I said.

His smile dropped and all warmth left the room.

"Good," he said. "Then let's have you back in tomorrow, first thing."

"Tomorrow?" I said. "It's my aunty's funeral tomorrow, sir. In the morning."

His expression didn't alter. It was as if I hadn't said anything at all.

"I'll let Chef Max know to expect you at seven a.m. sharp."

Chapter 17

A meaty arm blocked my exit through the corridor.

"No, it's okay," I told its owner. "I've just seen Ambrose."

He looked at my shoes, at their ragged laces and scuffs and the place where the sole had split from the leather. When his head raised up again, there was that leering, tonguey smile on his tiny pink mouth.

"He said I can start again tomorrow," I told him. "He said it was fine."

"We don't do second chances here, pal," he said. "This isn't Space Invaders. You don't get three lives."

"But he said because of the—"

His smell was still there.

"Your award? Yeah, I know about that," said Patrick. "Doesn't mean shit in here. Mate, you're not coming back in my kitchen and that's that."

Salami.

"No, my sauce. I think that's why. He liked my sauce. He said it was imaginative and contemporary and I think, well, I could make it for you if you like, I think you'll – "

He scowled me into silence.

"No one comes back. Once you've walked, you've walked."

"But you—"

He spoke over me, "I'll be watching that door tomorrow and if I see you in it, I'll push you right back out of it, into the fucking road, do you understand me?"

A shape filled the doorway at the end of the corridor. I stared over Patrick's arm, which was still preventing me from moving. There was light and noise from the kitchen and this great black silhouette. I knew it. I knew the curve of the skull. I knew the line of the neck.

"Do you understand me?" said Patrick, with increasing insistence. "Don't worry about what Ambrose said. You're not coming in tomorrow. You've gone. You walked. You've lost."

It was him! How could he have been present in the building without me sensing it? How could the ceiling not grow taller or the light burn brighter or the walls not bend out with the force of his extraordinary presence? How could the laws of nature treat him as if he was human, when he was Chef Max Mann?

He turned and he walked towards us. It would be fine, now, all this misunderstanding. Everything would go back to normal.

"Patrick?" he said.

And he was there, just there, talking to Patrick about a cod delivery. So close that I felt I could lick his breath right out of the air. I was shocked at how lifelike he looked. Exactly the same as he did on television, except somehow more compact and concentrated; drawn in startling detail. He had his name stitched onto the chest of his whites and the effect, perhaps perverse, was to imply humility; as if anyone needed to be told. His eyes appeared to have been planted right at the sides of his head, as if keeping out of the way of the great oaken nose that sprouted down the centre of his face, this magnificent organ that gave the impression of having such a history of extraordinary scents drawn up it that it had reacted by bolstering itself with layers of regrowth like new skin on a worn heel. As large as his eyes seemed to be, they had no particularly distinguishable colour; they just seemed watery, glassy and in a vaguely fish-like state of constantly searching for something; on the hunt for danger in the tiniest of details. His mouth was small, thin, and vertical creases lined both of his lips, as if he'd spent too many years sucking everything in his path onto that world-famous palate.

But there was one discomfiting way in which his real image varied from his famous one – the bags beneath his eyes, so leaden and swollen it was as if they were struggling to contain all the shadows that were seeping out of him. Taken in combination with his grey stubble and cropped hair, they gave his presence a crackle of dark instability that I wasn't expecting. Strangely, however, this didn't alter the central fact of Chef Max Mann. He seemed to have achieved that ultimate level of self-confidence in which every look, thought and movement is possessed of a perfect singularity of intent. There was no doubt, question or confusion in anything he did and that, of course, is as rare a quality in a man as it is attractive.

I couldn't suppress the loony grin that spread across my face. It didn't matter. I was with him now.

"I'm so pleased to meet you, Chef," I said, when they had finished.

He addressed Patrick.

"Who's that?" he said.

"An ex-apprentice," said Patrick. "He was here for about half an hour before service last week."

"Half an hour?" said Max.

"Forty minutes, tops. Then he walked."

Max grinned.

"A record!" he said.

"But I didn't walk," I said, being sure to smile. "That's okay, though. It doesn't matter. Ambrose said I can have another go. I can come in tomorrow, he said – " Max's face darkened. "He said I could come back."

Max blinked. He looked at me. He blinked again.

"Come back?"

"Not because of my award, because of the Young Saucier which I think you already know I'm going to win, it's because of the sauce that he tasted and I wanted you to know that I'm a hard worker and that you'll be pleased with me." My jaw was shaking. "I'm not disloyal. I'm probably the most loyal cook you'll ever work with, I can absolutely promise you that, Chef, all my life I have prided myself on being loyal and I've always wanted to be a cook, I've always felt most at home in a kitchen, actually I feel more at home in a kitchen than anywhere else and if there's one thing I am more than anything it's obedient, I've been training myself to be obedient all my life, Chef, and I know we'll work well together and I know, it's funny to say, but I've always thought we're a bit the same, you and me– "

"The same?" he said.

Patrick's lips rose over his yellow teeth.

"What I mean is, with your background, with your dad and everything with Speedy Sam's, well, it must have been hard for you to be taken seriously with all that, and you had to fight for it, and I have too, with my mum, you see, she never wanted me to be a chef, she wanted me to get a proper job–"

"You think we're the same?" he said.

I stopped.

"And we've both won the Young Saucier."

Nothing happened.

"I can cook," I said. "I can cook really well."

"He thinks he's an undiscovered genius," said Patrick. "He thinks he's doing us a favour."

They exchanged a look.

"Not a genius," I said. "But, I come from... my ancestors... I should tell you about my great-aunt Dorothy, in fact, that's what I wanted to ask you. I was just wondering if I might be able come in in the afternoon tomorrow. It's my aunt's funeral in the morning – her cremation – and my aunt – she's the one who taught me to cook so – "

"Stop," he said, softly. He held his hand up, and his smile took on a form that I'd never seen on the television.

"If Le Patron has really given you another chance, then so be it," he said. "*Bon*. I sense that Patrick and I will have a bit of fun, training you up."

"Thank you, Chef," I said.

Patrick snorted lightly.

"You're very welcome," he said. "But allow me to offer a little advice before it all begins. The trick of being a successful apprentice is to be unflappable, exactingly precise, consistent, hard-working and to never, ever make a mistake. And do you know what the catch is?"

"No, Chef."

"*Non*. You say '*non*, Chef'."

"*Non*, Chef."

"The catch is, there is no trick."

He looked me up and down.

"*Bon*," he said, evidently pleased with his little speech. When he turned his back to walk away, I thought I heard Patrick say, "Let the games begin..."

Chapter 18

I'd never known noise could have an effect like that; I was actually breathless. There was chopping, boiling, scraping, searing, doors slamming, crates dropping, clogs hammering, pots clattering, washing-up splashing and thudding and more and more and more chopping – a thousand blades hammering on a thousand surfaces. And then there were the voices: instructions, blunted syllables thrown like rabbit-punches and the constant calling of "*chaud*". I knew that was French for hot, of course, but the chefs let out the warning cry no matter what they were carrying as they passed behind you – plates, pans, produce. Having no windows didn't help – that feeling of being removed from time and the ordinary order of things. Nor did the continual heat and pressure, nor the smells.

By the time the lunch service was at full power, Max had been in the kitchen for two hours. He had begun the shift in the manner I would soon become accustomed to: emerging silently yet with vast resonance from the passageway at the top of the kitchen, glowing celestially in his starkly laundered whites. He would stand there for a moment, framed by the doorway, hands behind his back, before taking a deep sniff, as if he could detect, with his nose alone, everything that was happening before him.

The most senior staff would greet him respectfully with "Chef" and, if this was to be a good day, he would nod almost imperceptibly. Then came his tour, walking up and down the kitchen, peering over shoulders, picking up bits of produce and sending his inscrutable gaze deep into each piece.

Max's dominance was such that the kitchen effectively became a part of him; his consciousness extending from his skull and crawling out to encompass the whole space. The power of his presence was so strong that even if you couldn't see him you'd know when he was there.

We apprentices didn't move unless we had to. Not an inch out of place. We'd run to the toilet, having held it past the point of pain. Although a simple pasta lunch was prepared for the full-time chefs, for the apprentices food was nibbled on the job. Kathryn quietly let me know that there was a camping shop in nearby Covent Garden where Danno, the washing-up man, would stock up on Kendal Mint Cake and make a small profit dishing it out to the rest of us on the quiet.

That morning, I decided that basil was the answer. I would use it to take my mind off what was happening in that dismal crematorium in Kent. In front of me was a dewy mountain of bunches, each one composed of fifty-odd stems fastened with a red elastic band. My job was to remove each leaf by resting the top of the stem against the pad of my forefinger and cutting through it with a firm push of the thumbnail. The good, large leaves were to be used in a dish – I hadn't been told which and knew better than to ask – whilst the small and the bruised were to be turned into pesto.

I found myself rocking back and forth very slightly against the countertop. I was soothed in a small way by the knowledge that, despite everything, my parents were going to attend the short service at the Kent and Sussex Crematorium up at Benmall Hill Road. I thought back to the last time I had been there – when my grandmother died. I was about seven years old and I remembered feeling horrified at myself for not being more upset. My Nan was dead and I knew that the required emotion was devastation. But I felt nothing but a faraway calm when my mum yelped in distress as the coffin disappeared behind the curtain. And then that sensation of feeling utterly baffled by grown-ups: the sight of my mum and Uncle Paul sharing a joke in the car park at the very moment their mother's body was burning. They were laughing about something under that terrifying black finger of smoke and I wondered, then, if we might all be monsters.

As I chopped, I felt an urge to run to the toilet and let the tears out, like some shameful act of defecation. But I hadn't cried for almost a decade and I certainly wasn't about to start today. I looked around for a hot spoon or anything that I could press onto my skin to shock me out of the hurt.

I jumped as Patrick moved in behind me, so close we were almost touching. He pulled at the plastic tub that contained the rejected basil leaves; the ones I'd decided were good only for being crushed for pesto.

"Good enough, good enough, good enough," he said, stacking the leaves into a precarious little pile. "Do you have any idea how much basil's costing us at the moment? Are you trying to bankrupt us?"

I couldn't understand what he meant; couldn't believe that some of the leaves he was rescuing were good enough for King. There was what appeared to be a small semi-circular slug-munch out of one of them and a dark, wet bruise on another.

"*Non*, Chef," I said. "These I didn't think were perfect…"

He was so near that I could smell his reply as it came out of his mouth, meaty, rotting and sour.

"If this happens again, I'm marching you down the TSB and you can draw out the cash to cover the wastage. Do you know there are kids dying in Ethiopia? There are millions of bloated little fuckers who would claw your fucking eyes out for a lovely bit of basil. Don't waste it, you wasteful fucking racist."

"*Oui*, Chef," I said. "Sorry, Chef."

He walked off and I began gathering the leaves back up. Then, he stopped, waited and walked towards me again.

"Are you a racist?"

"*Non*, Chef," I said.

Shaking his head, he turned towards the grill station.

I dropped Patrick's basil in the "keep" box and tried to concentrate hard on the difficult logic of this new selection criterion. Ten minutes later, I felt the presence of Max as he moved in beside me. I watched his perfect fingernails sifting through the leaves. I couldn't believe it. He was helping me. *He* was helping *me*.

He tippedup the "keep" box and began to slowly, deliberately place all the leaves side-by-side on the steel surface.

"Tell me," he said, eventually. "Which culinary school have you joined us from?" He had made four rows by now, each one ten leaves in length.

"It's not really a culinary school, Chef," I said. "It's a college. West Kent. In Tonbridge."

He placed another leaf down.

"Your father. Employed?"

"*Oui*, Chef," I said.

And another leaf down.

"Has he always been in work?"

And another.

"*Oui*, Chef."

And another.

"Mother?"

And another.

"*Oui*, Chef. She's a social worker. My dad works in a factory. Margarine."

A pause.

"Money's tight?"

"Sometimes, Chef."

And another.

"I'm attempting to fathom your motives," he said. "What I'm wondering is, is he jealous? Is that why he's trying to sabotage my food? Perhaps he's jealous of the people who can afford to eat here?"

My hands were shaking, the black-green juice from the herbs staining my nails.

"*Non*, Chef," I said.

Silence again. He began straightening the leaves with his manicured fingers, so that all their stalks were at a perfect ninety degrees to the edge of my work surface.

"You know, you mustn't envy successful people for the lives they're able to lead. That's the way nature works, whether you approve of it or not. Some people just happen to possess admirable qualities. Some are born bright, brave and resilient. Others are born stupid, useless and poor." He paused. "As you well know. We all get what we deserve in life. It's no accident that the wealthy are the wealthy and the poor are the poor, no matter how much you or I may wish it otherwise."

I watched him pick up a damaged leaf – the one from earlier, with the slug munch in it – and put in the "reject" tub, where it had been in the first place, before Patrick had intervened. He lowered his voice to a menacing hiss.

"You are going to make my basil, grape and sweet-bread salad look and taste disgusting," he said. He leaned forward and whispered in my ear, "You're going to make my food taste like filthy, dirty, cremated old women. Is that what you want?"

"*Non*, Chef," I said.

He left. When he reached the pass, I heard Patrick let out a single laugh, like an auditory punch. Fifteen minutes after that, the *chef de cuisine* was back again. He tipped over my "reject" tub and picked out a leaf.

"The nasty little racist, I don't believe it: he's still trying to fucking bankrupt us."

And so it went. On and on and on. First Max then Patrick, then Max again. And as the kitchen worked harder and harder around me, as everyone else moved from job to job to job, they had me sorting and resorting basil, their threats and abuse becoming more pungent with every round.

Four hours into it, Max walked up to me and stood there, staring coldly as the silence slipped out of his mouth and wrapped around my throat. He slammed his fist, first into one pot and then into the other. I jumped both times, the noise so loud it cracked right through the racket that permeated the room. He stared some more, his thin lips lightly quivering with all the rage. It was then that I realised why Kathryn wore such a curious smile when she'd agreed with me that he never shouts. He didn't need to. Max Mann was an expert with silence. He used it like a master torturer, to create squirming, sweating, groaning discomfort; to generate the unique agony of the mind turned against itself: all the insecurities and monsters contained within it suddenly animated and growing with every empty second that passes. I felt like taking up the paring knife and drawing it across my arm, just to prove to him that I could take it. Behind him, Patrick's face was that of a six-year-old watching the climax of a magnificent firework display.

"If you don't get this right the next time," he said, "I will have you in the yard, polishing the cobblestones all night and back in here to start again first thing in the morning. Do you hear me?"

"*Oui*, Chef."

I turned and picked up the leaves which, by now, I knew intimately. I felt dizzy as I worked; faint. Speckles of yellow and red and blue flashed up before my eyes. I hadn't eaten in eight hours and hadn't drunk any water in three and the noise was like a waterfall of concrete blocks. I wanted to go home. I wanted my aunty.

My eyes darted to the water-filled pot in front of me in which there was a collection of knives. An idea presented itself to me. I could do it, too. I'd done it before, in times of far less distress than this. I had never seen it as "self-harm" – as an act of weakness. Rather, I'd got the idea during an RE lesson in which we were taught about a Catholic priest called Father Jean Vianney who used to fortify himself against temptation by wearing a belt of spikes and whipping himself with a metal scourge. My teacher, Sister Maria, proudly told us that Vianney's housekeeper would have to take a step ladder and mop the walls every single morning as they were splattered high with fresh spurts of blood. He was the strongest man I'd ever heard of. How could I not be impressed?

Nobody was looking. Nobody would notice. I picked out a paring knife and laid it casually on my chopping board. I pretended to trim a few stalks with it. Then, holding the tip of the blade between thumb and forefinger, swiped it into my arm. I felt my skin part and the sting as the tip touched into the flesh beneath it. Pulling my sleeve back over the cut, I dropped the knife back into the pot.

Half an hour later, Patrick came up with a fresh stock of basil and asked Kathryn to pick and sort it.

"Pathetic," he said to me as Kathryn started working through the new leaves, quickly and surely. "First day, easiest job, and you've set the whole kitchen back. The worst apprentice I've seen in five years, easily."

I looked at the pile of sorry herbs on the chopping board in front of me.

"What should I do next, Chef?" I asked.

"Sort your fucking leaves! Sort them and sort them again until you've worked out how to do it, you ugly fucking racist."

"*Oui*, Chef," I said.

He strode back towards Max at the pass, his words disappearing into the noise. "He's truly, properly useless this one, Chef. Maybe we should test him. Palate test."

So I began all over again. Soon I began to feel so faint that I wasn't sure I could carry on. Kathryn moved an inch closer and slowly, gently placed her pale, freckled hand on the back of mine. She squeezed just once, before pulling it back again. She didn't look up or give any other clue to anyone that she was comforting me.

I had to stop, momentarily, to gather myself.

* * *

At the end of service, when almost everyone else had cleaned down and dragged their wilting bodies home, Kathryn and Patrick remained, him finishing off some paperwork and her mopping down the floor over by the grill. As soon as Patrick had slunk towards the changing room, I stopped what I was doing and leaned against the countertop, rubbing the pain from my wrists. Kathryn left her mop and bucket where they were and approached. My focus hardened so that it was rigid on the floor.

"Is there something you wanted to say to me?" she said, leaning back, next to me, on the pass.

There were about a million things I wanted to say to her.

"Sorry," I said.

She put her hands behind her, onto the steel edge, and looked out into the dark, empty kitchen.

"Sorry?" she said.

"About hurting your elbow the other day. I didn't mean to."

"I was thinking more about how I finished your sauce and served it to Ambrose. He thought it was all right, you know."

"All right?" I said.

She touched her bottom lip with her tongue and looked away.

"That's what he told me."

"Thanks," I said. "Thank you for doing that."

I looked at my clogs; at how narrow my ankles looked inside them. *Skin and bone.*

"I wish I could say he thought you were a culinary genius and wanted to drive you down to Michelin HQ to insist on immediate delivery of three stars and a little badge with your name on it," said Kathryn. "But, you know, 'all right' for Ambrose is pretty good. You should be pleased."

I had been watching Kathryn. As far as I could tell, she never talked to anyone, not even when Max and Patrick weren't about and you could get away with it. Nobody really talked to her either.

"What's he like? Ambrose?" I asked.

"He's like a schizophrenic ghost, haunting himself."

" … "

"No?" she said, for once looking a little vulnerable. "He's obsessed with his own youth, that's what they say. Can't leave it alone. He grew up in France, after the war. That's how he got into his Grande Cuisine – the full Escoffier. Got a taste for it in Lyon, then made it fashionable in London in the fifties – late fifties. He was quite famous. Bit of a playboy. Everyone says he's a snake, but he seems decent enough to me. I heard he's been a bit grumpy about that new place in Charlotte Street. Rue St Jacques. It's all classic Parisian and it's looking like it's going to get starred. Andy, the pastry chef – he told me that Ambrose is planning something new along those lines. More traditional. Read into that what you will. If you ask me, it's not a bistro he's trying to build, it's a bloody time machine."

A tide of fatigue passed through me and I gave a deep arcing yawn. She watched me with a kind smile.

"Don't take it personally, what happened today," she said.

I remembered her hand on mine. It didn't seem possible.

"I couldn't work out what I was doing wrong," I said. "I tried. I tried so hard."

Maybe it wasn't. Maybe I had imagined it.

"But you weren't doing anything wrong, Killian. It's just what they do here. It's like I told you – it's a sport for them. They love to bully apprentices into quitting. That thing they say about never sacking any of us – it's like an in-joke. They don't sack us because they don't need to. I just – don't take what they do personally, okay? You seem like a nice guy and they appreciate 'nice' around here about as much as they appreciate Hawaiian pizza."

"But Max Mann." I said. "He wouldn't do it if it wasn't for a reason."

She gave me a look of baffled concern. "You think?"

"But everybody – " I began, and then stopped at an unwelcome memory – Patrick walking down the corridor. *Let the games begin.*

She turned and began clearing away my basil leaves which, by now, were torn and blackening. "Thanks, but Patrick said I had to finish them," I said.

She ignored me, scrunching the herbs into a damp ball.

"Fuck Patrick. He'll have forgotten all about this in the morning."

"But he's the boss."

"Well, the boss has left me with the keys and I have stuff to do for my mum and if I don't – "

She trailed off as she threw the leaves into an empty bin liner and the pots into the sink, ready for cleaning tomorrow. She walked off, leaving me alone, and I followed her into the changing room.

"Your mum," I said, as I let myself into my locker. "Does she live nearby?"

Kathryn lifted her home clothes into her arms and held them there in a slipping bundle.

"My mum?" Kathryn said. "Yeah, well, if you take a left out of here, keep going for about a hundred yards, then take a right, follow that through the city, take a left there, and you'll arrive at Number 3, None-of-your-Fucking-Business Avenue."

She disappeared into the toilet and closed the door behind her. The lock bolted. She said, "Let yourself out, will you?"

And as I slept, I heard the flies in all their gathering. I felt the Hunger rising. I heard the howling of the dogs.

And I saw him, from my place in the grass outside Dor. I saw the wise man, the finder man. He turned to look towards the garden. I pulled my head down and closed my eyes. I could feel it. The air was filthy with it. The old trouble. The held trouble. The trouble in the ground and in the attic and in the mortar. All of it stirred as I slept. All of it moved towards me.

And the finder man looked in my direction.

His eyes searched the grass with great Hunger.

Chapter 19

Early one morning a week or so into my time at King, a photographer from *The Face* magazine arrived to take pictures of the brigade, which would accompany an article about Max. When the chefs gathered for the shoot, I took the opportunity to study them closely and became transfixed. Their hair and faces were coated in a uniform layer of dimly shining grease; their chins and eye-sockets grew in unnatural directions; their noses were red and asymmetrical; their skin had turned the same lifeless green as the fluorescent lighting strips which they spent almost their entire waking lives beneath; and there were nicks and cuts and leery, random outcrops of beard-hair, the result of shaving hung-over at five a.m. every morning. They looked as if they'd just staggered in from some nuclear wilderness; a band of outlaws arrived to commit dark acts upon the trembling villagers.

Their appearance spoke of their utter commitment; they were giving everything for their calling. Their sacrifices were so deep that they had come to define the architecture of their appearance. The photographer was a lanky New Romantic with a pirate-costume jacket who couldn't pronounce his w's. He was visibly terrified and soon lost the nerve to actually direct his subjects, leaving them to lean threateningly against the counter and insult him in ways he could barely understand. As he blushed and snapped and quivered, all he knew was that these were swaggering bastards of the like he had not previously encountered, and he would never be allowed into the warm prison of their comradeship.

I knew this because it was precisely how all of us apprentices felt, every single day.

The brigade was more relaxed in the hours before Max arrived – there would be manly banter and occasional horseplay. But that all changed the moment Max appeared at the pass, as if we were trapped inside a held breath that would only be released at the end of the double shift – an unimaginably distant time in the future.

I'm sure that the chefs feared him equally, but he seemed to truly value their friendship. I noticed that, when a particularly brutal round of punishment had been meted out to one of us, he'd return to the pass with a whip-like smile and he'd sort of bounce around his strip of ground for a minute or two, enjoying the approval he'd glean from them all.

On my fourth shift, Max appeared looking five years older than he had the day before; paler, thinner, and yet more concentrated; honed somehow by the darkness. We didn't yet know it, but the *Evening Standard*'s weekly gossip column had run a piece that day about a "posh chef, famous for his gentlemanly nature, who doesn't welcome mention of his mother's tragic suicide. Rumours abound that her naturally gloomy demeanour was compounded by a secret addiction to barbiturates".

I wasn't aware of Max speaking at all until the tickets started coming in at the beginning of service. In the preceding hours, you could tell by the behaviour of the others that a new set of rules had silently clicked into place. Patrick kept a wide circle around him, assuming all of Max's usual responsibilities. Max himself seemed to just hang there, staring at the same page in a folder, then at the fingers of Carlo in the fish station (Carlo losing several shades of colour as he did so). You immediately thought, "That man should be in bed," but, of course, you knew that the best place for him was the kitchen.

But then came service. That was when he plugged himself in. Everything was double speed on Max's bad days and everything was worse. If some pastry was too dry, some sauce under-seasoned, some timing out by even a few seconds, it would start. First, of course, came the silence that always made you feel as if you had fallen through a hole in time. Then the climax, as he tried to remain composed, the muscles in his face tensed, and he began to stutter "N-n-n-n-n-n-no!", his lips tense and blueish; syrupy white balls of spittle in the corners of his mouth; veins in the backs of his hands like throbbing worms. You'd be desperate for him to erupt – just to explode and get it all over with – but he'd suck it all back inside himself. It was awful, like watching a balloon being inflated long past its popping point. And when it did come – that was when we were most at risk from getting hurt. Whilst he'd always leave the physical abuse to Patrick, his verbal attacks could inflict a violence that was far worse. Sometimes he'd hiss and whisper things that seemed designed to break you from the inside. On other occasions, he'd simply stare at you, assaulting you with his grotesque silence, the only clue to the rages within him his unyielding stare and a pale, sinewy look about his eyes, as if they'd been glued open.

Of course, even on his good days, Max actually cooked

nothing. His role was to stand at the pass at the top of the kitchen, calling orders in this strange squeaky voice, operating the machine that clanked and hissed and steamed beneath him. Patrick would plate up and Max would stand there, inspecting everything, perhaps adjusting a flower petal here or wiping at finger marks with his torchon. He'd prowl around the same square metre, sipping peppermint tea from his personal silver pot, continually running a comb through his sweat-sopping hair and issuing newly delivered orders to the brigade's "*Oui*, Chef" before inspecting the food whose constituent parts had made their way from disparate corners of the kitchen to their final triumphal coming-together on the plate in front of him. He'd also insist on seeing what came back from the dining room – each waitress would stand at the top of the pass with the dirty crockery, and if anything substantial had been left, he'd send her away with a disgusted flick of the arm. Not that his fury would ever be taken out on the girls or the Maître d'. Even when he did become cross with them, he was never intimidating, merely resorting to an "Oh come on, come on, come on, you can do better than this…". The glutinous fondness he had for his "girls" was undisguised. Indeed, the only time he ever seemed distracted was when his eyes followed one of his "terrifyingly beautiful" waitresses as she glided from the kitchen.

But if he didn't prepare any actual food, Max did cook one thing with the skill of a grand master: loyalty. I saw it happen on the first night. It was incredible; a kind of elemental magic. Unusually, there was a separate station for the cooking of fish, and the *chef de partie* who worked it was, aside from Max, the oldest worker in the kitchen. Carlo was a melancholy Italian divorcee – still heartbroken after the discovery of his ex-wife's various infidelities – who walked around as if he was still bent over his stove. His head was the shape of an upturned light bulb; his face bulging out from where his hat stopped, as if he'd been wearing it so long it had dictated the growth of his bones. From my place at the bottom of the kitchen, I could just about see Max admonishing him for overcooking four pieces of salmon.

"Are you trying to test me?" he said.

"*Non*, Chef."

"Are you trying to see whether I'm worth three stars?"

"*Non*, Chef."

"Don't you think I'm worth three stars?"

"*Oui*, Chef."

"I don't think you do. You think I'm lucky to have two."

"*Non*, Chef."

"Do you know what happens to cooks I dismiss from here?"

"*Oui*, Chef."

He moved in closer, his voice becoming quieter.

"*Oui* Chef, *oui* Chef, they end up working in hotel restaurants in Redcar making prawn cocktails for slum landlords. They become nothing. Do you know why? Because I make sure they become nothing. Do you really think you'll be able to stroll out of here and into the arms of Nico or Albert? It won't happen. I won't allow it. Do you want me to prove it, you amateur? You moron can't-cook-a-fucking-piece-of-f-f-fucking-salmon-fucking-schoolboy?"

"*Non*, Chef."

He smiled emptily. The corners of his eyes twitched with rage.

"No wonder Jacqueline took your boy. No wonder she tried to f-fuck every chef in here. You didn't know that, did you? She wanted a man who could take care of her, who could cook a simple piece of fish and she got lumbered with you, you Italian streak of piss, you fucking limp dick. You're pathetic, do you know that?"

"*Oui*, Chef."

I wasn't in a position to get a clear view of Carlo's face when all this was happening, but I saw it the next morning when Max gathered his men for their usual conference. Overnight, everything had changed. He put a hand on Carlo's shoulder and announced with a grin that crackled, hearth-like, with warmth and brotherhood, "And Carlo's given me his personal guarantee that he'll treat today's salmon with the precision for which he's so justly admired, haven't you, old boy?" And in that moment an alchemy took place that was as miraculous as anything that occurred in any pot, pan or oven. Carlo might have been up all night, cursing Max for his ingratitude, disloyalty and for stamping so hard on his already ruined heart. He might have sworn to himself he wouldn't tolerate the vile bastard for a second longer and that, as soon as the sun was up, he'd begin making enquiries about positions in Nico's kitchen. Every mote of pride in him – every small achievement he'd accrued in his three decades of kitchen work – might have collapsed under the impossible weight of Max's disapproval. And yet in that instant, as the king of King welcomed him back inside the cocoon of the brigade, you could tell that Carlo had done more than merely forgive him. Max had saved the banished Italian from everything he feared and you knew his gratitude felt endless.

Nothing like this happened with the apprentices. During one shift, I watched the trainee on the other side of Kathryn have perhaps the worst day of his life. At twenty-seven, Gregory was the oldest of all of us and it showed in all the good ways. He was more than six feet tall with long and delicate watchmaker's fingers. He was easily the best amongst us, his powerful, expressive hands working the blades and fragile ingredients seemingly of their own volition.

One of Gregory's responsibilities was cutting the fat from veal sweetbreads. As Max was passing behind him that afternoon, Gregory accidentally cut himself.

"Ach!" he said. "Shit."

Max stopped. He squinted over Gregory's shoulder.

"What have you done?"

"*Pardon*, Chef."

In the steel tub in front of him, two or three little drips of red were visible on the shining glands.

"You're bleeding on my sweetbreads." Max stared down the apprentice in all his wintery silence. Gregory pushed a thick squeeze of blood from his finger. Max didn't move.

"Give me your tunic," he said eventually.

"You want my... ?"

"Take it off. Give it to me. You will work the rest of this shift with your chest bare. During service you will assist Patrick on the sauté station. There's a lot of hot fat over there. There's a lot of fire. You will learn to be careful. You will *learn*. And if you make any more mistakes, I will have the rest of your uniform. Now give it to me."

Gregory glanced down the line, to see who was watching. Guiltily, I looked away. I could hear his poppers undoing and the small commotion of his disrobing. As he handed his top to Max, I could see the humiliation of his spotty back, his thick armpit hair and the domey paunch that sat above his trousers.

He worked like that all morning, before disappearing

into the fires of Patrick's domain. At the start of evening service, we heard Max hiss at him again.

"You," Max squealed.

We all turned around to see him staring directly at Gregory.

"Here."

The apprentice, his shoulders filmy with sweat, put his knife down, ran his beautiful hands down his torchon and walked to the pass. He was blinking madly with the tension as Max glowered coldly at him.

"Can you see this?" he said eventually.

Patrick was beside him, holding the nugget of offal.

"*Oui*, Chef." said Gregory, with an efficient nod.

"Can you see what's wrong with it?"

"*Oui*, Chef."

"Are you absolutely sure?" he said.

"*Oui*, Chef."

Patrick held it up to his eye, causing Gregory to pull his head back slightly.

"I'm not sure that you can," he said. "Because if you can see it now, why couldn't you see it earlier, when you were supposed to be trimming it?"

"*Oui*, Chef, I can see it, Chef."

"Chef Patrick, will you allow him to see it more clearly?"

He punched the hot ball of offal into Gregory's eye. The apprentice, trying not to make a cry, gasped horribly – it was an animal sound, more like a grunt – and slipped on the wet floor, banging his head on the counter with such force that the metal spoons on it clanked. I glanced at Kathryn to gauge her reaction. She looked as if she was very cold.

"Get up," said Max.

Gregory fumbled for the side of the counter and pulled

himself back up, his clogs slipping on the wet floor as they struggled for purchase.

"How long have you been cooking?" he asked.

"Ten years, Chef," Gregory said, trying desperately not to cry.

Once he was up, the young chef rubbed the injured side of his head and, as he did so, his arm apparently roused Max's curiosity.

"Show me your arms," he said.

He held them dumbly in front of him.

"You don't have enough burns to work in this kitchen," he said, with a withering sigh. He turned to Patrick. "Make him presentable, will you?"

"Certainly, Chef."

Using his torchon, Patrick picked up a set of metal tongs that had been resting in a hot pan and walked, grinning, towards Gregory, who now had terrible patches of drained white skin extending down from his eyes into his cheeks. It didn't take much. Patrick only had to tap the scorching metal onto his arm for all six foot-plus of him to collapse back to the floor in a mess of snivelling and crying. He began wailing, "I don't care what you do. I don't care any more. Do what you like. I don't care, I don't care, I don't care."

Max stood over him.

"This," he said, "is a defining moment. Now stand up. And *cook*."

Gregory didn't reply. He didn't even look at Max. He just scrabbled up again and walked back to his station, his still-terrified face running with tears and snot.

The next morning, Gregory had changed. There was no passion; no urgency; no life. The day after that, he didn't come in at all. Nobody commented upon his absence.

Chapter 20

After my first day, I was assigned yet again to basil duties. The moment Patrick handed me the crate, I felt an acute urge to run out of the door and back to my bedroom. But the work I did was unremarked upon and soon I was de-crusting bread and cutting it into squares for croutons; squeezing limes and lemons; peeling freshly boiled broad beans and then nicking-out the little cords that connected their two halves; filling *beurriers* for the tables and so on.

At the same time, I was busy going through the ancient retinue of pain that kitchen apprentices have known since the eighteenth century, when the first restaurants were opened after the French Revolution and the Reign of Terror, which drove all the aristocrats from the country, leaving their newly discharged cooks to wonder how to go about making a living. The bending down and the hours of tiny repetitive movements cause a very specific pain, like a knuckle pressing into your vertebrae at a single concentrated spot between the shoulder blades. Slowly, it ripples out into two great angel's wings of agony, spreading laterally and then down, down, as you go into your ninth hour, when it collects at the coccyx. It stays there, growing in pressure, as it begins to leak its leaden soreness into your

131

legs. Soon, the hurt encompasses your entire frame.

Only once, during those first two weeks, was I asked to prepare Ambrose's lunch again. As I was doing so, I became aware of Max observing me from a distance. Those great watery eyes examined me in a coolly fascinated way as I chopped my onions and leaned into the steam of my pan. My sauce was still five minutes away from being properly reduced when he finally approached and dipped a teaspoon into it.

"You're thickening with tomato purée?" he said, taking a step back so that I could continue cooking.

"*Oui*, Chef," I said. "And reducing. No roux."

I watched him taste it, his tongue slapping twice against the roof of his mouth and his throat moving with his swallow.

"*Bon, bon*," he said. "So you have been learning something here. *Bon*."

I glanced back into the pan, at the simmering, savoury red pool.

"Actually, Chef," I said. "I designed this sauce about a year ago."

There was a fleeting muscular twitch around his eyes. "Obviously, I think what you do here is amazing, though," I added quickly. "You and the Troisgros brothers and everyone. You revolutionised food back in the seventies."

He gave a smiling, quizzical expression.

"So – what?" he said. "What are you saying? It's dated, is it? What we do here?"

I was aware of his height beside me; the grandeur of the physical container which held his genius. He was wanted around the world, this man: legendary; famous; brilliant and brilliantly beside me; focused so intently on *me*. I had *so much* to tell him.

"No!" I said. "Not dated. Of course not. But, you know, nothing stays still, does it? I mean, do you ever think of what all this will turn into in the future? I mean, I love the freshness and the lightness that you do here and everything, but my aunt – well, I was brought up on rich French stews, Italian ragus – you know, fat and alcohol and wine. Have you ever thought about if you melded the two? The old and the new? I mean, it's like this sauce – it's not exactly healthy. It has butter and port in it. But it doesn't fill you up like an old-fashioned roux sauce and the flavour – the flavour's massive."

I could feel his breathing.

"You're going to teach me something about flavour?"

I could see all the colours of his stubble and I could see his skin, pale pink and pale yellow.

"*Non*, Chef," I said. "Definitely not. Absolutely not."

"You want me to believe that you came here, from your pitiful little college, already with all these skills?"

"But I did, Chef."

He gave a small, bitter snort and looked dismissively at my bubbling sauce.

"Go," he said. "Serve Le Patron. You've far more important things to be getting on with than making his lunch."

Five more minutes, and this sauce would be beautiful. But not now. It was too thin.

"It's not ready, Chef."

He leaned down so that his face met mine.

"Go. Now."

It wasn't even a sauce, yet. It was soup. Under-seasoned, under-cooked, useless watery broth. It was impossible to serve this to Ambrose. If this was presented to him as my best work, I would be –

"*Go.*"

— finished.

And I was at one end of a tunnel, looking down into a hot pan that was very far away. Way down there, I put my finger in the sauce as if to taste it. And I left it there, stopped in the heat. Stay, stay, stay.

Stop.

Stop.

Stop.

From my great distance, I could tell there was pain. But it was okay because I was in a different place. Miles and miles and miles away, the scalding, the burning, the agony building in the bone.

"Oh! Are you having some sort of tantrum?" Max smiled. "Oh, how utterly gripping. Do carry on."

He watched impassively. A silvery fly buzzed across his eye-line and settled on his tunic, right where he had his name stitched in cotton. He didn't move. My jaw began to shake. I whipped my finger out of the sauce and pushed it deep into my mouth.

"Now get upstairs."

When I came to collect Ambrose's dishes after lunch, he didn't even look up to greet me. As I picked up the plate, my thumb squelched into a great puckering slick of thin, leftover sauce.

* * *

It is probably hard to understand for someone who has not experienced kitchen life, but despite the vivid disappointment of having to serve Ambrose such a foul version of my sauce and despite the hunger, thirst, weakness and dread, there was also much to love.

Feeling so inextricably part of a team conjured a sense

of power and family that proved quickly addictive. My first seduction was by raw ingredients. Standing at my station with the morning air around me bursting with sizzles and blooming with wonderful scents heightened my awareness of the role I had to play in transforming these unprocessed lumps of this and that into dishes that would elevate some of the most cynical and celebrated diners on the planet into ecstasy. Leaves, roots and carcasses ceased being gently decomposing artefacts of nature and took on enchanted forms. The basil I worked with was no longer a wilting plant, but the greatest fragrance I'd known. I would breathe it in and let it play grand with my imagination – fresh, playful and innocent, it was a warm wind over summer fields; a pink Sicilian dawn; sunshine through the dress of the most beautiful girl in the village. Those leaves became precious things. And my job – our job – wasn't to slog repetitively for hours over a chopping board. It was to perform a kind of sorcery.

The second seduction was the struggle. The beauty of that struggle is something no culinary college can ever teach; the sense of service being like a malevolent force that exists as a humming, swelling mass on the other side of the umbilical corridor that connects kitchen to restaurant floor. As we worked through the night, we had no experience of individual diners, only the early jets of adrenaline that accompanied the first orders just after seven and then the urgency – always on the very edge of panic – as Max called more and more, the pressure building and building, and the brigade rising up and fighting back as the orders kept coming, the mind and the ears and the fingers working faster and faster, always concentrating, always watching yourself, always with your attention stretching tentacle-like to the others in the kitchen, pushing harder, pushing harder; and when we were winning, when the kitchen was communicating and the machine was fully powered, something happened. The machine became conscious; a sort of hive mind was generated. This is why it hurt so genuinely when you made a mistake. It was worse than letting your boss down. It was worse than letting your brigade down. You had sabotaged a part of yourself that you'd come to value more than anything else; the part that had become God. And when the final order was closed and service had gone well, we would look at each other – it would never be mentioned, what we'd just been through; it was all too strange and precious for that – we'd look at each other and we'd know.

Then there was the third seduction – the one I was to endure for the length of my life. When I recall how it grew, it seems to have come on both quickly and by infinitesimal degrees; with every shift, every service, every task, every minute and every breath it grew stronger, the feeling I had for that girl whose presence I had come to sense by instinct, as if it was fire.

Chapter 21

It was about nine and a half hours after Max had sent me upstairs, to Ambrose, with the watery sauce. He'd actually been in a decent mood since Thursday – he'd sat for an interview with *The Times* that had apparently gone well – but by ten p.m. any residual levity had deserted him. He pushed past me, causing me to slip with a tray of crabmeat, a small amount of which had spilled onto the floor. I crouched to pick it up and he hissed, "Idiot!" As I was down there, a heavy pan fell off the side and hit me on the back. It could only have been knocked onto me by Max. I collapsed into the mess, stunned and partially winded, and he bent down and whispered, "How do you like that for some old-fashioned, 1970s kitchen craft?"

Come the end of service, I was taking my frustrations out on my cleaning when Kathryn approached.

"What you doing tonight?" she said, leaning back on the counter.

"Going home," I said, pausing in the punishment that I was meting out on the world via my cloth. She'd taken off her cap and looked bright yet nervous, in a way that I had never seen before. But she looked beautiful too, in all the ways that I kept on finding myself remembering and imagining.

"Some of us are going for a Chinese, if you fancy it."

"I can't," I said. "I've got to get to the station. Last train."

Her smile broke down. She looked anxiously towards the approaching figure of a man – the chef with the chapped lips who had opened the door to me on the first day.

"Is he coming, then?" asked the man.

"Has to get the last train," said Kathryn.

"Why don't you stay at ours?" he said, wiping his hands down his flour-strewn whites. "You can kip on our sofa."

"But don't put yourself out," said Kathryn. "You know, get your train. Whatever you want." And then – I wasn't exactly sure – but she added something like, "Don't imagine that I give a fuck."

It wasn't until we were out of Gresse Street that I began to loosen up a little. I'd come to love stepping into the London night after service. The air in the kitchen was as hot and thick as tomato soup and the post-midnight city was the perfect antidote. And then there was everything else: the clubs, the stilettos, the preying minicabs, the mysterious open doorways that you only noticed after dark; the drunks, the punks, the city slicks, the ageing ska-boys, the red-laced Oi! boys and the odd stray New Romantic looking pale and vaguely terrified and in danger of tripping over his lacy cuffs. And above all this mess and mad theatre, the street lamps that cloaked everything in their dangerous, unreal light whispered in unison that the daytime world had gone away and under their watch you could try anything. Night-cast London was a constellation of a million sins and there was a thrill in walking amongst them; you could feel those sins bubbling into being around you, as sure as you could see the walls and windows and the orange-black sky. As a member of the team at King, I felt authentically part of it all; truly one of the city's people.

As we walked in the direction of Oxford Street, I made a decision to be cautious of Andy. He was walking alone, three paces ahead of us. I could guess what was going on: he was Kathryn's boyfriend, he had guessed how I'd begun to feel about her and he thought it was hysterical.

"I've been offered a job," Kathryn said, as we dodged some bin liners that were being tossed from the door of a Pizzaland. "Ambrose asked me today. It's my last day as an apprentice tomorrow. From Monday I'm an ouvrier."

She was wrapping her arms around herself, hugging out the cold. I had never seen her in her civvies before: she was in stonewashed jeans and, underneath her green and pink ski jacket, had on a plain white woollen turtleneck jumper.

"That's great," I said. "Fantastic."

"Cheers," she said, with a dismissive shrug. "I never thought they'd let me stay. I just thought Max was a sexist prick who thinks women are only good for carrying trays and sticking your fingers in. But when he told me, he actually smiled. He said, 'We have detected some trace of latent talent in you'."

"That's amazing," I said. "I hope I get asked."

Kathryn surprised me by looking thoughtfully concerned.

"I saw him laying into you today," she said.

I pushed my mouth into the shape of a smile.

"Well, it's all part of it, isn't it?"

"They gave me a hard time when I started," she said. "I cut into a tureen of chicken liver pâté before it was properly cooked and Max told me to eat the whole thing.

And, actually, it was delicious," she said. "I did have to take a couple of cheeky vomit breaks afterwards, though, but credit where it's due – Max's food tastes pretty good even when it's coming out again."

"Urgh," I said, with a laugh. "Has Patrick ever hit you or anything?"

She shook her head. "I'm a girl, you see," she said. "For some reason, they seem to believe that it's fine to torture female cooks in a million different ways, just so long as they're never struck by fist, foot or flying cutlery. Chivalrous of them, don't you think?"

We walked on in silence for a few moments, me frowning at the pavement and Kathryn pushing her hands ever deeper into the nestling blood-warmth of her coat. Even if she was telling the truth about the pâté, I thought, it goes to show that when Max gives you a hard time, it doesn't necessarily mean you won't make it through the six weeks. As long as Ambrose was happy, you had a chance. I wondered about my chance for a moment. I wondered what I'd do if I didn't make it.

"How often have you made Ambrose's lunches?" I asked.

"Oooh," she said. "Six or seven times now?"

"Shit, really?" I said. "I've only been asked twice. Didn't go very well the last time."

"I'm sure you'll get another chance. You deserve to." She looked at me. "You're quite talented."

Quite?

"Quite?"

"Quite."

Ten minutes later, we were all sitting down to duck pancakes and jasmine tea in an upstairs room at a Chinese restaurant which, I noted with a resonant pang of sadness, was next to the Asian grocer I'd once visited with Aunt Dorothy to buy Thai fish sauce and dried bonito flakes for a partially successful meatball experiment. The place was decorated with pictures of the Great Wall, stalking jungle tigers and Samantha Fox that had obviously been chopped out of used calendars. There was a locked door backed with a cracked mirror, a spread of damp in a ceiling corner and the musky-brown scents of hot oil, cigarette smoke and old, spilled beer. An elderly Asian man in a blue blazer, sitting by himself in the corner, kept sucking on barbecued ribs, licking his fingers then reaching under the table to scratch his crotch.

"Did you hear George Michael and his girlfriend were in tonight?" Andy said. He was pouring himself some tea and the pot was dribbling, a trickle of liquid running invisibly down the outside of the spout and re-emerging at its base, where it coalesced and fell, spreading into a translucent spill on the disposable paper tablecloth. I was attracted to the carefreeness of Andy's mess-making; the fact that here, in fantastic contrast to the place we spent so much of our time, it really didn't matter.

Kathryn tilted her head towards me. "Andy gets all the gossip. He's worked everywhere."

"Really?"

She was resting her left hand on the table, five or six inches closer to me than seemed strictly comfortable.

"He's trained in some of the best kitchens in London and Paris, with the best chefs." She looked at him. "You're working your way through the stations, aren't you?"

"Just learning pastry now." He waved his hands in front of me, like a stage magician casting a spell. "Mastering it."

I watched Andy bite into his pancake. A stray curl of spring onion shot from the end. I hadn't realised he had so much experience. I found myself sitting up, a little, in my seat. There were so many questions I wanted to ask him.

"Anyway. George Michael, if you're interested, ordered a deer and tangerine," he said, his mouth half full. "Apparently he paid more attention to his food than to his blonde. Max was delighted, naturally. He was out there like a shot, bidding him bon appetit. He's such a star-fucker. Well, he would be given half a chance. When it comes to fucking, Max mostly just concentrates on the wait staff."

I looked at Kathryn to gauge her reaction to this unlikely allegation. She raised her eyebrows in amused confirmation. Andy began trying to peel another papery pancake off the small stack with the tine of one of the forks that had been provided alongside the chopsticks. He turned to me. "Have you heard about his little accident? You know he's got one of them pregnant?"

"Really?" I said.

"This Russian girl," nodded Kathryn. "Wannabe actress or something. She had to quit work because she started to show. Max has paid for it to be 'dealt with'."

"That's good of him," I said.

"Oh yeah, very good," said Andy. "Paid her a fortune, apparently." He mimed someone picking up a telephone and spoke in an exaggerated Russian accent. "Hello? Is that Nigel Dempster? I got a leeeettle story for you... God, Nige would kill for a story like that."

What was he talking about?

"I wouldn't look so shocked, Killian," Kathryn said. "Max is a right terror. It's common knowledge. Did you know the waitresses aren't allowed to wear underwear? Unwritten rule. You should see them on the restaurant floor, bouncing around inside their tight little dresses. I can see why he does it. It's good for business. We could put six varieties of corned beef on the menu and we'd still be booked solid for the next year."

Andy leaned forward with a grin, savouring the delicious evil of what he was about to tell me.

"He has them round for parties over at Ambrose's," he said. "I went to one of them when I was working with Nico. They're bloody hideous. It's basically Max, the wait staff and all Ambrose's rich mates every Saturday night snorting coke and shagging. They'll be at it now, I guarantee it. Ambrose will be boring them shitless, reminiscing about his glory days in the 1950s – those faraway times when he could still get a hard-on. And Max? Well." He leaned in even closer. "Did you know he tries to whore the waitresses out to his powerful mates? I'm not joking. He tells them which fat millionaire is after them and makes it very clear he considers extra services to be part of their official duty. There was this gorgeous Lancashire girl, a couple of years ago, engaged to some fella or other. Tara – she was about nineteen. Some pissed-up old tycoon took a shine to her, and Max makes it clear what's expected. But she wouldn't have it. She told him she was getting married in a fortnight, so he tells her the only reason the waitresses work at King was because it gave them the chance to 'fuck themselves rich'. Tara was out of a job within the week. Bit of a dampener on the old wedding. Plenty of them have gone through with it though. Lots of them with him. I bet he's inching towards Ambrose's spare room with a new recruit as we speak."

As he'd been talking, I had been thinking about all the years I'd loved Max. The piles of interviews I'd kept in neat shoeboxes under my bed; the pictures from the *Radio Times* and the *Sun* that I'd glued to my wall; the video tapes of his television appearances. I remembered how I'd tried to mimic the way he sat and smiled and held himself about the shoulders.

"I don't think it's good, to be honest," I said, quietly. "To be talking about Max like this."

Andy looked comically alarmed. Kathryn peered down at her plate and, with her fingernails, tried to separate some strands of spring onion that hadn't been properly chopped through. The old Asian man was now drilling into his mouth with a toothpick with one hand and into the Stygian mines of his crotch with the other. Kathryn remained fiddling with her food, examining it intently.

"Here," said Andy, breaking the silence. "Look what I've got."

He waved an early copy of the next day's *Times* that he'd picked up from a seller outside Tottenham Court Road tube as he'd walked ahead of us. "Should've got a *Sun* as well," he said, clearing a space on the table, so he could flick through the paper. "They've got a story about some mystery business leader who was caught in an S&M club. Wouldn't it be amazing if it was Ambrose?" He looked up with another rascally grin. "You know they have to have a secret code word, those lot? That they say when the pain gets too much? I bet Ambrose's is 'Nouvelle Cuisine'. I'll tell you what mine would be: 'Shipham's Meat Paste'. That'd ruin the mood."

We laughed, more out of politeness than anything. Kathryn was blushing. It was odd – almost as if she felt as uncomfortable in the backwash of Andy's yabbering confidence as I did.

"Hey, what happened to that apprentice? The big one?" he continued, still turning pages.

"Gregory?" said Kathryn.

"Yeah, Max had his cunt helmet on for him this week, didn't he?"

"He left," Kathryn said, not meeting Andy's eye.

"He was a nice bloke," I said, "but he couldn't hack it."

Kathryn put her fork down.

"The poor man was in tears," she said. "Didn't you see him? He was like a cornered animal. But I suppose, yes, you're right – he couldn't hack it. Like the Yorkshire Ripper's victims couldn't hack having their brains caved in with a claw-hammer."

"But that's what it's like in fine-dining kitchens," I said. "They have to be like that, don't they? You know – drill out the weak ones."

"God, you sound like bloody *Max*," she said.

"Not all kitchens are like this, actually," said Andy. "King is easily the most brutal one in the country. Everyone knows it. Worst-kept secret in the business." He looked at Kathryn with an implied wink. "You've only got away with it because Max so clearly wants to fuck you."

"Piss off, Andy," she muttered.

She turned to me, unsmiling. "Max is an absolute *bastard*. I don't understand how you can defend him. If he didn't have so many mates in the press, I swear he'd have been exposed. He'd never have got away with all that 'gentleman chef' bollocks that Ambrose came up with."

"But it's because everyone's so loyal so him," I said. "The brigade would do anything for him."

Kathryn reared away from me just a fraction.

"It's sick. It's a disease these chefs have. It's an infectious mental illness."

"You don't get three Michelin stars by letting your standards slip," I said. "Max wants the best chefs. The toughest ones. The ones who are the most loyal. It might not be nice, but I don't expect many people who are obsessed with excellence are worried too much about nice. Doesn't mean they're not good people. They're exceptional and they have to make sure everyone who works for them is exceptional too."

"Gregory was the best apprentice in there," she said. "He's twice as good as me. The reason he's now saying he's going to quit cooking *for ever* is because of their vile game of knock-down-the-new-boy. Michelin stars are nothing to do with toughness; they're to do with talent and experience, and thanks to Patrick and your hero Max, that man is never going near a professional kitchen again. And don't give me that bullshit about loyalty. Loyalty's a con. It's a bloody trick of the devil. Loyalty's the real root of evil, not money. My dad was just like you," she said, her tone softening slightly. "He was a soldier. He was loyal to the queen, the country and the army. He was loyal to everyone. And look where loyalty got him."

I looked at Andy for help.

"Northern Ireland," he whispered.

"Oh," I said. I shifted in my seat; sat up. "Sorry. I'm sorry. But, what I'm saying is, everyone knows Max is nice. Everyone knows. I mean, it's just…" I trailed off as the logic of my argument evaporated from my mouth. Kathryn closed her eyes. Andy reached out across the table and patted my hand.

"Killian, dear," he said. "Learn when to shut up. We'll wait and see if you're so loyal to the big man by the end of your apprenticeship."

Kathryn placed her fingers over mine.

"Killian, listen, look at me."

I did as she asked and, even in the dimness, I could make out those crumbs of green and gold.

"Do you not see, in any of the tiniest parts of your naive, starstruck brain, that Max is just a bully?"

"But – "

"Think about it now. Don't speak for a moment. Think about it, then tell me the truth."

"He has to get – "

"Whatever you say next, don't you *dare* use the words 'standards', 'loyalty' or 'stars'."

I felt as if something critical, in my neck or eyes or head, was going to rupture.

"It's just, his kitchen," I swallowed. "I suppose it's true to say that it's not exactly what I was expecting. It's not what you think of, is it, when you think of Max Mann?"

To my alarm, my eyes had begun to feel dangerously heavy, my throat swollen and dry.

Andy picked up the steel pot and grinned into the weirdness. "Tea anyone?" He began to pour. "Max wants his third star, that's what's driving him insane. He wants that more than anybody has wanted anything in the history of bloody history. He's tormented by it. He's getting madder and madder by the day. He can't get through half the services without P-p-p-p-patrick." He put the pot down and continued flicking through his newspaper. Nobody spoke. "Here you go," he said finally. "Found it."

I listened as Andy read out excerpts that he thought were especially amusing, such as Max waxing lyrical about the personal philosophy that's earned him the nickname 'Gentleman'. "Most chefs believe you simply can't get the results if you mollycoddle staff. But I don't call it mollycoddling. It's more like support or nurture."

"He's campaigning for his OBE," said Kathryn. "Or his next date with Wogan."

"Oh, Jesus," Andy continued, "listen to this – 'and

Mann's famously benevolent management skills look as if they're paying off: although he refuses to be drawn as to whether he thinks he'll finally win his third Michelin star when the next guide is published in January, his face tells you what most in the industry already seem sure of: it's in the bag. Nevertheless, the chef is not without his detractors. Many agree that Nouvelle Cuisine, the style of cooking to which he's so firmly attached his name, is in its final throes, with predictions of its culinary death coming as soon as the end of 1986. Mann has always been a vocal critic of what he describes as traditional "fat cooking". Some say to keep up with the vagaries of gustatory fashion, he'll have to completely reinvent himself. Does the Gentleman Chef have what it takes?"

"I'm hearing that more and more, you know," Kathryn said. "Nouvelle Cuisine is becoming a bit of a joke. Even George Perry-Smith's got oxtail with grapes on his menu now."

Andy scratched the corner of his mouth thoughtfully.

"Maybe that's why Ambrose is planning on opening this 'Glamis' or whatever it's going to be called."

"Glamis?" I said to Kathryn.

"The new place. The bistro. That's what it's going to be called. Glamis."

Andy spoke over her: "Max has got to be a shoo-in for a third star this year. It'll be us and the Waterside Inn. Nico, probably not, poor fucker. God, I dread to think what it'll be like in the kitchen if Max doesn't get it. Most of the decent chefs I know reckon he doesn't deserve it and none of them in France would even dirty their mouths with his name. That's what he can't bloody stand."

Andy began gossiping about Alain Senderens buying the Lucas Carton, the incoming ("British!") senior chef

at Le Gavroche and Bruno Loubet's Gastronome One on the New Kings Road. But I was only half concentrating. I was aware, simply, that I'd made a mess of things. It was the first time I'd been invited anywhere. And yet I had the sense that I had ruined it. All I wanted to do, as Andy gassed happily, was disappear into a bathroom stall and busy myself with one of those knives.

And then something unexpected happened. Kathryn went to the toilet and Andy gave me the fully unrolled version of his mischievous smile.

"Who's a lucky boy then?" he said.

I didn't understand.

"Kathryn," he said. "You know, I've been living with that girl for eighteen months and this is the first time I have ever known her do anything even vaguely sociable."

"Oh," I said, uselessly.

"Well, it can't be *me,* can it?" he said. "The reason for this sudden interest in acting like an ordinary, friendly, functional human being? And if it's not me..."

Chapter 22

Kathryn and Andy lived in an upstairs flat in an old terrace in Brixton, nearly an hour's journey from the West End on the Number 3 bus. The walk from the stop was at once exhilarating and intimidating, with the drunks and the dealers and the pale faces hanging in doorways and corners, eyes skittering with dangerous intrigue over the landscape of tungsten and black. We passed a homeless man, camped out by a lamp post. He appeared to have an easel erected beneath a grimy bin-liner awning. "He's always here," said Kathryn, as an aside, once we'd passed him. "I'd love to know what he's painting."

Her front door was white and featureless – more like a fridge door – behind which a gloomy wooden staircase, cluttered with piles of telephone directories and old shoeboxes, led squeakily up two dark floors. We sat in a small lounge, on a sofa that was covered with a small Indian-looking throw. By my elbow was a brown monopedal ashtray with a retractable silver lid. There were no curtains, just lopsided office-style blinds, and a Van Gogh print with an Athena logo in the bottom corner, Blu-tacked straight onto the wall above the long-dead fireplace.

"Night-night you two," Andy said, after re-emerging from the kitchen with some tap water in a pint glass. He had that disreputable look again and I noticed a kiss of reddish pink appear faintly on each of Kathryn's cheeks. And then we were alone. A moment passed. Then another. I tried to think of something to say that wasn't to do with Max or the kitchen or her new job.

"Do you ever wonder," I asked, "what any of those extinct things might have tasted like?"

"Like a dinosaur?" she said.

"Exactly," I said. "I keep a list of things I have to eat before I die, and it makes me sad that there are all these, you know, *meats*, that are lost."

"You have a list?" she asked suspiciously.

"I do."

Her eyes brightened.

"I have a list too," she said.

"*You* have a list?"

"What, you thought you were the only one who had a list? The arrogance! At number one on mine is a giant tortoise."

"Aren't they extinct?" I said, laughing.

"Not sure."

"I want to try elvers," I said. "Have you heard of them?"

"Baby eels! What about ambergris? The most expensive food in the world. Charles II ate it on his eggs. It's whale snot or vomit or something. I prefer the sound of this Asian dish, have you heard of it? Son-in-Law Eggs?"

"Son-in-Law Eggs?" I replied, almost coming off my seat. "I can't believe you know about Son-in-Law Eggs. My aunt told me about them once. I'm *desperate* to try them. It's Thai, isn't it?"

"Whole eggs deep-fried in light batter and when you break into them—"

"– the warm yolk! Do you know they got their name because they're supposed to be so good that if a woman makes them for her son-in-law–"

"– he'll never leave her daughter."

By now I was so thrilled that I was on my feet.

"Let's get some now," I said. "Where can we get some?"

"Bangkok," she giggled. "But not London. Believe me, I've looked everywhere. And I've tried to make them. They're impossible."

"One day," I said, sitting back down, closer this time, my knee almost touching hers. "One day, let's cook them together."

"Okay," she said. "It's a plan."

When Kathryn got up to use the bathroom, I used the opportunity to examine the damage to my finger. As we'd been talking, I'd become increasingly conscious of the pain from when I'd placed it in the pan of hot sauce earlier. I gently unwrapped the bandage and winced at the sight of the white blister, pregnant with fluid, that was stuck on the end of it. I was blowing on the end of it when Kathryn returned.

"Oh my God, how did you do that?"

"Accident," I said. "I put it in a pan that had sauce in it."

"Bloody hell, how long for?" she said.

"I don't know," I said. I looked up at her. "I was annoyed. At Max. He said my sauce for Ambrose was finished and it wasn't. I kind of lost it a bit."

She sat down beside me. The room was lit only by a weak standard lamp in the corner, and its caramel light lay gently on her face.

"So, hang on," she said. "You did that *on purpose?*"

"No," I said. "God, no!" I laughed, and thought, I'm

saying "no" too much. "No, I'm not *mad*. No, no. I was using my finger to taste it. No, I think I was just so annoyed that I wasn't really feeling the pain. That's how it is when you get angry, isn't it?"

"Not really," said Kathryn, frowning quizzically.

She fetched an old grease-stained first-aid kit from a drawer in the kitchen and began to wrap a bandage around my finger. So that she could see what she was doing, she took a bobble from her pocket and tied her hair into a pony-tail. I could see the full stretch of her high, almost Nordic cheekbones. She had exposed, too, more of her birthmark than I had seen before. I looked at it. I wanted to touch it.

Holding my hand over her lap, she pulled the thin white material over the burn with the same purposeful delicacy with which she julienned mangoes. The stretching of my arm pulled my sleeve up a little, exposing a thrill of thin, crumbling needle-ish scabs from cuts on my wrist. I moved closer, so that my shirt covered them over. Our thighs, on the sofa, were touching.

"I'm sorry if I said the wrong thing about Max earlier," I said.

"You can say what you like about him. Your little crush on Max is nothing to do with me."

I took a moment to gather the courage to continue.

"I don't understand why he made me serve my sauce when he knew it wasn't ready," I said, carefully. "It seemed like... I mean, why would he do that?"

She smiled as she opened up a small safety pin and, with great care, leaned in and pierced the material. "You're an odd boy." She paused and smiled again. "You'll get it, though."

I looked at her neck, at the way the hem of her T-shirt lay over her collarbone and the dark canyons of shadow that fell down beneath it. As she held the end of the bandage in place in preparation for pinning it down, I tried to think of something else to say.

"I had a good time tonight," I said. She was nibbling the edge of her lip in concentration. "I can't remember the last time I went out for a meal. I never go out much."

She closed the pin and held my finger in hers for a moment.

"Billy-no-mates, are you?" she said.

I put my hand in my lap, curled my bandaged digit back into my palm and squeezed it as hard as I could.

"Me too," she said. "I think it's kitchens. They attract people like us. Things make sense when you're cooking, don't they? If you're good at your job, everyone likes you. If you're not, they don't. It's straightforward. Understandable. Not like out there." She waved dismissively towards the window.

"Were you moving about all those army bases when you were young?" I asked. "With your dad and everything? Is that why you didn't have many mates?"

"It wasn't to do with that, really," she said. "It was... I don't know."

It didn't seem possible that everything that was Kathryn was taking up the small space in front of me. The idea of her seemed so vast, and yet there she was. Just there.

"I don't usually talk to anyone either," I continued. "I find it hard, people. I don't know what to say to them so I mostly just don't say anything. Then they think I'm being arrogant or aloof or something." I braced myself. "For some reason," I said, "it's not so difficult with you."

She looked down at her lap. She was smiling. It was a good smile, I think. Self-conscious, definitely, but happy. A strange quiet fell over the room.

"You and Andy..." I said.

"This is his flat," she said. "And there's another girl here too. Jenny. She's a barmaid. Australian. We don't see much of her. She's still operating on Toowoomba time. Do you want a drink or something? Jenny's got some beers in the fridge."

Kathryn left to organise the drinks and I stood and browsed absent-mindedly through the pine bookshelves. I pulled out a tattered travel guide to Britain belonging, presumably, to the Australian. I'd just looked up Herstmonceux Castle when Kathryn returned with two cans of Hoffmeister, which she put down on the coffee table.

"I've got a house here," I said. I sat down beside her, and pointed to a black-and-white illustration of Herstmonceux. "A cottage. Well, sort of here. It used to be part of the grounds of the castle. Been in the family for hundreds of years and it's been left to me. It's a weird place. Dor Cottage, it's called. There was a witch lived there, once, they reckon. I'm going on Sunday – I'm moving in. It belonged to my aunt. My parents are pretty angry about me getting the place. My mum – at this rate, I don't think she's ever going to speak to me again." I turned so I could watch her closely. "Can I ask you something? You mentioned your mum, the other day..."

Kathryn sighed in such a way that I instantly regretted asking.

"Sorry–", I began.

"She's not well," she said.

"She's sick?"

"She's in a home. A kind of hostel."

She gazed at the dully shining top of an aluminium beer can. For a long moment, I was scared that she might cry.

155

"Are you okay?" I asked.

She shrugged, smally, without replying. Then, she said, "The place that she's in – I want to get her out of it. It's a shit-hole. That's kind of why I'm working so hard at the restaurant. It's…" She looked up at me. "I think, the people in that place, they don't treat her properly."

I wondered what would happen if I placed my hand on hers, just as she had done to me the other day. I could do that. Couldn't I?

Her skin felt cold. I let my hand lie there, my arm stretched uncomfortably, damp soaking out on my finger-tips. There was that kiss of reddish pink on her cheeks again and even though she was a year older than me, our proximity made me aware of her youth; of the simple clarity it afforded her skin and hair and neck; how her face could have been formed from a single, fresh drop of wax. I could feel the baying darkness outside and my heart beating inside and the seconds thumping past. She didn't mind, you see. She liked it. I looked at Kathryn's mouth. I shifted closer. I wasn't a child any more. I was here, in her flat. She had invited me here. We were touching. Not a boy, not any more. A *dog*, I leaned in towards her.

"What are you doing?" she said, rearing back. "For fuck's *sake*!"

"Sorry," I said. "Sorrysorrysorry. I'm sorry, I–"

She stood up and took a few steps back. "Forget it," she said. "You're just a stupid, silly man. You can't help it. Forget it. It's fine. Do you know what, though? I'm knackered. I'll get you a blanket and pillow and stuff."

There was a branding on my arm. A hot butcher's stink as my skin bubbled and melted.

Then I was outside in the grass of Dor, amongst the rain and dark soil. I felt the earth shift beneath me. It moved with all the trouble in all the surrounds.

I heard footsteps up by the cottage. I watched from the grass, through filthy air, as the finder man led the earl's man along the narrow path. He spoke quietly: "They say that she boils Feathers and Blood together using devilish Speeches and strange Gestures. She hath an Evil thing within her and the Devil attends her in the form of a Fly. She hath been heard to say that in her visions she sees four colours, red, yellow, green and black and that black is always Death."

The wet wind whipped his voice away.

There was something about a black book.

Something about mischief.

Something about devilish plants.

Chapter 23

I was straining in alert silence in the kitchen the next morning, when I finally heard it – a movement on the staircase. I dropped my basil leaves and went quickly, pushing my wet hands down my torchon and hurrying through the washing-up area towards the open door. By the time I got there, Ambrose had almost got away. He was high up, nearly at the well where the stairs turned ninety degrees. I could see his shiny brown shoes, his scarlet socks, the back of his trousers and his surprisingly plump bottom under the tail of his jacket.

"Um, Mr Rookwood," I said.

He stopped and peered back at me, over his shoulder, his hand gripping the banister, his white face floating in the gloom.

"I was just wondering if you wanted me to make your lunch today?"

"Not today, thank you," he said cheerily, and began moving again.

"Was it all right last week?"

"Not as good as I remembered, since you ask," he said, now just a voice disappearing into a lofty, dark echo.

Two hours later, I was cutting lemons into wedges; carefully removing the pith and pips with my paring knife – correcting all the ugly inconveniences of nature – when in my peripheral vision I noticed Carlo on his way to the fish station, delivering an eldorado of the very same butter that Max habitually promised millions never featured in his kitchens. I'd watched Carlo use it for his salmon, which was cooked *rosé à l'arête* – fried on one side before a hand grenade of French butter was thrown into the pan and a lid put on, which allowed it to steam in a hot mist of yellow fat. If anything could have given me cause to doubt Max, it was this incredible deceit. Although he did use Nouvelle Cuisine principles, the idea that he merely used water and 'Teflon pans' to achieve his two starred version of perfection was a fiction that had been sustained so long it was never even remarked upon in the kitchen.

By now, Kathryn, who had been working all morning in the walk-in freezer, was back next to me. I tried to catch her eye. All I wanted was one small, true smile, to tell me that I was forgiven.

"I can't believe how much butter Max uses," I said to her, trying to grin as naturally as I could. "I wonder what Nigel Dempster would have to say?" I made a telephone with my hand. "Hello? Is that Nigel Dempster? I have a story concerning Max Mann and four tonnes of French butter."

A cold swipe of air on the back of my neck. Somebody was behind me. God, no: *Max*. I braced myself for the assault. But he just walked past, as silently as he'd approached.

"Idiot!" whispered Kathryn, when he was safely gone. "Do you know what he'd have done if he'd heard you?"

I looked at her blankly. She said, "Keep your head down for the rest of service," and shook her head contemptuously. "God…"

It soon became apparent that Max was having one of his stuttering days. I was aware of him shuffling around at the pass, his apron tied tight around his waist. The bags beneath his eyes were like dead bat wings. He looked as if he hadn't slept and his gaze was snuffling around the place. But he wasn't looking at our hands to see what we were doing; instead he was inspecting our faces.

Later, Patrick told me that I would be helping to prepare one of Max's signature desserts, a light passion-fruit and lychee mousse that had a topping similar to that which you'd find on a crème caramel. My job was to sprinkle sugar over it, use a blowtorch to heat up a brand that had been moulded into the shape of a King logo and push it down, so the name of the restaurant was rendered in crisp, bubbling caramel. It wasn't easy. The brand was precisely the same size as the ramekins that the desserts were set in, and Max didn't want any excess sugar crystals visible on the surface. So how did you get them out? You couldn't tip the mousse. You couldn't blow on it. You couldn't fish them out with a spoon without disturbing the surface. The only way, I decided, was to sprinkle on the exact amount of sugar in the right places so that not a single crumb remained un-caramelised. The branding had to be done just before the dish was sent out, so it was still warm on the tongue.

The first desserts were usually plated at just after nine p.m. and immediately I had three to prepare. I began heating the brand with the blowtorch. Constantly aware of the sucking presence of Max at the pass, I dipped a tablespoon into the sugar and distributed it over the mousse surface in a thin drift. When I was sure the brand was sufficiently hot, I pushed it onto the sugar and watched carefully, my head no more than two inches away from the pudding.

Pulling it up, I raised the brand just in time. Perfect.

For the next mousse I sprinkled on a touch more sugar – I thought it could take it and I was right. The logo came up even better than before. I sprinkled yet more on the final dessert. In my mind, I saw Kathryn. I was beaming, telling her, "My mousses were great. You should've *seen* them."

And then I realised – too much sugar. I could tell that it was too much sugar.

"Where are my mousses?" Max was calling, his voice piercing through the noisy kitchen.

"Coming, Chef," I shouted.

I desperately tried to spoon off the excess without damaging the fragile surface of the pudding.

"Mousses, mousses, mousses! *Speeder!*"

I had another two desserts to prepare immediately and another five for three minutes after this. I pushed the brand in and it sizzled greedily. Perhaps if I held the heat there for a second longer, more of the stuff would melt. I smelled something rich, sharp, acid. A thin line of steaming black bubbles squeezed out from beneath the hot metal. I pulled the brand back.

It was burned – and fringed with excess sugar crystals. Ruined.

"Where are my mousses?" he called. "*Speeder! Speeder! N-now!*"

I placed them on a tray, lifted it carefully and made my way to the pass, the kitchen turning into a blur, the hellish noise seeming increasingly as if it was directed at me. I paced back to my station and sprinkled perfect dustings of sugar into the next two ramekins and began heating up the brand, holding it into the flame of the blowtorch until the dark steel lightened. I saw him through the hot, rising air. I saw him: his whole height, his whole fame, his whole majesty, walking towards my station with one of my desserts in his hand.

It was as if the air chilled as he stood in front of me, holding up a ramekin, his great nose rising in fury. He had a row of black hairs in each nostril, sprouting from a bed of broken blood vessels where, uncharacteristically, he'd failed to trim them.

"What do you call this, you fuck-eyed mudlark?" he asked, showing me the burned, crusted mess. "What do you c-call this? I'll tell you what I call it. A f-fucking cremation. What are you trying to do, you wretched pikey – send your dead aunt an offering?"

Underneath the scorched sugar, the mousse looked like Peach Melba Angel Delight. That had been one of my mum's favourites when she was a girl. Peach Melba Angel Delight with chocolate hundreds and thousands sprinkled on top of it.

"*Oui*, Chef," I said.

I wondered if Max Mann had ever eaten Peach Melba Angel Delight with chocolate hundreds and thousands sprinkled on top of it.

"Mistakes," he said. "I hate mistakes."

I imagined myself feeding it to him. Spooning it between his teeth; his lips closing over it. Gently cleaning away a smudge that had fallen onto his chin.

"Show me your arms."

I knew what was coming. I'd seen this before.

I pulled my sleeves up, bunching the material of my tunic securely into my elbows. I remembered the last time I'd eaten Peach Melba Angel Delight.

"You don't have enough burns to work in this kitchen."

I picked up the brand from where I had left it on the

pass. The edges were still whitened with heat; the dark steel of the word "KING" a light, wispy grey. I gripped my fingers around the plastic handle and brought it towards me, feeling the hotness of the metal as it approached my skin. Max's eyes followed what I was doing. They tracked my movements as I tracked his.

I imagined Max and my mother seated around a picnic table in a sunny garden, and me carrying in a vast dish of Angel Delight to them, pale and sculpted and wobbling and decorated in chocolate hundreds and thousands and Jelly Tots and chopped glacé cherries and popping candy. I would cut into it and there would be real peaches inside, peaches that had been macerated in Armagnac and Max would give a little clap and Mum a gasp of joy and I'd spoon it out onto silver plates.

For just the tiniest moment, the brand's contact against me felt cold. I pushed it in, hard, and then the agony and then nothing but pure white floating peace and the battle-field stench of scorching hair and skin.

There would be peaches inside that had been macer-ated in Armagnac and I would spoon it onto silver plates and give a little bow and Max would grimace and wretch and mock and my mum would say she didn't even like Peach Melba Angel Delight, it was disgusting, awful, baby food, full of chemicals and sugar and rot and those foul, soggy *peaches*...

I swallowed as a jolt of pain ran up my spine and made my upper lip twitch again and again and again. Max took a step back. He was even paler than before. A fly started turning noisy circles around his head. A single drop of sweat fell from his brow and onto the end of his nose.

He hit the brand out of my hand. It clattered to the floor.

"No more mistakes," he said, his voice shaking slightly.

"*Oui*, Chef," I said, bowing my head in deference at his retreating form.

On my arm, the word "KING" was tattooed in a grotesque scarlet logo, the edges of the letters bunched up and livid, a blister quickly forming. Andy, having seen what had happened, filled a bucket with cold water from the fish sink and forced my arm into it, whispering, "That was amazing. You nutter! I have never, ever seen anyone shut Max up like that. Are you totally bloody insane?"

I didn't reply. I just wanted to get back to my desserts.

Chapter 24

It was after one a.m. by the time I arrived at Dor Cottage, my eyes wired with exhaustion, my left arm in a loosening amateur bandage. I unlocked the heavy wooden door that opened straight into the lounge. Turning on the light, something caused me to pause. I had the strange experience of being alarmed by the scene, but for no obvious reason. The room felt as if it had been brooding in the darkness. There was Dorothy's green armchair and her little coffee table and the cat-print curtain that went across the TV cabinet. And there on the mantelpiece, a framed picture of me as a boy with raspberries on my fingers, oblivious to the loving gaze that she was sending towards me. It was a stage set for yet more magical lunches and warm, cloistered evenings with fennel-caramels and vanilla ice cream with salt and peanut butter and my great-aunt – all the props were poised expectantly, unaware of the disappearance of the essential actor.

Aware of my pulse and breathing, I paced through the shadows, straight to the kitchen. It seemed active, somehow, in its mad, toppling stillness. On the side, there was an open box of 40 PG Tips, a half-filled kettle, an old Sicilian cookbook and a Collins English-Italian pocket dictionary. I refilled the kettle and leaned against the counter, my eyes nervously tracking about the room. My forefinger tapped on the surface as the sound of the water roared into a boil. Mug of sugared black tea prepared, I carried it – slowly, defiantly – into the lounge and sat myself in the armchair. This is my house now, I thought to myself. Then I said it. "My house."

It wasn't long before the day caught up with me. My eyes became heavy and I welcomed it. As focus became harder to maintain, I lowered my still-full cup onto the carpet and rested my head against the worn, comfortable upholstery. I don't know how long I slept for – it may have been only minutes but it ended with a jolt. I lurched forward, letting out a small cry. I had no notion of any sound or movement – no evidence of the thing that had disturbed me so abruptly.

The sudden interruption from dreaming meant that I could still remember the contents of a kind of confused swirl of colliding nightmares. A mess of images and sounds: the night sky outside Dor, long ago, and a strange and frightening man whispering, walking up the path. I could recall, with all the substancelessness of a rapidly vanishing scent, dogs' mouths barking – white teeth and livid gums. And there was the voice of Dorothy, "Don't you ever go over that wall."

I rubbed my eyes. On the end of the arm of the chair there were two silver-grey flies. In the slithery light, I was revolted to see that they were mating. I stared at them for a drowsy moment. Still wreathed in the ghouls of my unconscious, I reached forward – quietly, gently, semi-awake – and I crushed the insects between my thumb and forefinger.

Chapter 25

S omething changed while I slept that night. As I'd taken myself upstairs the previous evening, I'd hesitated before going to bed in Aunt Dorothy's room at the front of the house. I had stood there on the buckled floorboards for some time, my hand stilled on the door handle. Why did the idea of it feel so much like a betrayal? I looked up and down the landing, the silence by now feeling so utter as to be deliberate. I wondered why the flaws of age always seem to give inanimate things human qualities; sagging walls becoming sagging cheeks, cracks becoming wrinkles.

I was being stupid. Weak. I stepped inside, turned on the light and set about clearing her things with a forced casualness. I took away the teacups and the Teasmaid; the tray with its dried fruits and its half-sized packet of dark chocolate McVities. The bed-sheets were stained with urine.

I slept as if unplugged and awoke filled with a reckless excitement, longing for the day to begin. I gathered some apple crates and some old newspapers from out the back and began to fill them with all the possessions, scattered about on shelves, hooks and cabinets, that made the place not mine: coats; shoes; a brass-handled walking stick; a collection of glass dogs and cats; a small pink-tinged photograph of Mum on a pebble beach – Hastings, probably. She looked so different, sitting there, grinning under the precarious English sun. I studied it for a while, before placing it back on the mantelpiece.

By half past ten, I had six full bin liners, the skins of which were beginning to stretch to a dangerous translucent grey. Without bothering to put my shoes on, I carried them carefully to the dustbin by the side of the house – the quickest route to which was via the front door. On my way back in, I stopped to admire the place, the warmth of the path's bricks soaking through my socks.

In a way, it was perfect, with its little white portico and satisfyingly fat chimney; ivy swarming up the walls and around the stumpy, nobly weathered front door. It was a reassuring scene; something about the harmony of the man-made and the natural managed to suggest that the world was ordered and rational and safe. If you were forced to name a single thing that was less appealing about the cottage, you'd probably pick out the small, deep-set windows that gave the building a defensive, furtive aspect. And then, of course, there was the garden.

Dorothy never seemed to relish spending time in the surprisingly mean patch of green that lay on Dor's eastern fringe. As a child, I'd long since given up asking her if we could play outside, as she'd unfailingly have "a much better idea" which would tend to involve desiccated coconut or chocolate drops or vanilla pods or, more likely, all three. It was a narrow and shaded space bordered, on the castle side, by a crudely built wall and was entirely empty bar the scrubby grass, some holly and rhododendron bushes and the shed that I used to spend entire afternoons in when I was young. Its walls unshaven with a million splinters, its uneven roof like a tinker's hat, it sat in a distant corner of the lawn like some banished relative, and I loved it. That shed had been my spaceship, my boat and, of course, my restaurant kitchen. I'll never forget the afternoon I discovered some dirty postcards wedged under a rickety work surface that someone had built in there, using dowelling for legs and a thin plank of eternally damp plywood.

It was out here that I had, for the first and only time, seen dread in Aunt Dorothy. She had been having some sort of baking crisis in the kitchen. Time had escaped her, and she'd forgotten to monitor my whereabouts. When she emerged out of the back door, drying her hands on a tea towel, I was scaling the brick garden wall, trying to see what was behind it. I had an odd memory of there being some strange statue over there – some stone monster or bird of prey bawling in a violent, retching pose.

"Get down!" she had shouted.

Seeing such terror on Dorothy's face had made me freeze. She ordered me down, then pulled me over her lap and proceeded to spank me with the full might of her strength.

"Never, never, never, never do that," she said. "Never, never, never go near this wall again."

She hit me so hard that she rocked back and forth, using the momentum of her body to give her strikes extra force. There was her face and the blue summer sky behind it and a rim of wet gathering in her left eye and then her right and then it spilled from the left, a tear that ran a faltering course, down past the creases and wrinkles in her skin.

I stood, remembering all this, with my hands on my hips and my feet square. I was about to go inside when I noticed something I'd never seen before. There was a small, dark window in the roof, peering out towards the clouds like a single, hooded eye. My arms collapsed by my sides. What was up there? An attic? How could I have never noticed it before? It didn't seem possible. Perhaps, because it was mine now, I was seeing the property with a kind of fresh proprietorial view. Whatever it was, I was certain I had always been completely unaware that... or had I? Although I had no recollection of the physical sight of this thing, the fact of its existence seemed somehow familiar in my memory's undercurrents. It was like recalling a childhood event, and being unsure whether it was something that had happened to me, or a scene from a television programme or perhaps even a dream. The attic in the cottage. Yes, of *course* there was an attic in the cottage.

I quickly gave up trying to understand it all. Besides, if it really was an attic, there was only one place the entrance could be. I strode up the path, flattening the weeds that were sprouting beneath the flagstones, and pushed open the back door. Just as I entered the kitchen, a cloud must have covered the sun as there was a sudden dip in the light. I ran up the stairs noisily and turned into the corridor, my neck craning upwards, waving away a couple of flies that were turning in circles at the end, just outside the sunny bedroom and – yes, my God, there it was – a recessed wooden square. A door in the ceiling like a sucked-back laugh. I wondered how long it had been since Dorothy had been able to get up there. Had she *ever* been up there?

I heaved the creaking apple crates filled with Dorothy's things up the stairs and left them in a pile on the floor beneath the entrance, ready to carry upwards. Then, wiping the hairlets of blond wood from my hands, I rushed to the shed to fetch a foldaway ladder.

The ladder's steps meowed irritably as I climbed towards the attic entrance. Once at the top, I gave each corner a firm thud with my fist and it opened surprisingly easily. I was so startled by what came out that I almost fell backwards onto the floor. The light! It was that time of day when the sun roared into the front bedroom, and as perfect as the windows in there were for capturing its rays, the attic was obviously even better placed. The light fell from the hole, as if a great store of it had been trapped up in the roof, building in weight for decades. It was a torrent of white and pale gold that broke apart as I squinted back at it, bursting into stars of red, blue and green.

Protecting my eyes with the back of my arm, I climbed up. As I sat myself down, I realised that the ground was covered with small, brittle balls that were crunching beneath my weight. When I looked at my palms, there was nothing left of the things but dust, with the odd fine little rod or thread amongst the grey smudge on my skin. Brushing it off, I waited, with my legs dangling towards the corridor below, until I became used to the brightness.

At first, it was impossible to make out anything at all. The attic seemed to be filled with large misshapen black forms that were lined up in a sulky parade. I realised that these were thick cloths that had probably been draped over whatever was underneath them in an effort to defend them against the sun's daily assault. Pushing myself to my feet, I saw there were more of the crispy balls on the ground. The place was blanketed in them. I leaned down to see what they were.

Flies. Fly carcasses. Thousands of them. So old that when any pressure was put on them they'd burst into a small puff of powder. Covering my nose with my sleeve, I crunched across them gingerly. In the eves, I could just make out the dried body of a bird and a couple of spider-webs so thick they looked like nests. I sniffed uncomfortably, my nostrils suddenly blocked, and pulled back the cloth that was directly in front of me, and a clatter of ancient insects hit the floor.

Recipe books. Some with glossy spines and titles such as *Sauces of Italy, Ancient and Modern.* But many more old enoughthattheirleatherbindingshadtakenondeeplymarinated shades of brown and red — the colours, suitably enough, of earth and blood. On each of the wooden shelves were handwritten labels saying "Italy". I tried to make out some titles in the earlier volumes: *De Re Coquinaria*; *Liber de Coquina*; *De Honesta Voluptate et Valitudine*. I pulled a book towards me and it struggled for a moment before finally giving way with sticky "tk". It was heavy and embossed with a golden spoon whose handle was the head of a serpent. It opened with a sound that was midway between a crack and a tut and its rough pages weren't laid out like any recipe book I'd seen before — no ingredients list or step-by-step method. Just dense paragraphs of arcane script in a language I couldn't understand.

It was only then that I grasped the proportions of the room I was standing in. It was a low space — my neck wasn't quite able to straighten at the ceiling's highest point — but the corridor of shelves had a surprising depth. I pushed the Italian book back into its space and removed more of the heavy cloths to reveal shelves labelled "France", "Spain", "Prussia & Scandinavia", "The Orient", "England", "The Americas". I peered into the "England" section and selected something entitled *The Forme of Cury*.

"For to make a formenty on a fichssday, tak the mylk of the hasel notis, boyl the wete wyth the aftermelk, til it be dryyd and take and colour yt wyth safron and the ferst mylk cast ther'to and boyle wel and serve yt forth."

"Serve yt forth," I muttered with a small shake of the head.

I gave *The Forme of Cury* back to its slot and removed the shroud from the neighbouring unit. On the wood, where previously there had been written the names of various culinary continents, was the word "Dor". The volumes on this shelf seemed to be homemade: some hard-bound notebooks that looked perhaps a hundred years old, some stapled and relatively modern, but others merely dishevelled piles of ancient rough-edged paper tied together with brittle yarn.

At the dark end of the corridor of books was a pile of boxes. The largest was a wooden trunk – oak, it looked like, with brass hinges that had dulled to the colour of moss. I bent down, brushed off a layer of petrified insects and pushed up on the lid, which yielded with an indignant groan. There was hay, and amongst that some heavy glass bottles – some brown, some greenish-clear, most with a moustache of dried earth around the thread at the top. They'd been labelled, each in a different hand, in fading watery ink, "Witch Bottle, discovered Aug 12th 1876, two ft beneath rosemary patch"; "Witch Bottle, March 31st 1845, 18" in earth beneath entrance gate, Dor Cottage"; "Witch Bottle, excavated March 10th 1869, 'neath thyme". I carefully lifted one from its bristly bed but it must have been already cracked because the top came away, soundlessly from its base. I let the pale, powdery soil empty on the floorboard. The was a knock, and then another – hard objects falling from the dirt. I picked one of them up and, in a horrible reflexive movement, threw it across the room with a "fuck!" that almost made me jump again, its sudden volume in the swaddling silence reminding me quite how alone I was. It was hair. Human, by the looks of it. Auburn curls tied in the middle and attached to something waxy.

The area where I'd thrown the thing was black and indistinct, and I stared into it, rubbing my fingertips on the denim of my jeans until they became reassuringly sore.

"Time for lunch," I muttered. But by now my eyes had warmed to the darkness and I could see an incongruously modern shoebox that had been stowed in the corner. Creeping over to it, and pulling it towards me, I opened the lid. It was full of... pictures... letters... newspaper clippings. On the top was a wedding portrait in a creamy card frame – black and white with the photographer's name embossed in partially flaked-off gold in the corner. I didn't recognise the groom, although he looked both kind and actually thrilled to be getting married, which is something, when I came to think about it, which you usually don't see in these sorts of photos. And next to him, humble bouquet in hand, beneath the Norman arch of an English country church...

Dorothy?

Chapter 26

I decided that the best thing would be to leave Aunt Dorothy's secrets where they were; to keep forgotten what was quite obviously intended to be forgotten. And yet I couldn't help noticing that I'd brought the shoebox down into the kitchen. I eyed it as I drank my tea, before announcing my surrender with those two words that precede untold millions of regrettable acts every day.

"Fuck it."

Lifting the wedding photograph out, I found a carefully folded newspaper cutting: an article from the *Sussex Messenger*. The headline read, "Popular Local Baker Announces Early Retirement". They'd pulled out a quote in bold in the middle of the text: "'A terrible shame,' Rosemary Pope, Castle Bakers."

"Popular local baker Dorothy Drake of Dor Cottage, Herstmonceux, announced last week that she will no longer supply the village bakery with her popular home-made cakes that are affectionately known to locals as 'Dotty Cakes'. Rosemary Pope, proprietor of Castle Bakers who sold the iced fancies, told a reporter from the *Sussex Messenger* that the news was, "A terrible shame".

"'We sell 300 Dotties every week and could easily do double that if only Mrs Drake had the time to bake them,' said Mrs Pope. 'We always find a little queue for them at 7 a.m. on Friday mornings when she makes her deliveries. We've no idea what she puts in them, but they're no ordinary fancies, I can tell you that. They're quite addictive. I've always told Mrs Drake she'd be a millionaire if she decided to sell the recipe to Mr Kipling.' When contacted by the *Sussex Messenger*, Mrs Drake declined to comment."

Beneath the article was a certificate of marriage to a Bryan Stanley Drake dated July 5th 1956. Next to that, divorce papers, filed eight and a bit years later. And then, in an immaculately opened envelope, a letter.

25th Nov, 1964

My Darling Dorothy,

I don't need to tell you again how deeply sorry I am for the way I have behaved. I have brought great shame upon you and I know you will find it impossible to ever forgive me. I cannot blame you for this, Dorothy, and find myself unable to say much in my defence. You know now that I did use that blasted herb for my own ends, reprehensible as they were.

I am currently staying with Mother in Portsmouth. As you can imagine, she was terribly sad to learn that our marriage has come to an end. When I confessed that it was down to my own adultery she was crushed.

My darling Dorothy, I am writing to you to make an appeal. I promise this will be the last you shall hear from me. I beg of you to remember the man I was before all this. I hope you remember that I was upstanding, moral and am still churchgoing.

We've had much fun (and made much profit) turning out Dotty Cakes for the past six years or so. I beg you to stop now. In fact, I go further. I propose that you allow me to build a wall that will extend the length of the garden and block out the Physic Garden completely. I know you could never bring yourself to destroy the garden itself. I ask only that you grant permission for me to build a high wall that is completely inaccessible to anyone.

I must furthermore confront a subject that we always failed to speak about properly. You might consider my addressing it now to be a fair measure of my desperation. Dorothy, you told me yourself that your relative was burned as a witch. I know that you noticed the change that seemed to come over the house when we started to harvest that herb. After long reflection, I have come to accept that, entirely by accident, we might have set off something evil in the place. Please understand that I am entirely sober-minded when I tell you that, in using those plants, I believe we invited into our home, in some form or guise, the Devil. I can only recommend the services of a local priest. Perhaps Father Demick could be trusted to act with the necessary discretion.

Please consider what I ask seriously. I await your reply.

Yours with all my love and tenderness,
Bryan.

Chapter 27

It was the mortar that gave it away. It looked lumpy and unfinished; you could see thumb-smears and casual licks that had petrified in the shapes they had been in on the day it had been built, presumably by this newly discovered uncle. The bricks weren't quite straight, the edges sticking out uncomfortably here and there. It was tall, though – the ladder was just about able to lift me to a clear view. Even though I was high up, I felt cowed by the elm forest whose blind distances stretched on towards the castle. I squinted into the velvet murk beneath. *Oh my God.* There were walls down there, almost as tall as this one, enclosing what appeared to be an abandoned garden about the size of the cottage again. They'd been built with the same ochre bricks as Dor, yet these were glum with damp and sickly with moss and lichen. Directly in front of me was an entrance – a wooden gate between stone pillars that were crowned by the screaming stone gargoyles that I remembered. The garden itself was strangely breathtaking; an ocean, moving slowly but with extreme violence. Silent crowds of nettles in the corners looked out onto a torment of weeds, thorns and tangles; vast clumps of dead-looking vegetation with dried stalks like ribcages a few leafy stems poking bravely through here and there. They looked like herbs, although not a variety I could remember seeing before.

"What the bloody hell are you up to?"

I turned towards the voice and, when I saw who it was, I climbed down the ladder so quickly I nearly twisted an ankle.

"Christ!" I said.

Kathryn seemed nervous, standing there at the garden gate, not sure whether to open it or not.

"Sorry," I said, brushing the dirt and brick crumbs from my hands. "I was just having a look – there seems to be an old garden back there."

"A garden? What sort of garden?"

"An overgrown one," I said, opening the gate. "Herbs, it looks like. What are you doing here?"

She shrugged in a way that suggested she was giving herself a little hug.

"I don't know. I was bored. Sitting around in that crap-hole of a flat with Andy in his pants, stinking of Babycham and Marlboro. Jenny brought some bloke back last night and he was in his pants too. I couldn't move for hairy thighs and ball bags. I thought, 'Sod this, I'll get in the car and go to the country'."

She managed to look me in the eye for the first time. I didn't know what to say. She glanced over her shoulder, towards Wartling Road.

"I just wanted to see the castle, really," she said. "I love castles. I think it's the military. It's in my blood." She turned back towards me. "I can piss off if you like."

"No!" I said. "Come in."

I led her through the gate. She paused to take in the house. "God, it's gorgeous, Killian."

"We can walk to the castle, if you like," I said. "It's ten minutes that way."

"What, right now?" she said, with an excited grin. "Cool. Go on then."

Wartling Road crept through the ancient fields of Sussex under a dim tunnel of trees, the sun just managing to sprinkle itself through the leaves above, attacking the shade with tiny arrows of pale light. We hadn't been walking down its crumbling tarmac edges for long before Kathryn gave me an uncertain look.

"I'm sorry if I was awful to you yesterday," she said.

"You weren't."

"I shouldn't have been so cross with you. I should've realised – men are kind of automatic, aren't they? Like moths, except it's not light bulbs, it's tits. You're all the same, really."

I smelled the smell of menthol cigarettes, back when I was young. I saw red fingernails pressing into the white filter and ash bunching up on my skin, then softly falling, like snowflakes, towards the carpet.

Kathryn looked at me: at my silence and colour.

"It's just – I have had bad experiences with men," she said. "To be frank about it, I've probably got a chip on my shoulder. So it's me that should be saying sorry, not you." She breathed out. "So I'm sorry. I'm trying really hard, Killian."

We continued in silence for what felt like too long.

"So anyway, I was worried about you," she said eventually. "After yesterday? You dashed off after work – your arm."

"I just wanted to get down here." I shrugged and lifted my bandage towards her. "It's fine now. Got some Savlon on it. It's just throbbing a bit. I quite like it when it throbs."

She glanced into the distance. "Why did you do it?"

"I don't know," I said. "I just wanted Max–"

"I don't know why you're so in thrall to him."

"Because he's the best."

"Is that what you think?"

When I thought of the Max that I used to love, and the Max I had known in recent weeks, I saw separate people. My image of him was like a double exposure, two not-quite-there men, neither fully resolving.

"I just want him to know I've got what it takes," I said.

"But, Killian, you don't need to … It's like you don't think you deserve your place in the kitchen. But you wouldn't be there if you didn't. You know, in this industry, you don't get anything unless you deserve it – jobs or customers or good reviews or stars. Whatever you get, you deserve."

"I know."

"I don't think you do."

She stopped and stood in front of me.

"You're going to be a huge success, Killian. You'll get a job, even if it's not at King, you'll get one and you'll become a head chef. What you did yesterday –" She began walking again. "Have you ever done anything like that before?"

"Not really."

"What about your finger that time? Was that on purpose? When you put it in the sauce?"

My mind felt crowded with answers, and yet it presented me with no answer at all. I wondered if we'd reached it now; if this was it, actually happening right as we were walking: the moment Kathryn realised that I was some sort of freak and stopped liking me.

"You don't need to impress anyone, you daft bastard," she said, eventually. "We can all tell you're talented. You've got the knife skills, the speed and it's… oh, you know, it's just the way you *are* around food, the way you touch it, the way you look at it, the way you talk about it, the way you pile those basil leaves so bloody perfectly in their bowls, the way you talk to those blackcurrants under your breath when they're not behaving. It's obvious. Anyway, you should be pleased. Max is giving you extra attention."

I felt a sudden lightness in my knees.

"Do you think so?" I said.

She started laughing.

"No," she said. "Not really. You're probably fucked."

We turned right onto the long castle drive, past the green domes of the observatory and on towards the magnificent pomp and portliness of Herstmonceux Castle. We talked about food – how, like me, she adored creamy sauces and four-hour stews prepared with whole bottles of red wine. It was the cooking of the ages that we loved: fat, alcohol and blood.

We meandered through the formal gardens and on towards the visitors' centre, on the outside wall of which was a mural that listed Herstmonceux's previous owners. I stopped and silently read down it: Idonea de Herst; Ingelram de Monceux; Maud de Monceux; Sir John Fiennes; Joan Dacre; Sir Richard Fiennes; Margaret Fiennes.

"You interested in all this?" Kathryn asked, her feet pointing in the opposite direction.

"Not really," I said. "My great-aunt – the one who died – she had this story about how the cottage was built hundreds of years ago for the cook of the castle's owner." I squinted at the list. "I'm not sure if I ever believed it. I can't remember what she said his name was, but it wasn't any of these. She might have been mistaken. My mum doesn't even think the cottage is that old. It's made of brick, you see."

"But so is the castle," said Kathryn.

"Yeah, and the castle was rebuilt in 1910. It *feels* old, the cottage. It definitely has that feeling about it. But maybe it isn't. I don't know."

Kathryn looked back at the castle, her nose squished with disappointment. I followed her into the small visitors' room where we browsed the photos and information in a half-bored silence.

"Here, Killian, look at this," she said, shortly.

I followed her nod to a small typed notice, on the green baize board in the corner.

"It was not until the middle of the 15th Century that a large building constructed wholly of brick appeared in Sussex: Herstmonceux Castle. Its sheer size necessitated making the bricks on the spot."

"Jesus," I said. "It *is* old."

Nearby, a typewritten list on white A4: "Owners of the manor of Herstmonceux".

I leaned into the small black type, scanned it carefully and stopped when I felt a thud, like something trying to break out of my chest.

"There he is," I said, pushing my finger against the line: "'1662: His son, Thomas Lennard, Lord Dacre, Earl of Sussex, 1654 – 1715'. That's the one my aunt told me about. Thomas Lennard. He had my ancestor burned as a witch."

It felt, suddenly, as if there was something prickly in the room with us. I looked over my shoulder and straightened up.

"Shall we go back and have some tea?" I said.

We spent the afternoon baking and half-watching videos – *Trading Places*, *Kramer vs Kramer*, some Kenny Everett rubbish. That night, I prepared one of my favourite ragus: the one Dorothy claimed was Catherine de Medici's preferred preparation: beef, pork and soffritto browned until it's all crackling angrily, then cooked until nearly scorched with a couple of tablespoons of tomato puree, then the milk, which the parched sauce always drank down with desperation, and then white wine, lemon juice and then another hour or two in a lazy oven with cinnamon, coriander, nutmeg and cloves. We ate in bleary silence and drank through three bottles of wine.

After the pasta, I plated some freshly baked rock cakes and sprinkled icing sugar over their golden, still-warm tops.

"I can't believe how beautiful this place is," said Kathryn, taking a bite of the cake and gazing at the beams on the ceiling. "I'd love to live somewhere like this. You're so lucky."

"I know," I said. "I feel a bit bad. My mum was pissed off that she didn't get it. I wonder if I shouldn't just let her have it, sometimes."

"But it was left to you..?"

Something distracted me. I looked down at my rock cake. Beneath the snow-like layer of icing sugar, something was twitching, lazily. I dismissed it. It must be nothing.

"My aunt had a thing about this place," I said. "She was convinced there are all these family secrets here. Things to do with the witch stuff. Dangerous stuff. I'm not sure what she was going on about. But this is definitely a weird place. You do get the feeling there are... sort of... I don't know. You probably think this is all nonsense, though? You don't believe in anything like that?"

Perhaps unconsciously, she touched the small silver crucifix around her neck.

"Well, I do pray, if that counts," Kathryn was saying.

"I pray every night. You're not allowed to laugh at that, by the way. Laughing is not okay when I'm telling you things like that."

The surface of my cake shifted again. Peering down, I brushed the jerking powder away. There was a raisin there, beneath the icing sugar. It was moving. I pulled the cake apart, a little, with the edges of my thumbs. It had red eyes and a silver body. A fly. It was there, in my cake, sliding its front legs against each other in a grotesque knitting motion.

"You're a Christian?" I asked.

"I don't know," said Kathryn. "I suppose so. My mum, a long time ago, studied theology. She taught me a lot of stuff that helped me understand it. Religion's not all it's cracked up to be. Organised religion, I mean. The Church – it has an amazing history. In a bad way. Horrible. Murder, genocide – the kind of stuff they don't really go into on *Songs of Praise*. But that's not to say I don't believe." She paused and shook her head dismissively, as if throwing the subject clear of her mind. "Anyway," she said. "These witch secrets or whatever they are. Why do they mean your mum didn't get the house?"

Gingerly, I put the cake back on the plate.

"She wanted to sell it and my aunt wouldn't let that happen. My mum was brought up in a pretty wealthy family but she married a working-class guy and I don't think she's ever got used to living on less. I think she only married him to piss my grandad off. Bit of rough, you know. But now they've run up debts, so they need money. But Dorothy seemed to think that selling Dor would be dangerous or something. I don't know why. To be honest, I think she was going a bit senile for a while there."

"What's she like, your mum?"

Kathryn had the most beautiful mouth; thin at the sides, her top lip gathering gently into a lovely, heavy, pink cushion of flesh. I wondered what my mum's mouth looked like when she was young. Had it been as pretty as Kathryn's?

"She's," I smiled uncertainly. "She's a social worker. You know, kind. Kind-hearted. Given-up-her-life-to-help-other-people sort of thing. She can be very, very loving, but she doesn't take a lot of shit from me or Dad. She's a bit like Max, in a weird way. She can get pretty angry."

"How angry?"

Memories flashed through my mind. Stills. Images.

"Oh," I shrugged.

I saw the backs of my mother's hands; the tips of her fingernails. With a mock-dismissive shake of the head, Kathryn asked, "She doesn't ever *hit* you or anything?"

I saw my mother's ankles as she walked away, their thin framework of muscle and sinew and vein.

"She doesn't mean it. She can be nice – she used to be nice, when I was a boy. And she always says sorry. Always. And I know why she does it – her dad used to beat her mum around and what with that and all the shit she sees in her job, it means she just doesn't like men very much and you can kind of understand her point. I mean, I don't want you to think – she's a good mum. She used to stick up for me when I got bullied. You know, she's so loyal, she'd do anything for her family. She just finds it hard to cope, that's all. And she's right about my dad – he's useless. When I was growing up, I had to take the slack with housework and everything, because my mum was always working and – I'd get things wrong and I'd be punished a bit sometimes. But it's done me good, in the long run. I'd never be able to cope with working at King if I hadn't been toughened up a bit."

I'd become so absorbed in what I was saying that I hadn't noticed that Kathryn's eyes had gone elsewhere. I'd lost her. But it was more than that. I could sense, in the tiny combinations of her muscles and mouth and breathing, that a kind of sadness had come into her. And then I remembered.

"Sorry," I said. I put my hand out to comfort her. I was deciding whether to touch her knee or arm or shoulder, but I just placed it down again, on my lap. "Your mum…"

She closed her eyes.

"I just miss her," she said. "She had a kind of a breakdown after my dad died and now she's sick with this fucking *thing*. She can't do anything. She can't go out. I try to see her when I can, but the hours – since I've been at King, I've hardly been able to visit her at all. She has bruises, sometimes. They say she falls and I know, sometimes, she gets violent with them. But you should see it – it's awful. She has to share a room with four other people and it stinks. It's filthy. I can't bear it. I asked Max if I could visit her, one time, when there was a problem, and he went crazy. Gave me this big fucking speech."

I put my hand out, tentatively, towards her. She took it, squeezed my fingers and placed it on her leg and then laughed bitterly. "I can't believe I'm letting you see me like this. I'm sorry if it's boring or anything, it's just—"

"Once, years ago, when I got upset, my aunt Dorothy told me I should close my eyes and paint a picture of heaven," I said. "It's obviously kind of childish, cheesy. But it works. I still do it sometimes. For years I imagined myself running a restaurant. Running King, actually."

"I still do," she smiled.

"You want to run King?" I asked.

She said. "Somewhere like that. Somewhere starred, at least. I can't think of any other way I can get Mum out of that place. To go private, it's hundreds of pounds a month."

"But you'll make it," I said. "Some day you'll be able to afford it."

"It's going to be years before I'm the executive chef of anywhere. And by then…"

Carefully at first, I put my arms around her. I felt her tears crush between our cheeks. "Do you know what upsets me most of all?" she said. "I can tell my mum thinks cooking is this shitty, nothing job. She'll never get to see where I'm working – how amazing it is. She'll never get to taste my food. And you should see the dirty *shit* they feed her on." She broke into soft sobbing and I held her as still as I could manage. She tightened her grip around my waist and I could smell her neck. I moved my nose towards it, towards the little mole that sat in the dusk of her creamy, shadowed shoulder and the lines in her skin, so fine that even Kathryn had surely never seen them, never been this close, never studied the curve of the back of her neck and that birthmark, so strange and sad, that disappeared down beneath the hem of her shirt and I was closer and closer –

She pulled away from me and said something that made this a moment for the stars.

"You're very special to me. And that's all I'm going to say."

I led her to the spare room and I left her to sleep, happily, alone.

Chapter 28

Behind my station, underneath the butchery block, was a row of four grouchy-looking polished-steel fridges. The door on the second fridge was broken. In order to close it properly, you had to pull it up on its hinges before pushing it to. In all the motion and ferocity of the kitchen, the chefs and apprentices frequently forgot about this uppity little eccentricity and simply dealt with this door as they did all the others – with a light heel-kick, at which point it would hit the frame with a thunk rather than a click.

The next morning, I was cutting the stalks off the blackcurrants when, deep beneath the layers of the chopping, clanking and sizzling, this dull clunk sounded. Without thinking or even moving my neck, I said, "Fridge door."

I heard the chef in question mutter, "He's got eyes in the back of his bloody head."

It was the apprentice Malcolm. He was standing there, with a tray of butter, looking at the door which was slowly gliding open as if compelled by a mischievous ghost. For a moment, I had no idea how I knew Malcolm hadn't shut it. But as my fingers and blade worked accurately and automatically on a blackcurrant, I realised that the cacophony that had made me so breathless on the first day had slowly come to make sense.

The menu might have looked like nothing more than a solemn list, but each one of those dishes had its own unique and violent song that had been filling the ears of the brigade for hours. Those songs combined to create a symphony; a secret music that every kitchen has its own version of, but which is possible to decipher only by total immersion. I could hear it now. There was the scrape and knock of the lamb racks being French-trimmed; there was the shik-shik-shik of the trout being de-scaled; there was the splash and clatter of Danno the pots man washing the bread tins in the sink. All in order; all in time; all correct and comforting. I'd developed the ability to hear the song of the kitchen using all my senses. I could smell the sweet herby richness of the rabbit stock reaching its simmer; feel the increase in heat as the grill station was fired up; sense the texture of the pressure in my gut and so read the mood of the kitchen. Now, after nearly six weeks of apprenticeship, my nose could tell me the time of day, almost to the nearest minute.

It wasn't long after this that I became aware of a silence that was overwhelming the top of the kitchen. Peering between the shelves, I could only see Max's back bending down to meet the face of one of his brigade.

"You've burned your finger?" I heard him say. "What am I supposed to do with a cook whose fingers don't work? What use is that to me? Do you think, when I pulled you out of that trough of mediocrity that is our apprentice brigade, that I did so because you were clumsy?"

I put my knife down and walked around the corner for a better view.

"Clearly, you need some supplementary training. *Bon. Bon.* You will have some. Let's have your tunic."

I could still only see his back. But Patrick – Patrick was looking down at the target of Max's ire and leering greedily, that spitty, pointed tongue resting on the inside edge of his lip.

"I'm sure you don't believe that I'll treat you differently because you're a girl," said Max. "This is, after all, the age of sexual equality."

I pushed past the apprentices and walked up behind Max, aware that the music of the kitchen – now slowed and loosened – was on the verge of collapsing since the conductor had become distracted. In the gap, between Max's arm and the tall steel wall, I glimpsed Kathryn slowly, defiantly, unbuttoning her tunic. Behind her, Patrick's tongue worked in little pumps, pushing out at his lower lip. The brigade threw excited glances between their work and the action.

She was doing it with the edge of her thumb, popping one white button out and then the next. I wondered which finger was burned. I wondered if she was in pain. The blue flames hissed and the hair on the back of Max's head was thin and wiry. Little white crumbs of dead skin hung inside it, here and there.

Max would stop her in a moment. I knew he would. Max wouldn't allow this to happen. He was testing her.

Then the bottom button was released, and Kathryn, chin down, cheeks blood-red, opened up her tunic. Patrick's tongue was free, half an inch of it poking from his mouth, his cigarette-stained teeth pushing down on it; his slimy taste buds like fur, like wet, grey velvet. The tunic hung from the end of Kathryn's fingers.

I'd never seen her stomach before. Her beautiful shoulders; the prominent mole on her right arm. I'd never seen the shape of her collarbone; her belly button, the soft curve of the peak of her hipbone. And now Patrick and Carlo and Simon and Chef Max Mann, they were all

seeing my own Kathryn, standing there in her smallness
and her secret perfection and her white, wash-dulled bra
and the smooth weight of the tops of her breasts.

I found myself pushing past Max. There wasn't much
room between Kathryn and him, but I got into the space
and I stood there in front of her and now nobody could
see her.

"Are you lost?" he said. "You belong in the cold pass,
not here with the g-grown ups. I suggest you get back
there, *tout de suite.*"

I could feel the warmth of Kathryn behind me; the
sound of her folding her arms over her chest. Her breath
was on the back of my neck, wet and fast. Max didn't
realise that he'd gone too far. He would realise, though,
when he was in a better mood. I undid my top button.

"If you want to test the limit of my patience," he said,
"please do carry on."

And then the next one. And then the next.

"But let me warn you, young man, there will be
consequences."

I pulled my tunic down, feeling the cotton run and
bump over my arms, and handed it to Kathryn. By the time
I turned back to face him, all the power had left Max's face.
His eyes were sinking down the skin of my torso. They
took in the scars on my chest; the scalds from the kettle;
the cigarette burns on my nipples; the raised furrows of
tissue from the whip-slashes of buckles and belts. In that
instant, Max saw two decades of motherly discipline cut
into the flesh of my body. And then, my own work, on
my arms and the soft sides of my stomach. From pencil
sharpener blades and razor blades and kitchen blades and
the broken glass of bottles of wine and whisky and gin.

He took it all in, the Gentleman Chef, his eyes stuttering

all over me, unable to disguise the horror, and for one beautiful moment the silence in his kitchen was mine. His jaw moved inside his skin, as if it was loose in there, this great slab of hinged bone all slack inside his face. I plucked Kathryn's tunic from his fingers.

"I don't have time for this childishness now," he said. "Once more, allow me to suggest that you go back to your station and get on with your work whilst I decide what to do with you. I'd do it now, if I were you."

I bowed my head before him.

"*Oui*, Chef. Sorry, Chef."

As Kathryn composed herself once more, Max turned to face the onlookers.

"Work," he hissed. "*Now.*"

* * *

Ten minutes later I found myself in Stephen Mews, alone with her. She had rushed up to me, urgently, with the news that Max and Patrick had left the kitchen for the back office – the rumour amongst the chefs was that something concerning Max had been spotted in the *Evening Standard* and it wasn't good.

"Come with me," she'd whispered. "Quick. Before they come back."

The kitchen door closed with a rattle over the sound of traffic and fussing pigeons and a stray newspaper page that was being blown across the ground. A day of sun was trying to lighten the courtyard's great grey walls. A tiny grain of heat and sparkle was reflected from each of the little cobblestones.

"Your chest," said Kathryn. Her head was cocked a little to the right and her face showed something like anger. "My God, Killian."

And then I realised. Of course, she had seen me now. She had seen my skin and my bone and the indelible tracks of my ugliness.

"It's disgusting," I said.

"Oh *no*, Killian."

With that, her expression fell open and she came towards me and took both my hands. There was a moment of hesitant tension. I could see her swallow; a fleeting glimpse of fear darted across her eyes. Then she put her arms around me. I yielded, gratefully, and she tightened her grip until I was held fast against her, my chin over her shoulder. She was pressing into me, her breasts against my ribs and her hot cheek into mine. Then she whispered, "It's not disgusting. Killian, I'm telling you, it's not disgusting *at all*."

I let my chin rest upon her shoulder and she said, "What you did in there, with Max – I can't believe you'd do something like that for me. And I just wanted to say, before I get too scared again, that I like you and I wanted to tell you, just in case you were interested or anything, and if you aren't, then can we just pretend this never happened? Please."

I moved my head back from where she'd been whispering. I would never have believed, when I met her on that first morning, that I would ever see her like this. All traces of sarcasm gone; nothing to her expression but openness and hoping.

"It's okay, Kathryn," I said. "It's fine, because I love you."

And with that, everything became automatic. Her lips came to mine and there began a kiss that dropped the floor, lifted the heavens and unmasked the universe. The courtyard, the kitchen, the city, the world – the whole of creation revealed itself to be nothing more than an elaborate stage set whose entire purpose had only ever been to guide the two of us into this moment.

"In that case… uh," she said, when it was over. "It's ridiculous. We've only known each other for… " She swallowed. "Anyway, sod it. I love you too."

Before I'd had the chance to absorb what she had said, she grabbed my hand tightly and led me towards the door. "Come on, before Max gets back."

We were lucky. Just a minute after I returned to my station, Max called down towards me.

"Er, Killian, do you have a moment?"

I followed him in struck silence into the dining room. There was a waitress, not yet changed, vacuuming in the corner by the window. Glasses were being polished and fresh orchids being placed in tall black vases. Even out here, everyone worked quietly; the hush a mixture of reverence, fear and self-importance.

Max nodded for me to sit at the table nearest the kitchen – Ambrose's favourite dining spot. He pulled out the chair opposite and sat, crossing his legs in that TV-AM way I had once so admired. I could see the place where his sock met his leg. I could see how thin his limbs were. Little spirals of dark hair curled on skin the colour of tripe.

"I was just a little concerned about your display earlier on," he said.

His tone was calm. He wasn't staring. In the dry melody of his voice, I was sure I could even detect the soft lift of a note of concern. Over his shoulder, the sommelier shot me an envious glance. I sat up bolt-straight.

"Sorry, Chef. I know discipline is important, Chef. And you do these things for a good reason. But that thing in particular…" I swallowed. My pulse lurched. "Maybe it's different with a woman."

His upper lip stiffened as he interrupted me.

"I am enquiring about the marks on your skin. Are you having problems at home?"

My colour rose as I decided to tell him what I'd once told Mr Callum, the PE teacher. "I was in a car accident when I was young. I was pretty cut up."

"And those fresh scabs on your arms? They are from a childhood incident too?"

"Just an accident at home, Chef. Nothing important."

"*Bon*," he smiled. "Good."

He stretched his left arm out on the table and stared at his manicured thumbnail for a moment.

"After my apprentices have been with me for some time, I like to take them to one side just to find out how they're getting on."

His grey eyes tracked up and down my face.

"Not finding it too tough?" he said.

"It's fine, Chef," I said. "I love it."

"Well, you must stop these petulant little displays of defiance. I run my kitchen as I do for a good reason. A less patient man than I would have fired you some time ago. But, as you know, we don't do that here."

"*Oui*, Chef."

A waitress I hadn't seen before walked by. I only saw her back as she glided past in regulation model fashion, one foot in front of the other, but that didn't prevent her leaving an impression. It held itself in the air for a tantalising moment, her static carnival – her shape, her movement, her posture, her sway, the way her wrists hung loose by her hips. And there was a scent: colourful and sherberty, its lovely fizziness fading very slowly beside us.

Max asked the Maître d', "Is that one new?"

"*Oui*, Chef?" she replied.

"She's wearing perfume."

"*Oui*, Chef", said the Maître d', before scurrying off obediently.

Perfume, I was to learn, wasn't permitted at King lest it interfere with the smell of the food. Max sat back in his seat and draped his hand over the chair next to him.

"That waitress," he said. "She looks a little like my first girlfriend, Grace."

He smiled and took a deep breath, filling himself with the memory.

"I'll let you into a secret. I used to be a very jealous boyfriend. Passionate, I used to tell myself, but that was a rather silly excuse. It was jealousy, pure and simple. Grace had had a boyfriend prior to me. I can't remember his name. I was – well, let me see – nineteen? Nineteen or twenty. Grace a little older. I'd somehow got it in my head that this ex-boyfriend had had the best of her. I think I'd seen a picture of her when she was sixteen, seventeen and… well, I realised that when a woman is fourteen or so she's too young to be really attractive. They can still look like an uncomfortable amalgam of Mum and Dad at that age, can't they? And by the time they're over thirty, say, they're past their best. Which means, logically speaking, there must be a point between those two ages when a woman is at her peak. There must be one afternoon, say, when her body and face are at their most sublime and everything else – her mood, her dress, the quality of the sun – coincides to make these few hours the ones in which she's at her most perfect. She'd never believe it, because to her it would have been the most wonderful day, but the truth is she'll never be as beautiful again as she has just been. It's terribly sad. It all drips away, doesn't it? I know it's not a very modish thing to say, but a woman's beauty is always her most prized possession, and for any female unfortunate enough to be born without it – well, that's a loss from which she never recovers."

By now the Maître d', without being asked, had delivered two espressos. Max took a sip of his, pushing his upper lip into his teeth and sucking it back as if to extract every last molecule of flavour from it.

"But anyhow, I became convinced, for some strange reason, that Grace had been at her most perfect when she was with her ex-boyfriend. And I just couldn't live with it. That was the first time I became obsessed with the idea of perfection. Luckily, nowadays, all that passion is directed at my food. Is that mango at its moment of perfect ripeness? Is that jus reduced to the exact point where any longer on the heat and it'll start to become syrupy? It's a much healthier way of expressing perfectionism, don't you think?"

I tried to think of something to say that wasn't "*Oui*, Chef".

"You could say the same about our job."

Underneath his top lip, Max slowly licked his teeth.

"How so?"

"Well," I said. "Is there a point where a chef is at his most talented? Is there one afternoon when he's cooking his best and he'd never believe it if you told him, because he thinks he's on fire, but he'll never be as good again?"

Max looked into the little cup that he was holding daintily in his thumb and forefinger.

"No, I wouldn't say so. Not at all," he said. "That's quite different. Quite, quite different."

There was a strange silence.

"Now why don't you tell me something about *your-self*?" said Max. "Are you courting? Getting along nicely with young Kathryn?"

"Well, I… I hope to."

He smiled back at me and a helpless grin broke out across my face.

"Good luck with that one," he said. "She's a fair cook. Pretty too. Bit straight-laced, though, it's always seemed to me. A bit sullen."

"I don't know," I said. "Maybe."

"Your mother must be pleased you're doing so well."

"Not really. She says that male cooks are just a bunch of Larry's."

He didn't respond.

"You know, Larry Graysons. Gays. She thinks I should be doing some good in the world. She thinks all the evil in the world is the fault of men. I think she expects me to do something about it."

His gaze had wandered above my head and seemed to settle on the front window of the restaurant. "Yes, of course," he said, unsmiling.

He sat forward abruptly, and his large eyes fixed onto mine.

"So, Killian. Now that we're friends again, why don't tell me what you know about the item on page 9 of today's *Evening Standard*."

I cleared my throat.

"Nothing," I replied. "I haven't seen it."

He moved closer; spoke more insistently.

"The report," he said, "apparently concerning me. My personal life. Information that must have come from this kitchen."

I shook my head.

"Come on, come on," he said, his voice thinning. "Don't be like that. You can talk to me. You can tell me. After all, I know full well who you socialise with. I've heard you myself, threatening to leak information to Nigel Dempster."

His mouth was smiling, but his eyes looked like holes in tarmac.

"It wasn't me," I said. "Honestly, Chef I wouldn't, I would never..."

Max stared at me for a long time. Two or three people walked past, not acknowledging us. And then, suddenly, he broke the spell.

"Very well," he said. "*Bon*. If it wasn't you, then I know what to do."

"Right," I said. "Good."

As we both moved to stand, our faces naturally broke contact. But, partly so I could remember the scene, I glanced back at him earlier than I otherwise might have done. He was wearing an expression so devoid of meaning, so utterly empty, it was startling.

* * *

A couple of hours later, Patrick called my name. He was holding the kitchen phone in his hand. "You're wanted in the office. Be quick."

I ran up the stairs with my head down. I knew which day this was and even though I had planned exactly what I was going to do, I could still feel a hot clamour rising in my chest and throat. I just wanted to be left alone to get on with my blackcurrants.

I knocked on the door and was summoned immediately.

"Well, look at the chef! Wonderful! Every inch the award winner." It was Mr Mayle, in a new-looking tan trench coat, paisley scarf and Oxford brogues that had been polished to a varnished mahogany. He'd dressed up, more smartly than I had ever seen him, in order to take me to the Young Saucier of the Year awards. The words evaporated from my tongue as he stood to greet me. Ambrose was sitting back in his chair, his usual red braces stretched over the foie-fed hillock above his hips, looking ostentatiously relaxed, as if keen to impress on his old friend that he was so much the king of his kingdom that its rule didn't even require him to sit up straight.

"I'm not going," I said. "I'm needed here. I'm sorry, sir. I'd forgotten you were coming. If you could collect my award…"

Mayle's hands squashed themselves in front of him. He looked crushed. Ambrose pulled himself up in his leather chair.

"Nonsense, Killian," he said. "This is a proud day for you and Robert. I'm sure the kitchen won't miss you."

"The kitchen will miss me, I think," I said. "We're an apprentice down now that Kathryn's been promoted."

Mayle took a step towards me and said, with beseeching eyes, "But please, Killian. Come on. I'm sure…"

"I'm sorry, sir. I've got to get back. Have a good time."

Chapter 29

By twelve o'clock that night, the brigade was beginning its final clean-down. All the steel units were being pulled from the walls and washed and tides of soapy water were pushed around our feet as the floor tiles were scraped, scrubbed, mopped and dried. It was the only part of the day in which we were allowed to chat, although it was mostly abusive banter which acted as both bonding glue and mettle-tester, with any crack in composure caused by the insults watched for and feasted upon. Still not fully used to the eighteen-hour shifts, it was easy to allow my exhaustion to overcome me. The others, I could tell, felt energised and victorious, having beaten back the forces of another double service.

That night, though, I was scrubbing my unit with even more determination than usual. I became aware of Ambrose coming into the kitchen, nose pinked and smile hardened by a night spent, presumably, entertaining friends and generally celebrating himself at his usual table.

"Attention!" he clapped. "Please, *mesdames*, *messieurs et gamins*. Don't stop what you're doing, but I'd appreciate it if you could give me as much attention as you can spare."

Everyone did as Le Patron had asked and popped their heads up. I paused, on my way back to the cleaning cupboard with a bucket, and noticed that someone was with him – Mr Mayle. He was holding a white presentation plate.

"Whilst you were all busy, Grosvenor House were doing their usual no doubt profoundly mediocre job of hosting the annual Young Saucier of the Year competition, a title that one or two of the wonderfully talented chefs present here have been shortlisted for in the past *and*, of course, the award our very own Max won years ago at the start of his long journey to international repute…"

The entire brigade had stopped. They could tell by the direction in which Ambrose kept looking that I was the winner. Carlo was smiling and nodding his head; the other apprentices spread their faces in expressions of simple astonishment. I dried my hands on my torchon and took a tentative step in the direction of Le Patron.

"It gives me great pleasure to announce the 1985 Young Saucier of the Year is our very own Killian Lone."

As I made my way towards Ambrose, the rest of the brigade began to clap. I watched my clogs slapping on the damp floor tiles and kept my head bowed, in an attempt at hiding the daft grin that had erupted across my face. As I got nearer, the appreciation of these marvellous men grew in strength and I began to feel as if I could hear every individual palm slapping another and I tried to hold the sound in my head, so that I could keep it for later and replay it again and again. Even Patrick was striking his muttony hands together. Everyone was doing so, except Max, who was leaning against the wall with the air of someone awaiting a late-running bus.

I shook Ambrose's cold right hand and took my plate from him, which was heavy and silly and brilliant. I tucked it under my arm and made a brief attempt at meeting the faces of the cooks, before dipping my chin again and grinning at my toes.

Beside Ambrose, Mayle stepped forward, flush-faced and wobbly on his heels. He had a Victorian-style pocket watch in his jacket. Its gold chain dangled as he spoke.

"I'd just like to say a few words to you all, if I may," he said. "I, like you, used to be a chef in a fine-dining restaurant. I was rather good at it, actually. I worked many long shifts for Ambrose, my business partner. And I have to tell you that I feel right at home being back. I could just dive right in there, right now, and grill off some beautiful filet mignon, sauté some gorgeous carrots in fine French butter, whip on a fresh rabbit stock, get a cassoulet bubbling or a fine lobster bisque."

Patrick sniggered. The smile vanished from my face.

"I suppose, looking at me now, it's probably hard to believe that the rather podgy old man that stands before you—"

To my left, Carlos muttered, "Can we go home now?" I tightened my grip on the plate and closed my eyes.

"—could have been a fine-dining chef in a restaurant of world repute. Even though I have been many years out of the kitchen, it still only feels like yesterday that I was doing double shifts, six days a week in clogs that were two sizes too big for me—"

Max shifted his weight against the wall and sighed.

"—not far from here, as a matter of fact, in a little side street just off Piccadilly. Anyhow, I digress. When young Killian here first walked through the door of my teaching kitchen, I must admit, I barely noticed him—"

I glanced at Max again. He looked back at me. A dark flurry of shame washed down the bones of my back.

"Great!" I said, placing my award beneath my knees.

"Thank you, Mr Mayle!" I started clapping my hands. He stopped talking. Patrick stood upright, a magnificent smile drawing his large, tired face upwards.

Mayle looked in my direction, as if to say, "What are you *doing?*" Patrick nodded his encouragement at me. I felt myself swell and rise and puff like a fast-baking loaf. "This is me," I said, still clapping, "saying, 'Shut the fuck up'."

The brigade ignited into laughter. It echoed off the tiles on the walls and off the suspended lights and the pots and the pans and the sinks and the ovens. Patrick let out a huge, spasmic guffaw and clapped his hands three times over his head. Mayle's jowls sagged. His fringe sat limp and damp and thinning on top of his sweaty head. His eyes sank to the floor.

"I also have a few words to say in gratitude to our young winner here."

The noise was killed instantly. It was Max.

"As you know," he began, his eyes moving around all the chefs, meeting them in turn. He looked thinner than ever, his hands rubbing warmth into themselves in front of him, all bony and crickety and slow. "I do not tolerate disloyalty in my kitchen. I expect, by now, you've all heard about the item in t-today's newspaper. Having conducted a thorough investigation this morning, and having been ably assisted by our talented young apprentice here, I have, this afternoon, dismissed Kathryn Riding for gross misconduct with immediate effect. Moreover, I will do my u-utmost," he twitched, with force, and stuttered, "t-to ensure she does not find meaningful employment in any serious kitchen again. That's all I have to say on the matter, apart from congratulations, Killian, for your prize, but more importantly for your brave show of loyalty today."

As one, the faces of the cooks in front of me took on a

long, hollow quality. For a moment, there was no sound at all. A drip of water bulged from a tap over an empty steel sink; a patina of blue light reflected off the plastic surface of a safety notice; a decapitated duck's head stared out from the top of an un-emptied waste bin. Someone at the back of the room blinked. For a second, we all just existed. And then, as if there had been a silent signal – bustle; the brigade operating without looking at me; without acknowledging that I even existed.

I strode down the length of the room and around the corner, into the pastry section. Andy was wiping down the sides of his sink.

"It wasn't me, Andy," I said.

He turned on the hot tap and the sound of water beating against metal filled the space. I watched as he slowly squeezed out his cloth beneath the stream. His knuckles bulged with the force of it.

"Did she go home?" I said. "Is she at the flat?"

He twisted the wet material into a tight spiral. A number of clear, bright trickles burst onto the draining board.

"She doesn't want to speak to you," he said. "Nor do I."

"It wasn't me, Andy," I said, suddenly wishing that I wasn't holding an award. "I didn't say anything. Tell Kathryn. Could you please tell Kathryn? I didn't say *anything*."

"Yeah, of course you didn't, mate," he laughed and, finally turned to face me. "I warned her about you. What is this thing you've got about Max? Have you got a crush on him or something?"

"I just want you to tell Kathryn," I said.

"She doesn't want to see you," he said. "Do yourself a favour. Piss off back to college. Nobody's going to want you here any more."

Chapter 30

I drove as fast as I could in Aunt Dorothy's old Peugeot, back to Dor. When I reached the cottage, I took the sledgehammer from the shed and tried to exorcise my rage by throwing it with furious strikes against my uncle's garden wall. I had a suspicion that what lay behind it was the "secret" Dorothy had warned me about.

It was more resilient than it appeared and the sharp knuckle of pain between my shoulder blades that I'd felt during my first shifts rose again, before spreading out and dropping to my lower spine. My neck stiffened, my arms throbbed, my fingers blistered. As the moon arced over my head and the elms gossiped in the forest around me, I relived all the aches of my six weeks at King, except this time I enjoyed them. Just before five, when the first rumours of dawn were becoming apparent behind the trees, the wall finally gave.

I stepped over the three-high lip of bricks that were too low to easily knock through. The space between the busted wall and the ancient gate was boggy and filled with a pointy kind of grass that was sticking up in spiny crowns. I pushed at the herb garden door. It was unpainted and of the same design as the one in the cottage, with its square-headed nails and heavy hinges, except these were so rusted they looked as if they were dissolving into the fabric of the wood. I shoved it with my shoulder, which just served to wedge it further into the earth behind it. It took almost ten minutes and all my remaining strength before I was able to squeeze myself inside.

By now, a blue haze was coming through the trees and the birds had begun their wild chorus. I trod slowly, careful not to let the brambles swallow my foot, and I tried to survey the garden. There was little contrast between the grey light and the thin dawn fog and it wasn't easy to see much detail. Perhaps it was just the angle I was viewing it at, but everything looked different from how it did before. The dead vegetation was all the same but there seemed to be more of the green shoots, with thick stems and fresh leaves, like flattened teardrops, every one a persuasive, plump green.

Flies buzzed over the garden, travelling in complex, busy directions. They seemed to inhabit an invisible airborne metro-polis, all en route to some essential desti-nation and then turning, immediately, to find another. They seemed convinced of their logic and yet there was a madness about their movements; a randomness and fervour that reminded me how much, as a child, I used to fear them. Waving them away, I rubbed a leaf from one of the plants and sniffed the pad of my thumb. I could only detect a faint earthy smell. Not one you'd necessarily associate with a herb, more a fungus or root. An early lick of dawn wind hit my cheeks as I picked a large leaf and put it in my mouth.

Immediately, my eyes dropped and I allowed the flavour to sink into my palate – that was the sensation, of it *sinking in*, soaking down into the roots of my taste buds, taking over my entire tongue and then gathering strength as it washed with a palpable kiss of pleasure down my throat.

There was a top note that carried a vague herby sweetness, not dissimilar to marjoram. But the booming, resonant flavours had more in common, in an obscure way, with some of the exotic foods I'd tried with Dorothy, like oysters, truffles and abalone. It was strangely organic, musky, intimate. A secret, adult taste.

And it was delightful. Incredible. Blissful. Like nothing I'd ever experienced before. Each morsel of leaf contained a complex symphony of pointillist glories that all coalesced into this heavenly whole. The deliciousness was so extreme that your instincts warned you off. It was as if some rogue God had taken the entire palette of gustatory pleasures and combined them for the purposes of mischief. It was a flavour that took ordinary beauty and violently challenged it; that took perfection and humiliated it.

My tongue, I realised, had actually begun to tingle. My palms were wet. I felt a gluey lurch of nausea and the dew of sweat on my forehead. Just as I was trying not to panic, the sickness in my belly lifted to be replaced by an effervescent heat that began to gather itself about my hips and pelvis.

And that's when it happened; this terrible sexual craving. I had never felt the pull so suddenly or so overpoweringly. There was very little I could do to satiate myself. I ran to the house and bolted the front door. Finding the bathroom, I did everything I could to relieve the maddening urge that had came over me.

I was eight again, at the foot of the stairs. Mary Dor was at the top. On the third step, in the centre, a clean, cold cup of milk. I reached for it. There was something in it; silvery, alive. I watched it for a moment. Struggling, whirring in circles, dancing its own death. I put the cup to my lips and drank. Mary watched. I felt the silvery thing crawling and buzzing as it went down.

Mary spoke. "Now it is done, so. Now you will no longer know the difference between God's miracles and the Devil's."

And she showed me her hands and her wrists were bound, tightly, with rope.

Up in the roof, I saw all the parts, the yellow, the red, the green and the black. Out amongst the elms, I could hear the children singing: "Earl's heart and earl's leafs and earl's lusts abounding. Earl's fires and earl's grace and earl's witch is burning."

And I knew that I was King of the Wastelands, King of the Hunger, King of the More and I knew that I could never stop them barking.

The old trouble, the quiet trouble, louder now, big and terrible and close.

Chapter 31

As I drove up the A21 towards London that morning, the fatigue and the strange night combined to make the world seem two-dimensional, as if it was all a projection that was running both too fast and too slow. As I drifted dazedly onto the M25, I couldn't stop thinking about the unbelievable flavour of that odd herb. If there was any way to harness it, to remove it from its goblinish effects, just imagine. I could make the most incredible sauce. And as for Dorothy – well, perhaps the long years in the cottage surrounded by all that sensed history had made her grow overly superstitious. The plant had some carnal, aphrodisiacal effect, some active component – that was obvious. But it wasn't magic. It was a product – and one which I would be fascinated to experiment with. First, though, I had to push through another day.

I walked into the locker room to find it choked full of silence. Everyone gave the impression they were concentrating extremely hard on what their fingers were doing: untying laces, fastening buttons, zipping up bags, sliding clogs onto feet. I dropped my rucksack onto the floor as Patrick passed by. "You're back, are you?" he said.

I didn't quite now how to respond.

"Still haven't had enough?" he continued.

"Of course not, Chef," I said.

"You've got a pair of bollocks, I'll give you that. You're hardly Mr Popular round here at the moment, you realise. Not after what happened with Kathryn."

"That was nothing to do with me," I said.

He gave a quick, powerless snort and walked away.

The previous week, I'd been charged with a new job: preparing the citrus for Max's signature dish, his deer and tangerine pie. Every morning, a new bag of thirty tangerines was delivered, twenty of which had to be juiced, the other ten segmented, deseeded and peeled for use in the garnish. Before they were squeezed, each piece of fruit had to be rolled with pressure on the chopping board, in order to loosen the summery liquid inside.

I'd just begun this process when Max walked up to me, the lid of his daily brand-new biro sticking like a medieval knight from the breast pocket of his dry-cleaned tunic. I instinctively looked at my hands to make sure there wasn't anything I could possibly be doing better.

"You," he said. "Stock rotation."

All the warmth from the previous day had evaporated. I placed the tangerine firmly on the chopping board so it wouldn't roll off and headed for the heavy, storm-coloured freezer door, where I found the protective coat and gloves to be missing from their hook.

"Does anyone know where the coat and the gloves for the freezer are?" I shouted into the kitchen.

I didn't see Patrick when he responded. I could only hear him.

"Fucking get on with it, dipshit."

I pulled down the steel lever and slid the door open. The shelves were filled with sacks of ice which was to be crushed and served in a bowl beneath the chilled melon soup. Above those were frozen peas and the steel tubs of sorbet and ice cream that I'd have to sort through and rotate, so the freshest was at the back. The light had a hollow, metallic quality and the place smelled of cold beef and rubber. The air in front of the recessed light was thick with cold. How could I possibly do this without gloves?

I crouched and began to pull the tubs onto the floor with my bare hands. There were glaces of nougat and walnut, Armagnac ice, sorbets of prickly pear, blackcurrant, acacia blossom, three types of apple and citrus – which was served in a halved and hollowed-out lemon.

The pain wasn't long in coming. It began as balls of low hurt deep inside my knuckles before spreading through the bones of my hands. My fingers started to sting as they stuck onto the icy metal containers; there was a constriction in my nostrils and a hardening in my sinuses that began to swell as if something was trying to break out of them.

The job took nearly twenty agonising minutes. All I wanted to do as I walked back into the kitchen was curl up in the toilet and push my hands between my legs for warmth, but I was desperate to know if someone had covered me on the tangerines, which should have been done by now. When I arrived back at my station, what I saw was Patrick stirring a small copper pan with his usual bullish intensity, wearing the thick orange freezer coat and black workman's gloves.

A crumble of laughter went through brigade and apprentices.

"You've got them…" I said. "You fucking…"

Patrick turned and pointed at me with his hot teaspoon which bled a quick trickle of sauce onto his clogs. His nose had reddened in the heat whilst the rest of his face remained the colour of beef dripping. His eyes looked tiny, as if they'd been shrinking away from the heat of the flames.

"Something you wanted to say, grass?"

I retreated back to my tangerines and picked up my knife from where I'd left it on the board. Something wasn't right. It was the quantity. There were supposed to be thirty pieces of fruit and... I made a quick count. Twenty-eight. I looked back towards Patrick. He'd gone – probably to take off the coat. I was aware of members of the brigade glancing at me; I could feel their flickers of attention like intermittent sparks of light.

Lunch service went by in a swimmy slick of time, the loss of Kathryn in my vicinity feeling ever more boundless with each hour. I managed to remain invisible until just after two p.m.

"You there," said Max.

I turned to see him standing at the top of the kitchen, the yellow glow from the pass casting cruelly over his cheekbones and sunken temples. He was holding up a large square black plate with the King logo on the side of it. It was smeared with a drying crust of reddy-brown sauce and there was something else on there as well: a dark nugget in the corner.

Max beckoned me with his manicured finger.

As I loped towards him, I could see it was a pip. A fresh, nearly-white tangerine pip.

"You have ruined my signature dish."

His tongue ran over his lower lip.

"Do you know who this plate belongs to?"

"*Non*, Chef."

He growled with bitter menace.

"Zsa Zsa fucking Gabor."

He jabbed a finger into my chest.

"Do you think you've made it, now that you've won that ridiculous prize? Do you think you can do what you like now?"

His fury generated a kind of electric field; a livid haze of energy through which his ugliest features became yet more grotesque.

"*Non*, Chef."

"*Non*, Chef, *non*, Chef…"

I stared back at him. I fixed all my muscles in place.

"Why did you sack Kathryn?" I said, quietly, my breaths becoming rapid and shallow. "Why did you do it?"

They were listening, the other chefs. They were pretending that they weren't, but they were.

"She was disloyal." His nostrils thinned. "Just as you told me."

"I didn't—"

He threw the plate at my feet and it smashed against my right ankle. I couldn't remember seeing him this furious before. His upper lip was quivering and lifting at the sides. He was actually baring teeth. When he spoke again it was in a whisper.

"You disgust me, do you know that? You make me feel unnerved." And then he left.

* * *

Two hours later I was cleaning celery in the between-service lull when Max approached in that severe, mincing way that I had learned to dread.

"Come," he said.

The corridor filled with the dull thump of clogs on antique carpet as I followed him. There was a boil on the back of his neck, nestling in the creases of yellowing skin, and his manicured nails appeared chewed. He opened the door to a large broom cupboard and nodded for me to enter. It was illuminated by a bare low-powered bulb and there were buckets and gloves and mousetraps and cockroach bait and white plastic bottles filled with cleaning chemicals. The light swung on its wire in response to the sharply closing door; the shadows of the mops and pots around us moving across the walls in an excitable, jeering dance.

In the middle, there was a wooden chair and a pile of sealed Tupperware boxes with a filthy torchon draped over them. Patrick was there, comfortable amongst the darkness and poisons, his smug smile pulled over his nibblish little teeth.

"Sit," said Max.

I did as I was told.

"Don't look so worried," he smiled. "It's the last day of your *stage* tomorrow, and this is just something we like to do with apprentices when they reach the end. A bit of fun. A tasting session. A palate test. You should consider yourself lucky, not everyone gets this treatment. Only special apprentices."

I gripped the seat, feeling the gritty dust on its underside.

"*Merci*, Chef."

"Special," he said, lightly. "And you *are* special, aren't you?"

I swallowed, my tongue dry, my throat tightening.

"*Non*, Chef," I said.

"Award winner!" he said, loudly. "Very confident young man. Confidence is good. But sometimes confidence can go too far. Tell me, what makes you think you can question me? What makes you think you can defy me in front of my brigade?"

"I'm sorry, Chef. I didn't —"

Max opened his hands up. The lines that ran across his palms were deep and red and purple against translucent skin.

"Don't panic," he said. "Don't worry. You poor thing, perhaps you misunderstand me when I say that I have never sacked an apprentice. Perhaps you took that to mean that you are somehow trapped here. But you must know – this is not a prison. You can leave at any time you want."

He looked enormous, looming over me like that. It is how I'd always imagined him – huge and all-powerful. Awesome in his height and presence.

"Do you understand?" he repeated.

"*Oui*, Chef."

"Now, I realise that you consider yourself a three-star apprentice and here at King we have cruelly made you wallow in the squalor of two, but still…"

"No, Chef– "

"Shut up," he said, his words popping out in a sudden punch of uncontrolled temper. "Now, sit back and concentrate. If you pass this test, Chef Patrick and I will not hesitate to congratulate you. But if you decide that you can't do it, if you want to leave, that's just fine. There's no shame in it. You can finish it at any time. Stand up and go. It really is that simple. Go. But if you do happen to decide to leave, you must not stop until you reach wherever it is you came from. Okay. *Bon*. So, Patrick's going to blindfold you."

I closed my eyes, my fingers gripping my seat ever harder, as the grimy torchon was knotted around my head.

"Tongue out," he said.

I heard Patrick move to my left. There was the brush of material, the popping of a lid, a chink of cutlery. I flinched as something tipped onto my tongue. It was lukewarm.

Waxy. I bit down and felt fat separate from flesh. The flavour was sweaty, salty and hollow and it was so greasy that my teeth slid about on it.

"Bacon," I said. "Raw."

Trying not to gag, I used my tongue to push the semi-masticated mush into a ball before forcing it into the back of my mouth and down.

"Streaky," I said. Then, remembering the style that was used at King. "Oak-smoked."

"Oak-smoked!" said Max, with a sarcastic laugh in his voice. "Oh, bravo."

I heard Patrick snigger.

"*Bon.* Very good. Next."

Despite the fact that my mouth was coated in a layer of thick slime, I could tell what the next ingredient was the moment it landed on my tongue.

"Chilli," I said. "Piri-piri."

There was a silence.

"He's very specific isn't he?" said Max, irritably.

I spent a moment trying to generate enough spit so that I could wash some of the intensity of the heat away. I heard the rustle of a packet as a film of feverish sweat soaked onto my brow and the water in my eyes threatened to well.

"No, don't cut it," I heard Max say. "Put it all in."

This one was even easier. These were my dad's favourites. Patrick was pushing it in quicker than I was able to chew. I was on the verge of choking, but luckily my saliva glands had been prompted to fire a wash of pre-vomit spit. I pumped my teeth on it as quickly as I could manage and smushy clags began to spill from the corners of my mouth and fall to my lap. The texture was the worst thing, like something verminous that had decomposed to the consistency of mash. There was an undeniable farty note in the background, which hung beneath the dominant flavours of fat, offal and old grey meat.

"Sausage," I said as soon as I was able. "Pork. Wall's."

It was the act of saying the name out loud rather than swallowing the thing that finally induced a gag as wide as a lion's roar. Strings of gastric phlegm hurled out and fell, splatting coldly down my chin.

I could do this. I had to.

"Ten out of ten so far," said Max.

If I could pull this off and just speak to Max; just make him understand; sit him down and explain how much I had loved him; tell him about the pictures on my bedroom wall. We could talk about what's happened, forget it all, reset it all...

"Next!"

I smelled the next one coming. The fact that my sinuses had been cleared out by the piri-piri meant that the savage bang of the old fish entrails entered my nostrils in a wave that was almost overwhelming. Patrick shovelled a heaped dessertspoon full into my mouth and they squished out into my cheeks, each slippery node, tube and lump picked out in vile detail by my tongue. It felt as if the tastes and textures were filling my head and I had to clamp my hand over my lips to force my system not to reject them and their flavours of stale blood and gut rot.

I wretched, twice. A layer of chilled sweat formed just below my eyes.

"Entrails," I said. "Herring."

"A little something to wash it down with?" said Max. "Purse your lips."

At first I thought it was olive oil. Then I felt the layer of carbon, tiny particles of black, and the flavours of scorch, fat and grime hit the back of my tongue.

"From the extractor fan," I said.

There was a silence.

"The extractor fan above the meat station."

Neither of them responded for a moment.

"Is that blindfold on properly?" Max asked.

Patrick gave the knot a sudden tug that threw my head back painfully.

"Looks like it."

"Hm," said Max. "Well, I suppose if you've been raised feeding from the trough, you are going to be familiar with the tastes of its fruits."

Patrick smirked. I became aware of more activity by the Tupperware near my feet.

"Don't bother with all that other stuff," Max said to Patrick. "Go straight to that one. No, not that. No. Right. Did you get some?"

"Yeah," said Patrick.

My stomach lurched as Max addressed me again.

"Tongue out, flat," he said. "No – flat. Flatter. Flat like a tray."

Somebody's fingers clamped my nostrils shut with a sharp pinch.

"Oh, God that's revolting," Max muttered. "Oh, you didn't..."

There was a hesitation.

"Go on," said Max.

"Yeah?" said Patrick.

"Go on."

I gagged once, twice, three times.

"No," I said, trying to block it by waving my hands to and fro.

"*Oui*," said Max, gripping the sides of my jaw with his thumb and forefinger. "Oh, *oui, oui, oui*. Tongue out."

A cheese biscuit was laid on my tongue. I pulled it in and crunched, barely believing this was happening. There it was, this gritty paste. Warm; the temperature of blood. My nose was released. I chewed. It stuck on my teeth. It was the particles that tipped me over. I felt a seed-like nugget, then something – a kernel of something – burst open.

The sounds that came from me then were not of my voicebox but from my gut. It was primal.

My nostrils were released. I heard them move out of the way. Cold, fizzing spasms ran up my cheeks and down my neck and I could feel sweat on my wrists. The vomit, when it came, was wetter than I expected and hot from the chilli.

"Uhh, the dirty fucking animal," said Patrick. "He's got it all over himself."

"Have you quite finished?" Max asked.

"It's shit," I said. "On a Ritz cracker." I took a guess. "Chef Patrick's shit." There was a surprisingly strong additional flavour, separate from that of the cracker. "And he's been eating cheese. Blue cheese. Roquefort?"

There was another silence.

"How the fuck did he know?" said Patrick.

Nothing seemed to happen for some time. There was a sound of movement, then material being moved about. It hit my chest first. Then Patrick adjusted himself and the hot, salty tasteless spray of urine hit me. I squeezed my mouth shut and closed my eyes hard behind the torchon. When it died down, after maybe ten seconds, I sensed that only Patrick was in the room.

"We can't have you in the kitchen in that state," he said. There was a hesitation. And when he spoke again, an undeniable tremor of concern in his voice. "Piss off home. Sort yourself out."

Having changed and washed my face, I took the bus

to Brixton and knocked on Kathryn's door. Nobody answered. I might have been freezing and filthy with cloying vomit and urine, but I wouldn't give up. I sat there on the step, my bony knees raised up to the level of my chin, and watched the people coming to and from the nearby market as the train rattled angrily across the bridge above us all. That peculiar man, the homeless painter, was busy beneath the lamp post just outside her door. I began to rock gently back and forth, my teeth clenching and releasing painfully on my tongue and my right heel bouncing up and down. I sat there, getting up every now and then to knock, for more than an hour.

Finally, the door opened an inch.

"Go away," said Kathryn.

I pushed and the chain scraped against the wood, the brass bolt clanking in its housing.

"I have to speak to you."

A ribbon of dull light fell on her nose. Her eyes were in darkness. I wanted to put my hand through the gap. I wanted to feel her.

"Why don't you go and sit on Max's doorstep?" she said. "You seem the stalkerish type. He lives in Chelsea, I think."

I moved my head about in an attempt to get a clearer view of her. "Kathryn, I didn't say anything. He's lying."

"No, it's my fault. I knew your career would always be more important than me. That's fine, you know, you go and be a good, loyal, successful boy. Just leave me the *fuck* alone whilst you're doing it."

She would see that I understood her, and that she understood me and the accident of us finding each other was something like a miracle. I had to make her know.

"But listen to me, we both want to be great as much as

each other," I said. "We both want to be executive chefs at King or somewhere. We'd both do anything for it. It's like, you know…" I tried to think of an example. "Like when you work a double shift instead of seeing your mum. I understand it, I get it."

"Cunt!"

The door slammed.

"No!" I kicked it. The sole of my shoe left a scuff of black rubber on the paintwork. "No! Kathryn!" I kicked it again and again. "Kathryn!"

I waited for another hour or so. There was nothing much to do, except to watch the homeless man. He was oddly dressed for a vagrant, in a mangy tweed suit with a bow tie over an old white shirt. I began to wonder what he was up to. He was sitting in a picnic chair, leaning forward under the homemade awning that he'd fashioned from some opened-out bin liners he'd taped together. Whatever he was working on, under there, he was evidently doing it with considerable care.

I examined him, from my place in the shadows. Suddenly, he looked directly at me.

"Sorry," I said. "I was just – "

"Drawing," he said.

The whites of his eyes had a yellow tint. There were three teeth missing from his lower jaw.

"I've seen you here before," I said.

"Every day, oh yes, indeed."

He looked proud; delighted to be in conversation.

"What do you draw?"

"Precious stuff. W-where we met," he said. "My wife and I."

"That's what you draw? Every day?"

He smiled wide and it was wet and foul – greys and

browns and blacks and livid swells of red. More like an infected wound than a mouth.

"Oh yes, indeed I do," he said. "Oh yes, indeed, very much I do, oh yes. Every day and every night. Always here, yes, indeed. Keep trying. Keep drawing. Never give up. Never never give up. Please," he gestured to what I now understood to be a covered easel. "Look."

I stood and peered carefully under the awning, and squinted at his pad. It was in pencil, and it was immediately clear that he had sketched the same scene countless times, one version over the top of the other. You could just about see two people in the middle of it all, in some sort of embrace. He'd drawn the lovers so often that they had become monstrous, dark lines scored onto dark lines, their eyes a torment of black layers. In several places, the pencil had gone right through the thick paper, leaving great gashes and rents.

"Oh yes, you see," he said, putting his head close to mine. "Perfect, you see. I do it again, all again and again and all over again. I have to make it perfect. Perfect, you see? Always and never, nothing else than perfect."

Chapter 32

I returned to Dor to find storm clouds boiling darkly, stretching in all directions over the elm forest. The whole place cowered under an atmosphere of bluster and hectoring. I couldn't remember ever seeing rain before in Dorothy's little sun-trap, and as I stepped over the lip in the wall and squeezed into the herb garden, I felt the first fat tears of what promised to be a dramatically wet few hours.

"*Christ*," I whispered to myself when I realised what had happened.

The cloud of flies had thickened and maddened. Their movements were too fast for the eye to follow and they seemed to have been attracted to and excited by the herbs. Hundreds more leaves had grown over night. Tribes of plants pushed themselves up through the spaces between the darkness. They rose with proud, keen and wobbling heads. I entered the humming zone of insects and began to pick. Flies hit my face repeatedly. After perhaps fifteen minutes, I felt a gust of warm air and the weather broke. I ran into the kitchen and, without stopping to remove my sodden coat, reached under the sink for some red onions and began chopping. As I was unscrewing the cap on the tawny port, the telephone rang.

"Killian?"

"Mr Mayle?"

Could it be him? The voice shared my teacher's biscuity timbre, but it seemed so graspless, so removed.

"I'm having to call now, because you haven't had the courtesy to get in touch," he said.

"Okay?"

"Well, it's your final day at King tomorrow and I don't yet know whether or not you'll be back at college on Monday. I contacted Ambrose but he wasn't much help. He had yet to speak with Max about it so was unsure. But I can only assume, as you're not there at the moment, that we will be seeing you?"

"I'm in," I said.

"You *are*?"

I gripped the receiver. "Of course," I said, with a lightly insulted laugh. "Max just gave me the afternoon off as a reward. A treat for all my hard work."

There was a moment of quiet.

"Well, congratulations," he said. Some of his warmth returned. I heard it and I felt it, too, lifting through my body. "I'll be sure to tell the class the good news. They'll be delighted for you."

I experienced a sudden and almost overwhelming fondness for him.

"Thanks for all your help, sir," I said. "It's all because of you."

I wished he was there with me now. I wished he could help me.

"Yes, well… Killian. Be careful. Don't…"

The drenched wind swiped at the roof above me. Glass shook in the panes. I stood there, alone.

"Yes," I interrupted him. "I know."

I finished preparing my sauce. This time, though, I

added just half of the small, teardrop-shaped leaf. At the moment it reached the correct consistency, I dipped my teaspoon in the sauce and blew on it. I was in such a state of urgency that extra space seemed to have been pushed between the seconds. I was actually aware of the time passing between the stuff hitting my tongue and the taste being detected.

My eyes were the first to go and then the back of my throat – a feeling of release as the pleasure of it caused muscles to involuntarily relax throughout my body. I groaned and grabbed onto the kitchen worktop as if to support myself. The most curious thing about it was that if you weren't looking for the herb, you wouldn't know it was there – this earthy, corrupt hum which was somehow redolent of young, intimate, sweated skin. It rang through all the sauce's extant layers, drawing out in each previously unknown depths of flavour. The port sang new hymns of cherries and strawberries; the tomatoes became prouder and juicier, the Worcester sauce took on a cavernous spice and tang. The whole thing become three-dimensional. It seemed to drench the palate and the lust it generated for more was thrilling; magical. But then, disaster: the heat and then the brutally gathering sexual urge.

I woke up twelve hours later in the place where I'd dropped off, on the bathroom floor. The alarm was sounding down the corridor in the bedroom.

I knew, as I scrubbed my skin in a madly steaming shower, that if I was to get this right, I had to think like a grown-up; separate the personal from the professional. This was *business*. Max had been as good as his promise: he had not dismissed me, given up on me, even when I had erred. Surely I had proved myself. I had survived the worst of his apprentice tests. I had done enough now. I had played their game and passed it. Surely I would be offered a job as full-time ouvrier.

Leaving the house for work, I tried not to notice what I was doing as I pushed the small, quietly dying leaf deep into my back pocket.

* * *

As I worked at my basil that morning, I tried to concentrate, but it was impossible not to think of Kathryn. I wondered what she'd think if I was told I hadn't proved worthy of a paid position in this kitchen. What would she think of me then? *Would* she think of me then?

I kept my eye on the station at which Ambrose's lunch was usually prepared at eleven thirty each day. The moment I saw Malcolm bending into the fridge beneath it, I walked purposefully up to him.

"Change of plan," I said. "Ambrose wants me to do his lunch today."

For all Malcolm's youth, he still managed to look five years younger than he actually was, with his silky blond hair on his upper lip and jaws.

"Says who?"

"Says Patrick," I said.

"Bollocks." He stood for a moment, holding a full steel milk jug. "Really?"

"You'll probably get a go tomorrow," I shrugged.

He hesitated.

"I don't think so."

What would Mr Mayle say if I was dismissed? What about Mark House? My mum? I grabbed Malcolm's wrist, circling its skin with my thumb and forefinger.

"*What are...?*" said Malcolm, looking down, half irritated, half confused. I squeezed.

Flashes. Cigarette smoke, menthol. Steam.

"*Argh!*"

"Not today," I said.

Just like your father.

"Get off!"

I squeezed it harder, pushing my nails in.

"Tomorrow," I said.

When it comes, when it happens, you have to be strong enough to be good.

I gave Malcolm's arm a final jerk. His milk jug dropped, clanged on the tiles and bounced once, its contents flying from its mouth in a small eruption of white and wet.

"Fuck!" he said. "You fuckin' freak." He rubbed at his skin. "That *hurt.*"

"Sorry, Malcolm, it's just what I've been told." I nodded towards my *mise-en-place*. "Could you give us a hand with that basil?"

As he loped off, I reached into the back of the fridge for my supplies. With them all laid before me, it was with a sense of sudden vertigo that I realised that *everything* depended on these modest ingredients. Everything, that onion. Everything, that bottle of sauce. Everything, that half-spent, crusty-lidded tube of tomato purée. I couldn't risk it. I had to use the herb in my sauce, just to make sure. I *had* to. It was obvious. And then, as I began to chop, it wasn't.

I could feel her around me. There was Dorothy, as I sweated off the onions and I added the port and the tomatoes and everything else. There was Dorothy, as I felt for the herb that I had put into my pocket that morning. There was Dorothy, as I hesitated over the pan and the steel and the fire. There was Dorothy as I left the herb undisturbed and decided, finally, to be good.

Chapter 33

"Oh," said Ambrose when I arrived with his heavy silver tray. "No Malcolm?"

"To be honest," I said, being careful not to slip on the loose, frayed rug. "It's my last day. I just wanted to see how you thought I'd got on."

Ambrose was leaning forward, holding a pair of half-moon spectacles between his thumb and forefinger.

"Oh, of course. Silly me," he said. "How could I forget that it's *you* who's in charge of what I eat for my lunch?"

I noticed the size of his desk. There were little carved elephant heads on its corners and its feet were fat and swollen like an old woman's ankles. I lowered the tray slowly and removed the cloche. Ambrose's eyes fell disappointedly to his lunch. He sighed and put his glasses down beside it.

"Reports on your *stage* have been less than satisfactory," he said. "I'm told there's a certain sloppiness. Tangerine pips left in pies and so on. That's not the end of the world in itself." He shrugged. "Could be nerves, youth… Sloppiness can sometimes be trained out of a cook your age. But, overall, Max describes you as mediocre."

"I'm not mediocre," I said, quietly.

"You did very well to win the Young Saucier and, I have to say, when you manage to make it properly, this sauce is good. But – " His face became and cold serious. "Chef Max tells me that there are questions as to its provenance."

"What?" I said.

"He says you purloined the recipe. Stole it."

"But *I* came up with this, at my aunt's house," I said, breathing heavily.

Ambrose gave an impatient shake of the head.

"If your thieving of the recipe wasn't enough of a mark against your name, Max tells me you have a poor palate. Palate, I'm afraid, is like character. It's just one of those things you're born with. You either have it or you don't and, it must be said, it would be highly unusual for a chap like you to have the sort of refined sensibilities that we insist upon here at King. Someone like you can have a very nice career in hotels, golf resorts, Trusthouse Fortes, that sort of thing. So," he glanced again at his cooling plate. "Cheer up and Godspeed. And by the way, if there are any reports in the *Evening Standard* that arouse our suspicions over the next six months, we'll know exactly where to direct our solicitors."

Over the endless moments during which Ambrose had been speaking, the two images of Max that I held in my head finally corresponded. Everything Kathryn had said about him was true. And, worse than that, he hated me. *Hated* me. Of course he did. An ominous weight gathered in my face. I remembered that afternoon at Sports Day, when Mark House pinned me to the floor and said what he had said about the person I'd loved. I could feel it again, the swelling in my throat. The choking.

"So I'm afraid that's that," said Ambrose.

I touched the corner of my eye. My finger came back wet.

"Are you okay?"

I nodded.

"Well, there's no use standing there looking sorry

231

for yourself," he said. "There's nothing you can do."

Max hated me. Of *course* he did.

"It's for the best, really. Stealing recipes, calling them your own. It's the kind of professional dishonesty that's usually an indicator of deeper troubles. Working at this level would only make them worse. Now go on, then. That's right. Goodbye."

I couldn't speak. I turned to leave.

"Don't think me cruel," he said. "It's just this business we're in. You understand, we can't have B-players like you and that girl at a place like King."

I stopped, midway down the carpet.

"What – Kathryn?" I said. "But she was good. You gave her a job."

"Her priorities were all wrong," he said, adding with a mutter, "Constantly blithering on about her bloody mother."

He picked up his knife and fork. I walked back to his desk and leaned over it to retrieve his plate.

"What *are* you doing?"

"Sorry, Ambrose," I said. "I'm really very sorry. I forgot to season your sauce."

He shrugged, his expression drenching me in contempt.

I could see my hand shaking as I placed the cloche back over his food. I ran carefully with the tray back to the kitchen. At the stove, I picked out the oval of fillet steak with my fingers and put it aside, before spooning as much of the sauce as possible back into a pan.

Unable to bare it any longer, I grabbed for a paring knife, pulled up my sleeve and enjoyed the tender resistance of my skin in the moments before it split. But it was too late to stop what was coming. I hadn't cried for so long and as I stood there, with the kitchen dancing obliviously behind me, a warm snake-head of wet made its tentative way down my left cheek as generous reserves of tears gathered beneath both eyes. I continued working, adding a splash more port, half a teaspoon of purée and subtle doses of all the necessary herbs, spices and condiments in order to inflate it back to its almost-cooked state so I could bring it all back down again to the point where its disparate flavours perfectly coincided.

I reached into my back pocket for the herb and tore off the tiniest crumb, flicking it from the pad of my thumb into the pan. It was greedily taken under and, in the strange state that had overcome me, I could almost detect something about the sauce change. My vision had taken on a zoomed-in quality: I could see the entire landscape of the sauce, the cool wet peaks and the hot valleys of its shifting topography. Under the flat white kitchen light it took on an unusual luminous quality. Eddies of steam appeared to arrange themselves as gaping mouths.

As I worked, my mind rebelled. Dorothy. That was it, now. I had defied her. It was done. Clearly I was not the good boy that she had believed in. But probably, you know, she was being over-protective. I was the grown-up now. Dor was mine. These herbs were mine. I would use them just this once, just to nudge me past this difficulty. They would secure me the job, which should have been mine anyway. Then, somehow, I could act to get Kathryn rehired. I would use the herbs only to do what *should* have been done in the first place. They would be a correction, a making-good. Yes, an act of justice.

Once the sauce was ready, I splashed water on my face to hide my crying and mounted the steps for what I realised might well be the last time.

"Here," I said to Le Patron on my return. "Sorry about that. All done now. Just perfect."

I turned to leave and, over my shoulder, said, "Goodbye, then. Thanks for giving me a go."

Ambrose peered irritably down at his plate. "Fine. Fine. Yes. Okay." He waved me away.

I closed the door behind me and waited at the top of the stairs; the music of the kitchen building exquisitely to its lunchtime crescendo without me coming from below. Nothing. I began walking down and stopped on the third step. I thought I had heard some chinking or knocking or... no.

Back at my station, I picked up my chopping board and took it to the corner sink with the pans where, despondently, I began blasting them with the hose. I thought, again, about West Kent. I wondered whether Kathryn would ever let me speak to her and, even if I could convince her of my innocence, whether she'd want to see me when I was nothing more than another shit student in a shit town in shit England.

With the noise of the water, I have no idea how I became aware that someone had walked up behind me.

"Ambrose?" I said, as I turned.

On the wall behind him was a large blue electric fly-killer. Its dense blue light fell over his neck and shoulders in a humming coating of ghostly material. Long shadows were thrown beneath his eyes, nose and chin. His parting had collapsed over his forehead. His hands hung limp by his sides, his mouth half open, his jaw moving slightly as if trembling. His chest rose and fell beneath his shirt.

"How did you make that sauce?" he said eventually.

I shrugged and glanced over at the station where I'd prepared it, as if to wake the snoozing memory.

"Just the usual way," I said. "Port, tomatoes, paprika, Worcester, fennel. I didn't get the seasoning quite right the last two times I made it for you. Actually, the last time, Max made me serve it to you ten minutes before it was ready so it was a bit sloppy."

Amrbose glanced at his shoes and frowned. The insect-killer flickered and buzzed as it sent its killing charge into a stray fly.

"Did he really?"

"Was it okay?" I asked. "Your lunch?"

All the life inside him was concentrated in his eyes. They pulsed with electricity and greed and possibility. But he didn't say anything at all. He just stood there in his red braces and his priceless white shirt. He just stood there by the sink and stared at me.

Chapter 34

Up in Ambrose's office, there was only the plate. I mean, there was everything else, of course – the obscene pictures, the stentorian desk, the mob of awards on the shelf – but the moment I walked through the door, my eyes focused exclusively on that black square of fine bone china. All that was left of his lunch was a faint ghostly brown hardness painted onto the plate's surface with finger smears, and a steak rind that had been sucked so clean it seemed stripped naked, lying prone and trembling and ravished on the rim.

Ambrose was in silhouette, standing by the window, hands behind his back and gaze cast towards the roofs of central London. His legs, meanwhile, were jiggling.

"Talk me through this sauce again," he said.

"It's just a case of treating the ingredients correctly," I said. "Not just bunging them in at a rough temperature. Sauces, it's more like pastry cooking. You need to be absolutely precise about your quantities, timings and temperatures. You have to know at exactly what level of heat each ingredient will yield its absolute best flavour – that's the secret. It's like science." I paused, worried that I was overcooking it a bit myself. "But I have practised a lot with that sauce, obviously. It's mostly practice."

Ambrose turned towards me, rubbing the tip of his tongue repeatedly over his lower lip, as if in an attempt to dig out some leftover flavour from beneath the surface of his skin. As he spoke, he kept losing control of his eyes, which would bounce between me and the plate before he could reassert his will and point them back out towards the window.

"And you could make it again, just like that?" he said. "You could do it again and again and again? It's consistency that marks the professional, you know. My chief concern is that you've made this for me two or three times now and it's ranged from very good to horrible... and now..."

"Of course," I said. "Of course I could. This sauce... " I shrugged "... this is nothing, really."

He glanced at his plate and blinked three times in quick succession. I noticed he had begun moving his lips almost invisibly against each other, like a man in the early stages of possession.

"Well, let's see, shall we?" he said eventually. "Let's go downstairs and make another. Come on, we'll do it together."

"Sure. Fine."

In the four seconds it took me to walk to the door I must have imagined and rejected at least half a dozen ways of extracting myself from this potentially disastrous situation.

"Damn," I said, stopping at the base of the stairs. I could see the shapes through the open kitchen door: the churn of dogs moving this way and that; the dance that accompanies the song. "I've used the last of the Worcester sauce. It's not a standard kitchen supply – I brought it in especially and it's all gone. I'll dash out and pick some up. I'll give you a knock when I'm back."

Ambrose moved to speak, his face darkening with questions.

"I just have to go to Mace," I smiled. "You're not going to come with me to Mace?"

"No," he said, snapping out of it. He waved me off with a fey flick of the hand. "Yes, you go."

I waited in a corner of Stephen Mews until I was sure he'd be back in his office, before sliding back through the kitchen to begin the sauce without him. It was all bubbling heartily, just a minute or so away from being at that quiltish consistency – so essential for a good sauce – that summons up the sense memories of being cosseted and caressed and soothed on cold evenings. I reached into my pocket for the leaf.

"Fuck it," I muttered.

I dropped in a double quantity, gave it a stir, poured the lot into a porcelain ramekin and finished it off with a couple of pinches of freshly ground black pepper. Perfect.

"I thought we were going to do that together?" said Ambrose when I walked into his office with my fragrant gift.

I held it forward, giving the scent a chance to take him.

"Have a taste," I said. "See what you think."

There was something of the obedient schoolboy about how perfectly he was sitting upright. I could see him as a nine-year-old, in his cap and shorts and mittens. He took a spoonful of the sauce and sniffed it. Shadows moved across the ceiling, cast by the traffic below. He moved in his seat. Silently, he swallowed another spoonful. Then another. He groaned.

"Is it okay?"

He looked as if he was going to cry with pleasure.

"I'm not entirely convinced it's the same as the last one," he began. "It's different somehow."

"It *is* the same," I said. "It's exactly the same."

He smiled again and moved his hand distractedly towards his crotch.

"Perhaps you'll give me five minutes whilst I finish some things. Then we can do it again. I'm just curious to know how you've made this, that's all. I'm sure you understand. My friend at the Young Saucier did tell me your concoction was good, but…" a greasy, grey toothed smile lashed out across his face. "You'll indulge a curious old gourmand?"

I couldn't understand it. I felt a sudden heat in my throat.

"You know, I've made this for you four times, Ambrose," I said. "Either you like it or you don't."

He looked up at me, his eyes lizardy and fierce.

"What I mean is," I said, "I don't want to be rude, but I don't work for you any more. If you give me a job, I'll make this sauce for you as often as you like. You can serve it on the menu. It's all yours. You can have it. I'm bored of it anyway. I've got much better sauces than this."

His antique wooden chair squealed as he crossed his legs. He glanced into the ramekin and pulled it just a little way towards him.

"You'll need to work on your consistency."

"I'll work on whatever you tell me to."

"And then there's Max. I'll be frank, if I may. Max's reaction to you was…" He swallowed. "The truth is, he doesn't want you anywhere near him. I mean, I don't know, exactly, what you did—"

I felt as if something hot and invisible was trying to push me over. My eyes lost focus momentarily.

"I don't care about Max," I said. "I won't work with him."

My legs began to fizz with weakness. Ambrose's gaze followed me as I pulled out a chair and sat down.

"Well then, what on earth are you suggesting then?" he said.

"Is it true you're opening a French place? Glamis?"

He reared back slightly.

"Dear me, you *are* well informed, aren't you?" There was a silence. He picked up a fat black fountain pen and put it down again. "Well, Glamis might work actually. Although I *am* concerned as to how you came to find out about it." He leaned forward, towards the ramekin which seemed to distract him. "May I ask who told you?"

I ignored him as he took another spoonful and gave a soft, involuntary groan. Behind him was a shelf of small silver statuettes of women: a naked adolescent with breasts like tender kisses; an adult woman weeping into her own arms; another with her hands in the air screaming at the gods. I surveyed them, emptily, my mind filled with thoughts that I'd never had before. New thoughts of Max.

"I'd want a senior position," I said.

"Don't be bloody ridiculous," he yelped. "You're an apprentice! You'd be lucky to be on the *line* in one of my kitchens!"

"I'm the best saucier you'll get."

"You're too young," he said. "You don't have the experience."

"What about Alain Ducasse? Two stars by twenty-seven."

"It's impossible, Killian. Absolutely impossible. I'm terribly sorry. I admire your ambition. You're more like Max than you probably realise, but I think this time you're letting your hunger for success cloud your powers of reason. But do not worry. You will have your moment. I'm certain I can find a place for you at the bistro."

"I want to be head chef."

He rose a little from his chair.

"You *can't* be head chef!" he said.

"Then I'll take my sauce to Nico."

"Oh fuck off," he shouted.

The rage sent him to his feet.

"How dare you?" he demanded. "Who in the name of God do you think you are?"

I leaned forward over his desk, picked up his fountain pen and scratched the phone number for Dor Cottage on his notepad.

"That's my number," I said.

Standing up, I reached over, intending to retrieve the ramekin, but the moment my fingers touched it, I changed my mind. I marched across the room, for the first time not intimidated in the slightest by his ridiculous slippery carpet, and just before I left, turned to deliver my final demand.

"And I want Kathryn to be my second."

Chapter 35

As I drove home, the sun was shining high over London. It was so hot in the city that you could smell the pavement, whilst out in the countryside the scent of trees and wildflowers was released into the air as if the whole of nature was being cooked on a low simmer. But as I neared Herstmonceux the weather changed dramatically. The further I travelled up the long track into the woodland clearing in which Dor nestled, the worse the storm became, my car wheels slipping in the mud and the rain forming a sheet of exploding water on my windscreen.

Turning off the ignition, I rubbed the mist from the window and surveyed my uncle's wall, now half destroyed and looking like a great, gaping smash-toothed mouth. I couldn't wait to finally obliterate the thing. Running through the rain, I decided it was too wet to launch my final attack on it and so determined instead to pay another visit to the attic.

The small door pushed open easily and I climbed the ladder into the loft. It was freezing and the storm was coming down onto the old roof like an assault. There was no wind; the only thing you could hear was the barrage, the relentless grey fall of rain. It must have been all over Kent and Sussex by now.

I spent perhaps an hour in the French section, hunting for dishes that might impress Ambrose if he did decide to give me a chance. After a time, I went to the section labelled "Dor". There were piles of old notebooks – some left by Dorothy, others by what must have been previous occupants. On the top shelf, in the furthest corner, I spotted the most gorgeous book of all. Black leather and with no decipherable title on the spine. I felt my narrow biceps strain as I took it down. Brushing the veil of dust and fly remains away with my sleeve, I read the words, *Index plantarum officinalium, quas ad materiae medicae scientiam promovendam, in horto, Dor Cotagium, Herstmonceux'*.

I opened it slowly. Every beautiful age-dried page was composed of hand-drawn illustrations of plants, each one crowded by closely rendered inky text. Page by page I turned and recognised, in amongst the etchings, many ordinary herbs. Marjoram, rosemary, meadowsweet, purslane – each was accompanied by descriptions that seemed to describe not their flavour, but their supposed medicinal properties. But the further I got into the book, the stranger its contents became. I stopped recognising many and then most of the plants, all of which were apparently once grown right here at Dor. Gradually, the sentences took on their own strange form, as if becoming affected, somehow, by the item they described. Eventually they ceased even to be written in straight lines. Instead they bulged and spread, sometimes following the contours of the particular herb they accompanied, sometimes following a logic all of their own. The result was a wonderful maelstrom of words that spoke of awe and magic and barely controlled terror.

I sat against the shelf and took my time with the index. Above my head, the rain crashed down ever harder as, beneath me, the cottage settled into its dark and favoured state. As the day fell away into night, I reached one of the final pages of the book. I felt myself gasp, a cloud of cold breath billowing visibly from my mouth. The picture in front of me – unmistakably, it was *my* herb, the one shaped like a teardrop. It was called 'Earl's Leaf'. The text was close and difficult to read. I strained to make out the words:

"*... must thereby be Warned that a Triumvirate of Plantes does grow in the Physic Garden of Dor Cottage that hold much Perille and Danger, causing vile Fites and Madnesses in each of man's distinct planes, Libido, Body and Spirite. If Takene together, these Plantes will cause Great Agonies and Death in Full Grown Men. Local Men and Women have been Bewitched by these same Herbes and Mary Dor Burned as a Witch on the Groundes of Herstmonceux Castle for the sin of Formenting same...*"

A sensation came over me, of being tiny in that attic; swallowed. I tracked down the text, fascinated by what I could make out of its discussion of my precious Earl's Leaf which, it said, causes "madness of libido" and "*... inflicts the Eater with a wicked and terrible desire to commit Foul Venereal Acts...*".

Turning the page, I came across a drawing of something called Cauter which was erect on a thick stem and had a tiny ball of thin thorns hanging from it. This would apparently cause a "madness of the body". The final of this "deadly triumvirate" of herbs, labelled Hindeling, had a stiff, five-petalled flower with a curling, tongue-like stamen which triggered a "madness of the mind". From what I could decipher, each one caused a different effect and, if taken together – according to the increasingly hysterical author of the book – they would kill.

Downstairs, I fetched my raincoat and the

sledgehammer from outside the back door. My boots were sucked into the mud as I made my way towards the hole in the wall. I stopped and peered in. In the torch's beam – it didn't seem possible. The Earl's Leaf was thick, leery and wild, almost reaching out towards me. I moved my torch around and saw other shapes in amongst the Earl's Leaf. There it was, thicker, shinier, with its white spikes and hanging head – the Cauter. And there in the distance – the purple, serpentine stamen of the Hindeling. I heard a sharp wooden groan from deep in the elm forest. It was thrilling to be amongst these plants that hadn't been seen for centuries. I stood there, in the rain, and laughed. The 350-year-old physic garden was *alive*.

I picked up the hammer and hurled it against the remaining bricks, which cracked and fell with satisfying ease. I soon got into a rhythm, my arms, legs and the rough wood-handled tool working in harmony. When the wall was finally down, I harvested an armful of Earl's Leaf. Trimming each tumescent stalk, I laid half the crop out in the kitchen and the other in the airing cupboard on sheets of newspaper to dry.

*   *   *

I was in the midst of some kind of nightmare when I was awoken by the telephone ringing.

"Good morning," said the voice in the receiver.

"Oh, Ambrose," I said. "Hi. Hello."

I looked at my watch. It was late – eight thirty a.m. I still had that peculiar sensation that accompanies nightmares: the inescapable feeling that you've been violated, somehow, by outside forces. I had the name "Mary" in my head and a memory of clawing, howling dogs.

"I've been considering our discussion and I have a

proposal to put to you. You should consider this to be a final offer, do you understand?"

"Yes," I said, still groggy.

"If this conversation comes to a close with anything other than you answering in the unqualified affirmative, the offer will be withdrawn immediately. Am I making myself clear?"

"Absolutely," I said.

"I have had a long conversation with a good friend of mine, a *patron* back in France. Claude tells me he made a young man about your age *chef d'cuisine* at a wonderful little restaurant, La Barriere de Clichy, a while back – Bernard Louiseau. You'll be pleased to hear it was a great success. Louiseau's down in Saulieu now and is thriving. So that is the position I am offering you. *Chef d'cuisine.*"

"Great…"

"However," he said, pausing for a moment, "you will be seconded by Chef Andrew Silverwood. It is Chef Andrew who will take ultimately responsibility for *all* aspects of the kitchen and the food. Unofficially, he will be your *chef de file*. For the avoidance of any potential unpleasantness down the road, I wish to also make it clear that your wage will be half that of Andrew's. Until he judges you to be sufficiently competent to take charge of the kitchen, you will not be carrying out the full duties of a head chef. You'll make your sauces and work on running the pass. If it emerges that you have the ability to call tickets and lead the brigade, and when you have learned to do it well, then of course we can renegotiate. Now then, Killian. All I want to hear from you is a single syllable. What's it to be?"

"So it will look like I'm in charge, but really it will be Andy?" I said.

"One syllable."

I made myself a promise. I would use the Earl's Leaf only when it was strictly necessary. I would honour Dorothy, as much as I reasonably could. I would be responsible. *Good.*

"Are you there?" said Ambrose.

"Yes."

"Yes you're there or yes you accept my offer?"

"Yes to both."

"Ah, the gratifying sound of a good man making the right decision. Excellent. Right. We need to discuss menus. It will be traditional bistro food, but tweaked in order to show off your sauces. You have more, I assume, than the one you prepared for me?"

"I do," I said. "And I have little twists on the French classics that I think you'll like. They'll be perfect for Glamis."

"I'll talk with Andy and we'll go over everything on Thursday afternoon. We'll meet at Glamis where you can prepare all your sauces for tasting. Don't let me down, Killian."

"Could I also have Kathryn?" I said. "I want Kathryn there."

"I thought I'd made myself clear. No conditions."

"Not as my second," I said. "Just on fish or meat. Please. She's brilliant and I'll work fantastically with her and Andy. She should never have been fired. You know that."

I listened to the humming telephone quiet.

"Oh, fine, fine," he said. "But if she gives any indication that her mind is with her damned mother, rather than with her work, then she's gone."

"And tell her that it was nothing to do with me. Please, Ambrose. Can you tell her what happened? Tell her it was Max, being a cunt."

There was a silence. When Ambrose spoke again, there was a world-weary note in his voice.

"The address is 11 Charlotte Street. Not far from King. I'll see you on Thursday."

I could see Mary in the kitchen, her rough cloth shawl and her hair, wet with steam and sweat, and her plum-blushed cheeks, and she was strong and young and handsome.

On the oaken table, she was laying out the Earl's herbs. Sheafs of freshly harvested stems with leaves like flattened teardrops. She squeezed one between her thumb and forefinger and breathed in the scent. Her tongue, pink and wet, pushed over her bottom lip and she smelled again. With a ball of twine, she began tying them together for drying.

Then footsteps up the path.

She stopped, her right ear angled up into the filthy air. To listen. To wait. To feel her heart in her chest.

Whispering outside: "They say she has an Evil thing within her and that the Devil attends her in the form of a Fly."

A hammering on the door. It shakes the Fly from where it was watching. It lifts and dances its spirals and circles. It's all around her as she listens through the filth.

A hammering again.

She drops the leaves and hurries up the stairs.

What about the fear? What about the burning? What about the trouble that's been breeding between the cracks in the beams and the cracks in the mortar and the cracks in the floor? What about the mischief that's been buried in the ground and is stirring? The old trouble, the family trouble, that old mischief come to find me.

Chapter 36

The first dish ever made at Glamis was grilled quail with sauce Bois Boudran – a herby, tangy French concoction, made with tomato compote, vinegar, chervil, chives and tarragon. I prepared it in the newly installed kitchen.

Andy was at the butcher's block, working on the quail. He barely lifted his head to greet me. He just motioned at the blue A4 folder that included the method for Bois Boudran, which I only took for the sake of appearances. I was already familiar with the recipe and I was thrilled: it would be perfect.

Over the previous three and a half weeks, I had been working through the nights, practising a variety of sauces without using Earl's Leaf. Although I had been pleased with how they had all tasted – and convinced that they would be entirely adequate for the purposes of an upmarket bistro – they were never quite enough. If I was to prove that Max had treated me unjustly then I would need dishes that were far beyond adequate. Beyond perfect was an absolute necessity. Moreover, if I wanted Kathryn to earn enough money to move her mother into humane accommodation, I realised that for me to take undue risks would be immoral. So I decided that, just for the time being, I would use a whisper of Earl's Leaf in each sauce.

Over those anxious days and heavy-lidded nights, I began to wonder if I might have exaggerated the herb's effect to myself – really, in a sense, it wasn't much more than a kind of seasoning. It lifted the flavours a little, that was all. When truly I thought about it, I decided that an untrained palate, in all likelihood, would barely be able to tell the difference – at least, not at the quantities I was using.

As I worked, I was surprised to find that I was thinking about Max as much as ever. I remembered finding a photo-graph, tucked into the cover of one of Aunt Dorothy's recipe books, of my parents enjoying a picnic in the grounds of Tonbridge Castle. They looked to be in their very early twenties and my dad had obviously said some-thing that amused Mum – her laughter was such that she was leaning backwards, her gaze so worshipful it felt almost improper. How could such evidently powerful love trans-mute so cleanly into hate? As I held that picture, years ago, I couldn't understand it. But now I had experienced some-thing of that nature myself. Where there had been wild adoration for Max, there was now a rage of equal force. I wondered if it was all made of the same essential mate-rial, if hate was just love in shadow. And I felt ashamed at how thoroughly my devotion to Max had spun its illusion around me. I couldn't rid myself of the thought that he had developed such a vigorous dislike of me. Of *me!* The one who had loved him more than anyone!

The mood in Dor seemed to alter itself as well. I couldn't work out the extent to which I was imagining things, but the upstairs room that had once been Dorothy's favourite had become, in some indistinct way, unwel-coming. I would go to sleep with the door and windows closed and still wake up to find flies buzzing over the bed.

I found myself more and more adept at reading the

different kinds of silence that were present in the house, as if they constituted a private language that was known only to me and the walls. Each version of quiet had its own pitch, texture and density. It was the density that I feared the most – that sense of crowding. I felt this, most commonly, in the kitchen and, of course, over the stairs.

* * *

As I worked in the Glamis kitchen that morning, I listened to the radio. The blank voice announced all the things that were going on out there: Neil Kinnock trying to isolate the far left of the Labour Party; Moscow warning Reagan against arming the Afghans; the Pentagon stepping up the use of lie detectors to determine employees' patriotism; Iraq bombing border villages in Iran; the Chinese leader Deng Xiaoping planning to make his country an "economic powerhouse" in the twenty-first century; George Bush meeting Thatcher to agree ideas on combating terrorism. There was something strange about it. It wasn't the same old news any more. It seemed different. It felt like the future.

When the moment came to drop the Earl's Leaf in, Andy was concentrating hard on cooking the quail, tongs in hand, bottom lip between his teeth, peering into the hazy heat. I retrieved an Old Holborn pouch which I'd cleaned out and filled with fresh Earl's Leaf. I watched the smallest pinch fall into the pan in front of me and disappear amongst the rest of the fragrantly glistening greenery. That would be enough. Just a breath of it.

"Quail'll be there in thirty seconds," Andy called. "Give it five minutes to rest."

"Yes, Chef."

When it was ready, Andy arranged the quail on one of the new white plates with some steamed vegetables that he'd finished in a little butter. I watched him taking charge of putting the dish together with his usual purring crafts-manship. Without meeting my eye, he held out his hand for me to pass him my pan of sauce. I ignored the gesture, and deliberately defying the Nouvelle Cuisine practice of saucing beneath the protein, I spooned it over the still-steaming bird.

Lifting the quail to one side, I made a kind of platform with the carrot spears and baby potatoes and put the meat back down on top it and drizzled another spoonful of sauce to repair the messy damage. It looked ridiculous, but that wasn't the point. I had made the dish mine.

"Okay?" I said.

Andy looked at the plate.

"If you want," he shrugged irritably.

I picked up the dish.

"Let's do this," I said, and led the way out onto the restaurant floor.

As it was a bistro, the dining space was larger than King's and the walls had been hung with dark-framed mirrors, decorated in gold leaf. The workmen were halfway through painting the ceiling a faux tobacco colour – Ambrose had given them the afternoon off, lest the fumes interfere with our tasting session – and there was a row of antique hat stands in the small corridor on which coats were to be hung. An exciting touch was the addition of an ostentatious "top table" that was constructed on a small platform and would be discreetly spotlit. There would be a twenty-per-cent surcharge for its use and, Ambrose predicted, would be highly in demand by newly minted City folk.

Still, all the decorators' best endeavours couldn't block out the deadening unromance of London that poured in through the windows that morning – the dreary dishwater light; the combustion farts of taxis and buses; the seagullish calls of a nearby newspaper seller. It was gloomy in the interior, too, as the bulbs hadn't yet been fitted. I could only make out the silhouette of Ambrose with his sleeves rolled up, leather-bound notebook on the table and cigarette on the go. And – he was with someone. Her hair, I noticed, was in a ponytail that had been tied low, from the base of her head. For some reason, it hurt me that she was wearing it in a style that I'd not seen before.

"Kathryn!" I said. "Great! How are you? You're here!"

She was leaning forward, her shoulders in a slump, her eyes cast down. She looked at me briefly before readjusting, quickly, to meet the eyes of Andy behind me.

"Yes, I am," she said.

I placed the plate down carefully in the middle of the table and grinned at her again.

"Presentation's a little off," Ambrose said, as I pulled out the chair next to Kathryn. "Why is it piled high like a tower? Nobody wants high food. They want it flat on the plate. They want to see what they're eating. And let's be more generous with this sauce please. This isn't King – we don't want too much china showing. We're supposed to be giving the impression of plenty. Right, come on ladies and gentlemen. The big moment is upon us. Who's going to say grace?"

I tried to coax Kathryn into smiling at Ambrose's joke. She sat there awkwardly, staring at the dish, her lips pushed together in a sad, swollen pucker as Ambrose tipped the beautifully browned bird off its platform and sliced into the breast. He pushed a piece of carrot onto his fork and then, with his knife, spread a generous layer of the green-flecked sauce over it. My heart made its presence felt on the inside of my ribs as I followed the parcel through the air, trailing a faint pall of steam, to be placed on the proprietor's much-feared tongue. He pulled the fork from his mouth. There was a moment, suspended. And then it happened. His eyes dropped. There was a single chew and silence. Then he chewed and chewed and finally swallowed. His unhealthy skin gave life to a fine drop of sweat, like blood from a pinprick, above his left eyebrow. He put his fork down gently, sat back, stared at the ceiling and spoke quietly.

"Good God."

Clearly bemused, Andy leaned forward and took a bite. As his jaws worked, a frown of intense concentration came over him, his eyes cast seriously towards his mouth.

"Fucking hell," he said, before he'd even swallowed. "Wow. How have you... ?"

I shifted uncomfortably. He pushed the plate towards Kathryn, dipping his little finger helplessly back into the unctuous green slick and tasting it again. Ambrose gave a little loinish "uh" and relaxed his neck completely, so that his head hung limply back.

"Try that," Andy told her. "It's unbelievable. Oh my God, Jesus Christ. It's amazing."

Feverish now, Andy stood up and put his hands on his hips, staring down at the plate with a ridiculous smile on his face, his black moustache crushed up between his lip and his nose. Ambrose's throat released another deeply satisfied post-coital grunt.

The change that came over Kathryn was something I will never forget. It was like watching a flower bloom into life. All the dour suspicion left her, her cheeks pinked and her eyes became alive and danced with admiration and pleasure and that intimate, thrilled, quasi-sexual shock that all cooks covet, that look that said I had touched her, I had given her pleasure and she couldn't help but crave for more.

"Mmmm," she said, modestly holding her hand to her mouth. "God, *mmmmm!*"

She took another bite. I noticed, with another small lurch of alarm, that her lips had pinked and swelled. I looked at the other two. The effect was less noticeable on them, but it was undeniably there.

Taking another dose of sauce, Ambrose chewed slowly and held it in his mouth for a time before reluctantly swallowing. He sat back and gazed adoringly in my direction.

"You have a first-class talent, Killian," he said. "Absolutely first class."

I shook my head and puffed out my cheeks, dismissively.

"Not really," I said.

"Oh, but you do. You have a way with flavour... You, you, you... as you say, you know just how to extract layers of flavour that I have never, in all my years in this silly business... It's like you can read the mind of the ingredients. It's like a second sight."

"Not really," I said again, sitting up. "Can you really...? I mean, it's not... It's just seasoning, really."

"What rot!" said Ambrose. Suddenly energised, he leaped to his feet and clapped his hands together, his expertly concealed kettle-drum belly bouncing like a bald extra head above his belt. "And this is just the first dish of the day! Ladies and gentlemen, I think we're going to have a success! A huge bloody success!"

"They'll be queuing round the block," said Andy, his mouth full again.

"Rubbish!" shouted Ambrose. "They'll be queuing round the block to get to the block where the fucking queue starts. They'll be rioting in the streets. Bravo, Killian! Bravo!"

* * *

That afternoon we ate our way through the entire menu. By the time we were done, no one seemed in any doubt about the sure success of Glamis.

"You've done really well," said Kathryn.

Ambrose and Andy had disappeared into the kitchen. Kathryn had lifted her ski jacket from the back of her chair and, looking towards the door, was pulling it on.

"Are you going?" I said.

I put my hands on my hips and tried to looked relaxed about things. Breezy.

"Stuff to do," she said. "Mum."

"You know – what Max said," I began. "It's not true, Kathryn." Relaxed and breezy. "He's a fucking liar." I could feel a vein pumping in my forehead. "I know you think I worship him, and you probably had a point, back then. But he lied about you and he lied about my sauce. And, you know, the whole reason I want to do this – the whole reason I asked Ambrose to hire you – is because I want us, me and you together, to show him how it's done. Nouvelle Cuisine is over. We'll prove it to him, and to everyone."

Relaxed and breezy and carefree. That's the way to do it.

"Blimey, you're keen," she said. "You've never even run a pass before."

A light above us began flickering. A yellowish pall blinked on and off over Kathryn's nose and cheeks and shoulders. Yellow and black, yellow and black, yellow and black, like wasps.

"Well, if you don't think I can do it…"

"I didn't say that."

"…why are you here?"

"Because I need a fucking *job*."

Relaxed and breezy and I could feel this sensation of *density* expanding behind my eyes and this restless, flapping urge in the joints of my fingers and the bones of my knees. The bulb flickered all over the white tablecloth. I sat back down and put my head in my hands. A passing motorbike rattled the window and I felt its vibrations in my elbows. I heard the chair next to me being pulled back and the sound of Kathryn sitting into it. She took my wrist and pulled it away from my face. For the first time since we were at King together, I saw the beginning of her vulnerable smile.

"Sorry, Killian," she said. "I'm sure you can do it."

I ignored her. She let me go and smoothed down the front of her jacket, which had puffed up with the action of her sitting.

"Max lied, you know," I said. "I didn't tell him anything."

"I know. Ambrose told me."

The bulb stopped flickering.

"So why are you being like this?" I said. "Why is it still weird between us?"

"I'm just nervous about it," she said. "You know, my life has been all over the place." A silver fly landed on the back of my hand. I watched its legs bend, its proboscis lower into one of my scabs. "I just want a piece of calm. A bit of peace. I don't know if us, being together – maybe it's not a good idea."

It started again, the maddening strobe, flashing on the walls and our skin and the marks on the tablecloth. It was enough to trigger a migraine. One of the cuts on my wrists began to itch. I scratched. As the fly zoomed off, small crumbles of dried blood fell onto a white napkin.

"But I didn't do anything wrong," I said, squinting.

"Breaking up with you made me realise how much…"

She looked away, briefly losing her thread. "I feel a lot for you, Killian. *A lot*. I can't go through anything like that again. It was too much." She hid her face in her hands. "You're too damaged, Killian. You're a fuck-up."

I reached out and touched her chin with my finger. Her skin felt smooth and cold and soft and she didn't move away. The corners of her mouth trembled slightly.

"Yes but, Kathryn, you're a fuck-up, too," I said, smiling. "We'll be fuck-ups together."

Nothing happened for a moment. I looked at her sitting there, utterly unable to fathom what she was thinking.

"I love you," I said.

"Don't make me cry," she said.

I took her hands in mine and squeezed them, rubbing my thumbs over the surface of her palms. I felt removed, as if I was looking down on us, huddled together under the failing bulb. I would have to remember this; to store the sensory information of what it felt like to touch her skin; to feel her narrow wrists; to breathe her out-breaths; to be so near to her face and body without her flinching. I'd have to save it, carefully and accurately, just in case.

"I promise, Kathryn," I said. "It will be worth it. I know it sounds a bit crazy, but I really believe in my sauces. I really think I can make Glamis a massive success. Then you can earn proper money and get your mum out of that awful home. Get her somewhere where they'll look after her properly."

She peered up at me.

"It's like you told me," I continued. "You don't get anything in the restaurant business unless you earn it. And I deserve this. So do you." I paused. "That's what I think, anyway. Maybe you don't. But can't we give it a go, just in case?"

She looked down again, still unresponsive. I whispered, "Max is over. We're going to make sure he is. We're going to fucking *destroy* him."

As she leaned over and put her arms around me, the bulb started going again. "Our success should be for our sake, not just to get back at him," she said.

"So…?"

She smiled. "But if I ever find myself having to put a Max mask on just to get your attention, there'll be trouble."

As soon as she was safely gone, I would climb onto the table, remove my shoe and, holding the chandelier with one hand, smash the flickering fucking lightbulb with the heel. I would savour the small calamity of sound and the sensation of hot glass falling all over me.

"I swear," I said. "There's nothing to worry about any more. Everything's going to be perfect."

Chapter 37

The media greeted the opening of Glamis with a level of expectation that the British restaurant world had never witnessed before. In the kitchen, we couldn't see the cameras and the lights and the crowd of more than two hundred that had amassed on the street to glimpse the arrival of the various celebrities that the *Sun*, the *Mirror*, the *Evening Standard*, the *Daily Mail* and even the *Guardian* and the *Daily Telegraph* had listed as attending. We could feel the excitement, though. We were all experiencing everything in sharper focus. Colours and smells and tastes became richer and time ticked by with a swagger that was palpable, as if the seconds themselves knew they were a part of history.

During the weeks in which the decorators had been finishing and Andy and I had perfected the menu, Ambrose had been squeezing all but the last drips of goodness out of his contacts book. He arranged for us to give confidential tastings to newspaper editors and food critics and other powerful entities on the strict condition that they wouldn't formally review the restaurant until it opened. It was a masterful plan. On a series of afternoons and evenings we cooked for everyone in London that mattered. Encouraged by the scent of exclusivity and secrecy that surrounded it, word bounced from critics to journalists to their influential friends.

Our most nerve-wracking night was a blustery Tuesday, when Barry Gruenfeld came for a meal. Gruenfeld, who was celebrated in the nation's kitchens for the gripping drama of his ugliness – his nose like a stamped frog, his lower lip sitting above his top one and his foul-smelling, rot-toothed smile – wrote a weekly column for the *Sunday Telegraph* and was easily the most feared critic in the country. Two years previously, Max Mann had had him evicted from King and – rumour has it – subsequently threatened him after he poked fun at the Gentleman Chef's appearance on the cover of the *Radio Times* with two fried eggs placed over his eyes. Ambrose was forced to hush the incident up with some senior publishing figure – a straight-forward enough task, given that the executive happened to be a regular at his debauched Saturday parties. Aware of these behind-the-scenes machinations and livid at his neutering, Gruenfeld had never forgiven Ambrose or Max. For more than two years, he'd used every excuse he could to snipe at King in print.

Initially, he refused to even take Ambrose's calls. But after several days, in which he suffered wave upon wave of thrilled gossip from his friends and colleagues, he finally relented. Of course, we fully expected Gruenfeld to feign disgust or lack of interest when he got here. What he did, on the night, was clear his throat, adjust his tie and, with a wide-eyed nervous politeness, ask for second helpings.

The rest of Ambrose's formidable business talents had been directed towards his network of kitchen informers. He tapped them all in an attempt to locate the most skilled young chefs in the country and then tempt them with the promise of long hours, low wages and a possible scintilla of reflected glory, all the while making it sound like the most astonishing deal imaginable. I blamed the fact he was only partly successful on Max working against us. The result was that we ended up with what must have been the youngest brigade in the country – only two were over twenty-six. I found myself in charge of my own apprentices, the best of which was a shy boy from Leeds named Marco who'd trained previously at the Box Tree in Ilkley and with the Rouxs. He was oddly attractive, with his long curly hair and the grave bags beneath his eyes that gave him a look of power and wisdom. He had an urgency and an instinct for graft that reminded me of myself. I liked Marco a lot. I believed he'd go far.

By the time opening night came around, we were already booked up for three weeks. Due in the restaurant for that first service were Phil Collins, Moira Stewart, Ian Botham, Nik Kershaw with his wife Sheri, Steve Davis, Keith Floyd, and three of Five Star along with a few actors from the new BBC TV show called *EastEnders*. And so, on the insistence of Ambrose, was Chef Max Mann.

As the hands on the large clock on the wall shifted thrillingly towards six p.m., I stood at the pass with Kathryn to my left and Andy to my right, and gathered the brigade around me. Everything in the kitchen was clean and perfect, including my chefs, their eyes direct, their hands folded obediently by their waists.

"Chefs," I said. "We have a lot to prove tonight. As most of you know, Glamis started out as nothing more than a side project for Ambrose – somewhere he could relive his wild Parisian days. As you can tell by all the noise outside, we're already punching considerably above our weight. It's not every 'local' bistro that gets three out of Five Star in on their opening night."

I paused to let this fact sink in.

"We've done this by creating a brilliant menu. But make no mistake, not everyone sitting out there in the restaurant wants us to succeed. Some actively want us to fail. You know who I'm talking about. Some of you have worked for him. One or two of you may still feel a little bit of loyalty to him. If so, you can take off your apron and walk out of that door right now, because I don't want you here."

Nobody moved.

"It's not just his silly 1970s food that has no place in this restaurant; it's his outdated way of running a kitchen. I'm going to make a promise to all of you right now. There will be no place in here for the kind of bullying that happens at King. Disrespect will not be tolerated in my kitchen, not from anyone. We will prove to Max Mann that you don't need to torment people to achieve the highest standards. I expect every cook here to want it badly enough to be their own drill sergeant. You should want it enough that you stop thinking about yourself, your wellbeing, your wants, when you're in here. You should walk in at seven every morning, slip into your clogs and become a part of Glamis. Everything you do should be for the restaurant. Because your career – everything that you work for – lives and dies by the restaurant. We need to prove to Max Mann that the days of Nouvelle Cuisine are over. The days of *Max Mann* are over! We're delivering to the people what they've always wanted – the luxury, the sensation, the richness, the *flavours*. We're taking the best of the past and the best of the present and, by doing so, we will become the future. And that future begins *right now!* So let's get him," I shouted. "Let's prove to Max that we can do it. Let's make a booking for the mad cunt's funeral–"

Kathryn squeezed my hand and glanced at me as if to say, "enough". Exchanging looks amongst themselves, the cooks scattered back to their stations. Minutes later, the Maître d' came in with the first orders.

"Okay, listen up," I shouted. "Two St Jacques, two foie, one bouillabaisse."

"Yes, Chef," came the response, gruff, stolid and resolute.

They snapped to it, necks bent and perfect.

"Is everyone with me?" I shouted.

"Yes, Chef!"

* * *

As much as I would have loved to have rejected every aspect of la Nouvelle Cuisine, it was obvious to me that this would have been foolish. I knew that if we were going to make a dent on the world culinary scene, we would have to be reasonably sparing with our butter and our cream (unlike Max who, no doubt, had begun cooking "the new style" – deglazing with water and thickening with carrot and onion purée and so on – but had clearly secretly reneged on that promise as part of his flagellating crawl towards his three-star dream). At Glamis, we would throw off the obvious pretensions, the gigantic plates, the meat-and-fruit combos, whilst keeping the essential architecture of the style – the freshness, the lightness, the reverence for the sanctity of the ingredient in its natural state. But we would bring to it the velvet luxury of Old Europe: truffles, foie gras and portions whose size verged on intimidating and which I insisted, mainly for reasons of stubbornness, upon arranging high on the plate as I had on the day of the tasting.

I also knew that we wouldn't be taken seriously if we didn't prepare everything in the modern way – to order, and from a standing, naked kitchen. And that had to include sauces. As well as running the pass (I had convinced Andy to let me try and, to my surprise, he relented with only a hint of complaint), it was my job to prepare them. I insisted that Kathryn hand me the pans in which she'd cooked plump 300-gram cuts of beef, lamb or veal and equally generous portions of Bresse chicken and woodcock, so that I could deglaze them and create the jus that would anoint the final dish at my own special sauce station. Even if I hadn't had that old tobacco pouch filled with Earl's Leaf secreted in my tunic, I would have insisted upon working this way.

I had no doubts about my wait staff, who had been mercilessly drilled by my stern and decidedly un-French Maître d', Ms Drusilla Langton-Grey — a bony, fifty-something spinster with aristocratic roots, alarming green eyeshadow and a seemingly endless appetite for fatty offcuts, which she'd scrounge by appearing abruptly at Kathryn's side at the sauté station, clicking her long fingernails like a hungry cricket and asking, in her deep, dry, upper-class tone, "Any trimmings, darling?"

When the *coup de feu* finally arrived, it was with a warm bloom of satisfaction that I found that the first table ordered two entrecôte with sauce Glamis — my award-winning sauce, which Ambrose had christened after the restaurant. As I took that pristine white ticket, I wondered, yet again, was using the Earl's Leaf somehow cheating? Did it count as such because it was unfair? What about all those customers at King who are celebrated by the world for their beauty or talent? We elevate them as if they've earned it. But you don't earn what you're born with; you steal it from God. If they were worthy of the gifts that had been passed down to them, then why wasn't I? Kathryn had been right. I deserved this.

And there it began, for the first time, the brand-new music of my kitchen. Following the first ticket there were two more orders for steak Glamis. Then three more – a run – and two for *tournedos Rossini* and two for *poularde à la vapeur*, then three chicken stuffed with truffles, foie gras and boned pigs' feet and then six *turbot à l'amiral*, which came with both a white wine sauce and a red, and then another steak Glamis and then the music reached a dangerous pitch, a kind of gnawing quiet broken by shouts of "behind" and shouts of "how long for…" and shouts of "fucking talk to me" and shouts of "where is it?" and then two turbot and a *poularde* and a cod for Table 12 and more pans go on and my wrist is burned, and then one Glamis, two cod and a Rossini and then have Table 9 had their starters yet and who's this plate for and the waiters, the waiters in their black trousers and their white aprons, they wait, they wait for me in a small queue and they try not to look at me and a woodcock à Glamis and a cod for Table 5 and is this the Glamis for Table 9 yes yes I think so and has 9 got their order yet then where's their fucking ticket and they try not to look at me but they stand there waiting for their food glancing at each other with raised eyes and whispering and ouch fuck my hand and is that over-reduced taste it taste it a little bit but fuck it and what do you want now can't you see I'm doing it I'm doing it just be patient fuck hang on where's that cod have we had the cod yet the cod the cod and there's Andy here's Andy what does Andy want it's not that bad –

"Come on!" I shouted to the brigade. "This isn't good enough, guys. Please! Come on!"

"We're fucked," Andy whispered. "We're completely fucked."

"We're not fucked," I said. "They'll just have to wait. It's good food. It's worth it."

As the minutes went by, and the trouble mounted, I forgot to worry quite so much about hiding the fact of the secret pouch in my apron. I only realised my mistake when I noticed Kathryn staring at me in bemusement.

"What?" I asked.

"Why are you sprinkling pocket fluff into your sauces?"

The world froze around me.

"That's a fucking stupid thing to say," I snapped.

And then the moment was broken, by, "I'm sorry, Chef." It was one of the waiters, his fringe fashionably wavy and extending from his hairline down to his left eyebrow, fingering a tray that had two plates of entrecôte on it, the deep crusted-brown trackmarks of its cooking still visible between the chubby red slides of sauce that I'd poured over it. "Is this for Table 7?"

"Yes, yes, yes," I said. "Just take it. Please."

"Wait," said Andy, approaching behind me. He pulled the tray back by its silver handles, the plates slipping a little on the purple paper liner, with its elaborate Glamis logo in gold art deco script.

"Fingerprints," he said, examining the china under the golden glow of the heat lamps. He pressed the back of his thumb down on the meat before closing his eyes. "It's cold." He checked the ticket. "And are you seriously telling me these are well done? They're still fucking farting."

"Fuck it," I said. "Damn."

Not wanting to lift my concentration from my pans, I quickly turned to Kathryn who was balancing a worryingly high pile of glistening meat on a metal sitting plate.

"It's under done, Kathryn. For fuck's sake!"

Fuck! I stirred one pan. I tasted another. I kicked the

steel wall of the unit by my feet so hard that my clogs rammed into my toes. Andy softened his face and placed his hands behind his back. What *was* he still doing here?

"Listen," he said. "Why don't I take over on sauces? You can concentrate on the pass, calling the orders. That's what you want to do, really, isn't it? Call the orders? That way you can keep on top of things and I can keep things moving along here."

In my peripheral vision, I could see a torchon, dangerously near to a burner.

"I can manage."

Was it smoking?

"Do you want me to call the orders then?" he said. "And you can concentrate on this?"

I glanced at it again. Andy followed my gaze, spotted the cloth and immediately lifted it away from the flame.

"I can manage, Andy," I said.

He leaned further in and whispered so closely that I felt a fleck of spit on my ear: "*Fucked.*"

By nine thirty p.m., no plate had left the kitchen for twenty minutes. I looked up from my station to see Ambrose in his checked suit, his purple lining flashing as he paced past the line of fractious waiters.

"What the fuck is going on?" he said, his eyes bouncing around the piles of pans and meat and the wet floor and the endless row of tickets that were hanging down in front of me.

"We're on it, Ambrose," I said. "Sorry. We're on it."

He took my arm and pulled me into the empty corridor that led to the changing rooms.

"Don't fuck this up, little boy," he said, his breath sour with wine and dry with tobacco. "I've put all my faith in you. I have risked my reputation telling the whole world and his mistress what a prodigy you are. There are people sitting within fifty feet of you right now who could break your career a thousand times over. And they will, believe me, if they don't get fed soon." He observed me over his pale nose and horsey nostrils. "Maybe this little factoid will help motivate you. There is only one person out there who is enjoying himself right now, and his name is Max Mann."

By the time I had slunk back, Andy was at the pass. He was calling out tickets, his voice magnificent with order and consequence. The brigade were answering him in kind. A fierce element had been introduced into the kitchen and everyone sounded, for the first time in more than an hour, hopeful. I bowed my head over my stove and tried to catch up, working for the rest of service in as much silence as was possible, avoiding the attentions of the brigade as best as I could. I made the sauces, for the rare and complex dishes that reached the heat lamps, most of which I didn't have the skill to cook myself, and watched Andy ride that pass like a cowboy on a bucking bull.

* * *

"Come, come," said Ambrose, sometime after eleven p.m., when all the diners had finished eating. I followed him down the short passageway and into the soothing dimness of the restaurant. After hours in the shadowless white of the kitchen, my eyes weren't yet used to the grainy light and I didn't have time to make out any individual faces in the crowd before Ambrose clapped three times and said, "Ladies and gentlemen, the best new chef in Britain, please welcome Mr Killian Lone."

They stood and cheered so loudly that the chandeliers began rocking on the ceiling. Their clapping was a million tiny cracks breaking the air; a dark rumble of stamping began rolling out from beneath it. There was something unnerving about the bedlam. Something desperate. They were a mob of maddened, straining people, palms hot, eyeballs wide, necks stretched and nostrils flaring. On and on and on it went. This wasn't a collection of men, women and dignitaries who'd just enjoyed a pleasant dinner. This was unnatural. They were *wild*. What had I done?

"Thank you all for coming," Ambrose shouted in an attempt to calm them down. But they continued, their stamping now synchronised, the cheers looping and colliding against whoops and whistles.

"Okay, okay, okay!" Ambrose shouted eventually. "Thank you, thank you, thank you. As I'm sure you all agree, the food here tonight was of an utterly sensational standard. And that is all thanks to this awesomely talented young man."

Where was he? Where was Max? The silhouette of the crowd was a great black monster in the gloom, spotted here and there with the fiery trails of cigarettes and cigars. It was impossible to pick him out. I stood there as Ambrose finished his speech. When it was over, and at the end of another, only marginally less ravenous applause, the beastly crowd came for me, and I was in it, swallowed inside its walls, surrounded by its arms and legs and wide, wet, licking mouths as they whispered and thanked and pushed napkins and menus and matchbooks on me to sign with my name.

"I'll leave you to it," Ambrose said as he escaped, unscathed through the middle of the thing.

"Where's Max?" I called after him.

"Gone."

I turned into the beautifully dressed mob and stared, entranced. For the first time it seemed so insanely possible: that I might, someday, have King, Dor, Glamis and all.

Chapter 38

The reviews that came in over the next couple of weeks were considerably better than spectacular. They listed the many wonders of Glamis in paragraph after adjective-choked paragraph. It was curious how the pleasure they'd clearly experienced from my sauces caused them to judge everything else with unfailing sympathy. The delays on the opening night and the mistakes I knew had gone out in every service – the sometimes sloppy presentation, the over-reduced sauces, the under-rested meat – were absent, forgotten entirely after the critics had tasted the magic of the crucial element. One even hailed our "confidence" in having only three desserts, when that paltry list was actually due to the fact that we hadn't, yet, found a full-time pastry chef. Admittedly, my lack of enthusiasm for that project was because I hadn't yet worked out the technicalities of successfully inveigling Earl's Leaf into puddings.

Ambrose would come in at eight thirty every morning, fattened with clucking pride and with an armful of newspapers, which he'd already pored through for references to Glamis. At first, he wanted me to read them out during my daily team talks, but I refused. I gathered my chefs around me for one specific purpose – to impress upon them that, although Andy was running the pass, I was in charge.

And, of course, to motivate them with my speeches about Max Mann. I'd work on these every day – ideas for the next morning's address would scrap messily for precedence in my head as I cooked.

Increasingly, I'd find my mind running helplessly with thoughts of him – hostile memories, strange fantasies and imagined conversations that, when I was alone in my small office, I'd sometimes speak out loud. When preparing a sauce for a dish I was particularly proud of, I'd picture him eating it and being so overcome with pleasure that he'd smile and shake me by the hand and then pull me to his breast in recognition of this connection between fellow journeymen.

At other times, I'd see him crumpled in humiliation at the flavour of my sauce Glamis. He'd throw his torchon to the ground, knowing he was beaten, knowing he'd made a mistake when he lied about me and made me eat shit, and then he'd fall to his knees and weep at this final failure and I'd comfort him, I'd stroke the back of his head and then, too late, too late, too late, old cunt, I'd take his head and throw it repeatedly to the floor, until I was healed completely by the blood and the silence.

One morning, before my team talk began, Ambrose read out a particularly mucilaginous review from Evan Parker-Scott in the *Daily Mail*. He ladled praise on this "prodigy of British cuisine" whose "incomparable gifts" would "finally put to rest the claims by our ancient enemy across the Channel that England is not a cooking nation", even going so far as to suggest I be awarded an OBE. When he had finally left, I addressed the brigade.

"We've had some great write-ups and I know you're all very pleased with yourselves," I said. "But I don't want us to be obsessing over the media. That's the trap our friend

Max has fallen into and look where it's got him. Self-obsessed, scared, fucking fried eggs on his eyeballs. And anyway, those reviews are of last week's dinners. Forget about them. That's why I've asked that all the framed cuttings be taken down from the walls of the corridor out there. I want every night's meals to be better than the ones before."

There was a silence as I tried to gather up their direct attention. There were eyes to the floor, eyes to the side, eyes to each other, eyes to folded hands. But no eyes on me. None.

"Okay?" I said.

"Yes, Chef," said one or two voices.

From behind me, Andy stepped forward.

"Thanks, Chef. That was great. All right, guys, great work this week but as Chef says, I know you can do better. Let's get to it."

"Yes, Chef!" they cried.

In those first few weeks, Michael Heseltine, Jonathan King and Mike Yarwood all made lucrative offers for me to cook in their homes. Barbara Windsor booked a table of eight to celebrate her divorce from Ronnie Knight. On one midweek evening, Princess Diana ate with some relative or other – at least we assumed it was a relative, as she was being generously affectionate with her guest and he definitely wasn't Prince Charles. I declined invitations to appear on *Pebble Mill at One*, *TV-AM* and *Food and Drink*. Our customers, meanwhile, became increasingly ravenous for our food, some trying to book themselves in every night for a week or more. We became fashionable with the young executives from the Manufacturers Hanover Trust or "Manny Hanny" – a glamorous bunch who some in Ambrose's circles had witheringly christened "young aspirational professionals" or "yaps". They all seemed to carry leather Filofaxes, drive BMWs and live in Stoke Newington. Before Glamis opened, Le Caprice, Garroway's and the Bombay Brasserie had all the lunchtime expense account business, but now they begged for space at our tables. Eventually they would become widely known as "yuppies", but to me, in those early weeks, they were a fascinating, beautiful and repellent new race.

But we couldn't feed them all. At one point, Ambrose had to step in to stop a black-market auction for tables. During the third week, our reservations book was stolen, and everyone listed in it was phoned up and offered thousands of pounds for their seat. Rumours of the strangely aphrodisiacal nature of our meals spread, too, with male yaps bringing beautiful dates in the evening and hoping for a bit of "Glamis luck", which rarely failed them. The *Daily Mail* ran a story about an expected generation of "Glamis babies" in nine months' time. It became ordinary for us to find young couples having sex up against the wall in Percy Passage, which ran near the building. We'd frequently find discarded lingerie on the dirty brick floor and, once, a pair of red braces that looked suspiciously similar to those worn by Le Patron.

Ambrose added fifty per cent to the prices and then another fifteen and it didn't make any difference. Despite my not working at the pass, he raised my wages from £2,750 a year to £5,500, the same level as Andy's. Beautiful girls began waiting for me at the kitchen door, but I was blind to them all. Kathryn and I were so busy, we barely had time to appreciate the brilliant love which had come to surround us. We would escape after service and kiss in the dark, my hands moving under her clothes as our forms moved anonymously in the passageway, next to whichever diners hadn't managed to make it home.

The success of Glamis and the success of my relationship with Kathryn seemed so intertwined as to be impossible to separate. But perhaps the greatest joy for me was seeing how it changed her. If Kathryn hadn't shown me that shard of compassion on my first day at King, in all likelihood, I would have only ever known the person that all the other chefs saw – a cold, sarcastic and tough young woman; just another wounded soldier of the kitchen. Working next to each other and fighting through the lunch and evening service as if we were battling our way through terrible gales, rapidly built foundations between us that felt grand and permanent. And all the time we had the awareness that our restaurant was growing, that with each of the day's twin victories Glamis was becoming more famous throughout the country and the security of our future was surer.

Whenever we weren't cooking, we'd huddle in my small office and talk. I'd sit on the already-broken Argos swivel chair and she'd perch on a cushion on top of the huge green iron safe and we'd gossip about customers and the brigade and rehearse the war stories that we imagined we'd one day be telling Wogan and Harty and maybe, if things carried on being this perfect, our children and grandchildren.

More than once, Andy caught us kissing. Whilst he feigned comic disgust at this, Kathryn appeared genuinely shamed. It was in front of Andy that she seemed to cling hardest to the old version of herself. But she was changing. I'd notice her smiling more and more in public; she even occasionally engaged other chefs in small talk in the lunch room. Although they were still slightly wary of her, I could tell they admired her. One or two of them even came to know her as *nice*.

Things soon became so frantic that, inevitably, tensions arose between us. I worried that she just wanted this less than me. Once she was earning enough for her mum to be taken care of properly, would her ambition slump? I became perhaps overly attentive to signs that she might not be truly committed. She complained, also, that I would regularly disappear back to Dor without her, the moment service finished. She didn't know it, of course, but I had no choice. It was vital that I tend the herb garden and gather and prepare a fresh batch of Earl's Leaf for the next day. So, naturally, Kathryn couldn't come with me. I could never risk her finding out my secret. If she or anyone else discovered it, I could only expect to be ruined.

Chapter 39

Kathryn had barely spoken a word since she'd arrived in the kitchen, eleven hours earlier. She was angry with me. It was her mother's birthday and I'd told her that, this being a Saturday, she couldn't take the time off to visit her. Actually, this was a half-lie. I had put into action a plan that I hoped might cheer her up.

Ambrose's fine idea of having a "Top Table" on a platform under discreet spotlights had, since the restaurant's opening, ended up mostly benefiting Ambrose. On the majority of weekend nights, he would reserve it for himself, and entertain notorious business leaders or celebrities or influential editors and critics. The other diners would ogle them enviously as they sat, elevated on their illuminated dais, wisps and trails of cigar smoke surrounding them like the traces of angels.

But I had made it clear that Ambrose was not to have the top table tonight. When he arrived, at getting on for our peak time, with a party of three and insisting that he have it, despite my pre-existing reservation, I knew that I had trouble.

"I'm sorry, Chef," said Drusilla, joining me at the pass. "I'm not sure what to do. You know what Mr Rookwood's like. He's very insistent when he's insisting on things."

I looked up at the clock.

"Oh, Jesus," I muttered. "Perfect timing."

I pulled my various pans off the burners and called over to Kathryn. "I might need your help with this one."

"What? *Now?*"

"Yeah, it's Ambrose."

She threw a basting spoon towards a tub of water. It missed, clattering against a steel butter pot.

"Oh, that's fine then, if it's Ambrose," she said.

"Look, I know you're pissed off with me today," I said. "But Ambrose is being unreasonable. There are diners booked on the top table already. I can't have him feeling humiliated. I think it'll help – a woman's touch."

"I can offer a woman's touch on his bloody jaw. Would that be helpful?"

As I walked onto the restaurant floor, Drusilla quietly explained the details of the issue. As I'd planned, the top table was empty and Ambrose was standing at the base of the steps that led to it. Three men in tuxedos loitered in the shadows behind him. I thought one of them looked like James Goldsmith, but I couldn't be sure. To my discomfort, when they realised it was me, they started peering nosily over his shoulder in my direction.

"Ah, Chef!" said Ambrose, running his thumb down one of his red braces. "You really shouldn't have been bothered with all this. There really is not a problem. For some unfathomable reason, Drusilla is telling me that there *is* a problem. But there's not a problem, is there?" He smiled his very particular smile that said "I'm not smiling".

"Sorry, Ambrose, but there's a reservation already for the top table," I said. "The thing is, Drusilla tells me these guests have already arrived. And it's quite important that they have this table. In fact, look, they're over there, by the door."

Kathryn, who was standing at my arm, looked towards the podium where Drusilla usually stood with her reservations book. There was a taxi driver there, the one that I'd hired. And there was a frail woman with her hair in a damp ponytail. She looked nervous, doubtful, overwhelmed, as if she couldn't believe she was in the right place.

"Mum?" Kathryn whispered. She clamped her hand over her mouth.

"Do you want to sit down?" I said to Kathryn, motioning towards the table. "One of those places is for you."

She looked up at me, a thick film of wet covering the surfaces of her eyes as she realised what was happening. Grabbing my arm, she whispered, "Thank you, Killian. *Thank you.*"

"I'm sure we can find your guests somewhere to sit," I said to Ambrose. "You understand, I know you do. It's Kathryn's mum's birthday today and she's here as my guest."

"Right," he said, and I saw the muscles in his jaw pump. "Of course. Yes."

Kathryn's mum was being led up the central isle which was specifically spotlit so that guests could be seen – especially the ones destined for the top table who, in order to reach it, had to walk its entire length. Except this time, with this diner, the effect appeared to be backfiring. A waiter was leading the way as Kathryn's mother, in her dirty coat and tracksuit trousers, shuffled towards us. In one hand she clutched an inhaler and a half-used pack of pocket tissues, in the other, a Swatch watch with a broken strap. As she inched painstakingly towards us, the chinkle of cutlery quietened, as did the chatter. I could see chins rise and mocking eyes pivot towards her. From a corner table, four yaps, with crisp shirts and mousse-sculpted hair, burst into laughter. Kathryn's mother dipped her head in shame. The effort she made, keeping the smile on her weak and yellowish face, was palpable.

I stepped forward, so that I was directly beneath a spotlight, and held my arms out towards her. An audible murmur moved through the darkness of the room. The diners, in their hushed luminous pools, gazed towards me and I could hear their whispers, *Killian, Killian, Killian,* the middle letters of my name jutting from the low, rolling sound like a thousand tiny legs.

"Mrs Riding," I said, loudly. "My very, *very* special guest. Happy birthday and welcome to Glamis. The best table in the house is ready for you, as is your extremely talented daughter."

As Kathryn stood and embraced her mum, I retreated back into the safety of the kitchen. Barely ten minutes had passed, but already the disappearance of Kathryn and I had had an effect. A dangerously long queue of tickets had built up and I was met by an ugly collage of irritated faces, all silently asking of me, "*What the fuck?*"

"Andy, can you take over the sauté station?" I said.

I had to work triple quick and, immediately, the wings of a terrible fluster began beating on my back. I had arranged my station in such a way that only Kathryn had a clear view of my cooking. But now Andy was beside me. Moreover, I had been in the job for long enough that most of what I did had become automatic. So what happened next was almost inevitable.

"What's that in your apron?" asked Andy.

He was staring at me. His tongs were held over a spitting veal fillet, the blue flame running hard beneath the blackened metal. I froze completely, my fingers in a damning sprinkle position directly over the top of a pan.

"What?" I said.

"You keep doing it," said Andy. "Taking something out of your pocket and putting it in the food."

A commis chef called Leon had moved in behind us, holding a tureen containing half set mousse. He was standing there, watching it all; listening.

"It's where I keep my pepper," I said. "I keep my pepper in here."

"But I can see your pepper," said Andy. "You've been adding pepper from the pot that's right there. So what's that in your apron?"

"It's pepper with a bit of ground clove in it. I put it in everything. For fuck's sake Andy, what's the matter with you?" I turned around. "Leon!" I shouted. "Fuck off before I boot you out of the fucking window."

I bent over my stove. Andy, in my peripheral vision, glanced back towards me, amused and bewildered and suspicious. He splashed some brandy into a veal pan, which he tipped into the flame to ignite into a whooshing cloud of pink and purple and ruby.

Chapter 40

"**H**ave you seen the *News of the World*? I wouldn't worry about it too much, but it is a little concerning. Never nice to feel there's disloyalty in the ranks."

It was Ambrose, calling from his home, eight days after the incident with Andy. I was alone in my office planning the motivational brigade talk about Max that I was to hold in half an hour's time. I pulled my chair closer to the desk.

"What's in it?"

"Oh, it's nothing really," he said. "Why don't you have a look? But don't overreact please. Call me back straight away if you want to discuss it."

I headed for the door, my walk turning into a run. Without stopping for my coat, I bolted out into the deserted Sunday morning streets which couldn't have been emptier if the Soviets had finally dropped the warhead we were forever being warned about. I bought a *News of the World* and began flicking as I walked back to the restaurant. It was right there, on page 4, a large photograph of me and the headline: "TEARS, RIVALRY AND SEXY INGREDIENTS: SECRETS OF GLAMIS REVEALED. Exclusive report by Bill Hastings."

I stood still on the pavement, only vaguely aware of the early buses and the colours of concrete and morning and the tarry city smell that was blowing over my face and fingers and through the cotton of my tunic.

"In stunning allegations that can be exclusively revealed today – which come from a source close to Killian Lone – the young London chef, who is the talk of the nation's gourmands, has been adding a sexy secret ingredient to his pricey dinners. Since the opening of his glitzy London restaurant, the so-called 'Glamis Effect' has become notorious amongst his well-to-do-diners, who include many of Britain's best-known stars of stage and screen, including Marc Almond, *Dr Who*'s Colin Baker and Stephen 'Tin Tin' Duffy. It's always been said that Lone's luxurious menu is so delicious that it gives anyone who eats it a raunchy aphrodisiac effect. But someone close to Lone has finally revealed his naughty habit. 'It's no secret that the punters who love Glamis food tend to get certain, shall we say, physical reactions,' says our source. 'Lone would have you believe it's all down to his genius. At his age? Come on, he must think we were born yesterday. Everyone in his kitchen is convinced there's some sort of trickery involved, possibly involving chemical pheromones bought from Soho sex shops.'

"In further claims that will rock the glamorous London restaurant scene, we can also reveal that Lone's famed skills as a top cook don't quite match his ability at the head of a professional brigade, a role that demands years of experience. 'The opening night was a disaster,' reveals our source. 'Killian got a big telling-off from the proprietor, Ambrose Rookwood and he was in tears. He had to give up running the kitchen completely and pass control to his second-in-command Andrew Silverwood. It's been like that ever since. Lone may be executive chef in name but he doesn't do much more than the sauces. He's lapping up all the glory, but everyone knows Andy's the one with the real talent.'

"Silverwood, 32, has trained at the altars of some of Europe's most celebrated chefs, most recently the legendary Max Mann, of the restaurant King – also part of the exclusive Rookwood Group of celebrity eateries. Our source reveals that it was Mann who taught Lone how to make the sauces, which, in the six weeks since the opening of Glamis, have already caused an international sensation, with reservations coming from as far away as Los Angeles, Cape Town and Tokyo and tables in the bistro being booked eight months in advance. It is also alleged that Chef Mann has confirmed to his staff his suspicions about Lone, calling his deadly Glamis rival a 'fraud'. 'Max told his brigade that Lone is 'Paul Daniels posing as Paul Bocuse', our source alleges, citing a world-famous French chef. 'His staff lapped it up'."

By the time I had run back to my office and picked up the phone, my throat felt as if it was blocked with wire wool.

"Bastards!" I shouted when Ambrose picked up.

"Calm down," he said. I looked around the room – at the files, the paperwork and the recipe books. I wanted to burn the whole lot of it. I wanted to go home. "Honestly, Killian, it doesn't matter. It's not going to affect the bottom line, I guarantee it. If one or two gullible readers stop coming, there are one or two thousand more waiting to replace them. Besides, the *News of the World* is not our market. Do you think the sort of idle rubbish that reads it would ever darken the doors of one of my restaurants?"

"It's not true," I said. "It's lies, all of it."

"Killian, my dear, of course it is," laughed Ambrose. "Drugs in the food. Even by the standards of the *News of the World* that's preposterous. You really don't need to deny it. I mean, pheromones?"

"And the thing about the tears! I wasn't crying. I can't have people – God! It's just bullshit. I'm going to sue them. I'm going to sue this fucker, Bill Hastings and I'm going to sue Max. Who is Bill Hastings, anyway? Do you know him?"

"Now, now, hang on there, young man," he said. "I can absolutely assure you that Max had nothing to do with this and I resent the implication. Max has been a close friend and colleague of mine for more than a decade and I know him to be an honourable man who always plays with a straight hand. He wishes you only the best."

I kicked the waste-paper bin, its contents spilling across the carpet.

"Bollocks," I said. "Why are you lying to me? Why are you *lying*?"

"Killian, you must calm down," he said. "Far more likely it's someone in your own brigade. It reeks of petty jealousy, the whole thing. The stink of envy fair rises off the page. It's probably one of the juniors trying to make an easy buck. Think about it – calmly. But in the meantime, you must trust me. I will look after you. I will back you, always. We will be fine. All will be forgotten come tomorrow."

The kitchen was in near silence that day, and that's just how I wanted it. I was distant from Kathryn and refused to entertain Andy with any contact. I removed myself from them all; returned to the sure comfort of my own embrace. During lunchtime service the wound from the branding I'd given myself in front of Max all those weeks ago began to itch. I had the word "King" seared in scar tissue on my arm and the temptation was to lock myself in the bathroom with a knife and slowly peel it off.

After the final diners had left the restaurant, I wandered back to my office. I sat there, alone, with my files and invoices and payslips and newspaper and magazine clippings from London and Paris and New York and Tokyo and Berlin and Helsinki and Toronto and Glasgow and Madrid and Washington and Lyon and Rome and Chicago and Dublin and Stockholm and Los Angeles, all of which said essentially the same thing – that Glamis was serving some of the best food in the world and the reason was that I, Killian Lone, was a genius. I scooped them up and dropped them in the waste-paper bin beneath my desk. It was too small so I stamped them in, harder and harder, angling my heel in, crushing them down, and then it fell over and my foot accidentally came down on the side and it cracked but it felt good so I leaned on my desk for support and did it again and again and then I became aware of a face peering around the door. It was Kathryn.

"Are you going to talk to me about it? Or do you want me to go?"

I stepped back from the explosion of plastic and paper on the floor. She came into the room and held me.

"Why don't you come back to mine later?" she said. "Day off tomorrow. Come on, you've had a face like an Eskimo's bollock all day."

Of course – she didn't realise it, but she had a point. I didn't have to fetch any Earl's Leaf for the next service, because Glamis didn't open on Mondays. I breathed out and shoved the mess under my desk with the side of my foot.

"Sure," I said. "All right."

* * *

Forty minutes alone with Kathryn in Dorothy's old car and, already, I had begun to feel better. The moment I closed the hollow wooden door of her flat, we rose up into a magnificent kiss. Because we had been working so hard, we hadn't really had any time alone, in private. We felt the build-up of that tension like some sort of supernatural force. First against the wall, where I found the gap under her woollen jumper and the bare cold skin of her slender waist, my hands running smoothly and bumping tantalisingly over the odd mark and mole and the mounds of her spine and up to the clasp of her bra which, eventually, I manoeuvred open. She pushed deeper with her tongue as my fingers slipped around the sides of the lace fabric and touched the tender weight of her breast. She took my arm and led me to the sofa, where we lay on the stained cushions, which began slipping out from under us as we moved. Her fingers began exploring the scars on my torso, picking over them slowly, carefully, deliberately. When she found the raised mark from the occasion, one Christmas, on which I'd cut the skin at the side of my stomach with a broken Bailey's bottle, she let out a quiet moan. I popped open the button on her jeans and thrilled at the hem of her thin cotton knickers and how they lay flat over the skin of her narrow pelvis. I went for the dark gap in between, but she tugged at my wrist, pulled it away and then... what was that? The lock. Keys turning. *Andy.*

"Hello, Killian – blimey," he said, smiling. He closed the door and then stopped to observe us on the sofa, Kathryn with half her shirt buttons undone, me with my belt hanging from my buckle. "Sorry, ha ha. Didn't mean to interrupt. Wasn't expecting to see you here."

He sat down next to me on the arm of the chair. I felt the cold he'd brought in with him from the street and picked up the faint scent of the upstairs of buses.

"It's going great, isn't it?" he said, lighting a Marlboro Red. "You must be pleased. Big man, eh?"

He took a series of short drags from his cigarette. For some reason, I briefly thought I could smell menthol in the smoke.

"Yeah, it's good," I said, sitting forward. "Thanks to you."

He had his leg crossed over his knee, just like Max did on the television, and was wearing brand-new 501s and box-fresh, all-white, high-top Air Jordans. His shoulders were strong and square inside his pastel-blue blazer; his moustache dense and manly and perfectly trimmed. Kathryn was using the opportunity of his addressing me to surreptitiously fasten up the rest of her buttons. That was that, then.

"So how do you think Max is taking it?" I said, looking up at him. "I bet he can't stand it, eh? And what about that Russian tart he's shacked up with? Jesus!"

Andy exhaled gently on the tip of his cigarette. It glowed and crackled obediently under his command.

"Yeah," he said, smiling blandly. "You've done so well. It's great."

"It's going pretty well, yeah," I nodded.

He took another puff and then cocked his head at me in a slightly exaggerated fashion.

"Hey, listen, mate," he said. "I was thinking. We should talk about refreshing the menu sometime. I think it's important that we keep things evolving, keep things fresh. You know, we have some very wealthy customers who eat at Glamis regularly. They don't want to have to keep choosing from the same list."

I sensed Kathryn next to me, nodding thoughtfully. There he was, perched on the sofa on one side. There she was, agreeing with him on the other. I shuffled forward, suddenly feeling as if I didn't have enough room.

"Well, they keep coming, don't they?" I said. "If they didn't like my menu, they'd stop, and that wouldn't be a big deal because there's a million more people who want to eat my food."

He nodded earnestly.

"That's right," he said. He was still nodding. Up and down went his large head. Up and down, serious-like, solemn-like, grave-like. Up and down it went, agreeing absolutely with everything I was saying. "But what about the press?" he said. "And the reviewers? And you can't forget Ambrose. He eats off our menu every day. I'm not saying we should rearrange everything just for him, but take a bit of advice from someone who knows. It's always best to keep the boss sweet."

"Fuck Ambrose," I said. "I'm making Ambrose a millionaire."

He studied the end of his Marlboro again, as if trying to fathom what was wrong with it. His knee was practically in my face. 'Big man.' *Big man?* I stood up.

"You know, Andy, I don't know where you get off, telling me my menu's no good."

Finally, he stopped gazing at his cigarette. He pursed his rosy, chubby, cracked lips. "That's not what I said."

I picked my way over to the other side of the coffee table. The end of my belt was still sticking out of my trousers. It was on the highest notch on the buckle, and the rest of it was jutting from my crotch, all flaccid.

"I'll change the menu when I feel like it," I said. "It's *my* menu."

Kathryn moved closer to him. "Come on, Kill," she said. "Andy's allowed to have an opinion. He does run the kitchen for you." Her eyes darted towards my flapping belt.

"Anyone can run a fucking kitchen!" I said. "It just takes a bit of practice. There's nothing amazing about working the pass, you know. Christ, read the papers! It's me they're going to give a star to when the guide comes out."

With shaking fingers, I ran the cheap band of leather back through the hoops of my trousers. They watched me carefully. They weren't laughing. I was pretty sure they weren't laughing.

"Anyway," I said. "It's not about me, is it? I just want to prove that Max is over. He treated me like crap, he treated Kathryn like crap. He's not getting away with it. His food's ridiculous. Guinea-fowl and mango? Fuck off. It's an embarrassment. Ambrose will get it eventually. Max is a liability. If King has any chance of not becoming a laughing stock by 1990, he needs to get rid of the nutter." I glanced at Kathryn. "We should take over that place."

"I reckon we should ignore Max, don't you?" said Andy. "Forget about him. It's not really about—"

But I spoke over him: "And now I've got enemies in my kitchen and I've got to deal with that." I drove my hands deep into the pockets of the flared corduroys that I'd had since I was fifteen. "I take it you saw that thing today? In the paper? I won't have enemies. I won't have disloyalty."

A silence crawled through the room. A breeze blew in from under the door. My too-short cords exposed my ankles and the cold air curled around them like the ghost of a cat. Andy hoisted a smile. "Such a good job you're doing with those sauces," he said, eventually. "They're amazing, really. Unbelievable."

The darning in my sock had gone and my toe was cold. It looked ridiculous, poking through the hole down there;

staring out at the world, all bald and pink and naked.

"Are you trying to tell me something?" I said to him.

"No!" he said.

"There's no fucking secret ingredient if that's what you're saying."

Andy tapped the head of his Marlboro into the shallow metal ashtray. "All right, matey, I know that," he said. "You need to calm down."

I saw the thin blue vein running up the bony framework of my mother's ankle as she left me alone. I saw her face – pale, beautiful and fascinated – through the steam of boiling water.

"I'm not your fucking matey," I said. "I'm your boss."

Andy stood, pushed out his cigarette and chuckled to himself.

"Going to your head enough is it?" he said, leaving towards the kitchen.

"You better be careful," I shouted after him. "All those little journo mates you hang out with. If I find out it was you that leaked–"

He stopped, just short of the doorway.

"Don't even go there," he said, shaking his head, as if struggling to absorb what I'd just said. "No, hang on," he said. "How *dare* you?"

Kathryn looked in his direction with a fragile, uncertain expression. I pointed, right in the direction of his face, my King scar itching, my ugly teeth showing, a silver-grey fly buzzing over the ashtray.

"You're on a warning," I said. "One more leak and you're gone."

Kathryn turned to me, aghast. "Killian!" she said.

As I addressed her, tiny cartwheels of spit flew in her direction. "I'm going home."

I walked out in my socks, my shoes hanging from my fingers, slamming the door behind me. By the time I was halfway down the stairs, Kathryn had appeared at the top.

"Come on," she said. "Don't go."

"It's just Andy," I said. "I don't trust him. He's not loyal."

"Are you sure you're not being unfair?" she said, walking down to meet me. "I don't think it was him. It's just not the kind of thing Andy would do."

"I mean anyway," I said. "It's crazy, what they're saying. Drugging the food! What with? Pheromones? Please! It's a joke."

She gave a shallow nod. I don't know exactly what I wanted her to do, but her reaction felt incomplete, unsatisfying.

"I'm not doing it, Kathryn," I said.

"I know," she said, weakly. She crossed her arms and looked at her feet. "Let's just not talk about it."

I made a show of idly scratching the back of my head.

"It was you that said, whatever I get I deserve it. You know, it meant a lot when you said that."

"You do deserve it," she said. "Of course you do."

"I mean, just imagine where we'll be in a year's time if things continue like they are. You'll be earning enough to keep your mum safe, in the best home in London, maybe even getting better."

She smiled at that. Her hands pushed around my waist and she gazed at me with shining eyes.

"It's really, actually possible, isn't it?" she said.

"Totally," I said. "I've just got to keep fighting. I need your back-up, though. I can't do it without you."

"Well, you've got it," she said. "You need to do whatever you need to, Kill. Just go out there and bloody grab it." She rested her head on my chest. "Listen, if you can't cope with Andy tonight, why don't I come back to the cottage with you?"

I glanced towards the exit.

"Oh, there's no point," I said. "I'm still in a crappy mood, to be honest. I'll be rubbish company. Why don't I call you tomorrow?"

As I drove back to the cold, strange cottage, I tried very hard to think about something that wasn't Max or Kathryn or the secret that was beginning to feel like a bruise that was ripening and yellowing and spreading out over everything.

Chapter 41

The *Restaurant Magazine* awards were held annually at the Café de Paris in the West End of London. It was the most glamorous fixture of the culinary year and, mainly due to the celebrity and minor royal guests, never failed to attract the attentions of the media – not to mention every working chef in the country. They all denied their interest, of course. It was fashionable in the kitchens of London to shrug at the mention of a nomination and, if you'd won anything in the past, to feign confusion, saying, "Did I? I'd forgotten all about it," perhaps adding, "For me, it's about the diners". The curious thing about that pose was how they would gossip about the event for months in advance. Contenders would hire the most expensive suits Moss Bros could supply and frequently react with such rage when the jury went the wrong way that walk-outs and even physical tussles were not uncommon.

Glamis wasn't nominated for any awards – we hadn't been open long enough – and that was fine with me. I was probably the only chef on the circuit who genuinely didn't want to attend. Whenever I was recognised – in the street or anywhere else – I experienced this shrinking, hunted feeling. So far, my refusal to make myself available to the media had had the opposite effect to that intended.

The less I spoke, the more they somehow found to write. However, Ambrose had made it clear that it was important I attend this ceremony, for fear of alienating people he felt it essential to remain on good terms with. Besides, I thought, the greatest chefs in Britain and much of Europe would be there. I would meet my heroes.

The awards were held on a Monday, because that was the day most fine-dining restaurants tended to be closed. Ambrose sent a courier to Glamis with clothes for Kathryn and me. Modest as ever, Kathryn went to change in the locker room whilst I climbed into the suit in my office. I felt odd and stiff and fraudulent, like an ugly picture that had been placed in a beautiful frame. My shoes were tight and made of thin, hard leather that gripped the skin of my heels as I pushed my feet in.

"Don't laugh," came a voice.

I looked up to find nobody there.

"Kathryn?" I said, standing up tentatively. "You can come in. I'm dressed."

There was a silence.

"I don't want to."

"Why not?" I craned my neck a little. "Come in!"

"It isn't supposed to be a fancy-dress party is it?" she said.

"No...?"

"So please explain – why am I dressed as a Cornetto?"

I stepped towards the door and tried to peep out into the corridor, the rim of leather on the backs of my shoes constricting irritably.

"Oh God!" she said, on hearing my approach. "If you laugh, I swear, I'll turn your balls into nut roast."

With a rustle and a blush, she moved into the room. It was a cocktail dress, black and Merlot red, that finished just above the knee. The sleeves were high and ruched into the shape of huge roses; there was a low scoop that revealed more of her décolletage than I was expecting. It was all finished off by an enormous satin bow that ran vertically up her left side, pinned in at the waist. I was dazzled. Kathryn scratched her face and bent her knee, awkwardly, as if she was desperate for the loo.

"Why aren't you saying anything? Oh God, you're embarrassed for me."

"You look incredible."

"Oh shut up." She pulled at its low, diving neck with both hands. "Does it show too much boob?"

"No."

"I look like a freak."

"If you could climb into my head and feel what I'm feeling now," I told her, "I promise you'd never be shy again."

"I'm not shy," she said, sighing in the way that she sighed when she wanted a hug but was too shy to say so.

"Why don't you wear your hair up?" I asked, when I'd put her down.

I lifted it over her birthmark but, as I did so, her face dropped, an unhappy pressure gathering on her lips. I ran my fingers gently over it.

"It's beautiful, though," I said.

"I'm not putting my hair up."

"All right," I said, kissing the dark purple shadow on her cheek. "It's okay."

A distant thud interrupted us. Ambrose emerged from the corridor like a 1950s Bond, in a spectacular tuxedo, scarlet bow tie and shining spats, hair fragrantly Daxed and his ever present, tight ruby ring stuck to his thumb like a boiled sweet that had been left too long in a pocket.

"Come on, kids. It's time."

I winced.

"Be brave," said Kathryn. "I'll look after you if you promise to look after me."

I let her take my hand and we walked the short distance to the venue in Coventry Street, my tight leather shoes scraping pain all over my heels. What made me more uncomfortable still was the man in the anorak who handed me a biro and an old Our Price receipt and asked for an autograph. Then the girl with the yellow exercise book. Then the woman with the diary. In the twenty minutes it took to walk from Glamis to the Café de Paris, I was stopped six times.

"Why do you look so shocked?" asked Ambrose as we rounded the corner, the celestial white glow of the venue's lights suddenly visible. "If you ever left that kitchen of yours, you might have noticed that you have become the most famous chef in Britain."

Then they saw us. It began with a single cry – "It's Lone!" – and it was as if someone had kicked a wasp nest full of glitter. There was an uproar of shouting and waving and flashing cameras. I stood, rooted in fright, on the red carpet that ran from the door like a tongue. I grabbed for Kathryn's hand as the mass of photographers, many of whom were on stepladders, called my name. I kept glancing back over my shoulder, not because I was looking for someone, but because I wanted to run away, down there, back down the alleyway, into the beautiful darkness. Ambrose placed his hand on my shoulder and squeezed, whilst a million tiny mosquitoes of light bombarded my face.

Eventually, we walked through the golden doors and managed to hustle a path through all the evening jackets and cocktail dresses and found a small space in the crowded lobby in which we could breathe. Ambrose said, "I really do appreciate your coming tonight. I know you're not comfortable with all this, but it's vital that you make the most of your celebrity – for Glamis and the Rookwood Group as well as yourself, of course. Max does a wonderful job of it, and it really does make an enormous difference."

I broke eye contact with him.

"Do we have to stay long?"

"Max is picking something up tonight. You should at least stay for that. We need some pictures of the two of you together, with Max holding his prize."

"It's just, I've not been sleeping too well…"

Ambrose turned to Kathryn, who was absent-mindedly chewing the inside of her lip.

"Kathryn, my dear, would you be kind enough to excuse us for just a moment?"

"Sure," she said, smiling emptily, visibly fazed by the restless thunder of hundreds of people trying to make themselves heard above each other.

"You wait here," he said. "We'll be back in a sniff."

Following in Ambrose's wake, I felt as if I was struggling through a narrow black corridor, with walls of dark pupils that clicked onto me a moment after I'd passed.

None of them wanted to be caught in the action of watching me, but I saw every one sliding in, blinking, crafty and quick. As we pushed towards a flight of stairs, a shameful urge grew in me. I wanted to grab hold of Ambrose's hand. I wanted him to look after me.

We went up a wide flight of empty stairs. There were golden statues of naked boys in dimly lit recesses and fake red flames flickering behind glass. We walked into a gent's bathroom. The walls were painted matt black and, by the sink, there were bottles of cologne and piles of perfectly folded handtowels made from fluffy cotton with "Café de Paris" stitched into them in golden thread.

"Are those real towels?" I said, amazed. "Aren't people just going to nick them?"

Ambrose disappeared into a toilet cubicle.

"Come on, then," he said, poking his head around the door.

"Ambrose, I don't really like things like this," I said, pulling the door closed behind me. "I don't want to stay too long."

He smiled broadly. One of his molars was made of metal.

"Well, let me help you enjoy yourself," he said. He removed a small silver case from his pocket, which had an elaborate engraving on its cover, and opened it with a click. There were a number of small paper parcels inside it, one of which he unwrapped carefully. It was powder, compacted so tightly that you could see the lines of the paper folds marked into its surface.

He slid a Platinum American Express card from a Burberry wallet and used it to push some of the powder onto the spotless black-tiled shelf above the cistern. I watched him arranging it into two lines of fine dust, his pushes and chops so practised he could have been a Michelin chef julienning a carrot.

He rolled up a grubby one-pound note and bent down to take his share, each particle of the stuff hesitating for a fraction of a second before rising up and disappearing high into his long nostrils.

"This will make you feel much better," he said, standing and sniffing repeatedly. He handed me the tubed note.

I hesitated, then copied what he'd done. I was surprised how easy it was – for some reason, I had always imagined snorting drugs would take some sort of practice. It stung my sinuses and a plasticky, chemically taste made itself known, along with a gammy numbness that began to spread down the back of my throat and tongue.

"It is speed?" I said, standing up.

"Oh dear God, no," he said, laughing. I watched carefully to see if any detectable change had come over him. "Oh bless you. Speed! Here…" He dropped two wrapped packets into my palm. "You'll be needing these."

I looked at them doubtfully.

"Trust me," he said. "It's a long night. You'll be wanting to, er, what's the phrase they're all using these days? Re-record, not fade away."

"Don't you care about getting caught?" I said, my hand still open in front of him.

"Not a chance of it. Money may not buy you happiness, Killian, my fine boy, but it does buy you freedom. Reach a certain level, as no doubt you will discover, and you'll find that the tapestry of life becomes a good deal richer with possibilities, especially in the realm of things to do for fun."

I felt nothing at all as we strode back down the magnificent stairs, except for slightly enormous. But there was a clamminess on my forehead and my socks had sprung wet with sweat. As we turned the corner, I looked again upon the crush below – the thick, smoking stew of champagne, mouths and eyes. I took a breath and savoured the sensation of air filling my lungs, my body, my brain. I could do this.

"Hi, hi, hi," I said as we went. Each time I said it to a different face, I noticed a different reaction. It was like ringing bells. Delight, embarrassment, respect, defiance, quick nods that were rippled through with complex veins of envy, alarm and fear. I saw fat hands on slender glass stems, scarlet fingernails lifting cigarettes to shining lips, spittle-flecked teeth in guffawing mouths, shirt collars pressed into scarlet, goosey throats and cocktail dresses with jewels that trapped rainbows and low-cut dresses that showed the skin, the smooth skin with the pearls and diamonds and the moles and the deep cleavage and the noses and the elbows and all the whispering words, all the hundreds of thousands of fluttering, skittering, whispering words, pointed at me: *there he is, there he goes, that's him, that's him, that's Killian Lone...*

"Where have you been?" said Kathryn when we found her.

"Just briefing Killian on protocol," said Ambrose, rising up on his toes with purring satisfaction. "Now – you two young things. Come with me."

I watched my feet as he guided us through the crowd, my shoes rubbing against my heel, my soles wet with sweat. They didn't suit me, those shoes. They weren't even mine. Hired for six pounds. Rented. Who else had walked in these shoes? Why were they wet?

"Killian!"

Ambrose's face was leering into mine.

"Allow me to introduce you to the editor of *Restaurant Magazine*. Craig Rolly, Killian Lone. Killian Lone, Craig Rolly."

"Fabulous to meet you at last, Chef Lone," he said, holding out his hand. "I've been following your career closely. Fascinating stuff. What a story. Meteoric, eh?"

I could see this Craig Rolly, with his triangular smiling mouth and his hair spiked high like the Russian out of *Rocky*. But I couldn't face him directly because I was transfixed by the man next to him. I was beginning to feel odd. There were stars running between my eyes and my brain. They were drying out my mouth.

"Hello, Max."

I looked at Max's shoes. They had buckles on them. *Buckles*. Look at the shoes, the shoes of Max Mann.

"I'm saying, it's amazing, the speed of your success," the editor repeated. "Max was just telling me…"

"You don't want to believe anything he tells you," I said.

Rolly glanced conspiratorially at Max, who responded with a snide, leonine smile. And there was a third man, in a loose suit of shiny grey, who snorted fatly at some private joke that had evidently been shared between them.

"And what's this one?" I demanded, pointing at him with my thumb.

"Bill," he said, holding out a hand like a boiled pork chop. "Bill Hastings, how do you do?"

"I know you," I said. "*News of the World*."

I glared at Max, as the light from the chandeliers above fell softly on his shark-wide eyes and arboreal nose. "Mate of yours, is it?"

I turned back to Kathryn who was occupying herself staring up at the ceiling. "He's the one that wrote that shit about me crying."

"What?" she replied, irritably.

"That shit about my sauces being drugged. You know? It's him. Bill Hastings."

Rolly leaned in, his cow-eyes heavy with champagne smugness. "I can assure you, Chef Max has been regaling us all with tales of your fantastic rise."

Max took an oyster from a passing waiter, who was carrying a reef of seafood in a deep ice-filled silver dish with carved cupid handles. "Would you believe," he said, "that Killian could barely strip a bunch of basil when he started under me?"

He opened his mouth, pushed out the tip of his tongue and let the shining mollusc slip in.

"I spent six weeks with Max," I shouted to the editor. "That's all. Six weeks. My aunt taught me how to cook, not him."

There was another voice, from behind, trying to get in. "Killian? Max?"

I turned to see Ambrose. A grease-sheen of sweat was visible over his forehead. Moisture sparkled from its creases. "Could I borrow you a moment, please?" He addressed the other two. "Sorry to interrupt, gentlemen. I'll have them back in a jiff."

The crowds parted once more as I followed the men, with Kathryn behind me, until we reached a clearing in a grubby corner by a fire exit. A white paper background had been erected, covered with the logos of Dom Perignon champagne, the company that had apparently sponsored the event. There was a white light that shone with such violence that it ached in the backs of my eyes. Just behind it was a cameraman, in an old blue polo shirt, loose jeans and sandals, and a woman in a wide shoulder-padded suit jacket in pastel blocks of yellow, green and red. I recognised her. She was from the television – Gillian something.

A crew member in fashionable brown oversized spectacles began clipping a microphone onto my lapel. I said to Kathryn, "That woman's from *Food and Drink*. My mum watches that."

"Your mum?" said the man, with a chummy smile.

"Yes," I said, a little embarrassed at his overhearing

me. He began attaching a wire to Max, who was standing beside me, grinning in his condescending way. "I was just saying," I continued feebly, "my mum watches this."

And then, we were on.

"I am joined by two London chefs who are very much the stars of this glittering occasion, Max Mann of the celebrity restaurant King and his young protégé Killian Lone of the superlative Glamis, which is fast becoming one of the hottest gourmet tickets in the world." The presenter turned to Max. "Max, you must be proud?"

"Oh, enormously so," he said. "I have just been saying, when young Killian here began at King he couldn't even strip a bunch of basil. Hard to believe, I know. But I was an early supporter of Killian's, despite several of my colleagues expressing doubts. I could see something in him and I'm glad I had my way. He took up a good deal of my attention, I must say, but I think all my hard work has been worth it."

"Worth it indeed," she smiled. "Killian, it sounds like you have the so-called Gentleman Chef a lot to thank for?"

There was all that light and the black box pointed at my face and there, just about visible in it all, the woman I knew from the television. I pointed my mouth towards the tiny microphone on my suit.

"My aunt taught me to cook," I said, loudly and slowly so that nothing could be lost. "And now I'm the most famous chef in England."

I squinted back into the light and heard Max chuckle. My jaw ached. My tongue felt fat and dry, like something sitting dead in my mouth. Stuff. I needed some more of that stuff. I had to get out of there. I blinked irritably into the light and turned around to find Ambrose. Where was he? I could see Kathryn, her face all jagged with alarm. She was shaking her head, mouthing, "No!"

"Well, he's certainly got the confidence!" the presenter was saying brightly.

"And all this amusing nonsense about his adding secret ingredients," Max continued. "Well, he should just allow your crew in to film him cooking. That would silence the doubters. What do you say, Killian?"

The silhouette of the woman seemed to be looking at me.

"Any time," I said, into the blackness, which smoked and glowed. "Any time whatsoever."

"Thank you, Killian, maybe we'll take you up on that exciting offer," said the presenter. "And Chef Max, we certainly wish you the best at the awards tonight."

He gave a little bow. "Thank you."

I plucked the microphone from my lapel. "Come on," said Kathryn. "Let's get a drink."

I was about to address Max again but Kathryn pulled me so hard that I felt it in the muscle of my forearm. She led me, quickly into the hot mass. They were a vast army of murmurers squashed into the building, all in black and sparkles, their heads pink, jowly and painted and shooting out bursts of ugliness and beauty that hit me as I passed. Every one fascinating, grotesque, the women arranged with such startling prettiness that my heart would groan with joy and sorrow as I saw each one. So many faces. Each one firing eyes at me, spelling out the words with their wet and sliding drunken tongues: *there he is, there he goes, that's him, that's him, that's Killian Lone…*

Kathryn took me to a quiet corridor that led to the kitchen. We sat on the floor as the stern tray-carrying waiters came and went above us. I rubbed my eyes. Everything was so confusing.

"What's wrong with you?" she said, trying to pull her legs inside her dress. "How did you get so drunk?"

"I'm not drunk," I said.

I looked crossly at my shoes. My heels were sore; the leather was pinching my toes and the elastic in the socks was too tight.

"Well, what's going on then?" she said. "*'I'm the most famous chef in England'?* Come on, Kill, that's not like you."

I bent forward to untie my laces, surprised at how relaxed I was feeling about the whole thing. "Jesus, did you see those photographers? All saying my name. Shouting it! I'm going to take my shoes off. Shall we get some whisky?"

Kathryn's grump lifted into a smile. She gave a naughty, delighted laugh.

"What are you doing?" she said. "You can't go shoeless."

"Shoes aren't compulsory."

"They are in the Café de Paris."

"It's like Ambrose told me, money doesn't buy you happiness, but it does enable you to fuck around with no shoes on."

"Ambrose didn't say that," she giggled, making a half-hearted, flirtatious attempt to swipe at my fingers.

"He did."

I pulled one shoe off and then the other, before dipping a hand into my jacket pocket.

"Here," I opened my palm to reveal one of the little parcels. "Do you want some?"

"What is it?"

"Almost certainly not speed."

Her laughter vanished.

"Have you taken cocaine?"

"Don't worry. I don't think it's done anything."

Her eyes rose in stung disappointment.

"Why did you do it?"

"Because... why not?"

"Because it's just not the kind of thing you do. You said you were going to look after me."

"But it was Ambrose."

"God, Killian. Please don't turn into one of *them*."

Her eyes fell to her knees. Pushing myself up off the floor, I said, "Anyway, since when have you been Miss bloody Goody Two Shoes?"

"I'm not Miss Goody Two Shoes...".

A flash of dirty light glinted from her crucifix.

"Oh God," I said. "Of course. Kathryn the Christian."

I watched in prickly confusion as she sprang to her feet and marched back into the noise. After a minute spent trying to gather myself together, I followed in her general direction in my socks, ordering a triple Bells at the bar, before heading back to the bathroom to start on the next wrap of cocaine.

I could feel it as I walked back downstairs. This was it – the best night of my life. Kathryn would be all right. *Everything* would be all right. I was donating my jacket to an elderly man with a large golden medallion in the shape of a chop when, around the corner, came Max.

"On your way to the snort traps?" I said, following him back up the steps.

He glanced at my socks and smiled in a way that was almost friendly.

"Shouldn't you be going to bed?" he said.

He was wearing a velvet bow tie, his shirt collar baggy on his cadaverous neck, the legs beneath his trousers so bony that the material hung from his waist as if he was on stilts. Enjoying a sudden rush of wellbeing, I reached up and put my arm around his shoulder.

"Max," I said, grinning. "Come on, Max Mann, man. Let's stop all this. Let's be friends, eh? Hey, 'Max Mann' – is that a made-up name? Because if it is, it's not a very good one, is it?"

He looked, anxiously, over his shoulder.

"Come on, man, we're equals now," I said. "It's over. Let's just get on with making great food and forget all this rivalry. Why are we tearing strips off each other?"

He nudged backwards, so that my arm slipped loose.

"I really have no idea what you're talking – "

"Yes, you do," I said. "All this! Leaking bollocks to the press–"

His face tilted in, just a fraction, just enough to gather the best of the darkness that was hovering about the stairs. The shadows worked gratefully over his lines and pock-marks and deep grey bags.

"You better watch what you accuse me of. If I find out I'm being slandered, lied about, I shall have no choice but to notify my solicitor."

"Stop talking to me like that, Max. Why are you talking to me like that? I've proved myself to you. I can do it, Max. I can cook. I'm tough enough. I'm as tough as you." I raised my arms and announced proudly, "I am a turnspit dog!"

Max whispered, "You're poisoning your guests with some kind of *additive* and you'll get found out. People aren't as stupid as you think. There will be proof. And the instant that there is, you're finished. I'll make sure of it. So make the most of your stolen moment. It won't last."

"You're telling me I won't last? Do you have any

idea what people say about your food? *Guinea-fowl and mango?* People are laughing at you, Max. Have you seen *Spitting Image* lately? They think you're hilarious. Take off your flared trousers, old man, and smell the future." I made a show of hungrily sniffing the air. "Hmmmm, smells like butter." I paused to feign the arrival of a sudden realisation. "Oh, but hang on, Max, you knew that didn't you? Do you think your mate Bill might be interested to hear how much of Echire's finest is used at King?"

He pushed me, with outstretched fingers, on the throat and I fell against the black painted wall behind me. Glancing quickly to check that we were alone, he spoke again, his voice in full whisper: "You have no idea how fragile your existence is. You have no idea how close you are to over."

"Tell me I'm talented."

"You're pathetic."

"Tell me I'm talented."

"You're ungrateful."

"Tell me I'm talented."

"You're needy. You're overrated. You're a fraud."

My head rang with it. My eyes began to swell.

"I'm not," I shouted. "I deserve it."

A couple passed by and Max stepped back. In the instant before he made his elegant way up the stairs and away from me, I saw his face lighten with victory.

Half an hour later I was back up there, forcing the remains of the first wrap up my nose. I leaned back on the wall and slid downwards, staring at the piss drips on the floor, waiting for the effect to hit. It didn't take long. I pushed myself to my feet and realised that I needed Kathryn.

I found her at the bar, looking more beautiful than

I'd ever seen her, ignoring a young Italian man with an expensive watch who was trying to engage her.

"I've been looking everywhere for you," I said, above the sound of the editor of *Restaurant Magazine* giving out awards on the stage. "Why did you walk off?"

"You were being a cock," she said. "But luckily for you I've since realised this whole building is filled with drunken idiot cock chefs and the prospect of making small talk with them is a very slightly more hideous prospect than listening to you tell the BBC what an amazing genius you are." She paused and, before I had the chance to respond, said, "God, you look like shit."

Inside my head, a grand nation of cherubim ejaculated simultaneously.

"Don't worry," I whispered. "I think it's worn off."

All of a sudden, I felt rather chatty.

"What would your secret word be then?" I said.

"Secret word?"

"You know, what Andy was saying when we went out that night – about the S&M people. They have a word they say for when the pain gets too much."

"Oh!" she laughed. "Hmm… well, yes… Pippin. My word would be pippin."

"That's not very sexy," I said.

"No, but it's a lovely word, don't you think? Pippin. A lovely word and a lovely apple. My favourite kind of apple. What would yours be?"

"If yours is pippin, mine is windfall," I decided. "I always feel sorry for those windfall apples. They get blown off the tree and then stamped into the ground, with all the bruises and the maggots. But they're perfectly good apples that have just been ignored by everyone and that's why they die. So it's a good word for the pain getting too much, if you think about it. Windfall apples live a life of pain."

Kathryn nodded wryly. "You're very much the apple philosopher tonight."

I pushed my fingertip down inside my collar. I hated this starched, neck-tightening shirt. It was the shirt of a Victorian headmaster; the shirt of a corpse. I took off my tie and stuffed it into my trouser pocket.

"I have to sit down," I said. "Why is everyone looking at me?"

"They're not," said Kathryn.

I unfastened the first three buttons of my shirt.

"Is it because I'm famous?"

She patted my hand. "Yes, dear."

Finally, the barman delivered my drink. I gifted him my tie, opened my throat and poured down the whisky. A jellyfish of nausea wrapped its tentacles around my stomach. I sniffed heavily and gripped the bar.

"I think this cocaine's off," I said.

"Shall we go and sit down?"

A field of coloured prickles shimmered in front of my eyes. Then the sickness passed and a new surge of power charged up my spine like beams of light. That was better. There was no past, there were no problems. There was only me and Kathryn and our jewel of a restaurant and our perfect future. I had done it. I had become magnificent.

"Are you all right, Kill? Your face has gone a bit berserk. Come on, let's sit down."

"There's something I have to tell you," I said. "I love you. I love you so much. I want to spend the rest of my life with you and, the restaurant – I want to do it properly. I've always known I could be a decent chef, Kathryn. But I want to do it on my own terms. I'm going to do it properly."

She glanced anxiously at the drunken man beside her.

"Pipe down," she said. "No gooey talk in public. I love you too."

She kissed me quickly on the chin. I felt it again: the surge.

"I don't need those herbs to cook, you know," I said. "I won the Young Saucier. That proves I deserve it."

"Herbs?" she said, a blade of irritation evident in her tone. "God, what are you *on* about? Why don't you shush, hey? Do you want another drink?"

A wave. A slump. A dead wind. I gripped the bar again.

"I think we need to go home," said Kathryn. "All that cocaine has made you poorly."

"Hang on," I muttered.

I felt in my trouser pocket for the second wrap and held it towards her.

"Have some with me. Go on," I said. "Every fucker in this room is on it, having fun. But you walk around sometimes like fun is kind of *beneath* you; like joy is a toy you used to play with when you were a kid but now you're too grown up for. You shouldn't look down on happiness. You shouldn't condescend to it – that's just such an *English* thing to do. Happiness, fun, excitement, joy – why don't you deserve that? Why don't *we*?"

"It's just—"

My words were coming fast now, and from a place I hadn't accessed before.

"Trying new things. Being foolish. Risky. Fearless. Standing up to the pain and saying, 'I fucking love the fucking pain'. I mean, pain? What is it? Humans are built for it. We need it. It's like muscles need to tear so they can grow. Pain is nothing to be frightened of. You go into it, and it's a bit dark, it's a bit scary, but it's just a corridor. And at the other end of the corridor is happiness. It's *always* happiness. And that's life, isn't it? That's the *whole thing*."

For a second, I forgot what I was talking about. Remembering, I eagerly grabbed Kathryn's arms and gave her the full sell.

"It'll be fine. It'll be amazing. You know, all that stuff you were telling me about going out and taking what you can get? Well what about taking some *life*? What about doing it now? With me? We deserve it. Don't we?"

She didn't respond. I was close and I knew it.

"We'll look back on this, one day, when we're old, when we're at the end. We'll look back on tonight and it will be the most brilliant memory."

She hesitated. Then she downed her vodka, plucked the wrap from my fingers and returned fifteen minutes later, looking wary and crafty and thrilled.

"My tongue's gone numb," she whispered, her eyes alive with adventure. "It tastes disgusting."

"So does vodka," I said, handing her an icy tumbler. "And I've got you a triple of that."

Talking, talking, talking. Running through the crowd, with my hand in hers. Knocking elbows and collapsing in smiles, curled up in a dark corner, laughing until we ached in our stomachs and in our throats. More to drink. Another package from Ambrose. More to drink. To the toilets again. Up the stairs. Falling down. All looking at me. Talking. Turning around at the bar and Kathryn's lost.

Where did she go? And who is he? Why is he looking at me? Where are my socks? I like being sockless. I like how it feels on my feet. So many intricate sensations. Where is Max? So wrong, Max Mann. He shouldn't have doubted me. He shouldn't have hated me, he should have liked me, he should have loved me. I'll take them off, the shirt buttons, the rest, one, two, three, four, now you'll all see the scars from the ovens, the scars from the cuts, the scars from the kettle, the burns on my nipples and there, off with the fucking shirt, you can have that, don't mention it, sir, and now you can see the fresh cuts on my arms, and the cuts on my ribs, all skin and bone, all cuts and love –

A stage. The stage. Beautiful, bright. And there's that man, that man with the Rocky hair from the magazine about restaurants.

"Ladies and Gentlemen, please welcome to the stage the winner of the 1985 Restaurant Magazine Lifetime Achievement award – from the legendary London restaurant King, the Gentleman Chef himself, Max Mann."

It all goes black. A single spotlight, over the lectern, hard and brilliant and sharp. It's waiting for him and they're cheering. They're cheering for *him*. My night. Fuckers, look. I'll make the fuckers look. Step onto the stage, one, two, three, I'll make the fuckers look at my skin and my bone and my scars and my love. He should have loved me.

Inside the spotlight. You can't see anything here. Blinding white on my skin. Smoke in the air. The stage cold and sticky beneath my feet. The lectern. There's a little support in the lectern. Like a shelf. Like a step. Okay, so, I'll step on it then. One foot on the lectern. Then the other. All those people. I'm on the lectern. On top! *My* night. Look at the people, all in their hundreds. Look at them looking at me.

The lectern is shaking. It might fall, into the crowd. My arms out to balance. Now they can see what I am. Centre stage, high up here, the army of black murmurers staring silent, *tamed*. My arms straight out, the spotlight on me, my skin and my bones and my scars and my cuts and there he is, there's my own Max, at the side of the stage, and I shout to him, I scream to him, "You should have loved me", and the lectern falls and I fall.

Later. Outside. A man with his arm around my shoulder. Asking about me. Friendly but not friendly. Asking about secrets; about secret ingredients. A journalist.

Shouting. I punch him. I'm kicked. In the ribs. In the head. In the back. I curl into myself. I need to sleep. I can't. Stuff. I need some more of that stuff.

Alone. Cold.

And then someone reaching down. Pale hands. Shaking fingers. A face. *Her*. I lift my head from the concrete and all I want to say, as she takes me in her arms, is *windfall, windfall, windfall*.

Chapter 42

I didn't sleep at all that night. I lay on Kathryn's sofa, empty of life. At around half past four in the morning I couldn't stand it any more. I tried to cry. I tried to force a break in the solidity that I had carried with me for years. But it wouldn't crack. I wanted tears. I wanted rupture. But I ended up just barking these ridiculous dry sobs that bottomed out into a thin, wounded cat whine.

I wanted to be clean again. I wanted purity for me and for Kathryn. This couldn't go on, this cheating. It was exactly what Aunt Dorothy had warned me about, and I'd failed her. Tomorrow, I would throw my pouch of Earl's Leaf away. As soon as I had the chance, I would burn the herb garden. And if that meant the end of Glamis, then that would be what it meant. Perhaps Kathryn would come with me to south-west France, where we would quietly continue our training. And we'd return to London in maybe five or six years and Ambrose could fund a new opening. Smaller than Glamis. Humble and simple and honest. I smiled as my plan unfolded itself. I felt a kernel of returning warmth in my chest.

I manoeuvred myself to a sitting position and thought about watching the television. The remote was nowhere to be seen and I didn't fancy the trek to the other side of the coffee table to switch it on. Besides, it would probably only be Ceefax or the Open University at this time of the morning. There was a pile of magazines near my feet. They looked like issues of *Restaurant Magazine*. Urgh. Just beneath the latest edition, though, there seemed to be something else. I pulled it out. A brochure.

Ten Pines House. It looked like a beautiful place. A gloried country mansion in a world of green and blue. I stared at the picture. I wished I could wake up in Ten Pines House. I could tell, from the broken spine and the state of the paper, that the booklet had been read often. One of the pages had had its corner bent over. I opened it up to see a nurse in angelic white assisting a woman who was climbing out of a swimming pool. Another picture showed a huge vase of colourful flowers sitting in a sunlit window and, just visible in the corner, a precisely made-up bed. The pillows looked plumply inviting, the sheets gentle and new. There were some numbers on the page, drawn in biro. Kathryn had written: £2,993 p.a. and underlined it.

For her mum. This must be where she wants to send her; her plan for when she earns enough money. You'd need to be the boss of somewhere, to afford that. *Chef de file*. The warmth in my chest vanished. I tried to stand but a wave of fizzing weakness struck me and I fell, help-lessly, back onto the sofa. Once recovered, I crawled on my hands and knees into the bathroom.

Using the sink to pull myself up, I opened the medicine cabinet, found a pink razor and, gathering as much force as I could muster, crushed it on the floor with the heel of my hand. Picking the blade out from the shards, I swiped it into the side of my stomach and watched the long lips of skin open up and begin to dribble. I swiped again, the adrenaline and the endorphins making me feel comforted and powerful.

There were only a few sheets of toilet paper left on the roll. I groaned at the realisation that I had to somehow make it to the kitchen and back with a tea towel. Staggering, leaning, crawling, I finally managed it when I noticed the sickly dawn light slithering through the bathroom blind and up the dirty white walls. I wondered what Dorothy would say if she could see me now. I pictured her, here with me. *"Oh, Kill, my love, my darling, what's happened?"* and she would soothe me and she would understand.

There were footsteps coming from Kathryn's bedroom. I felt as if my heart was too strong for my body; as if the power of its beats might shatter the rest of me. The rattle of the door handle sounded unnaturally loud. The lock, I noticed, was broken. I managed to throw myself against it, just in time.

"Killian?" she said. "Is that you?"

"Don't come in."

"Are you on the floor? What are you doing on the floor?"

"Go to bed."

"Let me *in*."

She shoved the door, hard. The handle hit the back of my head and I cowed away. She was barefoot, the faint blue light from the window shining ghost-like off her plain white nightshirt.

"Oh my God, Killian! Is that blood?"

It looked black, instead of red, in the dawn's haze.

"I was going to clear it up."

She crouched down to look at my cuts.

"What have you done?"

"Sorry," I said. "I'm sorry. I was going to clean it up."

She reached out and tenderly touched my wounds. Fascinated by what she was seeing, she asked, "Does it hurt?" She wobbled, slightly, and I realised that she was still drunk. "You're crazy," she said, smiling. She picked the blade up from the floor and touched it with her thumb. Staring at it, she quoted me from earlier: "And at the end of the darkness, there's always happiness." And then, "I want to try it."

"No," I said. I tried to take the blade from her but she pulled it away.

"You're right about me," she said, with a smile of vaguely cruel defiance. "I need to be more fearless. Pain is nothing to be frightened of."

"Don't," I said.

The fastest struggle and then "Ach!" She'd done it. I clasped my hand tightly around her wrist.

"No, Kathryn," I said. "Please don't do that. Please don't *ever*–"

Dropping the blade, she touched the place where she'd used it. She looked intense and detached and fascinated. She brought her fingers back and studied the translucent red stain on their tips. Then she put her hands on my jaw and kissed me, lowering me gently onto the tiles and the blood that had pooled on them. Running her hands down the scars on my torso, she groaned gently and then lifted her nightshirt over her head. Her breasts pushed softly onto me; her perfection pressing in on my ruined skin. She rolled, slightly, deliberately, into the blood, so it was on her: on her arms; on her ribs; on her breasts. I breathed slowly; exhausted; weightless in the pleasure, as she kissed down my neck and stroked with her tongue and her fingers across my scars. Not a single blemish was left without her gentle attention; not even the fresh ones.

She moved down further and further still until, eventually, she slid my boxer shorts down to my knees. I stared towards the ceiling as her mouth worked between my legs, my eyes unfocused, my hands gripping and releasing in an attempt to modulate the bliss. When she was finished, she pulled her nightshirt on, her back to me to hide her toplessness, before walking with a drowsy, contented slouch towards the kitchen.

"Go to bed," she instructed. "I'll sort the bathroom out."

Chapter 43

BAD BOY OF COOKING IN AWARDS UPROAR.
I moved the newspaper up to hide my face, grateful that I was in the hazy smoking carriage of the early-morning commuter train to London.

Fiery Protégé of Chef to the Stars Max Mann Steals ex-Boss's Big Moment.

My hands were shaking even more than they had been before I'd seen the huge picture of me on page 3 of the *Daily Mirror*. I looked deranged in the photo – topless, scarred, mouth half open, spotlit in the blackness of the Café de Paris stage and moments away from falling into the crowd from the lectern that I'd climbed, arms stretched out like some ghoulish, self-harming Jesus.

I'd spent the previous day in bed, back at the cottage. Earlier that morning, I'd forced myself to eat breakfast, following a long night in which I was still too strung out to sleep. I let myself in through the back door of Glamis and sat in my office for ten minutes with the light off, trying to turn all the noises and directions in my head into one firm and steady stream of awareness. When the phone rang, I jumped.

"Aha! The bad boy of cooking returns!" said Ambrose. "Bravo, Killian. Very well done. Excellent work. Bookings have gone wild. I know I told you to work the old image but, by golly, you have really excelled yourself."

"Thanks," I muttered, repetitively smoothing my eyebrow with my thumb.

"And the BBC have been on the phone. The *Food and Drink* people want to take you up on that offer. When can they come in to film? What shall I tell them?"

"I don't know."

"Fantastic opportunity. They're going to send Russell Harty. Good old Max for suggesting it. But, listen, I have to tell you – he is rather sore that you chose his moment for your little stunt. He'll get over it, but be kind to him, won't you? We're all on the same team, after all, and at the end of the day, you have a lot to thank him for."

The rage prickled down the back of my neck in fearful detail.

"Right," I said. "Okay."

As I was putting the phone down, the light turned on – a great scorching yellow burst of it like boiling water.

"Fuck," I said, squinting at the shadow in the doorway.

"Still suffering?"

It was Andy, leaning against the door frame with his arms folded, his fulsome lips bunched into a smirk, his heavy brows furrowed. I rested my forehead on a fisted hand in a way that I hoped he'd interpret as "fuck off".

"Bit of a shit service yesterday," he continued. "Bit of a shit two services, really."

I ignored him.

"Complaints," he said. "Food wasn't the same."

I couldn't work out what I hated the most: his nose, his eyes, his mouth or his hair.

"Well, what have you got to say for yourself?" I said.

"It's not my fault, Killian," he said, puffing himself up.

"I didn't do anything wrong."

All of it. I hated all of it.

"You know, it's funny," he continued. "I followed the recipes in the blue book precisely."

"Well, you can relax," I said. "I'm back now."

I folded my arms, aware of the lump in my apron pocket where a fresh pouch of Earl's Leaf had been secreted. Andy moved in and perched on the edge of my desk, his large buttock bulging through his trousers, his voice softening into a condescending smear.

"Killian, mate. Level with me. How are you making those sauces? What's in them?"

"I'm not 'mate', mate," I said. "I'm 'chef'. And I'm sorry if your ego's hurting. Obviously I can never have another day off for the rest of my life. Obviously this place needs me more than you realised."

"Listen, mate," he said. "Don't give me that. I know how to make sauces. I've been learning this shit for years. Hours and hours, shift after shift, bollocking after bollocking, cuts, burns, aching bones, exhaustion so bad you can't sleep, years and years and years of it, so much work that your body moulds around it, like they could give you an autopsy and pick out your chopping muscle and your stirring muscle and your bent spine and your eroded fucking wrists and say, 'yeah, that's a chef, I guarantee it'. I know what I'm talking about. I've *earned* the right to be here, and I've earned the right to tell you what I know – and I know this for a *fact*. Those recipes are not as you've written them down. They aren't right."

A shadow moved in from the corridor. Kathryn. She entered with a cautious half-grin. "Remembered how your legs work, have you?"

Her smile faded as her comment clattered, unwelcome, to the floor.

"What's going on?" she said.

"I don't know," I said, standing. "I think Andy's accusing me of something."

"What are you putting in those sauces?" he said. "Just tell us."

"Talent," I shouted. "Fresh fucking talent. Why is it so hard for you to believe that I am a good cook? Don't you believe any of the reviews? Don't you believe our waiting list?"

There was no blood in the tips of my fingers. There was no blood in me at all.

"Disloyal cunt!" I shouted. "Get out! You're fired."

"You're doing a very unwise thing," he said.

"Don't flatter yourself," I said. "You're not irreplaceable."

As he rounded the doorway, he muttered, "That's not what I meant."

Chapter 44

I sat down, slowly, behind my desk. Kathryn perched on its corner, where Andy had just been.

"You're not really going to sack him, are you?"

"If I can't get loyalty from my most senior chef, what's the point?"

She glanced at my pot of pens and said, "Loyalty isn't the answer to all your problems, Killian."

"It's the most important thing."

"But it's a lie, isn't it?" she said. "It's a compromise people make – people who are desperate to be loved. You're not like that, Killian. You don't need your arse kissed every day, like Max does. You don't need team players." She spoke the words as if they were fouling her tongue. "You need people who want to work hard for their own sake and who'll be brutally honest with you. And he was only being honest."

"What's wrong with being a team player?" I said.

"Team players?" Her face twisted. "Bland, middling, bullshitting, corporate kitchen politicians. You want lone rangers, people who do it for their own ego. Cooks who feel like knifing them*selves* in the heart if they make a mistake. That's Andy. You know, there's a reason communism doesn't work, Kill. Everybody has to work for the team, so nobody does any work at all."

She'd lost me, totally. "That's different," I said. "And, anyway, he was calling me a liar."

"He was asking about your sauces."

She met my eye and held it. My blood lurched. I refused to look away. There was a clatter, back in the kitchen. I was aware of the reflection of the light in her irises.

"There's nothing to ask about," I said.

She paused, and with a tentative look said, "Just talent."

"I mean, come on, what does he think? That man actually believes that I'm buying pheromones from a sex shop in Soho and dropping them in my food. Have you ever heard of anything as crazy as that? Think about it, though."

She looked down, apparently examining her thumbs.

"It does seem unlikely."

"He's delusional," I said. "I can't have someone with delusions working here. Imagine if he cracked completely and came for me with a fucking chopper," I laughed. "Imagine if he went for you?"

I tried to make her catch my smile, but she wouldn't.

"What's up?" I said.

"I just need reassuring, I think."

"Fucking..." I stood up. "Not you too?"

"Not about that," she said, quickly. "It's just, this is the right thing, isn't it?"

I wasn't sure what she meant.

"Of course it is," I said. "The way things are going, we'll have everything. Max is already halfway gone. I mean, the 'Lifetime Achievement' award – everyone knows what *that* means. He'll take his retirement, open up a monstrous pit in Las Vegas, cash his reputation in for good. And Ambrose will make me executive chef ove seeing both restaurants and that means it's up to me to appoint the *chef de file* of King. And that will be you. By this time next year. I promise."

She glanced into the empty corner. We sat like that for a while.

"I spoke to my mum this morning," she said, eventually. "She said she's fallen again. Hit her face. I could tell that someone was listening in, though. I just don't know what to do. Last time I complained, she told me not to. She begged me not to make a fuss about it. I'm sure they got their own back on her somehow. Seeing your mother frightened like that, it does something to you. I'd do anything—"

I stood in front of her and placed my hands on her shoulders.

"You have to trust me. We'll get what we want. We have to grab it. Take what we want. And then just pray it all works out. Which, you know, it will. It *has* to."

Shortly afterwards, she left the office and an hour later, I gathered the brigade.

"Right, quick announcement," I said. "Andy's gone. He's not coming back. I'll be carrying on with sauces and I'll also be running the pass. And a word of warning to you all. I will not have disloyalty in my team. Not a whisper of it."

I scanned the men as they looked back at me, their limbs arranged in angular discomfort, their faces rounded out variously with alarm, defiance and fear.

"The last time I ran the pass you let me down. That won't happen today. I want you to remember: every plate that goes out there, every bite of every dish is a judgement on me. It's my name that's above the door. It's my name that everyone wants to fail. When you're working in my kitchen, you are no longer you. You don't exist. You're my hands, you're my eyes, you're my brain, you're my body.

328

And be warned – I'm not the slightest bit afraid to punish myself, to draw blood, when I get things wrong."

I let them stand, for a moment, in the weirdness.

"We have made Glamis the greatest restaurant in the country; probably the world. We have a reputation to defend. Any mistakes and we lose it. There cannot be any mistakes. We must take perfection and better it. And if I hear any hint of d-disloyalty, you're going the same way as Andy. Okay? To work."

All day and all night, my anger radiated out through the room. At just after nine, I was about to dip my hand into my apron pocket when I was surprised by a presence that seemed to slide up to me, silently. It was our best apprentice, the shy boy from Leeds whose surname – something French or Italian – I could never remember. I only knew him as Marco.

"Don't fucking look at me," I told him.

Rather than shrinking back, as I had expected, he firmed up his shoulders and stepped towards me. Without thinking, I pushed him back, with both hands, and he fell against the steel unit behind him. He stood again, his face pinked, and balled his right fist. It was a blur; a mess; a panic; too quick for rational thought. Somehow, instinctively, I reached back for my paring knife. For a terrible moment, my fingertips touched the steel handle. I only realised what I was doing when I saw Marco's eyes widen. I pulled my arm back – as shocked as if I'd accidentally stuck it in the burner – then turned and announced to the kitchen, "No one fucking looks at me when I'm cooking. Do you understand? No one looks at me."

"Yes, Chef!"

That night was to be my finest service yet.

* * *

It was these days at Glamis that made me realise how badly my teacher, Mr Mayle, had been mistaken. Perhaps it said something about his failure as a chef that he believed the secret ingredient of unforgettable food was "humanity". My time at the restaurant also added depth and light to something I'd been thinking about for a while. It started after I'd seen a child psychologist on the *Nine O'Clock News* discussing the effects of spanking: "You must remember that every two-year-old, if they had the physical strength, would be a killer," she said. "They know they're dangerous – unconsciously, of course – and this can cause them great fear and distress. This is why all children need order and discipline. It's reassuring for them. Rules make them secure and therefore happy. And this doesn't really change as we grow into adults."

I had realised that what separates humankind from the animals is an incendiary combination of imagination and obedience. These are the qualities that built civilisation. And the mortar that holds them together – the infrastructure, the pipes, the circuitry – is loyalty. It takes someone with imagination to lead the masses into disciplined self-sacrifice, and if those masses are sufficiently loyal to him, the end result is progress, genius, magic; the end result is everything good about the world.

A correctly functioning kitchen is the human struggle in microcosm; ideal society in excelsis. Every cook in there wants to be the *chef de cuisine*, the man with the imagination. They want to depose him. But at the same time they are violently devoted to him. Their fidelity is felt in the most primitive way. They are in the sphere of a strong, powerful leader, a man of vision and control, a man who they instinctively know could make a difference to humanity, and so billions of years of human evolution kick in and they slot into place. They bend their necks, raise their eyes and say, as one, "Yes, Chef".

And through this subservience they become incredible cooks. Through this loyalty, self-sacrifice and pain, through the force with which they battle their wants, one or two might eventually prove themselves hardy enough to become like their leader. This is how it operates: accomplishment through loyalty, happiness through struggle, freedom through work.

So now I knew where Mayle had got it wrong, with his happy proclamations about humanity. I had been taught a lesson I swore never to forget, the hidden truth of all the Michelin kitchens in the world. The secret ingredient of unforgettable food is suffering.

Chapter 45

Driving home that night, I found myself taking risks I never had before. My foot taunted the accelerator pedal as I barrelled past junctions and lorries and around tight country corners. I was playing lightly with danger and it made me feel free. I would go faster and faster. I would take risks. And if the ground wasn't there to catch me, so be it. Notions of safety, of looking after yourself, of creeping through life constantly obsessing about arranging things just so that everything will always come out best for you – it all suddenly seemed so timid.

I pulled up outside Dor and walked through the tall, curling gates of the physic garden. The Earl's Leaf was surging forward in erect, willing clumps, and the other two herbs seemed to be doing better than ever, the snaking stamens of the Hindeling licking the air hungrily and the purple heads of the Cauter nodding in the wind. Flies zoomed madly here and there, a mathematical chaos of legs and wings and unfathomable purpose.

I harvested a fresh armful of Earl's Leaf and when I was back under the dull light of the kitchen, I noticed how much this room – the feeling of it – had changed. Whereas I used to remember the height and madness of the shelves and cupboards as tantalising and mysterious, now they seemed to loom in threat, casting great columns of darkness upon each other in some silent war of shadows. The jars and bottles lurked and plotted, spying down from their ceiling-bound eyrie; the mad contraptions had the air of torture devices. Perhaps the most dramatic shift of all, though, was in the disappearance of the warmth that had once seemed so unvanquishable. It was as if the chill that inhabited the stairs had leaked out and spread itself everywhere. The flies, at least, seemed to like it. They danced beneath the light, picked their way confidently over the table top and watched me with a jittery intensity from the cracks in the beams and in the mortar.

My task for the night was baking. I wanted to learn how to incorporate Earl's Leaf into a dessert. I knew, of course, that Dorothy's "Dotty Cakes" had softly bewitched the Herstmonceux villagers in the seventies, but I couldn't imagine how she'd done it because the way that Earl's Leaf worked with flavour seemed inherently savoury. There was a technical question too. It was one thing for the delicate plant to be added to a sauce right at the end of cooking, but dumping it in a dense, sticky dough and baking it in a hot oven? It would kill it off, surely.

I made twenty simple cupcakes, adding a little bit more of the herb into each. The first had a large crumb, about the size of a match-head, the last a dangerously powerful dose of five finely chopped leaves. After an impatient wait, I took Dorothy's old holly-patterned oven gloves, which were frayed and covered in scorched bruises, and pulled the trays out, allowing the fragrant steam to rise from the cracked, moist domes before breaking a nibble-sized chunk off the edge of the weakest cake. The taste was so incredible that I couldn't help but laugh. The Earl's Leaf had simultaneously lifted and darkened the complex vanilla, saffron and caramel flavours of the sponge. The plant also kept its aphrodisiac effect: I could tell that if I wanted to avoid problems, I should probably eat no more. It was amazing – the correct dose, it seemed, was just half a match-head.

I yawned so deeply that my jaw gave a painful click. Conscious, suddenly, of something indistinct in the silence, I looked around. A fly took off from a crack in a beam. Then, I heard a noise.

Tap, tap, tap.

I stopped. I heard it again.

Tap, tap, tap. A voice. *"Killian?"*

It couldn't be.

"Kathryn?"

I paced through the darkness of the kitchen and the lounge and turned the key in the old door. And there she was – her head cast down, her shoulders raised defensively against the weight of serious night that she'd just made her way through. Strands of loose hair were picked out by the weak light of the hallway. Her nose was wrinkled in distress, her arms folded in her favourite ski jacket, its pink and pale-green triangles of colour looking jarringly modern against the gruff brick and mean ceiling of the cottage's dwarfish entrance.

"Sorry to come, but I really want to talk to you," she said.

I followed her into the kitchen and she sat at the table, looking carefully into the darkness – by chance, towards the exact spot that Dorothy used to stand and stir and treat me to her amazing lessons. I pulled out the chair beside her.

"What happened today, with Marco," she said. "I don't like it, Kill. I don't like what's happening. Not just to you – to both of us."

I stood up.

"I'm running my kitchen, that's all I'm doing," I said. "I'm controlling it. I'm doing a good job. I'm getting excellence out of those cooks. I'm doing it for you."

She didn't respond. She just sat there, staring at the void that Dorothy had left. And then, very quietly, she said, "You're becoming a bit like *him*."

"Him? What?"

"Like Max."

"How could you even say that? That's like, the complete reverse of the truth. *I'm the one who's standing up to Max*. I'm the only one who can serve justice on that bastard. What don't you understand about that? He's a bully and a fraud. He doesn't care about food. It's all about his stars. His fame. His celebrity. And I'm going to take them all off him, because that's what he deserves, and put you in his kitchen. That's what justice is. That's a *good* thing. And if you're not going to help me, if you're going to be so disloyal as to…"

Kathryn pulled back in irritation at the word, the leg of her chair letting out a little yelp as it scraped on the floor.

"Disloyal? It's not about loyalty, Killian, it's about doing the right thing."

"I am doing the right thing!"

"And you want me to turn a blind eye to whatever it is you're doing?"

"I'm not doing anything except cooking."

"You're putting something in the food, Killian."

"*What?*"

"I see you doing it all the time. From your apron! I've just not…" She closed her eyes and shook her head. "And then, the other night, you said you were going to give up herbs. Then I remembered, when I came to visit the last time. You said there was a herb garden. Is that what it is? Are you growing some sort of drug out there?"

"You're doing it now," I said. "You're questioning me. It's disloyalty. How can I be with someone like this? How can you have no *integrity*?"

The wind took a strike at the chimney and, behind the thick glass of the range's doors, the flames flared and bowed.

"Do you really think loyalty and integrity are the same thing?" said Kathryn. "Killian, they're not. They're opposites. If you want to look for corruption, you've only got to look for loyalty. It's how powerful people get away with anything – businesses, the Church, governments, the bloody army. It's a con. Look at my dad. Loyalty made him believe that his life was worth sacrificing for his country. For his country! For Maggie bloody Thatcher! For some flag, some pattern on a cloth. It's the same all over Northern Ireland, loyalty to the Catholics, loyalty to the Protestants, loyalty to Britain, loyalty to the Republic. It's loyalty that means Americans are happy for their country to trigger a holocaust against the communists. It's the same in Leningrad and Moscow and Peking. Loyalty is a sin, Killian. It's corruption. It's a trick. It's evil."

"But you're supposed to be a Christian, aren't you?" I said. "You're loyal to your church."

"I don't go to church, Killian. Christ, what do you know about the Church anyway?" She took a moment to steady herself and said, more calmly, "I haven't been for years, if you must know. I don't agree with it. If you ask me, Adam eating the apple, that wasn't the original sin. The original sin was God demanding that the apple never be eaten in the first place, and then expecting that ridiculous order to be followed blindly, without question.

That's your loyalty, Killian. It's cruel and pointless and bullying and it leads to evil, always. And please don't lecture me on God. I know more about it than you do."

I shook my head slowly in the difficult silence that followed.

"So you hate the Church and what God said in the Bible is evil? And you're telling me that you're some expert? I mean, you're forgetting – it's loyalty that makes such amazing food."

"Why aren't you *listening* to me? It's loyalty that makes evil, Killian. It's loyalty that stops all the chefs that work at King not going to the police and reporting him for ABH, GBH." She paused. "You know, was it virtuous when you defended Max after he beat up Greg? Is it virtuous when you defend your mum who is clearly some kind of monster?"

I shouted then, my voice hard against the stone walls and floor, smashing at the warm memories of boyhood that still, despite everything, clung to this room, "Don't talk about my mum!"

Her chair pulled back further and she looked towards her feet, a wet string of hair hitting her freckled cheek as defeat or regret or exhaustion calmed her a little.

"You can't expect me to be loyal to you and your ridiculous, pointless feud against Max. It's not fair."

"But I'm fighting him on behalf of everyone!"

"Yes, he's a bully. Yes, he's an arsehole. But I'm here because I'm trying to say…" She shook her head and collapsed, slightly. "*Please* don't turn into one, Killian. Please. I love you. I love you so much. I don't want you to–"

I moved behind her, my shadow falling over her pale form, and touched her head. I sensed her body soften and she turned, arms raised. I pulled her off her chair and she stood, her face lying in the crook of my neck, her hair in my eyes, the weight of her on me, and I could see the delicate pores in her skin and feel her chest as she breathed. It was as if her embrace was a door that shut out everything that wasn't her.

I pressed my lips into her and she lifted her head.

"All right," I said. "I'm going to tell you the truth now. I am keeping a secret ingredient in my pouch. I'm surprised Andy didn't tell you, really. It's no big deal. It's just pepper with a bit of ground clove in it. Not quite enough so's you'd notice. But just enough to add a kind of meaty richness. I'm allowed a little trick or two, aren't I?"

"Ground clove?" she said, with a slight scrunch of the brow. "And that's all? *Clove?*"

"What's more likely?" I laughed. "That or I'm drugging the food?"

Finally, she smiled. We kissed with a bite and fury that had no room for all that had just happened. I became lost in it. It was as if the limits of our bodies had become porous. She lay back on the table and I unbuttoned her blue checked shirt and pulled it off one arm and then the other. Then, lifting her gently by the small of her narrow back, I unhooked her bra and she pulled my shirt over my head and we kissed again, her breasts pushing into my chest and her fingers tending to my scars; luxuriating in them. Then her jeans. Top button, next button, then white cotton tight over pale skin and then her hand pulling at my wrist, pulling me away. "No, no, Kill. Sorry. That's enough."

I stood up, my face stinging hotly, and looked at her half-naked body that was laid out before me, the dim light forming rich shadows over her stomach and breasts and her stretched, almond belly button and it was the most beautiful thing I'd ever seen and it was turning, curling away from me.

"For fuck's sake. Fuck!"

Anything. I would have done anything. I perched on the edge of the table and ran my hand over the candy-pink King scar on my left arm. She sat up, blushing, and crossed her arms clumsily over her chest.

"I'm a virgin too, you know," I said, softly. "You don't have to worry. It'll be our first time together."

She picked up her shirt and used it to cover herself.

"I want to wait."

"Don't tell me until you're married?"

"That's not such a ridiculous thing."

"Come on, Kathryn, it's not 1955. This is 1985. It's the future."

"It's just what I want to do," she said. "You understand, Kill, I know you do. It's not never. It's just not now."

I could imagine what my mum would think if she could see me now. I pictured her laughing, rocking back with pleasure, that squawk that bottomed out into a witchy cackle: "Look at it! All skin and no boner."

I walked over to the rack on the kitchen table. I deserved this. That's what Kathryn had said. I deserved everything I could get.

"Sorry," I said. "I'm sorry. Here, cheer up. Have a cake."

I threw it at her and she caught it, a happy, weary grin raising itself on her face. I picked up the still-warm cake I'd cautiously nibbled at earlier and glanced, with a sense of excited, guilty trepidation, at the empty space on the baking tray where the five-leafed version had been seconds earlier. There was an instant, just before she took her first bite, that I wished I hadn't done it.

"Hmm, it's good," she said. "Oh, it's so – hmm. I didn't realise how starving I was."

Another bite and her cheeks began to redden.

"Good cake," she muttered – quietly this time, almost to herself, and with a slight self-conscious pull.

She ate in silence, groaning her appreciation every now and then, crossing her legs tightly as she took the final bite, pushing it greedily into her mouth with the side of her finger. She gazed at the floor for a moment, then swallowed. Her tongue swept over her bottom lip, which had become full and red and glistening wet. As her legs tightened around themselves even further, I smiled at her disorientation.

"I love you, Kathryn."

She pushed her hands down her thighs, as if to dry her palms, as another deep groan of pleasure came from her throat. "That was amazing," she said, staring at her knees. When she looked back up, through damp strands of dark hair and bleeding mascara, her eyes had taken on a look of pleading. I moved towards her and she lifted her arms to receive me, her shirt dropping from her chest, her legs uncrossing. She whispered hungrily, "Show us your scars then."

And she was there, where they found her on that night and where they'd continued to find her every night since. She was there, in the place that the cottage held her. To repeat, to attempt to heal.

Mary, weak and wordless up sixteen steps. The finder man says, "Take off her black thrumb'd hat because I cannot abide to look at her."

She turned from the men and looked at me.

"Why didn't you stop them barking?"

And the finder man turned towards me, his wide jaw and small eyes and high stubble all set in ugly English dread.

"Who's there?" he said.

He could sense me as I watched him.

"Foul spirit, show thyself."

And I was the dog that he wanted.

I was King of the Wastelands.

King of the Mischief.

King of the More.

I was the red and the yellow and the black.

And I would never stop them barking.

Chapter 46

Sleep came, that night, in a thin layer. I kept breaking through its surface, disturbed by dreams and by joy and the unbelief: Kathryn – my Kathryn – was naked on the mattress beside me. I had decided to forgive what she'd said the night before. I loved her so much, how could I not? When she finally stirred, I was studying her ear, how it curled so perfectly, so tenderly, like young coral.

"What happened last night?" she murmured.

My arm, which I had draped over her chest just high enough that I could feel the kiss of her breasts on my skin, squeezed in. "Hmmmm," I replied, approvingly, and pushed my nose deeper into her neck so I could gorge once more on her dark and sweet pyjamary scent. She stiffened, her head lifting just a millimetre.

"What did you do to me?"

"What do you mean?"

She turned her head, dislodging me from the warm nest I'd made of her.

"Last night. What happened?"

"Last night was amazing, Kathryn. It was amazing."

She was looking down towards the sheet, her eyes disconnected.

"Do you think I'm an idiot?" she said "You must think I'm an idiot."

She stood, pulling the sheet up with her.

"I know what you did. You're a fucking nutcase," she said.

"No," I said. "Kathryn?"

She was a blur of frantic distress, picking up her clothe- from the stone floor, whilst with an awkward, angular desperation, trying to keep the sheet covering her body.

"Don't look at me!"

I lay still, confused and aware of her pulling her knickers up.

"What is it, Killian?" she said as she buttoned her Wranglers. "What did you put in that cake? What are you putting in the food?" She turned towards the window. "It's out there, isn't it?"

Standing unsteadily, I made a foolish attempt at hugging her; trying to push all her moving parts back together.

"Get away from me," she screamed.

She ran outside and, in the daylight, she saw the gates to the physic garden for the first time, with the weather-worn gargoyles; their shallow eyes and ancient teeth, straining in their static howls, commanding the skies above them. The sight stopped her momentarily before she went inside, her feet heaving further into black earth. It was all there for her to see – the lush and the misty space, rammed with baying plants and droning with insects. She picked a head of Cauter and sniffed it.

"No!" I shouted. "Don't!" I grabbed it off her. "Not that one – it's poisonous."

"Is this what you gave me? Is that what you've been using at Glamis?"

I tried, once more, to hold her. She pushed me away.

"What's wrong?" I said. "This is ridiculous. Kathryn, you don't understand – I love you."

The cold dawn wind came through elms and spread itself cruelly about us. The cottage watched through the open gate as she collapsed onto the turf and sobbed.

"What did you do to me? What did you do to me?"

Chapter 47

I arrived at Glamis late, and as soon as they saw me, every cook in the kitchen could tell how the day was going to pass. It amazed me, how I could manage the mood of my subordinates by controlling the look in my eye and the muscles in my face. The longer they searched in vain for some sign of my acceptance, the harder they worked to earn it. Throughout most of the service, none of them even had the courage to meet my gaze, and I remembered, with more bemusement than shame, how just a few weeks ago I had let this kitchen overwhelm me.

Everything was going perfectly. The diners were getting served promptly and, when I found mistakes, I had no trouble in letting the individual responsible know that such lapses were intolerable. Then, at the height of service, Drusilla the Maître d' gave a nervous little bow and said, "Mr McClaren wishes to send his compliments to the chef."

Everything was *fine*. But for some reason, I reacted by punching a silver cloche off the shelf above the pass with the heel of my hand. It bounced off the back wall and clanged onto the tiles. With the disorientating feeling that my rage had become something sentient and separate from me, I found myself shouting at her, "No more compliments to the chef! No more! I *never* want to hear another compliment to the *fucking* chef."

She gave another fluttering little bow before retreating. "Yes, Chef. Of course, Chef."

I watched Drusilla slip elegantly away and realised that I was panting. The backs of my hands were blotchy with red and white and I had a feeling of numbness and tightness over my temples and cheeks. I instructed Marco to take care of my duties, then went to the bathroom, locking the door of the toilet cubicle behind me and resting my head uncomfortably on the plastic pipe that led to the cistern. It wasn't long before I found myself picking, distractedly, at my scabs.

When I had imagined being in this position – when I had fantasised about being a world-renowned chef – I always seemed to conjure one particular image: me, at the pass, smilingly dressing a plate as friendly eyes looked on. I would be confident, at ease, popular with my brigade. But there was something wrong with my daydream; a disquieting flaw at its heart. That imaginary chef at that imaginary pass was not me. It could never be me. No matter how much I achieved in my career, I couldn't be that person. I wondered, as I sat there, if what I had thought had been a fantasy about success in the world had actually been a yearning for change in my soul.

I asked myself what Dorothy would have thought of everything I had done.

And that was it. That was enough.

* * *

During lunch service the next day, I watched the first few plates go out in a state of proud, paternal terror. I had prepared them honestly. I had not used any Earl's Leaf.

And there they went, my true children, sent out into the world towards uncertain fortune. My confidence gathered as an hour and then another passed by, apparently without anyone noticing. At about one fifteen, Drusilla was back.

"I'm sorry, Chef," she said, clacking those long finger-nails together nervously in front of her. "It's Mr Langeau. He's insisting it doesn't taste the same."

I put down the spoon I'd been holding and dried my hands slowly on my immaculate torchon. She clacked again.

"He's one of our regulars, Chef."

"Yes, I know that. What did he say?"

Her nostrils flared; her eyelids panicked.

"He says he won't pay fifteen pounds for five-pound food."

"Fucker," I said. "Okay. Don't worry, Drusilla. Give me a minute."

Just this once. To ease me in. I made Mr Langeau another entrecôte with sauce Glamis. I gave him a double dose of the leaf, to shut him up. But then another plate came back and then another. The fourth one, I smashed on the floor, the china and sauce flying towards Marco like shrapnel and napalm.

"You fucking useless prick," I shouted at him. "You're fucking all my food up."

"It's not me, Chef," he shrugged.

I looked at the congealing, returned plates that were piling up in front of me.

"Eat them," I said. "Take these plates, take them out into the restaurant, stand at the bar and eat what's on them."

"But, Chef!" he said.

"Drusilla!" I called the maitre d'. "Marco's hungry.

Gather these plates up. Help him with them. He's going to have his lunch at the bar."

I watched Marco, looking paler than ever, place his tongs to the side and walk into the restaurant, his hips moving with a defiant lumber and roll. When he came back, I thought, for a moment, that he might physically attack me.

When service was over, I closed the door of my office and phoned Kathryn.

"Hello? Hello?"

Her voice. I loved her voice.

"Killian?"

I loved her.

"Killian, is that you?"

I put the phone down.

* * *

The following morning, I arrived at work before anyone else. I hung my coat on the mahogany hat stand that I'd purloined from the restaurant and checked my watch: 06:35. Damn. Too early. I sat behind my desk and looked at the telephone. Probably I should leave it until seven. I browsed through the order book, distractedly. I looked at the time again: 06:39. Fuck.

At 06:48, I dialled her number. I counted: it rang eleven times before she picked up.

"Killian?" she said. "If that's you, you have to stop calling."

I tried to hear every detail of what was happening in her world; to absorb her through the receiver. I didn't move at all as I took in her soft crying.

"Killian, if you do this again, I'll call the police. I don't want to, but I will."

The phone clicked off and gave me its heartless,

electro-mechanic hum. I sat, in the room, and closed my eyes. Twelve minutes later, Ambrose called.

"I heard there were some issues yesterday?" he said. "With the food?"

I leaned forward as my stomach tightened painfully.

"Only a slight... Who told you?"

"Someone with your best interests at heart," he replied, a note of *don't-start* defensiveness pushing in his voice. "So what happened?"

"My eye was off the ball," I said. "It was my fault. Me and Kathryn–"

"And that's all?" Silence. "There was no other problem? Nothing you want to tell me about? Nothing I might find out about by some other means? Nothing that might damage my business? Nothing at all?"

"That's right."

"What?"

"Nothing at all."

"I don't want everything to fall to pieces now that you've fired Andrew."

"It was the right decision."

"You'd do well to remember who owns Glamis, Killian."

I glanced at the pile of framed reviews that I'd had removed from the walls of the corridor and that still sat on my office floor, leaning against a filing cabinet. I was struck by the staggering height of the pile.

"You'd do well to remember who's made it world famous, Ambrose."

"Well, it's not going to stay that way for long on the basis of last night's food."

I noticed, too, how dusty the precarious stack had become. It was amazing, the speed with which dust could gather; how remorselessly life shed its dead material.

"That won't happen again," I said. "That's a promise."

"Look," said Ambrose. "I have no idea what's going on between you and Kathryn and, frankly, I'm not interested. You mustn't let all this personal idiocy get in the way of your success. You must remain focused on the positive things. We just can't have this. Especially not now. For God's sake, between you and Max, the situation is—"

"Max?"

"Oh, his blasted girlfriend has done a runner."

"Has she?"

"Of course she has!"

"But he didn't really give a crap about her, did he? He was just keeping up appearances. She was pregnant and everything."

"Oh, if only that were true, Killian. You couldn't be more wrong. Max adored her. He was besotted. Obsessed. The first girlfriend who wasn't a pushover, that's what I think."

"Where's she gone?"

"Who knows?" he sighed. "Back to Russia, more than likely. Max is crushed, bless him. Between you and me, he's barely capable of leading that kitchen and these are important days. Critical. That's what I'm calling about, actually. I've just heard – the monks of Michelin will be at King any day. *L'Inspecteur* from the Avenue de Breteuil. The last thing I need is for the place to fall apart. In fact, I might need you to do me a favour."

Chapter 48

Ambrose's favour didn't come for another two weeks. During that time, I had to sack Drusilla. She kept *looking* at me. She was spying on me, of course she was – if not for Max, for Ambrose. If not for Ambrose, for the newspapers. Indeed, there was another Bill Hastings exclusive, clearly placed by Max. It excoriated the so-called "aggressive and terrifying" conditions of my kitchen whilst quoting a source "at the heart of Mann's operation" that described the heavenly conditions enjoyed by his brigade: "If only the young pretender had learned the lessons generously offered by the elder Gent: you don't have to be a bully to make good food."

Can there be anyone, in any trade, who has enough ambition to lead their field and yet who doesn't dance at the very edge of what's permissible? Ambition itself compels it; insists upon it. And so it was with me. All the pressures of the kitchen coalesced into a sharp beam of fury: *this* piece of veal; *this* fillet of cod; *this* sautéed carrot. When the weight of all the world is focused onto a single badly trimmed broad bean, the effect is indistinguishable from madness.

The fortnight passed in a smear of working and drinking and drugging. Despite what the newspapers implied, I wasn't having fun. I could sense the shadow of the wave on my back and a part of me wanted to drown.

In the elms, a small clearing. Mary, gagged, faint and soiled. Flames at her feet as the children sang, "Earl's heart and earl's leafs and earl's lusts abounding. Earl's fires and earl's grace and earl's witch is burning." The finder man called out his charges: "Witchcraft is the product of Carnal Lusts which is in Women Insatiable. Mary Dor did make for the Devil a work of Vile Bewitchment and destroyed the Soul of Full Grown Men by depriving them of Grace, inclining their Minds to inordinate Passions and delivering their Bodies up to the punishments for Sin…"

The silvery flesh flies crawled out from the cracks in the mortar and the cracks in the beams and the dark weight of the attic. They crawled over Mary's bed and her crucifix. They swarmed over the herbs that were piled on the kitchen table. They tizzed and crackled on the fire, dropping into the glowing coals, a stench like burning hair filling the cottage.

They broke in a great turning cloud above the garden. Flies amongst the elms. Flies over the men and women who had gathered in the forest to watch Mary Dor burn. Flies on their arms and cheeks and necks and covering their children. And as they screamed, flies in their mouths and down their throats and licking the sticky whites of their eyes.

And I saw it all.

And I knew that I was the red and the yellow and the black. And that black is always death.

Chapter 49

Before showering, I forced myself to study my face in the mirror. I touched the reddish-purple bags beneath my eyes, the areas of dry skin around my nostrils, the hair-thin network of cuts that extended from the sore edges where my lips met, some freshly descended crumbs from a cocaine nosebleed. I pulled back and took in the entirety of my reflection in all its hollow melancholy – the shaved head, the damaged eyelid, the wax and granite shades of exhaustion. Ninety minutes later, I was behind my desk, studying the news, hunting for references to Max when Ambrose called.

"This is it," he said, his voice confidential and excited. "I've just heard. Michelin. *L'Inspecteur*. He's coming to dinner at King tonight."

"How have you found that out?" I asked.

"I was wondering if you'd mind hopping over to Gresse Street to help out a little," he said, ignoring my question. "Just for the service."

I couldn't quite believe it.

"Oversee the sauces, perhaps," he continued, more cautiously now. "Just for an hour or two."

A blur of chefs in white tunics flitted past my open door, like nervous ghosts.

"Okay, so is Max going to come and give me a bit of help when it's my turn?" I said.

"That's hardly the point, Killian. Things at King –"

I stood up at my desk, the twisted cable tugging from the receiver and lifting the corner of the telephone off it.

"What about Glamis? What about *my* Michelin stars? Do you think Max gives one rocky bollock about that?"

"And what about *me*?"

I sat, slowly, back in my chair, cowed by this rare show of fury.

"Where's your fucking *loyalty*, man? Where's your gratitude? If you want to fuck off and start your own place then be my guest and fuck off. No one's going to go bankrupt without you, least of all me. We'll all have simpler, more enjoyable lives without you. You are bringing a downmarket tone to my group as it is. I don't care what you think of Max. Your ridiculous falling-out is of no interest to me. But the man is not well at the moment and I am asking you to do a favour for me. Just for one service. Just one. For God's sake, man, do you realise what it'll do to him if he doesn't get his third star? After the year he's had? Have you even thought about that for one moment? And you know full well that if Glamis isn't awarded any stars whatsoever it will have no effect on the bottom line. We'll still be drowning in bookings. It won't make a scrap of difference to the money we're making."

"And the same goes for Max. He's booked up for months!"

There was a silence.

"Isn't he?" I said.

Ambrose cleared his throat.

"I think it would be fair to say the winds are, perhaps, shifting just a little."

"Well, I just can't believe you're asking me this."

"Killian, you're the best saucier in Europe. Easily. Why wouldn't I want to tactically deploy my finest employee for the good of the group? And you must realise, it does you no good to put King and its reputation at risk."

"It doesn't make any difference to me whatsoever."

"Killian, you're not thinking cleverly enough. You're too hot-headed. I mean Max…" His voice took on an arachnid thinness. "You need to think long term about this. About your future and where it might lead."

My eyes skittered guiltily about the empty room.

"Two thirty," he said. "I want you there. Just to support him. Help him along a little."

I licked my lips with a dry tongue, feeling each crease and blister of their cracked surfaces.

"Two thirty," I said. "Fine."

"Oh, and Killian. The *Food and Drink* people want to come in on Friday. They couldn't get hold of you, they said. No one at Glamis would return their calls. I told them fine. I take it that that will not be a problem for any reason?"

I could tell, from the way he said it, that the wrong answer now would be dangerous.

"Well—"

"Good. Goodbye."

I looked at the receiver in the moments after I put it down. I watched as it goaded me and then, not even trying to resist, I picked it back up and phoned Kathryn. She was weeping before she even said hello this time. I listened for a few seconds, then gently hung up.

I sat there, staring at the backs of my hands, my mind comfortably disengaged. I found myself presented with an idea. And I believed it was a good idea – the *right* idea

– because of the silence. For months the noise in my head had been ceaseless: the anxieties would fade in and out, weaving their way between the imagined scenes with Max, the agonising over the herbs, the running of the brigade, the wondering about Dor – all these lines of logic, words moving through wires, conversations held with different versions of myself that would go here and there and back here again and end up, frequently, with one half shouting at the other half and my resorting to rocking in my chair or using the paring knife that I had taken to carrying around in my pocket, with its split little plastic cover over the blade.

I had once read that wind is nature's restless attempt at filling voids in the atmosphere, and that was just what the noise in my head had come to feel like: great blusters of dissonance that blew around up there. They were my brain's continual attempts at finding a solution, at thinking its way back to silence. And that's what I heard, when this idea presented itself. Calm. Peace. Nothing at all.

I looked up as Marco walked past my door.

"Marco!"

He reversed, popping his head in, a strand of curly hair slipping down over his eyes.

"Chef?"

"Something's come up. Can you take over for the rest of the day?"

"Yes, Chef," he said. "Not a problem."

I pulled my coat on, ran to my car and drove back to Dor.

Chapter 50

I walked past the crates of Perrier and over the discarded ring-pulls that were pressed into the cobbles and checked the inside of my apron pocket one more time. Yes, good. The three ancient gifts of Dor were still there. Then, with just one step, I was inside the music of King once again. In front of me was the line of fretful apprentices, their pink fingers on blue-grey steel surfaces, their blades flashing over basil and chervil and mango and tomato and raspberry and lime. I could sense the wave of thrilled alarm go through them as I passed and headed into that subterranean rectangle of smells and sounds and magic. There they were, all in place, the commis chefs, the first commis, the *demi chefs de partie*, the *chefs de partie*, working studiously, precisely, standing with their legs apart so they didn't have to bend so low over the counter, all of them in that peculiar state of concentrated determination that is so close to anger. The brigade looked so much a part of the kitchen, it was hard to believe that they all had different lives outside of it: different beds, different girlfriends, different histories in different towns.

None of them acknowledged my presence as I walked behind them, past the shelves stacked high with pans and dishes, the hissing stoves, the blue flames surging thickly through blackened steel burners, the dented grill trays, the rows of hanging cleavers and ladles and copper saucepans and the oven with the door that didn't quite close. If I was to take over this place for Kathryn, I realised we'd probably have a battle with them. But that was okay. If I found that any of these chefs lacked the loyalty to follow their new leader, I knew I had the teeth, the breeding, to deal with them. And, tonight, I had something else. Two pouches of herbs from Dor. It was still unclear to me what their effects might be. All I knew was what the book in the attic had said: that the Hindeling caused a madness of the mind, whilst the Cauter somehow affected the body.

I walked through to the restaurant floor where Max was sitting in a corner, the Maître d' pouring him a drink from his pot of peppermint tea. He was staring out of the front window as the waiters moved about him ironing fresh tablecloths for the evening. Down by his lap, he was holding a menu, the corners of which were shaking, very slightly, in his hands.

"Chef?" I said. His trance broken, he looked at me for a second, his eyes tracking over me.

"Good morning," he said.

"Ambrose said –"

"Yes, yes, I know why you're here." He put the menu down. "Such confidence he has in me."

I thought about the charming, confident Gentleman Chef that appeared on Wogan two years ago; the one I'd watched again and again on the video.

"Well, it's an important night," I said, softly.

His eyes flickered down. He appeared injured, somehow. Humbled. As bad as I knew his depressed days could be, I'd never seen him like this.

"Chef, I just wanted to say, I know you don't need

me here," I said. "I don't know why Ambrose has got it into his head that you do. But I suppose we might as well humour him."

His eyes tracked the menu. His top pocket, which usually held a brand new biro, hung empty.

"I'll go and make myself busy," I said. "I'm sure there's some prep I can help with. Tangerines or something."

"No pips," he said, without looking up.

"No pips," I replied with a smile.

For the next few hours, I was aware only of the squalls of murmur and laughter that were surely directed at me, gathering and then blowing themselves out as I passed by here and there. I was troubled more by the kitchen's haunted places: the stations at the cold pass where Kathryn and I had fallen in love; the freezer door where she had told me her name; even the corridor where I had first seen Max, feeling as if his presence was lit by rays that had escaped from heaven.

"Brigade," said Max when he emerged for service. He stood, leaning against the pass, the shadowless light falling greenish blue over his face. "Y-you all know how important tonight is for us."

He pointed his finger and panned it across the kitchen. I imagined that every one of his white-robed charges felt as I did – as if his cold, trembling digit had physically touched their skin.

"N-n-no mistakes. I don't care who you are, how long you've worked here. You will vanish. Out in the courtyard. G-gone."

"*Oui*, Chef."

His eyes flickered to each man in a pre-emptive strike of slithery accusation and I knew the fear they were feeling and I was desperate for them to know, despite their apparent contempt for me, that I was here to rescue them from this deathly man. He talked, his voice monotone and dry, and I saw his words as maths, as algebra, as lines of code – cold instructions from a dead machine, every one designed by a bloodless unit with only one function: to win and, by doing so, to make me fail.

When he was finished, I approached him. He seemed to have shut down, momentarily, and was just standing there alone, his limbs on hold, his gaze bland and unattached.

"I know you don't need any help on sauces, Chef," I said. "But I could just hang about in the general area, just in case."

I could feel my heart throb in the scabs on my arms. I knew: it all came down to now.

He glanced towards the cold pass, where the apprentices were working in anxious silence.

"You know, just the benefit of another set of eyes on a service like this. Can't do any harm."

He nodded, smally. A fly passed his eye-line. He batted after it rather feebly.

"Yes, fine," he said. "*Bon.*"

"Thank you, Chef," I said.

Then, behind me, a familiar voice: "Actually, I could really do with Killian in pastry tonight, Chef." It was Andy. I had heard he was back at King, but I was unprepared for the actual sight of him here, happily employed in Max's kitchen. I felt a jolt of ugly power. He was looking right past me – sleeves up, spatula in hand and a small thumb-smudge of icing sugar on his purposefully set jaw. Max returned Andy's request with an uncertain frown.

"Don't you think that would be a bit of a waste, Chef?" I said. "I'm best on sauces." I glared at Andy. I dared him to speak. "I mean, you know, sauces is what I'm best at. That's what I'm known for, isn't it?"

Max darkened, suddenly provoked. "*Non.*" He dismissed me with a small, limp wave. "Go with Andy."

* * *

I followed Andy into the pastry area, watching his bowed, slightly bouncy legs as they took me to the far end of the kitchen, around the corner from the sink where the fish was washed and de-scaled. I was effectively alone with him, amongst trays of empty pastry boats, a batch of freshly rinsed cumquats lined up on paper towels like miniature suns and, hanging from a shelf, tonight's special instructions – four birthdays and a golden wedding anniversary.

"So what do you want me to do?" I said.

He picked up his spatula from where he'd left it, next to the cumquats.

"Nothing at all. I want you here, out of harm's way."

It was having a strange effect on me, being back at King. My limbs felt gangly and awkward. My hands couldn't decide where to settle. Suddenly, I felt my age.

"How's Kathryn?" I said.

"I've not really seen her," he said. "I don't know what happened between you two, but she's barely spoken to anyone. She's with her mum today, I think."

I couldn't let myself be distracted by thoughts of Kathryn. I pictured those dogs, working the wheel.

"Ambrose has told me to help out on sauces tonight," I said, "so I might not be able to be in pastry for lo–"

He interrupted me. "You're staying here."

His environment had a magnifying effect on him. He appeared an absolute master of his workspace; the boundary between him and the kitchen seemed merely academic.

"Oh, you don't still believe those stories about me drugging people, do you?" I said. "It's like a conspiracy theory. Come on, mate," I smiled chummily. "You'll be accusing me of faking the moon landings next."

He didn't move. "If you try anything," he said, "I promise, I will make sure you regret it."

"Give over, Andy," I said. I put my hands on my hips. "Come off it, mate."

"With my contacts in the press," he said, "I could ruin your reputation for ever. Don't forget that."

I gave him a small, dismissive laugh.

"That's funny, is it?" he said. "You saw that Bill Hastings piece? The *News of the World*?" He gave a satisfied nod before adding, almost reluctantly, "On Max's instructions, of course."

I rubbed my eyes, resignedly and said, simply, "Cunt." I thought for a moment, as Andy became distracted by the tumble of flies that had invaded the space over his station. "And I bet it was you that leaked about Max too, wasn't it?" I said, as he shooed them off. "When I was at King? You're on a little power trip with all your journo mates, that's what this is all about. I'm sure it's very helpful, having all those contacts. The problem with you is that you don't care about anything but your career."

He giggled as if lightly amused by some passing gibberish.

"How dare you think you can cheat your way to the top? Do you have any idea at all how hard I've worked to get here? How hard Max has worked? How hard we've *all* worked?"

I took a step closer and lowered my voice. I would have to be careful.

"It's about justice. Everyone thinks he's so nice, 'The Gentleman Chef', but he's evil."

"But haven't you noticed? No one's leaving. We all stay here, don't we? Do you know why? We're loyal to him. One hundred per cent. We might bitch about him. We might hate him at the end of a rough service. But the truth is, we'd fucking die for him."

Above and between our words could be heard the delicious music of the chefs of King. That they made it so perfectly without me felt like an insult. He was right, wasn't he? They loved him.

"They hate him," I said. "Every one of them. You don't give a shit about Max. You're not loyal to him; he's just your leg-up to the next kitchen. You told tales in the press about him, for Christ's sake! Nice little thrill, was it, seeing it in the paper?" I shook my head. "And anyway, all he's doing is training another army of psychos who will open their own kitchens and then bully anyone they don't like into giving up. He's despicable. He's a virus."

Andy leaned forward, his lip curling spitefully, exposing his yellowy teeth.

"You just don't get it, do you, Killian?" he said. "You're the bad guy. *You're the bad guy.*"

I walked past him slowly, feigning confusion, and began washing my hands at a small sink, letting the fine little bubbles of soft warm water run soothingly over my skin.

"This is ridiculous," I said. "You've got some weird things in your head, mate."

With that, we began working and continued in silence, preparing soufflés and baking meringues. At about twenty to eight that evening, there was a sudden drop as Max clapped three times.

"H-he's here. The inspector. Table 7."

Soon afterwards, I heard the unmistakable sound of Max at full hiss at the top of the kitchen. I peered around the corner. Poor Carlo. He was getting it again. There was a queue of four waiters bunched up at the pass, none of whom seemed sure which trays they should be taking, all of them too terrified to interrupt and ask. I said, to no response, "I've never seen it like this. It's a mess. Is this what's it's been like?" I had to do it now. Even if I had to physically fight Andy, I had to do it now.

"I need the toilet," I said. "You're not going to stop me going to the toilet." He didn't lift his head from where he was bending over his tray of kiwi marzipan petits fours.

"Two minutes, and I'm breaking down the door."

I paced around the corner, past the washing-up area where Danno the pots man was aiming the flexible steel hose at a stack of heat-warped baking trays, out of the door and into the room beneath the stairs where Max and Patrick had given me my palate test. In amongst the cleaning products and miscellaneous mops and traps there was, I remembered, a box of spare pepper grinders. I closed the door, switched on the light, and fumbled noisily about the shelves. The fat plastic packets and metal cans and cardboard boxes were seemingly frozen in disapproving silence as I hunted.

It took too long to find them – they'd been moved to a bottom shelf, next to an old split case of damp-damaged scourers. Cursing silently, I unscrewed the top of a grinder, my eyes continually darting to the shut door as I tipped a pile of Cauter seeds into my palm. In the book I'd found in the attic, it had said that these dark little balls – which looked exactly like half-sized peppercorns, bar a slight purple tint – were what caused a "madness of the body", whatever that was. There were nine or ten of the pellets within each of the herb's spiny flowers and I had no idea what they would do as I filled the grinder and slipped out of the cupboard. I wasn't even wondering: my rational mind was still in its perfectly silent state.

Corralling all lessons I'd ever learned about remaining unnoticed, I crept back into the kitchen. I could tell that it was approaching its point of maximum stress. Like a ship's hull at the height of a storm, you could almost hear the walls creaking and groaning with the pressures that were bearing down on it. Up at the meat station, Patrick was a porcine hunk of sweat, fat and acne leaning over his sauté pans. He looked barely more alive than the animals he was cooking, the straining little white-heads poking like poisonous mushrooms through the fine copper hairs of his half-grown moustache. As I approached him, I realised that there were a couple of silvery flies in the air about me. No, there were more than that. Four, *five* of them, at least. Ignoring the insects, I scoped the little pinch-pots of sea salt and freshly cracked pepper he kept nearby and carefully knocked them onto the floor with my elbow. He was in such a well of concentration that he could only find the space to mumble, "Twat."

I tutted showily at my apparent clumsiness and ran with the empty receptacles to the store where the spare salt and pepper were kept. I refilled his pots with salt and a half-pepper, half-Cauter mix and placed them gently back at his side, before doing a small tour of the kitchen, helpfully refilling the salt and pepper of all the chefs, being generous with my grinds of the Dor seeds. By the time I was finished, I knew that hardly a dish would now go out that didn't have at least a dusting of my ancestor's herb either on it or in it.

Before making my way to the exit, I palmed a couple of

shredded Hindeling leaves and added them to a fresh brew of peppermint tea which I brought to Max. I placed the pot down on the pass and smiled at the sight of him sending his polar stare into the two guinea-fowl with caramel and mango that had just arrived in front of him.

"I've given Andy a help on pastry," I said, as he towelled a fingerprint off the side of a plate. "He was in trouble for a bit back there, believe it or not. Everything's motoring along perfectly now. And I've had a quick tour of the kitchen. You don't need my help at all. You've got an amazing team here." I began to untie my apron strings as he gave the dishes one final squinting examination. "You'll be fine, Max," I said. "With the Michelin guy, I mean. Easy."

I thought he was going to turn away, but he looked straight at me.

"You think?" he said. I felt myself automatically formulating a response that assumed he was being sarcastic. But something stopped me. "Yeah," I said, carefully. "Yes. For sure."

And then, watching the waitress pick up the tray, he wiped his hands against themselves and muttered, "Yes, well, good. Thanks."

"Sorry?"

He faced me, his rain-coloured eyes hopeful and open. The oxygen vanished from my throat.

"Thank you, Killian. For your help."

I had this insane urge to hold him, to push my head into his chest. I put my arm out to pick the teapot back up, but the Maître d' swooped in first and grabbed it, intending to pour him a cup. My hand lingered over the spout for a moment, enjoying the pain of the steam. I left, as quickly as was possible, before I had to watch him drink.

Chapter 51

I stalked out of the blue double doors, through the darkness of Stephen Mews and crossed Gresse Street with my head down. Hanging in the shadows by the post office over the road, a freezing wind blew around my face and, in it, I could smell cold concrete and the vague sweetly spiced waft of a distant cigarette, above the sickly yellow pong of fat and scorch that rose from my skin.

I had to wait, to watch. Above the silhouetted rectangular hedges I could see two oblongs of golden light – the windows into the dining room, the occasional shape of a beautiful waitress gliding with magnificent sex and ease around the tables, bending over the diners to serve. It was about half past eight when I became aware of the first strange noise. I crept forward, back over the road, so I could hear better. It was like a great, ribitting frog. I peered up at the window. An overweight man in a pinstripe suit and braces had begun hiccupping violently. An elderly woman at Table 3 looked on at him, making a great show of her shock at his apparent rudeness. Then, she let out a hiccup so powerful that it appeared to pull her a little way off her seat. Her narrow hand sprang to her mouth as her dining partner reached over to help her. It seemed that she was struggling for breath. I stepped back, nervously.

Shortly afterwards, a middle-aged diner in a tweed jacket and plum trousers stood up abruptly and walked, with all the haste that appearances would permit, towards the bathroom. Did he run the final few yards? Then a woman in a sequinned dress followed him. I watched as the initial intermittent hurry for the toilets became a small charge. A black vase fell on a tablecloth, spilling its water and partially ejecting a white orchid. A fork bounced onto the carpet. A chair tipped back.

Soon, the polite and sporadic disarray had deteriorated into general pandemonium. There were hiccups and dry heaving and demands for service and cries of outrage all merging together, discordant and confusing and muffled on the other side of the window. There were hands over mouths and torsos doubling up and then vomit – livid mauve-and-dun-coloured pulses of it – pouring between fat knuckles and delicate jewelled fingers, hitting crystal glasses and drenching cutlery. The waitresses reared in horror. Some began rushing around with towels, others crouched down by those who appeared especially helpless, but most just ran for the shelter of the kitchen. A woman in a peppermint-green skirt charged towards the bathroom in her heels, pushing a waitress out of the way, a light stain appearing on the back of her dress. All was hysteria. All was frenzy. All was terror. The air in the room had become hectic with hurtling insects. They appeared to be revelling in the bedlam, dancing above heads and settling greedily onto human fluids. I saw a man, dining alone, his face pale, his nose with an aristocratic bent, his suit ill-fitting old corduroy. He was at Table 7. The inspector! He looked about the room with mad alarm and then hunched forwards, as if struck powerfully on the neck, and exhaled a bright flume of bile. And then, a face in the background, staring in ashen despair directly at him. Max.

I pulled myself back into the shadows and retreated across the road to the safety of the dark post office. The restaurant's front door opened. A woman in a short red skirt burst out as if kicked from behind. She pushed her head as far over the steel railing as she could and held the base of her neck as a long hose of vomit emerged from her stretched mouth. It came and it came and it came and she fell to her knees, curled up like a baby lamb, as the eruptions faltered and she began coughing up phlegmy gobs of thick slurry, each one accompanied by gross abdominal tremors. I watched with fascinated detachment as she retched and whimpered, too exhausted to cry, too distressed to care about her tall stiletto tumbling down the steps, her chin coated in a sticky beard of filth, her hand grabbing weakly at her bottom, which – judging by her movements – was also now expelling liquid in curious pumping little spurts. Her sobs came out in time with her breaths and only when she wasn't desperately heaving out more of the weird fudgy matter from her throat. Soon, she began making a mysterious and inhuman groaning sound. Flies landed on her face. She was too weak to brush them away.

Ten minutes later, a taxi pulled up and a photographer jumped out. There were sirens. An ambulance. Then another, their red and blue lights stroking the surface of Ambrose's upstairs office window and the walls of the Bricklayer's Arms and the craning faces of the curious drinkers that were now bubbling through its doors. I crept away in the orange-cloaked darkness, tiny in the vast city, its endless glowing web of streets crawling out around me in all directions, all over the country and all over the floating world, and me just a pale nothing, just a slip of skin and bone, alone in the anonymous quiet.

Chapter 52

I arrived home to find Dor Cottage squatting in its square of night like a fat, satisfied toad, the moonlight reflecting in the dark eye of its attic window. It sat there and watched me, that great form of age and gathering mayhem, as I climbed out of the car and into the restless wind, the elms creaking around me. I stood there for a moment and tried to stare it down. I shouted, "Go on, then!" in its direction and paused nervously to see if anything would happen. It remained silent, scowling, insulted by the weather.

I let myself in and sat alone in the kitchen with an unscrewed bottle of Bell's whisky. The light laid itself over the contours of the glass and swam, as if panicking, inside the liquid. There was a thud from upstairs. I poured another large glass and drank it down. Nothing happened for a while. A repetitive knocking noise came from the lounge. It was the wind. It must be the wind. The sound abruptly stopped. I continued to drink. Feeling the whisky working its soft magic, I crawled on top of the table. I wouldn't take this. This was *my* house. I pulled myself to my feet and roared down at the space where she had stood.

"Aunty! Where are you? I can hear you." I paused. Nothing. "Please, Aunty! Aunty! I'm sorry. I'm *sorry*. I need you!"

A fly buzzed past and landed on my foot. Shaking it off, I climbed down from the table, lowering myself with unsteady legs. Another, different noise floated down from upstairs. Low, like the murmur of a faraway crowd.

I took a long draft of the whisky and waited, wondering what to do. I looked at the range, its dead black mass under the chimney, the holes where the spit used to be still visible in the fireplace walls. I looked at the surface of the old oaken table, the lines and notches that I'd known as a boy and that Dorothy must surely have known as a girl. I looked at the shelves and the jars and the prongs and the shredders and the pots and the small bale of drying Earl's Leaf on the sheets of newspaper that I'd gathered last week and hadn't managed to get through. I looked at everything in the room except the place that seemed to be inviting me; taunting me.

I stepped forward and peered into the darkness over the stairs. Another fly startled me, emerging from up there at speed and coming directly at me. I ducked to the side and followed its path as it disappeared towards the lounge. I wondered how many of them were in here, in this cottage? Studying me in their skittering way, from the beams and the cracks in the mortar? There was another noise from upstairs. It seemed to be coming from the attic.

I began climbing. When I finally reached the corridor, the murmuring had become even louder. It had a mechanistic quality about it. A sense of teeming. I came to a halt beneath the attic door.

It was creaking; groaning with a kind of weight. I looked up. Something came from the gap between the door and its frame. It popped out, darted through the air and went for the stairs. A fly. I squinted, looking closer. There were more of them: flies squeezing themselves out of the loft, their legs hauling their silvery bodies through and then, as they achieved their freedom, accelerating suddenly.

I retreated back to the lounge and tried to sleep in Dorothy's armchair, but ended up just drinking most of the whisky. I was roused from a bleary daze by the sound of the phone ringing, drunk enough that, momentarily, I didn't know what the noise was. I picked up the receiver.

"Kathryn?"

There was a sound amidst the static: a kind of swallowed gasp.

"Ambrose?"

"It's sad news, Killian," he said. "Terrible, awful news. I, er…"

I couldn't work out what was happening.

"Ambrose? Are you okay?"

"It's Max. He's dead."

There was a moment of blankness before my emotions caught up with what I had been told.

"But why? How?"

My mind scrabbled for sense. What had happened? The book had said three herbs taken at once would lead to death. Max had only had the Hindeling and that was supposed to do nothing more than cause some sort of "madness of the mind".

"It's not true," I said. "It can't be. It doesn't make sense."

"Oh, Killian, he hanged himself," said Ambrose. "There was the most horrific outbreak of food poisoning at King. Just unbelievable. Rivers of faeces and vomit. Beyond belief. Streams of it running across the floor. And flies — flies everywhere. I saw one old man, seventy years old at least, vomiting faeces. I can't imagine how it's happened." There was a pause. "I don't suppose you have any idea?"

"I left early," I said. "I just did a bit on pastry and left. I wasn't there for most of the night."

I heard static. I heard the wind. I heard my heartbeat.

"Your voice," said Ambrose, eventually. "Killian, you sound scared."

I heard that creaking noise again.

"Why are you scared, Killian?"

"It's, no – I'm sad."

"Patrick tells me you were tampering with the salt and pepper."

"I was refilling it."

"I'm going to have it tested."

"Why would you want to do that?"

"Your voice is shaking, Killian."

"I was helping Max," I said. "I was only trying to help."

"Killian Lone, you will listen to me now. I do not believe you weren't involved in this somehow. If this is true..." I stood there and listened breathlessly, as my silence made up his mind. "You have destroyed my business, you have destroyed my friend –"

Before Ambrose could finish, I put the phone down, then let the receiver hang. I dropped to the floor, where I let out a single, animal roar. I took my two largest knives from a kitchen drawer and walked outside, through the high gates and into the physic garden.

The old walls stretched on into the darkness, the elms rising behind them like a mob of sentinels, their straight trunks disappearing fearlessly up into the black heights. The plants, all arranged in their neat rows, bowed and whinnied under the pressure of the wind and looked as if they were joyously celebrating my arrival, each individual stem baying for attention. Through the crowding insects, I began swiping at their bases with my knives, grunting with each strike, the wind blowing them into my face, slices of leaf sticking to my wrists and arms and neck. My back ached and my hands complained at the pain of the cold as I pushed deeper and deeper in, cutting and pulling up roots, the smell of damp earth and chloroform steeping in the air.

Soon, my fingers were bleeding and my knives blunting. I realised I had only cut down perhaps a sixth of the plantation. I ran back inside and found, in a box in the bathroom, two old hairspray aerosols. I pulled a rusting can of Castrol out of the shed and splashed what was left of it as far as I could over the plants. Lighting a match in front of the spray, I sent a plume of red fire straight into the garden and it was quickly engulfed in a breathing monster of strange violet flame.

It was the noise of the car pulling up that finally made me halt. I looked around, half expecting the blue lights of police cars. But it wasn't the police. Small and trembling in the feral madness of the countryside, it was Kathryn.

I braced myself for the onslaught of fury. She took in the sight of the fire and ran for me, throwing her arms around me.

"What did you do?" she said.

"Nothing!"

"You killed him, Killian. You *killed* him."

"I thought he was stronger," I said.

She looked at me, a huddle of shivers and tears and wild feeling.

"I don't know what happened, Kathryn," I said.

Slowly, she let me have more and more of her weight. "You made me love you," she said, eventually, into my arm. "You made me love you. And now look."

I couldn't take any more. I collapsed, pulling her to the floor. We sat there, sprawled in the mud as I pushed my thumbs into her cheeks.

"You're the only one I can be normal with, Kathryn. You make me normal." I grabbed her face hard and tipped it. I forced her to look at me. "I don't know how it works, Kathryn. I tried. I tried really hard but I always got it wrong. I don't understand how anything works. Without you I'm awful."

I squeezed harder, feeling the bones of her skull under my thumbs. She looked back at me, her eyes fractured red. A long tear worked its way towards the soft boundary of her jaw. I squashed it in its passage.

"Do you think I'm bad? Do you think I'm a bad man? Kathryn, I'm scared."

I let go of her face and began to sob.

"I don't think there are bad people. It's just – ordinary people sometimes think themselves into bad places. They look like good places but they're not."

"I tried to be good. I tried to always choose the *right* thing to do. But how do you know? How do you tell?"

She closed her eyes.

"Stay there," I said. "Wait. I have to get something."

I pushed myself to my feet and staggered towards the raging herb garden, to the far right corner where the stems, still unburned, groaned and waved in fear of the approaching heat. Carefully choosing one fat specimen each of Hindeling, Cauter and Earl's Leaf, I made no attempt to bat away the flies which were humming around my head; circling and swooping and playing.

I kneeled back down in the mud, my knees damp and cold, and, taking her hands, I made myself smile.

"Kathryn, it's going to be okay," I said.

"No, it's not," she said. "How can it ever be okay? Everything could have been so good. Killian, I don't have anyone. And then *you*... I thought I could be happy. And now you've done what you've done and I can't be with you any more. I can't... I'm *nothing* again. I'm invisible."

I pressed her palms and gathered my courage as the heat made a noisy and sudden advance.

"Stop now," I said, gently. "It's okay. You're going to be okay. You know, I filled in the will ages ago. Dor is going to be yours. And I'll never leave you. I will prove to you that loyalty can be good. I'll always be with you. I promise."

I lifted the three leaves and put them in my mouth. I wasn't aware of any flavour, just a feeling of prickling numbness as I bit into them. Kathryn's gaze sharpened.

"What are you doing?" she said.

A dead sensation hit my throat. It sank past my heart and into my stomach. I slumped a little. Over at the cottage, there was a rising rattling noise, as if it was being bombarded from the inside, and then a crack of something breaking and a low, deafening hum.

Kathryn's eyes grew huge at the sight, her fingers tensing as her neck craned up in horror. A black column of flies coursed into the filthy sky, moving and twisting up and up. It swarmed into the coming dawn like smoke and then came for us, spreading over the physic garden, a hundred thousand insects landing, silver and black and red, on stems and leaves and the stone faces of the gargoyles and into the fire where they fizzed and singed.

"It's okay, Kathryn," I said. "It's okay, my love. Don't be scared. You're going to be happy now. I've made everything okay."

She wailed at the final realisation of what I had done. The sight of her doing so overwhelmed me. I wasn't ready yet. I had to see her happy.

"Smile for me," I said. "Please smile for me, just once."

"No, no, no, no," she sobbed. "Not this, Kill. Not this, *please*."

"Just *smile*, Kathryn. Once more." I tried to look happy for her. "You can promise me something. You'll make son-in-law eggs."

Impossibly, her eyes lifted and shone for a moment. But they fell with the realisation that I had now become too weak to speak. I knew that her hand on my face would be the last thing I would feel of her. I rocked softly back as it all drained away. Nine years of this pretence, this desperate game, this fantasy of strength – it left me as if it had never happened at all. I was eleven years old again. A boy, never a dog.

My breaths became forced, dragging at the back of my throat and catching in my chest. I attempted to keep my eyes open.

"We're fuck-ups, aren't we?" I whispered.

Kathryn, whimpering and shaking her head, stroked my face with her fingers. The tears running in trails down her cheeks and the flames glowing against her beautiful birthmark and chocolate-spray freckles, she forced a final smile. "Fuck-ups together," she said.

I fought, for as long as possible, to keep Kathryn in focus. I struggled to keep it all in view: her quick, smart mouth and her green- and gold-speckled irises and her rich brown hair all bunched in the rain. There she is, my wonderful girl. There she goes.

By the time Kathryn had gathered the courage to go into the house to call the ambulance, a gap in the dirt-coloured ceiling of cloud had opened up. When the sirens finally approached, a dart of dawn sun hit what remained of the top attic window. Two hours later, the herbs were reduced to sporadic blackened stems, the earth hot and black and giving out little eddies of smoke here and there. The morning's fresh light touched the stone gargoyles that guarded the physic garden. The elms fell silent.

On the day that Kathryn finally moved into the cottage, the kitchen seemed so warm and calm and beautiful, it felt as if its ancient walls were welcoming her arrival. Placing the first of her boxes on the table, she sat and wept a little. Then she climbed the stairs, gingerly opened the door of the front bedroom and closed the curtains against the tumult of light that was rushing in through the window and breaking against the walls. Laying herself on the bed, she sank into the deepest of sleeps. She dreamed of fire and knives and turnspit dogs; of boiling bones and blood under the fingernails of men.

Before the summer came to an end, she had a new wall built, higher than ever, to shutter in the gargoyles and barricade out the Earl's trees. The mischief became quiet. The old trouble slept. And Kathryn's life at Dor became one of stillness and distance and memory.

But our story never dimmed. It remained, ever present; waiting, watching; an unquiet frequency, a language of sighs that filled the rooms; an old tale remaining stubbornly unfinished.

And then, the long and wearying sickness; the same one that took her mother.

And now, her death. The walls of Dor Cottage breathing in.

An expectancy.

I can feel her coming now. I can feel our story finally coming to an end.

Acknowledgments

Many of the kitchen incidents in this book are based on real reported events. Sections of language and dialogue in the dream sequences were sourced from period material. I am hugely indebted to the great chefs Michel Roux Jnr and Guillaume Brahimi who granted me permission to work double shifts and interview chefs and apprentices at their restaurants Le Gavroche in London and Guillaume at Bennelong in Sydney. Needless to say, you won't find any of the gruesome events or characters that appear in these pages in their kitchens. Of all the books I read to research this novel, none was anywhere near as valuable as *The Perfectionist* by Rudolph Chelminski – a goldmine of insight as well as useful facts and observations. If you enjoyed the story of Killian Lone, then I urge you to track down his wonderful biography of the brilliant yet tormented chef Bernard Loiseau.

I am indebted to the array of talented writers who were kind enough to offer honest criticism throughout the four years that I worked on this manuscript. I owe thanks to Posie Graeme Evans and Lucy Dawson, undying gratitude to Rodge Glass and Edward Hogan and whatever it is that comes after that to my wonderful friend, Craig Pierce, who offered bracingly honest and insightful notes at no less than three separate stages – a truly heroic effort, and I have learned so much from it. Thank you.

Thanks also to Ann Eve, Jess Porter, Erin Kelly, Jonathan at The Bookseller Crow, John & Tam, Kirsten Galliott, Ross Jones, Emily Hayward Whitlock, Vanessa Beaumont, David Isaacs – one of the finest editors I've worked with – and all at Short Books in the UK and Allen & Unwin in Australia.

And very special thanks to my fantastic and fantastically patient agent Charlie Campbell, without whose wise counsel I would not have finished this book.

And bows, finally, to my beautiful and brilliant wife Farrah.

Will Storr is a longform journalist and novelist. His features have appeared in many magazines and broadsheet newspaper supplements in the UK and Australia, including the *Guardian Weekend*, the *Telegraph Magazine*, the *Observer Magazine*, *GQ* and the *Sydney Morning Herald (Good Weekend)*. He is a contributing editor at *Esquire* magazine. His radio documentaries have been broadcast on *BBC World*.

He has reported from the refugee camps of Africa, the war-torn departments of rural Colombia and the remote Aboriginal communities of Australia.

He has been named New Journalist of the Year and Feature Writer of the Year, and has won a National Press Club award for excellence. In 2010, his investigation into the kangaroo meat industry won the Australian Food Media award for Best Investigative Journalism and, in 2012, he was presented with the One World Press award and the Amnesty International award for his work for the *Observer* on sexual violence against men.

He is also a widely published photographer.